8TH EDITION

WASHINGTON REAL ESTATE PRACTICES

KATHRYN HAUPT

MEGAN DORSEY

DAVID JARMAN

JENNIFER GOTANDA

ROCKWELL PUBLISHING COMPANY

Copyright© 2013
By Rockwell Publishing, Inc.
13218 N.E. 20th
Bellevue, WA 98005
(425)747-7272 / 1-800-221-9347

Eighth Edition

ISBN: 978-1-939259-35-6

PRINTED IN THE UNITED STATES OF AMERICA

Completing a CMA. 130
The CMA Form. 133
The Problem of a Low Appraisal. 135

Chapter 5: Sales Techniques and Practices. 145

Listing Practices. 146
Prospecting for Listings 146
Listing Presentations. 151
Servicing the Listing. 155
Selling Practices. 162
Finding a Buyer 162
Showing Properties. 165
Making an Offer 166
Safety Issues 169
Real Estate Assistants 170

Chapter 6: Negotiating the Offer and Acceptance 177

Making an Offer to Purchase. 178
Preparing an Offer. 178
How Offers are Presented. 182
Multiple Offers 183
Backup Offers. 185
Revoking an Offer. 188
Counteroffers and Negotiations. 190
Accepting an Offer. 194
Communicating Acceptance. 194
Manner of Acceptance 195
Acceptance Cannot Change Terms. 196
Contract Amendments 196
Contract Rescission 196
Earnest Money Deposits 198
The Size of the Deposit. 198
The Form of the Deposit. 199
Handling a Deposit 201
Refund or Forfeiture of Earnest Money 204
Fair Housing Considerations 206

Chapter 7: Purchase and Sale Agreements 215

Requirements for a Valid Purchase and Sale Agreement. 216
Typical Provisions in a Residential Purchase and Sale Agreement. 217
Identifying the Parties. 223
Property Description. 225

Purchase Price and Method of Payment 226
Earnest Money 226
Included Items. 230
Conveyance and Title 230
Information Verification Period 231
Closing Date 231
Closing Agent 232
Closing Costs 233
Transfer of Possession 233
Default 236
Time is of the Essence 237
Addenda 238
Agency Disclosure 238
Lead-Based Paint Disclosures 238
Offer and Acceptance 241
Signatures 243
Vacant Land Purchase and Sale Agreements 243
Subdivision Regulations 243
Development and Construction Feasibility. 244
Zoning. 244
Percolation Test. 244

Chapter 8: Contingent Transactions **255**

How Contingencies Work 256
Termination or Waiver 256
Good Faith Effort Required 258
Basic Elements of a Contingency Clause 258
Types of Contingencies 259
Financing Contingencies. 259
Inspection Contingencies 264
Sale of Buyer's Home Contingencies. 269
Rescission 279

Chapter 9: Loan Qualifying. **287**

Preapproval 288
The Preapproval Process. 288
Prequalification 290
The Underwriting Process 290
Income Analysis 292
Net Worth 299

Credit Reputation 303
Low-Documentation Loans 306
Subprime Lending. 307
Choosing a Loan 308
Comparing Loan Costs 308
Other Considerations in Choosing a Loan 310
Predatory Lending 311

Chapter 10: Financing Programs **319**

Basic Loan Features. 320
Repayment Period. 320
Amortization. 322
Loan-to-Value Ratios 324
Secondary Financing. 325
Loan Fees 325
Fixed and Adjustable Interest Rates 326
Conventional Loans. 330
Conventional Loans and the Secondary Market. 331
Characteristics of Conventional Loans. 331
Underwriting Conventional Loans 336
Making Conventional Loans More Affordable. 341
Government-Sponsored Loan Programs 346
FHA-Insured Loans 347
VA-Guaranteed Loans. 353
Rural Housing Service Loans 359
Seller Financing. 360
How Seller Financing Works 360
Types of Seller Financing. 364
Other Ways Sellers Can Help 367

Chapter 11: Closing the Transaction and Real Estate Math **373**

The Closing Process. 374
Escrow 376
Steps in Closing a Transaction 377
The Real Estate Agent's Role in the Closing Process. 386
Closing Costs. 388
Costs and Credits 389
Estimating the Buyer's Net Cost. 391
Estimating the Seller's Net Proceeds 395
Federal Laws that Affect Closing 399
Income Tax Regulations. 399
Real Estate Settlement Procedures Act. 401

Real Estate Math 410
    Decimals and Percentages 410
    Area Problems. 412
    Percentage Problems. 416

Glossary **423**

Index **473**

REAL ESTATE AGENCY

BEFORE ACTING AS A REAL ESTATE AGENT

- Affiliation with a firm
- Planning and budgeting

REAL ESTATE AGENCY LAW

- Licensee's duties to all parties
- Agent's duties to the principal
- Legal effects of agency relationships

CREATING AGENCY RELATIONSHIPS

TERMINATING AGENCY RELATIONSHIPS

AGENCY DISCLOSURE REQUIREMENTS

- When disclosures must be made
- Acting in accordance with the disclosures
- Licensee acting as a principal

TYPES OF REAL ESTATE AGENCY RELATIONSHIPS

- Seller agency
- Buyer agency
- Dual agency
- Non-agency
- Licensees and subagency

INTRODUCTION

You have just closed your first sale. The seller was thrilled with the sales price; the buyers are happy to be moving into their dream house. Your branch manager is beaming with approval. Her office will now reach this month's sales goal, thanks to your sale. And you can't wait to take your commission check to the bank.

But wait! Now the buyer is talking to her attorney about breach of agency duties and threatening to cancel the contract because of undisclosed material facts. The Department of Licensing has notified you that it has received a complaint against you: the seller is claiming that you failed to disclose your agency status. Plus, the seller is refusing to pay the commission. Your branch manager is worried about a lawsuit, and she thinks that it's all your fault. What a disaster!

What went wrong? In this hypothetical situation, as sometimes in real life, there was confusion about agency relationships and what they meant for the real estate licensee. All real estate licensees—particularly new licensees—must understand the practical aspects of agency relationships, especially in today's complicated legal environment.

In this chapter, we will take a brief look at the steps a real estate agent must take to get her career off the ground, and then we will discuss real estate agency law, the ways in which agency relationships can be established and terminated, agency disclosure requirements, and the different types of agency relationships.

BEFORE ACTING AS A REAL ESTATE AGENT

As you know, before you can act as a real estate agent, you must first be licensed. In Washington, there are two types of individual real estate licenses—managing broker and broker.

- A **managing broker** is a person who performs—under the supervision of a designated broker—real estate brokerage services on behalf of a real estate firm. Managing brokers are experienced real estate licensees. To become a managing broker, a person must have been a licensed broker for at least three of the previous five years. He must also have completed additional real estate coursework and passed the managing broker's license examination.
- A **broker** is a person who performs brokerage services on behalf of a real estate firm, under the supervision of a designated or managing broker. No

previous real estate experience is needed to get a real estate broker license. Brokers who have been licensed for less than two years are subject to heightened supervision by their designated or managing broker.

Each real estate firm must also be licensed. Each firm is managed by a designated broker; the **designated broker** is a managing broker, and is ultimately responsible for all of the firm's activities.

A firm can establish one or more branch offices under the firm's name. Each branch is required to have a branch manager who—under the supervision of the firm's designated broker—will oversee the branch's activities. A branch manager must have a managing broker's license.

AFFILIATION WITH A FIRM

A licensee cannot perform any real estate services until she is affiliated with a real estate firm. When choosing which firm to work for, there are many factors to consider; there's a lot of variety among real estate companies, and it's important for an agent to find a good fit. When choosing a company, an agent must decide whether she would thrive in a high-pressure office or do better in a low-key atmosphere.

When comparing firms, here are some of the elements a new agent should examine:

- **Size.** A firm may be a small independent office sole proprietorship, or part of a national franchise that has thousands of agents and hundreds of offices.
- **Specialty.** Some companies work with all types of property and offer both traditional and nontraditional real estate services, including sales, property management, escrow, investment counseling, and mortgage brokerage services. Other companies are very specialized, handling only certain types of properties or certain types of transactions. For example, one particular commercial real estate firm might do nothing but tax-deferred exchanges, and one residential brokerage might focus strictly on subdivision sales.
- **Support services.** Some firms offer training and supervision far beyond the minimum required by law. Some firms have mentoring programs or in-house instructors. Others send new licensees to classes that help the agent get off to a good start. A firm may offer only basic office support, such as telephones, a fax machine, and membership in the local multiple listing service. Others provide more amenities, including conference rooms, centralized advertising services, and training on creating individual websites.

- **Commission structure.** Some firms pay their agents with commission splits (for instance, the agent may get 60% of the firm's share of the commission), and other firms charge their agents a substantial monthly desk fee, but let them keep 100% of the commissions they earn. Many firms use a combination of commission splits and desk fee.

EXAMPLE: The Joneses list their home with ABC Realty. They agree to pay the brokerage a commission equal to 6% of the sales price. They eventually accept a $400,000 offer presented by an agent working for Lakeside Realty. Sarah is the listing agent with ABC Realty. Luis is the selling agent who works for Lakeside Realty. The listing and selling offices are splitting the commission 50/50. ABC pays its affiliated agents on a 60/40 commission split. Lakeside Realty charges each agent a desk fee, but then pays each agent 90% of the commission. The commissions on this sale would be calculated as follows:

$24,000	Total commission paid by the Joneses
× .50	ABC's percentage of the commission
$12,000	ABC's share of the commission
× .60	Sarah's percentage of ABC's commission
$7,200	Sarah's share of the commission
$24,000	Total commission paid by the Joneses
× .50	Lakeside's percentage of the commission
$12,000	Lakeside's share of the commission
× .90	Luis's percentage of Lakeside's commission
$10,800	Luis's share of the commission

Note that a few firms treat their agents as employees and pay them salaries. However, most real estate agents are independent contractors, not employees. Under IRS rules, a person is generally considered to be an **independent contractor** if she sets her own work hours and receives compensation on a commission basis, rather than a fixed salary. In contrast, a person who receives a fixed salary and works within a defined work schedule is considered an employee. In a real estate firm, licensees are usually independent contractors and non-licensed staff are usually employees. While independent contractors typically aren't eligible for traditional employee benefits, like health insurance or retirement plans, Washington state does require real estate firms to pay workers' compensation insurance for all licensees. (Of course, being an independent contractor doesn't mean that a real estate licensee is his own boss. By law, every real estate licensee is required to work under the supervision of a designated broker or branch manager.)

PLANNING AND BUDGETING

Every licensee should approach his new real estate career as if he's starting a new business, because that's exactly what he's doing. A licensee who works as an independent contractor and who is paid on a commission basis is essentially operating his own business under the umbrella of his real estate firm. As with any new business owner, he should create a business plan, develop and follow a realistic operating budget, set up an accounting system (or hire an accountant), purchase all the necessary business equipment, and put aside enough cash reserves to pay his business expenses for at least six months.

Before even thinking about making that first cold call or listing presentation, every new licensee should prepare the following:

- a business plan that addresses both short-term and long-term goals and performance expectations;
- a budget that takes into account cash flow, gross income, business expenses, and personal expenses (mortgage payment, living expenses, retirement savings, etc.);
- a plan for building up financial reserves that will see the licensee through economic downturns;
- a list of start-up expenses, such as a computer, a smartphone, any business or accounting software, marketing materials (such as business cards and yard signs), association membership fees, insurance premiums, and professional fees (such as accounting or legal fees).

A licensee should be prepared to monitor his financial situation and make necessary adjustments to his budget on a regular basis. For instance, a lower-than-expected monthly income would require reducing expenses and/or finding ways to increase revenues.

REAL ESTATE AGENCY LAW

Now let's turn our attention to agency law. Agency law forms the basis for the real estate agent's relationship with her client. As you know, an **agent** is a person who has been authorized by a **client** to represent that client in dealings with third parties (sometimes called **customers**). A client may be a real estate seller, buyer, landlord, or tenant. Another word for client is **principal**.

> **EXAMPLE:** Sullivan asks Broker Harris to find a buyer for his house. Harris shows Sullivan's house to Brown, who makes an offer to purchase the house. Sullivan is Harris's client, or principal; Harris is Sullivan's agent; and Brown is the customer, or third party.

Would it make a difference if Harris were considered Brown's agent instead of Sullivan's agent? It would make a great deal of difference, because an agent owes a different set of duties to his principal than he owes to third parties.

Until 1997, Washington real estate agency relationships were governed by general agency law. Under general agency law, the duties owed by agents to their principals are called **fiduciary** duties. A fiduciary is a person who occupies a position of special trust in relation to another person. Fiduciary duties include the duties of reasonable care and skill, obedience and utmost good faith, accounting, loyalty, and disclosure of material facts.

In 1997, the Real Estate Brokerage Relationships Act went into effect in Washington. In real estate transactions, this law replaced fiduciary duties with statutory duties. These statutory duties are divided into two types: the general duties that a real estate licensee owes to any party, and the special duties that a real estate licensee owes only to his client (principal).

LICENSEE'S DUTIES TO ALL PARTIES

Traditionally, a real estate agent owed fiduciary duties to his principal, but owed third parties only the duty of honesty and fair dealing. And it was not always clear what the duty of honesty and fair dealing required of the agent. In many situations, the duty of honesty and fair dealing owed to a third party appeared to conflict with the agent's duties to his principal.

> **EXAMPLE:** A real estate agent is representing a seller who explained to the agent why he is moving: "I really hate this house. Even though there are a lot of windows, they all face north. It's so dark that I'm depressed all winter. Plus, there's no storage space and the neighbors are really loud."
>
> Now the agent is showing the house to a buyer who has confided to the agent that she suffers from SAD (seasonal affective disorder) and wants a house with lots of windows and light. Should the agent be loyal to the

seller and remain silent, or does his duty of honesty and fair dealing require him to disclose the seller's complaints about the lack of light?

Under Washington's real estate agency law, the general duty of honesty and fair dealing has been replaced by a statutory list of duties that are owed to any party a real estate licensee renders services to, regardless of which party the licensee represents. In fact, the licensee owes these duties even if she is not representing any of the parties.

EXAMPLE: Licensee Powell is helping a buyer and a seller complete a real estate transaction. She is not acting as either party's agent in the transaction; instead, she is acting as a facilitator. She has fully disclosed her non-agency status to both parties and is acting in accordance with that disclosure. Even though Powell is not acting as an agent, she still owes several statutory duties to both parties.

The statutory duties that a real estate licensee owes to any party involved in a transaction are:

- reasonable care and skill,
- honesty and good faith,
- presenting all written communications,
- disclosure of material facts,
- accounting,
- providing a pamphlet on agency law, and
- disclosing any existing agency relationship.

REASONABLE CARE AND SKILL. A real estate licensee is required to use the same degree of care and skill that would be expected of a reasonably competent real estate licensee. If a licensee harms a party because of carelessness or incompetence, he may be accused of negligence and held liable for the harm caused by that negligence.

HONESTY AND GOOD FAITH. A licensee must act toward any party with honesty and good faith. Making inaccurate statements or misrepresentations to prospective buyers or sellers is a breach of this duty. An intentional misrepresentation may constitute actual fraud, and even an unintentional misrepresentation may be considered constructive fraud. In either case, the party to whom the misrepresentation was made would have the right to rescind the transaction and/or sue the licensee (or her brokerage) for damages.

PRESENT WRITTEN COMMUNICATIONS. All types of written communications—including all written offers—to or from either party must be presented to the other party in a timely manner. This duty to present all offers continues even after the property is subject to an existing contract or the buyer is already a party to an existing contract.

> **EXAMPLE:** Seller Sanders has just accepted an offer from Buyer Barton. Garcia, a real estate licensee, receives another written offer for the same property from Buyer Bell. Garcia has a duty to present Bell's offer to Sanders, even though Sanders has already accepted Barton's offer.

DISCLOSURE OF MATERIAL FACTS. A licensee must disclose a material fact to a party if:

1. the licensee knows about it, and
2. it is not apparent or readily ascertainable by the party.

In most cases, a material fact requiring disclosure would be a **latent defect** in the property. A latent defect is a problem that would not be discovered by ordinary inspection.

Until Washington's real estate agency law went into effect, the term "material fact" was difficult for both real estate licensees and courts to define. In everyday situations, licensees simply had to use their best judgment to decide whether something would be considered a material fact requiring disclosure. Now, however, the real estate agency law provides a definition of "material fact." A **material fact** is information that has a substantial negative impact on the value of the property, on a party's ability to perform, or on the purpose of the transaction. The law goes on to specifically exclude certain types of information from this definition. It is not considered material if the property (or a neighboring property) was or may have been the site of a violent crime, a suicide or other death, drug- or gang-related activity, political or religious activity, or any other occurrence that doesn't adversely affect the physical condition of or title to the property.

> **EXAMPLE:** Agent Kipling is showing Buyer Green a home. Green has three children and wants a safe family home to live in. The home Kipling is

showing Green was the site of a brutal homicide-suicide three years ago. This information is not considered a material fact and need not be disclosed to Green.

However, if—in the example above—Green asked Kipling whether he was aware of any crimes that had occurred on the property, Kipling would have to answer honestly. Regardless of whether the information requested is a material fact, a licensee is obligated to answer questions honestly and in good faith.

Also, criminal activity is considered to be a material fact if it affects the physical condition of the property. For example, an illegal drug lab may leave behind dangerous chemical residues that substantially affect the condition of the property. So if a house has been used as a drug lab, that would have to be disclosed to prospective buyers.

Note that neither a licensee nor a seller has a legal duty to disclose the presence of a sex offender in the neighborhood. A buyer can readily obtain that information herself on the Internet.

In some situations a licensee may be required to make a disclosure concerning criminal activities because of a particular buyer's circumstances. But this type of disclosure is usually based on the duty of honesty and good faith rather than on the duty to disclose material facts.

EXAMPLE: In the past year, there have been several muggings in the neighborhood where the listed home is located. The victims were all frail, elderly women who were walking alone.

Potential buyers, a married couple with teenage children, tell the real estate agent that they plan on moving the wife's elderly mother into the home's spare bedroom. In this situation, the agent should disclose the muggings in the neighborhood. While it may not be a material fact according to the statutory definition, the licensee's duty of honesty and good faith requires her to disclose this information to the buyers.

Some states require real estate licensees to physically inspect the property and report their findings to the buyer. In Washington, however, the real estate agency law states that licensees do not have the duty to investigate any matters they have not specifically agreed to investigate. A licensee has no duty to inspect the property, investigate either party's financial position, or independently verify statements made by either party or any reasonable source.

FIG. 1.1   REAL ESTATE LICENSEE'S DUTIES

GENERAL DUTIES OWED TO ANY PARTY (INCLUDING THE PRINCIPAL)
- REASONABLE CARE AND SKILL
- HONESTY AND GOOD FAITH
- PRESENT ALL WRITTEN COMMUNICATIONS
- DISCLOSE MATERIAL FACTS
- ACCOUNTING
- AGENCY PAMPHLET
- AGENCY DISCLOSURE

AGENCY DUTIES OWED ONLY TO THE PRINCIPAL
- LOYALTY
- DISCLOSE CONFLICTS OF INTEREST
- CONFIDENTIALITY
- ADVISE PRINCIPAL TO SEEK EXPERT ADVICE
- GOOD FAITH AND CONTINUOUS EFFORT

ACCOUNTING. Real estate licensees must be able to account for all funds (or other valuables) entrusted to their care. These are referred to as **trust funds**. Licensees are required to report to their clients on the status of all trust funds on a regular basis. They must also avoid mixing, or **commingling**, trust funds with their own business or personal funds.

REAL ESTATE AGENCY LAW PAMPHLET. A licensee is required to give a pamphlet to each party she renders services to, which sets forth the provisions of Washington's real estate agency law, the Real Estate Brokerage Relationships Act. A party must receive the pamphlet before signing an agency agreement with the licensee, before signing an offer in a transaction handled by the licensee, before consenting to a dual agency, or before waiving any agency rights, whichever comes first.

AGENCY DISCLOSURE. In a real estate transaction handled by a licensee, before a party signs an offer, the licensee must disclose in writing to that party whether the licensee represents the buyer, the seller, both, or neither. Agency disclosure is discussed in more detail later in this chapter.

AGENT'S DUTIES TO THE PRINCIPAL

Whenever a real estate licensee acts as an agent in a transaction, a special set of duties comes into play, in addition to the general duties discussed above. If the licensee represents the seller, the agency duties are owed to the seller. If she represents the buyer, the agency duties are owed to the buyer. And if the licensee is acting as a dual agent, the agency duties are owed to both the seller and the buyer. (A **dual agent** is one who represents both the seller and the buyer in the same transaction.)

The special duties that an agent in a real estate transaction owes to the principal are:

- loyalty,
- disclosing conflicts of interest,
- confidentiality,
- advising the principal to seek expert advice, and
- a good faith and continuous effort to fulfill the goals of the agency.

LOYALTY. Real estate licensees must put the interests of their clients above their own interests and above the interests of any other party. Loyalty means that an agent must not make any **secret profits** from the agency. For example, it is a breach of agency duty for a licensee to list a property for less than it is worth, secretly buy it through an intermediary, and then sell it for a profit.

If a licensee is acting as a dual agent, this duty of loyalty is modified. It is not really possible to be loyal to two different principals with opposing interests; so a dual agent simply owes her principals the duty to take no action that is detrimental to either party's interests.

CONFLICTS OF INTEREST. Any conflicts of interest must be disclosed to the principal. For instance, the seller's agent must inform the seller if there is any relationship between the agent and a prospective buyer. And this disclosure must be made before the principal decides whether to accept the buyer's offer. If the buyer is a friend, relative, or business associate of the agent, or a company in which the agent has an interest, there may be a conflict of interest. The principal has the right to have this information when making his decision.

CONFIDENTIALITY. An agent may not disclose any confidential information about the principal, even after the agency relationship terminates. **Confidential**

information is defined in Washington's real estate agency law as information from or concerning a principal that:

1. was acquired by the licensee during the course of an agency relationship with the principal;
2. the principal reasonably expects to be kept confidential;
3. the principal has not disclosed or authorized to be disclosed to third parties;
4. would, if disclosed, operate to the detriment of the principal; and
5. the principal personally would not be obligated to disclose to the other party.

Information about latent defects must never be concealed on the grounds that the information is confidential. Because the principal would be legally obligated to disclose a latent defect to buyers, such information is by definition not confidential information. Agents should advise their clients that they (the agents) may be legally obligated to disclose certain types of information that the principal may have believed to be confidential.

EXPERT ADVICE. A real estate agent must advise the principal to seek expert advice on any matters relating to the transaction that are beyond the agent's expertise. For instance, if the principal has questions about the property's structural soundness, the agent should advise the principal to contact a home inspector.

GOOD FAITH AND CONTINUOUS EFFORT. A real estate agent has a duty to make a good faith effort to fulfill the terms of the agency agreement. This means an agent representing a seller must make a good faith and continuous effort to find a buyer for the property. An agent representing a buyer must make a good faith and continuous effort to find a suitable property for the buyer to purchase.

There are some specific limits on this duty. A seller's agent doesn't have to seek additional offers to purchase the property while the property is subject to an existing sales contract (although she still must present any additional offers that come in). A buyer's agent doesn't have to seek additional properties for the buyer to purchase while the buyer is a party to an existing sales contract. And a dual agent doesn't have to show a property if there is no written agreement to pay compensation to a dual agent in connection with that property.

LEGAL EFFECTS OF AGENCY RELATIONSHIPS

An agency relationship has other significant legal implications beyond the issue of agency duties. For a third party, dealing with an agent can be the legal equivalent of dealing with the principal. When an agent who is authorized to do so signs a document or makes a promise, it's as if the principal signed or promised.

Furthermore, under certain circumstances, if an agent does something wrong, the principal may be held liable to third parties for harm resulting from the agent's actions. This is called **vicarious liability**. Under Washington's real estate agency law, a seller or a buyer generally cannot be held vicariously liable for harm caused by his real estate agent. There are two exceptions to this rule, however. A principal may be liable for her real estate agent's actions if:

1. the principal participated in or authorized the act, error, or omission; or
2. the principal benefited from the act, error, or omission and a court determines that it is highly probable that the injured party would be unable to enforce a judgment against the agent.

To summarize, you can see how important it is to know which party you are representing in a real estate transaction. The existence of an agency relationship has an effect on all of the following concerns:

- the extent of the duties you owe to a particular party;
- whether your actions will be binding on a party; and
- whether, under some circumstances, another party may be held liable for your actions.

CREATING AGENCY RELATIONSHIPS

Under common law, real estate agency relationships could be formed in one of three different ways:

1. **Express agreement.** The principal appoints someone to act as an agent, and the agent accepts the appointment.
2. **Ratification.** The principal gives approval after the fact to acts performed by a person who was without authority to act for the principal.
3. **Estoppel.** It would be unfair to a third party to deny an agent's authority because the principal allowed the third party to believe there was an agency relationship.

Washington's real estate agency law changed the way real estate agency relationships are created. A written listing agreement (express agreement) is still the most common way to create an agency relationship between a firm and a property seller. However, the real estate agency law has had a significant impact on the creation of buyer agency relationships. Under this law, a licensee who performs real estate brokerage services for a buyer automatically becomes the buyer's agent, unless there is a written agreement to the contrary. Such a written agreement might be a listing agreement with the seller, a written dual agency agreement with both parties, a written subagency agreement with the seller, or a written non-agency agreement.

> **EXAMPLE:** Brenner, a prospective buyer, walks into Taylor Realty, where she begins talking to Agent Daley. Brenner tells Daley that she is looking for her first home. She tells him her general price range and the kind of house she wants. Daley goes to his computer, enters in some information, and gets a printout of homes that Brenner may be interested in. After making some phone calls, Daley and Brenner go and look at three of the homes.
>
> Under Washington's real estate agency law, Daley (acting for Taylor Realty) is Brenner's agent. This agency relationship was created automatically, because Daley is performing brokerage services for Brenner. Note, however, that Daley will not be Brenner's agent for a particular transaction if he has a previously existing written agency agreement with the home seller in question.

A real estate agency relationship is sometimes created inadvertently. This can happen if the seller's agent acts as if she's representing the buyer, leading the buyer to believe that the agent represents him instead of the seller. This is known as an **agency by implication**, because the agent's actions imply that she's the buyer's agent. To avoid unfairness to the buyer, the agent cannot deny the existence of this agency relationship. But since the agent is already representing the seller, this creates an inadvertent dual agency.

Inadvertent dual agency was once a common problem. But as we'll discuss shortly, both agency disclosure laws and Washington's real estate agency law have done much to prevent it.

TERMINATING AGENCY RELATIONSHIPS

An agency relationship may be terminated either by the actions of the parties or through the operation of law. Once an agency has been terminated, the agent is no longer authorized to represent the principal.

TERMINATION BY THE PARTIES

Since agency requires the consent of both the principal and the agent, they can end the agency relationship at any time. This may occur by mutual agreement, revocation, or renunciation.

MUTUAL AGREEMENT. In some cases, the principal and the agent simply agree to end the agency. If the agency was originally established with a written document, it's advisable to formally terminate it in writing, too.

REVOCATION. A principal may revoke an agent's authority at any time. Under some circumstances, however, the revocation may be a breach of contract. In that case, the principal may be liable to the agent for damages resulting from the breach of contract.

> **EXAMPLE:** Davidson decides she distrusts and dislikes the firm she listed her house with, but their exclusive listing won't expire for another two months. Even though Davidson could terminate the listing unilaterally, revoking the firm's authority to represent her, it would be much better if she could get the firm to agree to the termination instead. A unilateral revocation would be a breach of the listing agreement, and the firm could sue Davidson for the commission.

RENUNCIATION. An agent also has the right to terminate the agency relationship unilaterally, without the principal's consent. This is called renouncing the agency. Like revocation, renunciation may be a breach of contract, and the agent could end up owing the principal damages for the breach. But damages are usually not an issue when a real estate agent renounces an agency.

TERMINATION BY OPERATION OF LAW

An agency relationship can terminate by operation of law, without any action on the part of the principal or agent. This can happen as a result of the expiration of the agency, fulfillment of purpose, death or incapacity, or the extinction of the subject matter.

EXPIRATION. If an agency agreement has a termination date, the agent's authority to represent the principal terminates automatically when the expiration date arrives.

If there is no termination date, the agency will be deemed to expire within a reasonable time. How long a period is considered reasonable will depend on the circumstances and may be decided by a court.

Note that an agency agreement without a termination date can usually be ended by either party without liability for damages; unilateral termination does not represent a breach of the agreement. In some situations, however, the other party could ask for reimbursement of expenses incurred in the course of the agency.

FULFILLMENT OF PURPOSE. An agency relationship terminates automatically (before its expiration date) when its purpose has been fulfilled. A listing agreement, for example, is fulfilled when the sale of the listed property closes. The real estate agent's services are no longer needed.

DEATH OR INCAPACITY. A real estate agency also terminates if the principal dies or becomes legally incapacitated (mentally incompetent). As a general rule, the agent's authority to act on behalf of the principal ends at the moment the principal dies or is declared incompetent by a court, even if the agent is not informed of the event until later on.

EXTINCTION OF SUBJECT MATTER. If the subject matter of an agency is destroyed or otherwise ceases to exist, the agency terminates. For example, the subject matter of a property management agreement is the principal's property. If the principal sells the property, the agent's authority terminates.

AGENCY DISCLOSURE REQUIREMENTS

We began this chapter with an example of what can happen when there is confusion about agency relationships: loss of commissions, lawsuits, and disciplinary action. The best way to prevent confusion is with proper agency disclosure. Agency disclosure makes it clear to all parties who is representing whom, and it is required by state law.

WHEN DISCLOSURES MUST BE MADE

A real estate licensee must inform any party to whom she renders real estate services which party (or parties) she is representing in the transaction. The disclosure must be made to the buyer before the buyer signs the offer to purchase, and to the seller before she accepts the offer by signing it.

The disclosures must be in writing. They may be included in the purchase and sale agreement (as long as they are in a separate paragraph), or they may be made in a separate document. The parties' signatures on the agreement or the separate disclosure document show that they understand and accept the stated agency relationships.

Most standard MLS forms will contain the required disclosures. However, sometimes you must use a nonstandard form, such as when your sale involves a bank-owned property. The bank's required form may not include the necessary agency disclosure. In that case, you should use a separate agency disclosure form, such as the one shown in Figure 1.2. The disclosure form has a blank where the agent can name the party or parties (buyer, seller, or both) that he is representing, as well as blanks for the signatures of the buyer and the seller.

ACTING IN ACCORDANCE WITH DISCLOSURES

The disclosures mandated by state law are fairly straightforward. However, once the disclosures have been made, the licensee also must act in accordance with those disclosures. This may be more difficult than it sounds.

> **EXAMPLE:** Carville is the listing agent for Sharp's house. Carville discloses this fact, in writing, to Blaine, a potential buyer. But over the course of a few days, Carville begins acting more and more like Blaine's agent. He gives Blaine a lot of advice about making an offer and negotiating the best terms. Blaine begins to rely on Carville's advice, and by the time Blaine is ready to make an offer on Sharp's house, he feels confident that Carville is working in his (Blaine's) best interests.
>
> In this case, even though Carville properly disclosed his status as the seller's agent, his actions may imply an agency relationship with Blaine. This could create what is known as an inadvertent dual agency. In other words, Carville would be unintentionally representing the buyer as well as the seller in this transaction. If Blaine or Sharp later became dissatisfied with the transaction, either of them could accuse Carville of breaching his agency duties.

If a licensee's conduct is not consistent with her agency disclosure, she may be subject to disciplinary action by the Department of Licensing, and the following sanctions may be imposed:

- suspension or revocation of her real estate license;
- restriction and/or monitoring of her real estate activities;

FIG. 1.2   AGENCY DISCLOSURE FORM

Form 42
Agency Disclosure
Rev. 7/10
Page 1 of 1

AGENCY DISCLOSURE

Washington State law requires real estate brokers to disclose to all parties to whom the broker renders real estate 1
brokerage services whether the broker represents the seller (or lessor), the buyer (or lessee), both the seller/lessor 2
and buyer/lessee, or neither. 3

This form is for use when the transaction forms **do not** otherwise contain an agency disclosure provision. 4

THE UNDERSIGNED BROKER REPRESENTS: _____ 5

THE UNDERSIGNED BUYER / LESSEE OR SELLER / LESSOR ACKNOWLEDGES RECEIPT 6
OF A COPY OF THE PAMPHLET ENTITLED "THE LAW OF REAL ESTATE AGENCY" 7

_____ DATE _____ 8
Signature

_____ DATE _____ 9
Signature

_____ DATE _____ 10
Signature

_____ DATE _____ 11
Signature

BROKER _____ 12
Print/Type

BROKER'S SIGNATURE _____ 13

FIRM NAME AS LICENSED _____ 14
Print/Type

FIRM'S ASSUMED NAME (if applicable) _____ 15
Print/Type

SAMPLE

- a fine of up to $5,000 per violation;
- probation;
- the required completion of a relevant real estate course; and/or
- censure or reprimand.

LICENSEE ACTING AS A PRINCIPAL

If you are a licensee and are acting as a principal in a transaction—as either the seller or the buyer—you must make some special disclosures to the other party. You must disclose that you are licensed as a real estate agent in the state of Washington, that you are purchasing or selling the property for your own benefit, and that you intend to make a profit.

If you are a principal in a transaction, you should only represent yourself; do not try to act as an agent for the other party. Have your designated broker or branch manager review any contracts involved before you make or accept an offer. It is also a good idea to recommend that the other party seek independent legal advice and an independent appraisal.

Your brokerage firm may have specific office policies about buying or selling your own property. If so, you should become familiar with them and follow them.

TYPES OF AGENCY RELATIONSHIPS

Real estate transactions routinely involve more than one real estate agent. Here's an example. Some potential buyers visit a real estate office in the area of the city they are interested in. A licensee who works for that firm interviews the prospective buyers to find out what kind of a home they want and can afford, and then shows the buyers various suitable properties. Most firms belong to a multiple listing service, so the licensee will show the buyers not only homes that are listed directly with his own firm, but also homes that are listed with other MLS members. Meanwhile, other real estate agents may be showing these homes to other prospective buyers.

If the buyers become interested in a particular home, negotiations for the purchase of that home will involve the listing agent as well as the agent who has been showing properties to the buyers. In addition, other cooperating agents may have showed the home to other buyers who didn't want it or didn't offer enough for it. In order to understand the various agency relationships in this transaction, you must recognize which party each of the real estate licensees is representing.

There are four basic types of real estate agency relationships in Washington:

- seller agency,
- buyer agency,
- dual agency, and
- non-agency.

SELLER AGENCY

Seller agency is the traditional type of real estate agency.

EXAMPLE: Sterling, a property owner, has listed her home with Jenson. Jenson finds a buyer, Chang, who makes an offer on the home. Sterling accepts the offer. The sale closes, and Sterling pays a commission to Jenson. Sterling (the seller) is the principal, Jenson is the seller's agent, and Chang (the buyer) is a third party.

Before the real estate agency law was enacted, the majority of residential real estate agents in Washington acted as sellers' agents.

EXAMPLE: Suppose Jenson listed Sterling's home, but a licensee working for another real estate firm found the buyer for Sterling's home. Traditionally, not only Jenson, but the other licensee would have been considered Sterling's agents.

Under the old rules, any member of the multiple listing service who found a buyer for a listed property was presumed to represent the seller. The selling agent was considered to be a **subagent** of the principal (the seller). The buyer only had agency representation in the comparatively rare cases when the buyer and the selling agent had actually entered into a formal buyer representation agreement. So as a general rule, all of the agents involved in a transaction ordinarily represented the seller.

Now, however, under the terms of Washington's real estate agency law, an agent will generally represent the seller only if she is the seller's listing agent. In a typical listing agreement, the seller hires an agent to find a buyer who is ready, willing, and able to purchase the property on the seller's terms. In return for her services, the agent receives a commission (usually a percentage of the sales price).

SELLER'S AGENT'S DUTIES TO SELLER. As we discussed earlier, a real estate agent owes special duties to his principal, above and beyond the duties that he owes to any party. In general, a seller's agent must use his best efforts to promote the interests of the seller.

SELLER'S AGENT'S DUTIES TO BUYER. A seller's agent must always treat a prospective buyer with honesty and good faith, and must use reasonable care and skill in the transaction. But the seller's agent must not act as if she is representing the buyer. While the agent must fully disclose all the material facts and answer the buyer's questions honestly, the agent should not give the buyer advice, such as suggesting how much to offer for the listed property.

The seller's agent has the duty of confidentiality in regard to the seller; the agent must not disclose any confidential information obtained from the seller. However, the duty of loyalty to the seller requires the seller's agent to pass on to the seller any important information obtained from the buyer.

> **EXAMPLE:** Suppose that as Jenson shows Sterling's house to Buyer Chang, Chang says to Jenson, "Say, I really love this house. But there's no way I'm going to offer full price right off the bat. How about if I offer $5,000 below the listing price?"
>
> Or suppose Chang says, "This house is great! I'm going to offer full price. Of course, I did declare bankruptcy about a year and a half ago, so I don't know if I'll qualify for a loan. But it's worth a shot, right?"
>
> Or Chang might say to Jenson, "Wow! This house is really underpriced! I'm going to buy it for the full listing price, then turn around and sell it for $15,000 more than the owner is asking!"
>
> In each of these cases, Jenson would be obligated to pass Chang's comments on to the seller. Remember, Jenson must act in the best interests of his client, Sterling. But unless Jenson has made his responsibilities to Sterling absolutely clear to Chang, Chang may be surprised and upset to discover that Jenson has told Sterling things that Chang considered to be confidential information.

When a listing agent works closely with a buyer, the buyer may mistakenly assume that the agent is working on his behalf. Such a buyer might freely disclose vital information to the agent, expecting it to be kept confidential. The buyer is then shocked when the agent passes this information on to the seller, as the agent is obligated to do. Thus, it is imperative to make sure that the buyer understands that the listing agent is, in fact, the seller's agent. Again, the agent must fully disclose his status as a seller's agent and act in accordance with that disclosure. Otherwise, the situation could give rise to an inadvertent dual agency.

SERVICES TO BUYERS. There are many services that a seller's agent can provide to a buyer. In fact, many of these services actually promote the interests of the seller, because they increase the chances of a sale and then enable the sales transaction to close smoothly. These services include:

- discussing the buyer's housing needs;
- showing the property to the buyer;
- disclosing all pertinent information about the property (including material facts that adversely affect the property's value);
- answering questions about the property and the neighborhood;
- discussing financing alternatives;
- furnishing copies of documents that affect the property (such as CC&Rs and easements);
- explaining the process of presenting the offer, negotiation, and closing the transaction; and
- referring the buyer to other professionals, if necessary.

PRE-EXISTING RELATIONSHIPS. Ordinarily, a seller's agent can provide all of these services without creating an agency relationship with the buyer. However, sometimes the seller's agent has had a previous relationship with the buyer. In this situation it may be difficult for the agent to represent the seller's interests without feeling some loyalty to the buyer as well.

EXAMPLE: Sterling was so pleased with how Jenson found a buyer for her home, she wants Jenson to help her find another home. Jenson selects a suitable home that he has listed and shows it to Sterling.

Under the circumstances, it would be easy for Sterling to assume that Jenson is acting as her agent. But unless otherwise agreed, Jenson is the seller's agent, and he should emphasize this fact to Sterling. Jenson should disclose his agency relationship with the seller to Sterling, remind Sterling that he is obligated to tell the seller any material information Sterling reveals to him, and emphasize to Sterling that he will be representing the seller in all negotiations.

Note, however, that according to the real estate agency law, an agent cannot disclose confidential information about a principal even after the termination of the agency relationship.

EXAMPLE: During Jenson's earlier agency relationship with Sterling, he learned that Sterling has a substantial trust fund. As a result, when Jenson shows Sterling one of his own listings, he knows that Sterling can afford to pay full price for it. But this is confidential information that Jenson learned during their agency relationship. Therefore, Jenson cannot reveal it to the seller in the new transaction.

BUYER AGENCY

Under Washington's real estate agency law, the buyer is automatically represented by the licensee that the buyer is working with, unless there is a written agreement to the contrary (that is, the licensee has a written listing agreement with the seller, a written subagency agreement with the seller, a written dual agency agreement with both parties, or a written non-agency agreement). Thus, the majority of buyers are able to take advantage of the benefits of buyer agency. They can relax and divulge key information about their housing needs and financial condition, knowing their agents must keep these matters confidential.

EXPLAINING BUYER AGENCY TO BUYERS. When you disclose your agency status to a buyer you're representing, you can explain the benefits of the relationship by breaking them down into four categories:

- agency duties,
- objective advice,
- help with negotiations, and
- access to more properties.

AGENCY DUTIES. A buyer's agent owes agency duties to the buyer rather than to the seller. For many buyers, the loyalty and confidentiality owed to them by their agent is the most important benefit of a buyer agency relationship. Because of the duties of loyalty and confidentiality, a buyer's agent must put the buyer's interests ahead of her own interests, and any information the buyer discloses to the agent must be kept confidential.

EXAMPLE: Ashworth is a first-time home buyer. Donnelly is helping him find a home. Donnelly shows Ashworth a home he is very interested in. Its listing price is $259,000 and Ashworth could easily afford a home that costs $20,000 more. Donnelly must put Ashworth's interests before her own, so she encourages him to make an offer on the home, even though she would receive a larger commission if he purchased a more expensive property.

Ashworth is eager to buy the home and suggests making a full price offer. Donnelly suspects he could get the house for about $3,000 less than the listing price, so she advises him to offer $255,900. Even though Donnelly knows Ashworth is willing to pay the full listing price, she is obligated to keep this information confidential. If she had been the seller's agent, she would have been required to disclose this information to the seller.

OBJECTIVE ADVICE. Seller's agents develop expert sales techniques that are designed to convince the buyer to sign on the dotted line. Buyer's agents, on the other hand, are free to advise the buyer on the pros and cons of purchasing any given home.

EXAMPLE: The Whittiers looked very seriously at two homes before they purchased a third one. Their agent, Smith, gave them invaluable advice throughout the house-hunting process.

The Whittiers responded emotionally to the beautiful landscaping and gracious interior of the first home, and were immediately ready to make a full price offer. At Smith's urging, they looked into the property taxes, heating costs, and upkeep and realized immediately that the house would be too costly to maintain.

The second home they were interested in was much more affordable, but Smith made sure they got all the pertinent information about the structural condition of the house. Once they realized how much it would cost to replace the roof and what three previous termite infestations meant, they quickly decided against the purchase.

The third home seemed ideal, even after Smith helped them evaluate all the information about it. Because Smith was familiar with the housing market, he advised the Whittiers to offer $6,000 less than the listing price. Their offer was accepted and the transaction closed without a hitch. If it weren't for Smith's objective advice, they might have ended up with a property that wasn't right for them.

HELP WITH NEGOTIATIONS. While some buyers are happiest when they're dickering over a sales price, many buyers are decidedly uncomfortable negotiating for a home they want. They are afraid to offer full price, because they don't want to pay too much for the home. On the other hand, they are afraid to make an offer that's too low, for fear of offending the seller and ruining any chance of reaching an agreement. A buyer's agent is extremely useful during the negotiation phase. The agent can use her knowledge of the real estate market to help the buyer get the property on the best possible terms.

EXAMPLE: The Browns are first-time buyers. They have decided to make an offer on a starter home, but they are unsure about how much to offer. Their agent, Cohen, knows the going price for similar homes and suggests an amount for a strategic opening offer. She also discusses other important terms of the offer, such as the amount of the earnest money deposit, the closing date, and how the parties will divide the closing costs. With her help, the Browns are able to purchase the home on very favorable terms.

ACCESS TO MORE PROPERTIES. A buyer's agent who enters into a written representation agreement with the buyer will usually be compensated if the buyer purchases any home, even one that isn't listed with a firm. So a buyer's agent may pursue less traditional means of searching for properties, considering properties that are for sale by owner, properties with open listings, and properties in probate proceedings.

EXAMPLE: McHugh has very specific housing requirements. Among other things, he wants lake frontage, a boat ramp, an outbuilding to use as a shop, and fruit trees. A property with these features in McHugh's price range simply can't be found through the multiple listing service.

McHugh enters into a buyer representation agreement with Morris and agrees to pay a commission if Morris finds him a property that is not listed with the MLS. Morris scours legal notices for foreclosure, bankruptcy, and estate sales. He also carefully reviews "for sale by owner" (FSBO) ads on the Internet and in the newspaper. Finally, after driving through several lakeshore neighborhoods, he spots a FSBO that meets most of McHugh's requirements. McHugh makes an offer on the house and everyone is happy with the transaction.

BUYER REPRESENTATION AGREEMENTS. As we discussed previously, many buyer agency relationships will be created automatically under the terms of the real estate agency law. However, a buyer and a licensee may choose to enter into a written **representation agreement**. These agreements clearly describe the rights and duties of both parties. Naturally, the two most important duties are the agent's duty to use his professional expertise to locate a property for the buyer and negotiate the terms of the sale, and the buyer's duty to compensate the agent. Most buyer representation agreements contain other important provisions as well. These may include:

- the term of the agreement,
- general characteristics of the property the buyer wants,
- a price range for the property,
- any warranties or representations made by the agent, and
- how the buyer agency relationship will affect the agent's relationship with other property buyers and sellers.

An example of a buyer representation agreement is shown in Figure 1.3. This form states that the agency agreement does not create an agency relationship between the buyer and other licensees working for the same brokerage.

The buyer representation agreement shown in Figure 1.3 also provides that the agent may show the buyer properties listed with the agent's own firm. In that case, the supervising broker will become a dual agent. (See the section on in-house transactions in the discussion of dual agency later in this chapter.) In addition, the form states that no other brokers in the firm represent the buyer unless specifically appointed to do so.

The form has a section for the buyer to state whether this buyer agency agreement is exclusive or non-exclusive; if no box is checked, the agreement will be considered non-exclusive. The parties can also stipulate the geographic areas where the agent will look for properties for the buyer.

Another provision often found in buyer representation agreements is one regarding warranties and representations. Generally, the buyer agrees to be responsible for investigating and inspecting the property. The buyer's agent does not make any warranties or representations regarding the value of any property or its suitability for the buyer's purposes. Additionally, most forms provide that the buyer's agent will not assist in a transaction that is a distressed home conveyance unless agreed to in writing.

BUYER'S AGENT'S COMPENSATION. Naturally, real estate agents are concerned about how they will be compensated for their time and effort. The way a seller's agent is compensated is well-established: the seller agrees to pay the listing agent a percentage of the sales price when the property is sold. If another firm is involved in effecting the sale, the listing firm and the selling firm will split the commission.

The arrangements for paying a buyer's agent's fee are not so clear-cut. There are three common methods of compensating a buyer's agent:

- a seller-paid fee,
- a buyer-paid fee, and
- a retainer.

The buyer and the buyer's agent may agree to one of these methods, or a combination of two or more methods.

SELLER-PAID FEE. Under the terms of most listing agreements, the buyer's agent will be paid by the seller, as a result of a commission split. The seller pays the commission to the listing agent, and the listing agent then splits the commission with the buyer's agent. This arrangement is based on a provision found in most listing agreements that entitles any cooperating agent who procures a buyer to receive the selling agent's portion of the commission, regardless of who that cooperating agent represents. (The source of the commission does not determine the identity of the agent's principal.)

> **EXAMPLE:** Seller Forbes lists his property with Agent Webster. He agrees to pay Webster a commission of 7% of the sales price. The listing agreement includes a clause that entitles any cooperating licensee who procures a buyer to be paid the selling agent's portion of the commission.
>
> Agent Lopez is representing Buyer Brown. Brown offers $100,000 for Forbes's house and Forbes accepts the offer. When the transaction closes, the $7,000 commission paid by Forbes is split between Webster and Lopez. Accepting a share of the commission paid by the seller does not affect Lopez's agency relationship with the buyer.

Since the commission split arrangement does not change the amount of the commission the seller is obligated to pay, sellers rarely object to paying the buyer's agent's fee in this way. Most buyer representation agreements provide that the buyer's agent will be paid by a commission split when the buyer purchases a home that is listed through a multiple listing service.

BUYER-PAID FEE. Buyer representation agreements may also provide for a buyer-paid fee. The fee may be based on an hourly rate, an arrangement that turns the agent into a consultant. Alternatively, a buyer's agent may charge a percentage fee, requiring the buyer to pay the agent a percentage of the purchase price

FIG. 1.3   BUYER REPRESENTATION AGREEMENT

Form 41A
Buyer's Agency Agreement
Rev. 7/10
Page 1 of 2

BUYER'S AGENCY AGREEMENT

©Copyright 2010
Northwest Multiple Listing Service
ALL RIGHTS RESERVED

This Buyer's Agency Agreement is made this _____ between 1

_____ ("Real Estate Firm" or "Firm") 2

and _____ ("Buyer"). 3

1. **AGENCY.** Firm appoints _____ ("Selling Broker") 4
   to represent Buyer. This Agreement creates an agency relationship with Selling Broker and any of Firm's brokers 5
   who supervise Selling Broker's performance as Buyer's agent ("Supervising Broker"). No other brokers affiliated 6
   with Firm are agents of Buyer, except to the extent that Firm, in its discretion, appoints other brokers to act on 7
   Buyer's behalf as and when needed. Buyer acknowledges receipt of the pamphlet entitled "The Law of Real 8
   Estate Agency." 9

2. **EXCLUSIVE OR NON-EXCLUSIVE.** This Agreement creates a ❑ sole and exclusive; ❑ non-exclusive (non- 10
   exclusive if not checked) agency relationship. 11

3. **AREA.** Selling Broker will search for real property for Buyer located in the following geographical areas: 12
   _____ 13
   _____ (unlimited if not filled in) ("Area"). 14

4. **FIRM'S LISTINGS/SELLING BROKER'S OWN LISTINGS/DUAL AGENCY.** If Selling Broker locates a property 15
   listed by one of Firm's brokers other than Selling Broker ("Listing Broker"), Buyer consents to any Supervising 16
   Broker, who also supervises Listing Broker, acting as a dual agent. Further, if Selling Broker locates a property 17
   listed by Selling Broker, Buyer consents to Selling Broker and Supervising Broker acting as dual agents. 18

5. **TERM OF AGREEMENT.** This Agreement will expire _____ (120 days from signing if not filled in) or by 19
   prior written notice by either party. Buyer shall be under no obligation to Firm except for those obligations existing 20
   at the time of termination. 21

6. **NO WARRANTIES OR REPRESENTATIONS.** Firm makes no warranties or representations regarding the value 22
   of or the suitability of any property for Buyer's purposes. Buyer agrees to be responsible for making all inspections 23
   and investigations necessary to satisfy Buyer as to the property's suitability and value. 24

7. **INSPECTIONS RECOMMENDED.** Firm recommends that any offer to purchase a property be conditioned on 25
   Buyer's inspection of the property and its improvements. Firm and Selling Broker have no expertise on these 26
   matters and Buyer is solely responsible for interviewing and selecting all inspectors. 27

8. **COMPENSATION.** Buyer shall pay Firm compensation as follows: 28
   _____ 29
   _____ 30
   _____ 31

   a. **Exclusive.** If the parties agree to an exclusive relationship in Paragraph 2 above and if Buyer shall, during the 32
      course of this Agreement, purchase a property located in the Area, then Buyer shall pay to Firm the 33
      compensation provided for herein. If Buyer shall, within six (6) months after the expiration or termination of 34
      this Agreement, purchase a property located in the Area that was first brought to the attention of Buyer by the 35
      efforts or actions of Firm, or through information secured directly or indirectly from or through Firm, then Buyer 36
      shall pay to Firm the compensation provided for herein. 37

   b. **Non-Exclusive.** If the parties agree to non-exclusive relationship in Paragraph 2 above and if Buyer shall, 38
      during the course of or within six (6) months after the expiration or termination of this Agreement, purchase a 39
      property that was first brought to the attention of Buyer by the efforts or actions of Firm, or through information 40
      secured directly or indirectly from or through Firm, then Buyer shall pay to Firm the compensation provided for 41
      herein. 42

BUYER: _____   BUYER: _____

Form 41A
Buyer's Agency Agreement
Rev. 7/10
Page 2 of 2

BUYER'S AGENCY AGREEMENT
Continued

   c. **MLS**. Firm will utilize a multiple listing service ("MLS") to locate properties and MLS rules may require the 43
seller to compensate Firm by apportioning a commission between the Listing Firm and Firm. Firm will disclose 44
any such commission or bonuses offered by the seller prior to preparing any offer. Buyer will be credited with 45
any commission or bonus so payable to Firm. In the event that said commission and any bonus is less than 46
the compensation provided in this Agreement, Buyer will pay the difference to Firm at the time of closing. In 47
the event that said commission and any bonus is equal to or greater than the compensation provided for by 48
this Agreement, no compensation is due to Firm herein. If any of Firm's brokers act as a dual agent, Firm 49
shall receive the listing and selling commission paid by the seller plus any additional compensation Firm may 50
have negotiated with the seller. All such compensation shall be credited toward the fee specified above. 51

9. **V.A. TRANSACTIONS.** Due to VA regulations, VA financed transactions shall be conditioned upon the full 52
commission being paid by the seller. 53

10. **NO DISTRESSED HOME CONVEYANCE.** Firm will not represent or assist Buyer in a transaction that is a 54
"Distressed Home Conveyance" as defined by Chapter 61.34 RCW unless otherwise agreed in writing. A 55
"Distressed Home Conveyance" is a transaction where a buyer purchases property from a "Distressed 56
Homeowner" (defined by Chapter 61.34 RCW), allows the Distressed Homeowner to continue to occupy the 57
property, and promises to convey the property back to the Distressed Homeowner or promises the Distressed 58
Homeowner an interest in, or portion of the proceeds from a resale of the property. 59

11. **ATTORNEYS' FEES.** In the event of suit concerning this Agreement, including claims pursuant to the Washington 60
Consumer Protection Act, the prevailing party is entitled to court costs and a reasonable attorney's fee. The 61
venue of any suit shall be the county in which the property is located. 62

12. **OTHER AGREEMENTS (none if not filled in).** 63

_____ 64

_____ 65

_____ 66

Buyer has read and approves this Agreement and hereby acknowledges receipt of a copy. 67

_____	_____	_____	68
Buyer	Date	Firm (Company)	
			69
_____	_____	_____	
Buyer	Date	By: (Selling Broker)	
			70
_____			
Address			71
_____			72
City, State, Zip			
			73
_____			
Phone	Fax		
_____			
E-mail Address			

of the property as a commission. A third possibility is a flat fee—a specified sum that is payable if the buyer purchases a property found by the agent.

Many buyer representation agreements provide that the buyer's agent will accept a commission split if one is available, but that the buyer will pay the fee if the purchased property was unlisted (for example, if the property was for sale by owner).

RETAINER. Some agents insist on a retainer—a fee paid upfront—before agreeing to a buyer agency relationship. The retainer is usually non-refundable, but will be credited against any hourly fee or commission that the buyer's agent becomes entitled to.

DUAL AGENCY

As you know, a dual agency relationship exists when an agent represents both the seller and the buyer in the same transaction. A dual agent owes agency duties to both principals. However, because the interests of the buyer and the seller nearly always conflict, it is difficult to represent them both without being disloyal to one or the other.

> **EXAMPLE:** Woodman represents both the buyer and the seller in a real estate transaction. The seller informs Woodman that she is in a big hurry to sell and will accept any reasonable offer. The buyer tells Woodman that he is very interested in the house and is willing to pay the full listing price. Should Woodman tell the buyer about the seller's eagerness to sell? Should Woodman tell the seller about the buyer's willingness to pay full price?

In fact, it is really impossible for a dual agent to fully represent both parties. Thus, instead of the duty of loyalty, Washington law imposes on a dual agent the duty to refrain from acting to the detriment of either party.

Because of this, a dual agent should explain to both of her principals that neither of them will receive full representation. Certain facts must necessarily be withheld from each party; the dual agent cannot divulge confidential information about one party to the other party. For instance, the dual agent will not tell the buyer the seller's bottom line, nor will the dual agent tell the seller how much the buyer is willing to pay.

IN-HOUSE TRANSACTIONS. Nowadays, the context in which a dual agency is most likely to occur is in an in-house transaction. It's called an in-house transaction when the listing agent and the selling agent both work for the same brokerage firm. In this situation, the listing agent represents only the seller, and the selling agent represents only the buyer, but their designated broker is a dual agent, representing both parties.

> **EXAMPLE:** Werner, who works for Black Realty, has shown Miller several houses. Finally, Werner shows Miller a house listed by Nagano, who also works for Black Realty. Miller decides to make an offer on the house. Werner will continue to represent Miller; Nagano will continue to represent the seller; and Black Realty's designated broker will be considered a dual agent.

This arrangement is sometimes referred to as a **split agency**. It may also be called a **designated**, **assigned**, or **appointed agency**, referring to the fact that one agent in the brokerage is assigned or appointed to represent one party, while another agent with the same firm represents the other party.

DUAL AGENCY DISCLOSURE. Before acting as a dual agent, a licensee must have the informed written consent of both parties to the transaction. Acting as a dual agent without full disclosure and written consent is a violation of Washington's real estate license law, and may lead to disciplinary action. In his disclosure, the licensee must state that he will be acting as a dual agent. The terms of his compensation must also be revealed. The parties will then sign the confirmation of the agency disclosure in the purchase and sale agreement.

Real estate licensees should be extra careful with their disclosures in the context of dual agency. Buyers and sellers, eager to get on with the business of buying and selling a home, may agree to a dual agency without really understanding what it means. They may accept the agent's explanation at face value and sign a boilerplate disclosure form without question. Later, one party may feel that his or her interests were neglected and that agency duties were breached. This kind of disappointment often leads to legal action.

NON-AGENCY

For some real estate licensees who wish to avoid confusion over agency status, non-agency can be the answer. In some transactions—usually commercial transactions—real estate licensees act only as facilitators and refuse to assume any agency duties at all.

In a non-agency transaction, the licensee involved is usually referred to either as a **facilitator** or as an **intermediary**. The non-agent does not owe agency duties to either party, but still owes each party the general duties that a licensee owes to any party. There is no way for the licensee to avoid the general duties of disclosure, reasonable care and skill, honesty and good faith, and so on. Licensees must also provide the parties with the real estate agency law pamphlet. Naturally, the licensee's status as a non-agent and her rights and responsibilities must be fully disclosed to both parties.

There are various forms available that can be used when a licensee wants to act as a non-agent in a transaction. These forms will typically spell out the licensee's status as a non-agent, and include blanks for filling in the termination date of the relationship and the method of compensation.

LICENSEES AND SUBAGENCY

Throughout this chapter, we have discussed agency relationships between real estate licensees and clients without making a distinction between designated brokers and affiliated sales agents. Strictly speaking, however, only a designated broker acting on behalf of a real estate firm can have an agency relationship with a buyer or a seller. A real estate sales agent is not really the client's agent; instead, she is the agent of her firm and a **subagent** of the client.

A subagent is "an agent of an agent." An agent may hire a subagent with or without the permission of the principal. Under general agency law, if the principal authorizes the agent to employ a subagent, the principal may be held vicariously liable (along with the agent) for the acts of the subagent. If the agent hires a subagent without the principal's permission or knowledge, then the principal usually will not be liable for the subagent's acts; only the agent will be liable.

In real estate transactions, Washington's real estate agency law has limited a principal's vicarious liability for a subagent's actions in the same way that it has limited it for an agent's actions. As we discussed earlier, a principal (a seller or a buyer) can only be held vicariously liable for the actions of a real estate agent if the principal participated in, authorized, or benefited from the agent's actions. The same rule applies to a seller or buyer's liability for a subagent's actions.

In contrast, a real estate firm is legally responsible for the actions of all its affiliated sales agents. If someone involved in a real estate transaction suffers a loss because of a real estate agent's error, omission, or misconduct, the firm may be held liable.

CHAPTER SUMMARY

1. Whether or not there is an agency relationship, a real estate licensee owes these general duties to any party the licensee renders real estate services to: reasonable care and skill, honesty and good faith, presenting all written communications, disclosure of material facts, accounting, providing a pamphlet on agency law, and disclosing any agency relationship.

2. When a real estate licensee enters into an agency relationship, he owes his principal not only the general duties owed to any party, but also agency duties. These agency duties are loyalty, disclosure of conflicts of interest, confidentiality, advising the principal to seek expert advice, and a good faith and continuous effort to fulfill the terms of the agency agreement.

3. A seller agency relationship is usually created with a listing agreement. A buyer agency relationship is created by written agreement or by law. Under the terms of Washington's real estate agency law, a licensee automatically represents the buyer she is working with, unless there is a written agreement to the contrary.

4. Washington law requires agents to disclose to all parties which party they represent in the transaction. A disclosure must be made to each party before that party signs an offer to purchase. The disclosure must be in writing, and it may be a separate document or simply a provision that's included in the purchase and sale agreement.

5. A real estate licensee can represent the buyer, the seller, or both parties to a real estate transaction. Alternatively, the licensee may choose to act as a non-agent and represent no one.

CHAPTER QUIZ

1. A house has been the site of gang activity in the past. A buyer asks the agent if any gangs have been known to operate in the neighborhood. The agent says nothing about the gang activity in the house. What duty has the agent breached?

    a. The duty to disclose material facts

    b. The duty of reasonable care and skill

    c. The duty of honesty and good faith

    d. None; the agent acted properly

2. A real estate agent must do which of the following in order to disclose all material facts?

    a. Physically inspect the property

    b. Disclose latent defects the licensee knows about

    c. Investigate the financial position of both parties

    d. Actively search for material facts

3. The duty of accounting does not include which of the following responsibilities?

    a. To disclose the terms of the listing agent's compensation

    b. To be able to account for all funds or valuables entrusted to the brokerage

    c. To avoid commingling trust funds with the firm's business funds

    d. To report to clients on the status of all trust funds regularly

4. A real estate agent is required to give a buyer or a seller a pamphlet on Washington real estate agency law before any of the following events occur, except:

    a. the buyer or seller waives any agency rights

    b. the agent shows the buyer her listed property during an open house

    c. the buyer or seller consents to a dual agency

    d. the buyer or seller signs an agency agreement

5. In which of the following situations should the agent advise the principal to seek expert advice?

    a. A buyer asks her agent to help her look into properties that aren't listed with the MLS

    b. A buyer asks his agent for advice about whether a house is structurally sound

    c. A seller asks her agent for advice on whether she should accept an offer below the listing price

    d. A seller asks his agent for advice on what improvements to make so his house will sell for a better price

6. Which of the following is a limit on the duty to make a good faith and continuous effort to fulfill the goals of the agency?

    a. The buyer's agent doesn't have to seek additional properties for the buyer when the buyer has made an offer on a property

    b. The seller's agent doesn't have to present an offer if the seller already has a higher offer for the same property

    c. The seller's agent doesn't have to seek additional offers when the property is subject to an existing sales contract

    d. The seller's agent doesn't have to disclose material facts she learns after the sales contract has been signed

7. Whether or not you have an agency relationship with a party to a transaction does not affect:

    a. whether that party may be held liable for your actions

    b. the extent of the duties you owe to that party

    c. whether your actions will be binding on that party

    d. whether you have a duty to investigate the financial condition of the other party

8. Proper agency disclosure may be made:

    a. anywhere in the purchase and sale agreement

    b. in a separate document

    c. in a separate paragraph in the purchase and sale agreement

    d. Both b and c

9. Which of the following is not one of the four basic types of real estate agency relationships in Washington?

    a. Net agency

    b. Non-agency

    c. Dual agency

    d. Buyer agency

10. Which of the following situations involves a change from one type of agency relationship to another?

    a. A non-agent explains to the seller and the buyer that she is acting only as a facilitator in the transaction

    b. The buyer's agent receives the selling agent's share of the commission, even though the commission was paid by the seller

    c. After showing a buyer a number of other houses, the real estate agent shows the buyer one of her own listings and discloses that she is acting as the seller's agent in connection with this property

    d. A buyer representation agreement provides that the buyer's agent will accept a commission split if available, but otherwise the buyer will pay a commission

ANSWER KEY

1. c. The agent is not required to disclose the gang activity as a material fact, but by not responding truthfully to a specific question, the agent has breached the duty of honesty and good faith.

2. b. An agent is required to disclose any material facts of which she is aware, but she is not required to independently investigate the parties or the property.

3. a. The duty of accounting requires a licensee to account for all trust funds he holds. The licensee must keep the parties updated as to the status of the trust funds and avoid commingling them with his personal or general business funds. (The listing agent's share of the brokerage commission does not have to be disclosed to the parties.)

4. b. A real estate agent is not required to give a buyer a pamphlet on Washington real estate agency law before simply showing a listed house to a buyer.

5. b. The structural soundness of a house is a question that exceeds the expertise expected of a real estate agent. The agent should advise the client to consult with an expert on the subject.

6. c. The duty to make a good faith and continuous effort to fulfill the goals of the agency does not require the agent to seek additional offers or alternative properties once the client has entered into a purchase and sale agreement.

7. d. An agency relationship with one of the parties to a transaction doesn't create a duty to investigate the other party's financial condition.

8. d. The required agency disclosure may be made in the purchase and sale agreement or in a separate document. If it is incorporated into the purchase and sale agreement, it must be in a separate paragraph.

9. a. The basic types of real estate agency relationships in Washington are seller agency, buyer agency, dual agency, and non-agency.

10. c. When a real estate licensee works with a buyer, she is acting as the buyer's agent. However, that rule does not apply if there is an agency agreement to the contrary, such as a listing agreement with the property seller. In the situation described, the licensee is the buyer's agent until she shows the buyer one of her own listings. At that point, in connection with that property, she becomes the seller's agent. Note that receiving compensation from the other party does not affect a licensee's agency relationship with her client.

LISTING AGREEMENTS

TYPES OF LISTING AGREEMENTS

- Open listings
- Exclusive agency listings
- Exclusive right to sell listings

ELEMENTS OF A LISTING AGREEMENT

- Basic legal requirements
- Provisions of a typical listing agreement form
- Modifying a listing agreement

SELLER DISCLOSURE STATEMENT

- Disclosure requirements
- Timing and effect of disclosure
- When circumstances change
- Limitations on liability under the disclosure law

LISTING VACANT LAND

INTRODUCTION

When you begin your real estate career, your designated broker or branch manager will encourage you to obtain listings as soon as possible. Listing agreements can generate a lot of business activity, both for you and your brokerage firm:

- When a new "For Sale" sign shows up in a neighborhood, potential buyers start calling the office for more information. Even if they are ultimately not interested in that particular property, they may be interested in another listed property.
- When you hold an open house for the listed property, you meet potential buyers and sellers that you may be able to do business with in the future.
- And when the listed property sells, you get a portion of the commission, no matter who finds the buyer. Plus, a "Sold!" banner across your yard sign is good advertising for both you and your brokerage firm.

Obtaining your first listing is a positive and financially rewarding experience. You will learn a variety of techniques to help you get listings; these methods are thoroughly explained in courses and books on sales techniques. However, using a listing agreement properly and fulfilling the legal obligations imposed by that agreement are just as important as obtaining listings. If you are not thoroughly familiar with the terms of your listing agreement form and able to use it correctly, your career may get off to a very rocky start.

This chapter describes three different types of listing agreements, the elements of a valid listing agreement, and the standard provisions that are found in most listing agreement forms. It also discusses the seller disclosure statement form, which you will typically ask the sellers to fill out when you take their listing. The chapter ends with a section on listing vacant land.

TYPES OF LISTING AGREEMENTS

A **listing agreement** is a written employment contract between a property owner and a real estate firm. The owner hires the firm to find a buyer (or a tenant) who is **ready, willing, and able** to buy (or lease) the property on the owner's terms.

There are three different types of listing agreements:

- the open listing,
- the exclusive agency listing, and
- the exclusive right to sell listing.

OPEN LISTING AGREEMENTS

Open listings are rarely used in residential transactions these days, but you still need to understand how they work. Under an open listing, the seller is obligated to pay your brokerage a commission only if you are the **procuring cause** of the sale. The procuring cause is the person who is primarily responsible for bringing about the agreement between the seller and a buyer. To be the procuring cause, you usually must have personally negotiated the offer from the ready, willing, and able buyer.

An open listing is rarely in the best interests of either the real estate agent or the seller. Here are some of the disadvantages of open listings:

- A seller may enter into open listings with as many real estate firms as he wants. Only the firm whose affiliated licensee makes the sale is entitled to a commission; the other firms and their sales agents are not compensated for their time and effort. (If the seller himself makes the sale, he does not have to pay a commission to any of the firms.)
- Since a listing agent has little assurance of earning a commission from an open listing, she may not put as much effort into marketing the property.
- If two agents who work for competing firms negotiate with the person who ends up buying the property, there may be a dispute over which agent was the procuring cause.

Because of these problems, open listings are generally used only when a seller is unwilling to execute an exclusive agency or exclusive right to sell listing. Many multiple listing services don't accept open listings.

EXCLUSIVE AGENCY LISTING AGREEMENTS

In an exclusive agency listing, the seller agrees to list with only one brokerage, but retains the right to sell the property herself without being obligated to pay the firm a commission. The firm is entitled to a commission if anyone other than the seller finds a buyer for the property, but not if the seller finds the buyer without the help of an agent.

Exclusive agency listings are uncommon in residential transactions because they increase the chance of a commission dispute between the seller and the firm as to who was the procuring cause of the sale.

FIG. 2.1   TYPES OF LISTING AGREEMENTS

OPEN LISTING
- SELLER MAY GIVE OPEN LISTINGS TO SEVERAL BROKERAGE FIRMS
- LISTING FIRM COMPENSATED ONLY IF PROCURING CAUSE

EXCLUSIVE AGENCY LISTING
- SELLER GIVES LISTING TO ONLY ONE BROKERAGE
- LISTING FIRM COMPENSATED IF ANY AGENT FINDS A BUYER
- NO COMPENSATION IF SELLER FINDS A BUYER

EXCLUSIVE RIGHT TO SELL LISTING
- SELLER GIVES LISTING TO ONLY ONE BROKERAGE
- LISTING FIRM COMPENSATED IF ANYONE FINDS A BUYER

EXCLUSIVE RIGHT TO SELL LISTING AGREEMENTS

In an exclusive right to sell listing, the seller agrees to list with only one brokerage firm, and that firm is entitled to a commission if the property sells during the listing term, regardless of who finds the buyer. Even if the seller makes the sale directly, without the help of an agent, the brokerage is still entitled to the commission.

Not surprisingly, the exclusive right to sell listing is the type preferred by most firms. It provides the most protection for the listing firm, and the potential for conflict with the seller over who was the procuring cause is limited. The licensees involved in the transaction might disagree about who's entitled to the selling agent's share of the commission, but the seller will have to pay the listing firm in any event.

Because of these advantages, the great majority of residential listing agreements are exclusive right to sell listings.

ELEMENTS OF A LISTING AGREEMENT

When you go to your first listing appointment, you will take along the listing agreement form used by your office. It will probably be a form provided by your local multiple listing service or Association of Realtors®. Brokerage firms rarely use their own individual listing forms, and you certainly won't be expected to come up with one yourself. (If you did, you would be guilty of the unauthorized practice of law.) However, it is still important to know the basic legal requirements for a listing agreement. Later in the chapter we will look at the specific provisions of a typical listing agreement form.

BASIC LEGAL REQUIREMENTS

Washington law has four requirements for an enforceable listing agreement. Every listing agreement must:

- identify the property to be sold,
- include a promise to compensate the brokerage firm,
- specify the compensation, and
- be in writing and signed by the seller.

IDENTIFY THE PROPERTY. The property must be clearly identified in the agreement. Of course, it's best to use a legal description. A street address is useful, but not adequate by itself. After you fill in the property's street address, you should fill in or attach the property's legal description as well. If you do not have the property's legal description with you when you are filling out the form, you may go ahead and have the seller sign the agreement and then add the legal description later. To be on the safe side, you should write "Legal description to be provided by agent at a later date" into the blank for the legal description. Then make sure you really do add the description later. You can get the property's legal description from a title insurance company or from the seller's deed.

PROMISE TO COMPENSATE THE BROKERAGE. A listing agreement must include the seller's promise to compensate the brokerage. The conditions of payment should be clearly stated. For example, the seller could promise to pay the brokerage when a ready, willing, and able buyer has been found, or not until a contract is signed, or not unless a sale actually closes.

FIXED COMPENSATION. Not only must the listing agreement include a promise to compensate the brokerage, it must also state the compensation as a fixed figure. The commission is usually stated as a specified percentage of the sales price, but it may be a fixed dollar amount instead.

The commission cannot be based on the seller's net requirements; net listings are not legal in Washington. In a **net listing**, the seller stipulates a certain net amount that she wants from the sale of the property. If the sales price exceeds that net figure, the firm is entitled to keep the excess as its compensation.

> **EXAMPLE:** Warshaw wants you to sell her home. She wants to get $135,000 from the sale. She says you can have anything over that. In other words, if you can sell the property for $140,000, you get a $5,000 commission. If you sell the property for $150,000, you get a $15,000 commission.
>
> You cannot accept Warshaw's offer. She must agree to pay you either a flat fee or a percentage of the sales price.

Net listings are illegal because they give unscrupulous agents an opportunity to take advantage of clients who don't know the true value of their property.

IN WRITING. Washington's statute of frauds requires all listing agreements to be in writing and signed by the seller. Without a written, signed listing agreement, the firm can't sue for the commission. Note, however, that the writing requirement doesn't mean that you must have a formal listing agreement. Some notes jotted on a piece of paper could be sufficient.

> **EXAMPLE:** George runs into his old friend, Brad. Brad wants to put his house up for sale, and he's delighted to discover that George is now a real estate agent working for Hanson Realty. He'd like to list his property with George right away.
>
> George doesn't have a listing agreement form with him, so he jots down the following on a piece of paper: "I will pay Hanson Realty 6% of the selling price when he finds a ready, willing, and able buyer for the only piece of property I own—Hillshire Orchards—in Yakima County." Brad signs the paper. This would probably be enforceable in Washington, as long as Brad is legally competent.

PROVISIONS OF A TYPICAL LISTING AGREEMENT FORM

Of course, printed listing agreement forms contain more information than would be included in a handwritten note. Let's take a look at the many provisions found in a typical listing form.

In Washington and most other states, there is no single standard listing agreement form. Various forms are available through multiple listing services, professional associations, and general publishers of legal forms. Although these forms tend to have many common elements, there may also be significant differences

FIG. 2.2 EXCLUSIVE RIGHT TO SELL LISTING AGREEMENT FORM

Form 1A
Exclusive Sale
Rev. 6/12
Page 1 of 2

EXCLUSIVE SALE AND LISTING AGREEMENT

©Copyright 2012
Northwest Multiple Listing Service
ALL RIGHTS RESERVED

_____ ("Seller") 1

hereby grants to _____ , ("Real Estate Firm" or "Firm") 2

from date hereof until midnight of _____ ("Listing Term"), the sole and exclusive right 3

to submit offers to purchase, and to receipt for deposits in connection therewith, the real property ("the Property") 4

commonly known as_____ 5

in the City of _____ , County of _____ , State of Washington, Zip _____ ; 6

to be listed at $_____ and legally described as: LOT_____ , BLOCK _____ , 7

DIVISION _____ , VOL _____ , PAGE _____ 8

_____ . 9

1. **DEFINITIONS.** For purposes of this Agreement: (a) "MLS" means the Northwest Multiple Listing Service; and (b) "sell" 10
includes a contract to sell; an exchange or contract to exchange; an option to purchase; and/or a lease with option to 11
purchase. 12

2. **AGENCY/DUAL AGENCY.** Seller authorizes Firm to appoint _____ 13
as Seller's Listing Broker. This Agreement creates an agency relationship with Listing Broker and any of Firm's brokers 14
who supervise Listing Broker's performance as Seller's agent ("Supervising Broker"). No other brokers affiliated with 15
Firm are agents of Seller, except to the extent that Firm, in its discretion, appoints other brokers to act on Seller's behalf 16
as and when needed. 17

If the Property is sold to a buyer represented by one of Firm's brokers other than Listing Broker ("Buyer's Broker"), 18
Seller consents to any Supervising Broker, who also supervises Buyer's Broker, acting as a dual agent. If the Property 19
is sold to a buyer who Listing Broker also represents, Seller consents to Listing Broker and Supervising Broker acting as 20
dual agents. Seller acknowledges receipt of the pamphlet entitled "The Law of Real Estate Agency." 21

If any of Firm's brokers act as a dual agent, Firm shall be entitled to the entire commission payable under this 22
Agreement plus any additional compensation Firm may have negotiated with the buyer. 23

3. **COMMISSION.** If (a) Firm procures a buyer on the terms in this Agreement, or on other terms acceptable to Seller; or 24
(b) Seller directly or indirectly or through any person or entity other than Firm, during the Listing Term hereof, sells the 25
Property; and Seller closes the sale of the Property or defaults under an agreement to sell the Property, Seller will pay 26
Firm a commission of (fill in one and strike the other) _____% of the sales price, or $ _____ 27
("Total Commission"). From the Total Commission, Firm will offer a cooperating member of MLS representing a buyer 28
("Selling Firm") a commission of (fill in one and strike the other) _____% of the sales price, or $ _____ . 29
Further, if Seller shall, within six months after the expiration of the Listing Term, sell the Property to any person to 30
whose attention it was brought through the signs, advertising or other action of Firm, or on information secured directly 31
or indirectly from or through Firm, during the Listing Term, Seller will pay Firm the above commission. Provided, that if 32
Seller pays a commission to a member of MLS or a cooperating MLS in conjunction with a sale, the amount of 33
commission payable to Firm shall be reduced by the amount paid to such other member(s). Provided further, that if 34
Seller cancels this Agreement without legal cause, Seller may be liable for damages incurred by Firm as a result of such 35
cancellation, regardless of whether Seller pays a commission to another MLS member. Selling Firm is an intended third 36
party beneficiary of this Agreement. 37

4. **SHORT SALE / NO DISTRESSED HOME CONVEYANCE.** If the proceeds from the sale of the Property are insufficient 38
to cover the Seller's costs at closing, Seller acknowledges that the decision by any beneficiary or mortgagee, or its 39
assignees, to release its interest in the Property, for less than the amount owed, does not automatically relieve Seller of 40
the obligation to pay any debt or costs remaining at closing, including fees such as Firm's commission. Firm will not 41
represent or assist Seller in a transaction that is a "Distressed Home Conveyance" as defined by Chapter 61.34 RCW 42
unless otherwise agreed in writing. A "Distressed Home Conveyance" is a transaction where a buyer purchases 43
property from a "Distressed Homeowner" (defined by Chapter 61.34 RCW), allows the Distressed Homeowner to 44
continue to occupy the property, and promises to convey the property back to the Distressed Homeowner or promises 45
the Distressed Homeowner an interest in, or portion of, the proceeds from a resale of the property. 46

_____   _____
Seller   Seller

EXCLUSIVE SALE AND LISTING AGREEMENT
Continued

5. **KEYBOX.** Firm is authorized to install a keybox on the Property. Such keybox may be opened by a master key held by 47
members of MLS and their brokers. A master key also may be held by affiliated third parties such as inspectors and 48
appraisers who cannot have access to the Property without Firm's prior approval which will not be given without Firm 49
first making reasonable efforts to obtain Seller's approval. 50

6. **SELLER'S WARRANTIES AND REPRESENTATIONS.** Seller warrants that Seller has the right to sell the Property on 51
the terms herein and that the Property information on the attached pages to this Agreement is correct. Further, Seller 52
represents that to the best of Seller's knowledge, there are no structures or boundary indicators that either encroach on 53
adjacent property or on the Property. Seller authorizes Firm to provide the information in this Agreement and the 54
attached pages to prospective buyers and to other cooperating members of MLS who do not represent the Seller and, 55
in some instances, may represent the buyer. Seller agrees to indemnify and hold Firm and other members of MLS 56
harmless in the event the foregoing warranties and representations are incorrect. 57

7. **CLOSING COSTS.** Seller shall furnish and pay for a buyer's policy of title insurance showing marketable title to the 58
Property. Seller shall pay real estate excise tax and one-half of any escrow fees or such portion of escrow fees and any 59
other fees or charges as provided by law in the case of a FHA or VA financed sale. Rent, taxes, interest, reserves, 60
assumed encumbrances, homeowner fees and insurance are to be prorated between Seller and the buyer as of the 61
date of closing. 62

8. **MULTIPLE LISTING SERVICE.** Firm shall submit this listing, including the Property information on the attached pages 63
and photographs of the Property (collectively, "Listing Data") to MLS. Seller authorizes Firm and MLS to publish the 64
Listing Data and distribute it to other members of MLS and their affiliates and third parties for public display and other 65
purposes. This authorization shall survive the termination of this Agreement. Firm is authorized to report the sale of the 66
Property (including price and all terms) to MLS and to its members, financial institutions, appraisers, and others related 67
to the sale. Firm may refer this listing to any other cooperating multiple listing service at Firm's discretion. Firm shall 68
cooperate with all other members of MLS, or of a multiple listing service to which this listing is referred, in working 69
toward the sale of the Property. Regardless of whether a cooperating MLS member is the agent of the buyer, Seller, 70
neither or both, such member shall be entitled to receive the selling firm's share of the commission. MLS is an intended 71
third party beneficiary of this agreement and will provide the Listing Data to its members and their affiliates and third 72
parties, without verification and without assuming any responsibility with respect to this agreement. 73

9. **DISCLAIMER/SELLER'S INSURANCE.** Neither Firm, MLS, nor any members of MLS or of any multiple listing 74
service to which this listing is referred shall be responsible for loss, theft, or damage of any nature or kind whatsoever to 75
the Property and/or to any personal property therein, including entry by the master key to the keybox and/or at open 76
houses. Seller is advised to notify Seller's insurance company that the Property is listed for sale and ascertain that the 77
Seller has adequate insurance coverage. If the Property is to be vacant during all or part of the Listing Term, Seller 78
should request that a "vacancy clause" be added to Seller's insurance policy. 79

10. **FIRM'S RIGHT TO MARKET THE PROPERTY.** Seller shall not commit any act which materially impairs 80
Firm's ability to market and sell the Property under the terms of this Agreement. In the event of breach of the foregoing, 81
Seller shall pay Firm a commission in the above amount, or at the above rate applied to the listing price herein, 82
whichever is applicable. Unless otherwise agreed in writing, Firm and other members of MLS shall be entitled to show 83
the Property at all reasonable times. Firm need not submit to Seller any offers to lease, rent, execute an option to 84
purchase, or enter into any agreement other than for immediate sale of the Property. 85

11. **SELLER DISCLOSURE STATEMENT.** Unless Seller is exempt under RCW 64.06, Seller shall provide to Firm 86
as soon as reasonably practicable a completed and signed "Seller Disclosure Statement" (Form 17 (Residential), Form 87
17C (Unimproved Residential), or Form 17 Commercial). Seller agrees to indemnify, defend and hold Firm harmless 88
from and against any and all claims that the information Seller provides on Form 17, Form 17C, or Form 17 Commercial 89
is inaccurate. 90

12. **DAMAGES IN THE EVENT OF BUYER'S BREACH.** In the event Seller retains earnest money as liquidated 91
damages on a buyer's breach, any costs advanced or committed by Firm on Seller's behalf shall be paid therefrom and 92
the balance divided equally between Seller and Firm. 93

13. **ATTORNEYS' FEES.** In the event either party employs an attorney to enforce any terms of this Agreement and 94
is successful, the other party agrees to pay reasonable attorneys' fees. In the event of trial, the successful party shall be 95
entitled to an award of attorneys' fees and expenses; the amount of the attorneys' fees and expenses shall be fixed by 96
the court. The venue of any suit shall be the county in which the Property is located. 97

DATED THIS _____ DAY OF_____, _____ . Are the undersigned the sole owner(s)? ❑ YES ❑ NO   98

FIRM (COMPANY)_____   SELLER: _____   99

BY: _____   SELLER: _____   100

between them. You must be sure to learn the provisions of the specific form used by your brokerage firm.

The following is a general discussion of provisions likely to be encountered in a typical form, but any given form might omit some of these provisions and include others not discussed here. As an example, an exclusive right to sell listing form prepared by the Northwest Multiple Listing Service is shown in Figure 2.2.

BROKERAGE AUTHORITY AND LISTING PERIOD. The first lines in a listing agreement form usually identify the brokerage firm, establish the firm's agency authority, and specify the date on which the listing period will expire.

BROKERAGE NAME. Even though the listing agreement form is filled out and signed by an affiliated licensee, the listing agreement is actually a contract between the seller and the brokerage. Remember, only a brokerage may directly provide brokerage services to the public.

AGENCY AUTHORITY. The listing agreement gives the brokerage the authority to "submit offers to purchase." The firm is not given authority to sell the property. It is up to the seller to accept an offer and transfer the property to the buyer.

> **EXAMPLE:** You take a listing on Sorenson's house. Wilson is very interested in purchasing the house. She makes an offer that meets all of Sorenson's criteria. You do not have the authority to accept this offer; you only have the authority to present the offer to Sorenson. Sorenson can choose whether or not to accept the offer.

Typically, the listing agreement also gives the brokerage firm the authority to accept earnest money deposits from prospective buyers on behalf of the seller.

AGENCY RELATIONSHIPS. The listing form shown in Figure 2.2 allows the designated broker to appoint a particular agent as the listing agent. Both parties agree that the listing agreement creates an agency relationship between the seller, the firm, and the named agent (and only the named agent). There is no agency relationship between the seller and any other affiliated licensees of the brokerage. Any licensee working for a cooperating firm who finds a buyer for the property will not be the seller's agent, and may be the buyer's agent.

The form then goes on to describe the circumstances under which a dual agency situation may arise—when the property is sold to a buyer represented by the same firm and/or the same listing agent. The seller gives her consent to this dual agency situation. The seller also acknowledges that a dual agent is not permitted to give advice to either party to the detriment of the other party or to disclose confidential information from or about the other party. (Dual agency is discussed in Chapter 1.)

LISTING PERIOD. The term of the listing is virtually always included in the agreement. A termination date is especially important in an exclusive listing agreement, since an exclusive listing essentially prevents the seller from hiring other agents. However, unlike many other states, Washington does not require an exclusive listing agreement to include a termination date. In Washington, a listing agreement with no termination date will end after a reasonable time.

Of course, a listing agreement may terminate before its termination date even without a sale of the property. This can happen in a number of different ways.

The seller and the listing firm may terminate the listing by mutual agreement at any time. Alternatively, the seller may **revoke** the listing agreement by firing the agent whenever he wishes. The revocation would constitute a breach of contract, and the seller might be liable for any damages suffered by the listing agent. In many cases, a seller who revokes a listing agreement can be held liable for the commission.

On the other hand, the listing agent can **renounce** the listing agreement. Like revocation, renunciation would constitute a breach of contract, in which case the agent could be liable for the seller's damages resulting from the breach.

A listing agreement generally terminates before it expires if the seller dies or becomes incompetent. And if the listing firm loses its license, that will cause the listing to terminate. However, a listing will not terminate if the designated broker or the licensee who took the listing loses his license. The firm can appoint another designated broker (with appropriate notice to the Department of Licensing), or the Department could appoint a temporary designated broker to close pending transactions. If the licensee who took the listing loses his license, the firm will appoint another licensee to handle the listing.

PROPERTY DESCRIPTION. As we discussed earlier, a listing agreement must include a full and accurate description of the property—preferably a legal description. You should photocopy the description on a separate piece of paper and attach it to the listing agreement as Attachment A. Many counties provide online access to property records, allowing you to copy and paste legal descriptions.

COMMISSION. A listing agreement form usually includes a blank in which to fill in the percentage or amount of the commission. Commissions must be negotiable between the seller and the brokerage firm; it is a violation of antitrust laws for firms to set uniform commission rates. (See Chapter 3 for a discussion of antitrust laws and how they affect real estate licensees.)

Typically, a listing agreement also explains how and when the commission is earned. An exclusive right to sell listing form might provide that the listing agent will earn a commission if any of these events occur:

1. during the listing period, the listing agent (or another agent in the MLS) secures a buyer who is willing to buy on the exact terms specified by the seller in the listing agreement or on other terms acceptable to the seller (i.e., a ready, willing, and able buyer);

2. the seller sells, exchanges, or enters into a contract to sell or exchange the property during the term of the listing agreement; or

3. the seller sells the property within a certain period (e.g., six months) after the expiration date of the listing agreement to anyone who first became aware of the property through any advertising or other marketing activities of the listing agent (or other agents in the MLS).

EXTENDER CLAUSE. Number three on the list above is an example of an extender clause (sometimes called a "safety" or "carryover" clause). Occasionally, behind the listing agent's back, a buyer and a seller agree to postpone entering into a contract until after the listing expires, to save the cost of the brokerage commission. An extender clause prevents this strategy from working (unless the buyer and seller are willing to wait a long time).

Extender clauses differ from one listing agreement form to another. Sometimes the obligation to pay a commission after the listing has expired is triggered only when the property is sold to a buyer that the agent actually negotiated with during the listing period.

EXAMPLE: You have listed Baker's property. The extender clause in your listing agreement applies only to buyers you've negotiated with.

One buyer, Abrams, is very interested in Baker's property. You present her offer to Baker and spend a few days trying to negotiate the terms of the sale. Finally, Abrams decides that she is not willing to raise her final offer by the extra $1,000 that Baker wants, and she walks away from the property. Another buyer, Thornwood, sees your "For Sale" sign posted on the property and calls you on the phone to ask some questions about the property. You have no further contact with Thornwood, who does not sound very interested in the property after all.

Suppose Abrams buys the property after your listing agreement with Baker expires. Since you actually negotiated with Abrams, your extender clause applies and Baker owes you a commission. On the other hand, if Thornwood were to purchase the property during the extension period, Baker would not owe you a commission. Since you never actually negotiated with Thornwood, the extender clause does not apply.

Some extender clauses are more broadly worded and require the seller to pay a commission if the property is sold within the extension period to anyone who learned about it in any way that could be traced to the listing firm or the MLS.

EXAMPLE: Under this type of extender clause, if Thornwood were to buy Baker's property during the extension period, Baker would still owe you a commission. Even though you never actually negotiated with Thornwood, he learned the property was for sale because of your "For Sale" sign and then contacted you to find out more about the property.

Some extender clauses provide safeguards for the seller. For example, you may be required to give the seller a list of all the potential buyers you negotiated with during the listing period. Or the extender clause might state that a commission will not be due if the property is listed with another real estate firm during the extension period. This protects the seller from becoming liable for two commissions. Some extender clauses state that, in these circumstances, if the commission owed to the second listing agent is less than that owed to the first listing agent, the first listing agent is entitled to the excess amount.

EXAMPLE: Your listing agreement with Baker expires and Baker immediately lists the property with a new agent. Your listing agreement specified a 6% commission; the new listing agreement calls for a 5% commission. Shortly afterwards, Abrams (the buyer you negotiated with before your listing expired) purchases the property. Under the extender clause in your listing agreement, Baker owes a 5% commission to the new listing agent, but he also owes you a 1% commission.

SHORT SALES AND DISTRESSED HOME CONVEYANCES. In a short sale, the proceeds from a property's sale aren't enough to repay the debt secured by the property; nevertheless, the lender agrees to accept the sale proceeds and release the borrower from the debt. (Short sales are also discussed in Chapter 10.) When a potential short sale is being listed, Washington law requires the listing agent to give a seller a written disclosure explaining that the lender's approval of a short sale won't necessarily relieve the seller of liability for costs owed at closing, including the brokerage commission. This disclosure may be included in the listing form itself.

The listing form should also include a provision in which the seller warrants that her home is not distressed—that is, the seller's residence isn't in foreclosure or in imminent danger of foreclosure (we discuss the Distressed Property Law in Chapter 3).

ACCESS AND KEYBOXES. Listing forms typically give you the right to enter the property at reasonable times, so you can show it to prospective buyers. And since MLS members will be acting as cooperating agents—helping to find a buyer—they need a way to gain access to the property as well. Keyboxes are the most common method of facilitating access to listed properties when the owners are not home. Thus, MLS listing forms usually include a provision authorizing the installation of a keybox on the property and permitting MLS agents to enter and show the home. It's common to include a disclaimer of liability for any loss of or damage to the seller's property that may occur because of misuse of a keybox.

BROKERAGE'S RIGHT TO MARKET PROPERTY. Under the terms of many listing agreement forms, the seller agrees not to interfere with the firm's right to market the property. For example, if the seller leases the property, grants an option on the property, or enters into any other agreement that might interfere with selling the property, she will be liable for the full commission. The listing form may also emphasize the right of the firm to show the property at all reasonable times.

CLOSING COSTS. The listing form is also likely to provide that the seller will pay for a title insurance policy and certain other closing costs, such as the excise tax and part of the escrow fees. Keep in mind that these provisions in the listing agreement do not create any obligation to potential buyers. These are promises the seller makes to the brokerage, and failure to fulfill them can lead to liability only for the commission, not to any liability toward a buyer.

SELLER'S WARRANTIES. Most listing agreement forms include some warranties by the seller, which may include:

- a warranty stating that the seller has the right to sell the property on the terms stated in the listing agreement;
- a warranty stating that the information about the property included in the listing is accurate; and
- a warranty stating that there are no encroachments against the property and/or that the property complies with the applicable zoning regulations.

There is usually also a "hold harmless" clause to protect the brokerage. This clause states that the seller takes responsibility for the information given and will indemnify the firm against any losses caused by errors or omissions.

> **EXAMPLE:** You have listed Carr's property. You are unaware of the fact that the roof leaks, and the seller does not include this information in the listing agreement. The Bolts purchase the property, and when they discover the leaky roof, they sue both Carr and you. Since you relied on the information in the listing agreement and had no reason to doubt it, Carr is obligated to indemnify you against any losses you may suffer because of his omission.

MULTIPLE LISTING SERVICE PROVISION. Most listing agreements include a provision alerting the seller to the fact that you will be submitting the listing to your local multiple listing service. It reminds the seller that the information in the listing is not confidential—it will be circulated among the members of the MLS—and that the MLS assumes no responsibility for the accuracy of the information.

The MLS provision usually explains the relationship of the MLS members to the seller. Typically, listing agreements state that MLS members are considered "cooperating agents" and may act as the agent of the buyer, as the agent of the seller, or in some other capacity as agreed to by the parties. No matter who the selling agent represents, she will be entitled to the selling office's share of the commission.

DEPOSIT AS DAMAGES. Most purchase and sale agreements provide that if the buyer breaches the contract, the seller will be entitled to keep the earnest money deposit as liquidated damages. Listing agreements commonly provide that under those circumstances the seller will first use the deposit to reimburse the listing firm for any costs incurred; the seller and the firm will split the remainder of the deposit, with half going to the firm as compensation for their services.

ATTORNEYS' FEES. Many listing forms provide that if either the brokerage or the seller has to resort to a lawsuit to enforce the contract, the winner's attorneys' fees must be paid by the other party.

LISTING INFORMATION. Listing forms used by multiple listing services include one or more pages for information about the property, such as the listing input sheet shown in Figure 2.3. The purpose of a listing input sheet is to generate detailed information about the property and the listing that will be distributed on the MLS website. Much of the information is coded to make computer input easier.

All of the following basic information is typically required on a listing input sheet:

- property address,
- location of the property (according to a coded MLS map),
- architectural style of the home,
- listing price,
- identification of the listing agent,
- expiration date of the listing,
- age of the home,
- number of bedrooms and bathrooms,
- county tax ID number,
- selling agent commission,
- name of the occupant, and
- name and phone number of the owner.

The rest of the input sheet has spaces to fill in or boxes to check off to describe a wide variety of property features and amenities. There is also a place for information about any existing encumbrances and the annual property taxes.

SIGNATURES. A listing agreement should be signed by both parties, the listing firm and the seller. When you prepare a listing agreement form, you will sign on behalf of your firm. Write your firm's name (as licensed) on the line labeled "Firm (company)" and sign your own name on the "By" line underneath.

If more than one person owns the property, make sure all of them sign the form.

EXAMPLE: You are preparing a listing agreement for property owned by the Mastersons, a married couple. Unless both the husband and the wife sign the listing agreement form, the contract might turn out to be unenforceable.

FIG. 2.3 LISTING INPUT SHEET

NWMLS Form 1 Rev. 10/11
Copyright 2011
Northwest Multiple Listing Service
All Rights Reserved

RESIDENTIAL Exclusive Listing Agreement (page 1 of 3)
LISTING INPUT SHEET

PROPERTY 1
TYPE

ADDRESS

• Indicates Required information   ( ) Indicates Maximum Choice   *Indicates "Yes" By Default   **LISTING #**

• County   • City   • **ZIP** Code   + 4

• Area   • Community/District

Direction: ☐ N ☐ S ☐ E ☐ W ☐ NE ☐ NW ☐ SE ☐ SW

• Street # (HSN)   Modifier   • Street Name

Suffix   Post Direction
☐ Av Ct ☐ Blvd ☐ Ct ☐ Dr Ct ☐ Lane ☐ Place ☐ St Ct ☐ Terr   ☐ N ☐ S ☐ E ☐ W   Unit #
☐ Ave ☐ Cir ☐ Ct Av ☐ Hwy ☐ Loop ☐ Road ☐ St Dr ☐ Trail   ☐ NE ☐ NW ☐ SE ☐ SW
☐ Ave Pl ☐ Crt St ☐ Dr ☐ Junction ☐ Pkwy ☐ Street ☐ St Pl ☐ Way ☐ KPN ☐ KPS

LISTING

$
• Listing Price   • Listing Date   • Expiration Date   • Tax ID#   • Preliminary Title Ordered ☐ Yes ☐ No

LOCATION

Lot Number   Block   Plat/Subdivision/Building Name

• **MAP BOOK**
☐ Thomas ☐ RR-Jeff ☐ RR-Thurs ☐ RR-Clallam ☐ R A-Clark ☐ P-Grant ☐ P-Yakima ☐ Unknown   • Map Page   • Top Map Coord.   • Side Map Coord.
☐ RR-Kitsap ☐ RR-Mason ☐ RR-Lewis ☐ RR-Grays ☐ Totem ☐ P-Kittitas ☐ Yellow Pgs

PROPERTY INFORMATION

• Prohibit Blogging   • Allow Automated Valuation   • Show Map Link   • Internet Advertising   • Show Address to Public
☐ *Yes ☐ No   ☐ *Yes ☐ No   ☐ *Yes ☐ No   ☐ *Yes ☐ No   ☐ Yes ☐ No

• SOC (Selling Office Com.)   Selling Office Commission Comments (40 characters maximum)

• Year Built   • ASF - Total (Square   Lot Size (Square Feet)   Virtual Tour URL (Please included http://)

BROKER INFORMATION

• LAG   Broker Name and Phone   Listing Firm - ID#   Firm Name and Phone
Listing Broker ID#

Co Broker - ID#   CO Broker Name and Phone   Co Firm - ID#   Co Firm Name and Phone

LISTING INFORMATION

• Possession (3)   • Showing Information (10)
☐ Closing   ☐ Appointment   ☐ MLS Keybox   ☐ Power Off   • Senior Exemption
☐ Negotiable   ☐ Call Listing Office ☐ Other Keybox ☐ Renter-Call First $ ☐ *Yes ☐ No
☐ See Remarks   ☐ Day Sleeper   ☐ Owner-Call First ☐ Security System   • Tax Year   • Annual Taxes
☐ Sub. Tenant's Rights ☐ Gate Code Needed ☐ Pet in House ☐ See Remarks
                                                         ☐ Vacant

• Potential Terms (10)   Right of First Refusal ☐ Yes ☐ No   • Form 17 (1)
☐ Assumable   ☐ Farm Home Loan ☐ Owner Finance ☐ State Bond   ☐ Exempt
☐ Cash Out   ☐ FHA   ☐ Rehab Loan   ☐ USDA $ $ ☐ Not Provided
☐ Conventional ☐ Lease/Purchase ☐ See Remarks   ☐ VA   Monthly Rent Monthly HO Dues ☐ Provided

SCHOOL & OWNER INFO.

• School District   • Elementary School   Junior High/Middle School   Senior High School
(See Code List)

• Owner's Name   • Owner's Phone   • Occupant Type   • Occupant's Name
                                      (Owner/Presale/Tenant /Vacant)

• Phone to Show   • Owner's City and State   • 3rd Party Approval Required (2)   • Bank Owned/REO
                                                 ☐ None   ☐ Short Sale   ☐ Yes ☐ No
                                                 ☐ Other - See Remarks

INITIALS:
_____ Seller   _____ Date   _____ Seller   _____ Date   _____ Broker   _____ Date

NWMLS Form 1 Rev. 10/11
Copyright 2011
Northwest Multiple Listing Service
All Rights Reserved

RESIDENTIAL Exclusive Listing Agreement (page 2 of 3)
LISTING INPUT SHEET

PROPERTY **1**
TYPE

SITE INFORMATION

Listing Address: _____ **LAG #** _____

Lot Dimensions _____

Waterfront Footage (Feet) _____

Pool (1)
- ☐ Above Ground
- ☐ Community
- ☐ Indoor
- ☐ In-Ground

Zoning Code _____

Zoning Jurisdiction (1)
- ☐ City
- ☐ County
- ☐ See Remarks

Lot Topog./Veg. (7)
- ☐ Brush
- ☐ Dune
- ☐ Equestrian
- ☐ Fruit Trees
- ☐ Garden Sp.
- ☐ Level
- ☐ Partial Slope
- ☐ Pasture
- ☐ Rolling
- ☐ Sloped
- ☐ Steep Slope
- ☐ Terraces
- ☐ Wooded

View (6)
- ☐ Bay
- ☐ Canal
- ☐ City
- ☐ Golf Course
- ☐ Jetty
- ☐ Lake
- ☐ Mountain
- ☐ Ocean
- ☐ Partial
- ☐ River
- ☐ See Remarks
- ☐ Sound
- ☐ Strait
- ☐ Territorial

Waterfront (5)
- ☐ Bank-High
- ☐ Bank-Low
- ☐ Bank Medium
- ☐ Bay
- ☐ Bulkhead
- ☐ Canal
- ☐ Creek
- ☐ Jetty
- ☐ Lake
- ☐ No Bank
- ☐ Ocean
- ☐ River
- ☐ Saltwater
- ☐ Sound
- ☐ Strait
- ☐ Tideland Rights

Site Features (14)
- ☐ Arena-Indoor
- ☐ Arena-Outdoor
- ☐ Athletic Court
- ☐ Barn
- ☐ Boat House
- ☐ Cabana/Gazebo
- ☐ Cable TV
- ☐ Deck
- ☐ Disabled Access
- ☐ Dock
- ☐ Dog Run
- ☐ Fenced-Fully
- ☐ Fenced-Partially
- ☐ Gas Available
- ☐ Gated Entry
- ☐ Green House
- ☐ High Speed Internet
- ☐ Hot Tub/Spa
- ☐ Moorage
- ☐ Outbuildings
- ☐ Patio
- ☐ Propane
- ☐ RV Parking
- ☐ Shop
- ☐ Sprinkler
- ☐ Stable

Lot Details (7)
- ☐ Alley
- ☐ Corner Lot
- ☐ Cul-de-sac
- ☐ Curbs
- ☐ Dead End St.
- ☐ Drought Res Landscpe
- ☐ Hg. Voltage Line
- ☐ Open Space
- ☐ Paved Street
- ☐ Secluded
- ☐ Sidewalk
- ☐ Value in Land

BUILDING INFORMATION

• Sewer (2)
- ☐ Available
- ☐ None
- ☐ Septic
- ☐ Sewer Connected

Basement (3)
- ☐ Daylight
- ☐ Fully Finished
- ☐ None
- ☐ Partially Finished
- ☐ Roughed In
- ☐ Unfinished

• Parking Type (4)
- ☐ Carport-Attached
- ☐ Carport-Detached
- ☐ Garage-Attached
- ☐ Garage-Detached
- ☐ None
- ☐ Off Street

Aprvd # of Bedrooms (septic) _____

• Total Covered Parking _____

Builder _____

New Construction
- ☐ Completed
- ☐ Presale
- ☐ Under Construction

• Building Information (3)
- ☐ Addl. Dwelling
- ☐ Built on Lot
- ☐ Manufd. Home
- ☐ Modular
- ☐ Planned Unit Dev
- ☐ Zero Lot Line

• Style Code _____

Manufactured Home Model Name _____

Manufactured Home Serial No. _____

Manufactured Home Manufacturer _____

Environmental Cert (5)
- ☐ Built Green
- ☐ ENERGY STAR
- ☐ LEED
- ☐ Other - See Remarks
- ☐ Third Party Verif.

Foundation (3)
- ☐ Concrete Block
- ☐ Concrete Ribbon
- ☐ Post & Block
- ☐ Post & Pillar
- ☐ Poured Concrete
- ☐ See Remarks
- ☐ Slab
- ☐ Tie down

Building Condition (1)
- ☐ Average
- ☐ Fair
- ☐ Fixer
- ☐ Good
- ☐ Remodeled
- ☐ Restored
- ☐ Under Construction
- ☐ Very Good

• Roof (3)
- ☐ Built-up
- ☐ Cedar Shake
- ☐ Composition
- ☐ Flat
- ☐ Metal
- ☐ See Remarks
- ☐ Tile
- ☐ Torch Down

• Exterior (4)
- ☐ Brick
- ☐ Cement Planked
- ☐ Cement/Concrete
- ☐ Log
- ☐ Metal/Vinyl
- ☐ See Remarks
- ☐ Stone
- ☐ Stucco
- ☐ Wood
- ☐ Wood Products

Architecture (1)
- ☐ A-Frame/Dome
- ☐ Cabin
- ☐ Cape Cod
- ☐ Colonial
- ☐ Contemporary
- ☐ Craftsman
- ☐ Modern
- ☐ NW Contemporary
- ☐ See Remarks
- ☐ Spanish/SW
- ☐ Traditional
- ☐ Tudor
- ☐ Victorian

INTERIOR FEATURES

(Approximate Square Footage Excluding Garage)

Finished _____

Unfinished _____

• Square Footage Source _____

Total Number of Fireplaces _____

Leased Equipment _____

Water Heater Type _____

Water Heater Location _____

• Energy Source (4)
- ☐ Electric
- ☐ Natural Gas
- ☐ Oil
- ☐ Pellet
- ☐ Propane
- ☐ See Remarks
- ☐ Solar
- ☐ Wood

• Heating/Cooling (4)
- ☐ Baseboard
- ☐ Central A/C
- ☐ Forced Air
- ☐ Heat Pump
- ☐ High Efficiency
- ☐ Insert
- ☐ None
- ☐ Other-See Remarks
- ☐ Radiant
- ☐ Radiator
- ☐ Stove/Free Standing
- ☐ Wall

Floor Covering (5)
- ☐ Bamboo/Cork
- ☐ Ceramic Tile
- ☐ Concrete
- ☐ Fir/Softwood
- ☐ Hardwood
- ☐ Laminate
- ☐ Other Renewable
- ☐ See Remarks
- ☐ Slate
- ☐ Vinyl
- ☐ Wall to Wall Carpet

Interior Features (16)
- ☐ 2nd Kitchen
- ☐ 2nd Mstr BR
- ☐ Bath Off Master
- ☐ Built-in Vacuum
- ☐ Ceiling Fan(s)
- ☐ Dbl Pane/Strm Windw
- ☐ Dining Room
- ☐ Disabled Access
- ☐ FP in Mstr BR
- ☐ French Doors
- ☐ High Tech Cabling
- ☐ Hot Tub/Spa
- ☐ Jetted Tub
- ☐ Loft
- ☐ Sauna
- ☐ Security System
- ☐ Skylights
- ☐ Solarium/Atrium
- ☐ Vaulted Ceilings
- ☐ Walk-in Pantry
- ☐ Walk-in Closet
- ☐ Wet Bar
- ☐ Wine Cellar
- ☐ Wired for Generator

Appliances That Stay (10)
- ☐ Dishwasher
- ☐ Double Oven
- ☐ Dryer
- ☐ Garbage Disposal
- ☐ Microwave
- ☐ Range/Oven
- ☐ Refrigerator
- ☐ See Remarks
- ☐ Trash Compactor
- ☐ Washer

INITIALS: _____

| Seller | Date | Seller | Date | Broker | Date |

NWMLS Form 1 Rev. 10/11
Copyright 2011
Northwest Multiple Listing Service
All Rights Reserved

RESIDENTIAL Exclusive Listing Agreement (page 3 of 3)
LISTING INPUT SHEET

PROPERTY TYPE **1**

UTILITY/COMMUNITY   **Listing Address:**   **LAG #**

Community Features (7)
☐ Age Restriction ☐ Boat Launch ☐ Club House ☐ Pvt. Beach Access
☐ Airfield ☐ CCRs ☐ Golf Course

• **Water Source (3)**
☐ Community ☐ Private ☐ See Remarks ☐ Shares
☐ Individual Well ☐ Public ☐ Shared Well

Water Company _____   **Power Company** _____   **Sewer Company** _____

Bus Line Nearby _____
☐ Yes ☐ No   **Bus Route Number**

ROOM LOCATION

Level (1) U for Upper M for Main L for Lower S for Split G for Garage

Entry	U	M	L	S	**Kit w/o Eating Space**	U	M	L	**Extra Fin. Room**	U	M	L	G
Living Room	U	M	L		**Master Bedroom**	U	M	L	**Rec Room**	U	M	L	
Dining Room	U	M	L		**Bonus Room**	U	M	L	**Family Room**	U	M	L	
Kit with Eating Space	U	M	L		**Den/Office**	U	M	L					

No. of Bedrooms U____ M____ L____   **Utility Room** U____ M____ L____ G____

No. of Full Baths U____ M____ L____ G____   **Approved Accessory Dwelling Unit** U____ M____ L____

No. of ¾ Baths U____ M____ L____ G____

No. of ½ Baths U____ M____ L____ G____

REMARKS

Marketing Remarks. CAUTION! The comments you make in the following lines are limited to descriptions of the land and improvements only. These remarks will appear in the client handouts and websites. (500)

_____
_____
_____
_____
_____
_____
_____
_____

Confidential Broker-Only Remarks. Comments in this category are for broker's use only. (250)

_____
_____
_____

• **Driving Directions to Property** (200)

_____
_____
_____
_____

INITIALS: _____   _____   _____   _____   _____   _____
         Seller   Date   Seller   Date   Broker   Date

In some cases, the sellers are unsure of the names of all the owners. For example, this might happen if the property was inherited by several people, or if it is owned by a partnership. If the sellers seem at all uncertain, or if you simply want to double-check the ownership, you have three options:

1. get a copy of the deed or other title instrument from the seller,
2. check with a title company, or
3. check the county's tax records.

RECEIPT OF COPY. You are required by law to give a copy of any document you prepare to the parties at the time of signature. So a listing agreement form often includes the seller's acknowledgment of receipt of a copy of the agreement.

MODIFYING A LISTING AGREEMENT

Once a listing agreement (or any contract) has been signed, it can be modified only with the written consent of all of the parties.

> **EXAMPLE:** You and the Mastersons signed a listing agreement. Two days later, all of you decide to change the listing's expiration date. You've agreed that a 90-day listing would be more appropriate than a 60-day listing. So you cross out the old expiration date on the form and write in a new expiration date. To make this change legally effective, you must write your initials and the date beside the change, and both of the Mastersons must do the same.

In some cases it is acceptable to modify simple terms in a listing agreement by crossing out what was filled in and replacing it with new information (as long as both parties initial and date the change, as in the example above). However, it's a better practice to use an amendment form specifically designed for changing the terms of a listing agreement, such as the form shown in Figure 2.4. Of course, the amendment form must also be signed and dated by all parties to the original agreement.

SELLER DISCLOSURE STATEMENT

Some listing agreements include a clause that describes the seller's obligation to fill out a seller disclosure statement. Although the seller does not have to give the disclosure statement to the buyer until a purchase and sale agreement has

FIG. 2.4   LISTING AMENDMENT FORM

Form 18
Amendment to Exclusive Listing Agreement
Rev. 7/10
Page 1 of 1

AMENDMENT TO EXCLUSIVE LISTING AGREEMENT

Property Address: _____ 1

_____ 2

Seller: _____ 3

Listing No.: _____   Listed Price: $ _____ 4

Listing Firm: _____   Office No.: _____ 5

This amends the Exclusive Listing Agreement ("Agreement") dated _____ , 6

between _____ ("Seller") 7

and, _____ ("Firm") 8

concerning the property commonly known as _____ , 9

in the City of _____, County of _____, State of WA, Zip _____ . 10

SELLER AND FIRM AGREE AS FOLLOWS: 11

❏   **Price Change.** The listing price is changed to $ _____ . 12

❏   **Agreement Extended.** The Agreement is extended until midnight of _____ . 13
    If the Agreement expired prior to the parties' execution of this Amendment, the Agreement (and any prior 14
    Amendments thereto) are incorporated herein by this reference and this Amendment shall constitute a new 15
    Exclusive Listing Agreement.   16

❏   **Other:**   17

18

19

20

21

ALL OTHER TERMS AND CONDITIONS of the Agreement remain unchanged.   22

DATED THIS _____ DAY OF _____ , _____   23

FIRM (COMPANY)_____   SELLER _____   24

BY_____   SELLER _____   25

been signed, it's customary to have the seller fill it out and give it to the listing agent as soon as possible.

DISCLOSURE REQUIREMENTS

Washington requires sellers of residential property to give the buyer a disclosure statement when a purchase and sale agreement is signed. For the purposes of the disclosure law, a residential transaction is any transaction involving a dwelling with up to four units. Though certain types of transactions are exempt from the law, it generally applies to multifamily dwellings (with up to four units), new construction, properties for sale by owner, mobile homes sold with real property, and some condominium and timeshare sales.

As a real estate agent, you are not responsible for filling out the disclosure form; the seller is, and you should not do it for the seller. However, you must be familiar with the legal requirements so that you can explain them to the seller.

In the disclosure form, the seller is required to share her knowledge about the condition of the property, including the condition of the buildings and utilities, the existence of easements or other encumbrances, and other material information. A copy of the seller disclosure statement form is shown in Figure 2.5. The content of the form is prescribed by statute.

The disclosure form begins with instructions to the seller, along with a notice to the buyer explaining the form and the buyer's legal rights (which we'll discuss shortly). The part of the form that presents questions about the property is broken down into the following sections:

1. **Title.** This section asks questions about the seller's authority to sell the property; encumbrances that affect the title; easements, rights-of-way, boundary disputes, encroachments, CC&Rs, or other restrictions that affect use of the property; and any other elements (such as a written maintenance agreement, survey project, or zoning violation) that might affect title or use.
2. **Water.** The seller must disclose the source and condition of the household water supply, any water rights that go along with the property, and the condition of the sprinkler system.
3. **Sewer/on-site sewage system.** The form asks for information about the property's sewer or septic tank system, including what type of sewage disposal system is used. If it's an on-site system, there are questions to

FIG. 2.5   SELLER DISCLOSURE STATEMENT

Form 17 Seller Disclosure Statement Rev. 6/12 Page 1 of 5	**SELLER DISCLOSURE STATEMENT †** **IMPROVED PROPERTY**	©Copyright 2012 Northwest Multiple Listing Service ALL RIGHTS RESERVED

SELLER: _____ 1

† To be used in transfers of improved residential real property, including residential dwellings up to four units, new construction, condominiums 2
not subject to a public offering statement, certain timeshares, and manufactured and mobile homes. See RCW Chapter 64.06 and Section 3
43.22.432 for further explanations. 4

INSTRUCTIONS TO THE SELLER 5

Please complete the following form. Do not leave any spaces blank. If the question clearly does not apply to the property write "NA." If the 6
answer is "yes" to any asterisked (*) item(s), please explain on attached sheets. Please refer to the line number(s) of the question(s) when you 7
provide your explanation(s). For your protection you must date and initial each page of this disclosure statement and each attachment. Delivery 8
of the disclosure statement must occur not later than five (5) business days, unless otherwise agreed, after mutual acceptance of a written 9
purchase and sale agreement between Buyer and Seller. 10

NOTICE TO THE BUYER 11

THE FOLLOWING DISCLOSURES ARE MADE BY THE SELLER ABOUT THE CONDITION OF THE PROPERTY LOCATED AT 12
_____, 13
CITY _____, COUNTY _____ ("THE PROPERTY")14
OR AS LEGALLY DESCRIBED ON THE ATTACHED EXHIBIT A. SELLER MAKES THE FOLLOWING DISCLOSURES OF EXISTING 15
MATERIAL FACTS OR MATERIAL DEFECTS TO BUYER BASED ON SELLER'S ACTUAL KNOWLEDGE OF THE PROPERTY AT 16
THE TIME SELLER COMPLETES THIS DISCLOSURE STATEMENT. UNLESS YOU AND SELLER OTHERWISE AGREE IN 17
WRITING, YOU HAVE THREE (3) BUSINESS DAYS FROM THE DAY SELLER OR SELLER'S AGENT DELIVERS THIS 18
DISCLOSURE STATEMENT TO YOU TO RESCIND THE AGREEMENT BY DELIVERING A SEPARATELY SIGNED WRITTEN 19
STATEMENT OF RESCISSION TO SELLER OR SELLER'S AGENT. IF THE SELLER DOES NOT GIVE YOU A COMPLETED 20
DISCLOSURE STATEMENT, THEN YOU MAY WAIVE THE RIGHT TO RESCIND PRIOR TO OR AFTER THE TIME YOU ENTER 21
INTO A PURCHASE AND SALE AGREEMENT. 22

     THE FOLLOWING ARE DISCLOSURES MADE BY SELLER AND ARE NOT THE REPRESENTATIONS OF ANY REAL ESTATE 23
LICENSEE OR OTHER PARTY. THIS INFORMATION IS FOR DISCLOSURE ONLY AND IS NOT INTENDED TO BE A PART OF 24
ANY WRITTEN AGREEMENT BETWEEN BUYER AND SELLER. 25

     FOR A MORE COMPREHENSIVE EXAMINATION OF THE SPECIFIC CONDITION OF THIS PROPERTY YOU ARE ADVISED TO 26
OBTAIN AND PAY FOR THE SERVICES OF QUALIFIED EXPERTS TO INSPECT THE PROPERTY, WHICH MAY INCLUDE, WITHOUT 27
LIMITATION, ARCHITECTS, ENGINEERS, LAND SURVEYORS, PLUMBERS, ELECTRICIANS, ROOFERS, BUILDING INSPECTORS, ON- 28
SITE WASTEWATER TREATMENT INSPECTORS, OR STRUCTURAL PEST INSPECTORS. THE PROSPECTIVE BUYER AND SELLER 29
MAY WISH TO OBTAIN PROFESSIONAL ADVICE OR INSPECTIONS OF THE PROPERTY OR TO PROVIDE APPROPRIATE 30
PROVISIONS IN A CONTRACT BETWEEN THEM WITH RESPECT TO ANY ADVICE, INSPECTION, DEFECTS OR WARRANTIES. 31

Seller ❑ is/ ❑ is not occupying the property. 32

I.   SELLER'S DISCLOSURES: 33

    * If you answer "Yes" to a question with an asterisk (*), please explain your answer and attach documents, if available and not otherwise 34
publicly recorded. If necessary, use an attached sheet. 35

		YES	NO	DON'T KNOW	
1.	**TITLE**				36 / 37
A.	Do you have legal authority to sell the property? If no, please explain. .... ❑		❑	❑	38
*B.	Is title to the property subject to any of the following?				39
	(1) First right of refusal .... ❑		❑	❑	40
	(2) Option .... ❑		❑	❑	41
	(3) Lease or rental agreement .... ❑		❑	❑	42
	(4) Life estate? .... ❑		❑	❑	43
*C.	Are there any encroachments, boundary agreements, or boundary disputes? .... ❑		❑	❑	44
*D.	Is there a private road or easement agreement for access to the property? .... ❑		❑	❑	45
*E.	Are there any rights-of-way, easements, or access limitations that may affect the				46
	Buyer's use of the property? .... ❑		❑	❑	47
*F.	Are there any written agreements for joint maintenance of an easement or right-of-way? .... ❑		❑	❑	48
*G.	Is there any study, survey project, or notice that would adversely affect the property? .... ❑		❑	❑	49
*H.	Are there any pending or existing assessments against the property? .... ❑		❑	❑	50
*I.	Are there any zoning violations, nonconforming uses, or any unusual restrictions on the				51
	property that would affect future construction or remodeling? .... ❑		❑	❑	52
*J.	Is there a boundary survey for the property? .... ❑		❑	❑	53
*K.	Are there any covenants, conditions, or restrictions recorded against the property? .... ❑		❑	❑	54

PLEASE NOTE: Covenants, conditions, and restrictions which purport to forbid or restrict the conveyance, encumbrance, occupancy, or 55
lease of real property to individuals based on race, creed, color, sex, national origin, familial status, or disability are void, unenforceable, and 56
illegal. RCW 49.60.224. 57

SELLER'S INITIALS: _____ Date: _____ SELLER'S INITIALS: _____ Date: _____

Form 17
Seller Disclosure Statement
Rev. 06/12
Page 2 of 5

SELLER DISCLOSURE STATEMENT
IMPROVED PROPERTY
(Continued)

	YES	NO	DON'T KNOW	
				58
				59

2.   WATER   60
   A. Household Water
     (1) The source of water for the property is: ❑ Private or publicly owned water system   61
        ❑ Private well serving only the subject property *❑ Other water system   62
        *If shared, are there any written agreements? .... ❑   ❑   ❑   63
    *(2) Is there an easement (recorded or unrecorded) for access to and/or maintenance   64
        of the water source? .... ❑   ❑   ❑   65
    *(3) Are there any problems or repairs needed? .... ❑   ❑   ❑   66
    (4) During your ownership, has the source provided an adequate year-round supply   67
        of potable water? .... ❑   ❑   ❑   68

        If no, please explain: _____   69
    *(5) Are there any water treatment systems for the property? .... ❑   ❑   ❑   70
        If yes, are they: ❑ Leased   ❑ Owned   71
    *(6) Are there any water rights for the property associated with its domestic water supply,   72
        such as a water right permit, certificate, or claim? .... ❑   ❑   ❑   73
      (a) If yes, has the water right permit, certificate, or claim been assigned, transferred,   74
         or changed? .... ❑   ❑   ❑   75
      *(b) If yes, has all or any portion of the water right not been used for five or more   76
         successive years? .... ❑   ❑   ❑   77
    *(7) Are there any defects in the operation of the water system (e.g. pipes, tank, pump, etc.)? ❑   ❑   ❑   78
   B. Irrigation Water   79
     (1) Are there any irrigation water rights for the property, such as a water right permit,   80
        certificate, or claim? .... ❑   ❑   ❑   81
      *(a) If yes, has all or any portion of the water right not been used for five or more   82
         successive years? .... ❑   ❑   ❑   83
      *(b) If so, is the certificate available? (If yes, please attach a copy.) .... ❑   ❑   ❑   84
      *(c) If so, has the water right permit, certificate, or claim been assigned,   85
         transferred, or changed? .... ❑   ❑   ❑   86
    *(2) Does the property receive irrigation water from a ditch company, irrigation district, or other entity?....... ❑   ❑   ❑   87
        If so, please identify the entity that supplies water to the property: 88
        _____   89
   C. Outdoor Sprinkler System   90
     (1) Is there an outdoor sprinkler system for the property? .... ❑   ❑   ❑   91
    *(2) If yes, are there any defects in the system? .... ❑   ❑   ❑   92
    *(3) If yes, is the sprinkler system connected to irrigation water? .... ❑   ❑   ❑   93

3.   SEWER/ON-SITE SEWAGE SYSTEM   94
   A. The property is served by: 95
     ❑   Public sewer system ❑ On-site sewage system (including pipes, tanks, drainfields, and all other component parts)   96
     ❑   Other disposal system   97
     Please describe: _____   98
   B. If public sewer system service is available to the property, is the house   99
     connected to the sewer main? .... ❑   ❑   ❑   100

     If no, please explain: _____   101
  *C. Is the property subject to any sewage system fees or charges in addition to those covered   102
     in your regularly billed sewer or on-site sewage system maintenance service?............... ❑   ❑   ❑   103
   D. If the property is connected to an on-site sewage system: 104
    *(1) Was a permit issued for its construction, and was it approved by the local health   105
        department or district following its construction?................................... ❑   ❑   ❑   106

    (2) When was it last pumped? _____   107
    *(3) Are there any defects in the operation of the on-site sewage system?.............. ❑   ❑   ❑   108
    (4) When was it last inspected? _____   109
        By whom: _____   110
    (5) For how many bedrooms was the on-site sewage system approved? _____ bedrooms   111

SELLER'S INITIALS: _____   Date: _____   SELLER'S INITIALS: _____   Date: _____

Form 17	**SELLER DISCLOSURE STATEMENT**	©Copyright 2012	
Seller Disclosure Statement	**IMPROVED PROPERTY**	Northwest Multiple Listing Service	
Rev. 06/12		ALL RIGHTS RESERVED	
Page 3 of 5	*(Continued)*		

	YES	NO	DON'T KNOW	
E. Are all plumbing fixtures, including laundry drain, connected to the sewer/on-site sewage system?	❑	❑	❑	112 / 113 / 114
If no, please explain: _____				115
*F. Have there been any changes or repairs to the on-site sewage system?	❑	❑	❑	116
G. Is the on-site sewage system, including the drainfield, located entirely within the boundaries of the property?	❑	❑	❑	117 / 118
If no, please explain: _____				119
*H. Does the on-site sewage system require monitoring and maintenance services more frequently than once a year?	❑	❑	❑	120 / 121

NOTICE: IF THIS RESIDENTIAL REAL PROPERTY DISCLOSURE IS BEING COMPLETED FOR NEW CONSTRUCTION WHICH HAS NEVER BEEN OCCUPIED, SELLER IS NOT REQUIRED TO COMPLETE THE QUESTIONS LISTED IN ITEM 4 (STRUCTURAL) OR ITEM 5 (SYSTEMS AND FIXTURES). 122 / 123 / 124

4. STRUCTURAL 125

	YES	NO	DON'T KNOW	
*A. Has the roof leaked within the last 5 years?	❑	❑	❑	126
*B. Has the basement flooded or leaked?	❑	❑	❑	127
*C. Have there been any conversions, additions or remodeling?	❑	❑	❑	128
*(1) If yes, were all building permits obtained?	❑	❑	❑	129
*(2) If yes, were all final inspections obtained?	❑	❑	❑	130
D. Do you know the age of the house?	❑	❑	❑	131
If yes, year of original construction: _____				132
*E. Has there been any settling, slippage, or sliding of the property or its improvements?	❑	❑	❑	133
*F. Are there any defects with the following: (If yes, please check applicable items and explain.)	❑	❑	❑	134

❑ Foundations	❑ Decks	❑ Exterior Walls	135
❑ Chimneys	❑ Interior Walls	❑ Fire Alarms	136
❑ Doors	❑ Windows	❑ Patio	137
❑ Ceilings	❑ Slab Floors	❑ Driveways	138
❑ Pools	❑ Hot Tub	❑ Sauna	139
❑ Sidewalks	❑ Outbuildings	❑ Fireplaces	140
❑ Garage Floors	❑ Walkways	❑ Wood Stoves	141
❑ Siding	❑ Other _____		142

	YES	NO	DON'T KNOW	
*G. Was a structural pest or "whole house" inspection done?	❑	❑	❑	143
If yes, when and by whom was the inspection completed? _____				144 / 145
H. During your ownership, has the property had any wood destroying organism or pest infestation?	❑	❑	❑	146
I. Is the attic insulated?	❑	❑	❑	147
J. Is the basement insulated?	❑	❑	❑	148

5. SYSTEMS AND FIXTURES 149

	YES	NO	DON'T KNOW	
*A. If any of the following systems or fixtures are included with the transfer, are there any defects?				150
If yes, please explain: _____				151
Electrical system, including wiring, switches, outlets, and service	❑	❑	❑	152
Plumbing system, including pipes, faucets, fixtures, and toilets	❑	❑	❑	153
Hot water tank	❑	❑	❑	154
Garbage disposal	❑	❑	❑	155
Appliances	❑	❑	❑	156
Sump pump	❑	❑	❑	157
Heating and cooling systems	❑	❑	❑	158
Security system ❑ Owned ❑ Leased	❑	❑	❑	159
Other _____	❑	❑	❑	160
*B. If any of the following fixtures or property is included with the transfer, are they leased? (If yes, please attach copy of lease.)				161 / 162
Security System _____	❑	❑	❑	163
Tanks (type): _____	❑	❑	❑	164
Satellite dish _____	❑	❑	❑	165
Other: _____	❑	❑	❑	166

SELLER'S INITIALS: _____ Date: _____ SELLER'S INITIALS: _____ Date: _____

SELLER DISCLOSURE STATEMENT
IMPROVED PROPERTY
(Continued)

	YES	NO	DON'T KNOW	
*C. Are any of the following kinds of wood burning appliances present at the property?				167 / 168
(1) Woodstove?	❑	❑	❑	169
(2) Fireplace insert?	❑	❑	❑	170
(3) Pellet stove?	❑	❑	❑	171
(4) Fireplace?	❑	❑	❑	172
If yes, are all of the (1) woodstoves or (2) fireplace inserts certified by the U.S. Environmental Protection Agency as clean burning appliances to improve air quality and public health?	❑	❑	❑	173 / 174
D. Is the property located within a city, county, or district or within a department of natural resources fire protection zone that provides fire protection services?	❑	❑	❑	175 / 176
E. Is the property equipped with carbon monoxide alarms? (Note: Pursuant to RCW 19.27.530, Seller must equip the residence with carbon monoxide alarms as required by the state building code.)	❑	❑	❑	177 / 178
F. Is the property equipped with smoke alarms?	❑	❑	❑	179

6. HOMEOWNERS' ASSOCIATION/COMMON INTERESTS — 180

	YES	NO	DON'T KNOW	
A. Is there a Homeowners' Association?	❑	❑	❑	181
Name of Association and contact information for an officer, director, employee, or other authorized agent, if any, who may provide the association's financial statements, minutes, bylaws, fining policy, and other information that is not publicly available: _____				182 / 183 / 184
B. Are there regular periodic assessments?	❑	❑	❑	185
$ _____ per ❑ month ❑ year				186
❑ Other _____				187
*C. Are there any pending special assessments?	❑	❑	❑	188
*D. Are there any shared "common areas" or any joint maintenance agreements (facilities such as walls, fences, landscaping, pools, tennis courts, walkways, or other areas co-owned in undivided interest with others)?	❑	❑	❑	189 / 190 / 191

7. ENVIRONMENTAL — 192

	YES	NO	DON'T KNOW	
*A. Have there been any flooding, standing water, or drainage problems on the property that affect the property or access to the property?	❑	❑	❑	193 / 194
*B. Does any part of the property contain fill dirt, waste, or other fill material?	❑	❑	❑	195
*C. Is there any material damage to the property from fire, wind, floods, beach movements, earthquake, expansive soils, or landslides?	❑	❑	❑	196 / 197
D. Are there any shorelines, wetlands, floodplains, or critical areas on the property?	❑	❑	❑	198
*E. Are there any substances, materials, or products in or on the property that may be environmental concerns, such as asbestos, formaldehyde, radon gas, lead-based paint, fuel or chemical storage tanks, or contaminated soil or water?	❑	❑	❑	199 / 200 / 201
*F. Has the property been used for commercial or industrial purposes?	❑	❑	❑	202
*G. Is there any soil or groundwater contamination?	❑	❑	❑	203
*H. Are there transmission poles or other electrical utility equipment installed, maintained, or buried on the property that do not provide utility service to the structures on the property?	❑	❑	❑	204 / 205
*I. Has the property been used as a legal or illegal dumping site?	❑	❑	❑	206
*J. Has the property been used as an illegal drug manufacturing site?	❑	❑	❑	207
*K. Are there any radio towers in the area that cause interference with cellular telephone reception?	❑	❑	❑	208

8. LEAD BASED PAINT (Applicable if the house was built before 1978.) — 209

A. Presence of lead-based paint and/or lead-based paint hazards (check one below): — 210
  ❑   Known lead-based paint and/or lead-based paint hazards are present in the housing — 211
      (explain). _____ — 212
  ❑   Seller has no knowledge of lead-based paint and/or lead-based paint hazards in the housing. — 213
B. Records and reports available to the Seller (check one below): — 214
  ❑   Seller has provided the purchaser with all available records and reports pertaining to lead-based paint and/or lead-based paint hazards in the housing (list documents below). — 215 / 216
  _____ — 217
  ❑   Seller has no reports or records pertaining to lead-based paint and/or lead-based paint hazards in the housing. — 218

9. MANUFACTURED AND MOBILE HOMES — 219

If the property includes a manufactured or mobile home, — 220

	YES	NO	DON'T KNOW	
*A. Did you make any alterations to the home?	❑	❑	❑	221
If yes, please describe the alterations: _____				222
*B. Did any previous owner make any alterations to the home?	❑	❑	❑	223
*C. If alterations were made, were permits or variances for these alterations obtained?	❑	❑	❑	224

SELLER'S INITIALS: _____ Date: _____ SELLER'S INITIALS: _____ Date: _____

Form 17	**SELLER DISCLOSURE STATEMENT**	©Copyright 2012	
Seller Disclosure Statement	**IMPROVED PROPERTY**	Northwest Multiple Listing Service	
Rev. 06/12		ALL RIGHTS RESERVED	
Page 5 of 5	*(Continued)*		

10. FULL DISCLOSURE BY SELLERS   YES   NO   DON'T 225

    A. Other conditions or defects: KNOW 226

        *Are there any other existing material defects affecting the property that a prospective buyer   227

        should know about? .... ☐   ☐   ☐   228

    B. Verification   229

        The foregoing answers and attached explanations (if any) are complete and correct to the best of Seller's knowledge and Seller has 230
        received a copy hereof. Seller agrees to defend, indemnify and hold real estate licensees harmless from and against any and all claims 231
        that the above information is inaccurate. Seller authorizes real estate licensees, if any, to deliver a copy of this disclosure statement to 232
        other real estate licensees and all prospective buyers of the property. 233

        Date: _____   Date: _____ 234

        Seller: _____   Seller: _____ 235

NOTICES TO THE BUYER 236

SEX OFFENDER REGISTRATION 237

INFORMATION REGARDING REGISTERED SEX OFFENDERS MAY BE OBTAINED FROM LOCAL LAW ENFORCEMENT 238
AGENCIES. THIS NOTICE IS INTENDED ONLY TO INFORM YOU OF WHERE TO OBTAIN THIS INFORMATION AND IS 239
NOT AN INDICATION OF THE PRESENCE OF REGISTERED SEX OFFENDERS. 240

PROXIMITY TO FARMING 241

THIS NOTICE IS TO INFORM YOU THAT THE REAL PROPERTY YOU ARE CONSIDERING FOR PURCHASE MAY LIE IN 242
CLOSE PROXIMITY TO A FARM. THE OPERATION OF A FARM INVOLVES USUAL AND CUSTOMARY AGRICULTURAL 243
PRACTICES, WHICH ARE PROTECTED UNDER RCW 7.48.305, THE WASHINGTON RIGHT TO FARM ACT. 244

II. BUYER'S ACKNOWLEDGEMENT 245

    Buyer hereby acknowledges that: 246

    A.   Buyer has a duty to pay diligent attention to any material defects that are known to Buyer or can be known to Buyer by utilizing 247
         diligent attention and observation. 248

    B.   The disclosures set forth in this statement and in any amendments to this statement are made only by the Seller and not by any real 249
         estate licensee or other party. 250

    C.   Buyer acknowledges that, pursuant to RCW 64.06.050 (2), real estate licensees are not liable for inaccurate information provided by 251
         Seller, except to the extent that real estate licensees know of such inaccurate information. 252

    D.   This information is for disclosure only and is not intended to be a part of the written agreement between the Buyer and Seller. 253

    E.   Buyer (which term includes all persons signing the "Buyer's acceptance" portion of this disclosure statement below) has received a 254
         copy of this Disclosure Statement (including attachments, if any) bearing Seller's signature(s). 255

    F.   If the house was built prior to 1978, Buyer acknowledges receipt of the pamphlet *Protect Your Family From Lead in Your Home.* 256

DISCLOSURES CONTAINED IN THIS DISCLOSURE STATEMENT ARE PROVIDED BY SELLER BASED ON SELLER'S ACTUAL 257
KNOWLEDGE OF THE PROPERTY AT THE TIME SELLER COMPLETES THIS DISCLOSURE. UNLESS BUYER AND SELLER 258
OTHERWISE AGREE IN WRITING, BUYER SHALL HAVE THREE (3) BUSINESS DAYS FROM THE DAY SELLER OR SELLER'S 259
AGENT DELIVERS THIS DISCLOSURE STATEMENT TO RESCIND THE AGREEMENT BY DELIVERING A SEPARATELY SIGNED 260
WRITTEN STATEMENT OF RESCISSION TO SELLER OR SELLER'S AGENT. YOU MAY WAIVE THE RIGHT TO RESCIND PRIOR 261
TO OR AFTER THE TIME YOU ENTER INTO A SALE AGREEMENT. 262

BUYER HEREBY ACKNOWLEDGES RECEIPT OF A COPY OF THIS DISCLOSURE STATEMENT AND ACKNOWLEDGES THAT 263
THE DISCLOSURES MADE HEREIN ARE THOSE OF THE SELLER ONLY, AND NOT OF ANY REAL ESTATE LICENSEE OR 264
OTHER PARTY. 265

DATE: _____   DATE: _____ 266

BUYER: _____   BUYER: _____ 267

BUYER'S WAIVER OF RIGHT TO REVOKE OFFER 268

Buyer has read and reviewed the Seller's responses to this Seller Disclosure Statement. Buyer approves this statement and waives Buyer's right 269
to revoke Buyer's offer based on this disclosure. 270

DATE: _____   DATE: _____ 271

BUYER: _____   BUYER: _____ 272

BUYER'S WAIVER OF RIGHT TO RECEIVE COMPLETED SELLER DISCLOSURE STATEMENT 273

Buyer has been advised of Buyer's right to receive a completed Seller Disclosure Statement. Buyer waives that right. However, if the answer to 274
any of the questions in the section entitled "Environmental" would be "yes," Buyer may not waive the receipt of the "Environmental" section of 275
the Seller Disclosure Statement. 276

DATE: _____   DATE: _____ 277

BUYER: _____   BUYER: _____ 278

If the answer is "Yes" to any asterisked (*) items, please explain below (use additional sheets if necessary). Please refer to the line number(s) of 279
the question(s). 280

_____ 281

_____ 282

_____ 283

SELLER'S INITIALS: _____ Date: _____   SELLER'S INITIALS: _____ Date: _____

answer about its construction and upkeep, such as when the system was last inspected and pumped.

4. **Structural components.** This section of the form asks for information about the various structural components of the property, such as the roof and the foundation. The seller must also answer questions about any additions or remodeling; the settling or sliding of the structures; and various types of inspections, including pest inspections.

5. **Systems and fixtures.** This section lists several types of systems, fixtures, or appliances—such as the electrical system, the plumbing system, the hot water tank, the heating and cooling system, wood-burning appliances, and the security system—and asks if they have any defects. (Note: If the property is new construction that has never been occupied, sections 4 and 5 do not need to be completed.)

6. **Homeowners' association/common interests.** Here the seller lists information about the homeowners association (if any), assessments by the homeowners association, and any commonly owned areas.

7. **Environmental.** This section asks about soil or water problems, fill materials, damage caused by natural disasters, flooding, environmental hazards, the presence of shorelines or other critical areas, utility equipment, and radio tower interference with telephone reception.

8. **Lead-based paint.** This section requires disclosures concerning the possible presence of lead-based paint on the property if the house was built before 1978. (The federal lead-based paint disclosure law is discussed in Chapter 7.)

9. **Manufactured and mobile homes.** This section applies when the property being sold includes a manufactured or mobile home. The seller is asked about any alterations to the manufactured or mobile home.

10. **Full disclosure.** Finally, the form asks whether there are any other material defects affecting the property or its value that a buyer should be aware of.

Many of the questions in the disclosure form are marked with an asterisk. If the seller answers "Yes" to any of those questions, she is required to provide additional information at the end of the form or on additional sheets.

After answering the questions about the property, the seller is required to sign a verification provision. It states that the information provided is complete and correct to the best of the seller's knowledge. It also states that if the information is challenged as inaccurate, the seller will indemnify the real estate licensees and hold them harmless from claims based on the inaccuracy. The seller acknowledges receipt of a copy of the form and authorizes the real estate agent to distribute copies to other licensees and to prospective buyers.

The next section of the form is the buyer's acknowledgment. By signing this section, the buyer acknowledges that he has received the disclosure form and understands his rights and responsibilities—including the duty to look for problems with the property on his own behalf. The buyer also acknowledges that the disclosures were made by the seller, not by any of the real estate licensees.

At the end of the form are two waiver provisions. By signing one of these, the buyer can waive rights provided by the seller disclosure law. (Waiver is discussed below.) Note that if any answer to a question in the form's "Environmental" section is "yes," the buyer cannot waive receipt of that portion of the statement.

TIMING AND EFFECT OF DISCLOSURE

The seller must ordinarily give the buyer the disclosure statement within five days after the purchase and sale agreement is signed. (Note that the statement is for disclosure purposes only; it does not become part of the purchase and sale agreement.) The parties may agree in writing to a different deadline for delivery of the disclosure statement, or the buyer may waive the right to receive a completed statement by signing the waiver provision at the end of the form.

Within three business days after receiving a completed disclosure statement, the buyer can either "approve and accept" the disclosure statement or rescind the purchase and sale agreement. The choice between acceptance and rescission is completely up to the buyer. If he does not like the information in the disclosure statement for any reason, however trivial, he can rescind the agreement.

If the buyer decides to rescind the agreement, he must notify the seller or the seller's real estate agent in writing within the three-day period. The buyer will then be entitled to a full refund of the earnest money deposit.

If the seller fails to give the buyer a disclosure statement, the buyer can rescind the purchase and sale agreement at any time until closing.

WHEN CIRCUMSTANCES CHANGE

After the buyer accepts a disclosure statement, information may come to light that makes the disclosure statement inaccurate.

EXAMPLE: Stein and O'Neil signed a purchase and sale agreement. Stein filled out the seller disclosure statement and gave it to O'Neil within five days. O'Neil examined the statement, was satisfied with it, and decided to go ahead with the purchase. Two weeks later, Stein realizes that the roof leaks. The disclosure statement given to O'Neil is no longer accurate.

When newly discovered information makes the disclosure statement inaccurate, the seller may either give the buyer an amended disclosure statement, or else fix the problem so that the disclosure statement is made accurate once again. Note that if the new property information is discovered by the buyer or someone acting on the buyer's behalf (such as the buyer's home inspector), the seller does not have a duty to amend the disclosure report.

If the seller amends the disclosure statement, the buyer again has three days to either accept the amended disclosure statement or rescind the purchase and sale agreement.

EXAMPLE: Stein gives O'Neil an amended disclosure statement, this time listing the true condition of the roof. O'Neil, who has had second thoughts about buying the property anyway, decides to rescind the purchase and sale agreement.

If the seller chooses to fix the problem, the corrective action must be completed at least three days before closing, or else the closing date may be extended to allow for a three-day rescission period. Once the sale has closed, the buyer can no longer rescind, even if new information is discovered.

LIMITATIONS ON LIABILITY UNDER THE SELLER DISCLOSURE LAW

Washington's seller disclosure law specifically states that the information in the disclosure statement is based on the seller's actual knowledge of the property. The seller's answers to the questions are not to be considered representations made by the real estate agent. Furthermore, the statement is not a warranty from either the seller or the real estate agent. Neither the seller nor the real estate agent will be liable to the buyer for inaccuracies in the statement, unless they had personal knowledge of the inaccuracies.

On the other hand, the seller disclosure statement does not limit the responsibility of the seller and the real estate agent to disclose latent defects and other material facts to the buyer. Even if there is no question on the disclosure statement about a particular problem, the seller and the agent must disclose it if they are aware of it.

LISTING VACANT LAND

Some real estate transactions involve vacant land. In many cases, you will use the same listing agreement for vacant land as you do for single-family homes. However, the listing input sheet is likely to be quite different and, instead of a seller disclosure form, the seller will have to fill out a seller's property condition report for vacant land. A sample vacant land input sheet is shown in Figure 2.6.

While the terms of the vacant land listing agreement may be the same as those of the residential agreement, there are some special areas of concern. Vacant land is usually bought for development purposes. This means that the availability of utilities will be particularly important to the buyer. Zoning restrictions and drainage issues will also be of special interest. And the dimensions of the property itself often take on more importance with a vacant lot than with improved property. All of these items and more will be noted on the vacant land listing input sheet.

You also need to know that a seller is prohibited from offering a portion of a larger property for sale unless it has been platted and the plat has been recorded in the county where the property is located. Some counties allow property to be offered for sale after the preliminary plat is approved and prior to final approval and recording. Check local ordinances to determine the procedures in your county.

FIG. 2.6   VACANT LAND LISTING INPUT SHEET

NWMLS Form 5 Rev. 10/11
Copyright 2011
Northwest Multiple Listing Service
All Rights Reserved

VACANT LAND LISTING INPUT SHEET (page 1 of 2)

PROPERTY TYPE 4

• Indicates Required information   ( ) Indicates Maximum Choice   *Indicates "Yes" By Default   **LISTING #**

ADDRESS

• County

• City

• ZIP Code   + 4

• Area   –

• Community/District

• Street # (HSN)   Modifier

Direction
☐ N   ☐ S   ☐ E   ☐ W
☐ NE   ☐ NW   ☐ SE   ☐ SW

• Street Name

Post Direction
☐ N   ☐ S   ☐ E   ☐ W
☐ NE   ☐ NW   ☐ SE   ☐ SW
☐ KPN   ☐ KPS

Unit #

Suffix
☐ Av Ct   ☐ Blvd   ☐ Ct   ☐ Dr Ct   ☐ Lane   ☐ Place   ☐ St Ct   ☐ Terr
☐ Ave   ☐ Cir   ☐ Ct Av   ☐ Hwy   ☐ Loop   ☐ Road   ☐ St Dr   ☐ Trail
☐ Ave Pl   ☐ Crt St   ☐ Dr   ☐ Junction   ☐ Pkwy   ☐ Street   ☐ St Pl   ☐ Way

LISTING

$

• Listing Price   • Listing Date   • Expiration Date   • Tax ID#

• Preliminary Title Ordered
☐ Yes   ☐ No

LOCATION

Lot Number   Block   Plat/Subdivision/Building Name

• 3rd Party Approval Required (2)
☐ None   ☐ Other - See Remarks   ☐ Short Sale

• Bank Owned/REO
☐ Yes   ☐ No

• MAP BOOK
☐ Thomas   ☐ RR-Jeff   ☐ RR-Thurs   ☐ RR-Clallam   ☐ R A-Clark   ☐ P-Grant   ☐ P-Yakima   ☐ Unknown
☐ RR-Kitsap   ☐ RR-Mason   ☐ RR-Lewis   ☐ RR-Grays   ☐ Totem   ☐ P-Kittitas   ☐ Yellow Pgs

• Map Page   • Top Map Coord.   • Side Map Coord.

PROPERTY INFORMATION

• Owner's Name   • Owner's Phone   • Owner's City and State   Lot Size (Square Feet)

• Prohibit Blogging
☐ *Yes   ☐ No

• Allow Automated Valuation
☐ *Yes   ☐ No

• Show Map Link
☐ *Yes   ☐ No

• Internet Advertising
☐ *Yes   ☐ No

• Show Address to Public
☐ Yes   ☐ No

• SOC (Selling Office Com.)   Selling Office Commission Comments (40 characters maximum)   Virtual Tour URL (Please included http://)

BROKER INFORMATION

• LAG
Listing Broker ID#

Broker Name and Phone

Listing Firm - ID#   Firm Name and Phone

Co Broker - ID#   CO Broker Name and Phone

Co Firm - ID#   Co Firm Name and Phone

LISTING INFORMATION

General Zoning Classification (6)
☐ Agricultural   ☐ Forestry   ☐ Office
☐ Business   ☐ Industrial   ☐ Residential
☐ Commercial   ☐ Industrial-Light   ☐ Retail
☐ Farm & Ranch   ☐ Multi-Family   ☐ See Remarks

• Zoning Jurisdiction (1)
☐ City
☐ County
☐ See Remarks

Zoning Code

• Style Code

Restrictions (4)
☐ CC&R
☐ NO Manufactured Homes
☐ Manufactured Homes OK
☐ No Restrictions
☐ Timber Clause
☐ Unknown
☐ See Remarks

• Possession (3)
☐ Closing
☐ Negotiable
☐ See Remarks
☐ Sub. Tenant's Rights

• Form 17 (1)
☐ Exempt
☐ Not Provided
☐ Provided

• Sketch Submitted
☐ *Yes   ☐ No

$
Tax Year   Annual Taxes

• Potential Terms (10)
☐ Assumable   ☐ Owner Finance
☐ Cash Out   ☐ Rehab Loan
☐ Conventional   ☐ See Remarks
☐ Farm Home Loan   ☐ State Bond
☐ FHA   ☐ VA
☐ Lease/Purchase

Senior Exemption
☐ Yes   ☐ No

Right of First Refusal
☐ Yes   ☐ No

Assessment Fees (6)
☐ Electric   ☐ Road   ☐ Water
☐ Gas   ☐ School   ☐ See Remarks
☐ Parks   ☐ Sewer

Term Remarks (40 characters maximum)

INITIALS:
Seller   Date   Seller   Date   Broker   Date

NWMLS Form 5 Rev. 10/11
Copyright 2011
Northwest Multiple Listing Service
All Rights Reserved

VACANT LAND LISTING INPUT SHEET (page 2 of 2)

PROPERTY TYPE **4**

SITE INFORMATION

Listing Address: _____

LAG # _____

Quarter (Sec/Twn/Rng) _____

Lot Dimensions (Feet) _____

Waterfront Footage (Feet) _____

Reports/Documents Completed (9)
- ❑ CCRs
- ❑ Drainage
- ❑ Geotech
- ❑ Road Agreement
- ❑ Septic "As Built"
- ❑ Topographical
- ❑ Well Agreement
- ❑ Wetland Delineation
- ❑ See Remarks

Waterfront (5)
- ❑ Bank-High
- ❑ Bank-Low
- ❑ Bank Medium
- ❑ Bay
- ❑ Bulkhead
- ❑ Canal
- ❑ Creek
- ❑ Jetty
- ❑ Lake
- ❑ No Bank
- ❑ Ocean
- ❑ River
- ❑ Saltwater
- ❑ Sound
- ❑ Strait
- ❑ Tideland Rights

View (5)
- ❑ Bay
- ❑ Canal
- ❑ City
- ❑ Golf Course
- ❑ Jetty
- ❑ Lake
- ❑ Mountain
- ❑ Ocean
- ❑ Partial
- ❑ River
- ❑ See Remarks
- ❑ Sound
- ❑ Strait
- ❑ Territorial

Lot Details (7)
- ❑ Alley
- ❑ Corner Lot
- ❑ Cul-de-sac
- ❑ Curbs
- ❑ Dead End St.
- ❑ Hg. Voltage Line
- ❑ Open Space
- ❑ Paved Street
- ❑ Secluded
- ❑ Sidewalk

Improvements (10)
- ❑ Barn
- ❑ Boat House
- ❑ Cabana/Gazebo
- ❑ Cable TV Avail
- ❑ Dock
- ❑ Dwelling
- ❑ Fenced-Fully
- ❑ Fenced-Partially
- ❑ Garage
- ❑ Outbuilding(s)
- ❑ Shop
- ❑ Stable

Property Features (12)
- ❑ Brush
- ❑ Comm. Grade Timber
- ❑ Corners Flagged
- ❑ Dune Grasses
- ❑ Evergreens
- ❑ Garden/Fruit Trees
- ❑ Heavily Forested
- ❑ Irrigation
- ❑ Lightly Treed
- ❑ ORV Trails
- ❑ Partially Cleared
- ❑ Pasture Land
- ❑ Pond
- ❑ Recreational
- ❑ Riding Trails
- ❑ Stream/Creek

Topography (5)
- ❑ Cliffs
- ❑ Fill Needed
- ❑ Gullies
- ❑ Level
- ❑ Rolling
- ❑ See Remarks
- ❑ Sloped
- ❑ Swale

• Road Information (5)
- ❑ Access Easement
- ❑ County Maintained
- ❑ County Right of Way
- ❑ Gravel
- ❑ Paved
- ❑ Privately Maintained
- ❑ Recorded Maint. Agrm
- ❑ Trail Permit
- ❑ See Remarks

Road on which side of Property _____

Slopes Down to The (40 characters maximum) _____

Level (40 characters maximum) _____

UTILITY / SCHOOL / COMMUNITY

Community Features (7)
- ❑ Age Restriction
- ❑ Airfield
- ❑ Boat Launch
- ❑ CCRs
- ❑ Club House
- ❑ Golf Course
- ❑ Pvt. Beach Access

• Water (5)
- ❑ Available
- ❑ Community Well
- ❑ Drilled Well
- ❑ In Street
- ❑ Not Available
- ❑ On Property
- ❑ Private Well
- ❑ Share Available
- ❑ Shared Well
- ❑ Unknown
- ❑ Water Rights
- ❑ Well Site Approved

Water Jurisdiction _____

• Gas (1)
- ❑ On Property
- ❑ In Street
- ❑ Available
- ❑ Not Available

• Electricity (1)
- ❑ On Property
- ❑ In Street
- ❑ Available
- ❑ Not Available

• Sewer (2)
- ❑ Available
- ❑ In Street
- ❑ Not Available
- ❑ On Property

Septic System Installed
- ❑ Yes ❑ No

Septic Approved for # of Bedrooms _____

Soil Feasibility Test Available
- ❑ Yes ❑ No

Soil Test Date _____

Septic Design Applied For
- ❑ Yes ❑ No

Septic Design Apprv. Date _____

Septic Design Exp. Date _____

Septic System Type _____

Survey Information _____

Easements _____

• School District (See Code List) _____

Elementary School _____

Junior High/Middle School _____

Senior High School _____

REMARKS

Marketing Remarks. CAUTION! The comments you make in the following lines are limited to descriptions of the land and improvements only. These remarks will appear in the client handouts and websites. (500)

_____
_____
_____
_____
_____

Confidential Broker-Only Remarks. Comments in this category are for broker's use only. (250)

_____
_____
_____

• Driving Directions to Property (200)

_____
_____
_____

INITIALS: _____

Seller _____ Date _____ Seller _____ Date _____ Broker _____ Date

CHAPTER SUMMARY

1. The listing agreement is a contract between the seller and the real estate brokerage. The seller agrees to pay the firm a stated commission if a ready, willing, and able buyer is found during the listing period.

2. The three basic types of listing agreements are the open listing, the exclusive agency listing, and the exclusive right to sell listing. The type of listing determines the circumstances under which the firm is entitled to a commission.

3. A written listing agreement is an enforceable contract if it adequately identifies the property to be sold, includes a promise to pay a fixed compensation to the firm, and is signed by the seller.

4. The listing agreement should also state the terms of sale the seller will accept, the conditions under which the commission will be paid, the duration of the contract, and the seller's warranties regarding the accuracy of the information provided about the property.

5. A multiple listing service is a cooperative association of licensed firms and licensees who exchange information about their exclusive listings and help sell properties listed by other members.

6. An extender clause provides that the seller will be liable for the commission if the property is sold during a certain period after the listing expires to a buyer the listing agent dealt with during the listing period.

7. When entering into a purchase and sale agreement for residential property, the seller is required to give the buyer a seller disclosure statement, disclosing any problems that could affect the title or use of the property. On the basis of the information in the disclosure statement, the buyer may choose to rescind the purchase and sale agreement.

8. There are special listing input sheets and disclosure forms for vacant land listings. The listing agent must be aware of how development issues and regulations may affect the sale of vacant land.

Chapter Quiz

1. One disadvantage of an open listing agreement is that it:
   a. does not state the compensation as a fixed amount
   b. requires the listing agent to put more effort into marketing the property
   c. may lead to a dispute over which agent was the procuring cause, if the seller gives the listing to more than one brokerage
   d. prevents sellers from listing their property with as many real estate firms as they want

2. If John Dale is a licensed agent, which of the following written statements could be a valid listing agreement in Washington?
   a. I will pay John Dale a commission if he finds a ready, willing, and able buyer for my property within 90 days.—Signed, Adam Cook
   b. I will pay John Dale 6% of the selling price if he finds a ready, willing, and able buyer for my property, Morgan Manor, in Walla Walla, within 90 days.
   c. If John Dale can find a ready, willing, and able buyer for my property, Morgan Manor, in Walla Walla, I will pay him whatever portion of the sales price exceeds $120,000.—Signed, Adam Cook
   d. I will pay John Dale $5,000 if he finds a ready, willing, and able buyer for my property, Morgan Manor, in Walla Walla.—Signed, Adam Cook

3. A typical listing agreement form does not authorize the brokerage to:
   a. act as the agent of the seller
   b. accept earnest money deposits from prospective buyers on behalf of the seller
   c. accept an offer to purchase the property
   d. submit offers to purchase to the seller

4. In Washington, if an exclusive listing agreement does not include a termination date, when does the agreement end?
   a. After a reasonable time
   b. After 90 days
   c. After 60 days
   d. The agreement goes on indefinitely

5. If a firm renounces a listing agreement, the:
   a. seller will be liable for any damages suffered by the firm
   b. seller will be required to pay the commission
   c. senior managing broker in the firm's office can take over the listing
   d. firm could be liable for the seller's damages caused by the breach of contract

6. An extender clause (safety clause) might provide that:

   a. the seller must pay a commission if the property is sold within the extension period to a buyer you negotiated with during the listing period

   b. the seller may not owe you a commission if the property is listed with another firm during the extension period

   c. the provision may not be enforceable unless you give the seller a list of all potential buyers you negotiated with during the listing period

   d. All of the above

7. In listing agreements, sellers usually agree not to interfere with the firm's right to market the property. Which of the following would not interfere with that right?

   a. Granting an option on the property

   b. Refusing to allow a keybox to be installed on the property

   c. Entering into an agreement with a third party that prevents the brokerage from showing the property at reasonable times

   d. Leasing the property

8. The purpose of a listing input sheet is to:

   a. explain the agency relationships of MLS members to the seller

   b. allow the MLS to verify the accuracy of information about the listing

   c. gather information about the property for distribution by the MLS

   d. disclose information the seller is required to give to the buyer

9. With respect to the seller disclosure statement, which of the following statements concerning the buyer's rights is not true?

   a. If the buyer rescinds the purchase and sale agreement based on the disclosure statement, she gives up her earnest money deposit

   b. The buyer can rescind the purchase and sale agreement if she does not like something in the disclosure statement, no matter how trivial

   c. The buyer can only waive her rights in writing

   d. If the seller fails to provide a disclosure statement, the buyer can rescind the purchase and sale agreement at any time until closing

10. If the seller discovers new information that makes the seller disclosure statement inaccurate:

    a. the seller is required to take corrective action to fix the problem so that the disclosure statement is accurate again

    b. the seller does not have to give the buyer an amended disclosure statement if he can correct the problem so that the original statement is accurate again

    c. the buyer must accept any amended disclosure statement if she accepted the original disclosure statement

    d. the buyer may rescind the purchase and sale agreement after the sale closes

ANSWER KEY

1. c. Because a seller can give open listings to more than one brokerage, open listings can lead to disputes over which agent was the procuring cause of a sale.

2. d. A valid listing agreement must be in writing and must describe the property, include a promise of compensation, fix the amount of compensation, and be signed by the seller. Net listings (like the one in option c) are not legal in Washington.

3. c. Under the terms of nearly any listing agreement, an agent may submit offers to the seller, but only the seller can accept an offer. An agent cannot ordinarily accept an offer and create a contract that will be binding on the seller.

4. a. In Washington, a listing agreement that does not specify a termination date ends after a reasonable time.

5. d. Either party to a listing agreement, the firm or the seller, can unilaterally terminate the contract. This is called a renunciation if the firm terminates the contract, or a revocation if the principal terminates it. In either case, the termination may be a breach of contract, and the breaching party could be required to pay damages to the other party.

6. d. In addition to protecting the firm's commission for a specified period after the listing expires, an extender clause may also contain protections for the seller, such as the ones described in options b) and c).

7. b. The seller is not required to have a keybox installed, as long as she can make other arrangements that will allow the house to be shown.

8. c. The listing input sheet is filled in with information for the MLS to distribute to its members and use in listing the property. The MLS does not verify the information or take legal responsibility for it.

9. a. Within three days after receiving the seller disclosure statement, the buyer may rescind the purchase and sale agreement for any reason without penalty. If a disclosure statement is not provided, the buyer can rescind the agreement at any time until closing, but not after closing.

10. b. The seller has two choices. He can either give the buyer an amended disclosure statement, or else he can correct the problem to make the original disclosure statement accurate again.

CHAPTER

3

LISTING REGULATIONS

REAL ESTATE LICENSE LAW

- Commissions
- Ownership of a listing

DISTRESSED PROPERTY LAW

ANTIDISCRIMINATION LAWS

- Federal Fair Housing Act
- Washington antidiscrimination laws
- Complying with fair housing laws
- Americans with Disabilities Act

ANTITRUST LAWS AND LISTING PRACTICES

WASHINGTON UNFAIR BUSINESS PRACTICES AND CONSUMER PROTECTION ACT

ENVIRONMENTAL ISSUES

- Environmental laws
- Environmental hazards
- Real estate agent's responsibilities

INTRODUCTION

After a considerable amount of work, you now have a valid listing agreement signed by a seller. But do you know what would happen if the seller refused to pay your commission? Could you sue her? What should you do if the seller states that she doesn't want you to show the property to non-white buyers? Or what if you suspect there may be an environmental problem with the property?

A variety of laws affect real estate listing and marketing practices, and you'll need to be familiar with them if you're going to avoid some of the pitfalls of selling real estate. They include the real estate license law, antidiscrimination laws, antitrust laws, consumer protection laws, and environmental laws. In this chapter, we'll discuss the provisions of these laws that pertain to listing and marketing properties and to brokerage commissions.

REAL ESTATE LICENSE LAW

Washington's real estate license law includes rules concerning payment of brokerage commissions and the ownership and control of listings.

COMMISSIONS

As you know, a seller ordinarily pays the brokerage commission to the listing brokerage firm. In most cases, the listing firm then pays a share of the commission to its own affiliated licensee (the listing agent) and another share to the selling brokerage. The selling brokerage, in turn, pays a share of what it received to its own agent (the selling agent).

These steps are necessary because the license law allows a firm to share a commission only with another licensed brokerage or with one of its own affiliated sales agents. A firm may not pay any compensation directly to an agent who is affiliated with another brokerage. Payment must be made to that agent's firm, which then pays the agent.

> **EXAMPLE:** You work for Winston Realty. You found a buyer for a property that was listed by an agent working for Juarez Homes, Inc. When the sale closes, the seller pays Juarez Homes a $10,000 commission.
>
> Of that $10,000, Juarez Homes gets to keep $2,500 for itself. It will pay its own affiliated agent (the one who listed the property) another $2,500. It pays the other $5,000 to your firm, Winston Realty, because Winston Realty

is the selling firm. Winston Realty pays you $2,500, because you found the buyer. It would be unlawful for Juarez Homes to pay your $2,500 directly to you. Your compensation must come from your own firm.

Note that affiliated licensees aren't allowed to share their compensation with other licensees, whether they work for different firms or the same firm. If two licensees are going to split a commission, the split must be handled by their firm or firms.

A valid written agency agreement (either a listing agreement or a buyer representation agreement) is required before a firm can sue for a commission. Only the firm can sue the seller (or buyer, if appropriate) for the commission. An affiliated licensee can't sue a principal for a commission. However, if the firm fails to pay the licensee's share of the commission, the licensee can sue the firm for it.

OWNERSHIP OF A LISTING

Under the license law, only a brokerage can deal directly with the principal. Thus, even though a listing agreement is usually prepared and signed by a sales agent, the listing is in the name of the firm and belongs to the firm.

EXAMPLE: You work for Yamaguchi Realty now. You are making a listing presentation to Piper. He decides to list his property with you, and you and he both sign the listing agreement form. However, the listing is actually a contract between Yamaguchi Realty and Piper. When you sign the listing, you are signing it as an agent of Yamaguchi Realty.

Because the listing agreement is between the firm and the seller, if the sales agent goes to work for another firm, the listing stays with the original firm. (The same rule applies to all brokerage services contracts.)

EXAMPLE: You don't want to work for Yamaguchi Realty anymore, so you start working for Wilder Properties instead. Piper's listing agreement was with Yamaguchi Realty, not with you, so Yamaguchi Realty keeps the listing.

If a brokerage firm loses its license, all listing agreements with that brokerage are terminated. However, if the designated broker dies, goes out of business, or loses his license (but the firm remains licensed), the firm may appoint a new designated broker. The Department of Licensing may also appoint a temporary designated broker to close pending transactions.

DISTRESSED PROPERTY LAW

Concerns about foreclosure rates have dominated the public agenda in recent years, as a growing number of homeowners have been affected by the national mortgage and credit crisis. In 2008, Washington passed the Distressed Property Law to protect homeowners in financial distress from exploitive foreclosure rescue scams. This is a fairly complex law, but because it was amended in 2009 to exempt real estate agents from most of its provisions, it should not unduly impact most real estate licensees.

DEFINITIONS

Generally, the law imposes special duties on distressed home consultants. A **distressed home** is a personal residence that is in danger of foreclosure because the homeowner is delinquent on mortgage or tax payments. A **distressed home consultant** is defined as anyone who offers to help a homeowner stop or postpone the foreclosure sale, or arranges for the homeowner to lease or rent the home so he can retain possession of it.

If a person meets the definition of a distressed home consultant, she must enter into a formal contract with the homeowner, known as a **distressed home consultant agreement**. This agreement must include a full disclosure of the specific services that will be provided and the compensation the consultant will receive. The agreement also makes it clear that the consultant owes fiduciary duties to the homeowner, including the duty to disclose material facts, to use reasonable care, to do a full accounting, and the duty of loyalty.

MOST TRANSACTIONS EXEMPT

Generally, real estate licensees are not considered to be distressed home consultants when they are providing routine real estate brokerage services. However, this exemption from the law does not apply if a licensee actually participates in a **distressed home conveyance**. A distressed home conveyance is one where a buyer purchases property from a distressed homeowner (as defined by statute), allows the homeowner to continue to occupy the property for more than 20 days past the closing date, and promises to convey the property back to the homeowner or promises the homeowner an interest in or a portion of the proceeds from a resale of the property. If a licensee is participating in this type of transaction, he must complete a distressed home consultant agreement with the homeowner that describes the additional services that will be provided, as required by the distressed property law. An attorney should draft this separate agreement for the parties, and it should be attached as an addendum to the listing agreement. (Note that most MLS forms are not designed for this type of transaction and should not be used.)

Many standard listing agreement forms now include a clause stating that the licensee will not assist in a distressed home sale without a separate written agreement. You can see an example of this language in section four of the NWMLS Listing Agreement shown in Chapter 2 (Figure 2.2), entitled "Short Sale/No Distressed Home Conveyance."

Because of the 20-day occupancy rule, the buyer in a typical transaction will not be considered a distressed home consultant, even if the homeowner is behind on his mortgage payment. However, it's important to keep this time frame in mind. If a seller is allowed to stay in the property for longer than 20 days after closing, the buyer may unwittingly become a distressed home consultant, and the provisions of the distressed property law will then apply to him.

ANTIDISCRIMINATION LAWS

Fair housing laws and other antidiscrimination laws affect both how you obtain listings and how you market properties once they are listed. Before we discuss the impact of these laws on listing and marketing practices, let's review the basic provisions of the main federal and state antidiscrimination laws that apply in real estate transactions.

FEDERAL FAIR HOUSING ACT

The federal Fair Housing Act, part of the Civil Rights Act of 1968, makes it illegal to discriminate on the basis of **race**, **color**, **religion**, **sex**, **national origin**, **disability**, or **familial status** in the sale or lease of residential property, or in the sale or lease of vacant land for the construction of residential buildings. The law also prohibits discrimination in advertising, lending, real estate brokerage, and other services in connection with residential real estate transactions.

PROHIBITED ACTS. The Fair Housing Act prohibits any of the following actions if they are done on the basis of race, color, religion, sex, national origin, disability, or familial status:

- refusing to rent or sell residential property after receiving a bona fide offer;
- refusing to negotiate for the sale or rental of residential property, or otherwise making it unavailable;
- changing the terms of sale or lease for different potential buyers or tenants;
- using advertising that indicates a preference or intent to discriminate;
- representing that property is not available for inspection, sale, or rent when it is in fact available;
- discrimination by an institutional lender in making a housing loan;
- limiting participation in a multiple listing service or similar service;
- coercing, intimidating, threatening, or interfering with anyone on account of her enjoyment, attempt to enjoy, or encouragement or assistance to others in enjoying the rights granted by the Fair Housing Act.

The discriminatory practices known as blockbusting, steering, and redlining are also prohibited.

1. **Blockbusting.** This occurs when someone tries to induce homeowners to list or sell their properties by predicting that people of another race (or disabled people, people of a particular ethnic background, etc.) will be moving into the neighborhood, and that this will have undesirable consequences, such as lower property values. The blockbuster then profits by purchasing the homes at reduced prices, or (in the case of a real estate agent) by collecting commissions on the induced sales. Blockbusting is also known as **panic selling.**
2. **Steering.** This refers to channeling prospective buyers or tenants toward or away from specific neighborhoods based on their race (or religion, national origin, etc.) in order to maintain or change the character of those neighborhoods.
3. **Redlining.** This is a refusal to make a loan because of the racial or ethnic composition of the neighborhood in which the proposed security property is located. Rejection of a loan application must be based on objective financial considerations concerning the buyer or the property.

EXEMPTIONS. There are some exemptions from the Fair Housing Act. However, these exemptions are very limited and apply only rarely. And they *never* apply when a real estate agent is involved in a transaction.

ENFORCEMENT. The Fair Housing Act is enforced by the Department of Housing and Urban Development (HUD), through its Office of Fair Housing and Equal Opportunity. In a state such as Washington, where the state fair housing laws are very similar to the federal laws, HUD may refer complaints to the equivalent state agency (in Washington, the state Human Rights Commission).

When someone is held to have violated the Fair Housing Act, a court may issue an injunction ordering the violator to stop the discriminatory conduct. The violator may also be ordered to pay compensatory damages and attorney's fees to the injured party. In addition, the violator may be required to pay punitive damages to the injured party, or a civil penalty to the government. The civil penalty can range from a maximum of $16,000 for a first offense up to $65,000 for a third or subsequent offense.

WASHINGTON STATE ANTIDISCRIMINATION LAWS

Real estate agents must also comply with the state laws that prohibit discrimination. The Washington Law Against Discrimination and the real estate license law both include provisions designed to promote fair housing in this state.

WASHINGTON LAW AGAINST DISCRIMINATION. The Washington Law Against Discrimination declares that discrimination is a matter of state concern because it threatens the rights and privileges of state inhabitants and the foundations of a free democratic society. The Washington Law Against Discrimination is stricter than the federal Fair Housing Act. It covers a broader range of activities and protects more classes of people from discrimination.

The Washington law prohibits discrimination based on **race, creed, color, national origin, sex, sexual orientation, marital status,** or **familial status; sensory, physical, or mental disability;** the **use of a trained guide dog or service dog;** or **honorably discharged veteran or military status.** Note that those infected or perceived to be infected with **HIV** are protected from discrimination to the same extent that those with any other disability are.

UNLAWFUL DISCRIMINATORY PRACTICES. The Washington Law Against Discrimination is not just a fair housing law. It prohibits a wide range of discriminatory practices in employment, insurance, and credit transactions, places of public

FIG. 3.1   COMPARISON OF ANTIDISCRIMINATION LAWS

FEDERAL FAIR HOUSING ACT

- APPLIES ONLY TO RESIDENTIAL TRANSACTIONS
- PROTECTED CLASSES: RACE, COLOR, RELIGION, SEX, NATIONAL ORIGIN, HANDICAP, OR FAMILIAL STATUS
- NO EXEMPTIONS FOR TRANSACTIONS INVOLVING REAL ESTATE AGENTS

WASHINGTON LAW AGAINST DISCRIMINATION

- APPLIES TO ANY REAL ESTATE TRANSACTION
- PROTECTED CLASSES: RACE, CREED, COLOR, NATIONAL ORIGIN, SEX, SEXUAL ORIENTATION, MARITAL STATUS, FAMILIAL STATUS, DISABILITY, THE USE OF A GUIDE OR SERVICE DOG, OR HONORABLY DISCHARGED VETERAN OR MILITARY STATUS
- NO EXEMPTIONS FOR TRANSACTIONS INVOLVING REAL ESTATE AGENTS

accommodation and amusement (such as movie theaters, restaurants, hotels, beauty shops, and most other commercial enterprises), and in regard to all types of real property—not just residential property.

The state law prohibits discrimination in any real estate transaction, including the sale, appraisal, exchange, purchase, rental, or lease of real property; transacting or applying for a real estate loan; and the provision of brokerage services.

If based on discrimination against a protected class (race, creed, color, national origin, sex, sexual orientation, marital status, familial status, disability, the use of a guide or service dog, or honorably discharged veteran or military status), it is against the law to:

- refuse to engage in a real estate transaction;
- discriminate in the terms or conditions of a real estate transaction;
- discriminate in providing services or facilities in connection with a real estate transaction;
- refuse to receive or fail to transmit a bona fide offer;
- refuse to negotiate;
- represent that property is not available for inspection, sale, rental, or lease when it is in fact available;

- fail to advise a prospect about a property listing, or refuse to allow her to inspect the property;
- publish any advertisement, notice, or sign which indicates, directly or indirectly, an intent to discriminate;
- use any application form or make any record or inquiry which indicates, directly or indirectly, an intent to discriminate;
- offer, solicit, accept, or retain a listing with the understanding that a person may be discriminated against;
- expel a person from occupancy;
- discriminate in negotiating, executing, or financing a real estate transaction;
- discriminate in negotiating or executing any service or item in connection with a real estate transaction (such as title insurance or mortgage insurance);
- induce or attempt to induce, for profit, anyone to sell or rent by making representations regarding entry into the neighborhood of a person of a protected class (blockbusting);
- insert in a written instrument relating to real property, or honor or attempt to honor, any condition, restriction, or prohibition based on a protected class (any such provision in a deed or any other conveyance or instrument relating to real property is void); or
- discriminate in any credit transaction (whether or not it is related to real estate) in denying credit, increasing fees, requiring collateral, or in any other terms or conditions.

In short, just about every form of discrimination in real estate transactions or any services associated with real estate transactions is unlawful if it is based on someone's membership in any of the protected classes.

EXEMPTIONS. The Washington law has very few exemptions and, like the federal Fair Housing Act, it has none that apply to a real estate agent engaged in professional activity.

ENFORCEMENT. Washington's antidiscrimination laws are enforced by the Washington Human Rights Commission. A person who feels his rights have been violated in a real estate transaction may file a complaint with the Human Rights Commission within one year of the discriminatory action. The commission will investigate, and if it feels the complaint has merit, it will try to resolve the problem by conference, conciliation, and persuasion. If the problem remains unresolved, the commission can schedule a hearing before an administrative law judge. If the judge finds that there was unlawful discrimination, she may provide relief in the form of a cease and desist order, affirmative relief (such as requiring an apartment owner to give the next available apartment to the victim), compensatory damages, and/or a civil penalty.

Instead of pursuing an administrative remedy, the injured party may choose to have the attorney general bring a civil action against the alleged discriminator.

WASHINGTON REAL ESTATE LICENSE LAW. In addition to the federal and state laws already discussed, real estate licensees must comply with the antidiscrimination provisions of the license law and regulations.

Under the license law, a licensee's violation of any fair housing or civil rights law is grounds for disciplinary action. The Department of Licensing can suspend or revoke the license of a broker or managing broker who discriminates in sales or hiring activity against a member of a protected class, as well as impose a fine of up to $5,000 for each offense. The licensee could also be required to complete an educational course in civil rights laws and nondiscriminatory real estate practices. Violations of the license law are also punishable as gross misdemeanors.

COMPLYING WITH FAIR HOUSING LAWS

As you can see, these antidiscrimination laws cover a lot of territory. You must become familiar with their provisions and know what activities are prohibited. And you must remember that violating an antidiscrimination law does not require intent; if you do something that is considered discriminatory, you may be found guilty of violating the law even if you had good intentions.

EXAMPLE: You're giving a listing presentation at the seller's home. The sellers are from Central America and speak only limited English. You do not speak Spanish. During the listing presentation, you feel increasingly uncomfortable because of the communication barrier. When you finish your presentation, the sellers tell you they want to list their property with you right away. Somewhat sheepishly, you suggest that they may want to list their property with an agent who speaks Spanish. You explain tactfully that you have a very difficult time understanding them and believe that they would be happier with a Spanish-speaking agent.

They insist that they want to list with you. You tell them, in all honesty, that you think another agent would be able to give them better service. Your well-intentioned refusal to list their property could be regarded as discrimination on the basis of national origin, and you could be found guilty of violating federal or state antidiscrimination laws.

To help you avoid unintentional discriminatory acts, we will discuss some basic guidelines to follow when you list property and when you advertise the properties you list.

COMPLIANCE WHEN LISTING PROPERTY. When you are listing property, you should remember the following general rules.

Never say or imply that the presence of persons of a particular protected class (race, national origin, etc.) in a neighborhood could or will result in:

- lower property values,
- a change in the composition of the neighborhood,
- a more dangerous neighborhood, or
- a decline in the quality of the schools in the neighborhood.

EXAMPLE: Chadwick is making a listing presentation to Thompson, a homeowner who is considering selling her property but isn't sure this is the right time. During the presentation, Chadwick says to Thompson, "I hear your neighbor, Bowen, has an offer on his house from a minority couple. You know, it might be a good idea to get your house listed and an offer nailed down before any minority families move into the neighborhood. That way, you can get the best price for your house. If you wait until Bowen's house is sold—well, you just might not get as much for your house." This is an example of blockbusting. Chadwick has violated the antidiscrimination laws.

Remember that you can't refuse to list property in a market area served by your office because of the presence or absence of particular protected groups. Nor can you state or imply that a home will be more difficult (or easier) to sell based on the presence or absence of a particular group of people.

EXAMPLE: Norquist is discussing the listing price with the sellers. She tells them with enthusiasm, "Your house is in a great neighborhood! There aren't very many safe, white, middle-class neighborhoods left these days. Your home's really going to sell fast!" Norquist has just violated antidiscrimination laws.

Most agents would not act in an overtly discriminatory way; for example, they wouldn't raise the listing price because of the race of the prospective buyer. Yet some of these same agents might tell racial or ethnic jokes or make derogatory remarks about a particular group of people. Although these jokes or remarks don't necessarily indicate a willingness to actually discriminate in a transaction, a listener might assume that they do. And if an agent listens and says nothing while a seller, a buyer, or another agent makes discriminatory remarks or jokes, it can give the impression that the agent agrees with these discriminatory attitudes. Avoid participating in or going along with racial or ethnic slurs, no matter what the source.

Before taking a listing, be sure to discuss the fair housing laws with the seller, and tell the seller that you will strictly abide by those laws. Ask the seller to make a firm commitment to comply with the fair housing laws. If the seller refuses to do so, you should refuse to take the listing. The same holds true if the seller makes remarks that suggest that he might act in a discriminatory manner.

> **EXAMPLE:** You're making a listing presentation to the Boyds, a white couple who live in a predominantly white neighborhood. While you are discussing the listing terms, Mr. Boyd says, "You know, we certainly want the best price for our house. But we want you to be pretty careful who you show it to. We spent a lot of time fixing up this house. Hey, we raised our kids here. We don't really want to change the neighborhood. Our neighbors are good, traditional, hard-working folks. We don't want a buyer who would lower everybody else's property values. You know what we mean."
>
> Even though the Boyds don't come out and say so, they could easily be implying that they would not accept an offer from a buyer with a different racial or ethnic background. Their comments are red flags. You should discuss fair housing principles with them, emphasizing that equal opportunity is the law. If the Boyds seem uncomfortable with what you are saying, you would be wise to refuse to take the listing.

If you refuse a listing because you think the sellers would discriminate against potential buyers, you should immediately report it to your designated broker or branch manager.

In your relationships with potential sellers, be sure to provide equal service without regard to the seller's race, creed, color, religion, national origin, ancestry, sex, sexual orientation, marital status, familial status, age, or disability. You should always follow the same listing procedures no matter who your client is.

COMPLIANCE WHEN ADVERTISING PROPERTIES. After you list a property, your next step is usually to advertise it. Keep in mind that you need to avoid discrimination in the way you market the property.

Sometimes apparently innocent statements or actions may be interpreted as discriminatory. Suppose that you're preparing and mailing out a flyer about your listing. You could be accused of discrimination if:

- you send flyers only to neighborhoods where the residents are all predominantly of the same race or ethnic background as the seller;
- you send them to all the neighboring properties except those owned by people of a particular race or ethnic background; or
- the wording of the flyer suggests that the recipient can control the type of person who will buy the property.

EXAMPLE: Your flyer says that a neighbor can, by referring potential buyers, "uphold the standards of the community." But you fail to specify what community standards you're referring to. Unless you clearly describe these standards in nondiscriminatory language, a reader could infer that she can control the race or ethnic background of the buyer. Your flyer might be found to violate antidiscrimination laws.

As a real estate agent, you're likely to place many newspaper ads. Newspaper advertising has traditionally been one of the most common forms of advertising used by real estate agents. But your advertising strategies must avoid even inadvertent discrimination.

- Your choice of newspapers could constitute racial steering.

EXAMPLE: You have listed a home in a predominantly minority neighborhood. Your sellers are members of the minority group. You decide to advertise the property in the neighborhood weekly newspaper rather than the city newspaper or any other neighborhood weeklies. You feel this is the best choice, because you think other minority residents from the same neighborhood would be more interested in the home than residents of other neighborhoods. This is discriminatory.

- The choice of models you use in display advertising could also lead to charges of discrimination.

EXAMPLE: A licensee is the listing agent for a large, exclusive housing development. She advertises the homes in the development by putting display ads in the local paper. In every ad she places, the buyers and sellers are depicted only by white models, even though 38% of the city's population is

FIG. 3.2   FAIR HOUSING LOGO

non-white. The use of only white models could be grounds for a discrimination suit.

When pictures of people are used in display advertising, you should take all reasonable steps to make sure that the pictures give the impression that the housing is open to everyone.

- All your residential advertising should contain the Equal Housing Opportunity logo or slogan. Your brochures, circulars, business cards, direct mail advertising, and all other forms of advertising should also include the Equal Housing Opportunity logo or slogan.

ACTIONS THAT DO NOT VIOLATE FAIR HOUSING LAWS. Certain actions may initially appear to violate antidiscrimination laws, but in fact are not considered to be violations. Here are some examples.

- You may provide information required by a federal, state, or local agency for data collection or civil rights enforcement purposes.
- You may ask questions and provide information on forms in regard to marital status, in an effort to comply with the state's community property laws concerning the purchase, sale, or financing of real estate.
- You may ask questions or make statements as necessary to best serve the needs of a disabled person. This may include calling the attention of disabled clients or customers to particular buildings built or modified to meet their needs.

- You may use an affirmative marketing plan that tries to attract members of a particular group to an area or property that they might not otherwise be aware of. A brokerage or real estate board may also take affirmative steps to recruit minority employees or members.

  EXAMPLE: The developer of a large, moderately priced subdivision located on the fringes of the metropolitan area contacts you to assist in the sale of properties in the subdivision. The developer encourages you to target your marketing efforts toward recent immigrants who might be looking for affordable entry-level housing. In your area, most of the recent immigrants are non-white and live in a few older urban neighborhoods. You could devote extra effort to advertising in immigrant community newspapers or leafletting these neighborhoods, so long as you also advertised in other neighborhoods or in newspapers of wider circulation.

- You may truthfully answer questions about the racial composition of neighborhoods, even if this results in unintentional racial steering. If a buyer expresses a desire not to be shown homes in a particular neighborhood, even if the buyer makes that decision because of the race or other characteristics of the residents, you are not obligated to show them homes in that neighborhood.

  EXAMPLE: You are representing the Duvalls, who have only a limited amount of money to spend on their first home. You suggest a variety of neighborhoods where there are listings that fit their price range and other preferences, including the Greengate neighborhood. When Mr. Duvall asks about the people who live in Greengate, you truthfully respond that most of the residents belong to a particular immigrant group. Mr. Duvall says, "I'm not sure we'd feel comfortable there; we'd rather look in other areas." So long as you do not discourage the Duvalls from looking at properties in this neighborhood, you are not required to show the Duvalls houses in this area against their wishes.

AMERICANS WITH DISABILITIES ACT

To avoid discrimination and promote equal treatment, real estate licensees need to be familiar not only with the fair housing laws but also with the Americans with Disabilities Act. This federal law, which took effect in 1992, is intended to guarantee people with disabilities equal access to employment, goods, and services.

As we discussed, housing discrimination on the basis of disability is prohibited under the federal Fair Housing Act. The ADA has a broader application.

Under this law, no one may be discriminated against on the basis of disability in places of public accommodation or other commercial facilities. The law defines a **disability** as any physical or mental impairment that substantially limits one or more major life activities. (This is the same definition of disability that's used in the Fair Housing Act.)

Most significantly, this means places of public accommodation or other commercial facilities must be accessible to the disabled. Physical barriers to access must be removed, wheelchair ramps must be added, and restrooms and other facilities must be modified.

PLACES OF PUBLIC ACCOMMODATION. A wide variety of facilities open to the public, both publicly and privately owned, fall within the ADA's definition of public accommodation. Hotels, restaurants, retail stores, schools, theaters, and professional offices are all covered. For instance, the office of a real estate brokerage is open to the public and therefore must be accessible to people with disabilities. Even commercial offices that members of the public don't regularly visit, but that fall under the broader category of commercial facility, may need to be made accessible.

ADA REQUIREMENTS. If you deal with commercial or retail property often, it is particularly important to be familiar with ADA requirements. The person who owns, leases, or operates a place of public accommodation is legally responsible for the removal of barriers to accessibility, so you may need to advise clients about modifications that may be necessary on properties that they might purchase or lease.

Changes that the owner or tenant of a commercial property might need to make so that the building complies with the ADA include:

- creating an accessible entrance, by installing ramps, adding parking spaces, or widening doorways;
- providing access to goods and services within a building, by installing elevators, widening aisles, or adding Braille or raised-lettering signage;
- improving restrooms, by adding larger stalls, grab bars, or more easily-operated faucets and door handles; or
- relocating other features such as drinking fountains or pay phones so they are more easily reached.

Note that barrier removal is required only in public areas, and is not required where it is not "readily achievable." For example, the owner of a small, independently owned two-story retail business would not necessarily be required to install an elevator to the second story. However, the business would be required to make other accommodations to serve a disabled customer, such as having a salesperson bring items down to the customer on the first floor.

NEW CONSTRUCTION. If you are representing someone who plans to build a new building, you should be aware that all new construction of places of public accommodation or other commercial facilities must comply with ADA requirements.

Model homes are not ordinarily required to meet ADA requirements. However, if a model home is also serving as a sales office for a subdivision or complex, then the area used as a sales office would be considered a place of public accommodation.

ANTITRUST LAWS AND LISTING PRACTICES

As you go about the business of obtaining listings and negotiating listing terms, you must be aware of the restrictions imposed by federal antitrust laws. The purpose of antitrust laws is to foster fair business practices among competitors. These laws are based on the belief that free enterprise and healthy competition are good both for individual consumers and for the economy as a whole.

The most important federal antitrust law is the **Sherman Antitrust Act**, which was passed in 1890. The Sherman Act prohibits any agreement that has the effect of unreasonably restraining trade. This includes a **conspiracy**, defined in the law as two or more business entities participating in a common scheme, the effect of which is the unreasonable restraint of trade.

The Sherman Act doesn't apply only to monolithic computer companies and oil companies. Since 1950, antitrust laws have also applied to the real estate industry. In a landmark case, the United States Supreme Court held that mandatory fee schedules established and enforced by a real estate board violated the Sherman Act (*United States v. National Association of Real Estate Boards*).

The penalties for violating antitrust laws are severe:

- if an individual is found guilty of violating the Sherman Act, he can be fined up to one million dollars and/or sentenced to ten years' imprisonment; and
- if a corporation is found guilty of violating the Sherman Act, it can be fined up to one hundred million dollars.

To avoid violating antitrust regulations, you need to be aware of four types of prohibited activities. These are:

- price fixing,
- group boycotts,
- tie-in arrangements, and
- market allocation.

PRICE FIXING

Price fixing is defined as the cooperative setting of prices or price ranges by competing firms. Real estate firms can run afoul of the law against price fixing by setting, or appearing to set, uniform commission rates.

> **EXAMPLE:** Members of a local organization of real estate agents decide that they should all insist on 7% commissions. They arrange for 7% to be pre-printed in all their listing forms, and when potential sellers question the commission rate, the real estate agents say, "It's the same rate everybody charges." This would be considered a blatant case of illegal price fixing.

One of the best ways to avoid the appearance of price fixing is to scrupulously avoid discussing commission rates with competing agents. (Note that it's a discussion between *competing* agents that is dangerous—it's all right for a designated broker to discuss commission rates with her own sales agents.) The only exception to this general rule is that two competing designated brokers may discuss a commission split in a cooperative sale. In other words, designated brokers who represent the buyer and the seller may discuss how they will split the sales commission.

Even casually mentioning that you're changing your commission rate could lead to antitrust problems.

> **EXAMPLE:** A prominent designated broker attends a meeting of the local real estate agents' organization. He's asked to give a brief speech about his firm's sales goals. In the middle of his comments, he mentions that he's going to raise his firm's commission rate, even if nobody else raises theirs. The profitability of his firm depends on it.
>
> These statements could be interpreted as an invitation to conspire to fix prices. If any other members of the agents' organization follow his lead and raise their rates, they might be accused of accepting his invitation to fix prices.

As this example illustrates, an agent doesn't have to actually consult with other agents to be accused of conspiring to fix commission rates. Merely mentioning, among competing agents, an intent to increase rates could be enough to lead to an antitrust lawsuit.

When you are taking a listing, it is important to emphasize to the seller that the commission rate is freely negotiable. You should never imply that commission rates are set by law or by your local MLS or Board of Realtors®. Don't mention the rates of competing agents, either.

EXAMPLE: Harris is making a listing presentation to Bell. When Bell asks Harris about the commission, Harris casually says, "Oh, the commission rate is 7%." When Bell asks if she has to pay a 7% commission, Harris replies, "All the agents around here insist on a 7% commission. In fact, if you decided to pay a smaller commission, I'm not even sure that the MLS would accept the listing." Harris has violated the antitrust laws.

GROUP BOYCOTTS

Antitrust laws also prohibit group boycotts. A **group boycott** is an agreement between business competitors to exclude another competitor from fair participation in business activities. For example, an agreement between two or more real estate agents to exclude another agent from fair participation in real estate activities would be a group boycott. The purpose of a group boycott is to hurt or destroy a competitor, and this is automatically unlawful under the antitrust laws.

A group boycott doesn't have to be based on a formal arrangement or carried out by a large group of people.

EXAMPLE: Barker and Jaffrey, two real estate agents, meet to discuss an offer on a house. After discussing the offer, they begin talking about the business practices of a third agent, Hutton. Barker, angry with Hutton because of a past business transaction, claims that Hutton is dishonest. Barker says, "That sleazy jerk! I'll never do business with him again!" Jaffrey laughs. Barker then says, "You know, I've stopped returning Hutton's calls when he's asking about my listings. You should do the same thing. With any luck, the guy will be out of business in a few months." Jaffrey, who also disapproves of Hutton, agrees. Barker and Jaffrey could be found guilty of a conspiracy to boycott Hutton.

It's one thing to think another agent is dishonest or unethical and to choose to avoid her. It's another matter entirely to encourage other agents to do the same. You should never tell clients or other agents not to work with a competing agent because (for example) you have doubts about that agent's competence or integrity. (If you have evidence of an agent's incompetence or dishonesty, you should report this to the licensing authority.)

It would also be considered a group boycott if a multiple listing service refused to allow an agent to become a member because he had a different kind of fee schedule. For example, an MLS can't refuse membership to a brokerage firm just because it charges a small flat fee for a listing, rather than a percentage of the sales price.

TIE-IN ARRANGEMENTS

Another type of business practice that antitrust laws prohibit is a tie-in arrangement. A **tie-in arrangement** is defined as an agreement to sell one product only on the condition that the buyer also purchases a different (or "tied") product.

EXAMPLE: Fisher is a subdivision developer. Tyler, a builder, wants to buy a lot. Fisher tells Tyler that he will sell him a lot only if Tyler agrees that after Tyler builds a house on the lot, he will list the improved property with Fisher.

The type of agreement described in this example is known as a **list-back agreement**. List-back agreements are not unlawful. But requiring a lot buyer to enter into one as a condition of the sale is a tie-in arrangement and violates the antitrust laws.

Another danger area for real estate agents is agreeing to manage property only if the owner agrees to list that property with you.

EXAMPLE: Dahl, a licensee, is negotiating a property management agreement with Heinz, a property owner. Dahl wants to include a clause in the agreement that provides that if Heinz ever decides to sell the managed property, he will list the property with Dahl. If Dahl tells Heinz that she'll enter into a management agreement only if it includes this listing clause, Dahl is violating the antitrust laws.

MARKET ALLOCATION

Market allocation occurs when competing agents divide up the market by agreeing not to sell certain products or services in certain areas, or agreeing not to sell to certain customers in particular areas. Market allocation between competing agents is illegal, as it limits competition.

As with group boycotts, it's the collective action that makes market allocation illegal. An individual agent is free to determine the market areas in which she wants her brokerage to specialize; similarly, she can allocate territory to particular affiliated licensees within her brokerage. It's allocation of territory between competing firms that is considered group action and therefore a violation of antitrust law.

> **EXAMPLE:** Cecilia of ABC Realty assigns Ava to handle all incoming customers in the luxury home market, and assigns Paxton to all incoming customers in the vacant land market. This practice does not violate antitrust law.
>
> However, if Cecilia of ABC Realty and Carson of XYZ Realty agree to allocate customers so that ABC Realty will handle all luxury homes and XYZ Realty will handle all vacant land, this would violate antitrust law.

WASHINGTON UNFAIR BUSINESS PRACTICES AND CONSUMER PROTECTION ACT

The Washington Unfair Business Practices and Consumer Protection Act (commonly called the Consumer Protection Act) prohibits the same anticompetitive practices as the federal antitrust laws, including price fixing, group boycotts, tie-in arrangements, and market allocation. Beyond this, the Consumer Protection Act is a comprehensive law that bans "unfair or deceptive acts or practices in the conduct of any trade or commerce." Although the real estate industry is primarily regulated through the license law, it is also covered by the Consumer Protection Act.

So a real estate agent's failure to disclose material facts to a customer (or a conflict of interest to a client) would violate both the real estate license law and the Consumer Protection Act. For example, if you know that a commercial property that you have listed lacks commercial potential, but you fail to inform potential buyers, you might be liable to the buyer for damages under the Consumer Protection Act. (Despite the name, the Consumer Protection Act covers both consumer and commercial transactions.)

The Consumer Protection Act also prohibits misleading and deceptive advertising. An advertisement for a property that misrepresents its features, or an ad for brokerage services containing false information, would be a violation of this law.

This has particularly been an issue where advertisements for land development promotions have misled consumers about the acceptability of the lots for sale.

> **EXAMPLE:** Cunningham publishes an ad in a newspaper, offering inexpensive mountain-view lots in a new subdivision in eastern Washington. He neglects to mention that no utilities are available at the home sites, and that the ground is too dry to grow anything without installation of an irrigation system. Even if consumers bought the lots sight unseen, Cunningham could be required to give refunds to dissatisfied purchasers, or to pay for installation of utilities and other site improvements.

The Consumer Protection Act also applies to the sale of new homes. Under the act, the builder/seller of a new home gives the buyer an implied warranty of habitability. Latent defects that affect the safety and livability of the house violate the implied warranty, and the buyer could sue the builder/seller because of the defects.

> **EXAMPLE:** The Vaughn family purchases a house in a large new subdivision, Carlisle Ridge. After winter rains, it becomes clear that the foundation is unstable and rapidly settling, causing large cracks in the interior walls of the house. This is a fundamental defect affecting the safety of the house, and the Vaughns have grounds for a suit against the developer of Carlisle Ridge. The developer may be required to pay for the cost of repairs, or the Vaughns may be allowed to rescind the purchase.

In a situation like the one in the example, if a real estate agent was involved in the sale of the property and knew of the latent defects, the buyers might be able to sue the agent as well as the developer under the Consumer Protection Act.

A private party suing under the Consumer Protection Act may recover damages, court costs, and attorney's fees, and the court is allowed to triple the damages award. The state may also bring suit against a company or individual under this law.

ENVIRONMENTAL ISSUES

As we mentioned in Chapter 2, the seller disclosure statement calls for the disclosure of environmental hazards. Because of the growing concern about environmental hazards related to real estate—even residential real estate—it's worthwhile to discuss some of those hazards and the laws related to them. While you aren't expected to be an environmental expert, you should have a basic understanding of the environmental problems facing property owners and buyers today.

ENVIRONMENTAL LAWS

A number of federal and state environmental laws affect real estate agents and property buyers and sellers. We will just highlight a few of the most important laws.

NATIONAL ENVIRONMENTAL POLICY ACT. The National Environmental Policy Act (NEPA) requires federal agencies to provide an **environmental impact statement** (EIS) for any action that would have a significant effect on the environment. NEPA applies to all types of federal development, such as construction projects, the building of highways, and waste control. NEPA also applies to private uses or developments that require the approval of a federal agency in the form of a license, a permit, or even a federal loan. In these cases, federal agencies may require submission of an EIS before approving the use or development.

An EIS should disclose the impact of the development on energy consumption, sewage systems, school population, drainage, water facilities, and other environmental, economic, and social factors.

STATE ENVIRONMENTAL POLICY ACT. Washington has its own version of NEPA, the State Environmental Policy Act (SEPA). SEPA requires an environmental impact statement for all acts of state and local government agencies that may have a significant effect on the quality of the environment.

SEPA applies not only to developments by state and local agencies, but also to private developments that require the approval of state, city, or county government agencies. For instance, SEPA requirements must be met before a city or county can give approval for rezones, variances, conditional use permits, or building permits.

SHORELINE MANAGEMENT ACT. The purpose of Washington's Shoreline Management Act is to protect shorelines by regulating development within 200 feet of a high water mark. The act applies to coastal shorelines, to the shores of lakes larger than 20 acres, and to streams that flow at a rate in excess of 20 cubic feet per second.

Developers of shoreline property are required to obtain a **substantial development permit** from the local city or county government before beginning any work. A development is considered "substantial" if its value exceeds $6,416, or if it would materially interfere with the normal public use of the water or shoreline. (The state will adjust the dollar amount threshold for inflation again in 2017.)

Someone who violates the Shoreline Management Act may be fined up to $1,000 per day while the violation continues. A court may also order that the shoreline be restored to its original condition—even if this means the complete removal of any buildings or improvements.

Since there is so much shoreline in Washington, the Shoreline Management Act affects a large amount of property. Anyone purchasing shoreline property needs to consider what impact this law may have on their plans for the property.

CERCLA. One of the most important environmental laws is the federal Comprehensive Environmental Response, Compensation, and Liability Act (CERCLA). CERCLA concerns liability for environmental cleanup costs and has dramatically changed the way property buyers view potential environmental liability.

CERCLA is best known for its creation of a multibillion-dollar fund called **Superfund**. The purpose of Superfund is to clean up hazardous waste sites. CERCLA also created a process for identifying the parties who are responsible for cleanup costs. Cleanup costs may include the cost of cleaning up the site where the waste was released, as well as any neighboring properties that were contaminated.

The parties responsible for the cleanup may include both present and previous landowners. In some cases, the current owners of contaminated property may be required to pay for the cleanup even if they did not cause the contamination. A buyer who is considering purchasing property that may have been contaminated should consult an environmental engineer and/or an attorney specializing in environmental law.

Clean Water Act. Of particular concern to land developers is the federal law protecting **wetlands**—swamps, marshes, ponds, and similar areas where the soil is saturated for part of the year. Section 404 of the Clean Water Act makes it illegal for a private landowner to fill or drain wetlands on his property without obtaining a permit from the Army Corps of Engineers. Violations may be punished with an order to restore the wetlands, civil penalties, and even criminal sanctions.

The presence of a wetland is not necessarily a complete barrier to the development of a property, though. A landowner may fill a wetland for development if she creates or restores new wetlands elsewhere, so that there is no net loss of wetland area. Alternatively, the landowner may purchase the right to develop in wetland areas by paying into a government fund that is used to develop new wetlands elsewhere.

ENDANGERED SPECIES ACT. The purpose of the Endangered Species Act is to conserve habitats that shelter endangered or threatened species. There are dozens of listed species within Washington, many of which make their habitat primarily on private lands.

As with wetlands, however, the presence of an endangered species on a property does not completely bar development; private landowners may develop land supporting listed species if they agree to a Habitat Conservation Plan and undertake conservation measures. Landowners who agree to a plan and carry it out won't be required to take additional steps later on, even if the environmental circumstances change.

As a real estate agent, you should be familiar with the basic requirements of these environmental laws. And you should not hesitate to refer prospective buyers of developable land to the U.S. Environmental Protection Agency, the U.S. Fish and Wildlife Service, or the Washington Department of Ecology if they have any questions as to whether these laws may limit how they can use the land.

ENVIRONMENTAL HAZARDS

Now let's take a look at some of the more common environmental hazards that real estate agents need to know about.

ASBESTOS. Asbestos was used for many years in insulation on plumbing pipes and heating ducts, and as general insulation material. It can also be found in floor tile and roofing material. In its original condition, asbestos is considered relatively harmless; but when asbestos dust filters into the air, it can cause lung cancer. Asbestos becomes a hazard in two ways: when it gets old and starts to disintegrate into a fine dust, and when it is damaged or removed during remodeling projects.

There are three methods of dealing with the presence of asbestos:

1. enclosure (this involves placing an airtight barrier between the asbestos and the rest of the space);
2. encapsulation (this involves covering the asbestos with an adhesive that will permanently seal in the asbestos fibers); or
3. removal.

Each of these three methods should only be undertaken by an experienced professional.

UREA FORMALDEHYDE. Until 1982, urea formaldehyde was used in foam insulation. It was banned because of the risk of illness caused by the formaldehyde gas released from the foam insulation. Urea formaldehyde foam insulation (UFFI) is not found in most American homes. If a home does contain UFFI, the health department can test the amount of formaldehyde gas being released from the insulation. UFFI can be removed, but new insulation and wall siding will have to be installed.

Urea formaldehyde may also be found in the adhesives used in pressed wood building materials, which are widely used in furniture, kitchen cabinets, and some types of paneling.

Urea formaldehyde may cause cancer, skin rashes, and breathing problems. However, it emits significant amounts of dangerous gas only in the first few years. Older urea formaldehyde materials are not considered dangerous.

RADON. Radon, a colorless, odorless gas, is actually present almost everywhere. It is found wherever uranium is deposited in the earth's crust. As uranium decays, radon gas is formed and seeps from the earth, usually into the atmosphere. However, radon sometimes collects in buildings. For example, radon may enter a house through cracks in the foundation or through floor drains. Exposure to dangerous levels of radon gas may cause lung cancer.

There are three ways to lower radon levels in a home:

1. sealing the holes and cracks that allow the gas to enter the home;
2. increasing ventilation to dilute the gas, especially in the areas where radon enters, such as the basement or crawl spaces; and
3. pressurizing the home to keep the gas out.

LEAD-BASED PAINT. Lead, though useful for many things, is extremely toxic to human beings. Children are especially susceptible to lead poisoning because they absorb it more quickly and have a more adverse reaction to its toxicity. Lead damages the brain, the kidneys, and the central nervous system.

The most common source of lead in the home is lead-based paint. Many homes built before 1978 contain some lead-based paint. (Lead is now banned in consumer paint.) As lead-based paint deteriorates, or if it is sanded or scraped, it forms a lead dust that accumulates inside and outside the home. This dust can be breathed in or ingested, increasing the risk of toxic lead exposure.

FIG. 3.3   ENVIRONMENTAL HAZARDS

ENVIRONMENTAL HAZARDS THAT MAY AFFECT HOMES

- ASBESTOS
- UREA FORMALDEHYDE
- RADON GAS
- LEAD-BASED PAINT
- UNDERGROUND STORAGE TANKS
- WATER CONTAMINATION
- ILLEGAL DRUG MANUFACTURING
- MOLD
- GEOLOGIC HAZARDS: LANDSLIDES, FLOODING, SUBSIDENCE, AND EARTHQUAKES

If there is lead-based paint in a home, it can be either eliminated or covered with non-lead-based paint. This requires special equipment and training; homeowners should not try to handle lead-based paint on their own.

Under some circumstances, a seller or landlord is required by law to make disclosures concerning lead-based paint to prospective buyers or tenants. This disclosure law is discussed in Chapter 7.

UNDERGROUND STORAGE TANKS. Underground storage tanks are found not only on commercial and industrial properties, but also on residential properties. A storage tank is considered underground if 10% of its volume (including piping) is below the earth's surface. Probably the most common commercial use of underground storage tanks is for gas stations. Chemical plants, paint manufacturers, and other industries use underground storage tanks to store toxic liquids. In the residential setting, older homes used underground storage tanks to store fuel oil.

The principal danger from underground storage tanks is that they eventually grow old and begin to rust, leaking toxic products into the soil or, even more dangerously, into the groundwater.

Removing underground storage tanks and cleaning up the contaminated soil can be time-consuming and expensive. Both federal and state laws regulate the removal of storage tanks and the necessary cleanup.

WATER CONTAMINATION. Water can be contaminated by a variety of agents, including bacteria, viruses, nitrates, metals such as lead or mercury, fertilizers and pesticides, and radon. These contaminants may come from underground storage tanks, industrial discharge, urban area runoff, malfunctioning septic systems, and runoff from agricultural areas. Drinking contaminated water can cause physical symptoms that range from mild stomachaches to kidney and liver damage, cancer, and death.

If a homeowner uses a well as a water source, it should be tested by health authorities or private laboratories at least once a year. If well water becomes contaminated, a new well may have to be dug.

ILLEGAL DRUG MANUFACTURING. If property has been the site of illegal drug manufacturing, there may be substantial health risks for the occupants. The chemicals used to manufacture certain illegal drugs are highly toxic, and the effects of the contamination can linger for a long time.

If property is currently being used to manufacture illegal drugs, it can be seized by the government. This can occur even if the owner has no knowledge of the illegal drug activity.

> **EXAMPLE:** Meyers owns a single-family home that has been used as a rental property for several years. Unknown to Meyers, the current tenants are manufacturing illegal drugs in the basement of the home. The property could be seized by the government, even though Meyers knows nothing about the drug activity.

Of course, a property should not be listed or sold until any conditions that may subject the property to seizure have been eliminated.

MOLD. Mold is a commonplace problem, especially in damp parts of houses such as basements and bathrooms. For most people, the presence of mold does not cause any adverse effects. However, for people who are allergic to mold or who have respiratory problems, the presence of mold may render a house unlivable. You may hear references to "toxic mold," which is something of a misnomer; certain varieties of black mold can be particularly problematic for those who are sensitive to mold, but generally do not pose any more of a health hazard for most people than other types of mold.

Mold can never be completely eliminated, but it can be controlled by cutting off sources of moisture. Mold that is already growing can be removed by scrubbing with a water and bleach solution. Carpet or tile that is affected by mold may need to be removed and thrown out.

Awareness of mold has increased greatly in recent years, as a result of some high-profile lawsuits against builders or insurance companies, as well as news reports about contamination of public buildings, such as schools and government offices. "Mold contingencies," where sale of a property is contingent upon not finding mold during the inspection process, are sometimes written into purchase and sale agreements.

Mold problems that you're aware of should be treated as a latent defect and disclosed to prospective buyers. You should also disclose any knowledge of previous incidents of flooding or water damage, since that can start the growth of mold. Bear in mind that mold may grow out of sight, inside walls or heating ducts, and will not necessarily be discovered in an inspection, so your disclosure is particularly important.

GEOLOGIC HAZARDS. Geologic hazards are a significant concern for many property owners in Washington, especially in the western part of the state.

LANDSLIDES. Probably the most costly geologic problem affecting homeowners is landslides. It's quite common for a house to be built close to the top of a cliff overlooking a body of water, in order to take advantage of the view. However, the weight of the house on unstable soil, particularly after heavy rainfall, can cause ground movement downhill, damaging the foundation or even tearing the house apart.

When you're dealing with a property located on or near a steep slope, you should always look for signs of ground movement. Active soil erosion, cracking, dipping, or slumping ground, and tilting trees are all indicators of slide activity. A property owner may take corrective steps, such as building retaining walls or rockeries, but they are expensive and unlikely to completely solve the problem.

If you see any evidence of landslide activity, it may be wise to consult with a geologist, in order to assess the magnitude of the problem. In addition, if you have listed a property where there is any evidence of ground movement, that should be considered a latent defect and disclosed to potential buyers.

FLOODING. Flooding can also be a serious problem for property owners. Whenever property is located in a flood plain—in the low-lying, flat areas immediately adjacent to a river—there is cause for concern. A prudent agent will check for signs of previous flood damage to structures, particularly in basements and foundations. An agent listing a flood-prone property should disclose frequent flooding as a latent defect.

SUBSIDENCE. Another potential geologic problem is subsidence, the collapse of ground into underground cavities. This can occur naturally, but only in areas of particularly porous bedrock. In most cases, subsidence is caused by man-made cavities. It may happen when forgotten underground storage tanks collapse, or when underground tanks have been removed but the soil has not been properly replaced. It is most common where mining has occurred. Over 50,000 acres of abandoned coal mines underlie parts of western Washington, so before engaging in new construction in rural areas where coal mining once occurred, it may be advisable to obtain maps from state or local governments that depict old mines.

EARTHQUAKES. The most potentially destructive geologic problem is also the least predictable and least controllable: earthquakes. Because this is a regional problem, rather than one that affects one or a few properties, there is not much sense in disclosing general earthquake hazards to potential buyers.

However, steps can be taken to protect buildings against earthquakes. In fact, seismic retrofitting can make a property more desirable and increase its value. The most important step in this process involves bolting elements of a home's wood frame to the underlying foundation. Many contractors are able to perform this type of work, and information about seismic retrofitting is widely available from state and local government agencies.

REAL ESTATE AGENT'S RESPONSIBILITIES

As you make your listing presentation and later prepare offers to purchase, you have two major responsibilities in regard to environmental issues:

1. to recognize potential environmental hazards, and
2. to recommend that the seller obtain the advice of an environmental attorney or other environmental expert.

If you are representing a seller whose property has environmental problems, it is better to have an attorney draft the appropriate disclosures instead of doing it yourself—if only to lessen your own liability. And if you represent buyers who are interested in purchasing a property with environmental problems, you need to make sure that they understand the potential risks of such a purchase. These risks should be explained to them by their attorney.

Naturally, contaminated property should change hands only after the cleanup has been completed. But even then, under federal environmental laws, the buyers may be assuming more potential liability than they are aware of. As the new owners of the property, the buyers may be held responsible for any additional cleanup costs, even though they had nothing to do with the contamination.

CHAPTER SUMMARY

1. The real estate license law imposes certain restrictions on your listing activities. As a licensee, you can be paid your commission only by your own brokerage. You can't be paid by other firms or other licensees, or by the principal. And you may not sue the principal for a commission; only the firm may sue the principal.

2. A listing agreement belongs to the listing firm. It is a contract between the property seller and the firm; you sign the listing agreement only as an agent of your firm. Should you stop working for the listing firm, the listing remains with the firm. You can't take it with you to your new firm.

3. Under the state's distressed property law, if a licensee meets the definition of a distressed home consultant (which would be rare), she must have a distressed home consultant agreement with the distressed homeowner (seller). She will also owe specific fiduciary duties to the distressed homeowner.

4. The federal Fair Housing Act prohibits discrimination based on race, color, religion, sex, national origin, disability, or familial status. The Washington Law Against Discrimination prohibits discrimination based on race, creed, color, national origin, sex, sexual orientation, marital status, familial status, veteran or military status, or sensory, physical, or mental disability, or the use of a trained guide dog or service dog. Both laws apply to real estate agents acting in their professional capacity *without exception*.

5. While dealing with potential clients and taking listings, you need to scrupulously follow all fair housing laws. Never imply that the presence of a particular group of residents will change property values or other characteristics of a neighborhood. Never refuse to list a property because of a protected characteristic (such as the race or ethnic background) of the home seller. Avoid making any kind of discriminatory slur, including telling racial or ethnic jokes or passively listening to them. You should also review fair housing laws with the seller before taking a listing. If you think the seller may discriminate against potential purchasers, you must refuse to take the listing.

6. When you advertise listed properties, make sure that all your advertising complies with fair housing laws. Never send flyers or choose advertising media based on discriminatory ideas, and make sure any models included in ads are not used in a discriminatory manner. Remember to include the fair housing logo or slogan in your ads.

7. Antitrust laws prohibit price fixing, group boycotts, tie-in arrangements, and market allocation. To avoid charges of price fixing, you should never discuss your commission rates with competing agents, and you must be sure to explain to the seller that the commission rate is fully negotiable. Never use a listing agreement form that has a commission amount or rate already filled in.

8. You should be familiar with the basic provisions of several environmental laws, including the National Environmental Policy Act, the State Environmental Policy Act, the Shoreline Management Act, and the Comprehensive Environmental Response, Compensation, and Liability Act (CERCLA). CERCLA is particularly important, because it may impose liability on property owners for the cost of cleaning up hazardous substances, regardless of fault.

9. The environmental hazards you need to be aware of include asbestos, urea formaldehyde, radon, lead-based paint, underground storage tanks, water contamination, and the effects of illegal drug manufacturing. You must be able to recognize potential environmental hazards in a listed property, and be prepared to advise the seller to consult an environmental professional.

CHAPTER QUIZ

1. Agent Jackson and Agent Robinson work for the same real estate firm, Stellar Properties. They've both worked closely with a particular buyer. When that buyer finally purchases a house, Stellar Properties receives the selling agent's share of the commission and pays Jackson half of it. Jackson then gives half of her share of the commission to Robinson. This is:

    a. legal, because once a commission share has been paid to a licensee, she is entitled to do whatever she wants with it

    b. legal, because agents are allowed to share compensation if they work for the same firm

    c. illegal, because a firm can share a commission only with another licensed firm

    d. illegal, because a commission split must be handled by the firm or firms involved

2. Generally speaking, a real estate licensee will not be considered a distressed home consultant (and subject to the distressed property law requirements) unless:

    a. he helps a buyer purchase a home that will foreclose soon

    b. he helps a seller sell her home before a foreclosure sale

    c. he personally participates in a distressed property transaction

    d. the buyer delays taking possession until she sells her current home

3. Although the federal Fair Housing Act and the Washington Law Against Discrimination are similar, one significant difference between them is that:

    a. only the Washington law allows an award of damages

    b. the Washington law applies to a wider range of real estate transactions than the Fair Housing Act

    c. the Fair Housing Act covers all types of real property, while the Washington law covers only housing

    d. the Washington law allows an exemption for real estate agents engaged in professional activity

4. Which of the following is not an example of illegal steering?

    a. An agent working with a buyer who has a disability calls his attention to a property with modifications that meet his needs

    b. An agent avoids showing an unmarried buyer houses in neighborhoods where most residents are married couples with children

    c. An agent working with a white couple only shows them homes in predominantly white neighborhoods

    d. An agent working with a minority couple only shows them homes in predominantly minority neighborhoods

5. Your advertising for residential properties should always include:

    a. models from the same ethnic group as the residents of the neighborhood you are advertising in

    b. models of a different ethnic background than the residents of the neighborhood you are advertising in

    c. the Equal Housing Opportunity logo or slogan

    d. a specific explanation of the standards of the community

6. Which of the following actions is most likely to be considered discriminatory?

    a. When a white buyer asks about the racial composition of a neighborhood, an agent truthfully answers that it is predominantly minority

    b. The listing agent for a home in a predominantly minority neighborhood decides to advertise only in the neighborhood newspaper because he thinks other minorities are most likely to be interested in the home

    c. A brokerage uses a marketing plan to let minority buyers know about properties in predominantly white neighborhoods that they might not otherwise be aware of

    d. A white couple expresses a desire not to be shown homes in a minority neighborhood, and their agent complies with their request

7. Which of the following is an example of price fixing?

    a. A listing agent and a selling agent discuss a commission split in a cooperative sale

    b. An agent making a listing presentation tells the seller that she is asking for a 7% commission, but emphasizes that the commission is negotiable

    c. A designated broker holds a staff meeting with her sales agents to discuss commission rates for the office

    d. A designated broker is having lunch with two other designated brokers and mentions that he is raising his commission rate, but there is no further discussion of the matter

8. The Consumer Protection Act does not:

    a. make property owners responsible for the cost of cleaning up hazardous waste even if they did not cause the contamination

    b. prohibit misleading and deceptive advertising

    c. apply to the real estate industry

    d. prohibit the same anticompetitive practices as federal antitrust law

9. Which environmental law requires developers to obtain a substantial development permit before beginning work?

    a. Shoreline Management Act

    b. Endangered Species Act

    c. National Environmental Policy Act

    d. Clean Water Act

10. As a real estate agent, what is your responsibility with respect to environmental issues?

    a. Recognizing potential hazards and recommending that your clients obtain expert advice

    b. Making sure that an environmental impact statement is provided to the buyer

    c. Deciding what corrective action needs to be taken to solve the problem

    d. All of the above

ANSWER KEY

1. d. Two agents working for the same firm may split a commission, but the commission split must be handled by their firm. A licensee can only receive a commission through her firm.

2. c. Most real estate licensees are exempt from the provisions of the distressed property law when they are providing routine real estate brokerage services. However, if a licensee actually participates in a distressed property transaction, he may be considered a distressed home consultant.

3. b. The Washington Law Against Discrimination covers all real estate transactions, not just residential transactions. It also specifically prohibits a broader range of activities and protects more classes of people than the Fair Housing Act.

4. a. An agent can legitimately bring properties that are specially suited to the needs of a disabled buyer to the buyer's attention.

5. c. Regardless of what type of advertising you use to market a home, it should always include the Equal Housing Opportunity logo or slogan.

6. b. Advertising can be considered discriminatory if it appears only in a publication directed toward the minority neighborhood where the property is located. The advertising should also appear where it will be seen by a broader section of the population.

7. d. Any communication between competing designated brokers about prices, even if they do not explicitly decide to cooperate in fixing prices, could be seen as an invitation to engage in price fixing.

8. a. The Consumer Protection Act overlaps significantly with federal antitrust law and the real estate license law. Liability for cleanup of hazardous waste is determined under CERCLA and other environmental laws.

9. a. Under the Shoreline Management Act, developers must obtain a substantial development permit before starting work on property within 200 feet of a high water mark.

10. a. If there are environmental issues concerning a property, you should always recommend that your clients seek expert advice from an environmental engineer or attorney.

4

EVALUATING AND PRICING PROPERTY

THE AGENT'S ROLE IN PRICING PROPERTY

VALUE

- Types of value
- Value vs. price or cost

COMPETITIVE MARKET ANALYSIS

- Analyzing the seller's property
  - Neighborhood analysis
  - Site analysis
  - Building analysis
  - Design and layout
  - Design deficiencies
- Choosing comparable properties
- Making adjustments to the comparables
- Estimating market value
- Completing a CMA
- The CMA form

THE PROBLEM OF A LOW APPRAISAL

INTRODUCTION

How quickly your listing sells, or whether it sells at all, depends largely on the listing price. How is a competitive listing price determined? If your seller insists on listing her home at a ridiculously inflated price, should you simply take the listing and hope for the best?

In this chapter, we will discuss the listing agent's role in evaluating and pricing a seller's home, the dangers of setting a listing price too high, the concept of value, and how to complete a competitive market analysis.

THE AGENT'S ROLE IN PRICING PROPERTY

It is your seller's responsibility—not yours—to decide on a listing price for his home. But the average seller does not have the knowledge or expertise to arrive at a realistic price. Your seller will depend on you for information and advice about this important decision. Without your expertise, the seller could easily underprice or overprice his property. Either of these mistakes could have serious consequences for you and for the seller.

EXAMPLE: Jeffries is listing his home with you. He asks you for advice on setting a listing price, but you tell him that the price is up to him.

Jeffries has noticed a few houses in his neighborhood that have been for sale for many months. He believes the houses haven't sold because they are overpriced. He thinks his house is comparable to these other houses, but he wants a quick sale. So Jeffries sets his listing price by deducting $10,000 from the listing price of the other houses. He ends up listing his house for $320,000.

Jeffries's house is actually very appealing and sells quickly at that price. When his house is appraised, he discovers to his dismay that it was actually worth about $350,000. He's very angry—he just lost $30,000 and he considers it entirely your fault. If he decided to sue you, you could lose your commission and might even have to pay additional damages as well.

On the other hand, suppose that when Jeffries sets his listing price, he thinks his house is worth much more than it really is. With a listing price of $390,000, his house languishes on the market for several months. Finally, your listing agreement expires and Jeffries decides to list the property with another firm. Because of an inflated listing price, Jeffries waited in vain for a sale, you wasted a good deal of effort trying to sell an overpriced house, and your reputation in the neighborhood suffered as your "For Sale" sign faded and was then removed without a "SOLD!" banner.

Your ability to suggest a competitive listing price is one of the most important services you can provide a seller. Your advice on a listing price will generally take the form of a **competitive market analysis** (CMA). A CMA compares your seller's house to other similar houses that are on the market or have recently sold. The listing or sales prices of those other houses helps the seller set a realistic listing price for her own house.

A CMA is similar to an appraisal, but it is not an appraisal. As the listing agent, your role is very different from that of an appraiser. Your job is to provide the seller with information about the sales prices of similar homes. This is the information that is contained in your CMA. The seller uses this information to decide how much to ask for her property.

An appraiser, on the other hand, uses his professional experience to estimate the property's market value as of a specific date. The appraiser usually does this for a lender, to help the lender set a maximum loan amount for the loan applicant who wants to buy the property. The appraiser bases this estimate on a wide variety of data, including general social and economic data. An appraisal is much more complex than a competitive market analysis and is based on more information.

VALUE

The value of a home has many consequences for the owner. The value largely determines not only how much it costs to purchase the home, but also the financing, the property tax assessment, the insurance coverage, the potential rental rate, the eventual selling price, and the income tax consequences of its sale.

To estimate the value of a home, you need a general understanding of the concept of value. First of all, keep in mind that value is created by people. It is not so much the intrinsic qualities of an item that make it valuable, but rather our attitudes toward it. For example, if it were to begin raining gold instead of water, gold would become a nuisance and its value would disappear. Yet its intrinsic qualities would be the same whether it was a rare and precious metal or a too-common nuisance.

TYPES OF VALUE

Appraisers distinguish between several different types of value. A property's value can vary depending on which type of value is in question in a given situation. For example, **value in use** is the subjective value placed on a property by someone who owns or uses it. By contrast, **value in exchange** (commonly referred to as **market value**) is the objective value of a property in the eyes of the average person. The difference between these two types of value is one reason the seller needs your help in setting a listing price.

> **EXAMPLE:** Darnell owns a large old house that has been in his family for generations. Because of the history of the house, it is very valuable to Darnell. In other words, its value in use is very high. Yet if an objective third party were considering buying the house, she would not be willing to pay very much for it. The plumbing is poor, the wiring is old, and the design is very outdated. The property's value in exchange is not nearly as high as its value in use.

Real estate agents are concerned with value in exchange, or market value. Here is the most widely accepted definition of market value, taken from the Federal National Mortgage Association (Fannie Mae):

> *The most probable price which a property should bring in a competitive and open market under all conditions requisite to a fair sale, the buyer and seller each acting prudently and knowledgeably, and assuming the price is not affected by undue stimulus.*

VALUE VS. PRICE OR COST

When you're estimating the value of property, always remember that there's an important distinction between market value and market price. **Market price** is the price actually paid for a property, regardless of whether the parties to the transaction were informed and acting free of unusual pressure. Market value, as you've seen, is what should be paid if a property is purchased and sold under all the conditions requisite to a fair sale.

Another related concept is that of cost. **Cost** is the amount of money that was paid to acquire the property and build the structures on it. A property's cost, value, and price may all be different.

> **EXAMPLE:** A developer paid $35,000 for a parcel of vacant land and then spent $100,000 to build a house on the land. After the house was completed, the property was worth $150,000. But the developer needed some fast cash, so he sold the property at the "fire sale" price of $140,000. The cost of the house was $135,000, the value of the house was $150,000, and the price of the house was $140,000.

The basis for a good listing price for a home is its market value, not its original cost or purchase price. And the real estate agent's best tool for estimating market value is a competitive market analysis.

COMPETITIVE MARKET ANALYSIS

Although a competitive market analysis is not the only way to arrive at a listing price, there's a lot to recommend it. It has two key advantages over the "eyeball" approach to setting a listing price: it's reliable, and it's easy to explain.

With the eyeball approach, the real estate agent simply walks through the seller's house, observes its features, and then mentally compares them to features he's observed in other houses. The agent then decides on what he feels is a competitive price. A price reached in this way can be far from the true market value. Not only that, the agent does not have any data to support his conclusion if the seller questions him about it.

An estimate of value based on your gut feelings is especially problematic when the seller is expecting to get more for her property than it's worth. Unless you can back up your "low" estimate with facts and figures that are easy to understand, you will lose credibility as well as the seller's good will. So it's important to have a simple method of valuing property that is easy to apply and to explain.

In a formal appraisal, the appraiser may estimate the property's value by applying these three methods:

1. **Cost approach to value.** Estimating how much it would cost to build a similar structure, and then subtracting the depreciation that has accrued.
2. **Income approach to value.** Estimating value based on the income the property could potentially generate.
3. **Sales comparison approach to value.** Estimating value by comparing the property to similar properties that have recently sold.

The first two methods can be complicated, time-consuming, and difficult for a seller to understand. The third method, the sales comparison approach, is much simpler to use and easier for the seller to understand. In addition, the sales comparison approach is considered the most reliable method for appraising residential property. As a result, real estate agents have borrowed the sales comparison method of appraisal and modified it for their own use. This modified sales comparison method is called competitive market analysis, or CMA.

With a CMA, you estimate the value of your seller's property by comparing it to similar nearby properties that have sold recently or are for sale. CMAs are effective because an informed buyer acting free of pressure will not pay more for a particular property than she would have to pay for an equally desirable substitute property. Thus, if the seller is objective, he will base the listing price on the prices recently paid for similar properties in the same area.

The steps involved in completing a CMA include:

1. collecting and analyzing information about the seller's property,
2. choosing the comparable properties,
3. comparing the seller's property to the comparables and adjusting the value of the comparables accordingly, and
4. estimating a realistic listing price for the seller's property.

There are many computer programs available to help you prepare a CMA. (Your managing broker's office or your MLS is likely to have one you can use.) However, even though these programs simplify the tasks considerably, you must still have a firm understanding of the principles underlying the process.

ANALYZING THE SELLER'S PROPERTY

The first step is to gather and study information about the seller's property. Naturally, you should pay the most attention to the elements that have the greatest impact on value. These elements fall into three categories:

1. the property's neighborhood,
2. the property (or site) itself, and
3. the improvements on the property.

As you collect information about the seller's property (sometimes called the **subject property**), keep in mind that you will need to gather the same information about the properties you choose as comparables.

NEIGHBORHOOD ANALYSIS. Few factors have as great an impact on a property's value as its location, or neighborhood. A neighborhood is an area that contains similar types of properties; it may be residential, commercial, industrial, or agricultural. Its boundaries may be determined by physical obstacles (such as highways and bodies of water), land use patterns, the age and value of homes or other buildings, and the economic status of the residents.

Neighborhood characteristics set the upper and lower limits of a property's value. A high-quality property cannot overcome the adverse influence of a poor neighborhood. And the value of a relatively weak property is enhanced by a desirable neighborhood.

Here are some specific factors to look at when gathering data about a residential neighborhood:

1. **Percentage of homeownership.** Is there a high degree of owner-occupancy, or do rental properties predominate? Owner-occupied homes are generally better-maintained and less susceptible to deterioration.

2. **Vacant homes and lots.** An unusual number of vacant homes or lots suggests a low level of interest in the area, which has a negative effect on property values. On the other hand, significant construction activity indicates strong interest in the area.

3. **Conformity.** The homes in a neighborhood should be reasonably similar in style, age, size, and quality. Strictly enforced zoning and private restrictions promote conformity and protect property values.

4. **Changing land use.** Is the neighborhood in the middle of a transition from residential use to some other type of use? If so, the properties may be losing their value.

5. **Contour of the land.** Mildly rolling topography is preferable to terrain that is either monotonously flat or excessively hilly.

6. **Streets.** Wide, gently curving streets are more appealing than narrow or straight streets. Streets should be hard-surfaced and well maintained.

7. **Utilities.** Does the neighborhood have electricity, gas, water, sewers, and telephones? What about cable television and high-speed Internet access?

8. **Nuisances.** Not surprisingly, nuisances (odors, eyesores, industrial noises or pollutants, or exposure to unusual winds, smog, or fog) in or near a neighborhood hurt property values.

9. **Reputation.** Is the neighborhood considered prestigious? If so, that will increase property values.

10. **Proximity.** How far is it to traffic arterials and to important points such as downtown, employment centers, and shopping centers?

11. **Schools.** What schools serve the neighborhood? Are they highly regarded? Are they within walking distance? The quality of a school or school district can make a major difference in property values in a residential neighborhood.

12. **Public services.** How well is the neighborhood served by public transportation, police, and fire units?

13. **Governmental influences.** Does zoning in and around the neighborhood promote residential use and insulate the property owner from nuisances? How do the property tax rates compare with those of other neighborhoods nearby?

You can use a form (on paper or on a computer) such as the one shown in Figure 4.1 to record your neighborhood information. (Some CMA software may gather neighborhood information from your local MLS or other sources.) Of course, as you gain more experience, you will become familiar with all of the neighborhoods in your area and their distinguishing characteristics. Before long, you will be able to gauge the effect of the neighborhood on a property's value as soon as you hear where the property is located.

SITE ANALYSIS. Studying the site of the subject property means collecting information about the following factors:

1. **Width.** This refers to the lot's measurements from one side boundary to the other. Width can vary from front to back, as in the case of a pie-shaped lot on a cul-de-sac.

2. **Frontage.** Frontage is the length of the front boundary of the lot, the boundary that abuts a street or a body of water. The amount of frontage can be an important consideration if it measures the property's access or exposure to something desirable.

3. **Depth.** Depth is the distance between the site's front boundary and its rear boundary. Greater depth (more than the norm) can mean greater value, but it doesn't always. For example, suppose Lot 1 and Lot 2 are the same, except that Lot 2 is deeper; Lot 2 is not necessarily more valuable than Lot 1. Each situation must be analyzed individually to determine whether more depth translates into greater value.

4. **Area.** Area is the total size of the site, usually measured in square feet or acres. Comparisons between lots often focus on the features of frontage and area.

    Commercial land is usually valued in terms of frontage; that is, it is worth a certain number of dollars per front foot. Industrial land, on the other hand, tends to be valued in terms of square feet or acreage. Residential lots are measured both ways: by square feet or by acreage in

FIG. 4.1   NEIGHBORHOOD DATA FORM

NEIGHBORHOOD DATA

Property adjacent to:

NORTH_____Plum Boulevard, garden apartments_____

SOUTH_____Cherry Street, single-family homes_____

EAST_____14th Avenue, single-family homes_____

WEST_____12th Avenue, single-family homes_____

Population: __ increasing   __ decreasing   _x_ stable

Life cycle stage: __integration   _x_ equilibrium   __disintegration   __rebirth

Tax rate: __ higher __lower _x_ same as competing areas

Services: _x_ police   _x_ fire   _x_ garbage   __other: _____

Average family size: _3.5_____

Occupational status: _White collar; skilled trades_____

Distance from:

Commercial areas _3 miles_____

Elementary school _6 blocks_____

Secondary school _1 mile_____

Recreational areas _2 miles_____

Cultural centers _3 miles_____

Places of worship _Methodist, Catholic, Baptist_____

Transportation _Bus stop 1 block; frequent service to downtown_

Freeway/highway _10 blocks_____

Typical Properties	Age	Price Range	Owner-occupancy
Vacant lots: 0%			
Single-family homes: 80%	20 yrs	$175,000-$200,000	93%
Apartments, 2- to 4-unit: 15%	10 yrs		
Apartments, over 4 units: 5%	5 yrs		
Non-residential: 0%			

Nuisances (odors, noise, etc.) _None_____

Environmental hazards (chemical storage, etc.) _None_____

most instances, but by front foot when the property abuts a lake or river, or some other desirable feature.

Under certain circumstances, combining two or more adjoining lots to achieve greater width, depth, or area will make the larger parcel more valuable than the sum of the values of its component parcels. The increment of value that results when two or more lots are combined to produce greater value is called **plottage**. The process of assembling lots to increase their value is most frequently part of industrial or commercial land development.

5. **Shape.** Lots with uniform width and depth (such as rectangular lots) are almost always more useful than irregularly shaped lots; a standard shape is more versatile for building purposes. This is true for any kind of lot—residential, commercial, or industrial.

6. **Topography.** A site is generally more valuable if it is aesthetically appealing. Rolling terrain is preferable to flat, monotonous land. On the other hand, if the site would be costly to develop because it sits well above or below the street or is excessively hilly, that lessens its value.

7. **Position and orientation.** How a lot is situated relative to the surrounding area influences its value. Consider whether the site has a view, and how much sunshine it gets during the day. And is it sheltered, or exposed to the elements and/or to traffic noise?

8. **Title.** Of course, any title problems will have an adverse effect on the value of the property. When you examine the site, look for signs of easements or encroachments. If a utility company has an easement across the rear portion of the property, for example, this would reduce the value of the property in comparison to a similar property with no easement.

You may want to use a worksheet such as the one shown in Figure 4.2 to record the information you gather about the site.

BUILDING ANALYSIS. After examining the neighborhood and the site of the seller's property, the next step is to examine the improvements built on the property. For the typical residential property, this means a house and garage, and perhaps a garden shed or workshop. Here are some of the primary factors to analyze.

1. **Construction quality.** Is the quality of the materials and workmanship good, average, or poor?

FIG. 4.2   SITE DATA FORM

SITE DATA

Address   10157 - 13th Avenue

Legal description   Lot 6, Block 4, Caldwell's Addition, vol. 72, pg. 25

Dimensions 50' x 200'   Shape Rectangular

Square feet 10,000   Street paving Asphalt

Landscaping Adequate   Topsoil Good

Drainage Good   Frontage (Street)

Easements Utility S 15'   Corner lot__ Inside lot_x_ View__

Encroachments Fence on west property line?

Improvements: _x_ Driveway   _x_ Sidewalks   _x_ Curbs   __ Alley

Utilities: _x_ Electricity   __ Gas   _x_ Water   _x_ Sewers   _x_ Storm drains
            _x_ Telephone   _x_ Cable TV   _x_ High-speed Internet

---

2. **Age/condition.** How old is the home? Is its overall condition good, average, or poor? Depending on the condition, the effective age of the home may be more or less than its actual age.

3. **Size of house (square footage).** This includes the improved living area, excluding the garage, basement, and porches. (Note that an appraiser will exclude the square footage of any addition that was built without a valid permit when she is appraising the property.)

4. **Basement.** A functional basement, especially a finished basement, contributes to value. (However, the amount a finished basement contributes to value is often not enough to recover the cost of the finish work.)

5. **Number of rooms.** Add up the total number of rooms in the house, excluding bathrooms and basement rooms.

6. **Number of bedrooms.** The number of bedrooms has a major impact on value. For instance, if all else is equal, a two-bedroom home is worth considerably less than a three-bedroom home.

7. **Number of bathrooms.** A full bath is a wash basin, toilet, shower, and bathtub; a three-quarter bath is a wash basin, toilet, and either a shower or tub. A half bath is a wash basin and toilet only. The number of bathrooms can have a noticeable effect on value.

8. **Air conditioning.** The presence or absence of an air conditioning system is important in hot regions.

9. **Energy efficiency.** With rising energy costs, an energy-efficient home is more valuable than a comparable one that is not. Energy-efficient features, such as double-paned windows, good insulation, and weather stripping, increase value.

10. **Garage or carport.** An enclosed garage is generally better than a carport. How many cars can it accommodate? Is there work or storage space in addition to space for parking? Is it possible to enter the home directly from the garage or carport, protected from the weather?

11. **Design and layout.** Is the floor plan functional and convenient? Are the design and layout attractive and efficient, or are there obvious design deficiencies that will decrease the value of the home? (We'll discuss design and layout in more detail in the next section of the chapter.)

You might want to use a form such as the one shown in Figure 4.3 to record the information you gather about the quality and condition of the improvements.

DESIGN AND LAYOUT. A well-designed house is one that is the right size, shape, and configuration to produce the maximum value. Here are some questions to ask yourself as you examine the design of a house.

GENERAL DESIGN. The number of bedrooms in a house usually determines which buyers will consider purchasing it. Keep in mind the family size of those potential buyers as you evaluate the house.

In relation to the number of bedrooms, is the house large enough overall? Are there enough bathrooms, and an adequate number of closets? Is there a separate family room, children's playroom, or other recreational space? Is there sufficient work space in the kitchen and laundry room, and is there storage space for cleaning and gardening tools? Are there enough windows and natural light, especially in the kitchen and other work or recreational spaces?

LIVING ROOM AND FAMILY ROOM. How large are the living room and the family or recreation room (if any)? Will the shape of each room and the available wall space accommodate the furniture that will probably be placed in it?

DINING ROOM OR DINING AREA. Is the dining area convenient to the kitchen and large enough for the number of people who will be eating there?

KITCHEN. Is the kitchen convenient to an outside entrance and to the garage or carport? Is there adequate counter and cabinet space?

FIG. 4.3   BUILDING DATA FORM

BUILDING DATA

Address ___10157 - 13th Avenue___

Age __7 years__   Square feet __1,350__

Number of rooms __6__   Construction quality __very good__

Style __ranch__   General condition __very good__

Feature	Good	Fair	Bad
Exterior: brick, frame, veneer, stucco, alum	x		
Foundation: slab, bsmt, crawl sp.	x		
Garage: attached, 1-car, 2-car, 3-car	x		
Patio, deck, porch, shed, other		x	
Interior (general condition)	x		
Walls: drywall, wood, plaster	x		
Ceilings	x		
Floors: wood, tile, lino, concrete, carpet		x	
Electrical wiring	x		
Heating: electric, gas, oil, other	x		
Air conditioning None			
Fireplace(s) None			
Kitchen	x		
Bathroom(s) 2 full	x		
Bedroom(s) 3	x		

Additional amenities __Large windows in living areas__

Design advantages __Convenient, sunny kitchen__

Design flaws __Inadequate closets in the two smaller bedrooms__

Energy efficiency __Insulation, weather-stripping, storm windows__

Location	Living Rm	Dining Rm	Kitchen	Bedrms	Baths	Family Rm
Basement						
First floor	x	x	x	3	2	None
Second floor						
Attic						

Depreciation:

Deferred maintenance __Normal wear, except for deck railings__

Functional obsolescence __No family room__

External obsolescence __None__

BEDROOMS. How large are the bedrooms? Is there a master bedroom that's significantly larger than the other bedrooms? Are the bedroom closets big enough? Where are the bedrooms located in the house? It's better for the bedrooms to be located apart from the living room, family room, kitchen, and other work or recreational spaces.

BATHROOMS. There should be at least two bathrooms if the house has more than two bedrooms. In many areas, particularly in newer houses, a private bathroom off the master bedroom is standard. Are there windows or ceiling fans in the bathrooms to provide adequate ventilation?

DESIGN DEFICIENCIES. Here is a brief list of some of the most common design deficiencies to watch out for:

- The front door opens directly into the living room.
- There's no front hall closet.
- The back door is difficult to reach from the kitchen, or from the driveway or garage.
- There's no comfortable area in or near the kitchen where the family can eat informally.
- The dining room is not easily accessible from the kitchen.
- The stairway leading to the second story is off of a room rather than in a hallway or foyer.
- A bathroom or some of the bedrooms are visible from the living room or foyer.
- The family room or recreation room is not visible from the kitchen.
- There is no direct access to the basement from outside the house.
- The bedrooms are not separated by a bathroom or closet wall (for soundproofing).
- It's necessary to pass through one of the bedrooms to reach another bedroom.
- Outdoor living areas (such as a patio or deck) are not accessible from the kitchen.

CHOOSING COMPARABLE PROPERTIES

You now know a great deal of information about the seller's property. The next step in your CMA is to choose comparable properties that have recently sold and others that are now for sale. (These properties are called **comparables** because they have the same or nearly the same characteristics as the seller's property.) By evaluating the sales prices or listing prices of these comparable properties, you will be able to estimate a reasonable listing price for the seller's property.

As you choose your comparables, you will refer to various sources of information. You will need to obtain comprehensive market data, which includes the listing and sales prices of properties in the seller's neighborhood, the financing terms of the sales transactions, and the physical characteristics of the properties. The most reliable source of sales information is the multiple listing service. An MLS usually requires active members to assemble and share complete records of transactions, showing not only listing prices but also other useful data such as consummated sales, financing terms, and length of time on the market. Other sources of information include:

- real estate search websites, such as Zillow and Trulia;
- real estate advertisements in the local newspapers (this provides listing prices only);
- other licensees, loan officers, escrow officers, or anyone else actively involved with the local real estate market; and
- practical, everyday experience gained from previewing properties in a neighborhood over time.

Comparable properties must be truly comparable to the subject property in the areas of greatest importance, which are listed below. In choosing your comparables, these are the areas you should focus on. If a potential comparable is a listed property or a recently expired listing, you will be concerned with two key factors:

1. **Location of comparable.** We already mentioned how important location is to the value of a home. Ideally, a comparable property should be in the same neighborhood as the seller's property. If you can't find enough comparables in the seller's neighborhood, you can choose comparables from similar neighborhoods nearby.

    Even if your comparable is located in the same neighborhood as the seller's home, you may have to take into account differences in value due to location *within* a neighborhood.

    EXAMPLE: Two identical properties located one block apart in the same neighborhood may have very different values if one of the properties borders a lake and the other does not. The values of the properties could also differ if one is located on a busy main avenue, while the other is on a quiet side street.

    If a comparable is in an inferior neighborhood, it is probably less valuable than the subject property, even if structurally identical. The opposite is true of a comparable from a superior neighborhood.

2. **Physical characteristics.** To qualify as a comparable, a property should have physical characteristics that are similar to the subject property, including size, style, layout and design, construction materials, and condition of the building.

If the comparable has recently sold, you will also be concerned with the following factors, in addition to location and physical characteristics:

3. **Date of comparable sale.** The sale should be recent. The comparison is more reliable if the sale occurred within the last six months, and sales more than one year old should not be used at all. Older sales aren't reliable enough because market conditions (such as sales prices, interest rates, and construction costs) change over time. If the comparable you're considering sold between six months and one year ago (or even more recently in a rapidly changing market), you may have to make adjustments for the time factor, allowing for inflationary or deflationary trends or other changes in the market since the sale of the comparable.

4. **Terms of sale.** How was the sale financed? If the financing terms did not affect the price paid for the property, the financing is referred to as cash equivalent. If the buyer used a standard conventional loan to finance the sale of the home, the financing would be considered cash equivalent. But if the financing terms were unusual, they may have affected the sales price of the comparable.

    Nonstandard financing can take a variety of forms, from seller financing to an interest rate buydown (see Chapter 9). In some cases, the effect of a special financing arrangement may be fairly obvious.

    EXAMPLE: The buyer's lender is charging $3,000 in discount points. The seller is going to pay the points to help the buyer qualify for the loan. The purchase price the buyer has agreed to pay is about $3,000 more than he would otherwise have paid, to compensate the seller for paying the points. In this case, the effect on the sales price equals the amount paid by the seller.

    Other cases are not so clear-cut. In a sale that involves seller financing, for instance, the buyer may benefit in any of several ways. A below-market interest rate, a small downpayment, reduced (or zero) loan fees, and easier loan qualification are some of the possible benefits of seller financing.

Calculating the effect of nonstandard financing on price is rarely a simple task. If you don't feel comfortable making those calculations, it may be best to find another comparable with cash equivalent financing terms.

5. **Conditions of sale.** This factor concerns the motivations of the buyer and seller in a particular transaction. A sale can be used as a comparable only if it took place under normal market conditions: it was an arm's length transaction (between unrelated parties), neither party was acting under unusual pressure, both parties acted prudently and knowledgeably and in their own best interests, and the property was exposed on the open market for a reasonable length of time. If a sale did not take place under normal conditions, the price paid is not a reliable indicator of market value, because the buyer and seller were acting under the influence of forces that do not affect the market in general.

EXAMPLE: Morgan has been transferred to another city, and she's due to begin her new job in four weeks. Her employer is paying for her moving expenses and has also offered to make up the difference between the market value of her house and any reasonable offer that is made in the first three weeks. Morgan can accept a low offer just to make a quick sale, since she won't personally lose any money on the transaction. This seller is not typically motivated, so this transaction should not be used as a comparable.

MAKING ADJUSTMENTS TO THE COMPARABLES

Now that you have chosen your comparable properties, you must compare each one to the seller's property. The comparison is made on the basis of the same elements you used to choose the comparables in the first place: 1) location, 2) physical characteristics, 3) date of sale, and 4) terms of sale. (The conditions of sale have already been taken into account, because a sale that did not take place under normal conditions would not be used as a comparable.) Before, you used these elements to weed out noncomparable properties. Now you'll use them to make minor adjustments in the sales prices or listing prices of the comparables.

Of course, the more similar the comparable, the easier the comparison. A comparable that is identical in design, neighborhood, site characteristics, and condition that sold under typical financing terms the previous month would give you an excellent indication of the market value of the subject property with no adjustments necessary. However, except in some new housing developments, you're not likely to find comparables that are so similar to the seller's property. Instead, there will nearly always be at least a few significant differences between the comparables and the seller's property. So you'll have to make the proper adjustments to the value of the comparables.

> **EXAMPLE:** You've found a comparable that's very similar to the subject property, except that it has three bedrooms and the subject property has only two. The comparable recently sold for $189,000. If you know that a third bedroom is worth approximately $4,000, you'll subtract $4,000 from the sales price of the comparable. This adjusted price reflects the difference in the number of bedrooms.

One of the greatest challenges of completing a CMA is determining the value of the differences between the comparables and the subject property. How do you know how much an extra bedroom or bathroom, or proximity to a good elementary school, is really worth?

Sometimes, you can find reliable data on the value of certain home features for your area on the Internet or as part of your CMA computer program. At other times, placing a value on individual features will be a matter of careful research and comparison.

> **EXAMPLE:** You have two properties, A and B. They are virtually identical except that A has one bathroom and B has two. A sold for $247,000 and B sold for $253,500. Since the number of the bathrooms is the only real difference between the two properties, the value of the second bathroom is about $6,500.

By comparing many different properties in this way, you will be able to place a particular value on several different features. Of course, in the real world you may not find properties with only one distinguishing feature, like the one in our example. But with time and experience you will able to place a value on each of the many features that differ from one property to another.

The chart in Figure 4.4 illustrates how you can estimate the value of individual features. As you examine the chart, note that a few of the properties had no variables, so they were used as the standard against which the value of each distinguishing feature was measured.

Remember that it's the sales or listing price of the comparable that is adjusted to indicate the probable market value of the subject property. Never try to make the adjustments to the value of the subject property. If a comparable lacks a feature that the subject property has, *add* the value of the missing feature to the

FIG. 4.4   FINDING THE ADJUSTMENT VALUE FOR INDIVIDUAL FEATURES

Features	Comparables							
	A	B	C	D	E	F	G	H
Sales price	$192,500	$187,000	$192,500	$196,500	$199,000	$192,500	$188,500	$177,500
Location	Riverbend	Riverbend	Riverbend	Riverbend	Riverbend	Riverbend	Riverbend	Wood Hill
Age	8 yrs	7 yrs	8 yrs	6 yrs	8 yrs	7 yrs	6 yrs	7 yrs
Lot size	75 x 200	80 x 200	75 x 200	75 x 200	100 x 200	75 x 200	75 x 200	80 x 200
Construction	frame	frame	frame	frame	frame	frame	frame	frame
Style	ranch	ranch	ranch	ranch	ranch	ranch	ranch	ranch
No. of rooms	7	7	7	8	7	7	6	7
No. of bedrooms	3	3	3	4	3	3	2	3
No. of baths	2	1	2	2	2	2	2	2
Square feet	1,300	1,300	1,300	1,425	1,300	1,300	1,250	1,300
Exterior	good	good	good	good	good	good	good	good
Interior	good	good	good	good	good	good	good	good
Garage	2-car, att.	2-car, att.	2-car, att.	2-car, att.	2-car, att.	2-car, att.	2-car, att.	2-car, att.
Other	basement	basement	basement	basement	basement	basement	basement	basement
Financing	80% S/L	80% S/L	90% S/L	90% S/L	80% S/L	90% S/L	90% S/L	90% S/L
Date of sale	8 wk.	7 wk.	6 wk.	8 wk.	5 wk.	7 wk.	6 wk.	9 wk.
Typical house value	$192,500	$192,500	$192,500	$192,500	$192,500	$192,500	$192,500	$192,500
Variable feature		1 bath		4 bdrm.	larger lot		2 bdrm	poor loc.
Adjustment value for variable		$5,500		$4,000	$6,500		$4,000	$15,000

Sales Price Adjustment Chart

comparable's price. If a comparable has a feature that the subject property lacks, *subtract* the value of the feature from the comparable's price. The completed comparison chart shown in Figure 4.6 illustrates this process.

ESTIMATING MARKET VALUE

After making all the required adjustments for varying features, you will have an adjusted market value figure for each comparable. You'll use these figures to estimate the market value of the seller's property. To do this, you have to evaluate the reliability of each comparable. The comparables that are most like the subject property (and consequently have the fewest adjustments) offer the most reliable indication of market value.

EXAMPLE: You have found three comparables with the values shown in Figure 4.5. Obviously, Comparable C has a significant number of variables (differences between the comparable and the subject property), which makes it less reliable as a comparable. Comparables A and B are much more similar to the subject property, with A being most like it. Therefore, the market value of A should be given the most weight and C the least. In this situation, you might estimate the market value of the seller's property to be about $228,000.

Of course, when you're estimating market value to help the seller set a realistic listing price, you don't need to provide an exact figure. You can give the seller a range of figures, such as "between $227,000 and $229,000." It's then up to the seller to choose the listing price he wants.

FIG. 4.5   COMPARABLES

Comparables			
	A	**B**	**C**
Selling price	**$232,500**	**$241,750**	**$251,800**
Extra bedroom	-$6,000	-$6,000	-$6,000
Two-car garage			-$4,300
Large lot			-$6,500
Aluminum siding		-$5,750	
Final value	**$226,500**	**$230,000**	**$235,000**

FIG. 4.6   COMPARABLE SALES COMPARISON CHART

Comparable Sales Comparison Chart					
Features	**Subject Property**	**Comparables**			
		1	**2**	**3**	**4**
Sales price		$191,750	$196,500	$187,000	$188,500
Location	quiet street				
Age	7 years				
Lot size	80 × 200				
Construction	frame			+$6,000	
Style	ranch				
Number of rooms	7		−$5,000		
Number of bedrooms	3			+$4,000	+$4,000
Number of baths	2	+$5,500			
Square feet	1,400				
Exterior	good				
Interior	good				
Garage	2-car attached				
Other improvements		−$5,000			
Financing					
Date of sale			−$3,000		
Net adjustments		**+$500**	**−$8,000**	**+$10,000**	**+$4,000**
Adjusted value		**$192,250**	**$188,500**	**$197,000**	**$192,500**

COMPLETING A CMA

Let's walk through the process of completing a competitive market analysis for a hypothetical property. Although the steps we will follow are the same ones you'll use when preparing CMAs in real life, the data we'll be using is simplified. The actual CMAs you'll prepare will usually involve more complex data and a greater number of variables.

Suppose some prospective sellers have asked you for advice on how much their house could sell for in the current market. They'll give you the listing if they're happy with the suggested price.

Your first step is to gather information about the sellers' house, the subject property. You walk through the house with the sellers, taking notes. You observe the property's amenities and defects; you also discuss the sellers' motivation for selling and their time parameters. When you leave, you drive through the neighborhood, noting the benefits and drawbacks of the area. You look for other properties that are on the market or that have recently sold.

After viewing the property, talking with the sellers, and studying the neighborhood, you have the following information: The house is located in Cedar Hills, which is a small, stable, middle-income neighborhood three miles north of the business district of Jeffersville. The house has three bedrooms, two full bathrooms, a dining room, and a large, well-landscaped back yard. It's a two-story house with a double garage. The house is four years old and in excellent condition.

The next step is to select comparable properties and gather information about them. You browse the computer database of your MLS and probably check some real estate search websites. You find several potential comparable properties, walk through the ones that are currently for sale, and drive by the properties that have sold or that have expired listings. After analyzing them as to date of sale, location, physical characteristics, and terms and conditions of sale, you choose the comparables listed in Figure 4.7. Like the sellers' property, all of them are located in the Cedar Hills neighborhood, have two stories, and are in excellent condition.

In preparing a CMA, remember that sales prices are better indications of value than listing prices. Sales prices represent what buyers were actually willing to pay in this marketplace. Listing prices are more likely to represent the ceiling of values in the area, since buyers rarely pay more for a property than the asking price, unless the market is exceptionally competitive.

FIG. 4.7   COMPARABLES FOR CEDAR HILLS CMA

- **COMPARABLE A:** 3 BEDROOMS, 2 BATHS, DINING ROOM, 3-CAR GARAGE, LARGE BACK YARD, 3½ YRS OLD. SOLD 5 MONTHS AGO FOR $345,500.

- **COMPARABLE B:** 4 BEDROOMS, 2 BATHS, DINING ROOM, 2-CAR GARAGE, LARGE SIDE YARD, 4 YRS OLD. SOLD 2 MONTHS AGO FOR $347,700.

- **COMPARABLE C:** 3 BEDROOMS, 3 BATHS, LARGE BACK YARD, 3-CAR GARAGE, 3½ YRS OLD. NO DINING ROOM. SOLD 7 MONTHS AGO FOR $341,000.

- **COMPARABLE D:** 3 BEDROOMS, 3 BATHS, 2-CAR GARAGE, LARGE BACK YARD, 5 YRS OLD. NO DINING ROOM. CURRENTLY LISTED FOR $349,500.

- **COMPARABLE E:** 4 BEDROOMS, 2 BATHS, DINING ROOM, 3-CAR GARAGE, LARGE BACK YARD, 4 YRS OLD. LISTING EXPIRED 2 WEEKS AGO; PRICE WAS $373,500.

Next, you compare the comparables you've chosen to your sellers' property. Of course, there are differences between the subject property and the comparables that will require some adjustments, including:

1. a double garage versus a three-car garage,
2. three bedrooms versus four bedrooms,
3. two bathrooms versus three bathrooms, and
4. the presence or absence of a dining room.

Before you can make the appropriate adjustments for these differences, you must determine the adjustment value of each distinguishing feature. After checking your sources, you find four pairs of properties that provide the information you need.

1. Two houses are nearly identical to one another, except that one has a double garage and the other has a three-car garage. One sold for $378,700 and the other for $385,500. From this you conclude that a three-car garage is worth approximately $6,800 more than a double garage.

2. Two other houses are nearly identical except that one has three bedrooms and the other has four. The first sold for $353,000 and the other for $364,500. So you conclude that a fourth bedroom is worth about $11,500.

FIG. 4.8   ADJUSTED VALUES FOR COMPARABLES

	Comparables				
	A	B	C	D	E
Market value	$345,500	$347,700	$341,000	$349,500	$373,500
Three-car garage	-$6,800		-$6,800		-$6,800
Fourth bedroom		-$11,500			-$11,500
Third bathroom			-$13,200	-$13,200	
Dining room			+$6,200	+$6,200	
Total adjustments	-$6,800	-$11,500	-$13,800	-$7,000	-$18,300
Total adjusted value	$338,700	$336,200	$327,200	$342,500	$355,200

3. Two more houses are nearly identical except that one has three bathrooms and the other has only two. The first sold for $374,750 and the other sold for $361,550. The third bathroom is apparently worth about $13,200.

4. Finally, two other houses are nearly identical except that one has a dining room and the other does not. The one with the dining room sold for $327,000 and the other for $320,800. Thus, the dining room is worth about $6,200.

Based on these other sales, you have a general idea of how each of the variables should be valued. Now you make the adjustments for each of these features, as shown in Figure 4.8.

You now have the adjusted market values for the five comparables and can formulate an opinion of the subject property's market value. First you consider the reliability of each comparable. Comparable C has the most distinguishing features and thus the most adjustments, so it is the least reliable. Comparables A and B each have only one adjustment, but the variable between Comparable A and the subject property (the three-car garage) is less important to the property's overall value. Comparable A is probably the most reliable; but note how close the market values of A and B are anyway. Comparable D has not yet sold, so its listing price can be considered the ceiling of value. The listing on Comparable E expired, so its price was evidently unreasonable in current market conditions. Overall, you decide that a reasonable estimate of market value for the subject property is $338,000.

You present your estimate of value and give the sellers a range of reasonable listing prices—from $336,000 to $339,000. You explain the supporting data to them, discussing each comparable and how it affected your estimated price range. Impressed with your professional competence, the sellers give you their listing. They decide on a listing price of $338,500, a price you all feel comfortable with.

THE CMA FORM

When you prepare a CMA and present it to the seller, it is helpful to use a standard CMA form such as the one shown in Figure 4.9.

This form is easy to use and to explain. A major advantage is that it shows the seller what buyers can pay, will pay, and will not pay for a home in her neighborhood. The form also helps you plan your presentation in a logical sequence. Of course, as with any form, it is only useful if the information contained in it is current.

The form has spaces for up to 15 homes that are comparable to the seller's property. Of course, the more similar they are to the seller's property, the more likely the seller is to accept your estimate of value.

The first section of the form calls for homes that are for sale now. Their prices represent what a buyer could pay for a similar home today on the open market. Select the homes (up to five) that are the most comparable to the seller's home. For each one, list the address, age, style, number of rooms, number of bedrooms and baths, condition, financing terms, date listed, and other characteristics.

The next section is for homes that have sold in the past 12 months. These show what buyers have actually paid for similar homes. You should choose the five homes that are the most recent and most comparable to the seller's property, and fill in the pertinent information. Of course, the most important information is how much the comparable sold for and the terms under which it sold.

The next section deals with listings that have expired in the past 12 months. These represent what buyers would not pay for a similar home in this market. List all of the information called for on the form.

Other items to be filled in on the form include the subject property's location, strong points, and drawbacks; market conditions; financing; and general comments.

FIG. 4.9 COMPETITIVE MARKET ANALYSIS FORM

Competitive Market Analysis

Subject Property Address: 458 Maple

Address	Price	Age	Lot Size	Style	Exterior	No. of Rooms	Sq. Ft.	No. of Bedrms	Baths	Garage	Condition	Other Impr.	Terms	$ per sq. ft.	List Date	Date Sold
Subject	$161,500	7 yrs	80 x 150	ranch	wood	7	1,350	3	2	1-car, att.	excellent	—	cash	$120		
Current Listings																
291 Maple	$160,000	8 yrs	70 x 140	ranch	wood	6	1,250	3	1	1-car, att.	excellent	basement	cash	$128	July	
175 Main	$159,700	12 yrs	70 x 140	ranch	brick	7	1,350	3	2	1-car, att.	good		cash	$118	Aug.	
389 - 5th	$161,500	10 yrs	80 x 150	ranch	brick	7	1,420	3	2	2-car, att.	good	basement	cash	$113	Aug.	
995 Merrit	$156,000	5 yrs	80 x 150	ranch	wood	6	1,415	2	2	1-car, att.	good		cash	$110	June	
Recently Sold																
256 Oak	$157,500	10 yrs	80 x 140	ranch	wood	7	1,270	3	2	2-car, att.	good		cash	$124	March	May
1156 Larch	$156,000	6 yrs	80 x 150	ranch	brick	6	1,400	3	1	1-car, att.	excellent		cash	$111	Feb.	April
1052 - 8th	$150,250	7 yrs	80 x 140	ranch	brick	7	1,300	3	2	1-car, att.	good		cash	$116	April	June
Expired Listings																
2782 Cherry	$166,800	6 yrs	80 x 150	ranch	wood	6	1,150	2	2	1-car, att.	good		cash	$145	Jan.	
10012 - 7th	$169,800	4 yrs	80 x 140	ranch	brick	7	1,300	3	2	2-car, att.	excellent		cash	$131	March	

Location: centrally located, convenient to business center and public transportation	General Comments:
Assets: excellent condition, professionally landscaped yard	
Drawbacks: no basement	
Market Conditions: market is very competitive, sales price within 2% of market value	Company: Smith Realty
Financing Terms: cash	Agent: Susan James
Probable Market Value: $161,500	Phone: 555-8811

All the information you have gathered and analyzed about the seller's property and the comparable properties should be presented to the seller during your listing presentation, along with your explanation of how this information indicates market value. The information presented in the form can correct any misconceptions the seller has regarding the current market conditions in his neighborhood. It should help the seller take a realistic approach to pricing.

THE PROBLEM OF A LOW APPRAISAL

In spite of your best efforts to help sellers choose a listing price based on the market value of their home, you're likely to run into the problem of a low appraisal from time to time.

A low appraisal is an appraiser's estimate of value that is significantly lower than the price a seller and a buyer have agreed on. They've entered into a purchase and sale agreement at a sales price that both parties are pleased with. But when the property is formally appraised for the buyer's lender, the appraiser concludes that the property is not worth as much as the buyer has agreed to pay.

A low appraisal puts the sale in serious jeopardy. If the transaction is contingent on financing, the buyer doesn't have to complete the sale if the appraised value turns out to be less than the agreed price. Not surprisingly, buyers are reluctant to pay more for a home than a professional appraiser says it is worth. And even when a buyer would like to go ahead with the purchase in spite of the low appraisal, she may not be able to afford to do so. The purchase loan is based on the sales price or the appraised value, whichever is less, so a low appraisal means a smaller loan—and a bigger downpayment.

EXAMPLE:

1. Buyer is prepared to make a 10% downpayment and obtain a 90% loan.

2. Sales price is $210,000.

3. Appraisal is issued at $200,000.

4. Maximum loan amount is 90% of $200,000.

$200,000	Appraised value
× 90%	Loan-to-value ratio
$180,000	Maximum loan amount

Because of the low appraisal ($10,000 less than the sales price), the loan amount is limited to $180,000. The buyer expected to make a $21,000 downpayment ($210,000 sales price × 90% = $189,000 loan). But the buyer would now have to make a $30,000 downpayment ($210,000 − $180,000 loan = $30,000) to pay the $210,000 price.

The easy solution to the problem of a low appraisal is for the seller to lower the sales price to the appraised value. But the seller may not be willing to do this; once a seller has become accustomed to a certain sales price, he'll be very reluctant to give it up.

Sometimes the buyer and seller will agree to a compromise price between the appraised value and the original sales price. More often, this solution runs up against both the seller's reluctance to lower the price and the buyer's reluctance (or inability) to pay any more than the appraised value.

Because of these problems, when there's a significant gap between the sales price and the appraised value, the most likely result is termination of the sale. It's the real estate agent's job to help the parties avoid this outcome whenever possible.

In some cases the agent should ask the lender to reconsider the appraised value, in the hope that it will be increased to a figure more acceptable to the buyer and seller. This is called a request for reconsideration of value.

REQUEST FOR RECONSIDERATION OF VALUE

Although appraisers try to be objective, subjective considerations are a part of every appraisal. In the end the appraiser's conclusions are only an opinion of value. When you get a low appraisal and you genuinely believe the appraiser is mistaken, you can appeal the appraisal by submitting a request for reconsideration of value to the lender. With the proper documentation, you may be able to get the appraised value increased, possibly to the figure the buyer and seller originally agreed on.

EVALUATING A LOW APPRAISAL. The sooner you find out about a low appraisal, the better. After the appraiser has inspected the seller's property, ask a representative of the lender (for example, the loan officer) to call you with the results of the appraisal as soon as they are received. Don't try to get the results directly from the appraiser; she has a fiduciary relationship with the lender and is not allowed to divulge information about the appraisal to others without the lender's permission.

If the appraisal comes in low, ask the loan officer for the following information:

1. the final value estimate,
2. the value indicated by the sales comparison method, and
3. the addresses of the comparables the appraiser used.

This is the essential information, because the sales comparison analysis is the heart of a residential appraisal, the part that the appraiser really relies on when estimating market value.

Evaluate the appraiser's comparables and update your competitive market analysis. Then decide if a request for reconsideration of value is a realistic option. You will have to support your request with at least three comparable sales (not listings) that indicate a higher value estimate is in order. If you're going to convince the lender that your comparables are more reliable than the appraiser's, yours must be at least as similar to the subject property as the appraiser's are.

If you believe the lender is likely to grant a request for reconsideration, your next step is to prepare the request and a cover letter.

PREPARING A RECONSIDERATION REQUEST. Some lenders have their own form for requests for reconsideration of value. If so, you should use their form (in fact, you may even be required to). Otherwise, you can prepare your own. It makes sense to present your information in the same format as the Sales Comparison Analysis section of the Uniform Residential Appraisal Report form. Make four columns for the properties, with the subject property in the first column and the three comparables to the right.

Write a cover letter making your request and attach your competitive market analysis to it. The cover letter should be simple and very polite; do not criticize the appraiser.

Sometimes appraisers don't use the best information available, and when they don't, their findings can be successfully challenged. If your request for reconsideration of value contains well-researched, properly documented information and is presented in a professional manner, your chances of success are good.

Keep in mind that federal and state law prohibits anyone with an interest in a real estate transaction from inappropriately influencing the appraiser. The law prohibits a licensee from (among other things) providing an appraiser with an anticipated value, conditioning the payment of the appraiser's fee on the appraisal result, or otherwise encouraging a specific outcome. Violation of this law is grounds for disciplinary action. However, the law specifically permits asking an appraiser to:

1. consider additional information about the property,
2. provide further detail or explanation for the appraiser's conclusion, or
3. correct any factual errors in the appraisal report.

CHAPTER SUMMARY

1. It is the seller's responsibility to establish a listing price. However, your sellers will rely on you for advice about listing prices. Your advice will usually take the form of a competitive market analysis, which presents information about similar properties that are currently for sale or that have sold recently in the seller's neighborhood.

2. While there are many different types of value, you will be most concerned with market value, which should be the basis for the seller's listing price. Market value is defined as the most probable price that a property should bring in under normal market conditions. (Remember to distinguish value from price and cost. Price is what a buyer actually paid for a property, and cost is what was paid to purchase a property and build an improvement on it.)

3. When you estimate the value of a seller's property, your first step is to collect and study information about the property. Your information will come from a neighborhood analysis, a site analysis, and a building analysis. As you study the house itself, you should pay particular attention to its design and layout. Once you have a clear picture of all the features, amenities, and drawbacks of the seller's property, you can choose your comparables.

4. Comparables are properties in the seller's neighborhood (or a similar neighborhood) that are similar to the seller's property and that are currently for sale or have sold recently. Once you've picked your comparables, you'll note the differences between the comparables and the seller's property and adjust the value of the comparables accordingly. Features that a comparable property lacks are taken into account by adding the value of the missing feature to the comparable's price. Features that a comparable property has that the seller's property lacks are taken into account by deducting the value of the feature from the comparable's price. You'll then use the adjusted prices of the comparables as the basis for a reasonable price range for the seller's property.

5. You may present your CMA to the seller by filling out a CMA form on paper or using CMA software. Giving the seller a form that provides all the key information will enable the seller to understand your presentation more easily.

6. A low appraisal is one that concludes the property is worth less than the buyer has agreed to pay for it. If the sale is contingent on financing, the buyer won't be required to complete it. In some cases, you can appeal a low appraisal by submitting a request for reconsideration of value to the lender.

CHAPTER QUIZ

1. The value of an item comes primarily from the:
   a. average of its cost and its market price
   b. intrinsic qualities of the item
   c. perceptions and attitudes people have about the item
   d. rarity of the item

2. A competitive market analysis (CMA) is an effective way to estimate value because:
   a. an informed buyer acting free of pressure will not pay more for a property than she could pay for another property that is equally desirable
   b. a buyer will never pay more than market value for a property
   c. it takes more neighborhoods into account when evaluating the property
   d. the income method of appraisal is the most reliable way to value residential property

3. Which of the following is true about neighborhood characteristics?
   a. The boundaries are defined by the county planning board
   b. Neighborhood characteristics set the upper limit of value for the properties located there
   c. Neighborhood characteristics do not affect the value of vacant lots located there
   d. A neighborhood's effect on property values is determined by the most expensive properties located there

4. What kind of topography is considered most desirable for a residential neighborhood?
   a. Level
   b. Sloping
   c. Gently subsiding
   d. Mildly rolling

5. A bathroom with a wash basin and toilet, but no shower or tub, is a:
   a. half bath
   b. three-quarter bath
   c. full bath
   d. design deficiency

6. Which of the following is a common design deficiency?

   a. More bathrooms than bedrooms

   b. Front door opens directly into living room

   c. Bedrooms are not visible from living room

   d. Kitchen too close to garage

7. Which of the following is an example of "normal market conditions"?

   a. The seller of the property is the buyer's uncle, but both the buyer and the seller are being advised by attorneys

   b. The seller of the property is the buyer's aunt, but the buyer and the seller are represented by agents working for different firms

   c. The seller is relocating to take a new job, so she lets her employer take care of selling the house for her

   d. The seller finds a buyer after the property has been on the market for two months and the buyer has been looking in this area for some time

8. In a CMA, which of the following elements may make it necessary to adjust the prices of the comparables?

   a. Date of sale

   b. Value in use

   c. Cost

   d. Conditions of sale

9. To prepare a CMA for your seller's property, you choose three properties as comparables. You make all the necessary adjustments to reflect how the comparables differ from the subject property. Comparable A has an adjusted value of $311,000. Comparable B has an adjusted value of $327,500. Comparable C has an adjusted value of $314,000. How do you arrive at an estimate of the value of the subject property?

   a. Take the average of the adjusted values of the comparables

   b. Let the seller choose between the three values to set a listing price

   c. Evaluate the reliability of each comparable and use that as a basis for deciding on a suggested price

   d. Choose the value of the comparable property with the fewest adjustments

10. To have the best chance of succeeding with a request for reconsideration of value, you should use:

    a. exactly the same comparables as the appraiser

    b. the income approach to value

    c. only currently listed properties as comparables

    d. comparable sales that are at least as similar to the subject property as the appraiser's comparables

ANSWER KEY

1. c. Value is created by people. Our perceptions and attitudes do more to determine the value of an item than the characteristics of the item itself.

2. a. A CMA is a modified form of the sales comparison method of appraisal. It is based on the assumption that a buyer will not want to pay more for a property than she could pay for a similar comparable property.

3. b. Neighborhood characteristics set both the upper and lower limits of a property's value.

4. d. Mildly rolling terrain is usually considered preferable, both as a neighborhood characteristic and for the property site itself.

5. a. A bathroom with only a wash basin and a toilet is considered a half bath.

6. b. It's considered a design deficiency when the front door of a house opens directly into the living room, without any sort of front hall or entryway.

7. d. A sale under normal market conditions is one in which the parties were unrelated, neither party was acting under unusual pressure, both parties acted prudently and knowledgeably and in their own best interests, and the property was exposed on the open market for a reasonable length of time.

8. a. If a comparable did not sell recently, it may be necessary to make an adjustment to take into account changes in the market since the date of sale. Sales more than one year old should not be used as comparables; in some cases, the limit may be six months.

9. c. You have to evaluate the reliability of each comparable to estimate the market value of the subject property. The comparables that are most like the subject property offer the most reliable indication of market value.

10. d. To persuade the lender to accept your estimate of value over the appraiser's, you need to select comparable sales that are at least as similar to the subject property as the appraiser's comparables.

5

SALES TECHNIQUES AND PRACTICES

LISTING PRACTICES

- Prospecting for listings
  - Farming
  - Cold calls
  - Expired listings
  - For sale by owners
  - Referrals
- Listing presentations
- Servicing the listing

SELLING PRACTICES

- Finding a buyer
- Showing properties
- Making an offer

SAFETY ISSUES

REAL ESTATE ASSISTANTS

INTRODUCTION

To be successful, a real estate agent must list properties, find buyers for properties, or both. Finding a seller or finding a buyer is the main way to earn a commission. Therefore, listing and selling practices are the lifeblood of a real estate career. This chapter reviews the basic steps of listing a property, and the basic steps of finding a buyer for a property. It also covers the ways in which an assistant, licensed or unlicensed, can help an agent with listing and selling practices.

LISTING PRACTICES

A listing agent's job involves more than just filling out a listing agreement form and waiting for a buyer to come along. First, you must work to locate listing prospects. Then you must convince prospective sellers to list their property for sale with you. Once you have entered into a listing agreement with the seller, you'll need to continue to service the listing. This includes preparing the property, marketing the property, and communicating with the sellers about the work you're doing and the progress you're making.

PROSPECTING FOR LISTINGS

Agents should be familiar with a number of listing sources and activities that can generate listings. These include:

- farming,
- cold calls,
- expired listings,
- for sale by owners, and
- referrals.

FARMING. Farming is a technique that involves choosing a neighborhood where you wish to concentrate your activities, and then becoming a well-known name in that neighborhood.

> **EXAMPLE:** Marty Thompson is a new real estate agent. He needs to generate some listings, so he decides to "farm" an area. He decides that the area he knows best is his own neighborhood—a development containing about 350 homes. He starts out by sending an introductory letter to every home,

introducing himself and describing the services he can offer. He follows up the letter with a personal visit, leaving a refrigerator magnet with his name, web and email address, and phone number at each home. He occasionally sends a newsletter to each home in the neighborhood. The newsletter contains neighborhood news, such as who's graduating from high school or who offers babysitting services, as well as information on local property values and market trends. He hosts periodic neighborhood socials, and holds a barbeque in the summer. He visits each home during the holidays, dropping off a calendar pre-printed with his name and other contact information. Soon, whenever neighborhood residents think about listing their homes, they immediately think of their neighbor, Marty Thompson.

By farming an area effectively and consistently, an agent can reasonably expect a constant supply of listings.

Many agents choose their "farm" based on three factors. The first factor is **diversity**—diversity of floor plans, square footage, exteriors, amenities, and values. Diversity guarantees that a variety of buyers will be attracted to the area. The second factor is **affinity**. An agent will be more successful if she chooses an area that feels comfortable. An agent should be enthusiastic about her "farm." The third factor is **turnover**. A neighborhood that is too stable will not offer many opportunities for listings. On the other hand, an area with a lot of recent turnover may be ready for a dry spell. An area with a steady stream of new listings is ideal.

Many licensees are enthusiastic proponents of farming, and it can be very successful. Other agents, however, are not comfortable farming and prefer to use other methods to generate listings.

COLD CALLS. The **cold call** technique is also popular with agents. This method involves calling homeowners on the telephone and asking whether they are interested in selling their homes or if they know someone who is. The homeowners who are called may be chosen randomly, or may be part of a systematic plan (such as calling all of the homeowners in a particular area).

Cold calling works only if the agent is willing to make a great many calls. Cold calling is often referred to as a "numbers game." One hundred calls may generate one listing appointment. As with farming, many agents feel that cold calls are a waste of precious time, or they feel uncomfortable with the process. Other agents, however, are very successful generating listings through cold calls.

An agent making cold calls probably doesn't think of himself as a telemarketer, but he is bound by some of the same laws as other telemarketers. An agent may not call individuals who have registered with the DO-NOT-CALL registry maintained by the Federal Trade Commission. It is the agent's responsibility to obtain an updated copy of the registry. Even when contacting persons not on the registry, an agent must always honor requests not to be called again, may not block Caller ID, and may not call outside permissible calling hours.

EXPIRED LISTINGS. Real estate agents often keep an eye on listings that are about to expire. Expired listings are often opportunities in disguise. There are many reasons why a listing might not have sold: it was not marketed properly, minor repairs should have been made that were not, or the price was not reduced when it should have been. If so, a fresh approach may generate both the listing and a quick sale. (If the listing did not sell because the owners were not motivated, there is probably little that another agent can do to move the property.)

After a listing has expired, the new agent can approach the homeowners and see if they are interested in relisting their property. Note that these sellers may be wary of signing another listing agreement because they have just had one negative experience with a real estate agent.

Agents must never try to convince sellers to terminate an existing listing so that the seller can switch to another agent. Agents should also exercise extreme caution when discussing a previous agent's actions. Criticizing another agent's selling efforts is unprofessional. Instead, agents should focus on what they can do for their clients.

FOR SALE BY OWNERS. Another way to obtain listings is to call sellers who are trying to sell their homes on their own. Calling "for sale by owners" (FSBOs) can be very effective, as these homeowners have already decided to sell their homes. All the agent needs to do is convince the FSBO that the agent can do a better job selling the home, in a shorter period of time, and for a higher sales price with a greater net return.

Agents keep track of FSBOs by noting "for sale" signs or reading newspaper or online classified ads. Some agents will contact any FSBO, while others have a more systematic approach, such as only contacting those in a certain price range.

Agents approach FSBOs in a number of different ways. One approach includes sending several letters to the homeowner. These letters include helpful advice on selling a home. Another approach is to deliver free "service packages" to FSBOs. These packages include forms, helpful hints and articles on selling a home, and sample settlement instructions. Some agents may simply phone for an

FIG. 5.1   LISTING INFORMATION FORM

Listing Information	
Property:	
Seller name:	
Seller address:	
Seller phone: (H)	(W)
Date listed:	Date expires:
List price:	Estimated market value:
Seller wants to move by:	

First Loan	**Second Loan**
Lender:	Lender:
Phone:	Phone:
Loan type: [ ] conventional [ ] FHA [ ] VA [ ] seller	Loan type: [ ] conventional [ ] FHA [ ] VA [ ] seller
Balance: $ [ ] verified	Balance: $ [ ] verified
Monthly payment: $	Monthly payment: $
Interest rate: [ ] fixed [ ] adjustable	Interest rate: [ ] fixed [ ] adjustable
Assumable:	Assumable:
Assumption fee:	Assumption fee:
Seller's terms:	Seller's terms:

30-Day Marketing Strategy	
[ ] Submit to MLS	[ ] Meet with seller
[ ] Install lock box	[ ] Collect all agent business cards
[ ] Install for sale sign	[ ] Discuss agents' comments
[ ] Key at office	[ ] Review market value estimate
[ ] Office tour date	[ ] Other:
[ ] MLS tour date	[ ] Other:
[ ] Submit ad	[ ] Other:

Suggestions for Showing Property Better

appointment or knock on the door. The key to any approach is to convince the homeowner that selling real estate is a complicated business that an agent can do better and faster.

Even agents who shy away from FSBOs will contact one if they have a particular buyer in mind. Under those circumstances, an agent can call the FSBO and ask for a one-party listing. A **one-party listing** is a listing agreement that is valid only in regard to one particular buyer. FSBOs may be initially skeptical of agents who request one-party listings. They may not believe the agent actually has a particular buyer in mind. However, they will often agree to a one-party listing if they are convinced that there is a legitimate prospect.

REFERRALS. Perhaps the most effective way to get listings is through referrals. Referrals may come from other real estate or finance professionals, such as attorneys, accountants, mortgage brokers, or escrow officers; these people are often happy to recommend prospects to a real estate agent, with the expectation that the agent might return the favor by referring clients who might need their services. Referrals may also come from satisfied clients or customers, in the form of repeat business or word-of-mouth.

Seeking referrals is really no different from the sort of **networking** any job-seeker uses. The first step is for an agent to contact friends, family, professionals whose services he uses, and other people in the community, and inform them of the services the agent provides. The goal is to create an endless chain of recommendations: if an agent receives two referral prospects from a friend, the agent should contact those two referral prospects and try to garner another two referrals from each of those prospects. If an agent tries out every link in the chain, the potential for hundreds of listings exists.

It may be particularly helpful for an agent to cultivate the friendship of influential persons in his neighborhood or community. These **centers of influence** can be a fruitful source of referrals, since they tend to have many acquaintances, some of whom might need an agent's services. When thinking of centers of influence, people often think of professionals such as attorneys, doctors, or public officials, but they can just as easily be store owners, bartenders, bank tellers, or anyone who interacts with a wide variety of people.

A key source for meeting centers of influence and other useful contacts is local community service groups. Many of the most successful agents build their referral networks through membership in groups such as churches, the PTA, the Chamber of Commerce, political organizations, or fraternal groups. An agent should focus on deeper involvement in only one or two organizations, rather than superficial involvement in a wide number of groups. An agent's main focus, at first, should be on the group's mission rather than aggressively seeking referrals; the referrals will come naturally as one becomes more deeply involved in the community.

An agent should always maintain a referral file, preferably using a contact management database. These programs will allow an agent to generate either mass or personalized mailings, and can even remind an agent when it is time to write or call in order to maintain steady contact.

LISTING PRESENTATIONS

Once a prospective seller has been located, a **listing presentation** may be necessary to convince the seller to list the property with the agent. Many sellers "shop around" for a real estate agent by asking two or three agents to make a listing presentation. That way, sellers can judge the strengths and weaknesses of different agents before making a final choice. Thus, it is important for the agent to come across as professional and well-prepared at the listing presentation; otherwise, the listing may go to someone else.

Even if an owner needs no convincing and is ready to list, the agent may want to use a listing presentation as an opportunity to discuss pricing. It's important to ensure that the owner is willing to put the property on the market at a competitive price.

BEFORE THE PRESENTATION. As soon as an agent has an appointment to make a listing presentation, he should begin preparing for it. A variety of tasks should be completed prior to the listing appointment, including:

- researching the property,
- visiting the property,
- completing a competitive market analysis, and
- preparing a marketing plan.

RESEARCH THE PROPERTY. Basic information about the property should be gathered, including the legal description, a plat map, tax information, and ownership information. This information often can be obtained from a local title company at no charge.

Visit the property. The agent should ask the owner if he can stop by to inspect the property prior to the listing appointment. During this visit, the agent counts and measures rooms, notes any special features (such as a gourmet kitchen or a dazzling view), and gets a general impression of the soundness of the construction. The agent also drives through the neighborhood to get a general feel for the area. Are neighboring homes well-kept? Are there nearby parks? How close are the schools?

Complete a competitive market analysis. Once the agent has become familiar with the home and the neighborhood, it's time to complete a competitive market analysis. As you will recall from Chapter 4, a CMA is a comparison of the prices of homes that are similar in location, style, and amenities to the subject property. The purpose of a CMA is to help the seller set a realistic listing price—it is only by comparing the prices of similar homes that a seller can establish a reasonable price for her own home.

Three types of properties are used to prepare a CMA:

1. homes that are for sale now,
2. homes that have recently sold, and
3. homes whose listings have expired.

The prices of homes that are currently for sale tell the seller what a buyer could pay now for a similar home on the open market. The prices of homes that recently sold tell the seller what a buyer did pay for a similar home. And expired listings tell the seller what a buyer would not pay for a similar home. Note that the prices paid for properties are better indications of value than list prices, because sales prices represent what buyers were actually willing to pay in a competitive market situation. List prices represent the ceiling of values in the area—generally, buyers will balk at paying more than the list price.

Many offices have their own software and/or forms to help agents prepare their CMAs. An example of such a form is shown in Figure 4.9.

Marketing plan. The agent should be prepared to discuss all the different ways she plans to promote the seller's property to prospective buyers. Most marketing plans will include a combination of traditional marketing practices (such as MLS listings and "For Sale" signs), as well as newer marketing practices (such as Internet-based advertising and virtual tours of the home).

Listing Appointment. The agent should arrive at the seller's home armed with the CMA, a marketing plan, a listing agreement form, a net proceeds to seller form

FIG. 5.2   LISTING PRESENTATIONS

WHAT TO BRING TO YOUR LISTING PRESENTATION

- COMPETITIVE MARKET ANALYSIS
- MARKETING PLAN
- LISTING AGREEMENT FORM
- AGENCY RELATIONSHIP PAMPHLET
- NET PROCEEDS TO THE SELLER FORM
- INFORMATION ON THE AGENT'S BACKGROUND AND EXPERIENCE

(discussed later in this chapter), an agency relationship pamphlet, and information about the agent and the agent's company. These items will help the agent explain the listing process to the seller and help the seller set a listing price. But the listing presentation is more than just an exchange of information; it is also the best opportunity the agent has to gain the seller's confidence and build rapport with the seller.

PRESENT THE CMA. A major benefit of a real estate agent's services is her ability to help establish a realistic listing price. The seller is probably more interested in hearing the agent's opinion of the value of the seller's home than any other piece of information.

All the information that was gathered and analyzed for the CMA should be presented to the seller, along with an explanation of how that information helps determine market value. A CMA form enables the agent to present the information in an orderly, easily understood manner. Plus, a CMA form makes it clear that the agent's estimate of value is based on facts, not personal opinion.

When the agent discusses value, it is best to focus on objective criteria: size, number of rooms, age, location, and terms of sale. This way, the seller (and the agent) won't get sidetracked with subjective issues, such as the fact that it took three years to complete the fancy deck, or cost hundreds of dollars to purchase just the right plants for the rock garden.

Agents often present three figures to the seller. The first figure is the general price range. The second figure is a suggested listing price, which is typically higher than the estimated selling price, to leave room for negotiation. The third figure is what the agent believes the property will actually sell for—the estimated selling price. The estimated selling price should be close to the property's market value.

During the discussion of listing prices, the agent should emphasize that it is the seller, not the agent, who will ultimately decide the listing price. The agent can offer opinions and advice, but it is the seller who must set the price.

Many owners expect to receive more for their property than it is worth because of market misinformation, inflated expectations of value, or the owner's personal attachment to the property. The information presented in the CMA can correct any misconceptions the seller has regarding current market conditions in his neighborhood, and force a more realistic approach to pricing.

PRESENT MARKETING PLAN. The agent should present the marketing plan to the buyer. The agent may show the sellers a sample flyer, so they can see what type of marketing materials the agent would provide. The agent should explain each step in the marketing process, so the sellers will know what to expect. For instance, the agent might explain to the sellers that open houses rarely generate a buyer for the home, but they do provide valuable feedback as to pricing and presentation.

PROVIDE BACKGROUND INFORMATION. Sellers want to know something about the agent making the presentation and the agent's company. The agent should be prepared to discuss the success rate of the real estate company, its membership in the local MLS, and how the MLS operates. Information about the agent's career is also important, including number of years of experience, any awards or achievements that have been earned, and the amount of education completed.

LISTING AGREEMENT. The agent should review the listing agreement with the seller. This includes showing the seller the form, reviewing its basic terms, and asking for and answering any questions the seller may have. It's a good idea to leave a copy of the form with the seller for a closer reading. (Of course, if the seller signs the agreement, the license law requires leaving a copy. Listing agreements are discussed in Chapter 2.)

AGENCY DISCLOSURE. As we discussed in Chapter 1, an agent needs to let all parties know whom she represents, in order to most effectively represent her client. When the listing agreement is signed, an agency relationship between the seller and the listing agent is automatically formed. The listing agreement is an express agreement between the agent and the principal (one of the ways in which an agency relationship can be created).

Even though the agency relationship is formed automatically, the listing agent should still inform the seller that she will be representing the seller, and representing only the seller. Upon the signing of the listing agreement, the listing agent should provide the seller with a copy of the pamphlet explaining the provisions of Washington's Real Estate Brokerage Relationships Act.

NET PROCEEDS TO SELLER. Along with the listing price, sellers are very interested in their net proceeds. They want to know how much cash they will walk away with after the sale has closed and all the expenses have been paid. Agents often use a "net proceeds to seller" form to arrive at the seller's bottom line. Of course at this point, the expenses can only be estimated, but it is possible to arrive at a fairly accurate figure. The steps for determining the net proceeds are discussed in Chapter 11, and a net proceeds to seller form is shown in Figure 11.5.

SERVICING THE LISTING

Once the listing has been taken, the work of servicing the listing begins. This includes helping prepare the property for showing, marketing the property, and maintaining ongoing communication with the seller. In some cases, servicing the listing also includes modifying the original listing agreement.

PREPARING THE PROPERTY. It is a rare house that is in prime condition and ready to go on the market. Most homes need at least some work, and many need a lot of work. At a minimum, homes must be cleaned thoroughly before they are shown to prospective buyers. Many homes also need some minor repairs.

Both interiors and exteriors should be clean, freshly painted (if possible), and tidied up. Curb appeal—how a property looks from the street—is important. First impressions are often lasting impressions. Home interiors should be decorated in neutral colors. Closets should be cleaned and organized—bulging closets indicate a lack of storage space. All fixtures should work properly. Leaky faucets, squeaking doors, creaking floors, broken fences, or torn window screens should all be repaired.

Renovations can also make a home more marketable. For example, sellers can often expect to recoup more than 100% of what they spend on minor kitchen renovations.

The following are some tasks that should be completed before a home is shown. Some of these items need to be done on a regular basis to keep the property in top condition during the listing period:

- mow and water lawns;
- weed flower beds;
- plant extra flowers or shrubs (after removing all dead or damaged plantings);
- prune the trees and shrubs;
- rake up all old leaves and other debris;

- cover bare ground with bark chips or gravel;
- pressure wash the roof and replace any missing shingles;
- mend broken fences or railings;
- clean up porches and decks;
- repaint when necessary (especially trim);
- remove children's toys and bikes from walkways and driveways;
- straighten up the garage and shed;
- fix broken door and window screens;
- replace or fix the mailbox;
- remove any old vehicles;
- clean and remove clutter from rooms;
- reorganize the closets, basement, attic, and other storage spaces;
- repaint any brightly colored walls in a neutral shade;
- replace any old or outdated carpeting and wallpaper;
- repair any cracks in the walls;
- fix leaky faucets;
- put new hardware on drawers and cabinets; and
- oil squeaky doors.

SECURITY. The seller should remove any small items of value, such as jewelry or coins, and keep them in a safety deposit box for the duration of the listing period. It may also be a good idea to rearrange or otherwise secure any delicate pieces of furniture or artwork.

KEYS AND KEYBOXES. The seller must provide the agent with a copy of keys to the property, which are generally stored in a lockbox attached to the front door.

MARKETING THE PROPERTY. Real estate agents market listed properties in many ways. One of the most important (and first) marketing activities occurs when the agent submits the listing to the MLS. Typically, this is done right after the listing agreement is signed. All the other MLS members become aware that the property is for sale and can begin looking for prospective buyers.

"For sale" signs are also an extremely effective form of marketing. Many prospective buyers drive around areas they are interested in, looking for "for sale" signs. If they see a property they are interested in, they follow up with a phone call to their agent.

Flyers containing information about the property should be prepared and left in an obvious spot in the house (such as a kitchen counter, or a table in the entryway). That way, whenever any agent shows the home to a prospect, all the pertinent information about the house is close at hand. Flyers may also be placed in an information box attached to the "for sale" sign in front of the home.

The flyer should include the price, terms of sale, the number of bedrooms and bathrooms, and other pertinent features. It may also include a photograph or sketch of the property.

Many listed homes are advertised in a newspaper or other periodical. **Newspaper ads** are usually classified ads—small text-only ads that appear in the classified section of the newspaper. Often, properties are advertised more to make the real estate office's phone ring than to sell the subject property. It is a rare buyer who sees an ad for a property and instantly wants to purchase that house. The buyer is more likely to call about the ad, find out the house isn't exactly right, and talk to the agent about other properties. For many agents, advertising is a very important way to bring in potential buyers for all of their listed properties.

Of course, the Internet has become an important tool in real estate advertising. Large brokerages and real estate organizations maintain **websites** with color photographs, video clips, and detailed information on listed properties. Many smaller offices and individual agents also maintain their own websites. Prospective buyers can search these websites to get a sense of what is currently available on the market. If they find something that interests them, they can get in touch with an agent using the contact information on the website.

Real estate agents must be aware of many restrictions on real estate advertising, both state and federal. Some restrictions involve the truthfulness of the ad; others involve making full disclosure. These laws apply to both traditional print ads and Internet advertising. The Washington State Real Estate Commission has issued guidelines for the use of Internet advertising and Internet social media.

Regardless of the marketing tools you use, you should always be sure that the money you spend on marketing activities is cost-effective. The key factor in any marketing strategy is to measure the dollars spent against the outcome achieved. Many agents find it helpful to keep a log of their marketing efforts. For example, an agent who spends $100 sending an email flyer about a new listing to 5,000 licensees will want to keep track of how many of those flyers result in showings, calls, offers, and/or sales. In her local market, she may find that the same $100 is better spent on an ad in the community newspaper.

Keeping track will help you determine which marketing strategies work best for a particular type of property in your area.

LICENSE LAW RESTRICTIONS. According to the real estate license law, all advertising must be truthful and not misleading. Most advertising must also include the brokerage firm's name as licensed; an ad that does not state the firm's name is a "blind ad" and a violation of the license law. (If a real estate agent is advertising his personally owned property, the firm's name need not be included but the ad must disclose that the owner is a real estate licensee.) If an agent is using the name of a franchise service, the ad must include the brokerage's name as well as the franchise name.

TRUTH IN LENDING ACT. The federal Truth in Lending Act also contains provisions that apply to advertising. Generally, anyone placing a consumer credit advertisement must comply with the provisions of the act. This includes real estate agents who advertise private homes for sale.

Prior to passage of the act, an advertiser might have disclosed only the most attractive credit terms, thus distorting the true costs of the financing. For example, the advertisement could have described low monthly payments ("$450 a month") without indicating the large downpayment necessary to qualify for that payment level. The act now requires the advertiser to include such pertinent details.

If an advertisement contains any one of several terms specified in the act, that ad must also include certain disclosures. The specified terms trigger the disclosures. In other words, if the advertiser uses a trigger term in the advertisement, the disclosures must be made; if the advertisement does not use a trigger term, no disclosures need be made. Trigger terms for real estate advertisements include:

- the amount of the downpayment (e.g., "20% down");
- the amount of any payment (e.g., "Pay less than $1,700 per month");
- the number of payments (e.g., "260 monthly payments");
- the period of repayment (e.g., "30-year financing available"); and
- the amount of any finance charge (e.g., "1% finance charge").

EXAMPLE: Agent Simms places a classified ad that reads "Fantastic buy! Three-bedroom, two-bath house in the Wildwood neighborhood. Buyer can assume seller's VA loan. Payments are only $1,525 a month!"

This ad contains a trigger term, the amount of the monthly payment, so certain other loan terms must also be included in the ad.

If any trigger terms are used in the advertisement, all of the following disclosures must be made:

- the amount of the downpayment;
- the terms of repayment; and
- the annual percentage rate, using that term spelled out in full.

The **annual percentage rate** (APR) is the relationship of the total finance charge to the amount of the loan, expressed as an annual percentage. The APR takes into account both the interest rate and the various fees charged by a lender to make a loan, such as the loan fee.

Some examples of phrases that would not trigger the required disclosures are:

- "No downpayment,"
- "8% Annual Percentage Rate loan available here,"
- "Easy monthly payments,"
- "Adjustable-rate financing available,"
- "VA and FHA financing available," and
- "Terms to fit your budget."

> **EXAMPLE:** Returning to the previous example, Agent Simms decides that he does not want to clutter up the ad with a lot of disclosures, so he rewrites the ad to read: "Fantastic buy! Three-bedroom, two-bath house in the Wildwood neighborhood. Buyer can assume seller's VA loan and take advantage of low monthly payments." This ad complies with the requirements of the Truth in Lending Act; no additional disclosures are required.

Advertising is also subject to fair housing laws. See Chapter 3 for a full discussion of this topic.

HOLDING OPEN HOUSES. As with advertising, most open houses do not result in immediate sales. Some real estate experts have estimated that the odds are 250 to 1 that someone walking into an open house will buy the property. The big advantage of open houses is finding prospective buyers that may be interested in other listed homes or prospective sellers who are ready to list their own homes.

The basic steps to holding an open house include arranging a day and time with the sellers when they can be out of the home, advertising the open house, preparing informational packets about the property, making sure the home is ready for showing, setting up open house directional signs, putting out a guest log, staying at the property during the scheduled open house hours, and following up with thank-you notes to those visitors who signed the guest log.

SETTING THE DAY AND TIME. Sellers should never remain in the house during an open house, so it is important for the agent to choose a day and time when it is convenient for the sellers to be away from their home. If a seller questions the need to be absent during an open house, the agent must tactfully explain that most buyers do not feel comfortable looking at a home when the owner is present.

ADVERTISING. After the date is set, the open house can be advertised in the newspaper and on the Internet. The ad for the open house should target a specific audience. For example, an ad for a small two-bedroom home might be written to appeal to young couples or retirees.

Flyers are often sent to neighbors. Neighbors may know of someone in the market for a home, or may be interested in listing their own home (potential sellers like to know which agents are active in their neighborhood).

Flyer packets can be given to interested prospects who tour the home. These packages generally include a flyer about the home, the agent's business card, flyers on other listings in the area, and information about the agent.

PREPARING THE HOME. For an open house to accomplish anything, the listed property must be in top condition. The home should be sparkling clean, the rooms brightly lit and fresh-smelling. All clutter should be put away. The grounds should be mowed, trimmed, and tidied. Some sellers need an extra nudge to get their homes in shape for an open house. But for that all-important first impression, order and cleanliness are a must.

DIRECTIONAL SIGNS. "Open house" signs with arrows that point prospects in the right direction should be placed at strategic locations. Never count on a prospect's ability to find an address. Show the prospects how to get there, or they may not show up at all.

GUEST LOGS. Guest logs are used to keep track of who views the property. A guest log can be a source of new leads as well as a security measure. Of course, not every prospect will want to sign the log; it is usually a mistake to try to push everyone to sign in.

PRESENCE DURING OPEN HOUSE HOURS. An agent should never leave an open house early, even if business is slow. Sellers are not very happy to come home to an empty house when they are expecting a positive report from an enthusiastic agent. Prospects that arrive at the property after the agent has left are sure to be disappointed and wary of dealing with that agent in the future. If an emergency arises and the agent must leave early, he should call another agent for backup. If business is slow, an agent can work on other aspects of the business during open house hours, such as calling FSBOs.

Of course, when the open house is over, it is imperative to lock up the home properly if the sellers have not yet returned.

FOLLOW UP. Agents generally follow up on the leads who signed the guest log, in the form of a thank-you card or a personal note. It is especially important to keep any promises that were made. For instance, if an agent promised to go to a prospect's home and perform a CMA, it is vital that he do so.

SHOWING THE PROPERTY. Open houses occur only occasionally—usually when the property is first listed. And, as mentioned earlier, open houses rarely generate sales. The way most properties are sold is by showing them to individual prospects. Showing homes will be discussed in more detail later in the chapter.

LISTING MODIFICATIONS AND EXTENSIONS. Sometimes a property is listed at a price that both the real estate agent and seller believe reasonable, yet weeks pass without significant interest. This may be due to a slow real estate market, or may reflect a changing market. For example, if comparable homes have subsequently been put on the market at lower prices, this may decrease the interest in your listing. Of course, it's also possible that the listing simply was overpriced in the first place.

If this happens, the agent should meet with the seller to discuss the situation and reevaluate the listing price. The seller may be resistant to the idea of lowering the price, so the agent should be prepared with data on new listings or comparable sales. Proof of the marketing efforts may also be helpful, such as flyers or advertisement clippings.

Modifications to a listing agreement such as a change in listing price should be made using an appropriate form. (Listing agreement modifications are discussed in Chapter 2. A sample modification form is shown in Figure 2.4.)

If the listing expiration date approaches and no sale is scheduled to close, the agent will want to obtain a listing extension. As with a listing modification, this involves meeting with the seller to discuss the efforts the agent has made and reasons why the property has not yet sold.

A listing agreement extension should also be made using a separate form. The modification form shown in Figure 2.4 can be used for this purpose.

COMMUNICATING WITH THE SELLER. An important aspect of servicing the listing is communication with the seller. Even though the agent's efforts will be focused on marketing the property, it's important to remain in contact with the seller. Informing the seller of what to expect and providing regular progress reports reassures the seller that the agent is working hard, and reduces the chance of any misunderstandings.

The agent should provide the seller with regular updates summarizing the number of inquiries and/or showings on the property, and any advertising used. The reports may also include copies of advertisements for the property, and any comments from other agents or prospective buyers.

SELLING PRACTICES

Just as a listing agent must work to obtain and market listings, a selling agent must find prospective buyers. Once a prospective buyer is found, the buyer's agent must choose appropriate properties to show her, and work to maximize the appeal of those homes.

FINDING A BUYER

Buyers can be categorized in roughly four ways:

- first-time buyers,
- trade-up buyers,
- empty-nesters, and
- retirees.

First-time buyers are the novices—typically they know little about buying a home, have limited funds, and are looking for smaller homes. They have lots of questions about buying a home and often rely on a parent or older friend for advice. Sometimes a parent will be helping to finance the home, by giving the son or daughter some money towards a downpayment or by co-signing the loan.

Trade-up buyers are selling one house in order to purchase a newer and/or larger house. They are more experienced at buying a home, have a better idea of what they want, and rely less (if at all) on the advice of parents or friends. Because they are selling their present home, they usually can make a fairly large downpayment on their new home.

Empty-nesters are couples whose children have left home. These buyers no longer need all the space available in a large family home. They typically look for smaller homes that require less upkeep. Often, these buyers can afford a hefty downpayment, using the equity they have in their present home.

FIG. 5.3   WORKSHEET TO TRACK LEADS

Seller Prospect	
Name:	
Address:	
Phone: (H) (W)	
Reason for Selling:	
Must Sell By:	

Property Data	
Location:	
Age:	Family Room:
Lot size:	Square Footage:
Style:	Garage:
Bedroom:	Fireplace:
Bathroom:	Heating:
Dining Room:	Condition:
Asking Price: Estimated Value:	
Existing Financing:	
Minimum Net to Seller:	

Buyer Prospect	
Name:	
Address:	
Phone: (H) (W)	
Must Take Possession By:	

Property Desired	
Location:	Family Room:
Style:	Square Footage:
Bedroom:	Garage:
Bathroom:	Fireplace:
Dining Room:	Other:
Price Range: Maximum Downpayment: Maximum Mortgage Payment:	
Comments:	

Retirees are also looking for smaller, easily maintained homes. Monthly payments may be a concern, because retirees have a fixed income. They may be interested in condominium units or other attached housing.

All types of buyers are found through some of the techniques previously discussed, such as advertising and open houses. Many buyers call real estate agents after seeing a "for sale" sign posted on an attractive property, which is why most agents post their personal "name rider" on signs. Others find properties by browsing websites. And still others simply call or visit a real estate office because they want an agent to show them some properties. These "call-ins" or "walk-ins" are helped by the agent who is "working the floor" at the time.

Floor duty is the practice of assigning one agent to handle all the telephone calls and office visits for a specific period of time. If those calling or visiting do not ask to speak with a particular agent, the agent on floor duty can help them and, hopefully, retain them as customers. Some agents find it helpful to use a prospect form (such as the one shown in Figure 5.3) while they are on floor duty. With a prospect form, an agent can quickly jot down the pertinent information about callers or walk-in customers, be they potential buyers or potential sellers.

Some agents find buyers from a roster of people who contact their community's Chamber of Commerce. People interested in moving to a new area often contact that area's Chamber of Commerce for information. Some of those people can be turned into buyers by enterprising agents.

Regional or national companies often transfer workers from office to office. Transferees need agents to help them with both sides of the move: selling their present home and helping them to buy a home in a new community. Many real estate offices specialize in relocation or have relocation programs. These programs can be a lucrative source of business.

DETERMINING NEEDS. Once an agent has found a prospective buyer, she must assess his housing needs. Determining a buyer's needs is a two-step process. First the agent helps the buyer determine how much he can afford, and then the agent must help the buyer define specific housing requirements (such as number of bedrooms and bathrooms).

To determine the price range of affordable homes, real estate agents used to **prequalify** the buyer: apply basic underwriting rules to the buyer's income to arrive at an estimate of how big of a loan she would likely qualify for. However, today's real estate agents are better off advising the buyer to get **preapproved** by a lender. When a lender preapproves a buyer, it agrees to loan her up to a specified amount of money, as long as the home she chooses meets the lender's standards.

The preapproval process is discussed in more detail in Chapter 9, but for now, it is enough to know that showing buyers homes they cannot afford is extremely counterproductive. It wastes the time of both the buyer and the agent, and it needlessly disappoints the buyer. There is probably nothing so discouraging to a buyer as getting excited about a dream home, only to discover that it is completely out of his price range. Suddenly other, more affordable housing loses its appeal, and the buyer may despair of ever finding the right home for the right price.

Buyers usually know what kind of home they want. The difficult part is prioritizing their needs.

EXAMPLE: Stan and Nancy Cook meet with Agent Sandin to discuss their housing needs. The Cooks have two children and a lot of out-of-town guests. They tell Agent Sandin that they need a four-bedroom, two-bathroom house. They need a large kitchen, a family room, at least one fireplace, a three-car garage, a large yard, and room for a kennel for their three dogs. "And a laundry room," says Stan. "And a tool shed," Nancy adds.

Agent Sandin knows there's no way he is going to find a house with all of these attributes in the price range the Cooks can afford. After asking a lot of questions and listening carefully to the Cooks' answers, Agent Sandin says, "It sounds like four bedrooms, two bathrooms, and a large kitchen are the three most important criteria. The fourth item is room for your dogs, and the fifth is a large family room. Is that right?" After a moment's thought, the Cooks readily agree. Now Agent Sandin can begin looking for a house that fits their needs.

Sometimes creative problem-solving can help meet a housing need.

EXAMPLE: Agent Sandin has found what he thinks is the perfect home for the Cooks, but it has only three bedrooms instead of four. However, the den could easily double as a guest room, especially since there is a third bathroom right off the den. The Cooks are more than willing to compromise on the guest bedroom and are delighted with a third bathroom.

An agent should never try to manipulate a buyer into considering a property just because that agent listed the home. If buyers feel they are being pressured to view homes that don't meet their needs, they will quickly find another agent who is more willing to accommodate them. If buyers sense a conflict of interest, they might even pursue disciplinary measures.

SHOWING PROPERTIES

The ability to show property effectively is vital to a successful real estate career. An agent should always take the time to research and plan his efforts, in order to make showings as efficient and useful as possible. Thorough preparation includes developing sales speeches and keeping current with the local market and general real estate trends.

SELECTING LISTINGS. When choosing properties to show a prospective buyer, only pick homes the buyer can afford. An agent can lose a sale by showing a buyer homes that are priced too high. Buyers should be preapproved (or at least prequalified) to determine their affordable price range. However, sometimes buyers choose to pay less on housing than they can afford. An agent must respect the buyer's wishes—it is up to the buyer to decide how much to spend on a home.

Don't show too many houses on one trip. After five or six houses, most buyers begin to tire and may forget or confuse impressions and details. It does no good to show a home to a buyer who is not going to remember it.

PREVIEWING THE PROPERTIES. Before taking buyers on a showing, the agent should always preview the listed homes and research the area. Knowing a home's best and worst attributes in advance allows the agent to choose what to highlight and what to downplay during the showing. It also helps the agent prepare to handle any objections that might be raised by the buyers.

Learning the local streets and planning a route will help avoid the embarrassment of getting lost. It's also a good idea to become familiar with school district boundaries and to know the location of neighborhood shopping and recreational facilities.

INSIDE THE HOMES. It's important to read the buyer's signals. The buyer will let the agent know, either verbally or by body language, how she feels about the house. It's important for the agent to listen to what the buyer says and pick up any nonverbal cues. Is this the kind of house the buyer loves? Hates? The buyer's reaction to one house will help the agent pick out the next house to show the buyer.

The agent should give the buyers a chance to picture themselves in the home. Most buyers need to picture themselves in a house before they will make an offer on it. In order to do this, they need some time to themselves. Agents don't have to talk nonstop during a showing. A little silence can be an effective sales tool.

MAKING AN OFFER

Once a buyer has found a house that she would like to buy, the selling agent's next step is to prepare an offer. To purchase real estate, an offer must be made in writing. Once the offer has been signed by the seller, the offer forms a binding purchase and sale agreement. (We will discuss offers and the purchase and sale agreement in greater detail in the next two chapters.)

OFFERS AND COUNTEROFFERS. Agents are required to submit any offer to the seller, even if that offer seems unreasonable. It is the seller who decides whether to accept an offer, not the real estate agent.

When a buyer's agent prepares a written offer, it should be passed on to the listing agent, who then presents it to the seller. Typically, once an offer is presented to the seller, a period of negotiation begins. This is perhaps one of the most valuable services an agent can provide: shepherding the parties through the process of making offers and counteroffers, and helping the buyer and seller reach an agreement that satisfies them both.

NEGOTIATION. When presenting the offer, agents often present the most positive aspects first, and then the more negative aspects. This prevents the seller from immediately rejecting the offer before the seller has had a chance to listen to and carefully consider all the terms. Even if the seller is unwilling to accept a negative term (such as a low sales price or a quick closing date), the seller is more likely to counter with another offer than to reject the buyer outright.

During the negotiation process, agents should remember to maintain their professionalism and avoid hostility between the parties. They must also give the parties copies of any documents they sign when they sign them. This means that the buyer must get a copy of any offer as soon as it is signed, the seller must get a copy of any counteroffer as soon as it is signed, and both parties must get a copy of the final purchase and sale agreement as soon as it is signed.

MULTIPLE OFFERS. In an active real estate market, it is likely that more than one offer will be submitted to a seller. In such a situation, the listing agent should present all offers to the seller as they come in, without presenting them in a prejudicial fashion. The seller has the option of rejecting all offers, accepting one offer, making a counteroffer to one offer, or accepting one offer and making a contingent backup counteroffer to another offer.

Ultimately, the seller's decision when faced with multiple offers will hinge largely on the amount offered as a sales price, but there are ways to help a buyer's offer stand out from the crowd. Because a home sale is an emotional as well as financial decision, many owners will give some weight to a personal appeal from the buyers. Some selling agents, in a tight market, will have prospective buyers write a brief statement about themselves and why the seller's house appeals to them. Sellers often feel some reluctance to sell, and are likely to feel better about selling to someone they "know," who has articulated their appreciation and enthusiasm for the property.

EXAMPLE: A prospective buyer might write a statement such as this: "We are a young married couple looking to purchase our first house, as we are planning to start a family and will need more room as our family grows. My husband is an accountant with an investment firm, and I am a veterinarian. You might say we're both animal lovers; we have several dogs, as well as some smaller pets, and love that your house has a large yard for the dogs to play, as well as ample kennel space in the utility room. We were also won over by the lush landscaping and the terrific school district."

Also bear in mind that most buyers are interested in other properties as well, and—especially in a tight market—it can be helpful to tell a seller about other properties that the buyer is interested in. Not only does this remind the sellers that their house is competing against other properties, it also helps reassure the sellers that their house will be appreciated.

EXAMPLE: A selling agent might inform the sellers: "The buyers were undecided between your home and a nearby property on Willow Way. While that property had a fourth bedroom and was about the same price, they opted for your property because they thought your home was in better condition, requiring less touching-up before they move in, and because they loved the big yard and the well-maintained landscaping."

It is best for all buyers to be preapproved ahead of time before making an offer, and this is even more important in a competitive market. Formal preapproval by a lender distinguishes a buyer as being serious about making a purchase, and eases some of the concerns a seller might have about the buyer's ability to obtain the necessary financing. If a seller has to choose between two otherwise equal offers where one buyer is preapproved, the seller is likely to choose the preapproved buyer.

AGENCY DISCLOSURE. Remember that Washington state law requires an agent to inform any party to a transaction which party that agent represents. This disclosure must be made to the buyer before the buyer signs the offer to purchase, and to the seller before the seller signs the offer to accept it. The disclosure must be made in writing, either as part of the purchase and sale agreement or as a separate document. Many times, the selling agent will have explained his agency status to the buyer at the time they signed a buyer agency agreement prior to looking at houses—but the selling agent, during the negotiation process, must still remember to disclose to the seller that he represents the buyer and only the buyer.

Safety Issues

Throughout the listing and selling process, real estate agents must be conscious of safety and security issues.

Real estate agents must take care to protect the safety of clients and customers. For example, agents should never show buyers homes that are in the middle of construction. Instead, agents should arrange to have the contractor show the buyer the home. Construction sites are dangerous places, and can present grave hazards. This is particularly true if the buyer is accompanied by young children.

Real estate agents should also take precautions to secure a seller's possessions during open houses or when showing the property. Sellers should be warned to remove valuable items from the home prior to showing. Agents should never leave prospects unattended in a home and should encourage all visitors to sign a log. Agents should be especially wary when a couple attends an open house and one partner keeps the agent occupied while the other partner disappears into another part of the house—this behavior is a signal that trouble may be brewing. And, naturally, agents must be sure to leave the property securely locked.

Keys and keyboxes pose special hazards. Agents must make every effort to keep house keys in a safe place, and to make sure that keyboxes are as secure as possible. For example, when a licensee terminates affiliation with a firm, the designated broker must be sure to notify the MLS immediately so that the agent's keybox code can be deactivated.

Real estate agents must also be conscious of their own safety. Because real estate agents often work alone with virtual strangers, extra precautions should be taken. While physical violence is rare, instances do occur.

If at all possible, agents should work in pairs when showing properties or holding open houses. If that is not possible, agents should ask their customers to meet them at their offices. This avoids the dangers of meeting a stranger at an empty house. And when meeting with customers for the first time, it is wise to ask for photo ID.

Customers who call up and insist on meeting the agent at the property because they are pressed for time, or who "simply cannot" leave a number where they can be reached are poor risks. Legitimate customers are generally willing to reschedule appointments and are also happy to comply with personal safety rules. Remember, if the agent and the customer meet for the first time at the property rather than the office, the customer is also at risk. The customer is also meeting a stranger (the real estate agent) at a deserted property. If the agent explains that it is in everyone's best interest to meet first at the office, most customers will readily agree.

When agents are showing properties, they should leave word with their office as to where they are going and when they will return. They can also arrange to check in with someone on a regular basis. A phone should always be available for emergencies during open houses, and keeping a cellular phone handy is a good safety measure.

In areas where crime is a problem and agents are worried about their personal safety, most local police departments are happy to provide training and give advice on ways to foster personal safety.

REAL ESTATE ASSISTANTS

Depending on the amount of business a real estate agent handles, she may decide to hire a real estate assistant. Many administrative and other tasks can be delegated to an assistant, freeing up more time for the agent to spend working face-to-face with clients. An assistant may work on a part-time or full-time basis, and is typically paid on a salary or salary-plus-commission basis.

Under the license law, many of the day-to-day activities performed by a real estate agent require a real estate license. Unlicensed assistants may not:

- show properties, answer questions, or interpret information about the property, price, or condition;
- interpret information about listings, titles, financing, contracts, closing, or other information relating to a transaction;
- fill in legal forms or negotiate price or terms;
- hold or disburse trust funds; or
- perform any act with the intent to circumvent, or which results in the circumvention of, real estate licensing laws.

For this reason, when hiring a real estate assistant, an agent may want to consider hiring another real estate licensee.

For a variety of reasons, many licensees choose to work as real estate assistants instead of working as agents. For example, a new licensee might want more experience before taking on full-scale agent responsibilities. Working as an assistant gives the licensee a chance to become more familiar with the business and to benefit from the knowledge and guidance of a mentor. A licensee might choose to work as an assistant because he can't afford to work full-time on a commission basis until he is more established and has a dependable stream of income. And some licensees simply find that they are not comfortable performing the marketing and sales duties associated with being an agent. Working as a real estate assistant allows them to limit their negotiation and sales responsibilities while remaining in the business.

If the agent decides to hire an assistant who is not a real estate licensee, both the agent and assistant must take care to ensure that none of the assistant's activities require a license.

TYPICAL DUTIES OF A REAL ESTATE ASSISTANT

A real estate agent may delegate any of a variety of tasks and responsibilities to a real estate assistant, depending on how much experience the assistant has, and whether she is a real estate licensee. Office procedures and business practices will vary from firm to firm, but the following is a discussion of some of the duties a real estate assistant might be expected to fulfill.

OFFICE ADMINISTRATION. Whether licensed or not, most real estate assistants will be expected to help with basic office administration tasks. Real estate transactions generate a significant amount of paperwork; for example, the license law requires real estate firms to keep transaction records for a minimum of three years after closing. A transaction folder might include a listing agreement, purchase and sale agreement, modifications or addenda to those agreements, and a settlement statement. By the time the transaction is completed, the folder might also hold photographs, disclosure forms, offers to purchase, an appraisal, escrow papers, and closing documents. An assistant will likely be responsible for organizing and filing these documents accordingly. If any documents must be duplicated and distributed to different parties, this task might also fall to an assistant.

In addition to handling paperwork, an assistant may answer and direct phone calls, and greet current or prospective clients visiting the office. When handling inquiries, an assistant can provide general information about listings, but should refer more complicated questions to the agent.

UPDATING INFORMATION. When a real estate agent takes a listing, the information should be given to the MLS as soon as possible. In addition, listing status changes must be updated with the MLS. If the listing information is not kept current, another agent may end up wasting time considering or showing a home that is no longer available. Failing to report a pending or closed sale is not only unprofessional, but may also subject the listing agent to a penalty. For example, some multiple listing services or professional organizations may impose fines for failing to report listing status changes within a certain period of time. An assistant can be invaluable in helping an agent to submit listing information to the MLS. However, depending on the requirements of the particular MLS, this task may require a real estate license.

If the agent maintains a website with listing information, it must also be updated regularly. Advertising homes that are no longer available (or failing to advertise homes that have come on the market) is unprofessional, as well as a violation of the DOL's guidelines on maintaining websites. If a prospective buyer is interested in a listing advertised on the agent's website, she will not be impressed to learn that it actually sold two months ago.

CLIENT COMMUNICATION. Keeping in contact with clients is essential to a successful real estate business, but can be extremely time-consuming. A busy agent might be able to handle exchanges with current clients, such as answering questions or providing updates. But the agent may not have time to stay in touch with former and prospective clients, even though this type of contact is an important component of marketing.

An agent may choose to delegate this work to an assistant, who may or may not be licensed. For example, an unlicensed assistant might be responsible for preparing and sending mass mailings of newsletters, seasonal cards, or other promotional materials.

APPOINTMENTS AND OPEN HOUSES. Even the most organized agent may need help managing a busy schedule. An unlicensed assistant can coordinate the agent's appointments and remind the agent of upcoming meetings and showings.

However, an unlicensed assistant may not actually show properties, answer questions, or interpret information regarding property, price, or condition.

A licensed assistant would be able to take on more responsibility. For instance, a licensed assistant could show homes and then actually write up an offer in the real estate agent's absence. As a real estate licensee, the assistant would have fewer limitations on the duties he could assume.

CHAPTER SUMMARY

1. Listing properties is a vital part of a real estate agent's business. Listings can be found by farming, by making cold calls, by approaching expired listings and FSBOs, and through referrals.

2. Before making a listing presentation, the agent should research the property, visit the property, and prepare a competitive market analysis and marketing plan. At the listing presentation, the agent will present the competitive market analysis and marketing plan, tell the seller about the services the agent will provide, review the listing agreement, and discuss the net proceeds to the seller.

3. Once the listing is obtained, the agent must service the listing. This means advising the seller on preparing the property, advertising the property, holding an open house, and showing the home. If the listing does not sell, the listing agent and seller may agree to a listing modification or extension.

4. Agents need to find buyers for properties as well as listing properties. Buyers can be found by advertising, by holding open houses, and by working floor duty. When a prospective buyer is found, the agent needs to determine the price range of affordable homes and to prioritize what the buyer wants in a home.

5. The agent must comply with certain license law restrictions on presenting offers and counteroffers. When making offers in a competitive market, it is important for a selling agent to paint a picture of the buyers and sell the buyers to the sellers; it is also important for buyers to be preapproved for financing.

6. An agent must be aware of a number of safety issues. Agents need to protect the physical safety of their clients and customers, protect the possessions of sellers, and protect themselves from danger.

7. An agent may need to hire a real estate assistant in order to make better use of her time. An assistant can help with a number of activities, such as maintaining files, updating listing information, communicating with clients, and setting up open houses. An agent must be careful that an unlicensed assistant does not perform any tasks that require a real estate license.

CHAPTER QUIZ

1. Agent Kalliwaki spends one hour every day randomly calling 20 homeowners to ask if they are interested in selling their homes. This practice is known as:

   a. farming

   b. cold calling

   c. FSBO-ing

   d. showing

2. Which of the following may be used in a competitive market analysis?

   a. Recently sold homes

   b. Current listings

   c. Recently expired listings

   d. All of the above

3. A homeowner wants to list his property for $245,900. The agent informs the homeowner that five similar homes have recently sold for around $235,000, there are five similar homes currently listed for around $239,000, and two similar, recently expired listings were priced at around $244,000. Which of the following statements is true?

   a. The upper ceiling of value is around $239,000

   b. The recently sold homes are the best indicators of value

   c. $245,900 is too high, because buyers refused to purchase similar homes for $244,000

   d. All of the above

4. An agent is using a franchise name in his advertisements. The agent:

   a. is violating the real estate license law

   b. must also include his firm's name in the advertisement

   c. must note that the agent is a licensed member of the franchise

   d. None of the above

5. The following ad is placed in a local newspaper: "Fixer-upper going cheap. Two-bedroom, one-bathroom. Good foundation and plumbing, but needs a lot of TLC. Seller offers financing with small downpayment." This ad:

   a. violates the Truth in Lending Act

   b. must include the APR of the seller financing

   c. complies with the Truth in Lending Act

   d. must include the interest rate of the seller financing

6. Open houses:

    a. are often held to generate potential buyers for other listings

    b. should be conducted with the sellers present

    c. are held just before the listing is submitted to the MLS

    d. are a good way to determine what repairs need to be completed before the house will sell

7. Agent Brown receives two offers on the same house in the same hour. One offer is full price; the other is $25,000 below the listing price.

    a. Brown must submit both offers to the seller immediately

    b. Brown need submit only the most advantageous offer to the seller

    c. Brown has the authority to accept the best offer on behalf of the seller

    d. Brown must submit the best offer immediately, but can wait until the following day to submit the less advantageous offer

8. Now that the Knolls' last child has gone off to college, they are looking for a smaller house with easier upkeep. They can afford a significant downpayment using the equity from their current house. The Knolls would be considered:

    a. first-time buyers

    b. trade-up buyers

    c. empty-nesters

    d. retirees

9. Which of the following is not a safety precaution that agents should take?

    a. Warn sellers to remove valuable items from the home prior to showing

    b. Request that customers meet them at the property rather than at their office

    c. Work in pairs when showing properties or holding open houses, when possible

    d. Leave word with the office where they are going and when they will return

10. Which of the following activities should an unlicensed real estate assistant not perform?

    a. Maintain information in transaction folders

    b. Prepare flyers for mass mailings

    c. Coordinate appointments

    d. Advise buyers about obtaining financing

ANSWER KEY

1. b. Cold calling is an unsolicited inquiry, usually by phone, made to a home-owner in order to obtain a listing.

2. d. Recently sold listings, current listings, and expired listings are all used in a CMA.

3. d. All of the options are true. Recent sales always provide the best indicators of value, and recently expired listings are likely to have been priced too high.

4. b. An agent advertising under the name of a franchise must also include his firm's name in the advertisement.

5. c. The ad complies with the Truth in Lending Act as no trigger terms are used.

6. a. People who walk into open houses rarely buy that particular home, but they are often interested in having the agent show them other homes.

7. a. Both offers must be submitted to the seller immediately. It is up to the seller to decide which offer to accept, not the agent.

8. c. The Knolls would be considered empty-nesters, since their children have moved out and they are looking for a smaller, easier-to-maintain property.

9. b. To be safe, agents should request that clients meet them at the brokerage office first, rather than at an empty house.

10. d. An unlicensed real estate assistant should not answer questions about financing; this should be done only by licensees.

NEGOTIATING THE OFFER AND ACCEPTANCE

MAKING AN OFFER TO PURCHASE

- Preparing an offer
- How offers are presented
- Multiple offers
- Backup offers
- Revoking an offer

COUNTEROFFERS AND NEGOTIATIONS

ACCEPTING AN OFFER

- Communicating acceptance
- Manner of acceptance
- Acceptance cannot change terms

CONTRACT AMENDMENTS

CONTRACT RESCISSION

EARNEST MONEY DEPOSITS

- Size of the deposit
- Form of the deposit
- Handling a deposit
- Refund or forfeiture

FAIR HOUSING CONSIDERATIONS

INTRODUCTION

When a buyer finds a house he wants and decides to make an offer on it, what happens next? How and when are offers presented to a seller? What is your role as negotiator? What if you're representing the seller instead of the buyer?

In this chapter, we will discuss preparing and presenting an offer to purchase, negotiating terms, and the point at which an offer becomes a binding contract. We will also explain the procedures for handling the earnest money that customarily accompanies an offer.

MAKING AN OFFER TO PURCHASE

You're helping your buyers—a married couple—look for a house that meets their needs: at least 1,800 square feet, three bedrooms, two baths, a large kitchen, and a double garage, in the $320,000 price range. After you've shown them several houses that fulfill these requirements, the buyers find one they are really interested in. You can tell, because they linger there a little longer, ask specific questions ("How old is the roof?" "How far is it to the elementary school?"), and mentally "move in" to the house, visualizing where their own furniture would go. They may make plans to come back and see the house again, perhaps bringing a third party—such as a parent or a more experienced friend—to examine the property with them.

After the buyers have had a chance to look at the property on their own and discuss it between themselves, you review the property's features and benefits and how well it meets their housing needs. All their objections are overcome, and they are now ready to make an offer to purchase the house. They ask you to write up their offer for them and present it to the seller.

PREPARING AN OFFER

Under the statute of frauds, an offer to purchase real property must be in writing and signed by the offeror (the buyer). The statute of frauds is the law that requires certain types of contracts to be in writing.

An offer to purchase residential property is usually written up on a standard purchase and sale agreement form (see Chapter 8). It must set forth all of the essential terms of the buyer's offer, including the purchase price, the amount of earnest money the buyer is willing to provide as an indication of good faith, how he will pay the purchase price, and the proposed closing date. It's important to include all of the terms on which the buyer is willing to purchase the property, because once the document is signed by both the buyer and the seller, it becomes a binding contract—their purchase and sale agreement.

What if a buyer wants to make an offer that is unrealistically low or contains too many conditions? As an agent, your job is to represent the client's best interests—naturally, this includes getting the best price possible, but it also includes helping write an offer that will be considered seriously by the seller. This is especially important in a situation where a seller is receiving multiple offers. (We'll discuss multiple offers in greater detail later in this chapter.)

Typically, price is the most important element of an offer, but other factors can make an offer more or less attractive to the seller. The seller wants to get the best price for his home, but is also interested in a smooth, problem-free transaction. Anything the buyer can do to demonstrate greater commitment to the purchase will be viewed favorably by the seller. For example, offering an unusually large earnest money deposit shows the seller that the buyer's interest in the property is sincere.

Similarly, accepting an offer with few or no contingencies assures the seller of a greater chance of the sale closing smoothly. Submitting a "clean offer" with no conditions is ideal. Preapproval by a lender also makes an offer more attractive, since the buyer's ability to obtain financing is guaranteed. An all-cash offer is even better (although admittedly rare), as loan approval becomes completely unnecessary.

You may need to assist the buyer in restructuring an offer to make it more attractive to the seller. For example, if the buyer wants to make a lowball offer, you may need to explain that the seller is not likely to take the offer seriously and may in fact be offended. However, as the buyer's agent, you must always make sure that the offer submitted reflects what is best for the buyer. Never encourage the buyer to eliminate an important contract condition or to make an offer higher than what he can afford.

WHO CAN PREPARE AN OFFER. Whose job is it to prepare the offer to purchase? A buyer could write her own offer; it is always legal (although generally not advisable) for the parties to a transaction to draw up their own contract. Or an attorney at law could draft the buyer's offer for her. What about you, the real estate agent? Can you prepare the buyer's offer?

When someone draws up a contract on behalf of others, he is considered to be practicing law. Only licensed attorneys may practice law, so as a general rule, contracts must be drafted by an attorney. However, there is an exception to this rule: real estate agents may prepare routine purchase and sale agreements using standard forms that were originally written and approved by attorneys with expertise in real estate law. But even this exception is limited. As a real estate agent, you may only fill out a purchase and sale agreement form in connection with a transaction that you are handling. And you cannot charge a separate fee (in addition to your share of the brokerage commission) for completing the forms.

Note that when you fill out a contract form, you will be held to the same standard of care that is required of a lawyer. If, through negligence, you make a mistake, you may be liable for any harm suffered by the buyer or the seller because of that mistake.

Also, remember that you are only allowed to fill in the blanks on a standard form. Writing special clauses to insert into the pre-printed form or advising the parties on the legal effect of certain provisions may constitute the unauthorized practice of law, which is a criminal offense.

REVIEWING THE OFFER. After filling out the purchase and sale agreement form, check it over to see if it's complete and accurate. Then go over the form with the buyers, to make sure they understand and are satisfied with all of the terms. If they have questions about the legal consequences of particular provisions, refer them to a real estate lawyer.

When you review the financial aspects of the offer, it is helpful to use a "Buyer's Estimated Net Cost" worksheet to calculate the buyers' closing costs and show them approximately how much cash they'll need to close the transaction if the seller accepts their offer. (See Figure 11.4 in Chapter 11.)

After going through the offer with the buyers, have them sign it, and then immediately give them a copy of the signed form. At this point, the buyers will usually give you an earnest money deposit (discussed later in this chapter), which you will turn over to your designated broker.

LEGAL REQUIREMENTS. In addition to being in writing and signed, a buyer's offer must meet certain other basic legal requirements to serve as the basis for a binding contract. To be valid, the offer must be definite and certain in its terms, not vague or incomplete. If you fill out the purchase and sale agreement form properly, including the price, the closing date, and all of the other important terms, the buyer's offer will meet this requirement.

A valid offer must also clearly express a willingness to enter into a contract. Again, a standard purchase and sale agreement will fulfill this requirement.

WHEN TO SEEK ADVICE. In filling out a purchase and sale agreement form, there are three key areas where problems most often occur:

- **Property description.** The property must be correctly described for the offer (and the subsequent sales contract) to be enforceable. A full legal description is not required, but one should be used whenever possible.

- **Method of payment.** The offer must state how the buyer intends to pay the purchase price. Will the buyer obtain institutional financing, pay cash, or take advantage of seller financing?

- **Contingencies or special arrangements.** If the offer is contingent (on loan approval, on inspection results, or on the sale of the buyer's current residence, for example), the contingency provision must clearly state the circumstances under which the contingency will be considered fulfilled. And any special arrangements that the buyer wants to make, such as taking possession before the closing date, need to be spelled out in the offer.

These are areas you should pay extra attention to, but of course all of the terms of the offer are important. When you feel there may be a problem with one of the terms of the buyer's offer, or if you think you may have made a mistake, ask your designated broker or branch manager for advice right away. Remember, you are preparing the offer as an agent of your firm, so your designated broker wants it to be problem-free.

Occasionally your designated broker or branch manager will instruct you to get in touch with a real estate attorney. (Larger brokerages often have a legal staff of their own.) You should also consult an attorney in any of these situations:

- You have a question and your designated broker or branch manager is not available.
- Because of special terms in the offer, you can't use a pre-printed purchase and sale agreement or addendum. (Remember, you may not draft an agreement or even a simple clause.)
- You need legal documents, such as an easement or a road maintenance agreement, to be prepared.

HOW OFFERS ARE PRESENTED

It's usually the listing agent who presents an offer to the seller. (After all, it is the listing agent who represents the seller.) But the buyer's agent can also play an important role. We'll look at the presentation of a buyer's offer to a seller first from the buyer's agent's point of view and then from the listing agent's.

BUYER'S AGENT'S ROLE. If you are the buyer's agent and the listing agent is going to present the offer to the seller, you should thoroughly explain the offer to the listing agent first. You may even want to go along when the listing agent meets with the seller, so that you can answer questions about the buyer or the offer.

> **EXAMPLE:** The terms of your buyers' offer include paying cash for the seller's home and closing the transaction within 15 days. Because a cash sale is so unusual, you want to be there when the listing agent presents the offer to the seller. The seller might be suspicious of the buyers and want to know who they are, where they got their cash, and why they want to close the transaction so quickly. You can relieve the seller's concerns by explaining the situation: the buyers recently received a large inheritance, and they want to move into a new house quickly because they are expecting their first baby soon. Making this explanation in person may be more effective than simply asking the listing agent to relay the information.

If the buyer is especially likable, or in a situation that could evoke sympathy, it may be a good idea to ask the buyer to prepare a personal letter to give to the seller. Though financial considerations will be the primary basis for the seller's decision, he may view the offer more favorably if he thinks about the buyer as a real person rather than in the abstract.

Note that if you go along when the offer is presented to the seller, you must disclose your agency status to the seller.

Naturally, you'll give the seller the opportunity to discuss the offer privately with the listing agent. Whatever the seller decides to do about the offer, it is your job to convey that decision to the buyer.

LISTING AGENT'S ROLE. If you are the listing agent and receive a written offer to purchase, you should arrange to meet with the seller to discuss the offer right away. Any and all offers to purchase that you receive must be presented to the seller as soon as possible.

When you meet with the seller, you should go over all of the terms and conditions of the offer and make sure the seller understands them. When there is more than one seller, it's a good idea to give each of them a copy of the offer. For instance, if the sellers are a married couple, make a photocopy of the offer so that each spouse can have a copy to look at as you discuss it. Then go through the offer line by line, answering the sellers' questions. It is especially important to discuss the following provisions:

- the proposed closing date and date of possession;
- the list of included items (any personal property that would be transferred to the buyers along with the real property);
- any contingencies (such as whether the buyers need to sell their own house first); and
- any obligations the sellers would have to fulfill before closing, such as completing repairs or cleanup.

If the sellers have legal questions, recommend that they consult an attorney. Do not try to answer legal questions yourself.

The sellers may ask questions about the buyers—who they are, whether they can afford the home, and how motivated they are to buy. If you have any personal information about the buyers, be sure to avoid describing them in terms that might lead to a violation of the fair housing laws. Certain characteristics—race, national origin, religion, and so on—should not be mentioned.

When you review the financial aspects of the sale, it's helpful to use a "Seller's Estimated Net Proceeds" worksheet, which will make it easier to calculate the selling costs and the amount of cash the sellers can expect to receive at closing. (See Figure 11.5 in Chapter 11.)

MULTIPLE OFFERS

Sometimes a seller has more than one offer to consider at the same time. Two or more offers may come in simultaneously, or an additional offer may come in while the seller is considering an earlier one. The listing agent must present every offer received to the seller, even if the seller has already decided to accept another offer.

EXAMPLE: You are the listing agent. You presented an offer to the sellers two days ago and they've been considering it very seriously. This morning they told you that they're almost sure they will accept it. They just want a little more time to think it over.

A few minutes ago, a buyer's agent faxed you another offer on the sellers' house. This offer is not nearly as attractive as the first one. Even so, you are required to present the new offer to the sellers right away. You can't wait around to see whether they accept or reject the first offer.

In competitive real estate markets, multiple offers are not uncommon. From a seller's point of view, multiple offer situations are desirable. Competing buyers may eliminate contingencies and increase offer amounts to make their offers more attractive. The final sales price is likely to be driven up. For these same reasons, buyers usually try to avoid multiple offer situations.

BUYER'S AGENT'S ROLE. If you represent a buyer in a multiple offer situation, your goal is to work with the buyer to make the offer as attractive as possible, without compromising too much. Depending on your client's financial situation, this may mean increasing the amount of the earnest money deposit, or perhaps offering an unusually short closing period. As discussed in the previous chapter, a written statement or letter from the buyers may be helpful. Lender preapproval is almost a requirement; the seller is far less likely to consider an offer from an unapproved buyer if a similar offer has been submitted by an approved buyer. You may be able to find out from the seller's agent if the seller wants any special terms or concessions. For example, if the seller wants to sell quickly but remain in the home for an extra six months, you could add a sale-leaseback clause to your client's offer.

Make sure that any terms and concessions are really worth it to your client. It's easy for an anxious buyer to get caught up in a bidding war, and he may want to offer more than he can afford, or agree to unreasonable seller demands.

LISTING AGENT'S ROLE. On the other hand, if you represent the seller in a multiple offer situation, your goal is to ensure that the seller accepts an offer that maximizes her profit but minimizes the chance that the sale will fall through.

One possible pitfall of a bidding war can occur if the price is driven up beyond what the home is truly worth. The seller may accept the highest offer but see the deal fall through when the buyer's lender appraises the house for less than the offered amount. Or the sale may fail for a different reason, and when the seller begins the negotiating process again, she may have inflated expectations of her home's value.

It is the listing agent's job to explain to the seller that simply accepting the highest offer isn't necessarily the wisest move. It may make more sense, for example, to choose a lower, all-cash offer over a higher offer requiring lender approval.

When faced with multiple offers, a seller has a number of options. The seller may decide to:

- reject all of the offers,
- accept one of the offers and reject the others,
- make a counteroffer on one offer and reject the others, or
- accept one offer and make a contingent counteroffer on another.

The last of these alternatives, the contingent counteroffer, brings us to the subject of backup offers.

BACKUP OFFERS

Some buyers are so interested in a particular house that they are willing to make a backup offer—an offer that's contingent on the failure of a previous sales contract.

EXAMPLE: You showed Clark's house to Lenihan a week ago, and this morning Lenihan called to say he wants to make an offer on it. You contact the listing agent and learn that the seller has already signed a purchase and sale agreement. Your client, Lenihan, is extremely disappointed. You explain that he can make a backup offer that is contingent on the failure of the first contract. He agrees to this, and you submit Lenihan's backup offer to the listing agent.

A listing agent is not only required to present additional offers received while the seller is already considering an offer, he must also present offers that come in after the seller has signed a contract, up until that sale actually closes. However, when an offer is submitted after the seller has signed a contract, it should be made contingent on the first sale's failure to close. Attaching a backup addendum such as the one shown in Figure 6.1 to the second buyer's offer is the best way to accomplish this.

CONTINGENT COUNTEROFFER. Suppose you're representing a seller who has already signed a purchase and sale agreement, and another buyer makes an offer. The seller is interested in accepting this as a backup offer, but it isn't contingent on the failure of the first contract. You should advise the seller to make a

FIG. 6.1   BACKUP OFFER ADDENDUM

Form 38A
Back-up Addendum
Rev. 8/11
Page 1 of 1

"BACK-UP" ADDENDUM TO PURCHASE AND SALE AGREEMENT

The following is part of the Purchase and Sale Agreement dated _____   1

between _____ ("Buyer")   2

and _____ ("Seller")   3

concerning _____ (the "Property").   4

1. **Property Already Sold.** Seller has previously sold the Property pursuant to a purchase and sale agreement   5
   dated _____ ("First Sale"). Seller reserves the right to change or amend the terms of the First Sale.   6

2. **Back-Up Agreement Subject to First Sale.** This "Back-Up Agreement" is subject to the First Sale. Seller is not   7
   obligated to sell to Buyer, unless the First Sale fails to close.   8

3. **Notice - If First Sale Fails to Close.** Seller shall give notice to Buyer within 3 days of learning that the First Sale   9
   will not close ("First Sale Failure Notice").   10

4. **Closing.** If the First Sale fails to close, this Back-Up Agreement shall be closed _____ days (60 days if not   11
   filled in) from the date of delivery of the First Sale Failure Notice.   12

5. **Expiration of Back-Up Agreement.** If Seller has not given the First Sale Failure Notice within _____ days   13
   (60 days if not filled in) after mutual acceptance of this Back-Up Agreement, this Back-Up Agreement shall   14
   terminate.   15

6. **Termination by Buyer.** Buyer may terminate this Back-Up Agreement any time prior to receiving the First Sale   16
   Failure Notice.   17

7. **Time.** For the purposes of computing time (except for paragraph 5 above), all timelines in this Back-Up   18
   Agreement, including the deposit of Earnest Money, shall begin on the date of delivery of the First Sale Failure   19
   Notice.   20

8. **Other.**   21

                                                                                                       22
                                                                                                       23
                                                                                                       24
                                                                                                       25
                                                                                                       26
                                                                                                       27
                                                                                                       28
                                                                                                       29
                                                                                                       30
                                                                                                       31

_____   _____   _____   _____
Buyer   Date   Seller   Date

_____   _____   _____   _____
Buyer   Date   Seller   Date

contingent counteroffer. The counteroffer will repeat the buyer's offer but add a contingency clause regarding the first contract.

EXAMPLE: Your sellers have accepted an offer from the Browns. The Browns' offer is for the full listing price, but it's by no means certain that the Browns will qualify for the financing they need to complete the purchase. So when you present an offer from Finney, the sellers are very interested. Finney's offer is for $4,000 less than the Browns' offer, but Finney will undoubtedly qualify for the necessary loan.

The sellers want to accept Finney's offer as a backup offer. However, Finney's offer does not include a clause that makes it contingent on the failure of the first agreement. So you advise the sellers to make a counteroffer. They offer Finney the same terms set forth in his original offer, but they include a backup addendum making the sale to Finney contingent on the failure of the sale to the Browns. Finney accepts the sellers' counteroffer. Now if the Browns fail to qualify for financing, the sellers will have a binding contract with Finney.

BACKUP OFFERS AND BREACH OF CONTRACT. If a seller were to accept a second offer without a backup contingency clause, she would end up obligated under two different purchase and sale agreements. Because one contract couldn't be fulfilled without breaching the other, the seller would be liable for breach of contract to the potential buyer who didn't get the property.

EXAMPLE: Returning to the previous example, suppose your sellers accepted Finney's offer without adding the contingency provision. They would then be obligated to sell the property both to Finney and to the Browns. Obviously, the sellers can only transfer the property to one of the buyers. So if the sale to the Browns closed, Finney could sue the sellers for breach of his contract.

Never try to convince a seller to break an existing agreement in order to accept another offer, even if the second offer is much better. If you were to do that, you could be found guilty of a tort (a civil wrong) called "tortious interference with a contractual relationship." You could be held liable for damages caused by the breach of contract.

EXAMPLE: Now suppose that Finney's offer is substantially better than the Browns' offer. Finney is offering $5,000 more than the listing price, will pay all of the closing costs, and is sure to qualify for the necessary financing. The sellers would be better off with this offer, and so would you (your commission would be larger because of the higher purchase price). But you should not suggest that the sellers breach their contract with the Browns in order to accept Finney's offer. If you did, the Browns could sue you for damages, and you could also lose your real estate license.

If your clients express an interest in breaching a contract in favor of another offer, you should strongly recommend that they talk to a real estate attorney before taking any action.

NOTICE TO BACKUP BUYER. When a seller has accepted a backup offer and the first sale fails to close, the seller must notify the backup buyer that their purchase and sale agreement is now a binding contract. The seller can use a form such as the one shown in Figure 6.2 to notify the backup buyer that the first sale has failed.

REVOKING AN OFFER

A buyer can revoke an offer to purchase at any time before the seller properly communicates his acceptance of the offer. When the offer is accepted, a binding contract is created, and the buyer can't back out without breaching it.

Even if an offer gives the seller a specific length of time to consider it, the buyer can revoke the offer sooner than that, as long as she acts before the seller sends his acceptance.

EXAMPLE: Grant offers to buy Rush's house for $215,000. The offer states that it will terminate in 48 hours. If the 48 hours pass without an acceptance, Grant's offer will terminate automatically. But if Grant changes her mind about buying the house before that (for example, 30 hours after making the offer) and Rush has not yet accepted it, Grant is free to revoke the offer. Rush cannot force her to keep the offer open for the full 48 hours.

If a time limit is not stated in the offer, it will terminate after a reasonable amount of time.

EXAMPLE: Now suppose that Grant's offer to Rush doesn't have a termination date. Rush doesn't respond to the offer for weeks. Finally, six weeks after receiving the offer, Rush notifies Grant that he's accepting it. It's too late, however. It's not reasonable to expect that an offer to purchase a house

FIG. 6.2   NOTICE TO BACKUP BUYER

Form 38B
Notice to Back-Up First Sale Fail
Rev. 8/11
Page 1 of 1

©Copyright 2011
Northwest Multiple Listing Service
ALL RIGHTS RESERVED

**FIRST SALE FAILURE NOTICE
TO BACK-UP BUYER**

The following is part of the Purchase and Sale Agreement dated _____ 1

between _____ ("Buyer") 2

and   _____ ("Seller") 3

concerning _____ ("the Property"). 4

Pursuant to Paragraph 3 of the "Back-Up" Addendum (Form 38A), Seller gives notice to Buyer that the First Sale 5
failed to close ("First Sale Failure Notice"). This "Back-Up Agreement" is now a firm agreement for sale of the 6
Property. 7

_____   _____ 8
Seller   Date   Seller   Date

will be kept open for six weeks. If Grant has changed her mind about buying, she's no longer bound by her offer.

Counteroffers and Negotiations

Unless a buyer has made an offer that matches all of the seller's terms, there is likely to be some negotiation. In fact, negotiation is the norm rather than the exception. Sellers don't generally expect full-price offers, and buyers aren't surprised when the seller rejects their first offer and counters with another offer. The most common objections to initial offers are regarding:

- the price offered,
- the size of the earnest money deposit,
- the proposed closing date and date of possession,
- which furnishings or fixtures are included in the sale, and
- financing terms.

If the seller decides to counter the buyer's offer with another offer, you may be able to make the seller's changes on the original purchase and sale agreement form.

Example: Gordon has offered Lamont $275,000 for her house, with a closing date of June 16. He is making an earnest money deposit of $1,500. Lamont is pleased with nearly all of the terms of Gordon's offer, but she wants a larger deposit—$6,500. Lamont's agent simply crosses out the $1,500 earnest money figure on the form submitted by Gordon and writes in $6,500. Lamont initials the change, and her agent presents the counteroffer (the revised purchase and sale agreement form) to Gordon.

For simple changes such as the one in the example, this might work just fine. But it's usually better to use a separate counteroffer form, such as the one shown in Figure 6.3, especially when the changes are numerous or complicated. Otherwise the purchase and sale agreement may become confusing and, as a result, unenforceable.

On the counteroffer form in Figure 6.3, you identify the original offer by filling in the date it was signed by the buyer, the property description, and the names of the buyer and seller.

The counteroffer states that all of the terms of the original offer are acceptable to the seller, except for the changes noted. The form has lots of room to fill in the

FIG. 6.3   COUNTEROFFER FORM

Form 36
Counteroffer Addendum
Rev. 8/11
Page 1 of 1

©Copyright 2011
Northwest Multiple Listing Service
ALL RIGHTS RESERVED

**COUNTEROFFER ADDENDUM
TO REAL ESTATE PURCHASE AND SALE AGREEMENT**

All terms and conditions of the offer (Real Estate Purchase and Sale Agreement) dated _____ ,   1

concerning _____ (the "Property"),   2

by, _____ , as _____   3

and the undersigned _____ , as _____   4

are accepted, except for the following changes.   5

❑   **The Purchase Price** shall be $ _____   6

_____   7

❑   **Other.**   8

9

10

11

12

13

14

15

16

17

18

19

20

21

22

23

24

25

26

27

This counteroffer shall expire at 9:00 p.m. on _____ (if not filled in, two days after it is delivered),   28
unless it is sooner withdrawn. Acceptance shall not be effective until a signed copy is received by the counterofferor,   29
their broker or at the licensed office of their broker. If this counteroffer is not so accepted, it shall lapse and the   30
Earnest Money shall be refunded to Buyer.   31

All other terms and conditions of the above offer are incorporated herein by reference as though fully set forth.   32

_____   _____   _____   _____
Signature   Date   Signature   Date

The above counteroffer is accepted.

_____   _____   _____   _____
Signature   Date   Signature   Date

Reprinted courtesy of Northwest Multiple Listing Service. All rights reserved.

new terms the seller is proposing. There's space for setting a deadline, to indicate how long the buyer has to consider the counteroffer before it will terminate. The counteroffer is then signed by the seller and presented to the buyer for approval or rejection.

When your seller decides to make a counteroffer, be sure to explain that the counteroffer will terminate the original offer and all of the buyer's obligations under that offer.

> **EXAMPLE:** Returning to the previous example, suppose that Gordon rejects Lamont's counteroffer. He doesn't want to make a $6,500 earnest money deposit. In that case, Gordon has no further obligation to Lamont. That's because Lamont's counteroffer had the same effect as a rejection of Gordon's original offer would have had: it terminated the offer. So when Gordon refuses to pay a larger deposit, Lamont can't simply change her mind and decide to accept Gordon's original offer. His offer has already been terminated by rejection. If Gordon still wants to buy the property, he can renew his offer; however, if he no longer wants to buy it (or buy it on the terms he originally offered), he is not obligated to do so.

If you are presenting a counteroffer to a buyer, review every term the seller has altered. You may want to prepare another "Buyer's Estimated Costs" worksheet if the counteroffer changes the buyer's costs. If the buyer decides to accept the counteroffer, have him sign the counteroffer form. Then notify the seller that the counteroffer has been accepted.

In some cases, the parties will trade counteroffers back and forth a number of times. The negotiation process can be frustrating or even nerve-wracking. As always, maintain your professionalism and do what you can to keep the parties from becoming hostile. Refrain from making negative comments about either party. It's your responsibility to serve the best interests of your client, and a transaction that satisfies both parties is in your client's best interests, whether you're representing the buyer or the seller.

Don't forget to give the parties copies of any documents they sign when they sign them. Each party who makes a counteroffer should get a copy of it immediately after signing it, and both parties should get a copy of the final purchase and sale agreement as soon as it is signed.

FIG. 6.4   WITHDRAWAL OF OFFER OR COUNTEROFFER

Form 36A
Offer/Counteroffer Withdrawal
Rev. 7/10
Page 1 of 1

©Copyright 2010
Northwest Multiple Listing Service
ALL RIGHTS RESERVED

WITHDRAWAL OF OFFER OR COUNTEROFFER

The following is part of the Purchase and Sale Agreement dated _____ 1

between _____ ("Buyer") 2

and _____ ("Seller") 3

concerning _____ (the "Property"). 4

TO: ❑   SELLER **AND** LISTING BROKER   5
           ❑   BUYER **AND** SELLING BROKER   6

THE ATTACHED ❑ OFFER OR ❑ COUNTEROFFER IS WITHDRAWN AND THE EARNEST MONEY SHOULD 7
BE RETURNED TO BUYER. 8

9

DATED: _____

_____ 10

_____ 11

RECEIPT OF THE ABOVE IS ACKNOWLEDGED AT _____ ON _____ 12

_____ 13

_____ 14

Reprinted courtesy of Northwest Multiple Listing Service. All rights reserved.

Like any offer, a counteroffer can be revoked at any time until the other party accepts it. A form such as the one shown in Figure 6.4 can be used to withdraw a counteroffer.

ACCEPTING AN OFFER

When an offer (or a counteroffer) is accepted, a contract is formed and the parties are legally bound by it. There are three rules to keep in mind concerning the acceptance of an offer.

The acceptance:

1. must be communicated to the person who made the offer,
2. must be made in the specified manner, and
3. cannot change any of the terms of the offer.

COMMUNICATING ACCEPTANCE

To be effective and create a valid contract, the offeree's acceptance must be communicated to the offeror. (The offeree is the person to whom the offer was made, and the offeror is the person who made it.) A seller may have decided to accept a buyer's offer, but until the seller informs the buyer that the offer has been accepted, the buyer can still revoke it.

> **EXAMPLE:** White is selling his home. Hathaway makes an offer to buy it, and White's agent presents the offer to White.
>
> In the meantime, Hathaway finds another house she likes better. She immediately notifies White that she's revoking her offer.
>
> White protests, claiming that he had already signed Hathaway's offer before she revoked it. But since White hadn't given the signed contract to Hathaway yet, the acceptance was not communicated. As a result, Hathaway still had the right to revoke the offer.

MAILBOX RULE. Acceptance of an offer may be communicated in a number of ways. When the seller's acceptance is delivered to the buyer in person, acceptance is deemed to take place at the time of delivery. But there are times when a seller may use the mail to notify the buyer of an acceptance. In this situation, the "mailbox rule" applies: the acceptance creates a binding contract when the seller drops it in the mailbox, even though the buyer will not receive it right away. The mailbox rule has been extended to other similar methods of communication, such as faxed messages.

Many purchase agreement forms have a provision that trumps this rule, however. For example, the Northwest Multiple Listing Service purchase agreement form states that delivery, regardless of the method used (mail, email, fax, etc.) is effective only upon personal receipt.

Communication to Agent. Acceptance is also considered to be communicated when the seller delivers it to the buyer's agent, even before the buyer's agent relays the acceptance to the buyer.

Manner of Acceptance

Because a contract to purchase real estate must be in writing, an offer to purchase real estate must be accepted in writing. A spoken acceptance does not create an enforceable contract.

Example: Adams submits a written offer to purchase Baker's property. Baker finds the offer very attractive, so she immediately calls Adams and accepts the offer over the phone. Two hours later, Baker receives an even better offer. Baker can still withdraw her acceptance of the offer because the acceptance wasn't in writing.

Sometimes an offer calls for a particular manner of acceptance. If so, the acceptance must be made in the specified manner to be binding.

Example: Wallace offers to buy Sanchez's property. But Wallace is leaving town shortly, so he includes the following provision in the offer: "This offer shall become a binding contract when written acceptance is hand-delivered to my attorney at 437 First Avenue, Suite 312." Sanchez can only accept the offer by having the acceptance hand-delivered to Wallace's attorney at the specified address.

If the offer does not call for a particular manner of acceptance, it may be accepted by any reasonable medium of communication. A medium is considered reasonable when it is the same one that was used by the buyer, it is one that is customarily used in similar transactions, or it has been used by the parties in previous transactions. For instance, if the buyer sent the offer to the seller by email, it's reasonable for the seller to send the acceptance to the buyer by email. (Note that if you email offers and acceptances, it's a good idea to get signed originals from both parties.)

ACCEPTANCE CANNOT CHANGE TERMS

To create a contract, the seller must accept the buyer's terms exactly as offered. The seller can't modify the terms of the offer or add any new terms. An acceptance with modifications is actually a counteroffer, not an acceptance.

CONTRACT AMENDMENTS

When an offer to purchase (or a counteroffer) is accepted in the proper manner, a contract is created. The terms of the contract can't be changed without the consent of both parties.

If the buyer and seller agree to modify their contract, you should use a separate form instead of writing the changes on the original purchase and sale agreement form. For example, amendments to the Northwest Multiple Listing Service purchase and sale agreement form are made with the optional clauses addendum shown in Chapter 7 (Figure 7.4).

The form used for an amendment should identify the original contract, provide space to write in the changes, and require the signatures of both parties. The signed amendment form should be attached to the original agreement. Each party should be given a copy of the amendment as soon as he or she signs it.

When you're filling out a form to amend a contract, remember that writing a special provision for the parties would be considered the unauthorized practice of law. When a transaction requires a special provision, ask your designated broker or branch manager. She is likely to have one or more standard clauses drafted by lawyers that are appropriate for your transaction.

CONTRACT RESCISSION

Sometimes both the buyer and the seller change their minds, and they agree to rescind or cancel their contract. The parties are always free to terminate their contract by mutual agreement. To do this, the buyer and the seller should sign a rescission agreement, which officially terminates the purchase and sale agreement. An example of a rescission form is shown in Figure 6.5.

A rescission agreement should describe how the earnest money deposit will be handled. When a purchase and sale agreement is rescinded by mutual agreement, the buyer and the seller may agree to let the listing and selling firms split the deposit in lieu of receiving the commission. Technically, the seller is still

FIG. 6.5   RESCISSION AGREEMENT FORM

RESCISSION OF PURCHASE & SALE AGREEMENT

This Rescission is made by _____ ("Buyer")   1

and _____ ("Seller"),   2

parties to a real estate purchase and sale agreement for the property whose address is   3

_____ , Washington, ZIP _____   4

(the "Property") dated _____ (the "Agreement").   5

1. **RELEASE.** The parties agree that the Agreement between them and all other agreements or   6
undertakings between them in respect to the Property are hereby rescinded; and each releases   7
the other and all real estate firms and brokers involved with this sale from any and all present or   8
future liability thereunder and/or in connection with said sale, other than as set forth hereinafter,   9
provided, that nothing herein shall be construed to terminate any existing agency relationships or   10
agreements unless otherwise agreed in writing.   11

2. **EARNEST MONEY.** The party holding the earnest money is authorized and directed to   12
immediately disburse the earnest money as follows: 13

_____   14

_____   15

_____   16

3. **COMMISSION IF SOLD IN FUTURE.** If Seller shall, within six (6) months after the date hereof,   17
sell said property to Buyer or someone acting on Buyer's behalf, Seller shall pay Listing Firm a   18
commission of (check one) ❑ $ _____ or ❑ _____% of   19
the sales price, less any portion of the above earnest money retained by Listing Firm. Provided if   20
a commission is paid to another member(s) of a multiple listing service in conjunction with such a   21
sale, the amount of commission payable to Listing Firm shall be reduced by the amount paid to   22
such other member(s). "Sell" means a Purchase and Sale Agreement signed during said six   23
months, regardless of when it closes.   24

_____   _____   25
Buyer's Signature   Date   Seller's Signature   Date

_____   _____   26
Buyer's Signature   Date   Seller's Signature   Date

_____   _____   27
Selling Firm   Listing Firm

_____   _____   28
Selling Broker's Signature   Date   Listing Broker's Signature   Date

liable for the brokerage commission, but the firms are usually willing to share the earnest money instead.

For the firms' protection, a rescission agreement form may have an extender clause similar to the ones that appear in listing agreements. Under this type of provision, if the seller enters into a new purchase and sale agreement with this same buyer within a specified period (such as six months) after rescinding their original agreement, the seller will be required to pay the firms their full commission.

Rescission agreements are also used when a purchase and sale agreement terminates because a contingency has not been fulfilled. This is discussed in Chapter 8.

Earnest Money Deposits

An important part of helping a buyer make an offer to purchase a home is handling the earnest money deposit. It's traditional for the buyer to give the seller earnest money (sometimes called a good faith deposit) as evidence of the buyer's good faith intention to buy the property on the terms he has offered.

There's no law that requires a buyer to give the seller an earnest money deposit, but virtually every seller will expect one. A seller does not want to take her home off the market for weeks, possibly months, unless the buyer is actually going to follow through on his promise to buy the property. Since the buyer will usually forfeit the deposit if he backs out, the deposit gives the seller some assurance that the buyer really is ready, willing, and able to buy the property.

The Size of the Deposit

There is no "standard" deposit amount or percentage. In fact, the size of the earnest money deposit usually depends on the buyer's circumstances. A buyer who is planning on making a large cash downpayment generally won't have any trouble making a substantial deposit; the deposit will simply be applied toward the downpayment when the sale closes. On the other hand, if the buyer is planning to finance the purchase with a no-downpayment VA loan, he may not have enough cash for a big deposit.

As a general rule, the deposit should be large enough to give the buyer an economic incentive to complete the transaction. It should also be large enough to compensate the seller for the time and expense involved in taking the house off the market if the buyer fails to complete the transaction.

EXAMPLE: Bernhardt offers to buy Warren's property for $250,000. He makes a $250 deposit. Two weeks later, Bernhardt finds another property he likes more than Warren's for only $240,000. He decides to walk away from his contract with Warren, forfeit the $250 deposit, and purchase the other property.

Under the terms of the purchase and sale agreement, Warren can keep the deposit as payment for his time and trouble. But in this case, the deposit was too small to serve its purpose. The $250 deposit was not enough money to convince Bernhardt to honor his contract, nor was it enough to compensate Warren for taking his property off the market for two weeks.

THE FORM OF THE DEPOSIT

A real estate agent who accepts an earnest money deposit from a buyer is required by law to tell the seller the amount of the deposit and what form it is in. Is it cash, a money order, a personal check, a cashier's check, a postdated check, or a promissory note? If you fail to disclose this information to the seller, you may be subject to disciplinary action. You may also face disciplinary action if you don't tell the seller that the earnest money check bounced or that the note was not paid. In addition, the seller could sue you for damages if you fail to make the proper disclosures and then the buyer does not come through with the deposit.

EXAMPLE: You're the listing agent for Peterson's house. When Thompson makes an offer, he tells you that he'll give you a $5,000 earnest money deposit. However, he explains that he can't write the earnest money check until he has transferred funds into his checking account. He assures you that he'll bring you a check tomorrow. He asks you to present the offer to Peterson right away.

When you present the offer, you tell Peterson that Thompson is making a $5,000 deposit, but neglect to mention that he hasn't given you the check yet. You could be subject to disciplinary action for failing to disclose this information.

Peterson accepts Thompson's offer without asking to see the check. She assumes that you already have it and will give it to your brokerage firm, in the usual way.

The next day, Thompson puts you off for one more day. The day after that, he refuses to give you the check and tells you he's decided to back out of his contract with Peterson. Now not only are you subject to disciplinary action, but Peterson could sue you and your firm for the money she should have received as compensation for Thompson's breach of contract.

Now let's consider the advantages and disadvantages of the different forms an earnest money deposit can take.

PERSONAL CHECKS. Most buyers make their earnest money deposit with a personal check. The check should be made payable to either the escrow agent or to the brokerage that will deposit the check if the buyer's offer is accepted.

> **EXAMPLE:** You work for Hadley Realty. Your buyer, Morrison, is making an offer and writing a personal check for the earnest money. He should make the check payable to Hadley Realty, not to you.

Some firms require a cashier's check or a money order instead of a personal check. You should ask your designated broker or branch manager whether it is company policy to accept personal checks.

Sometimes a buyer will want to use a postdated check, which can't be deposited until the date on the check. Before you accept it, you should check your firm's policies. Some won't accept postdated checks. If you do accept a postdated check, you must tell the seller. It's wise to make this disclosure in writing.

As an alternative to using a postdated check, the buyer may choose to make a small earnest money deposit with the offer and include a provision in the offer that she will make an additional deposit within a certain period of time.

> **EXAMPLE:** Hassam wants to make on offer on a home. She has a certificate of deposit that will mature in ten days, and she's planning on using those funds for the downpayment. Right now, however, she only has enough cash available to make a $300 earnest money deposit. She doesn't want to cash in her certificate of deposit before it matures, because she would have to pay a penalty for early withdrawal. Instead, she gives you a $300 check with her offer and agrees in writing to make an additional earnest money deposit in the amount of $1,500 in ten days.

CASH. Sometimes a buyer will offer to make the earnest money deposit in cash. But accepting an earnest money deposit in cash may increase the chance of loss or improper handling.

> **EXAMPLE:** A buyer wants to make an offer for a property on Friday night. He gives you a cash earnest money deposit of $1,200. You can't turn the cash over to your firm until Monday. What do you do with the cash over the weekend? You can't deposit it in your own account (that would be com-

mingling trust funds with personal funds), but you will be responsible if the cash is lost or stolen.

Your brokerage may have a policy against accepting cash deposits. Once you explain some of the problems with a cash deposit, most buyers are willing to use a money order or a check instead of cash.

If you do take a cash deposit, you must turn it over to the firm in its original cash form. You may not deposit it into your account and then write a check against the deposit. Nor may you purchase a money order or a cashier's check with the cash.

PROMISSORY NOTES. Although it's risky to accept a promissory note as an earnest money deposit, sometimes a seller is willing to do so. When you tell the seller that the deposit is in the form of a note, be sure he understands the risk. Should the buyer refuse to pay the note when it comes due, a lawsuit would be the only way to collect the money owed.

A form that can be used for an earnest money note is shown in Figure 6.6. This form provides that failure to pay the note as agreed will be considered a breach of the purchase and sale agreement as well as a default on the note. It also provides that if it is necessary to sue the buyer to collect on the note, the buyer will have to pay reasonable attorney's fees and court costs.

PERSONAL PROPERTY. In unusual cases, a buyer may want to use an item of personal property as an earnest money deposit. For instance, you might encounter a buyer who wants to use stock certificates, bonds, or a boat as part or all of the deposit. It is up to the seller to decide whether to accept such an item as a deposit. The parties and your firm will have to arrange an appropriate method of safekeeping for the item in question.

HANDLING A DEPOSIT

When a buyer gives you an earnest money deposit, you're required to turn it over to your firm as soon as possible. How the firm handles the deposit is governed partly by the trust fund procedures set forth in the real estate license law, and partly by the terms of the purchase and sale agreement (the buyer's offer). Since most earnest money deposits take the form of a personal check, we'll focus on the procedures for handling a check.

FIG. 6.6   EARNEST MONEY PROMISSORY NOTE FORM

Form 31
Earnest Money Promissory Note
Rev. 7/10
Pages 1 of 1

EARNEST MONEY PROMISSORY NOTE

$ _____   _____ , Washington 1

FOR VALUE RECEIVED, _____ ("Buyer") 2

agree(s) to pay to the order of _____ (Selling Firm or Closing Agent) 3

the sum of _____ Dollars 4

($ _____), as follows: 5

❑   within 3 days following mutual acceptance of the Purchase and Sale Agreement. 6

❑   * _____ . 7

This Note is evidence of the obligation to pay Earnest Money under a real estate Purchase and 8

Sale Agreement between the Buyer and _____ ("Seller") 9

dated _____, Buyer's failure to pay the Earnest Money 10
strictly as above shall constitute default on said Purchase and Sale Agreement as well as on this Note. 11

If this Note shall be placed in the hands of an attorney for collection, or if suit shall be brought to collect 12
any of the balance due on this Note, the Buyer promises to pay reasonable attorneys' fees, and all 13
court and collection costs. 14

Date: _____ 15

                    BUYER   _____ 16

                    BUYER   _____ 17

* "On closing" or similar language is not recommended. Use a definite date. 18

HOLDING OR DEPOSITING THE CHECK. Many purchase and sale agreements provide that the firm may hold the earnest money check, without depositing it, for a certain amount of time or until a certain event occurs. For instance, the agreement may provide that the firm is to hold the check until the seller accepts the offer. The agreement then requires the firm to deposit the earnest money into its trust account within a specified number of days after the seller's acceptance. If the seller rejects the offer, the check is returned to the buyer. If the seller makes a counteroffer that the buyer rejects, the buyer may ask for his check back. If the buyer accepts the seller's counteroffer, the firm must then deposit the check into its trust account within the specified number of days. If the buyer decides to reject the counteroffer and make another counteroffer, the brokerage should continue to hold the check until there is an acceptance or a final rejection.

Alternatively, a purchase and sale agreement may provide that the earnest money check is to be given to a third party, such as an escrow company or an attorney. In that case, the firm is required to deliver the buyer's check to the designated person within the specified number of days. The firm should obtain a dated receipt for the deposit to keep in its files.

If the purchase and sale agreement does not have a provision that calls for holding the check undeposited or turning it over to a third party, the law requires the check to be deposited into the firm's trust account by the end of the first banking day after receipt.

TRUST ACCOUNTS AND INTEREST. If the earnest money check is for $10,000 or less, the firm must keep it in a pooled trust account identified as a housing trust fund account, with interest paid to the Department of Licensing. If the check is for more than $10,000, it is usually placed in a separate trust account, with the interest paid to the buyer (unless the parties choose to have it kept in the pooled account). Before the buyer's check can be deposited into a separate account, the buyer must complete IRS form W-9.

FIRM'S RESPONSIBILITIES. Generally, the firm that receives the earnest money is the one responsible for handling the funds properly. Thus, the selling firm is usually the one who is required to deposit the funds, deliver them to the designated third party, or hold them until the seller accepts the offer. Usually, the deposit is first given to the buyer's agent, who is supposed to turn the deposit over to her designated broker as soon as possible. Every firm is responsible for setting up office procedures for handling deposits. For example, a designated broker should give his sales agents instructions on what to do if they receive an earnest money deposit when the office is closed.

Bounced or Stopped Checks. After the firm deposits an earnest money check into the appropriate trust account, problems can still arise. The check may fail to clear, or the buyer may stop payment for some reason.

> **Example:** On Tuesday, Green made an offer on Bowen's property. He gave you a $1,000 personal check for the earnest money, and you immediately turned it over to your designated broker.
>
> Wednesday morning, your designated broker deposited the check into her trust account. Wednesday evening, Bowen rejected Green's offer, so Green asked for a refund of his deposit. Thursday morning, your designated broker wrote Green a $1,000 check from her trust account.
>
> On Friday morning, the bank calls your designated broker to inform her that Green's check failed to clear his bank due to insufficient funds. Now Green has your firm's $1,000, your firm's trust account is overdrawn, and your designated broker may face disciplinary action for the shortfall.

To prevent this type of problem, the purchase and sale agreement can include a provision that requires the buyer to wait until his check clears before requesting a refund of the earnest money deposit. Of course, if the agreement provides that the firm will hold the deposit until the seller accepts the offer, this problem is avoided altogether.

Refund or Forfeiture of Earnest Money

If the buyer and seller have signed a purchase and sale agreement, but the sale fails to close, the earnest money will either be returned to the buyer or forfeited to the seller. The circumstances under which it will be refunded or forfeited should be stated clearly in the purchase and sale agreement. This is the best way to prevent a dispute between the buyer and the seller over who is entitled to the deposit.

Typically, the buyer is entitled to a refund of the deposit if:

- the seller rejects the offer;
- the buyer withdraws the offer before it is accepted;
- the buyer rescinds based on information in the seller disclosure statement or discovers a material inaccuracy concerning the property; or
- the seller accepts the offer, but a contingency provision is not fulfilled, so the contract is terminated.

EXAMPLE: Lindor and Jones have a purchase and sale agreement that's contingent on Lindor obtaining a conventional loan to finance the purchase. Lindor applies to three lenders, but they all reject his loan application. The contingency hasn't been fulfilled, so the contract is terminated, and Lindor is entitled to a refund of the deposit.

On the other hand, the deposit will generally be forfeited to the seller if the buyer simply changes her mind and backs out of the sale. Most purchase and sale agreements provide that the deposit will be treated as liquidated damages in the event of a breach of contract. If the buyer defaults, the seller will keep the deposit as liquidated damages rather than suing the buyer for actual damages.

In Washington, there is a statutory limit on liquidated damages in real estate transactions. When a buyer's earnest money deposit is treated as liquidated damages, the amount that the buyer forfeits cannot exceed 5% of the purchase price of the property.

Before the earnest money is disbursed to either the seller or the buyer, the firm should get the parties to agree to the disbursement in writing. If they disagree as to which of them is entitled to the deposit, the firm must give written notice to both parties of the intent to distribute the funds within 30 days.

Remember, it is the brokerage firm—not you—who is responsible for disbursing earnest money deposits. If a buyer or seller has questions about how the deposit will be handled, always refer her to your designated broker or branch manager. Never try to answer these questions yourself.

FIG. 6.7   EARNEST MONEY RULES

BUYER'S EARNEST MONEY DEPOSIT

- MUST BE DEPOSITED INTO TRUST ACCOUNT BY END OF FIRST BANKING DAY AFTER RECEIPT, UNLESS OTHERWISE AGREED

- $10,000 OR LESS: MUST BE KEPT IN POOLED ACCOUNT, WITH INTEREST PAID TO STATE HOUSING TRUST FUND

- MORE THAN $10,000: MAY BE KEPT IN SEPARATE ACCOUNT, WITH INTEREST PAID TO BUYER

- IF BUYER DEFAULTS, AMOUNT FORFEITED CAN'T EXCEED 5% OF PURCHASE PRICE

Some purchase and sale agreements provide that any expenses already incurred that were to be paid at closing will be deducted from the earnest money before it's forfeited to the seller. Also, listing agreements typically provide that the seller will pay half of the remainder of the deposit to the listing firm and selling firm in place of their commission.

Fair Housing Considerations

As you prepare offers and negotiate counteroffers, you must be sure to avoid discrimination based on race, color, religion, national origin, sex, disability, familial status, or marital status. The potential for discriminating against a buyer begins with your first meeting. Even before you show the buyer a house, prepare an offer, or negotiate a sale, you could engage in discriminatory conduct.

It's important to remember that you do not have to intend to discriminate in order to violate a state or federal fair housing law. Acting in a discriminatory manner, or with a discriminatory effect, is enough.

> **Example:** A potential buyer walks into your firm's office. In broken English, with a heavy accent, he tells you he is interested in looking at homes. He is from China, and you have a lot of trouble understanding him. You suggest that he find an agent who speaks some Chinese, because you genuinely believe an agent who knows his language will be able to help him better. You could be held to have discriminated against this buyer and violated the fair housing laws, even though your intentions were good. In this situation, engaging (or offering to engage) the assistance of a translator might have been a better option.

A wide array of actions toward home buyers are considered discriminatory under federal and Washington fair housing laws. These include:

- refusing to receive or failing to transmit a bona fide offer;
- refusing to negotiate for the sale of property, or otherwise making it unavailable;
- changing the terms of the sale for different potential buyers;
- discriminating in providing services or facilities in connection with a real estate transaction;
- representing that a property is not available for inspection or sale when it is in fact available;

- failing to advise a prospect about a property listing;
- using any application form or making any record or inquiry which indicates, directly or indirectly, an intent to discriminate; and
- discriminating in negotiating or executing any service or item (such as title insurance or mortgage insurance) in connection with a real estate transaction.

You should never refuse to show a buyer a particular house because of the buyer's race or another characteristic protected under the fair housing laws. Any buyer who asks to see a particular property should be shown the property.

EXAMPLE: You have shown Hernandez, a Hispanic buyer, several houses. Hernandez asks to be shown a particular house that he noticed online. He thinks it might be just the place he's looking for. From office rumors, you know that the seller will probably refuse to accept an offer from any minority buyer. You are anxious to avoid a confrontation, so you tell Hernandez that the seller has already accepted an offer and the house is no longer available. You have just discriminated against Hernandez by representing that the property is not available when in fact it is.

As explained in Chapter 3, steering refers to channeling prospective buyers or tenants toward or away from specific neighborhoods based on their race (or national origin, religion, etc.) in order to maintain or change the character of those neighborhoods.

EXAMPLE: Your office has thirteen white agents and four African-American agents. African-American buyers are directed to the African-American agents, who are "encouraged" to show them properties only in the one neighborhood in the city that is mainly African-American. This is done on the principle that these buyers would be more comfortable living there. Your real estate office is guilty of steering.

You must also be sure to treat all buyers the same in terms of client and customer services. It would obviously be discriminatory to ignore minority prospects when they enter your office, or to refuse to drive them to see the listed houses that interest them (if that's a service you ordinarily provide).

Because so many actions could be considered discriminatory, it's important to develop sales practices that will ensure your compliance with fair housing laws.

Here are a few guidelines to follow when interviewing buyers, showing homes, and presenting and negotiating offers:

- Never imply that a person of a particular race, color, religion, national origin, etc., will have a harder time getting financing.
- Always offer to show your prospects all the listed properties in your market area that meet their objective criteria. Don't make assumptions about a buyer's housing needs or neighborhood preferences based on stereotypes.
- Be sure to treat all prospects equally when setting up showings, making keys available, setting appointments to present offers, or conducting negotiations.
- Report any suspected discriminatory act or statement on the part of a seller to your designated broker or branch manager immediately. Ask him (or a lawyer, if necessary) what you should do about a rejection that seemed to be based on discriminatory reasons.

CHAPTER SUMMARY

1. As a real estate agent, you may fill out a standard purchase and sale agreement form, but only for a transaction you are handling, and you cannot charge a separate fee for the service. You may not draft special clauses or give advice about the legal effect of provisions in the form. If you have any questions or concerns when filling out a form, you should talk to your designated broker or a real estate attorney.

2. All offers to purchase, regardless of their merit, must be presented to the seller. You must even present offers received after the seller has already accepted another offer. (These backup offers should be made contingent on the failure of the first sales contract.) Offers are usually presented by the listing agent. You must disclose your agency status before presenting an offer to purchase.

3. When a seller "accepts" an offer with a few modifications, the seller is actually rejecting the offer and making a counteroffer. When a party wants to make a counteroffer, it is best to use a special counteroffer form. When you present a counteroffer, be sure to explain each term that has been changed and discuss the financial ramifications of the changes.

4. If an offer does not have a time limit, it will terminate after a reasonable period of time. An offer can be revoked at any time up until it is accepted. To be effective, the acceptance must be communicated to the person who made the offer. An offer to purchase real property must be in writing. The acceptance also must be in writing, and any other stipulations about the manner of acceptance must be complied with.

5. When an offer is properly accepted, a binding contract is created. It cannot be modified without the written consent of both parties. The parties may mutually agree to terminate the contract, although the seller may still owe the firm the sales commission. If the contract is terminated, the parties should sign a rescission agreement.

6. You must disclose the amount and the form of the buyer's earnest money deposit to the seller and also disclose any problems with the deposit. Most deposits are personal checks, but they may also be in the form of cash, a money order, a cashier's check, a promissory note, or personal property.

7. Earnest money must be deposited in the firm's trust account within one banking day of receipt unless the purchase and sale agreement provides otherwise. Sometimes the agreement provides that the deposit is to be turned over to a third party, or that the firm is to hold the earnest money check un-cashed until the seller accepts the offer. If the sale closes, the earnest money will be credited against the buyer's downpayment. If the sale fails to close, the earnest money will either be returned to the buyer or forfeited to the seller, depending on the circumstances.

8. In showing homes, preparing offers, and negotiating sales, be sure you do not discriminate against the buyers you're working with. Discrimination does not have to be intentional to violate fair housing laws.

CHAPTER QUIZ

1. Which of the following statements about an offer to purchase real property is true?

    a. The offer needs to be in writing, but the acceptance does not

    b. Both the offer and the acceptance must be in writing

    c. Neither the offer nor the acceptance needs to be in writing, but the deed to transfer title must be in writing

    d. The offer does not have to be in writing, but the acceptance must include all of the terms of the offer

2. Which of the following statements about preparing an offer to purchase is true?

    a. The buyer cannot write her own offer without engaging in the unauthorized practice of law

    b. A real estate agent may write special clauses for the parties as long as they are inserted into a pre-printed form written and approved by attorneys

    c. A real estate agent may not prepare an offer if he represents one of the parties

    d. A real estate agent is held to the same standard of care as a lawyer when preparing an offer

3. A contingent counteroffer would be appropriate when:

    a. the seller has already signed a purchase and sale agreement, and then receives an attractive offer from another buyer

    b. the seller wants to accept the buyer's offer, but modify some of the terms

    c. the buyer wants to accept the seller's counteroffer, but isn't sure if he'll qualify for financing

    d. the seller has received multiple offers and wants to withdraw her previous counteroffer to one buyer and accept another buyer's offer

4. The seller's acceptance would be effective (so that the buyer could no longer withdraw his offer) in all of the following situations, except:

    a. the seller accepts the buyer's offer over the phone

    b. the seller uses a fax machine to transmit her acceptance

    c. the seller sends her acceptance in the mail, but with delivery confirmation

    d. the seller sends her acceptance via telegram

5. Once it has been signed by both the buyer and the seller, a purchase and sale agreement can be modified only if:

    a. a contingency clause is not fulfilled

    b. the buyer accepts the seller's counteroffer in writing

    c. both parties agree to the modifications in writing

    d. the seller failed to disclose certain information he was legally required to disclose

6. Which of the following is least likely to be found in a rescission agreement?

   a. An extender clause

   b. A notice to backup buyer

   c. An agreement to allow the listing and selling firms to share the earnest money deposit in lieu of a commission

   d. The signatures of both parties

7. After accepting an earnest money deposit from a buyer, you are required to tell the seller:

   a. what form the deposit is in

   b. whether the buyer actually has paid you the deposit funds

   c. the amount of the deposit

   d. All of the above

8. If you accept cash as an earnest money deposit, you:

   a. must turn the deposit over to the firm in its original cash form

   b. should use the cash to purchase a certified check, to prevent the funds from being lost or stolen

   c. should have the buyer's receipt notarized

   d. may face disciplinary action for violating the real estate license law

9. Many purchase and sale agreement forms have a provision allowing the firm to hold the earnest money check without depositing it for a specified period. One advantage of this is that:

   a. it gives the seller more time to consider the offer

   b. the firm can simply return the check to the buyer if the offer is rejected

   c. it ensures that the buyer has sufficient funds in her account

   d. the check can be postdated by a week or more

10. If the buyer forfeits the earnest money deposit as liquidated damages for breach of the purchase and sale agreement:

   a. the full amount of the deposit will be split between the selling firm and the listing firm in lieu of a commission

   b. any amount in excess of 5% of the purchase price must be refunded to the buyer

   c. any amount in excess of $10,000 must be refunded to the buyer

   d. the seller will be entitled to keep the entire amount, less any expenses incurred by the listing firm

ANSWER KEY

1. b. The statute of frauds requires both an offer to purchase real property and the acceptance of the offer to be in writing.

2. d. When filling out a contract form, a real estate agent is held to the same standard of care that is required of a lawyer.

3. a. A contingent counteroffer allows a seller to accept a second offer, contingent on the failure of the first contract.

4. a. In order to form a contract to purchase real estate, the acceptance must be made in writing. Telephone communication is not a valid form of acceptance. The mailbox rule would apply to all of the other situations listed.

5. c. Once a contract has been formed, the terms of the contract can't be changed without the written consent of both parties. The parties may agree to amend the contract for any reason.

6. b. A contract rescission agreement should be signed by both parties and describe how the earnest money deposit will be handled. It may include an extender clause for the licensees' protection. If the seller has accepted a backup offer, the notice to the backup buyer will be handled separately.

7. d. A real estate agent who accepts an earnest money deposit is required to disclose the amount and form of the deposit to the seller. The agent must also inform the seller if the earnest money check bounces, the funds have not actually been paid, or a promissory note is not been paid.

8. a. If you accept an earnest money deposit in cash, you must turn the cash over to your firm so that it can be placed in the trust account in cash. Although accepting an earnest money deposit in cash increases the chance of loss or improper handling, it is not in itself grounds for disciplinary action.

9. b. Purchase and sale agreements often allow the firm to hold the earnest money check without depositing it until the seller accepts the offer. This makes it easier to return the earnest money to the buyer if the offer is rejected.

10. b. If the buyer breaches the purchase and sale agreement, no more than 5% of the purchase price can be retained as liquidated damages. After expenses incurred by the firm have been deducted, the seller usually keeps half of the remainder and gives the listing firm the other half. The listing firm will usually split this portion with the selling firm.

7

PURCHASE AND SALE AGREEMENTS

REQUIREMENTS FOR A VALID AGREEMENT

PROVISIONS IN A RESIDENTIAL AGREEMENT

- Identifying the parties
- Property description
- Purchase price and method of payment
- Earnest money
- Included items
- Conveyance and title
- Information verification period
- Closing provisions
- Transfer of possession
- Default
- Time is of the essence
- Addenda
- Agency disclosure
- Lead-based paint disclosures
- Offer and acceptance
- Signatures

VACANT LAND PURCHASE AND SALE AGREEMENTS

INTRODUCTION

We've discussed a variety of techniques that will help you find potential buyers, show properties, and negotiate offers. Your designated broker or branch manager will undoubtedly give you training in these matters. However, learning the functions of a purchase and sale agreement and understanding its provisions are just as important to your career. If you make a mistake in filling out a purchase and sale agreement form, you could face the loss of your commission, a lawsuit by the buyer or the seller, and disciplinary action. This chapter describes the requirements for a valid purchase and sale agreement, the provisions typically found in a residential purchase and sale agreement form, and some of the addenda commonly used in residential transactions. At the end of the chapter, we'll look at a purchase and sale agreement for vacant land.

REQUIREMENTS FOR A VALID PURCHASE AND SALE AGREEMENT

When a buyer is ready to make an offer, he may not understand why it's necessary to fill out a purchase and sale agreement form. After all, the buyer figures, it's just an offer. Why not just jot down the important part—the sales price—on a piece of paper? If the seller's interested, they can agree on the details later.

There are two main problems with that approach. First, the seller can't decide whether the buyer's offer is acceptable unless all of the material terms of the proposed transaction have been set forth. Anything from the amount of the earnest money to the date set for closing could affect the seller's decision.

Second, when the seller signs the buyer's written offer, agreeing to the buyer's terms, a contract is formed. The purpose of the contract is to hold the buyer and seller to their agreement until the sale is ready to close. But the contract won't be enforceable unless it includes all of the terms that are legally required for a valid purchase and sale agreement.

A purchase and sale agreement must meet the basic legal requirements for any contract. The parties must be competent, and there must be mutual consent (offer and acceptance), a lawful objective, and consideration (the seller's promise to sell and the buyer's promise to buy).

In addition, a purchase and sale agreement must:

1. be in writing;
2. identify the parties and describe the property;

3. state the price and method of payment;
4. provide for the payment of utilities and the proration of taxes, insurance, and liens;
5. state the type of deed and the condition of title;
6. list the liens or other encumbrances the buyer will assume or take title subject to;
7. describe any conditions or contingencies (such as a financing contingency); and
8. state the time for delivery of title and possession.

While these are the minimum requirements for validity, most purchase and sale agreement forms are quite detailed. It is important for the agreement between the parties to be stated fully and accurately; anything that isn't made clear at the outset can give rise to a dispute later on, and might prevent the transaction from closing.

TYPICAL PROVISIONS IN A RESIDENTIAL PURCHASE AND SALE AGREEMENT

There is no one purchase and sale agreement form that all real estate agents must use. A variety of forms are available from multiple listing services, other professional organizations, and legal form publishers. As an example, Figure 7.1 shows the residential purchase and sale agreement form that the Northwest Multiple Listing Service (NWMLS) uses. Of course, you need to become familiar with the terms of the purchase and sale agreement form that is used in your office. Our discussion will be an overview of the provisions found in most purchase and sale agreement forms.

To fill out a purchase and sale agreement form, you need to be able to answer these questions:

1. What information needs to be filled in?
2. Which provisions are pertinent to this transaction?
3. Which provisions should be crossed out?
4. What other provisions need to be attached to the form as addenda?

Remember that contract forms should always be filled in completely. If an entry doesn't apply to the transaction, write in "N/A," rather than leaving the space blank.

FIG. 7.1   RESIDENTIAL PURCHASE AND SALE AGREEMENT FORM

**RESIDENTIAL REAL ESTATE PURCHASE AND SALE AGREEMENT
SPECIFIC TERMS**

1. **Date:** _____   **MLS No.:** _____

2. **Buyer:** _____

3. **Seller:** _____

4. **Property:** Tax Parcel No(s).: _____ (_____County)
   Street Address: _____ Washington _____
   Legal Description: Attached as Exhibit A.

5. **Included Items**: ❑ stove/range; ❑ refrigerator; ❑ washer; ❑ dryer; ❑ dishwasher; ❑ hot tub; ❑ fireplace insert; ❑ wood stove; ❑ satellite dish and operating equipment; ❑ security system; ❑ attached television(s); ❑ attached speaker(s); ❑ other _____

6. **Purchase Price:** $ _____

7. **Earnest Money:** (To be held by ❑ Selling Firm; ❑ Closing Agent)
   Personal Check: $_____; Note: $_____; Other (_____): $ _____

8. **Default:** (check only one) ❑ Forfeiture of Earnest Money; ❑ Seller's Election of Remedies

9. **Title Insurance Company:** _____

10. **Closing Agent:** ❑ a qualified closing agent of Buyer's choice; ❑ _____

11. **Closing Date:** _____

12. **Possession Date:** ❑ on Closing; ❑ Other _____

13. **Offer Expiration Date:** _____

14. **Services of Closing Agent for Payment of Utilities:** ❑ Requested (attach NWMLS Form 22K); ❑ Waived

15. **Charges and Assessments Due After Closing:** ❑ assumed by Buyer; ❑ prepaid in full by Seller at Closing

16. **Agency Disclosure:**   Selling Broker represents: ❑ Buyer; ❑ Seller; ❑ both parties; ❑ neither party
    Listing Broker represents: ❑ Seller; ❑ both parties

17. **Addenda:** _____
    _____
    _____
    _____

Buyer's Signature	Date	Seller's Signature	Date
Buyer's Signature	Date	Seller's Signature	Date
Buyer's Address		Seller's Address	
City, State, Zip		City, State, Zip	
Phone No.	Fax No.	Phone No.	Fax No.
Buyer's E-mail Address		Seller's E-mail Address	
Selling Firm	MLS Office No.	Listing Firm	MLS Office No.
Selling Firm's Assumed Name (if applicable)		Listing Firm's Assumed Name (if applicable)	
Selling Broker (Print)	MLS LAG No.	Listing Broker (Print)	MLS LAG No.
Phone No.	Firm Fax No.	Phone No.	Firm Fax No.
Selling Broker's E-mail Address		Listing Broker's E-mail Address	

Form 21
Residential Purchase & Sale Agreement
Rev. 12/12
Page 2 of 5

©Copyright 2012
Northwest Multiple Listing Service
ALL RIGHTS RESERVED

RESIDENTIAL REAL ESTATE PURCHASE AND SALE AGREEMENT
GENERAL TERMS
Continued

a. Purchase Price. Buyer shall pay to Seller the Purchase Price, including the Earnest Money, in cash at Closing, unless 1
otherwise specified in this Agreement. Buyer represents that Buyer has sufficient funds to close this sale in accordance 2
with this Agreement and is not relying on any contingent source of funds, including funds from loans, the sale of other 3
property, gifts, retirement, or future earnings, except to the extent otherwise specified in this Agreement. 4

b. Earnest Money. Buyer shall deliver the Earnest Money within 2 days after mutual acceptance of this Agreement to 5
Selling Broker who will deposit any check to be held by Selling Firm, or deliver any Earnest Money to be held by Closing 6
Agent, within 3 days of receipt or mutual acceptance, whichever occurs later. If the Earnest Money is held by Selling 7
Firm and is over $10,000.00 it shall be deposited into an interest bearing trust account in Selling Firm's name provided 8
that Buyer completes an IRS Form W-9. Interest, if any, after deduction of bank charges and fees, will be paid to Buyer. 9
Buyer shall reimburse Selling Firm for bank charges and fees in excess of the interest earned, if any. If the Earnest 10
Money held by Selling Firm is over $10,000.00 Buyer has the option to require Selling Firm to deposit the Earnest 11
Money into the Housing Trust Fund Account, with the interest paid to the State Treasurer, if both Seller and Buyer so 12
agree in writing. If the Buyer does not complete an IRS Form W-9 before Selling Firm must deposit the Earnest Money 13
or the Earnest Money is $10,000.00 or less, the Earnest Money shall be deposited into the Housing Trust Fund 14
Account. Selling Firm may transfer the Earnest Money to Closing Agent at Closing. If all or part of the Earnest Money is 15
to be refunded to Buyer and any such costs remain unpaid, the Selling Firm or Closing Agent may deduct and pay them 16
therefrom. The parties instruct Closing Agent to provide written verification of receipt of the Earnest Money and notice of 17
dishonor of any check to the parties and Brokers at the addresses and/or fax numbers provided herein. 18

Upon termination of this Agreement, a party or the Closing Agent may deliver a form authorizing the release of Earnest 19
Money to the other party or the parties. The party(s) shall execute such form and deliver the same to the Closing Agent. 20
If either party fails to execute the release form, the other party may make a written demand to the Closing Agent for the 21
Earnest Money. If only one party makes such a demand, Closing Agent shall promptly deliver notice of the demand to 22
the other party. If the other party does not object to the demand within 10 days of Closing Agent's notice, Closing Agent 23
shall disburse the Earnest Money to the party making the demand. If Closing Agent complies with the preceding 24
process, each party shall be deemed to have released Closing Agent from any and all claims or liability related to the 25
disbursal of the Earnest Money. The parties are advised that, notwithstanding the foregoing, Closing Agent may require 26
the parties to execute a separate agreement before disbursing the Earnest Money. If either party fails to authorize the 27
release of the Earnest Money to the other party when required to do so under this Agreement, that party shall be in 28
breach of this Agreement. Upon either party's request, the party holding the Earnest Money shall commence an 29
interpleader action in the county in which the Property is located. For the purposes of this section, the term Closing 30
Agent includes a Selling Firm holding the Earnest Money. The parties authorize the party commencing an interpleader 31
action to deduct up to $500.00 for the costs thereof. 32

c. Included Items. Any of the following items, including items identified in Specific Term No. 5 if the corresponding box is 33
checked, located in or on the Property are included in the sale: built-in appliances; wall-to-wall carpeting; curtains, 34
drapes and all other window treatments; window and door screens; awnings; storm doors and windows; installed 35
television antennas; ventilating, air conditioning and heating fixtures; trash compactor; fireplace doors, gas logs and gas 36
log lighters; irrigation fixtures; electric garage door openers; water heaters; installed electrical fixtures; lighting fixtures; 37
shrubs, plants and trees planted in the ground; and other fixtures; and all associated operating remote controls. If any of 38
the above Included Items are leased or encumbered, Seller shall acquire and clear title at or before Closing. 39

d. Condition of Title. Unless otherwise specified in this Agreement, title to the Property shall be marketable at Closing. 40
The following shall not cause the title to be unmarketable: rights, reservations, covenants, conditions and restrictions, 41
presently of record and general to the area; easements and encroachments, not materially affecting the value of or 42
unduly interfering with Buyer's reasonable use of the Property; and reserved oil and/or mining rights. Monetary 43
encumbrances or liens not assumed by Buyer, shall be paid or discharged by Seller on or before Closing. Title shall be 44
conveyed by a Statutory Warranty Deed. If this Agreement is for conveyance of a buyer's interest in a Real Estate 45
Contract, the Statutory Warranty Deed shall include a buyer's assignment of the contract sufficient to convey after 46
acquired title. 47

e. Title Insurance. Seller authorizes Buyer's lender or Closing Agent, at Seller's expense, to apply for the then-current 48
ALTA form of Homeowner's Policy of Title Insurance for One-to-Four Family Residence, from the Title Insurance 49
Company. If Seller previously received a preliminary commitment from a Title Insurance Company that Buyer declines 50
to use, Buyer shall pay any cancellation fees owing to the original Title Insurance Company. Otherwise, the party 51
applying for title insurance shall pay any title cancellation fee, in the event such a fee is assessed. If the Title Insurance 52
Company selected by the parties will not issue a Homeowner's Policy for the Property, the parties agree that the Title 53
Insurance Company shall instead issue the then-current ALTA standard form Owner's Policy, together with 54
homeowner's additional protection and inflation protection endorsements, if available. The Title Insurance Company 55
shall send a copy of the preliminary commitment to Seller, Listing Broker, Buyer and Selling Broker. The preliminary 56
commitment, and the title policy to be issued, shall contain no exceptions other than the General Exclusions and 57
Exceptions in the Policy and Special Exceptions consistent with the Condition of Title herein provided. If title cannot be 58
made so insurable prior to the Closing Date, then as Buyer's sole and exclusive remedy, the Earnest Money shall, 59

Initials: BUYER: _____ Date: _____ SELLER: _____ Date: _____

BUYER: _____ Date: _____ SELLER: _____ Date: _____

RESIDENTIAL REAL ESTATE PURCHASE AND SALE AGREEMENT
GENERAL TERMS
Continued

unless Buyer elects to waive such defects or encumbrances, be refunded to the Buyer, less any unpaid costs described 60
in this Agreement, and this Agreement shall thereupon be terminated. Buyer shall have no right to specific performance 61
or damages as a consequence of Seller's inability to provide insurable title. 62

f. **Closing and Possession**. This sale shall be closed by the Closing Agent on the Closing Date. If the Closing Date falls 63
on a Saturday, Sunday, legal holiday as defined in RCW 1.16.050, or day when the county recording office is closed, 64
the Closing Agent shall close the transaction on the next day that is not a Saturday, Sunday, legal holiday, or day when 65
the county recording office is closed. "Closing" means the date on which all documents are recorded and the sale 66
proceeds are available to Seller. Seller shall deliver keys and garage door remotes to Buyer on the Closing Date or on 67
the Possession Date, whichever occurs first. Buyer shall be entitled to possession at 9:00 p.m. on the Possession Date. 68
Seller shall maintain the Property in its present condition, normal wear and tear excepted, until the Buyer is entitled to 69
possession. Seller shall not enter into or modify existing leases or rental agreements, service contracts, or other 70
agreements affecting the Property which have terms extending beyond Closing without first obtaining Buyer's consent, 71
which shall not be unreasonably withheld. If possession transfers at a time other than Closing, the parties agree to 72
execute NWMLS Form 65A (Rental Agreement/Occupancy Prior to Closing) or NWMLS Form 65B (Rental 73
Agreement/Seller Occupancy After Closing) (or alternative rental agreements) and are advised of the need to contact 74
their respective insurance companies to assure appropriate hazard and liability insurance policies are in place, as 75
applicable. 76

RCW 19.27.530 requires the seller of any owner-occupied single-family residence to equip the residence with a carbon 77
monoxide alarm(s) in accordance with the state building code before a buyer or any other person may legally occupy 78
the residence following the sale. The parties acknowledge that the Brokers are not responsible for ensuring that Seller 79
complies with RCW 19.27.530. Buyer and Seller shall hold the Brokers and their Firms harmless from any claim 80
resulting from Seller's failure to install a carbon monoxide alarm(s) in the Property. 81

g. **Section 1031 Like-Kind Exchange**. If either Buyer or Seller intends for this transaction to be a part of a Section 1031 82
like-kind exchange, then the other party shall cooperate in the completion of the like-kind exchange so long as the 83
cooperating party incurs no additional liability in doing so, and so long as any expenses (including attorneys' fees and 84
costs) incurred by the cooperating party that are related only to the exchange are paid or reimbursed to the cooperating 85
party at or prior to Closing. Notwithstanding the Assignment paragraph of this Agreement, any party completing a 86
Section 1031 like-kind exchange may assign this Agreement to its qualified intermediary or any entity set up for the 87
purposes of completing a reverse exchange. 88

h. **Closing Costs and Prorations and Charges and Assessments**. Seller and Buyer shall each pay one-half of the 89
escrow fee unless otherwise required by applicable FHA or VA regulations. Taxes for the current year, rent, interest, 90
and lienable homeowner's association dues shall be prorated as of Closing. Buyer shall pay Buyer's loan costs, 91
including credit report, appraisal charge and lender's title insurance, unless provided otherwise in this Agreement. If any 92
payments are delinquent on encumbrances which will remain after Closing, Closing Agent is instructed to pay such 93
delinquencies at Closing from money due, or to be paid by, Seller. Buyer shall pay for remaining fuel in the fuel tank if, 94
prior to Closing, Seller obtains a written statement as to the quantity and current price from the supplier. Seller shall pay 95
all utility charges, including unbilled charges. Unless waived in Specific Term No. 14, Seller and Buyer request the 96
services of Closing Agent in disbursing funds necessary to satisfy unpaid utility charges in accordance with RCW 60.80 97
and Seller shall provide the names and addresses of all utilities providing service to the Property and having lien rights 98
(attach NWMLS Form 22K Identification of Utilities or equivalent). 99

Buyer is advised to verify the existence and amount of any local improvement district, capacity or impact charges or 100
other assessments that may be charged against the Property before or after Closing. Seller will pay such charges that 101
are encumbrances at the time of Closing, or that are or become due on or before Closing. Charges levied before 102
Closing, but becoming due after Closing shall be paid as agreed in Specific Term No. 15. 103

i. **Sale Information**. Listing Broker and Selling Broker are authorized to report this Agreement (including price and all 104
terms) to the Multiple Listing Service that published it and to its members, financing institutions, appraisers, and anyone 105
else related to this sale. Buyer and Seller expressly authorize all Closing Agents, appraisers, title insurance companies, 106
and others related to this Sale, to furnish the Listing Broker and/or Selling Broker, on request, any and all information 107
and copies of documents concerning this sale. 108

j. **FIRPTA - Tax Withholding at Closing**. The Closing Agent is instructed to prepare a certification (NWMLS Form 22E or 109
equivalent) that Seller is not a "foreign person" within the meaning of the Foreign Investment In Real Property Tax Act. 110
Seller shall sign this certification. If Seller is a foreign person, and this transaction is not otherwise exempt from FIRPTA, 111
Closing Agent is instructed to withhold and pay the required amount to the Internal Revenue Service. 112

k. **Notices**. In consideration of the license to use this and NWMLS's companion forms and for the benefit of the Listing 113
Broker and the Selling Broker as well as the orderly administration of the offer, counteroffer or this Agreement, the 114
parties irrevocably agree that unless otherwise specified in this Agreement, any notice required or permitted in, or 115
related to, this Agreement (including revocations of offers or counteroffers) must be in writing. Notices to Seller must be 116

Initials: BUYER: _____ Date: _____ SELLER: _____ Date: _____
BUYER: _____ Date: _____ SELLER: _____ Date: _____

Form 21
Residential Purchase & Sale Agreement
Rev. 12/12
Page 4 of 5

©Copyright 2012
Northwest Multiple Listing Service
ALL RIGHTS RESERVED

RESIDENTIAL REAL ESTATE PURCHASE AND SALE AGREEMENT
GENERAL TERMS
Continued

signed by at least one Buyer and shall be deemed given only when the notice is received by Seller, by Listing Broker or 117
at the licensed office of Listing Broker. Notices to Buyer must be signed by at least one Seller and shall be deemed 118
given only when the notice is received by Buyer, by Selling Broker or at the licensed office of Selling Broker. Receipt by 119
Selling Broker of a Form 17, Disclosure of Information on Lead-Based Paint and Lead-Based Paint Hazards, Public 120
Offering Statement or Resale Certificate, homeowners' association documents provided pursuant to NWMLS Form 121
22D, or a preliminary commitment for title insurance provided pursuant to NWMLS Form 22T shall be deemed receipt 122
by Buyer. Selling Broker and Listing Broker have no responsibility to advise of receipt of a notice beyond either phoning 123
the party or causing a copy of the notice to be delivered to the party's address shown on this Agreement. Buyer and 124
Seller must keep Selling Broker and Listing Broker advised of their whereabouts in order to receive prompt notification 125
of receipt of a notice. 126

l. **Computation of Time.** Unless otherwise specified in this Agreement, any period of time measured in days and stated 127
in this Agreement shall start on the day following the event commencing the period and shall expire at 9:00 p.m. of the 128
last calendar day of the specified period of time. Except for the Possession Date, if the last day is a Saturday, Sunday 129
or legal holiday as defined in RCW 1.16.050, the specified period of time shall expire on the next day that is not a 130
Saturday, Sunday or legal holiday. Any specified period of 5 days or less shall not include Saturdays, Sundays or legal 131
holidays. If the parties agree that an event will occur on a specific calendar date, the event shall occur on that date, 132
except for the Closing Date, which, if it falls on a Saturday, Sunday, legal holiday as defined in RCW 1.16.050, or day 133
when the county recording office is closed, shall occur on the next day that is not a Saturday, Sunday, legal holiday, or 134
day when the county recording office is closed. If the parties agree upon and attach a legal description after this 135
Agreement is signed by the offeree and delivered to the offeror, then for the purposes of computing time, mutual 136
acceptance shall be deemed to be on the date of delivery of an accepted offer or counteroffer to the offeror, rather than 137
on the date the legal description is attached. Time is of the essence of this Agreement. 138

m. **Facsimile and E-mail Transmission.** Facsimile transmission of any signed original document, and retransmission of 139
any signed facsimile transmission, shall be the same as delivery of an original. At the request of either party, or the 140
Closing Agent, the parties will confirm facsimile transmitted signatures by signing an original document. E-mail 141
transmission of any document or notice shall not be effective unless the parties to this Agreement otherwise agree in 142
writing. 143

n. **Integration and Electronic Signatures.** This Agreement constitutes the entire understanding between the parties and 144
supersedes all prior or contemporaneous understandings and representations. No modification of this Agreement shall 145
be effective unless agreed in writing and signed by Buyer and Seller. The parties acknowledge that a signature in 146
electronic form has the same legal effect and validity as a handwritten signature. 147

o. **Assignment.** Buyer may not assign this Agreement, or Buyer's rights hereunder, without Seller's prior written consent, 148
unless the parties indicate that assignment is permitted by the addition of "and/or assigns" on the line identifying the 149
Buyer on the first page of this Agreement. 150

p. **Default.** In the event Buyer fails, without legal excuse, to complete the purchase of the Property, then the following 151
provision, as identified in Specific Term No. 8, shall apply: 152

    i. **Forfeiture of Earnest Money.** That portion of the Earnest Money that does not exceed five percent (5%) of the 153
    Purchase Price shall be forfeited to the Seller as the sole and exclusive remedy for such failure. 154

    ii. **Seller's Election of Remedies.** Seller may, at Seller's option, (a) keep the Earnest Money as liquidated damages 155
    as the sole and exclusive remedy available to Seller for such failure, (b) bring suit against Buyer for Seller's actual 156
    damages, (c) bring suit to specifically enforce this Agreement and recover any incidental damages, or (d) pursue 157
    any other rights or remedies available at law or equity. 158

q. **Professional Advice and Attorneys' Fees.** Buyer and Seller are advised to seek the counsel of an attorney and a 159
certified public accountant to review the terms of this Agreement. Buyer and Seller agree to pay their own fees incurred 160
for such review. However, if Buyer or Seller institutes suit against the other concerning this Agreement the prevailing 161
party is entitled to reasonable attorneys' fees and expenses. 162

r. **Offer.** Buyer shall purchase the Property under the terms and conditions of this Agreement. Seller shall have until 9:00 163
p.m. on the Offer Expiration Date to accept this offer, unless sooner withdrawn. Acceptance shall not be effective until a 164
signed copy is received by Buyer, by Selling Broker or at the licensed office of Selling Broker. If this offer is not so 165
accepted, it shall lapse and any Earnest Money shall be refunded to Buyer. 166

s. **Counteroffer.** Any change in the terms presented in an offer or counteroffer, other than the insertion of the Seller's 167
name, shall be considered a counteroffer. If a party makes a counteroffer, then the other party shall have until 9:00 p.m. 168
on the counteroffer expiration date to accept that counteroffer, unless sooner withdrawn. Acceptance shall not be 169
effective until a signed copy is received by Seller, by Listing Broker or at the licensed office of Listing Broker. If the 170
counteroffer is not so accepted, it shall lapse and any Earnest Money shall be refunded to Buyer. 171

Initials: BUYER: _____ Date: _____ SELLER: _____ Date: _____

        BUYER: _____ Date: _____ SELLER: _____ Date: _____

RESIDENTIAL REAL ESTATE PURCHASE AND SALE AGREEMENT
GENERAL TERMS
Continued

t. **Offer and Counteroffer Expiration Date**. If no expiration date is specified for an offer/counteroffer, the offer/counteroffer shall expire 2 days after the offer/counteroffer is delivered by the party making the offer/counteroffer, unless sooner withdrawn. [172][173][174]

u. **Agency Disclosure**. Selling Firm, Selling Firm's Designated Broker, Selling Broker's Branch Manager (if any) and Selling Broker's Managing Broker (if any) represent the same party that Selling Broker represents. Listing Firm, Listing Firm's Designated Broker, Listing Broker's Branch Manager (if any), and Listing Broker's Managing Broker (if any) represent the same party that the Listing Broker represents. If Selling Broker and Listing Broker are different persons affiliated with the same Firm, then both Buyer and Seller confirm their consent to Designated Broker, Branch Manager (if any), and Managing Broker (if any) representing both parties as dual agents. If Selling Broker and Listing Broker are the same person representing both parties then both Buyer and Seller confirm their consent to that person and his/her Designated Broker, Branch Manager (if any), and Managing Broker (if any) representing both parties as dual agents. All parties acknowledge receipt of the pamphlet entitled "The Law of Real Estate Agency." [175][176][177][178][179][180][181][182][183]

v. **Commission**. Seller and Buyer agree to pay a commission in accordance with any listing or commission agreement to which they are a party. The Listing Firm's commission shall be apportioned between Listing Firm and Selling Firm as specified in the listing. Seller and Buyer hereby consent to Listing Firm or Selling Firm receiving compensation from more than one party. Seller and Buyer hereby assign to Listing Firm and Selling Firm, as applicable, a portion of their funds in escrow equal to such commission(s) and irrevocably instruct the Closing Agent to disburse the commission(s) directly to the Firm(s). In any action by Listing or Selling Firm to enforce this paragraph, the prevailing party is entitled to court costs and reasonable attorneys' fees. Seller and Buyer agree that the Firms are intended third party beneficiaries under this Agreement. [184][185][186][187][188][189][190][191]

w. **Cancellation Rights/Lead-Based Paint**. If a residential dwelling was built on the Property prior to 1978, and Buyer receives a Disclosure of Information on Lead-Based Paint and Lead-Based Paint Hazards (NWMLS Form 22J) after mutual acceptance, Buyer may rescind this Agreement at any time up to 3 days thereafter. [192][193][194]

x. **Information Verification Period and Property Condition Disclaimer**. Buyer shall have 10 days after mutual acceptance to verify all information provided from Seller or Listing Firm related to the Property. This contingency shall be deemed satisfied unless Buyer gives notice identifying the materially inaccurate information within 10 days of mutual acceptance. If Buyer gives timely notice under this section, then this Agreement shall terminate and the Earnest Money shall be refunded to Buyer. [195][196][197][198][199]

Buyer and Seller agree, that except as provided in this Agreement, all representations and information regarding the Property and the transaction are solely from the Seller or Buyer, and not from any Broker. The parties acknowledge that the Brokers are not responsible for assuring that the parties perform their obligations under this Agreement and that none of the Brokers has agreed to independently investigate or confirm any matter related to this transaction except as stated in this Agreement, or in a separate writing signed by such Broker. In addition, Brokers do not guarantee the value, quality or condition of the Property and some properties may contain building materials, including siding, roofing, ceiling, insulation, electrical, and plumbing, that have been the subject of lawsuits and/or governmental inquiry because of possible defects or health hazards. Some properties may have other defects arising after construction, such as drainage, leakage, pest, rot and mold problems. Brokers do not have the expertise to identify or assess defective products, materials, or conditions. Buyer is urged to use due diligence to inspect the Property to Buyer's satisfaction and to retain inspectors qualified to identify the presence of defective materials and evaluate the condition of the Property as there may be defects that may only be revealed by careful inspection. Buyer is advised to investigate whether there is a sufficient water supply to meet Buyer's needs. Buyer and Seller acknowledge that home protection plans may be available which may provide additional protection and benefit to Buyer and Seller. Brokers may assist the parties with locating and selecting third party service providers, such as inspectors or contractors, but Brokers cannot guarantee or be responsible for the services provided by those third parties. The parties agree to exercise their own judgment and due diligence regarding third-party service providers. [200][201][202][203][204][205][206][207][208][209][210][211][212][213][214][215][216]

Initials: BUYER: _____ Date: _____ SELLER: _____ Date: _____
         BUYER: _____ Date: _____ SELLER: _____ Date: _____

Also, a form must be used only for its intended purpose. For instance, the form in Figure 7.1 is intended for residential sales only. It shouldn't be used for any other type of transaction.

IDENTIFYING THE PARTIES

We generally refer to the parties to a purchase and sale agreement as the buyer and the seller. But in many transactions there's more than one buyer and/or more than one seller.

You must make sure that everyone who has an ownership interest in the property signs the contract. If any owner fails to sign it, the buyer may only be able to enforce the sale of a partial interest in the property, or the contract may not be enforceable at all.

> **EXAMPLE:** A property is owned by three cousins who inherited it from their grandfather. One of the cousins has lived in South America for several years, and the other two cousins have managed the property. When they ask you to handle the sale of the property, you must be sure that the third cousin will be available to sign the sales contract, either in person or through a representative (such as an attorney in fact). Otherwise, a buyer would only be able to purchase a partial interest in the property. (Note that the absent cousin must also sign the listing agreement.)

You should also consider whether everyone who is signing the contract has contractual capacity. If one of the parties is a minor (younger than 18) or mentally incompetent, the contract should be signed by that party's legal guardian. Otherwise, the purchase and sale agreement will be either voidable or void.

MARITAL PROPERTY. Find out whether or not each buyer or seller who is going to sign the purchase and sale agreement is married. If so, have that party's spouse sign the agreement too. In Washington, when community real property is bought or sold, both spouses must join in the contract.

> **EXAMPLE:** Henry and Deborah's house is community property. They've been talking about selling it for some time. While Deborah's out of town, Henry decides to surprise her. He signs a purchase and sale agreement with the Bentleys, agreeing to sell their house for $225,000. When Deborah comes home and hears the news, she's aghast. She believes their house is worth much more than $225,000, and she isn't ready to move so soon. Deborah

can call off the sale, because the house is community property and she didn't sign the contract.

Although a married person can sell his or her separate property without the spouse's consent, it's often difficult to know when real property owned by a married person is community property or separate property. It's not your job to determine the status of the property, so it's always best to get both spouses to sign all documents related to the transaction. If they have questions about the separate or community status of their property, they should consult an attorney.

In addition, if an agent knows there is a pending divorce action that may have an impact on a transaction, she should consult her managing broker or an attorney to make sure that all signed agreements are enforceable, and that the transaction will close. It is in the interests of all parties to make sure that there are no outstanding disputes that would prevent the sale from closing.

When filling in the names of a married couple, state each name separately; for example, "Edward K. Hardy and Joanna T. Hardy, a married couple."

OTHER FORMS OF CO-OWNERSHIP. When property is owned as a tenancy in common or in joint tenancy, all of the owners must sign the purchase and sale agreement in order to convey full ownership to the buyer. However, an individual tenant in common or joint tenant can convey her own interest without the consent of the other owner(s).

BUSINESS ASSOCIATIONS AS PARTIES. When one of the parties to the contract is a partnership, the names of all of the general partners (and their spouses) and the name of the partnership itself should appear in the contract. For both partnerships and corporations, the company's address and the state in which it is organized or incorporated should also be shown.

For partnerships, corporations, and other types of associations, legal authority to enter into the transaction must be established. Before closing, the escrow agent (or other closing agent) will require documentation proving that a partner or a corporate officer has authority to sign on behalf of the association. The documentation could be in the form of a power of attorney or a resolution of the board of directors. If there's any doubt about who needs to sign the documents, it's best to get the advice of a lawyer.

ESTATES AND TRUSTS. When property that is part of an estate is sold, the personal representative or executor of the estate must sign the purchase and sale agreement and other documents. To sell property that is part of a trust, the trustee must sign the documents.

BANKRUPTCY AND FORECLOSURE. If a buyer is purchasing property from a seller who is involved in personal bankruptcy proceedings, she should be prepared for a more complicated selling process. The property can be sold only with the approval of the bankruptcy court, is typically sold subject to existing liens and encumbrances, and is often sold without title insurance or any warranties.

A property that is on the verge of mortgage foreclosure can be sold, but the transaction may be subject to the approval of the foreclosing lender, especially if it's a short sale (the proceeds won't be enough to pay off the loan balance). Even if the lender's approval is not required, the transaction may meet the criteria of a distressed home sale, and the provisions of the Distressed Property Law may apply (see Chapter 3). Agents dealing with these types of transactions should always consult their designated broker and/or an attorney for advice on the appropriate way to proceed.

ATTORNEYS IN FACT. If a party to a contract is unavailable or unable to sign the contract documents, a personal representative may be authorized to sign on his behalf. Authorization to sign for someone else is granted by a written document called a **power of attorney**. The authorized person is referred to as an **attorney in fact**. The power of attorney is valid only while the person who granted it is still alive and mentally competent.

When an attorney in fact signs for another person, she usually signs that person's name and then writes her own name beneath it:

Michelle H. Plunkett
by Sarah R. Johnson, her Attorney in Fact

In a sale you're involved in, if an attorney in fact is going to sign any of the documents, ask to see a copy of the power of attorney and verify its validity by checking with the person who granted the power.

PROPERTY DESCRIPTION

To be enforceable, a purchase and sale agreement must have an unambiguous description of the property. A complete legal description should always be used. The street address is not enough. Tax numbers are subject to change, and the description in the tax statement might be incomplete.

There usually isn't enough room for the property's legal description on the form, so an addendum containing the description should be attached. (The form already provides for this.) If the legal description is complicated, photocopy it from the seller's deed or get a photocopy from a title company. That way, you'll avoid the transcription mistakes that commonly occur when a legal description is copied by hand.

PURCHASE PRICE AND METHOD OF PAYMENT

The full purchase price, including any mortgages or other liens that the buyer is going to assume, should be stated in the agreement. For example, if the buyer is going to assume the seller's mortgage, which has a remaining principal balance of $147,000, and also give the seller $35,000 in cash at closing, then you should fill in $182,000 as the purchase price on the purchase and sale agreement form.

Most residential purchase and sale agreements are contingent on financing; in other words, the agreement will not be binding unless the buyer is able to obtain a loan. This requires a contingency provision, which is typically set forth in an addendum to the agreement. The financing contingency may specify the downpayment the buyer is willing to make and other terms of the loan he will apply for. The contingency may also state the buyer's duty to make a good faith effort to obtain financing. Financing contingencies are discussed in Chapter 8, and an example is shown in Figure 8.1.

Some transactions are financed completely or partially by the seller. The seller may accept a cash downpayment with a real estate contract or a deed of trust for all or part of the remainder of the purchase price. In that case, the interest rate, payment amount, and other terms for the seller financing must be included in the purchase and sale agreement, and a copy of the financing document forms (the real estate contract, or the promissory note and deed of trust) that the parties will be executing must be attached to the agreement. When a transaction involves seller financing, the parties should use an addendum such as the payment terms addendum shown in Figure 7.2. (For more information about seller financing, see Chapter 10.)

EARNEST MONEY

The purchase and sale agreement form states how the deposit will be handled. As we explained in Chapter 6, the agreement should also state whether the deposit is in the form of cash, a money order, a check, or a promissory note.

FIG. 7.2   PAYMENT TERMS ADDENDUM

Form 22C
Payment Terms Addendum
Rev. 7/10
Page 1 of 3

**PAYMENT TERMS ADDENDUM
TO PURCHASE AND SALE AGREEMENT**

©Copyright 2010
Northwest Multiple Listing Service
ALL RIGHTS RESERVED

The following is part of the Purchase and Sale Agreement dated _____ 1

between _____ ("Buyer") 2

and _____ ("Seller") 3

concerning _____ (the "Property"). 4

1. **General Financing Terms.**   5

Buyer shall pay the Purchase Price as follows: 6

　　i.   Down payment, including Earnest Money, at Closing $ _____ . 7

　　ii. Buyer shall assume the following obligations $ _____ 8

　　iii. Buyer shall pay the balance of the Purchase Price ($ _____) in monthly installments 9
　　　　of $ _____, or more at Buyer's option, including _____% interest from the date of 10
　　　　Closing, on or before the _____ day of each month, commencing: ❑ 30 days following 11
　　　　the Closing; or ❑ _____.   12

2. **Method of Payment.** (Check applicable box)   13

　A. ❑   **NOTE AND DEED OF TRUST**   14

　　i.   **Security.** The indebtedness shall be evidenced by a Promissory Note and a ❑ first; ❑ second; 15
　　　　❑ third (first, if not filled in) Deed of Trust, as set forth below.   16

　　ii. **Due Date.** The balance of principal and accrued interest shall be due and payable ❑ _____ 17
　　　　years from the date of Closing ❑ on _____.   18

　　iii. **Default and Default Interest.** During any period of Buyer's default, the principal shall bear interest at 19
　　　　the rate of _____ % per annum (18% if not filled in) or the maximum rate allowed by law, 20
　　　　whichever is less, during any period of Buyer's default. A late charge of $ _____ or 21
　　　　_____ % of any installment payment (5% of the payment if neither is filled in) shall be added to 22
　　　　any payment more than _____ days late (5 days if not filled in). If Buyer has not cured any default 23
　　　　within _____ (30 days if not filled in) after written notice, Seller may declare all outstanding sums 24
　　　　immediately due and payable.   25

　　iv. **Promissory Note.** Buyer agrees to sign at Closing the then current version of LPB Form 28A 26
　　　　(Promissory Note), which must be attached to this Agreement.   27

　　v.   **Deed of Trust.** Buyer agrees to sign at Closing the then current version of (check applicable box): 28

　　　　a. ❑ LPB Form 22 (Deed of Trust) securing the Property, which must be attached to this Agreement; 29
　　　　　　or   30
　　　　b. ❑ LPB Form 22A (Deed of Trust with Due on Sale and Due Date) securing the Property, which 31
　　　　　　must be attached to this Agreement. The parties agree to initial the Due on Sale clause, which 32
　　　　　　provides: "The property described in this security instrument may not be sold or transferred without 33
　　　　　　the Beneficiary's consent. Upon breach of this provision, Beneficiary may declare all sums due 34
　　　　　　under the note and Deed of Trust immediately due and payable, unless prohibited by applicable 35
　　　　　　law."   36

　　vi. **NOTE**: If the Property is primarily for agricultural purposes, then a non-judicial foreclosure/forfeiture 37
　　　　remedy is available only by using a real estate contract.   38

Initials: BUYER: _____   Date: _____   SELLER: _____   Date: _____
　　　　　BUYER: _____   Date: _____   SELLER: _____   Date: _____

**PAYMENT TERMS ADDENDUM
TO PURCHASE AND SALE AGREEMENT**
Continued

B. ❑ **REAL ESTATE CONTRACT** 39

   i. **Real Estate Contract.** The parties agree to sign the then current version of current LPB Form 44 (Real 40 Estate Contract), which must be attached to this Agreement. The parties agree to initial the following 41 Optional Provisions in LPB Form 44 if the corresponding box is checked: 42

      ❑ Substitution and Security on Personal Property 43
      ❑ Alterations 44
      ❑ Due on Sale 45
      ❑ Pre-Payment Penalties on Prior Encumbrances 46
      ❑ Periodic Payments on Taxes and Insurance (The payments during the current year shall be 47 $_____ per _____) 48

   ii. ❑ **Cash Out.** The entire balance of principal and interest shall be due and payable: ❑ _____ 49 years from the date of Closing ❑ on _____ . 50

C. ❑ **SELLER WRAP OF EXISTING LOAN.** 51

   i. **Default and Default Interest**. The unpaid principal balance shall, at Seller's option, bear interest at the 52 rate of _____ % per annum (18% if not filled in) or the maximum rate allowed by law, 53 whichever is less, during any period of Buyer's default. From the payments by Buyer to Seller, Seller 54 will pay the monthly payments of $_____ due on an existing loan by 55 _____ (the lender) having an approximate present principal 56 balance of $_____ with interest at _____ % per annum computed on the 57 unpaid principal and secured by the Property. Such balance remains the obligation of the Seller and 58 Seller agrees to pay such obligation in accordance with its terms and conditions. Buyer shall have the 59 right to remedy any default on the underlying obligation, provided Buyer is not in default to the Seller, 60 and all sums so paid shall be credited to Buyer's payments to Seller. 61

   ii. **Type of Loan.** Buyer and Seller agree to sign, at Closing, the form ❑ Real Estate Contract; 62 ❑ Note and Deed of Trust, securing the Property which must be attached to this Agreement. 63

   NOTE: The parties must select and complete either the Note and Deed of Trust or Real Estate Contract 64 section of this Addendum. 65

D. ❑ **CASH DOWN TO EXISTING LOAN.** 66

   i. **Type of Loan**. Buyer agrees to assume, at Closing, an existing ❑ Deed of Trust; ❑ Mortgage; 67 ❑ Real Estate Contract securing the Property and to pay the balance of the Purchase Price in cash, 68 including Earnest Money, at Closing. The assumed loan ❑ is; ❑ is not an Adjustable Rate Mortgage 69 (ARM). The monthly payments could increase or decrease if the assumed loan is an ARM. 70

   ii. **Loan Amount and Payments**. The assumed loan has a principal balance of approximately 71 $_____ and is payable in monthly installments of approximately 72 $_____ including interest at _____ % per annum computed on the declining 73 principal balance, and including ❑ real estate taxes ❑ hazard insurance. Seller shall pay any 74 delinquencies at Closing. 75

   iii. ❑ **Seller Warranty – Loan is Assumable**. Seller warrants that the assumed loan is assumable 76 provided that Buyer complies with and agrees to abide by any requirements or conditions imposed by 77 the holder of the assumed loan. 78

   iv. ❑ **Buyer Review Period**. This Agreement is conditioned upon Buyer's review of the assumed loan. 79 Unless Buyer gives written notice to Seller of Buyer's disapproval of the assumed loan within 80 _____ days (5 days if not filled in), this contingency shall be deemed satisfied (waived). 81

   v. ❑ **Seller Review Period**. Seller understands that when a loan is "assumed," Seller may remain liable 82 to pay the holder of the assumed loan if the Buyer fails to do so. This Agreement is conditioned upon 83 Seller's review of the terms of the assumed loan. Unless Seller gives written notice to Buyer of Seller's 84 disapproval of the terms of the assumed loan within _____ days (5 days if not filled in), this 85 contingency shall be deemed satisfied (waived). 86

Initials: BUYER: _____ Date: _____ SELLER: _____ Date: _____
       BUYER: _____ Date: _____ SELLER: _____ Date: _____

Form 22C
Payment Terms Addendum
Rev. 7/10
Page 3 of 3

**PAYMENT TERMS ADDENDUM
TO PURCHASE AND SALE AGREEMENT**
Continued

3. **Other Terms.** (Check all that apply).   87

    A. **PAYMENTS TO COLLECTION ACCOUNT.**   88

        i. **Collection Account.** Buyer's payments to or on behalf of Seller shall be made to a contract collection   89
account at _____ (the "Collection Account"),   90
❑ to be established and paid for by Buyer and Seller equally; or ❑ to be established and paid for as   91
follows: _____ (established and paid for equally if not filled in).   92

        ii. ❑ **Escrow.** The Collection Account shall also serve as escrow for a request for reconveyance or   93
fulfillment deed (as applicable), which shall be fully executed by Seller at Closing and held by the   94
Collection Account pending payment of funds as provided for herein and shall be released to Buyer   95
when full payment of funds due and owing have been received by the Collection Account.   96

        iii. ❑ **Taxes and Insurance.** Payments to the Collection Account shall be applied to ❑ real property   97
taxes; ❑ insurance, which amounts may change due to adjustments in taxes and insurance premiums.   98

    B. ❑ **SELLER'S REVIEW OF BUYER'S FINANCES CONTINGENCY.** This Agreement is conditioned upon   99
Seller's review and approval of (i) ❑ Buyer's credit report; (ii) ❑ Buyer's income tax returns for the prior   100
_____ years (3 years if not filled in); (iii) ❑ verification of Buyer's employment from Buyer's employer;   101
and (iv) ❑ other _____, which approval(s) shall not be   102
unreasonably withheld. Buyer will provide Seller with all applicable information including a credit report (if   103
applicable) within _____ days (5 days if not filled in) of mutual acceptance. Unless Seller gives written   104
notice to Buyer of Seller's disapproval of the applicable conditions within_____ days (2 days if not   105
filled in) of the date the information is due, this contingency shall be deemed satisfied (waived).   106

    C. ❑ **TITLE INSURANCE.** Buyer agrees to pay the costs of a lender's standard title insurance policy insuring   107
Seller's security interest.   108

    D. **ATTORNEY REVIEW.**   109

        i. Seller understands that Seller's security interest in the Property may be inferior to a third party's   110
interest in the property, such as a lender. Seller understands that the total amount of indebtedness on   111
the Property should not exceed the Purchase Price. Seller is advised to seek the counsel of an   112
attorney to review the terms of this Agreement.   113

        ii. **Seller Attorney Review.** This Agreement is conditioned upon review and approval by counsel for   114
Seller. Unless Seller gives written notice to Buyer of Seller's disapproval of this Agreement within   115
_____ days (5 days if not filled in), this contingency shall be deemed satisfied (waived).   116

        iii. **Buyer Attorney Review.** This Agreement is conditioned upon review and approval by counsel for   117
Buyer. Unless Buyer gives written notice to Seller of Buyer's disapproval of this Agreement within   118
_____ days (5 days if not filled in), this contingency shall be deemed satisfied (waived).   119

    E. **CONSENT OF HOLDER OF UNDERLYING OBLIGATION.** If there is an existing Deed of Trust, Real   120
Estate Contract or other encumbrance which is to remain unpaid after Closing and its terms require the   121
holder's consent to this sale, Buyer agrees to promptly apply for such consent upon mutual acceptance of   122
this Agreement. This Agreement is subject to the written consent of the holder of the underlying obligation   123
within _____ days (15 days if not filled in) after the mutual acceptance of this Agreement. If the   124
holder's written consent to this Agreement is not obtained by such date, this Agreement shall terminate, and   125
the Earnest Money shall be refunded to Buyer.   126

Initials: BUYER: _____ Date: _____ SELLER: _____ Date: _____

           BUYER: _____ Date: _____ SELLER: _____ Date: _____

In most cases, the purchase agreement provides that the buyer will give her agent a personal check for the deposit after the seller accepts the offer. The agreement directs the agent either to deposit the money in the firm's account or to deliver it to the escrow agent.

INCLUDED ITEMS

An "included items" paragraph states that certain items are included in the sale unless otherwise noted in the agreement. The list usually includes carpeting, built-in appliances, window coverings, air conditioning equipment, shrubs, and so forth. Even without this provision in the agreement, many of the items listed would be considered fixtures or attachments and included in the sale, but the provision helps prevent disputes over this issue.

If the seller wants to remove an item listed in the provision or exclude an item that would normally be considered real property, you can attach an addendum specifying that the item is excluded from the sale. Similarly, if an item that is not listed in the provision will be included in the sale, you can attach an addendum stating that the item is included. Many forms provide a list of boxes that can be checked to include items that are not usually considered fixtures, but which are often included in the sale, such as a washer, dryer, or refrigerator.

CONVEYANCE AND TITLE

A purchase and sale agreement form includes provisions pertaining to the conveyance of the property and the condition of title. The type of deed that the seller will execute in favor of the buyer (ordinarily a statutory warranty deed) is specified. There is usually a clause in which the seller agrees to provide marketable title, free of undisclosed encumbrances, with a standard coverage title insurance policy. The seller also agrees to pay off any liens at closing (if not before), unless the buyer is assuming or taking title subject to an existing lien. Any unusual encumbrances that will remain after closing must be disclosed in the purchase and sale agreement.

Many agreements go into some detail about what will be considered marketable title. For example, an agreement might say that CC&Rs that apply to the entire neighborhood or subdivision will not make the title unmarketable, nor will easements that do not significantly interfere with the buyer's use of the property (an easement for underground wiring, for instance). There will be no problem if encumbrances of that type show up as exceptions on the preliminary title report. However, if the title report reveals other undisclosed encumbrances (such as an access easement that would interfere with the buyer's use of the property) and the seller cannot remove them before closing, then the title will be considered unmarketable and the buyer can refuse to go through with the purchase.

If the seller is a party to a legal action—such as a bankruptcy, a divorce, or a foreclosure action—the seller may not be able to convey clear title. This is a material fact and should be disclosed to the buyer. If the buyer has questions about the legal ramifications of the seller's court proceedings, the buyer should consult an attorney.

INFORMATION VERIFICATION PERIOD

The purchase and sale agreement may also contain a provision giving the buyer a certain amount of time to verify information about the property. During that period, the buyer should verify the facts provided by the seller and listing agent in the property listing, the seller disclosure statement, and any advertising. If the buyer finds any material inaccuracies, she has the right to terminate the agreement within the verification period. Alternatively, she may choose to waive that right and go ahead with the sale.

CLOSING DATE

The closing date is the date when the proceeds of the sale are disbursed to the seller, the deed is delivered to the buyer, and all the appropriate documents are recorded. The purchase and sale agreement usually sets a specific date for closing. A lender will be able to recommend a suitable date, based on conditions in the local finance market.

In setting a closing date, it's important to consider how long it will take to meet any conditions that the purchase and sale agreement is contingent on (see Chapter 8) and any obligations it imposes. For example, the buyer may have to apply for a loan, which will involve an appraisal and a complete credit check. The seller may have to arrange to clear away liens and could be required to make some repairs. The chosen closing date must allow enough time for the parties to fulfill these conditions and obligations.

If the closing date is approaching and repairs have not been completed, a loan approval has not been obtained, or some other contingency has not yet been satisfied, the parties may want to change the closing date by executing a written extension agreement. The purchase and sale agreement will terminate on the date set for closing, so try to get an extension agreement signed as soon as possible. Failure to extend the closing date may result in an unenforceable agreement. A special form may be used for an extension agreement, or you can simply use a general amendment form in states that the parties agree to defer the closing to some later date.

> **EXAMPLE:** Gopal is buying Harrison's home. The closing date is June 4. On June 2, Gopal's lender informs Gopal that because of unforeseen circumstances, his loan costs have increased significantly. Thus, the annual percentage rate on his loan will be higher than the rate the lender quoted at the time of application, and (by law) the lender must give Gopal a new disclosure statement. The lender gives Gopal the new disclosure statement on June 3. Since this new statement must be given to Gopal at least three days before closing, Gopal and Harrison must change their closing date to June 4. Gopal and Harrison can use a Regulation Z Addendum to their purchase and sale agreement to extend their closing date.

On the other hand, if all conditions and obligations have been fulfilled well before the date set for closing, the buyer and seller may agree to move the closing date up. This amendment should also be in writing and signed by both parties.

CLOSING AGENT

The buyer should designate an escrow agent or other closing agent in the purchase and sale agreement. In many cases, the escrow department of the buyer's lender serves as the closing agent.

Closing agents may perform a wide variety of tasks, such as ordering title insurance, arranging for liens to be paid off and released, and preparing documents on behalf of both the buyer and the seller. They also hold funds and documents in escrow for the parties, distributing them only when specified conditions have been fulfilled. (Escrow instructions and the closing process are discussed in Chapter 11.)

A federal law called the Foreign Investment in Real Property Tax Act (FIRPTA) applies to some transactions in which the seller is a nonresident alien.

FIRPTA requires the buyer to withhold a certain percentage of the proceeds the seller realized from the sale and turn that money over to the Internal Revenue Service. This is ordinarily handled by the closing agent on the buyer's behalf. The purchase and sale agreement may include a provision concerning compliance with this law. (Many residential transactions are exempt from FIRPTA. See Chapter 11.)

CLOSING COSTS

The purchase and sale agreement should state which party is responsible for paying the escrow agent's fee (typically, it is split between the parties) and certain other closing costs (such as costs connected with the buyer's loan). In addition, the agreement should set forth how certain property expenses (taxes, homeowners association dues, etc.) and income (rent from tenants) will be shared. These are ordinarily prorated as of the closing date, unless otherwise agreed.

TRANSFER OF POSSESSION

Most purchase and sale agreement forms have a space for filling in the date of possession, when the seller will relinquish possession of the property to the buyer. The seller usually agrees that the property will be maintained in its present condition until the buyer takes possession.

Possession is normally transferred to the buyer at closing. Sometimes the buyer wants to take possession a few days or even a few weeks earlier, or the seller wants a few extra days to vacate the property.

> **EXAMPLE:** Jenkins is buying Hahn's home. The sale will close on October 17. However, the sale of Jenkins's current home will close on September 10. Jenkins wants to move into Hahn's home on September 10 to avoid the nuisance of moving twice. Hahn agrees to move out by September 10.

If possession is transferred before (or after) the closing date, the parties should execute a separate rental agreement. An example of a rental agreement that can be used for occupancy before closing is shown in Figure 7.3. This agreement sets forth the dates of occupancy, the rental rate, and other terms that will govern possession during the rental period.

Transfer of possession to the buyer before closing may cause trouble for the seller if the sale fails to close. If the buyer/tenant refuses to vacate the property

FIG. 7.3   RENTAL AGREEMENT FORM

Form 65A
Rental Agreement - Prior
Rev. 7/10
Page 1 of 2

RENTAL AGREEMENT
(Occupancy Prior to Closing)

©Copyright 2010
Northwest Multiple Listing Service
ALL RIGHTS RESERVED

Notice: NWMLS recommends that sellers do NOT give a buyer a right to occupy the property prior to closing.
All sellers are urged to consult with a lawyer before entering into a Rental Agreement that provides a buyer with occupancy prior to closing.

Date: _____   1

Tenant(s) _____   2

agree(s) to rent from Landlord _____   3

the property commonly known as _____   4

in_____ County, Washington (the "House") on the following terms and conditions: 5

1.   **RENT.** The rent shall be $_____ per _____. Landlord acknowledges receipt of the first   6

_____ rent. Future rents shall be payable on the _____ day of each _____, one   7

_____ in advance, commencing on _____. Rent shall be payable to _____   8

at _____ .   9

Tenant is entitled to possession on _____ .   10

This Agreement shall terminate on _____. If Tenant purchases the House from   11
Landlord, then this Agreement shall terminate on Closing of the sale. At the time of Closing, advance rent paid to   12
Landlord shall be pro-rated on a daily basis, and Tenant shall be credited with any unused portion thereof. If this   13
Agreement is terminated prior to the termination date set forth in this paragraph, then any advance rent shall be   14
pro-rated on a daily basis, and the unused portion refunded to Tenant immediately upon Tenant's vacating the   15
House.   16

2.   **INSURANCE.** Landlord agrees to keep the House insured against fire and other normal casualties. All proceeds   17
of any such policy shall be payable to Landlord alone. Landlord shall have no responsibility for insuring anything   18
in or on the Property which belongs to Tenant.   19

3.   **UTILITIES.** Tenant agrees to pay for all utilities, including garbage collection charges, during the term of this   20
Agreement.   21

4.   **IMPROVEMENTS.** Tenant shall not be entitled to make any improvements or alterations in the House, including   22
painting, during the term of this Agreement without the express written permission of Landlord. In the event this   23
Agreement terminates for any reason other than Tenant's purchase of the House, Tenant will return the House to   24
Landlord in as good a condition as it presently is, ordinary wear and tear excepted.   25

5.   **LANDLORD - TENANT ACT.** This Agreement is subject to the provisions of the Residential Landlord - Tenant   26
Act, RCW 59.18 and the Unlawful Detainer Statute, RCW 59.12. If Tenant and Landlord have entered into a   27
purchase and sale agreement for the purchase of the House, then a default under that purchase and sale   28
agreement shall constitute a default under this Agreement, and Landlord shall be entitled to all remedies provided   29
for in the Residential Landlord-Tenant Act, RCW 59.18, including but not limited to the exercise of all eviction   30
proceedings authorized by RCW 59.12.   31

6.   **SUBLETTING OR ASSIGNMENT.** Tenant may not sublet the House and may not assign Tenant's rights under   32
this Agreement.   33

7.   **CITY OF SEATTLE RENTAL AGREEMENT REGULATION ORDINANCE.** If the House is located within the City   34
of Seattle then a copy of a summary of city and state landlord/tenant laws is attached. Tenant hereby   35
acknowledges receipt of a copy of the summary.   36

8.   **TIME.** Time is of the essence in this Agreement.   37

_____   _____   _____   _____
Landlord   Date   Tenant   Date

_____   _____   _____   _____
Landlord   Date   Tenant   Date

Form 65A
Rental Agreement - Prior
Rev. 7/10
Page 2 of 2

RENTAL AGREEMENT
(Continued)

9. RELEASE OF REAL ESTATE FIRMS. Landlord and Tenant release all real estate firms and brokers involved 38
with this Agreement and any purchase and sale agreement between Landlord and Tenant relating to the House, 39
and agree to indemnify all real estate firms and brokers from any and all claims arising under this Agreement. 40

10. ATTORNEYS' FEES. In the event either party employs an attorney to enforce any terms of this Agreement and is 41
successful, the other party agrees to pay reasonable attorneys' fees. In the event of trial, the amount shall be as 42
fixed by the court. 43

11. SMOKE DETECTOR. Tenant acknowledges and Lessor certifies that the Property is equipped with a smoke 44
detector(s) as required by RCW 43.44.110 and that the detector(s) has/have been tested and is/are operable. It is 45
Tenant's responsibility to maintain the smoke detector(s) as specified by the manufacturer, including replacement 46
of batteries, if required. In addition, if the Property is a multi-family building (more than one unit), Lessor makes 47
the following disclosures: 48

(a) The smoke detection device is ❑ hard-wired ❑ battery operated. 49
(b) The Building ❑ does ❑ does not have a fire sprinkler system. 50
(c) The Building ❑ does ❑ does not have a fire alarm system. 51
(d) ❑ The building has a smoking policy, as follows: 52
_____ 53

    ❑ The building does not have a smoking policy 54
(e) ❑ The building has an emergency notification plan for occupants, a copy of which is attached to this 55
    Agreement. 56
    ❑ The building does not have an emergency notification plan for occupants. 57
(f) ❑ The building has an emergency relocation plan for occupants, a copy of which is attached to this 58
    Agreement. 59
    ❑ The building does not have an emergency relocation plan for occupants. 60
(g) ❑ The building has an emergency evacuation plan for occupants, a copy of which is attached to this 61
    Agreement. 62
    ❑ The building does not have an emergency evacuation plan for occupants. 63

Tenant hereby acknowledges receipt of a copy of the building's emergency evacuation routes. 64

12. LEAD-BASED PAINT. If the Property includes housing that was built before 1978, then the Addendum entitled 65
"Disclosure of Information on Lead-Based Paint and Lead-Based Paint Hazards" (NWMLS Form 22J or 66
equivalent), must be attached to this Agreement unless this lease/rental transaction is exempt from all applicable 67
federal regulations. 68

13. MOLD DISCLOSURE. Tenant acknowledges receipt of the pamphlet entitled "A Brief Guide to Mold, Moisture, 69
and Your Home." 70

_____ _____ _____ _____
Landlord   Date   Tenant   Date

_____ _____ _____ _____
Landlord   Date   Tenant   Date

in accordance with the terms of the rental agreement, the seller might have to take legal action to evict him. Note that in the rental agreement in Figure 7.3, the Northwest Multiple Listing Service recommends against transferring possession to the buyer before closing and advises sellers to consult a lawyer before entering into such an arrangement.

While early transfer of possession may put the seller at risk, delayed transfer of possession may pose other problems for the parties. If a buyer allows a seller to remain in the home for more than 20 days after closing, he could risk turning the transaction into a distressed property conveyance (see discussion of the Distressed Property Law in Chapter 3). Of course, for this law to apply, the subject property would have to be a distressed property—one that is in danger of foreclosure. But if the property is a distressed home and the transfer of possession will be delayed, both the seller's agent and the buyer's agent should advise their clients to consult an attorney.

DEFAULT

A purchase and sale agreement usually states the remedies available to the buyer or the seller if the other party defaults, and explains how the earnest money deposit will be treated in case of default.

The default provision in the NWMLS form shown in Figure 7.1 gives the parties two options: the seller's sole remedy may be to keep the earnest money deposit as liquidated damages, or the seller may be allowed to choose what remedy to pursue. The possible remedies would include keeping the deposit, suing the buyer for damages, or suing for specific performance.

LIQUIDATED DAMAGES. Under Washington law, no more than 5% of the property's sales price can be treated as liquidated damages in a purchase and sale agreement. So if the buyer's earnest money deposit was more than 5% of the price, the seller will be required to return the excess to the buyer if the buyer forfeits the earnest money.

At one time Washington law required the liquidated damages provision in a residential purchase and sale agreement to be initialed by the buyer and the seller, to show that each of them was aware of the provision and specifically consented to it. Otherwise, the provision would be unenforceable and the buyer's deposit could not be treated as liquidated damages. This requirement was repealed; it's no longer necessary for the parties to initial the liquidated damages provision.

DISPOSITION OF EARNEST MONEY. A purchase and sale agreement may provide that if the buyer is entitled to have the earnest money deposit returned, the closing agent may first deduct expenses that have already been incurred on the buyer's behalf.

If the buyer forfeits the earnest money to the seller, the listing firm is usually entitled to half of the money the seller receives (but not more than the firm would have been paid as a commission if the sale had closed). This is usually provided for in the listing agreement rather than the purchase and sale agreement (see Chapter 2). In practical terms, this usually means that the seller gets half of the deposit, the listing firm gets 25% of the deposit, and the selling firm gets 25% of the deposit.

> **EXAMPLE:** Bowen agreed to sell her house to Wilder for $175,000. The earnest money deposit was $10,000. Now Wilder has defaulted on the purchase and sale agreement by backing out of the transaction with no legal excuse.
>
> Under the terms of the agreement Bowen is entitled to keep Wilder's earnest money deposit as liquidated damages. However, the law allows a seller to keep no more than 5% of the sales price. In this case, that's $8,750 ($175,000 × 5% = $8,750), so Bowen must return $1,250 to Wilder ($10,000 − $8,750 = $1,250).
>
> When she listed her property, Bowen agreed to give 50% of any forfeited earnest money deposit to the listing firm, Cunningham Realty. As a result, Bowen and Cunningham Realty each get $4,375. Under the terms of a commission split agreement, Cunningham Realty is required to split its share with the selling firm. Thus, each of the firms ends up with $2,187.50.

ATTORNEY'S FEES. A purchase and sale agreement typically includes an attorney's fees provision. Under this provision, if one party has to sue the other party to enforce the contract, the prevailing party's attorney's fees and related expenses must be paid by the losing party.

TIME IS OF THE ESSENCE

A purchase and sale agreement usually states that "time is of the essence of this agreement." This phrase doesn't simply mean that the parties hope the sale progresses as quickly as possible; it means they are legally required to meet all deadlines set in the agreement. Performance on or before the specified dates (not just within a reasonable time thereafter) is considered one of the essential terms of the agreement. Failure to meet any of the deadlines is a breach of contract.

ADDENDA

A provision headed "Addenda" indicates whether there are attachments to the purchase and sale agreement that contain additional contract provisions. The attachments might include one of the addendum forms we've already discussed, such as the payment terms addendum, or any of a number of others. The optional clauses addendum, shown in Figure 7.4, is used in many transactions. To incorporate the addenda into the agreement, the names of the forms should be listed in the space provided and attached to the main document, and the parties must sign or initial and date each page of the attachments.

Sometimes a purchase and sale agreement form has a paragraph called "Additional Provisions," where the parties may include any other terms that are not covered in the agreement or by a formal attachment. If the additional provisions are at all complicated or unusual, an attorney should draft them. As we've discussed, real estate agents are not allowed to write complicated clauses for inclusion in a purchase and sale agreement.

AGENCY DISCLOSURE

As we discussed in Chapter 1, Washington law requires real estate licensees to give the parties a written agency disclosure statement. A listing agent must inform both the buyer and the seller which party (or parties) she is representing in the transaction. If there is a selling agent as well as a listing agent, the selling agent must also disclose this information. The disclosures must be made to the buyer before the buyer signs the offer to purchase, and to the seller before the seller signs the buyer's offer. The disclosures must be in writing, and they must appear either in the purchase and sale agreement or in a separate agency disclosure form.

LEAD-BASED PAINT DISCLOSURES

Residential purchase and sale agreements have a disclosure provision or addendum concerning lead-based paint. In transactions that involve housing built before 1978, federal law requires the seller to disclose information about lead-based paint on the property to potential buyers. Many of the homes built before 1978 contain some lead-based paint. The paint is usually not dangerous if properly maintained, but if it deteriorates and is ingested, it may cause brain damage and organ damage in young children.

FIG. 7.4 OPTIONAL CLAUSES ADDENDUM

Form 22D
Optional Clauses Addendum
Rev. 12/12
Page 1 of 2

©Copyright 2012
Northwest Multiple Listing Service
ALL RIGHTS RESERVED

OPTIONAL CLAUSES ADDENDUM TO
PURCHASE & SALE AGREEMENT

The following is part of the Purchase and Sale Agreement dated _____ 1

between _____ ("Buyer") 2

and _____ ("Seller") 3

concerning _____ (the "Property"). 4

CHECK IF INCLUDED: 5

1. ☐ **Square Footage/Lot Size/Encroachments.** The Listing Broker and Selling Broker make no representations 6
concerning: (a) the lot size or the accuracy of any information provided by the Seller; (b) the square footage of 7
any improvements on the Property; (c) whether there are any encroachments (fences, rockeries, buildings) on 8
the Property, or by the Property on adjacent properties. Buyer is advised to verify lot size, square footage and 9
encroachments to Buyer's own satisfaction within the inspection contingency period. 10

2. ☐ **Title Insurance.** The Title Insurance clause in the Agreement provides Seller is to provide the then-current ALTA 11
form of Homeowner's Policy of Title Insurance. The parties have the option to provide less coverage by selecting 12
a Standard Owner's Policy or more coverage by selecting an Extended Coverage Policy: 13

    ☐ **Standard Owner's Policy.** Seller authorizes Buyer's lender or Closing Agent, at Seller's expense, to 14
apply for the then-current ALTA form of Owner's Policy of Title Insurance, together with homeowner's 15
additional protection and inflation protection endorsements, if available at no additional cost, rather than 16
the Homeowner's Policy of Title Insurance. 17

    ☐ **Extended Policy.** Seller authorizes Buyer's lender or Closing Agent, at Seller's expense to apply for an 18
ALTA or comparable Extended Coverage Policy of Title Insurance, rather than the Homeowner's Policy 19
of Title Insurance. Buyer shall pay the increased costs associated with the Extended Coverage Policy, 20
including the excess premium over that charged for Homeowner's Policy of Title Insurance and the cost 21
of any survey required by the title insurer. 22

3. ☐ **Property And Grounds Maintained.** Until possession is transferred to Buyer, Seller shall maintain the 23
Property in the same condition as when initially viewed by Buyer. The term "Property" includes the building(s); 24
grounds; plumbing, heat, electrical and other systems; and all Included Items. Should an appliance or system 25
become inoperative or malfunction prior to transfer of possession, Seller shall either repair, or replace the 26
same with an appliance or system of at least equal quality. Buyer reserves the right to reinspect the Property 27
within 5 days prior to transfer of possession to verify the foregoing. Buyer and Seller understand and agree 28
that the Listing Broker and Selling Broker shall not, under any circumstances, be liable for the foregoing or 29
Seller's breach of this clause. 30

4. ☐ **Items Left by Seller.** Any personal property, fixtures or other items remaining on the Property when 31
possession is transferred to Buyer shall thereupon become the property of the Buyer, and may be retained or 32
disposed of as Buyer determines. However, Seller shall clean the interiors of any structures and remove all 33
trash, debris and rubbish from the Property prior to Buyer taking possession. 34

5. ☐ **Utilities.** To the best of Seller's knowledge, Seller represents that the Property is connected to a: 35

    ☐ public water main; ☐ public sewer main; ☐ septic tank; ☐ well (specify type) _____ ; 36

    ☐ irrigation water (specify provider) _____ ; ☐ natural gas; ☐ telephone; 37

    ☐ cable; ☐ electricity; ☐ other _____ . 38

6. ☐ **Insulation - New Construction.** If this is new construction, Federal Trade Commission Regulations require 39
the following to be filled in. If insulation has not yet been selected, FTC regulations require Seller to furnish 40
Buyer the information below in writing as soon as available: 41

WALL INSULATION: TYPE: _____ THICKNESS: _____ R-VALUE: _____ 42

CEILING INSULATION: TYPE: _____ THICKNESS: _____ R-VALUE: _____ 43

OTHER INSULATION DATA: _____ 44

Initials: BUYER: _____ Date: _____ SELLER: _____ Date: _____

BUYER: _____ Date: _____ SELLER: _____ Date: _____

**OPTIONAL CLAUSES ADDENDUM TO
PURCHASE & SALE AGREEMENT**
Continued

7. ☐ **Leased Property.** Buyer acknowledges that Seller leases the following items of personal property: 45

☐ propane tank; ☐ security system; ☐ satellite dish and operating equipment; ☐ other_____ 46

Buyer shall assume the lease(s) for the selected item(s) and hold Seller harmless from and against any 47
further obligation, liability, or claim arising from the lease(s), if the lease(s) can be assumed. 48

8. ☐ **Homeowners' Association Review Period.** If the Property is subject to a homeowners' association or any 49
other association, then Seller shall provide Buyer a copy of the following documents (if available from the 50
Association) within _____ days (10 days if not filled in) of mutual acceptance: 51

   a. Association rules and regulations, including, but not limited to architectural guidelines; 52

   b. Association meeting minutes from the prior two (2) years; 53

   c. Association Board of Directors meeting minutes from the prior six (6) months; and 54

   d. Association financial statements from the prior two (2) years. 55

If Buyer, in Buyer's sole discretion, does not give notice of disapproval within _____ days (5 days if not 56
filled in) of receipt of the above documents or the date that the above documents are due, then this 57
homeowners' association review period shall conclusively be deemed satisfied (waived). If Buyer gives timely 58
notice of disapproval, then this Agreement shall terminate and the Earnest Money shall be refunded to Buyer. 59

9. ☐ **Excluded Item(s).** The following item(s), that would otherwise be included in the sale of the Property, is 60
excluded from the sale ("Excluded Item(s)"). Seller shall repair any damage to the Property caused by the 61
removal of the Excluded Item(s). Excluded Item(s): 62

_____ 63

_____ 64

10. ☐ **E-mail Transmission.** E-mail transmission of any signed original document, and retransmission of any 65
signed e-mail transmission, shall be the same as delivery of an original, provided that the document is sent to 66
both Selling Broker and Selling Firm or both Listing Broker and Listing Firm at the e-mail addresses below. At 67
the request of either party, or the Closing Agent, the parties will confirm e-mail transmitted signatures by 68
signing an original document. 69

  70

_____   _____
Selling Broker E-mail Address   Listing Broker E-mail Address

_____   _____ 71
Selling Firm Authorized E-mail Address   Listing Firm Authorized E-mail Address

11. ☐ **Home Warranty.** Buyer and Seller acknowledge that home warranty plans are available which may provide 72
additional protection and benefits to Buyer and Seller. Buyer shall order a one-year home warranty as 73
follows: 74

   a. Home warranty provider: _____ 75

   b. Seller shall pay up to $_____ ($0.00 if not filled in) of the cost for the home warranty, together 76
      with any included options, and Buyer shall pay any balance. 77

   c. Options to be included: _____ 78

      _____ (none, if not filled in). 79

   d. Other_____. 80

12. ☐ **Other.** 81

  82

  83

  84

Initials: BUYER: _____ Date: _____ SELLER: _____ Date: _____

        BUYER: _____ Date: _____ SELLER: _____ Date: _____

The seller of a dwelling built before 1978 must do all of the following:

- disclose the location of any lead-based paint in the home that he is aware of;
- provide a copy of any report concerning lead-based paint in the home, if the home has been inspected;
- give buyers a copy of a pamphlet on lead-based paint prepared by the U.S. Environmental Protection Agency; and
- allow buyers at least a ten-day period in which to have the home tested for lead-based paint.

Specific warnings must be included in the purchase and sale agreement, along with signed statements from the parties acknowledging that the requirements of this law have been fulfilled. The signed acknowledgments must be kept for at least three years as proof of compliance. An addendum like the one in Figure 7.5 may be used to satisfy these legal requirements.

AGENT'S RESPONSIBILITIES. A real estate agent is required to ensure that the seller knows her obligations under the lead-based paint disclosure law and fulfills those obligations. It is also the agent's responsibility to make sure that the purchase agreement contains the required warnings, disclosures, and signatures.

PENALTIES. Sellers and real estate agents who fail to fulfill their obligations under the lead-based paint disclosure law may be ordered to pay the buyer treble damages (three times the amount of any actual damages suffered by the buyer). Civil and criminal penalties may also be imposed.

OFFER AND ACCEPTANCE

A purchase and sale agreement form includes space in which to set a deadline for acceptance of the offer. The manner in which the seller is required to communicate acceptance may also be specified. In the NWMLS form, for example, the seller's acceptance is not effective until a copy of the agreement signed by the seller is received by the buyer, by the selling agent, or at the selling agent's office.

A purchase and sale agreement may also set a deadline for the buyer's acceptance of a counteroffer. Remember that a counteroffer isn't an acceptance, so the buyer isn't contractually bound unless he accepts the seller's counteroffer.

FIG. 7.5   LEAD-BASED PAINT DISCLOSURE FORM

Disclosure of Information on Lead-Based Paint and/or Lead-Based Paint Hazards

Lead Warning Statement

Every purchaser of any interest in residential real property on which a residential dwelling was built prior to 1978 is notified that such property may present exposure to lead from lead-based paint that may place young children at risk of developing lead poisoning. Lead poisoning in young children may produce permanent neurological damage, including learning disabilities, reduced intelligence quotient, behavioral problems, and impaired memory. Lead poisoning also poses a particular risk to pregnant women. The seller of any interest in residential real property is required to provide the buyer with any information on lead-based paint hazards from risk assessments or inspections in the seller's possession and notify the buyer of any known lead-based paint hazards. A risk assessment or inspection for possible lead-based paint hazards is recommended prior to purchase.

Seller's Disclosure

(a) Presence of lead-based paint and/or lead-based paint hazards (check (i) or (ii) below):

  (i) _____ Known lead-based paint and/or lead-based paint hazards are present in the housing (explain).

  _____

  (ii) _____ Seller has no knowledge of lead-based paint and/or lead-based paint hazards in the housing.

(b) Records and reports available to the seller (check (i) or (ii) below):

  (i) _____ Seller has provided the purchaser with all available records and reports pertaining to lead-based paint and/or lead-based paint hazards in the housing (list documents below).

  _____

  (ii) _____ Seller has no reports or records pertaining to lead-based paint and/or lead-based paint hazards in the housing.

Purchaser's Acknowledgment (initial)

(c) _____ Purchaser has received copies of all information listed above.

(d) _____ Purchaser has received the pamphlet *Protect Your Family from Lead in Your Home.*

(e) Purchaser has (check (i) or (ii) below):

  (i) _____ received a 10-day opportunity (or mutually agreed upon period) to conduct a risk assessment or inspection for the presence of lead-based paint and/or lead-based paint hazards; or

  (ii) _____ waived the opportunity to conduct a risk assessment or inspection for the presence of lead-based paint and/or lead-based paint hazards.

Agent's Acknowledgment (initial)

(f) _____ Agent has informed the seller of the seller's obligations under 42 U.S.C. 4852(d) and is aware of his/her responsibility to ensure compliance.

Certification of Accuracy

The following parties have reviewed the information above and certify, to the best of their knowledge, that the information they have provided is true and accurate.

Seller	Date	Seller	Date
Purchaser	Date	Purchaser	Date
Agent	Date	Agent	Date

SIGNATURES

Of course, space is provided for each party's signature. The buyer's signature makes the form an offer to purchase, and the seller's signature turns it into a binding contract. On many forms, the listing and selling agents are also supposed to sign and fill in the names of their brokerages.

With some purchase and sale agreement forms, when the seller signs the form to accept the buyer's offer, the seller is also agreeing to pay the real estate commission. This gives the firm a safety net, in case the listing agreement was invalid for some reason. The clause in the purchase and sale agreement satisfies the statute of frauds and allows the firm to sue the seller for the commission, if necessary.

VACANT LAND PURCHASE AND SALE AGREEMENTS

The purchase and sale agreement shown in Figure 7.1 should be used only for improved residential property—land and a house. If your buyer is making an offer on vacant land, use a vacant land purchase and sale agreement instead, such as the one shown in Figure 7.6.

Many of the provisions of a vacant land purchase and sale agreement are similar or identical to those of a residential agreement. As is the case with residential purchase agreements, agents should be careful when completing Form 25, making sure to check every box that is appropriate. Other common mistakes agents make when using this form include inadequate descriptions of the property or incomplete payment terms, or a failure to attach a note and deed of trust if seller financing is a part of the transaction. Now let's discuss some of the provisions that are unique to vacant land agreements.

SUBDIVISION REGULATIONS

Before land can be subdivided and developed, various procedural requirements must be met. One of these requirements is submission of a plat to the planning commission for approval. A plat is a map that shows the location and boundaries of proposed lots, streets, and public areas within the subdivision, as well as the availability of public services. Many vacant land purchase and sale agreements have provisions that address the platting requirements for the land. If the property is already platted, the plat number must be part of the property's legal description.

DEVELOPMENT AND CONSTRUCTION FEASIBILITY

The cost of developing the property is crucial in any decision to buy vacant land, so a provision concerning development and construction costs is typically included in the purchase and sale agreement. The agreement shown in Figure 7.6 states that it's the buyer's responsibility to determine whether the property can be platted, developed, and built upon, and what it will cost to do so. The buyer is supposed to fill in the number of days it will take to verify this information. To gather the necessary information, the buyer should consult the county and/or city and various utility districts. The feasibility provision goes on to list some of the specific information the buyer should find out about, including applicable building moratoriums, special building requirements, environmental concerns, growth mitigation restrictions or fees, plat approval requirements, and utility connection charges.

Unless the buyer gives the seller notice within the stated number of days, the buyer is deemed to be satisfied with the feasibility and cost of development and construction. If the buyer notifies the seller that he is not satisfied, the agreement will terminate and the earnest money will be refunded (less any unpaid costs).

ZONING

The property's zoning designation may be disclosed in the purchase and sale agreement. The zoning controls what type of use may be made of the vacant land, so proper disclosure is imperative. Real estate agents have been held liable to buyers for misrepresenting the property's zoning designation on the purchase and sale agreement form.

PERCOLATION TEST

When vacant land is sold for development, if the property isn't served by a sewer system, the seller may have to provide the buyer with the results of a percolation test (often called a perc test). This is required in some Washington counties and not in others. Purchase and sale agreement forms used in counties where a perc test is required may include a provision concerning the requirement.

FIG. 7.6   VACANT LAND PURCHASE AND SALE AGREEMENT

Form 25
Vacant Land Purchase & Sale
Rev. 12/12
Page 1 of 5

©Copyright 2012
Northwest Multiple Listing Service
ALL RIGHTS RESERVED

VACANT LAND PURCHASE AND SALE AGREEMENT
SPECIFIC TERMS

1. **Date:** _____ MLS No.: _____
2. **Buyer:** _____
3. **Seller:** _____
4. **Property:** Tax Parcel No(s).: _____ (_____ County)
    Street Address: _____ Washington _____
    Legal Description: Attached as Exhibit A.
5. **Purchase Price:** $_____
6. **Earnest Money:** (To be held by ❏ Selling Firm; ❏ Closing Agent)
    Personal Check: $ _____; Note: $_____; Other (_____): $ _____
7. **Default:** (check only one) ❏ Forfeiture of Earnest Money; ❏ Seller's Election of Remedies
8. **Title Insurance Company:** _____
9. **Closing Agent:** ❏ a qualified closing agent of Buyer's choice; ❏ _____
10. **Closing Date:** _____
11. **Possession Date:** ❏ on Closing; ❏ Other _____
12. **Offer Expiration Date:** _____
13. **Services of Closing Agent for Payment of Utilities:** ❏ Requested (attach NWMLS Form 22K); ❏ Waived
14. **Charges and Assessments Due After Closing:** ❏ assumed by Buyer; ❏ prepaid in full by Seller at Closing
15. **Subdivision:** The Property: ❏ must be subdivided before_____; ❏ is not required to be subdivided
16. **Feasibility Contingency Expiration Date:** ❏_____ days after mutual acceptance; ❏ Other_____
17. **Agency Disclosure:**   Selling Broker represents: ❏ Buyer; ❏ Seller; ❏ both parties; ❏ neither party
                            Listing Broker represents: ❏ Seller; ❏ both parties
18. **Addenda:** _____
    _____
    _____
    _____
    _____

Buyer's Signature	Date	Seller's Signature	Date
Buyer's Signature	Date	Seller's Signature	Date
Buyer's Address		Seller's Address	
City, State, Zip		City, State, Zip	
Phone No.	Fax No.	Phone No.	Fax No.
Buyer's E-mail Address		Seller's E-mail Address	
Selling Firm	MLS Office No.	Listing Firm	MLS Office No.
Selling Firm's Assumed Name (if applicable)		Listing Firm's Assumed Name (if applicable)	
Selling Broker (Print)	MLS LAG No.	Listing Broker (Print)	MLS LAG No.
Phone No.	Firm Fax No.	Phone No.	Firm Fax No.
Selling Broker's E-mail Address		Listing Broker's E-mail Address	

SAMPLE

Reprinted courtesy of Northwest Multiple Listing Service. All rights reserved.

Form 25
Vacant Land Purchase & Sale
Rev. 12/12
Page 2 of 5

VACANT LAND PURCHASE AND SALE AGREEMENT
GENERAL TERMS
Continued

a. **Purchase Price.** Buyer shall pay to Seller the Purchase Price, including the Earnest Money, in cash at Closing, unless 1
otherwise specified in this Agreement. Buyer represents that Buyer has sufficient funds to close this sale in accordance 2
with this Agreement and is not relying on any contingent source of funds, including funds from loans, the sale of other 3
property, gifts, retirement, or future earnings, except to the extent otherwise specified in this Agreement. 4

b. **Earnest Money.** Buyer shall deliver the Earnest Money within 2 days after mutual acceptance of this Agreement to 5
Selling Broker who will deposit any check to be held by Selling Firm, or deliver any Earnest Money to be held by Closing 6
Agent, within 3 days of receipt or mutual acceptance, whichever occurs later. If the Earnest Money is held by Selling 7
Firm and is over $10,000.00 it shall be deposited into an interest bearing trust account in Selling Firm's name provided 8
that Buyer completes an IRS Form W-9. Interest, if any, after deduction of bank charges and fees, will be paid to Buyer. 9
Buyer shall reimburse Selling Firm for bank charges and fees in excess of the interest earned, if any. If the Earnest 10
Money held by Selling Firm is over $10,000.00 Buyer has the option to require Selling Firm to deposit the Earnest 11
Money into the Housing Trust Fund Account, with the interest paid to the State Treasurer, if both Seller and Buyer so 12
agree in writing. If the Buyer does not complete an IRS Form W-9 before Selling Firm must deposit the Earnest Money 13
or the Earnest Money is $10,000.00 or less, the Earnest Money shall be deposited into the Housing Trust Fund 14
Account. Selling Firm may transfer the Earnest Money to Closing Agent at Closing. If all or part of the Earnest Money is 15
to be refunded to Buyer and any such costs remain unpaid, the Selling Firm or Closing Agent may deduct and pay them 16
therefrom. The parties instruct Closing Agent to provide written verification of receipt of the Earnest Money and notice of 17
dishonor of any check to the parties at the addresses and/or fax numbers provided herein. 18

Upon termination of this Agreement, a party or the Closing Agent may deliver a form authorizing the release of Earnest 19
Money to the other party or the parties. The party(s) shall execute such form and deliver the same to the Closing Agent. 20
If either party fails to execute the release form, the other party may make a written demand to the Closing Agent for the 21
Earnest Money. If only one party makes such a demand, Closing Agent shall promptly deliver notice of the demand to 22
the other party. If the other party does not object to the demand within 10 days of Closing Agent's notice, Closing Agent 23
shall disburse the Earnest Money to the party making the demand. If Closing Agent complies with the preceding 24
process, each party shall be deemed to have released Closing Agent from any and all claims or liability related to the 25
disbursal of the Earnest Money. The parties are advised that, notwithstanding the foregoing, Closing Agent may require 26
the parties to execute a separate agreement before disbursing the Earnest Money. If either party fails to authorize the 27
release of the Earnest Money to the other party when required to do so under this Agreement, that party shall be in 28
breach of this Agreement. Upon either party's request, the party holding the Earnest Money shall commence an 29
interpleader action in the county in which the Property is located. For the purposes of this section, the term Closing 30
Agent includes a Selling Firm holding the Earnest Money. The parties authorize the party commencing an interpleader 31
action to deduct up to $500.00 for the costs thereof. 32

c. **Condition of Title.** Unless otherwise specified in this Agreement, title to the Property shall be marketable at Closing. 33
The following shall not cause the title to be unmarketable: rights, reservations, covenants, conditions and restrictions, 34
presently of record and general to the area; easements and encroachments, not materially affecting the value of or 35
unduly interfering with Buyer's reasonable use of the Property; and reserved oil and/or mining rights. Monetary 36
encumbrances or liens not assumed by Buyer, shall be paid or discharged by Seller on or before Closing. Title shall be 37
conveyed by a Statutory Warranty Deed. If this Agreement is for conveyance of a buyer's interest in a Real Estate 38
Contract, the Statutory Warranty Deed shall include a buyer's assignment of the contract sufficient to convey after 39
acquired title. If the Property has been short platted, the Short Plat number is in the Legal Description. 40

d. **Title Insurance.** Seller authorizes Buyer's lender or Closing Agent, at Seller's expense, to apply for the then-current 41
ALTA form of standard form owner's policy of title insurance from the Title Insurance Company. If Seller previously 42
received a preliminary commitment from a Title Insurance Company that Buyer declines to use, Buyer shall pay any 43
cancellation fees owing to the original Title Insurance Company. Otherwise, the party applying for title insurance shall 44
pay any title cancellation fee, in the event such a fee is assessed. The Title Insurance Company shall send a copy of 45
the preliminary commitment to Seller, Listing Broker, Buyer and Selling Broker. The preliminary commitment, and the 46
title policy to be issued, shall contain no exceptions other than the General Exclusions and Exceptions in said standard 47
form and Special Exceptions consistent with the Condition of Title herein provided. If title cannot be made so insurable 48
prior to the Closing Date, then as Buyer's sole and exclusive remedy, the Earnest Money shall, unless Buyer elects to 49
waive such defects or encumbrances, be refunded to the Buyer, less any unpaid costs described in this Agreement, and 50
this Agreement shall thereupon be terminated. Buyer shall have no right to specific performance or damages as a 51
consequence of Seller's inability to provide insurable title. 52

e. **Closing and Possession.** This sale shall be closed by the Closing Agent on the Closing Date. "Closing" means the 53
date on which all documents are recorded and the sale proceeds are available to Seller. If the Closing Date falls on a 54
Saturday, Sunday, legal holiday as defined in RCW 1.16.050, or day when the county recording office is closed, the 55
Closing Agent shall close the transaction on the next day that is not a Saturday, Sunday, legal holiday, or day when the 56
county recording office is closed. Buyer shall be entitled to possession at 9:00 p.m. on the Possession Date. Seller shall 57
maintain the Property in its present condition, normal wear and tear excepted, until the Buyer is entitled to possession. 58
Seller shall not enter into or modify existing leases or rental agreements, service contracts, or other agreements 59
affecting the Property which have terms extending beyond Closing without first obtaining Buyer's consent, which shall 60
not be unreasonably withheld. 61

Initials: BUYER: _____ Date: _____ SELLER: _____ Date: _____

BUYER: _____ Date: _____ SELLER: _____ Date: _____

Form 25
Vacant Land Purchase & Sale
Rev. 12/12
Page 3 of 5

VACANT LAND PURCHASE AND SALE AGREEMENT
GENERAL TERMS
Continued

f. **Section 1031 Like-Kind Exchange.** If either Buyer or Seller intends for this transaction to be a part of a Section 1031 62
like-kind exchange, then the other party shall cooperate in the completion of the like-kind exchange so long as the 63
cooperating party incurs no additional liability in doing so, and so long as any expenses (including attorneys' fees and 64
costs) incurred by the cooperating party that are related only to the exchange are paid or reimbursed to the cooperating 65
party at or prior to Closing. Notwithstanding the Assignment paragraph of this Agreement, any party completing a 66
Section 1031 like-kind exchange may assign this Agreement to its qualified intermediary or any entity set up for the 67
purposes of completing a reverse exchange. 68

g. **Closing Costs and Prorations and Charges and Assessments.** Seller and Buyer shall each pay one-half of the 69
escrow fee unless otherwise required by applicable FHA or VA regulations. Taxes for the current year, rent, interest, 70
and lienable homeowner's association dues shall be prorated as of Closing. Buyer shall pay Buyer's loan costs, 71
including credit report, appraisal charge and lender's title insurance, unless provided otherwise in this Agreement. If any 72
payments are delinquent on encumbrances which will remain after Closing, Closing Agent is instructed to pay such 73
delinquencies at Closing from money due, or to be paid by, Seller. Buyer shall pay for remaining fuel in the fuel tank if, 74
prior to Closing, Seller obtains a written statement as to the quantity and current price from the supplier. Seller shall pay 75
all utility charges, including unbilled charges. Unless waived in Specific Term No. 13, Seller and Buyer request the 76
services of Closing Agent in disbursing funds necessary to satisfy unpaid utility charges in accordance with RCW 60.80 77
and Seller shall provide the names and addresses of all utilities providing service to the Property and having lien rights 78
(attach NWMLS Form 22K Identification of Utilities or equivalent). 79

Buyer is advised to verify the existence and amount of any local improvement district, capacity or impact charges or 80
other assessments that may be charged against the Property before or after Closing. Seller will pay such charges that 81
are encumbrances at the time of Closing, or that are or become due on or before Closing. Charges levied before 82
Closing, but becoming due after Closing shall be paid as agreed in Specific Term No. 14. 83

h. **Sale Information.** Listing Broker and Selling Broker are authorized to report this Agreement (including price and all 84
terms) to the Multiple Listing Service that published it and to its members, financing institutions, appraisers, and anyone 85
else related to this sale. Buyer and Seller expressly authorize all Closing Agents, appraisers, title insurance companies, 86
and others related to this Sale, to furnish the Listing Broker and/or Selling Broker, on request, any and all information 87
and copies of documents concerning this sale. 88

i. **FIRPTA - Tax Withholding at Closing.** The Closing Agent is instructed to prepare a certification (NWMLS Form 22E or 89
equivalent) that Seller is not a "foreign person" within the meaning of the Foreign Investment In Real Property Tax Act. 90
Seller shall sign this certification. If Seller is a foreign person, and this transaction is not otherwise exempt from FIRPTA, 91
Closing Agent is instructed to withhold and pay the required amount to the Internal Revenue Service. 92

j. **Notices.** In consideration of the license to use this and NWMLS's companion forms and for the benefit of the Listing 93
Broker and the Selling Broker as well as the orderly administration of the offer, counteroffer or this agreement, the 94
parties irrevocably agree that unless otherwise specified in this Agreement, any notice required or permitted in, or 95
related to, this Agreement (including revocations of offers or counteroffers) must be in writing. Notices to Seller must be 96
signed by at least one Buyer and shall be deemed given only when the notice is received by Seller, by Listing Broker or 97
at the licensed office of Listing Broker. Notices to Buyer must be signed by at least one Seller and shall be deemed 98
given only when the notice is received by Buyer, by Selling Broker or at the licensed office of Selling Broker. Receipt by 99
Selling Broker of a Form 17 or 17C (whichever is applicable), Public Offering Statement or Resale Certificate, 100
homeowners' association documents provided pursuant to NWMLS Form 22D, or a preliminary commitment for title 101
insurance provided pursuant to NWMLS Form 22T shall be deemed receipt by Buyer. Selling Broker and Listing Broker 102
have no responsibility to advise of receipt of a notice beyond either phoning the party or causing a copy of the notice to 103
be delivered to the party's address shown on this Agreement. Buyer and Seller must keep Selling Broker and Listing 104
Broker advised of their whereabouts in order to receive prompt notification of receipt of a notice. 105

k. **Computation of Time.** Unless otherwise specified in this Agreement, any period of time measured in days and stated 106
in this Agreement shall start on the day following the event commencing the period and shall expire at 9:00 p.m. of the 107
last calendar day of the specified period of time. Except for the Possession Date, if the last day is a Saturday, Sunday 108
or legal holiday as defined in RCW 1.16.050, the specified period of time shall expire on the next day that is not a 109
Saturday, Sunday or legal holiday. Any specified period of 5 days or less shall not include Saturdays, Sundays or legal 110
holidays. If the parties agree that an event will occur on a specific calendar date, the event shall occur on that date, 111
except for the Closing Date, which, if it falls on a Saturday, Sunday, legal holiday as defined in RCW 1.16.050, or day 112
when the county recording office is closed, shall occur on the next day that is not a Saturday, Sunday, legal holiday, or 113
day when the county recording office is closed. If the parties agree upon and attach a legal description after this 114
Agreement is signed by the offeree and delivered to the offeror, then for the purposes of computing time, mutual 115
acceptance shall be deemed to be on the date of delivery of an accepted offer or counteroffer to the offeror, rather than 116
on the date the legal description is attached. Time is of the essence of this Agreement. 117

Initials: BUYER: _____ Date: _____ SELLER: _____ Date: _____

BUYER: _____ Date: _____ SELLER: _____ Date: _____

Form 25
Vacant Land Purchase & Sale
Rev. 12/12
Page 4 of 5

VACANT LAND PURCHASE AND SALE AGREEMENT
GENERAL TERMS
Continued

l. **Facsimile or E-mail Transmission.** Facsimile transmission of any signed original document, and retransmission of any 118
signed facsimile transmission, shall be the same as delivery of an original. At the request of either party, or the Closing 119
Agent, the parties will confirm facsimile transmitted signatures by signing an original document. E-mail transmission of 120
any document or notice shall not be effective unless the parties to this Agreement otherwise agree in writing. 121

m. **Integration and Electronic Signatures.** This Agreement constitutes the entire understanding between the parties and 122
supersedes all prior or contemporaneous understandings and representations. No modification of this Agreement shall 123
be effective unless agreed in writing and signed by Buyer and Seller. The parties acknowledge that a signature in 124
electronic form has the same legal effect and validity as a handwritten signature. 125

n. **Assignment.** Buyer may not assign this Agreement, or Buyer's rights hereunder, without Seller's prior written consent, 126
unless the parties indicate that assignment is permitted by the addition of "and/or assigns" on the line identifying the 127
Buyer on the first page of this Agreement. 128

o. **Default.** In the event Buyer fails, without legal excuse, to complete the purchase of the Property, then the following 129
provision, as identified in Specific Term No. 7, shall apply: 130

    i. **Forfeiture of Earnest Money.** That portion of the Earnest Money that does not exceed five percent (5%) of the 131
    Purchase Price shall be forfeited to the Seller as the sole and exclusive remedy available to Seller for such failure. 132

    ii. **Seller's Election of Remedies.** Seller may, at Seller's option, (a) keep the Earnest Money as liquidated damages 133
    as the sole and exclusive remedy available to Seller for such failure, (b) bring suit against Buyer for Seller's actual 134
    damages, (c) bring suit to specifically enforce this Agreement and recover any incidental damages, or (d) pursue 135
    any other rights or remedies available at law or equity. 136

p. **Professional Advice and Attorneys' Fees.** Buyer and Seller are advised to seek the counsel of an attorney and a 137
certified public accountant to review the terms of this Agreement. Buyer and Seller agree to pay their own fees incurred 138
for such review. However, if Buyer or Seller institutes suit against the other concerning this Agreement the prevailing 139
party is entitled to reasonable attorneys' fees and expenses. 140

q. **Offer.** Buyer shall purchase the Property under the terms and conditions of this Agreement. Seller shall have until 9:00 141
p.m. on the Offer Expiration Date to accept this offer, unless sooner withdrawn. Acceptance shall not be effective until a 142
signed copy is received by Buyer, by Selling Broker or at the licensed office of Selling Broker. If this offer is not so 143
accepted, it shall lapse and any Earnest Money shall be refunded to Buyer. 144

r. **Counteroffer.** Any change in the terms presented in an offer or counteroffer, other than the insertion of the Seller's 145
name, shall be considered a counteroffer. If a party makes a counteroffer, then the other party shall have until 9:00 p.m. 146
on the counteroffer expiration date to accept that counteroffer, unless sooner withdrawn. Acceptance shall not be 147
effective until a signed copy is received by Seller, by Listing Broker or at the licensed office of Listing Broker. If the 148
counteroffer is not so accepted, it shall lapse and any Earnest Money shall be refunded to Buyer. 149

s. **Offer and Counteroffer Expiration Date.** If no expiration date is specified for an offer/counteroffer, the 150
offer/counteroffer shall expire 2 days after the offer/counteroffer is delivered by the party making the offer/counteroffer, 151
unless sooner withdrawn. 152

t. **Agency Disclosure.** Selling Firm, Selling Firm's Designated Broker, Selling Broker's Branch Manager (if any) and 153
Selling Broker's Managing Broker (if any) represent the same party that Selling Broker represents. Listing Firm, Listing 154
Firm's Designated Broker, Listing Broker's Branch Manager (if any), and Listing Broker's Managing Broker (if any) 155
represent the same party that the Listing Broker represents. If Selling Broker and Listing Broker are different persons 156
affiliated with the same Firm, then both Buyer and Seller confirm their consent to Designated Broker, Branch Manager 157
(if any), and Managing Broker (if any) representing both parties as dual agents. If Selling Broker and Listing Broker are 158
the same person representing both parties then both Buyer and Seller confirm their consent to that person and his/her 159
Designated Broker, Branch Manager (if any), and Managing Broker (if any) representing both parties as dual agents. All 160
parties acknowledge receipt of the pamphlet entitled "The Law of Real Estate Agency." 161

u. **Commission.** Seller and Buyer agree to pay a commission in accordance with any listing or commission agreement to 162
which they are a party. The Listing Firm's commission shall be apportioned between Listing Firm and Selling Firm as 163
specified in the listing. Seller and Buyer hereby consent to Listing Firm or Selling Firm receiving compensation from 164
more than one party. Seller and Buyer hereby assign to Listing Firm and Selling Firm, as applicable, a portion of their 165
funds in escrow equal to such commission(s) and irrevocably instruct the Closing Agent to disburse the commission(s) 166
directly to the Firm(s). In any action by Listing or Selling Firm to enforce this paragraph, the prevailing party is entitled to 167
court costs and reasonable attorneys' fees. Seller and Buyer agree that the Firms are intended third party beneficiaries 168
under this Agreement. 169

Initials: BUYER: _____ Date: _____ SELLER: _____ Date: _____

        BUYER: _____ Date: _____ SELLER: _____ Date: _____

Form 25
Vacant Land Purchase & Sale
Rev. 12/12
Page 5 of 5

VACANT LAND PURCHASE AND SALE AGREEMENT
GENERAL TERMS
Continued

v. **Feasibility Contingency.** It is the Buyer's responsibility to verify before the Feasibility Contingency Expiration Date 170
identified in Specific Term No. 16 whether or not the Property can be platted, developed and/or built on (now or in the 171
future) and what it will cost to do this. BUYER SHOULD NOT RELY ON ANY ORAL STATEMENTS concerning this 172
made by the Seller, Listing Broker or Selling Broker. Buyer should inquire at the city or county, and water, sewer or 173
other special districts in which the Property is located. Buyer's inquiry should include, but not be limited to: building or 174
development moratoriums applicable to or being considered for the Property; any special building requirements, 175
including setbacks, height limits or restrictions on where buildings may be constructed on the Property; whether the 176
Property is affected by a flood zone, wetlands, shorelands or other environmentally sensitive area; road, school, fire and 177
any other growth mitigation or impact fees that must be paid; the procedure and length of time necessary to obtain plat 178
approval and/or a building permit; sufficient water, sewer and utility and any service connection charges; and all other 179
charges that must be paid. Buyer and Buyer's agents, representatives, consultants, architects and engineers shall have 180
the right, from time to time during the feasibility contingency, to enter onto the Property and to conduct any tests or 181
studies that Buyer may need to ascertain the condition and suitability of the Property for Buyer's intended purpose. 182
Buyer shall restore the Property and all improvements on the Property to the same condition they were in prior to the 183
inspection. Buyer shall be responsible for all damages resulting from any inspection of the Property performed on 184
Buyer's behalf. If the Buyer does not give notice to the contrary on or before the Feasibility Contingency Expiration Date 185
identified in Specific Term No. 16, it shall be conclusively deemed that Buyer is satisfied as to development and/or 186
construction feasibility and cost. If Buyer gives notice this Agreement shall terminate and the Earnest Money shall be 187
refunded to Buyer, less any unpaid costs. 188

w. **Subdivision**. If the Property must be subdivided, Seller represents that there has been preliminary plat approval for the 189
Property and this Agreement is conditioned on the recording of the final plat containing the Property on or before the 190
date specified in Specific Term 15. If the final plat is not recorded by such date, this Agreement shall terminate and the 191
Earnest Money shall be refunded to Buyer. 192

x. **Information Verification Period and Property Condition Disclaimer.** Buyer shall have 10 days after mutual 193
acceptance to verify all information provided from Seller or Listing Firm related to the Property. This contingency shall 194
be deemed satisfied unless Buyer gives notice identifying the materially inaccurate information within 10 days of mutual 195
acceptance. If Buyer gives timely notice under this section, then Agreement shall terminate and the Earnest Money 196
shall be refunded to Buyer. 197

Buyer and Seller agree, that except as provided in this Agreement, all representations and information regarding the 198
Property and the transaction are solely from the Seller or Buyer, and not from any Broker. The parties acknowledge that 199
the Brokers are not responsible for assuring that the parties perform their obligations under this Agreement and that 200
none of the Brokers has agreed to independently investigate or confirm any matter related to this transaction except as 201
stated in this Agreement, or in a separate writing signed by such Broker. In addition, Brokers do not guarantee the 202
value, quality or condition of the Property and some properties may contain building materials, including siding, roofing, 203
ceiling, insulation, electrical, and plumbing, that have been the subject of lawsuits and/or governmental inquiry because 204
of possible defects or health hazards. Some properties may have other defects arising after construction, such as 205
drainage, leakage, pest, rot and mold problems. Brokers do not have the expertise to identify or assess defective 206
products, materials, or conditions. Buyer is urged to use due diligence to inspect the Property to Buyer's satisfaction 207
and to retain inspectors qualified to identify the presence of defective materials and evaluate the condition of the 208
Property as there may be defects that may only be revealed by careful inspection. Buyer is advised to investigate 209
whether there is a sufficient water supply to meet Buyer's needs. Brokers may assist the parties with locating and 210
selecting third party service providers, such as inspectors or contractors, but Brokers cannot guarantee or be 211
responsible for the services provided by those third parties. The parties agree to exercise their own judgment and due 212
diligence regarding third-party service providers. 213

Initials: BUYER: _____ Date: _____ SELLER: _____ Date: _____

BUYER: _____ Date: _____ SELLER: _____ Date: _____

CHAPTER SUMMARY

1. A properly executed purchase and sale agreement is a binding contract that holds the parties to the terms of their agreement until all conditions have been fulfilled and the transaction is ready to close.

2. The parties to a purchase and sale agreement are the buyer(s) and the seller(s). All parties must have contractual capacity. Everyone with an interest in the property must sign the agreement. The spouse of any married seller or buyer should also sign.

3. Every purchase and sale agreement must have an adequate description of the property, specify the total purchase price and the method of payment, set a closing date and date of possession, and state by what type of deed and in what condition title will be conveyed.

4. Purchase and sale agreements almost always contain a "time is of the essence" clause, which makes the closing date a material term of the contract. Closing must take place on or before the date stated in the agreement, unless the parties agree in writing to an extension.

5. In Washington, a purchase and sale agreement should include an agency disclosure paragraph, stating that the real estate agents involved in the transaction have made the required disclosures concerning which party or parties they were representing.

6. In most cases, the purchase agreement provides that the buyer will give her agent a personal check for the deposit after the seller accepts the offer. The agreement directs the agent either to deposit the money in the firm's account or, commonly, deliver it to the escrow agent.

7. A vacant land purchase and sale agreement should be used when a buyer makes an offer to purchase unimproved property. Provisions regarding subdivision, development feasibility, and zoning are important in a transaction involving vacant land.

CHAPTER QUIZ

1. If the seller is a minor, the purchase and sale agreement should be signed by:
   a. the seller's husband or wife
   b. both the seller and the seller's spouse
   c. the seller's legal guardian
   d. both the seller and the seller's attorney in fact

2. The purchase price stated in the purchase and sale agreement should include:
   a. mortgages or other liens being assumed by the buyer
   b. seller financing
   c. any loan amount contingent on buyer obtaining financing
   d. All of the above

3. The buyer usually gives the earnest money deposit to either the escrow agent or the:
   a. selling agent
   b. seller
   c. listing agent
   d. escrow agent

4. The "included items" paragraph is used to:
   a. disclose the encumbrances on the property
   b. list the documents that are being attached to the agreement
   c. determine how closing costs will be allocated
   d. specify what fixtures or other property will be part of the sale

5. In choosing a closing date, you should take into account all of the following except:
   a. when the next installment of the property taxes will be due
   b. how long the seller needs to make any necessary repairs
   c. whether the buyer needs to sell her current home
   d. the time needed to clear away any liens

6. Which document should be prepared if the buyer plans to take possession before the closing date?
   a. Rental agreement
   b. Sale of buyer's home contingency
   c. Bump notice
   d. Backup offer

7. Under federal law, the seller of a home built before 1978 must:
   a. remove all lead-based paint from the property
   b. have the home inspected for lead-based paint
   c. provide a copy of any report about lead-based paint in the home
   d. repaint any areas where lead-based paint was used

8. Which of the following might interfere with the seller's ability to convey clear title to the property?
   a. The existence of fixtures on the property
   b. An easement for underground wiring
   c. The seller is going through a divorce
   d. CC&Rs that apply to the entire neighborhood

9. The Foreign Investment in Real Property Tax Act applies to a transaction if which of the following is not a U.S. citizen or resident alien?
   a. Real estate agent
   b. Buyer
   c. Closing agent
   d. Seller

10. All of the following provisions are unique to a vacant land agreement except:
    a. development and construction feasibility
    b. default provisions
    c. property's subdivision status
    d. drainage test

ANSWER KEY

1. c. If one of the parties to a contract is a minor (under 18 years of age), the contract should be signed by that party's legal guardian.

2. d. The purchase price stated in the agreement should be the full price being paid for the property, including the downpayment, any mortgages or liens the buyer is assuming, and any part of the price that the buyer is financing.

3. a. In most cases, the buyer will give the earnest money deposit to the selling agent (and the deposit will be held in trust or delivered to an escrow agent by the selling agent).

4. d. The "included items" paragraph lists items that are included in the sale unless otherwise noted. (Many of the items listed would be considered fixtures or attachments to the real property and included in the sale even without this provision.)

5. a. In setting a closing date, it's important to consider how long it will take the parties to fulfill their obligations and satisfy any contingencies in the purchase and sale agreement.

6. a. If the parties plan to transfer possession of the property either before or after the closing date, they should sign a rental agreement that includes rental terms and rate.

7. c. The seller of a home built before 1978 must provide a copy of any report concerning lead-based paint in the home and disclose the location of any lead-based paint that he is aware of.

8. c. If the seller is a party to a legal action, such as a divorce or bankruptcy, the seller may not be able to convey clear title to the property.

9. d. FIRPTA applies to some transactions in which the seller is a nonresident alien rather than a U.S. citizen or resident alien.

10. b. All of the provisions are unique to vacant land transactions with the exception of the default provisions, which are the same in both the residential purchase and sale agreement and the vacant land agreement form.

CONTINGENT TRANSACTIONS

HOW CONTINGENCIES WORK

- Termination or waiver
- Good faith effort required
- Basic elements of a contingency clause

TYPES OF CONTINGENCIES

- Financing contingencies
  - Financing terms and deadlines
  - Loan cost provisions
  - Lender-required inspections
  - Appraisal provisions
  - Seller financing
- Inspection contingencies
  - Approval or disapproval of inspection report
  - Opportunity to repair vs. buyer's satisfaction
  - Neighborhood review
  - Code violations
  - "As is" sales
- Sale of buyer's home contingencies
  - Elements
  - Bump clauses

RESCISSION

INTRODUCTION

In many cases a buyer wants to make an offer on a house, but does not want to become bound by a contract with the seller unless a particular event occurs first. For instance, the buyer may need to get a purchase loan approved, or she may want to have the house inspected by an expert. However, the buyer doesn't want to wait until that event occurs before making an offer on the house—by that time, the seller might have sold the property to someone else. In this situation, the buyer needs to make her offer conditional or contingent on the occurrence of the event in question.

To help a buyer prepare a contingent offer, you need to know how contingency clauses work, the essential elements of a contingency, the common types of contingencies, and the various pre-printed forms you can use to establish a contingency.

HOW CONTINGENCIES WORK

Many purchase and sale agreements are enforceable only if a certain event occurs. The event is called a **contingency**, or a **condition** of the sale. If the specified event occurs, then both the buyer and the seller are bound to carry out the terms of their contract. If the specified event does not occur, the agreement may be terminated and, in most cases, the buyer is entitled to a refund of the earnest money deposit.

TERMINATION OR WAIVER

A contingency provision is typically included in a contract for the benefit of one of the parties rather than both of them. If the contingency is not fulfilled—if the specified event does not happen—the benefiting party has two choices. He may:

1. terminate the contract without penalty, or
2. waive the condition and proceed with the contract.

Only the benefiting party has the right to choose between terminating the contract or waiving the condition. If the benefiting party is willing to waive the condition, the other party cannot refuse to go through with the sale because the condition has not been met.

EXAMPLE: Suppose a purchase and sale agreement is contingent on the buyer obtaining a fixed-rate conventional loan with a $20,000 downpayment within 30 days of the seller's acceptance of the offer. This contingency benefits the buyer. It protects the buyer from being forced to complete the purchase if he can't get the financing he needs.

If the buyer gets the loan within the 30-day period, he is obligated to buy the seller's property. If the buyer got the loan but refused to purchase the property anyway, the seller would be able to keep the buyer's earnest money deposit as liquidated damages or (depending on the terms of their agreement) sue the buyer.

On the other hand, if he doesn't get the loan, the buyer can take one of two courses of action. He can give the seller notice that the condition has not been met, terminate the agreement, and get the deposit back. Alternatively, he can waive the financing contingency and go ahead with the transaction. This would mean that he would have to come up with the purchase price from some other source by the closing date, or else forfeit his deposit.

If the buyer decides to go ahead with the purchase, the seller cannot then refuse to complete the transaction because the condition was not met. Since the condition was included in the purchase and sale agreement for the benefit of the buyer, only the buyer can choose whether to waive the condition or terminate the sale.

In the unusual case when a contingency clause benefits both parties to a contract, the condition can be waived only with the consent of both parties. In other words, if the condition is not met, either party would have the option of terminating the contract.

FOR THE BUYER'S BENEFIT. Contingency provisions in a purchase and sale agreement are usually for the benefit of the buyer. They protect the buyer from becoming obligated to go through with the purchase if something doesn't work out in her own situation, or if it turns out that the property is unsuitable in some way—for instance, because it can't be subdivided, or it's infested with termites, or the well water is contaminated. Common contingency provisions in real estate transactions concern the buyer's financing (as in the example above); the sale of property the buyer currently owns; a satisfactory pest, soil, septic, well, or structural inspection; obtaining approval for a rezone, variance, or subdivision from the local planning commission; or the issuance of some sort of license needed to operate an establishment (such as a liquor license).

Good Faith Effort Required

Whenever a contract contains a contingency clause, the benefited party has an implied legal obligation to make a reasonable, good faith effort to fulfill the contingency.

> **Example:** Hanson's agreement to purchase Moore's house is contingent on Hanson getting a 30-year, 90%, fixed-rate loan at 6% interest. Three days after signing the agreement, Hanson decides she doesn't want to buy Moore's property after all, and she doesn't even bother to apply for a loan. Hanson then tells Moore that she's terminating the contract because the contingency hasn't been fulfilled, and she demands the return of her earnest money.
>
> However, Hanson had a legal obligation to make a reasonable effort to get a loan. Because she didn't fulfill that obligation, she has breached the purchase and sale agreement and is not entitled to a refund of her deposit.

If the responsible party does not make a good faith effort to satisfy the contingency, then it is dropped from the contract. That party is bound by the contract even though the condition has not been met. Under these circumstances, as in the example above, the seller could keep the deposit if the buyer failed to go through with the purchase.

Although the obligation to make a good faith effort to fulfill a condition is always implied in the contract, the contingency clause should spell out that obligation. For example, the Northwest Multiple Listing Service financing contingency addendum, which we'll discuss later in this chapter, includes the following clause:

> *If Buyer has not waived this financing contingency, and is unable to obtain financing after a good faith effort then, on Buyer's notice, this Agreement shall terminate. The Earnest Money shall be refunded to Buyer...*

Basic Elements of a Contingency Clause

Any type of contingency provision, whether it's a financing contingency, an inspection contingency, or some other type, should contain all of the following elements:

1. A clear statement of exactly what the condition is and what has to be done to fulfill it.

2. The procedure for notifying the other party of either satisfaction or waiver of the condition.
3. A deadline by which the condition must be met or waived.
4. The rights of the parties if the condition is not met or waived by the specified date.

While it's important to know the elements a contingency clause should have, you shouldn't try to draft one yourself. As with the purchase and sale agreement itself, you should use a pre-printed, attorney-approved contingency form that can be attached as an addendum to the agreement. If you were to write your own provision instead of using a pre-printed form, that would probably be considered the unauthorized practice of law.

TYPES OF CONTINGENCIES

In purchase and sale agreements for residential transactions, three types of contingency clauses are very common. These are financing contingencies, inspection contingencies, and contingencies concerning the sale of the buyer's home.

FINANCING CONTINGENCIES

Most residential purchase and sale agreements are contingent on whether the buyer can obtain the financing needed in order to be able to pay the seller the agreed price. Standard contract forms may either include a financing contingency clause in the purchase and sale agreement itself, or require an addendum that sets forth the terms of the financing contingency.

The primary purpose of a financing contingency is to allow the buyer to be released from the agreement and get the deposit back if she can't get the necessary financing.

A financing contingency usually states the type of financing the buyer will apply for, sets deadlines for the loan application and fulfillment or waiver of the contingency, specifies the notice periods, and describes how lender-required inspections and repairs will be handled.

FINANCING TERMS. The financing terms set forth in the contingency clause may be general or specific. In this regard, the parties have conflicting interests. The buyer may want the contract to be contingent on a specific and very favorable financing arrangement, one that is as affordable as possible. On the other hand, the seller—who wants to hold the buyer to the agreement, or to keep the deposit if the buyer backs out—would prefer a financing contingency that simply calls for an institutional loan that's typical for the current marketplace. The seller probably won't agree to a financing contingency that specifies a below-market interest rate or unusually low loan fees, because it's much less likely that the buyer will be able to obtain that type of financing.

Figure 8.1 shows the financing addendum designed for use with the Northwest Multiple Listing Service purchase and sale agreement that appears in Chapter 7 (Figure 7.1). The financing terms set forth in this addendum are fairly general. In the first paragraph, you're supposed to indicate the type of financing the buyer will seek, and state the amount of the buyer's downpayment. The buyer is required to apply for a loan to pay the balance of the purchase price.

A more specific financing contingency could stipulate any or all of these additional terms for the buyer's loan: the interest rate, and whether the rate is fixed or variable; the loan term and whether the loan will be fully or partially amortized; and the maximum monthly payment amount. Again, a very specific financing contingency is ordinarily to the buyer's advantage and the seller's disadvantage.

Many financing contingencies state which party will pay the costs and fees associated with the loan application; this is usually the buyer's responsibility.

FINANCING TIMELINES. A financing contingency usually states that the buyer must apply for the loan within a certain number of days. In addition, the contingency provision may establish a time period after which the seller may give notice of his right to terminate their agreement. Once the buyer receives this notice, she has three days to decide whether to waive the contingency; if she chooses not to waive it, the seller may terminate the agreement.

LOAN COST PROVISIONS. The financing contingency usually allows the parties to negotiate whether the seller will pay any of the buyer's loan or closing costs. In addition, the contingency often includes special provisions concerning FHA, VA, and RD (rural development) financing. The regulations that govern these financing programs prevent the buyer from paying certain loan and closing costs, so the seller agrees to pay these costs if the buyer is applying for an FHA, VA, or RD loan. FHA, VA, and RD transactions also require special provisions concerning the property appraisal.

FIG. 8.1   FINANCING CONTINGENCY ADDENDUM

**FINANCING ADDENDUM TO
PURCHASE & SALE AGREEMENT**

The following is part of the Purchase and Sale Agreement dated _____ 1

between _____ ("Buyer") 2

and _____ ("Seller") 3

concerning _____ (the "Property"). 4

5

1. **DOWN PAYMENT/LOAN APPLICATION.** 5

   a. **Loan Application.** This Agreement is contingent on Buyer obtaining the following loan or loans to purchase 6
   the Property (the "Loan(s)"): ❑ Conventional First; ❑ Conventional Second; ❑ Bridge; ❑ VA; ❑ FHA; ❑ Rural 7
   Development ("RD"); ❑ Home Equity Line of Credit; ❑ Other _____ (the 8
   "Financing Contingency"). Buyer shall pay ❑ $; or ❑ % of the Purchase Price _____ 9
   down, in addition to the Loans and to make written application for the Loans to pay the balance of the 10
   Purchase Price and pay the application fee, if required, for the subject Property within _____ days 11
   (5 days if not filled in) after mutual acceptance of this Agreement. If not waived, the Financing Contingency 12
   shall survive the Closing Date. 13

   b. **Waiver of Financing Contingency.** If Buyer (i) fails to make application for financing for the Property within 14
   the agreed time; (ii) changes the type of loan without Seller's prior written consent; or (iii) changes the lender 15
   without Seller's prior written consent after the agreed upon time to apply for financing expires, then the 16
   Financing Contingency shall be deemed waived. For purposes of this Addendum, "lender" means the party 17
   funding the loan. 18

2. **SELLER'S RIGHT TO TERMINATE.** 19

   a. **Right to Terminate Notice.** At any time _____ days (30 days if not filled in) after mutual acceptance, 20
   Seller may give notice to Buyer that Seller may terminate the Agreement at any time 3 days after delivery of 21
   that notice (the "Right to Terminate Notice"). NWMLS Form 22AR may be used for this notice. 22

   b. **Termination Notice.** If Buyer has not previously waived the Financing Contingency, Seller may give notice of 23
   termination of this Agreement (the "Termination Notice") any time following 3 days after delivery of the Right 24
   to Terminate Notice. If Seller gives the Termination Notice before Buyer has waived the Financing 25
   Contingency, this Agreement is terminated and the Earnest Money shall be refunded to Buyer. NWMLS Form 26
   22AR shall be used for this notice. 27

3. **LOAN COST PROVISIONS.** Seller shall pay up to ❑ $; or ❑ % of the Purchase Price _____ 28
   ($0.00 if not filled in), which shall be applied to Buyer's Loan(s) and settlement costs, including, but not limited to 29
   prepaids, loan discount, loan fee, interest buy down, financing, closing, or other costs allowed by lender. If this 30
   sale is contingent on Buyer obtaining an FHA, RD, or VA loan, Seller shall also pay up to $300.00 for that portion 31
   of Buyer's Loan and settlement costs that the Lender is prohibited from collecting from Buyer under FHA/RD/VA 32
   regulations. If this sale is contingent on Buyer obtaining a VA loan, Seller shall also pay the full escrow fee for the 33
   closing of this Agreement. 34

4. **EARNEST MONEY.** If Buyer has not waived the Financing Contingency, and is unable to obtain financing after a 35
   good faith effort then, on Buyer's notice, this Agreement shall terminate. The Earnest Money shall be refunded to 36
   Buyer after Buyer delivers to Seller written confirmation from Buyer's lender confirming (a) the date Buyer's loan 37
   application for the subject property was made; (b) that Buyer possessed sufficient funds to close; and (c) the 38
   reasons Buyer's application was denied. If Seller terminates this Agreement, the Earnest Money shall be refunded 39
   without need for such confirmation from Buyer's lender. 40

5. **INSPECTION.** Seller agrees to permit inspections required by Buyer's lender, including but not limited to 41
   structural, pest, heating, plumbing, roof, electrical, septic, and well inspections. Seller is not obligated to pay for 42
   such inspections unless otherwise agreed. 43

Initials: BUYER: _____ Date: _____ SELLER: _____ Date: _____

BUYER: _____ Date: _____ SELLER: _____ Date: _____

Form 22A
Financing Addendum
Rev.12/12
Page 2 of 2

**FINANCING ADDENDUM TO
PURCHASE & SALE AGREEMENT**
Continued

6. **APPRAISAL LESS THAN SALE PRICE.** 44

    a. Notice of Low Appraisal. If Buyer's lender's appraised value of the Property is less than the Purchase Price, 45
Buyer may, within 3 days after receipt of a copy of lender's appraisal, give notice of low appraisal, which 46
notice shall include a copy of lender's appraisal. 47

    b. Seller's Response to Notice of Low Appraisal. Seller shall, within 10 days after Buyer's notice of low 48
appraisal, give notice of: 49

        (i) A reappraisal or reconsideration of value, at Seller's expense, by the same appraiser or another appraiser 50
acceptable to lender, in an amount not less than the Purchase Price. Buyer shall promptly seek lender's 51
approval of such reappraisal or reconsideration of value. The parties are advised that Buyer's lender may 52
elect not to accept a reappraisal or reconsideration of value; 53

        (ii) Seller's consent to reduce the Purchase Price to an amount not more than the amount specified in the 54
appraisal or reappraisal by the same appraiser, or an appraisal by another appraiser acceptable to 55
lender, whichever is higher. (This provision is not applicable if this Agreement is conditioned on FHA, VA, 56
or RD financing. FHA, VA, and RD financing does not permit the Buyer to be obligated to buy if the Seller 57
reduces the Purchase Price to the appraised value. Buyer, however, has the option to buy at the reduced 58
price.); or 59

        (iii) Seller's rejection of Buyer's notice of low appraisal. 60

    If Seller timely delivers notice of reappraisal, reconsideration of value, or consent to reduce the Purchase 61
Price, and Buyer's lender accepts Seller's response, then Buyer shall be bound by Seller's response. 62

    c. Buyer's Reply. Buyer shall have 3 days from either Seller's notice of rejection of low appraisal or, if Seller 63
fails to respond, the day Seller's response period ends, whichever is earlier, to (a) waive the Financing 64
Contingency or (b) terminate the Agreement, in which event the Earnest Money shall be refunded to Buyer. 65
Buyer's inaction during this reply period shall result in termination of the Agreement and return of the Earnest 66
Money to Buyer. The Closing date shall be extended as necessary to accommodate the foregoing times for 67
notices. Buyer's waiver of the Financing Contingency constitutes waiver of this Paragraph 6. 68

7. **FHA/VA/RD - Appraisal Certificate.** If this Agreement is contingent on Buyer obtaining FHA, VA, or RD 69
financing, notwithstanding any other provisions of this Agreement, Buyer is not obligated to complete the 70
purchase of the Property unless Buyer has been given in accordance with HUD/FHA, VA, or RD requirements a 71
written statement by FHA, VA, RD or a Direct Endorsement lender, setting forth the appraised value of the 72
Property (excluding closing costs). Buyer shall pay the costs of any appraisal. If the appraised value of the 73
Property is less than the Purchase Price, Paragraph 6 above shall apply. 74

    Purpose of Appraisal. The appraised valuation is arrived at only to determine the maximum mortgage FHA, VA, 75
or RD will insure. FHA, VA, or RD do not warrant the value or the condition of the Property. Buyer agrees to 76
satisfy himself/herself that the price and condition of the Property are acceptable. 77

8. **EXTENSION OF CLOSING TO ACCOMMODATE REQUIREMENTS OF REGULATION Z OF THE TRUTH IN** 78
LENDING ACT. In the event the Annual Percentage Rate ("APR") of Buyer's Loan(s) varies from the APR initially 79
disclosed to Buyer in the Good Faith Estimate provided by Buyer's lender(s) by .125% or more in the case of a 80
fixed rate loan or .250% in an adjustable rate loan, the Closing Date shall be extended for up to four (4) days to 81
accommodate the requirements of Regulation Z of the Truth in Lending Act. This paragraph shall survive Buyer's 82
waiver of the Financing Contingency. 83

Initials: BUYER: _____ Date: _____ SELLER: _____ Date: _____

        BUYER: _____ Date: _____ SELLER: _____ Date: _____

EARNEST MONEY. The financing contingency will also state the seller's obligation to return the earnest money to the buyer if the purchase agreement is terminated because the buyer's loan application is denied. To receive a refund of the earnest money, the buyer must provide the seller with a written confirmation from the buyer's lender stating that the buyer's loan application was denied and the reasons for the denial.

LENDER-REQUIRED INSPECTIONS. Before approving a loan application, many lenders require the property to be inspected, so a financing contingency may describe how a lender-required inspection will be handled. The contingency will state that the seller agrees to allow this type of inspection. It will also say whether the seller will pay for the inspection (usually not).

If the inspection report says that repairs are needed, the lender may require the repairs to be completed as a condition of loan approval. If the seller opts not to pay for these repairs, the buyer can cancel the agreement without losing the good faith deposit.

APPRAISAL PROVISIONS. Because the buyer's loan amount depends in part on the appraised value of the property, the financing contingency usually addresses the parties' options in the event of a low appraisal. Typically, the contingency will provide that if the appraised value is lower than the price the buyer agreed to pay, the seller must either obtain a reappraisal that matches or exceeds the agreed price, or else reduce the price to the appraised amount. Otherwise, the buyer can terminate the purchase and sale agreement without forfeiting the earnest money.

Note that if there is a low appraisal in an FHA or RD transaction, the buyer can't be required to go through with the purchase even if the seller is willing to reduce the price (although the buyer may choose to buy the property at the reduced price). If the seller can get a reappraisal that indicates the property is worth the originally agreed price, the buyer will be obligated to proceed with the transaction; but the FHA and RD programs require this reappraisal to be made by the same appraiser who initially submitted the low appraisal.

See Chapter 4 for a more general discussion of the low appraisal problem.

TRUTH IN LENDING ACT. Under the federal Truth in Lending Act, if the annual percentage rate (APR) on the buyer's loan differs significantly from the APR that was initially disclosed to the buyer in the good faith estimate, the lender must disclose this change to the buyer at least three days before closing. The financing contingency may contain a provision that will extend closing by up to four days, if necessary, to accommodate this requirement. This provision remains effective even if the buyer waives the financing contingency.

SELLER FINANCING. If the seller is going to provide the buyer's financing, the purchase and sale agreement normally won't have a financing contingency. A different type of addendum, such as the payment terms addendum in Chapter 7 (Figure 7.2), should be used to set forth the terms of the seller financing. The financing forms that are going to be used—the real estate contract, or the promissory note and deed of trust—must also be attached to the purchase and sale agreement. It will be a breach of contract if the seller fails to provide financing on the agreed terms.

INSPECTION CONTINGENCIES

Another very common type of contingency in residential purchase and sale agreements is an inspection contingency. (See Figure 8.2.) The contract may be made contingent on one or more expert inspections of the property: for example, a structural inspection, a geological inspection, a hazardous substances inspection, and/or a pest control inspection.

An inspection contingency should establish:

- which party is responsible for ordering and paying for the inspection,
- when and how the buyer will give the seller notice of disapproval of the inspection report,
- whether the seller has the option of making repairs, and
- a time limit for reinspection by the buyer if the seller makes repairs.

APPROVAL OR DISAPPROVAL. Most inspection contingencies provide that if the buyer fails to notify the seller that he disapproves the inspection report before the deadline, the buyer will be deemed to have approved the report.

If the buyer disapproves the inspection report, the seller may be given the opportunity to repair the problems noted in the report. If so, the seller will have a certain period—three days, for example—to notify the buyer whether she will make the requested repairs. If the seller chooses to make the repairs, the purchase and sale agreement becomes binding and the buyer must go ahead with the purchase.

The seller's repairs are generally subject to reinspection and approval by the same inspector who prepared the original report. The reinspection is usually paid for by the buyer.

FIG. 8.2   INSPECTION CONTINGENCY ADDENDUM

Form 35
Inspection Addendum
Rev. 8/11
Page 1 of 2

INSPECTION ADDENDUM TO PURCHASE AND SALE AGREEMENT

The following is part of the Purchase and Sale Agreement dated _____ 1

between _____ ("Buyer") 2

and _____ ("Seller") 3

concerning _____ (the "Property"). 4

1. ☐ **a. INSPECTION CONTINGENCY.** This Agreement is conditioned on Buyer's subjective satisfaction with 5
inspections of the Property and the improvements on the Property. Buyer's inspections may include, at 6
Buyer's option and without limitation, the structural, mechanical and general condition of the improvements 7
to the Property, compliance with building and zoning codes, an inspection of the Property for hazardous 8
materials, a pest inspection, and a soils/stability inspection. 9

Buyer's Obligations. All inspections are to be (a) ordered by Buyer, (b) performed by inspectors of Buyer's 10
choice, and (c) completed at Buyer's expense. Buyer shall not alter the Property or any improvements on the 11
Property without first obtaining Seller's permission. Buyer is solely responsible for interviewing and selecting 12
all inspectors. Buyer shall restore the Property and all improvements on the Property to the same condition 13
they were in prior to the inspection. Buyer shall be responsible for all damages resulting from any inspection 14
of the Property performed on Buyer's behalf. 15

BUYER'S NOTICE. This inspection contingency **SHALL CONCLUSIVELY BE DEEMED WAIVED** unless 16
within _____ days (10 days if not filled in) after mutual acceptance of this Agreement (the "Initial 17
Inspection Period"), Buyer gives notice (1) approving the inspection and waiving this contingency; (2) 18
disapproving the inspection and terminating the Agreement; (3) that Buyer will conduct additional 19
inspections; or (4) proposing repairs to the property or modifications to the Agreement. If Buyer disapproves 20
the inspection and terminates the Agreement, the Earnest Money shall be refunded to Buyer. If Buyer 21
proposes repairs to the property or modifications to the Agreement, including adjustments to the purchase 22
price or credits for repairs to be performed after closing, the parties shall negotiate as set forth in paragraph 23
1.c, below. The parties may use NWMLS Form 35R to give notices required by this Addendum. 24

ATTENTION BUYER: If Buyer fails to give timely notice, then this inspection contingency shall be deemed 25
waived and Seller shall not be obligated to make any repairs or modifications. 26

b. Additional Inspections. If an inspector so recommends, Buyer may obtain further evaluation of any 27
item by a specialist at Buyer's option and expense if, on or before the end of the Initial Inspection Period, 28
Buyer provides Seller a copy of the inspector's recommendation and notice that Buyer will seek additional 29
inspections. If Buyer gives timely notice of additional inspections, Buyer shall have _____ (5 days if 30
not filled in) after giving the notice to obtain the additional inspection(s) by a specialist. 31

c. Buyer's Requests for Repairs or Modifications. If Buyer requests repairs or modifications under 32
paragraph 1.a above, the parties shall negotiate as set forth in this paragraph. All requests, responses, and 33
replies made in accordance with the following procedures are irrevocable for the time period provided. 34

(i) Seller's Response to Request for Repairs or Modifications. Seller shall have _____ days 35
(3 days if not filled in) after receipt of Buyer's request for repairs or modifications to give notice that 36
Seller (a) agrees to the repairs or modifications proposed by Buyer; (b) agrees to some of the repairs or 37
modifications proposed by Buyer; (c) rejects all repairs or modifications proposed by Buyer; or (d) offers 38
different or additional repairs or modifications. If Seller agrees to the terms of Buyer's request for repairs 39
or modifications, this contingency shall be satisfied and Buyer's Reply shall not be necessary. If Seller 40
does not agree to all of Buyer's repairs or modifications, Buyer shall have an opportunity to reply, as 41
follows: 42

(ii) Buyer's Reply. If Seller does not agree to all of the repairs or modifications proposed by Buyer, 43
Buyer shall have _____ days (3 days if not filled in) from either the day Buyer receives Seller's 44
response or, if Seller fails to respond, the day Seller's response period ends, whichever is earlier, to (a) 45
accept the Seller's response at which time this contingency shall be satisfied; (b) agree with the Seller 46
on other remedies; or (c) disapprove the inspection and terminate the Agreement, in which event the 47
Earnest Money shall be refunded to Buyer. 48

Initials: BUYER: _____   Date: _____   SELLER: _____   Date: _____

BUYER: _____   Date: _____   SELLER: _____   Date: _____

Form 35
Inspection Addendum
Rev. 8/11
Page 2 of 2

INSPECTION ADDENDUM TO PURCHASE AND SALE AGREEMENT
Continued

ATTENTION BUYER: These time periods for negotiating repairs or modifications shall not repeat. The 49
parties must either reach a written agreement or Buyer must terminate this Agreement by the Buyer's Reply 50
deadline set forth in paragraph 1.c.ii. Buyer's inaction during Buyer's reply period shall result in waiver of this 51
inspection condition, in which case Seller shall not be obligated to make any repairs or modifications 52
whatsoever AND THIS CONTINGENCY SHALL BE DEEMED WAIVED. 53

d. Repairs. If Seller agrees to make the repairs proposed by Buyer, then repairs shall be accomplished at 54
Seller's expense in a commercially reasonable manner prior to the Closing Date. In the case of hazardous 55
materials, "repair" means removal or treatment (including but not limited to removal or, at Seller's option, 56
decommissioning of any oil storage tanks) of the hazardous material at Seller's expense as recommended by 57
and under the direction of a licensed hazardous material engineer or other expert selected by Seller. Seller's 58
repairs are subject to reinspection and approval, prior to Closing, by the inspector who recommended the repair, 59
if Buyer elects to order and pay for such reinspection. If Buyer agrees to pay for any repairs prior to closing, the 60
parties are advised to seek the counsel of an attorney to review the terms of that agreement. 61

e. Oil Storage Tanks. Any inspection regarding oil storage tanks or contamination from such tanks shall be 62
limited solely to determining the presence or non-presence of oil storage tanks on the Property, unless otherwise 63
agreed in writing by Buyer and Seller. 64

f. Licensed Home Inspector. If the person performing the inspection is required to be licensed under Chapter 65
18.280 RCW, then that person must be so licensed. 66

2. ON-SITE SEWAGE DISPOSAL SYSTEMS ADVISORY. Buyer is advised that on-site sewage disposal systems, 67
including "septic systems," are subject to strict governmental regulation and occasional malfunction and even 68
failure. Buyer is advised to consider conducting an inspection of any on-site sewage system in addition to the 69
inspection of the Property provided by this Form 35 by including an appropriate on-site sewage disposal 70
inspection contingency such as NWMLS Form 22S (Septic Addendum). 71

3. ☐ NEIGHBORHOOD REVIEW CONTINGENCY. Buyer's inspection includes Buyer's subjective satisfaction 72
that the conditions of the neighborhood in which the Property is located are consistent with the Buyer's 73
intended use of the Property (the "Neighborhood Review"). The Neighborhood Review may include Buyer's 74
investigation of the schools, proximity to bus lines, availability of shopping, traffic patterns, noise, parking and 75
investigation of other neighborhood, environmental and safety conditions the Buyer may determine to be 76
relevant in deciding to purchase the Property. If Buyer does not give notice of disapproval of the 77
Neighborhood Review within _____ (3 days if not filled in) of mutual acceptance of the Agreement, 78
then this Neighborhood Review condition shall conclusively be deemed satisfied (waived). If Buyer gives a 79
timely notice of disapproval, then this Agreement shall terminate and the Earnest Money shall be refunded to 80
Buyer. 81

4. ☐ PREINSPECTION CONDUCTED. Buyer, prior to mutual acceptance of this Agreement, conducted a 82
building, hazardous substances, building and zoning code, pest or soils/stability inspection of the Property, 83
and closing of this Agreement is not conditioned on the results of such inspections. Buyer elects to buy the 84
Property in its present condition and acknowledges that the decision to purchase the property was based on 85
Buyer's prior inspection and that Buyer has not relied on representations by Seller, Listing Broker or Selling 86
Broker. 87

5. ☐ WAIVER OF INSPECTION. Buyer has been advised to obtain a building, hazardous substances, building 88
and zoning code, pest or soils/stability inspection, and to condition the closing of this Agreement on the 89
results of such inspections, but Buyer elects to waive the right and buy the Property in its present condition. 90
Buyer acknowledges that the decision to waive Buyer's inspection options was based on Buyer's personal 91
inspection and Buyer has not relied on representations by Seller, Listing Broker or Selling Broker. 92

Initials: BUYER: _____ Date: _____ SELLER: _____ Date: _____

BUYER: _____ Date: _____ SELLER: _____ Date: _____

FIG. 8.3   INSPECTION RESPONSE FORM

Form 35R
Inspection Response for Form 35
Rev.7/08
Page 1 of 1

INSPECTION RESPONSE FOR FORM 35

©Copyright 2008
Northwest Multiple Listing Service
ALL RIGHTS RESERVED

The following is part of the Purchase and Sale Agreement dated _____ , 200 _____

between _____ ("Buyer")

and _____ ("Seller")

concerning _____ ("the Property")

I. BUYER'S RESPONSE OR REQUEST FOR REPAIRS OR MODIFICATION.

☐ Buyer's inspection of the Property is approved and the inspection contingency is satisfied.

☐ Buyer's inspection of the Property is disapproved and the Agreement is terminated. The Earnest Money shall be refunded to Buyer.

☐ Buyer gives notice of an additional inspection. The inspector's recommendation is attached. The time for Buyer's response to the initial and additional inspection is extended as provided in paragraph 1(b) of Form 35.

☐ Buyer requests the following modifications and/or repairs. If Seller agrees to these modifications or repairs, the inspection contingency shall be deemed satisfied.

_____
_____
_____
_____
_____
_____
_____

| Buyer | Date | Buyer | Date |

If Buyer requests modifications and/or repairs, this Form 35R and any other addenda or notice pertaining to the modifications and/or repairs and amendment to the Agreement related to or resulting from the request for modifications and/or repairs shall become a part of the Agreement.

II. SELLER'S RESPONSE TO BUYER'S REQUEST FOR REPAIRS OR MODIFICATION.
Seller acknowledges receipt of Buyer's request for modification or repair, and responds as follows:

☐ Seller agrees to all of the modifications or repairs in Buyer's request for modification or repair. The inspection contingency is satisfied, the parties agree to proceed to Closing as provided in the Agreement, and Buyer's reply, below, is not necessary.

☐ Seller offers to repair only the following conditions:

_____
_____

☐ Seller rejects all proposals by Buyer.

☐ Seller rejects all proposals by Buyer, but proposes the following alternative modifications or repairs:

_____
_____
_____

| Seller | Date | Seller | Date |

III. BUYER'S REPLY TO SELLER'S RESPONSE.

☐ Buyer accepts Seller's response and agrees to proceed to Closing as provided in the Agreement.

☐ Buyer rejects Seller's response. Buyer disapproves of the inspection and this Agreement is terminated. The Earnest Money shall be refunded to Buyer.

☐ Buyer rejects Seller's response, but offers the attached alternative proposal for modification or repair. Buyer acknowledges that the inspection contingency will be waived unless Buyer and Seller reach written agreement or Buyer gives notice disapproving the inspection and terminating the Agreement before the deadline in paragraph 1(c)(ii) of the inspection contingency (NWMLS Form 35).

| Buyer | Date | Buyer | Date |

If the seller decides not to make the requested repairs, the buyer then must choose whether to waive the condition and proceed with the transaction, or else terminate the purchase and sale agreement.

Sometimes a seller responds to the buyer by offering to make only some of the requested repairs, or by offering to modify their contract in some way (for example, by lowering the purchase price). It is then up to the buyer to accept or reject the seller's offer. The parties may go back and forth in this way several times before a compromise is reached or the buyer decides to give up and terminate the contract.

OPPORTUNITY TO REPAIR VS. BUYER'S SATISFACTION. After the buyer receives an inspection report, whether he's required to give the seller an opportunity to make repairs will depend on the terms of the inspection contingency that they included in their purchase and sale agreement.

If an inspection contingency form provides that the seller must be given an opportunity to make repairs if she chooses to do so, the form will typically require the buyer's requests for repairs to be based on specific problems revealed in the inspection report. The seller may be entitled to a copy of the relevant parts of the report that justify the buyer's requests. If the report shows that the inspector didn't find any problems, then the buyer is usually required to go ahead with the transaction.

Other inspection contingency forms have no such requirements. For example, the Northwest Multiple Listing Service inspection contingency addendum, shown in Figure 8.2, allows the buyer to terminate the transaction without offering the seller a chance to make repairs. It makes the purchase and sale agreement contingent on the buyer's subjective satisfaction with the inspection report. After reviewing the report, the buyer may choose to ask the seller to make repairs or to modify their contract; but the buyer is under no obligation to continue with the transaction if he has changed his mind about buying the property. He can withdraw even if the inspection report indicates that there are no problems with the property whatsoever. In fact, the seller isn't entitled to see a copy of the report if the buyer doesn't want to show it to her.

NOTIFICATION FORM. The NWMLS inspection addendum form has a corresponding notification form, which is shown in Figure 8.3. The buyer uses this form to give the seller notice of her approval or disapproval of the inspection report. The buyer also uses the notification form to request repairs if she chooses to do so, and the seller will use the same form to respond.

NEIGHBORHOOD REVIEW. In addition to inspecting characteristics of the property itself, the buyer may also want to inspect the neighborhood. The NWMLS inspection addendum contains a neighborhood review contingency, which gives the buyer an opportunity to perform a neighborhood review, looking at characteristics such as schools, public transportation, and traffic patterns. The buyer has three days to notify the seller that he disapproves of the neighborhood; otherwise the contingency is waived.

CODE VIOLATIONS. Sellers should be aware that if an inspection reveals violations of the building code or other laws, public authorities could order them to correct the violations, whether or not the sale to the buyer proceeds.

"AS IS" SALES. Of course, a buyer might want to purchase the seller's property "as is," without having any expert inspections done. If so, the inspection addendum form shown in Figure 8.2 has a waiver provision that can be checked. In this provision, the buyer acknowledges that his decision to waive his inspection options was based on his own inspection of the property, not on any representations made by the seller or the real estate licensees.

SALE OF BUYER'S HOME CONTINGENCIES

Unless you're helping them buy their first home, your buyers will usually have to sell their current home before buying a new one. For one thing, they probably need to sell their current home to generate the cash for the downpayment on the new home. Also, few buyers can afford the mortgage payments on two houses at the same time. For both of these reasons, it's very common to make the sale of the buyer's current home a condition of the contract for the purchase of the new home.

Depending on the terms of the purchase and sale agreement, this condition may actually be a "hidden contingency." In other words, the agreement may be contingent on the sale of the buyer's home even though that contingency is not expressly stated in the agreement.

> **EXAMPLE:** Wilder has agreed to purchase Greenbaum's home. The sale is contingent on financing: unless Wilder obtains a purchase loan from an institutional lender, the contract will not be binding.
>
> When Wilder applies for a loan, she doesn't have enough cash for the downpayment she'll be required to make. She plans to sell her current home to get the necessary cash. The lender processes the application and approves the loan on the condition that Wilder obtain the necessary cash

FIG. 8.4 SALE OF BUYER'S PROPERTY CONTINGENCY ADDENDUM

Form 22B
Buyer's Property Contingency Addendum
Rev. 8/11
Page 1 of 2

**BUYER'S SALE OF PROPERTY CONTINGENCY ADDENDUM TO
PURCHASE & SALE AGREEMENT**

The following is part of the Purchase and Sale Agreement dated _____ 1

between _____ ("Buyer") 2

and _____ ("Seller") 3

concerning _____ (the "Property"). 4

1. **CONTINGENT ON SALE OF BUYER'S PROPERTY.** This Agreement is contingent on Buyer selling Buyer's 5
   property at _____ 6
   City of _____ , State of _____ (the "Contingency Property") 7
   on or before _____ (if not filled in, 45 days after mutual acceptance of this Agreement) (the 8
   "Contingency Period"). Buyer shall list the Contingency Property for sale on a multiple listing service in the area 9
   serving the property with a licensed real estate firm within 5 days after mutual acceptance of this Agreement. If 10
   Buyer fails to do so, this contingency shall be deemed waived and paragraph 7 below shall apply. If Buyer has not 11
   sold the Contingency Property or given written notice waiving this contingency by the end of the Contingency 12
   Period, then this Agreement shall terminate and the Earnest Money shall be refunded to Buyer. 13

2. **WHEN SELLER'S CONSENT IS REQUIRED ON SALE OF THE CONTINGENCY PROPERTY.** Buyer must 14
   obtain Seller's written consent before Buyer accepts any offer for the sale of the Contingency Property that: 15
   (a) is contingent on the sale or closing of that (second) buyer's property; and/or 16
   (b) has a closing date less than 30 or more than 45 days from the date of mutual acceptance of the offer on the 17
   Contingency Property. 18
   If Buyer accepts any such offer without Seller's written consent, this Agreement shall terminate and the Earnest 19
   Money shall be forfeited to the Seller. 20

3. **LOAN APPLICATION.** If this Agreement is contingent on Buyer obtaining financing pursuant to Form 22A 21
   (Financing Addendum), Buyer shall make written application for the Loan(s) (defined in Form 22A) and pay the 22
   application fee, if required, for the subject Property ☐ within _____ days (5 days if not filled in) after mutual 23
   acceptance of this Agreement, or ☐ within _____ days (5 days if not filled in) after Buyer satisfies the 24
   contingency in this Addendum ("Satisfaction") (from mutual acceptance if neither box checked), for the Loan(s) to 25
   pay the balance of the purchase price. If Buyer is not required to apply for the Loan(s) until after Satisfaction, the 26
   timelines in Form 22A shall not begin until Satisfaction. This paragraph 3 supersedes the requirement for Buyer's 27
   loan application in Form 22A. 28

4. **EARNEST MONEY RETURN.** If the sale of the Contingency Property fails to close through no fault of Buyer 29
   before expiration of the Contingency Period in paragraph 1, then this contingency shall be reinstated until the 30
   Contingency Period has expired. If the sale of the Contingency Property fails to close through no fault of the 31
   Buyer after expiration of the Contingency Period, then this Agreement shall terminate and the Earnest Money 32
   shall be refunded to Buyer, provided, however, that the Buyer shall have the sole privilege and option of 33
   proceeding with the consummation of this Agreement without regard to the failure of the sale of the Contingency 34
   Property to close and provided further that if Buyer chooses to proceed with this Agreement without having sold 35
   the Contingency Property, then paragraph 7 below shall apply (and in the case of new construction, paragraph 8 36
   shall apply). Notwithstanding the computation of time and manner of giving notice set forth in this Purchase and 37
   Sale Agreement, Buyer must give notice to Seller within 12 hours of learning that the sale of the Contingency 38
   Property has failed or as soon thereafter as reasonably practicable, but in no event later than 24 hours. Such 39
   notice must be given regardless of whether Buyer chooses to proceed with this Agreement. Such notice may be 40
   given by telephone to Listing Broker or to Seller, or by such other method by which notice will be received within 41
   12 hours, including, but not limited to, facsimile transmission or electronic transmission. If Buyer does not give 42
   such notice within the foregoing time limit, then Buyer shall be in default and the Default and Attorneys' Fees 43
   clauses in the Agreement shall apply. For the purposes of this Addendum, the terms "sell," "selling" and "sold" 44
   shall mean that Buyer has entered into a valid and enforceable agreement for the purchase and sale of the 45
   Contingency Property. 46

Initials: BUYER: _____ Date: _____ SELLER: _____ Date: _____

BUYER: _____ Date: _____ SELLER: _____ Date: _____

Form 22B
Buyer's Property Contingency Addendum
Rev. 8/11
Page 2 of 2

**BUYER'S SALE OF PROPERTY CONTINGENCY ADDENDUM TO
PURCHASE & SALE AGREEMENT**
Continued

5. **PROPERTY REMAINS ON MARKET.** It is agreed that Seller may keep the Property on the market and continue 47
    to show it until Seller has received notice that Buyer has entered into an agreement to sell the Contingency 48
    Property or Buyer waives this contingency. If prior to that time, Seller accepts another offer to purchase the 49
    Property, Seller shall give written notice that Seller has accepted the new offer and shall give Buyer _____ 50
    days (5 days if not filled in) or by the expiration of the contingency in paragraph 1, whichever is earlier (the "Bump 51
    Period") to waive this Contingency or this Agreement shall terminate and the Earnest Money shall be refunded to 52
    the Buyer. Seller's notice shall be on NWMLS Form No. 44, Bump Notice, or otherwise meet the requirements of 53
    this Addendum, and Buyer's reply shall be on NWMLS Form No. 46, Bump Reply, or otherwise meet the 54
    requirements of this Addendum. 55

6. **CONTINGENCY SATISFIED OR WAIVED.** Buyer must give notice to Seller within 2 days of entering into an 56
    agreement to sell the Contingency Property (i.e., the contingency is "satisfied"). If Buyer gives notice that Buyer 57
    has entered into an agreement to sell the Contingency Property or that Buyer waives this contingency before 58
    expiration of the Bump Period, Buyer shall have the continued right and obligation to purchase the Property (see 59
    paragraph 7 below). 60

    IF THE CONTINGENCY PROPERTY HAS BEEN SOLD, BUYER'S NOTICE SHALL BE VOID UNLESS 61
    ACCOMPANIED BY A COPY OF ALL PAGES OF THE PURCHASE AND SALE AGREEMENT FOR THE 62
    CONTINGENCY PROPERTY. 63

7. **NEW CLOSING DATE; BUYER'S WAIVER.** If the Contingency Property is sold and this contingency is satisfied, 64
    the sale of the Property shall be closed 3 days after the closing of the sale of the Contingency Property. If Buyer 65
    waives this contingency, the sale of the Property shall close 30 days after the date of Buyer's waiver. BY 66
    WAIVING THIS CONTINGENCY, BUYER ALSO WAIVES ALL OTHER CONDITIONS IN THE PURCHASE AND 67
    SALE AGREEMENT (INCLUDING, WITHOUT LIMITATION, ANY FINANCING OR OTHER CONTINGENCY). IF 68
    BUYER THEREAFTER FAILS TO CLOSE THIS SALE WITHIN 30 DAYS FOR ANY REASON, BUYER SHALL 69
    BE IN DEFAULT. 70

8. **CLOSING DATE FOR NEW CONSTRUCTION.** If the Buyer waives the above contingency without having sold 71
    the Contingency Property, and, at the time of the waiver, the Property which is the subject of this Purchase and 72
    Sale Agreement is not completed with a Certificate of Occupancy (CO) or its equivalent has not been issued by 73
    the applicable government authority, then Buyer shall close within _____ days (5 days if not filled in), of 74
    notice from Seller to Buyer that a Certificate of Occupancy, or equivalent, has been issued or within 30 days of 75
    waiver, whichever is later. 76

9. **CLOSING DATE.** The Closing Date set forth in this Addendum shall supersede the Closing Date set forth in the 77
    Agreement. 78

10. **OTHER.** 79

80

81

82

83

84

85

86

87

88

89

90

Initials: BUYER: _____ Date: _____ SELLER: _____ Date: _____

BUYER: _____ Date: _____ SELLER: _____ Date: _____

before closing. If Wilder is unable to sell her home before the closing date set in her contract with Greenbaum, she won't have the cash for the downpayment and the lender will refuse to fund the loan. Thus, the sale of Greenbaum's home is actually contingent on the sale of Wilder's home, even though this contingency was not stated in their purchase and sale agreement.

Naturally, it's important to state the terms of any contingency clearly rather than leave it unstated or hidden behind another contingency. The seller needs to be aware of all the contingencies of the sale before he can make an informed decision about whether or not to accept the buyer's offer. This is particularly important when the buyer must sell her own property before completing the purchase. If this contingency is not made clear to the seller, the seller may believe that the buyer has a much better chance of getting a loan than she actually does. If the transaction doesn't close because the buyer is unable to sell her home (and thus get the loan), the seller could claim that by failing to disclose the hidden contingency, you misrepresented the buyer's financial ability to complete the purchase.

ELEMENTS. Some purchase and sale agreements have pre-printed clauses to fill out in order to make the offer contingent on the sale of the buyer's home. Or an addendum may be used, such as the one shown in Figure 8.4. In any case, the contingency provision should address the issues that exist with any contingency (how a party fulfills the contingency, relevant deadlines, method of notifying the parties, and what happens if a party fulfills or waives the contingency). In addition, with a sale of buyer's home contingency, the parties need to state what will happen if the seller gets another offer during the contingency period.

ACCEPTANCE OR CLOSING. There are two ways to set up this type of contingency provision. The sale can be made contingent on the buyer's acceptance of an offer to buy his current home, or on the closing of the sale of his current home. The seller will usually prefer to base fulfillment of the contingency on the buyer's acceptance of an offer. That way, the seller doesn't have to wait until the buyer's sale closes to know whether she and the buyer have a binding contract. If the buyer doesn't get an acceptable offer for his house within a certain period—for example, 30 days—then his agreement with the seller can be terminated.

From the buyer's point of view, it's preferable to base fulfillment of the contingency on the actual closing of his sale and the receipt of enough cash from that sale to close the transaction with the seller.

EXAMPLE: Whitfield is offering to buy Mayer's home for $189,000, with a $19,000 downpayment. The purchase and sale agreement will be contingent on the sale of Whitfield's current home.

Whitfield wants the contingency clause to be written so that the condition will be fulfilled only if the sale of his home actually closes within 90 days and he nets enough cash to make his $19,000 downpayment. He's afraid of what would happen if the condition were fulfilled when he accepted an offer for his home, but that sale failed to close for some reason. He wouldn't be able to go through with his purchase of Mayer's home (because he wouldn't have the money for the downpayment). As a result, Whitfield would be in default on the purchase and sale agreement, and he would forfeit his earnest money deposit to Mayer.

On the other hand, Mayer wants the contingency clause to be written so that the condition will be fulfilled if Whitfield accepts an offer on his current home within 30 days of signing the purchase and sale agreement with Mayer. Mayer doesn't want to wait up to 90 days to see whether Whitfield's sale is actually going to close. He wants to know that they have an enforceable contract much sooner than that. Otherwise, he would rather wait for another offer.

Many contingency forms try to address both of these conflicting needs. For instance, the form shown in Figure 8.4 states that the contingency will be fulfilled when the buyer accepts an offer on his house. However, if the sale of the buyer's house fails to close through no fault of the buyer, the purchase and sale agreement will terminate and the earnest money deposit will be refunded to the buyer.

Another way the buyer can handle this problem is by applying to a lender for a **swing loan** (also called a bridge loan or gap loan). This loan will provide the buyer with the funds to close the purchase of the new house. It creates a lien against the old house, and the buyer will pay it off whenever the sale of the old house eventually closes.

DEADLINES. The conflicting interests of the buyer and the seller are also apparent when you fill in the time periods in this type of contingency clause or addendum. The buyer will want as much time as possible to fulfill the contingency, so that her house can be sold for the highest possible price. The seller, on the other hand, will usually want the present transaction to close as soon as possible, so that he'll have the money from the sale more quickly. So the parties must agree on a compromise that will give the buyer a reasonable length of time to market her house without delaying the resolution of the present transaction (either a successful closing or the failure of the condition) for too long.

It's extremely important to make sure that the dates in the contingency clause agree with the other dates in the purchase and sale agreement. For example, the contingency should not give the buyer 120 days to sell her home if the current sale is supposed to close within 90 days.

BUMP CLAUSES. When a purchase and sale agreement is contingent on the sale of the buyer's home, it's common to include a provision that gives the seller the right to keep the house on the market and to accept another offer. This provision, known as a "bump clause," may be used with any type of contingency, but is most commonly used with offers that are contingent on the sale of the buyer's home. That's because this contingency tends to involve greater uncertainty and a longer wait than other types. While you can usually predict whether a buyer will be able to get a loan or whether a pest inspection will be satisfactory, it's harder to predict whether a buyer will be able to sell his home by a certain date on terms that will generate a certain amount of cash.

A bump clause helps reconcile the buyer's need for time to sell his current home with the seller's need for a timely resolution of her contingent contract with the buyer. A bump clause may also solve the problem of whether to make the contract contingent on the buyer's acceptance of an offer or on the closing of the sale of the buyer's home. Essentially, a bump clause allows the seller to accept an uncertain offer without having to take her property off the market.

The contingency addendum in Figure 8.4 includes a bump clause. This bump clause states that the seller will continue to actively market her property until the buyer notifies the seller that the contingency has been satisfied or waived. If the seller receives a second offer during this period, the seller will notify the buyer of her intention to accept the second offer. The buyer is given a short period of time—the default period is five days—to notify the seller that the contingency has been either satisfied or waived. Otherwise, the transaction will terminate and the deposit will be returned to the buyer.

SECOND BUYER'S ADDENDUM. Before the seller sends the first buyer a bump notice, the seller may require the second buyer to waive any contingencies the second sales agreement is subject to. This will protect the seller against bumping one contingent buyer in order to enter into a contract with another contingent buyer, and ultimately losing both buyers. A form such as the one shown in Figure 8.5 can be used for this purpose. This second buyer's addendum states that the

FIG. 8.5   SECOND BUYER'S ADDENDUM

NWMLS Form 39
Second Buyer's Addendum
Revised 04/01
Page 1 of 1

SECOND BUYER'S ADDENDUM

©Copyright 2001
Northwest Multiple Listing Service
ALL RIGHTS RESERVED

The following Addendum is part of the Purchase and Sale Agreement dated _____ , 200 ____   1

(the "Second Sale Agreement") between _____ ("Second Buyer")   2

and _____ ("Seller")   3

concerning _____ ("the Property").   4

1. **PROPERTY SUBJECT TO PRIOR CONTINGENT SALE.** Second Buyer acknowledges that the Property is subject to a   5
prior purchase and sale agreement (the "Prior Sale") between Seller and _____   6
("First Buyer"). The Prior Sale is contingent on First Buyer's entering into an agreement for the sale of First Buyer's   7
property ("the Contingency Property") on or before _____ . The Prior Sale gives Seller the right to con-   8
tinue marketing the Property and provides that if Seller receives another offer on the Property that is acceptable to   9
Seller, then written notice of Seller's intent to proceed to Closing on the second offer may be given to First Buyer on   10
NWMLS Form No. 44 Notice to Remove Contingency or its equivalent (the "Bump Notice"). If, after receipt of the   11
Bump Notice, First Buyer does not give timely notice that (i) First Buyer has sold the Contingency Property or (ii) that   12
First Buyer waives the Sale of Property Contingency, then the Prior Sale will terminate, and this Second Sale   13
Agreement may proceed to Closing.   14

2. **PROPERTY SUBJECT TO PRIOR CONTINGENT SALE.** Before a Bump Notice is given to First Buyer, Second   15
Buyer shall **waive** the contingencies checked below. The Bump Notice shall not be given to First Buyer until Seller has   16
received written notice of Second Buyer's waiver or satisfaction of all the contingencies checked below.   17

☐ a. Second Buyer's approval of a "Seller Disclosure Statement" (e.g., NWMLS Form No. 17).   18

☐ b. Second Buyer's approval of the written results of (i) a general and structural inspection of the Property, (ii) an   19
inspection of hazardous materials, and (iii) any other inspection of the Property or the improvements on the   20
Property, including but not limited to roof, pest, soils/stability and septic/drainfield inspections.   21

☐ c. Second Buyer's approval of a review of the neighborhood's conditions to determine if the Property can be   22
used in a manner consistent with Second Buyer's intended use.   23

☐ d. Second Buyer's approval of a Condominium Resale Certificate (e.g., NWMLS Form No. 27).   24

☐ e. Second Buyer's financing condition, if any.   25

☐ f. Second Buyer's approval of _____   26

3. **BUMP NOTICE TO BE GIVEN UPON RECEIPT OF SECOND BUYER'S WAIVER.** Within _____ days (24 hours   27
if not filled in) of Seller's receipt from Second Buyer of written notice that **all** contingencies checked in paragraph 2 of   28
this Addendum have been satisfied or waived, a Bump Notice shall be given to First Buyer pursuant to NWMLS   29
procedures for giving Bump Notices. Seller shall inform Second Buyer of the results of any notice Seller receives from   30
First Buyer in response to the Bump Notice. **If Second Buyer attempts, without legal cause, to withdraw or cancel**   31
this Second Sale Agreement after the Bump Notice, then Second Buyer shall be in breach of this Second Sale   32
Agreement and the Default and Attorneys' Fees provisions of this Second Sale Agreement shall apply.

4. **FIRST BUYER'S CONTINGENCY WAIVED.** If First Buyer responds to the Bump Notice by giving notice that First   34
Buyer will remove or satisfy First Buyer's Sale of Property Contingency and/or that First Buyer will proceed with the   35
purchase of the Property, then this Second Sale Agreement shall terminate, the Earnest Money shall be refunded to   36
Second Buyer, and Seller and Second Buyer shall have no further obligations to each other.

5. **FIRST BUYER'S CONTINGENCY NOT WAIVED.** If First Buyer responds to the Bump Notice by giving notice that   38
Buyer will **not** remove the Sale of Property Contingency and/or that First Buyer will **not** proceed with the purchase of   39
the Property, then the Prior Sale shall terminate and this Second Sale Agreement shall close according to the terms   40
and conditions set forth in the Second Sale Agreement.

6. **THIS ADDENDUM CONTROLS.** All other terms and conditions of the Second Sale Agreement remain in full force   42
and effect. In the event of conflict between the terms of this Addendum and any other term of this Second Sale   43
Agreement, this Addendum shall control.   44

Initials: BUYER: _____ DATE: _____ SELLER: _____ DATE: _____   45

BUYER: _____ DATE: _____ SELLER: _____ DATE: _____   46

FIG. 8.6   BUMP NOTICE (FROM SELLER TO FIRST BUYER)

Form 44
Bump Notice
Rev. 7/10
Page 1 of 1

NOTICE TO REMOVE CONTINGENCY
(Notice that Seller has accepted another offer.)

©Copyright 2010
Northwest Multiple Listing Service
ALL RIGHTS RESERVED

TO: _____ FROM: _____ 1
SELLING FIRM NO. 1   BRANCH   LISTING FIRM   BRANCH

_____ _____ 2
SELLING BROKER   LISTING BROKER

_____ _____ 3
ADDRESS   ADDRESS

_____ _____ 4
CITY   CITY

_____ _____ 5
PHONE   FAX   PHONE   FAX

Under the Purchase and Sale Agreement dated _____ 6

_____ "Buyer" 7
FIRST BUYER'S NAME

agreed to purchase from _____ "Seller" 8

the Property located at _____ , 9
STREET

_____ Washington. 10
CITY

The Agreement includes a "Buyer's Sale of Property Contingency" Addendum (Form 22B) which provides that if Seller 11
accepts another offer to purchase the Property, Seller shall give notice that Seller has accepted the new offer. 12

NOTICE IS HEREBY GIVEN that Seller has accepted another offer. 13

Unless Buyer gives notice before expiration of the Bump Period that Buyer has waived or satisfied (by selling the 14
Contingency Property) said contingency, the Agreement shall terminate. 15

Attached is NWMLS Form No. 46 "Notice from Contingent Buyer to Seller" for Buyer's convenience in replying to this notice. 16

17

Listing Firm send copy to: 18

_____ _____
SELLING FIRM NO. 2   SELLER   DATE

19

_____ _____
SELLING BROKER NO. 2   ADDRESS

20

_____ _____
ADDRESS   CITY

21

_____ _____
PHONE   FAX   PHONE   FAX

INSTRUCTIONS: 22

1. **THE LISTING FIRM MUST:** 23
   A. Deliver Form 39 Second Buyer's Addendum to the Second Selling Firm on or before mutual acceptance of 24
      the second offer. 25
   B. Prepare (fill in) this form. 26
   C. Attach a Form 46 Bump Reply. 27
   D. Deliver a completed Form 44 (this Form) and Form 46 to the First Selling Firm. 28
   E. Send a copy of the completed Form 44 to the Second Selling Firm. 29
   F. Phone the First and Second Selling Firms and advise that the above has been done. 30

2. **THE FIRST SELLING FIRM MUST** make every effort to notify the First Buyer that this notice has been received. 31
   The above deadline for reply is effective regardless of whether (or when) the First Selling Firm notifies the First 32
   Buyer. 33

FIG. 8.7   BUMP REPLY (FROM FIRST BUYER TO SELLER)

NOTICE FROM CONTINGENT BUYER TO SELLER

Buyer: _____   1

Seller: _____   2

Property: _____   3

_____   4

(NOTE: Use this box to reply to NWMLS Form 44 Bump Notice.)   5

❑   1.   **SELLER'S NOTICE RECEIVED.** In response to Seller's notice that Seller has accepted another   6
offer on the Property (the "Bump Notice"), Buyer hereby gives notice as follows: 7

❑   A.   **BUYER'S PROPERTY SOLD - CONTINGENCY SATISFIED.** Buyer has accepted an offer   8
on Buyer's property which is not contingent on sale of another property and which calls for   9
closing no less than 30 days or more than 45 days from the date Buyer accepted the offer   10
or which has otherwise been consented to by Seller. **Attached hereto is a copy of the**   11
complete purchase & sale agreement. Buyer understands this notice is not effective if the   12
purchase and sale agreement is not attached. The Property shall now be removed from the   13
market. If the sale of Buyer's property fails to close, Buyer will give notice to Seller within 12   14
hours of learning that the sale of Buyer's property has failed, as required by NWMLS Form   15
22B, Buyer's Sale of Property Contingency Addendum.   16

❑   B.   **BUYER'S PROPERTY NOT SOLD - CONTINGENCY WAIVED.** Even though Buyer has   17
not accepted an offer on Buyer's property, Buyer hereby waives that contingency and   18
agrees to close this sale within 30 days of the date of this notice to Seller (or whatever other   19
time limit is specified in Paragraph 8 of the Buyer's Sale of Property Contingency   20
Addendum to the Agreement). Buyer understands that by waiving this contingency, **BUYER**   21
WAIVES ALL OTHER CONTINGENCIES (INCLUDING FINANCING AND INSPECTION   22
CONTINGENCIES). The Property shall now be removed from the market.   23

❑   C.   **CONTINGENCY NOT WAIVED.** Buyer does not waive the contingency. The Agreement is   24
terminated and the Earnest Money shall be refunded to Buyer.   25

NOTICE FROM CONTINGENT BUYER TO SELLER
Continued

(NOTE: Use this box when there has not been a Bump Notice.) 26

☐ **2. NO NOTICE RECEIVED FROM SELLER - BUYER'S PROPERTY SOLD - CONTINGENCY SATISFIED:** Buyer has accepted an offer on Buyer's property which is not contingent on the sale of another property and which calls for closing in no less than 30 days or more than 45 days from date of acceptance or which has otherwise been consented to by Seller. **Attached is a copy of the complete purchase & sale agreement for sale of Buyer's property.** Buyer understands this notice is void if it is not attached. If the sale of Buyer's property fails to close, Buyer will give notice to Seller within 12 hours of learning that the sale of Buyer's property has failed, as required by NWMLS Form 22B, Buyer's Sale of Property Contingency. 27 28 29 30 31 32 33 34

Acknowledgement of Receipt from Buyer

_____ 35
Buyer

_____
Date Received

_____ 36
Date

_____
Name of Listing Firm

_____ 37
Address

_____
Signature

_____ 38
City   Phone

INSTRUCTIONS: 39

1. **THE FIRST SELLING FIRM MUST:** 40
   A. Prepare (fill in) this form. (Remember: If 1A or 2 is checked, the appropriate documents <u>must be attached</u>, 41 or this Notice is <u>void</u>). 42
   B. Have this form signed by the First Buyer. 43
   C. Send this form to the Listing Firm, and phone the Listing Firm to advise that this has been done. 44
   D. If a Bump Notice (Form No. 44) was given, deliver a copy to the Second Selling Firm, <u>and phone the Second</u> 45
      <u>Selling Firm</u> to advise that this has been done. 46

2. **THE LISTING FIRM MUST:** 47
   A. Sign and date it in the "Acknowledgment of Receipt from Buyer" box. 48
   B. Notify the Seller by phone and/or deliver a copy signed by Buyer to the Seller. 49

3. **IF A BUMP NOTICE HAS BEEN GIVEN,** <u>the Second Selling Firm</u> notifies the Second Buyer by phone and/or 50
   delivers a copy to the Second Buyer. 51

property is subject to a first sales agreement that is contingent on the buyer selling his current home. It goes on to say that before the seller sends the first buyer a bump notice, the second buyer must waive all the contingencies checked off on the form.

After the seller receives the second buyer's waiver, the seller will send the first buyer the bump notice and then notify the second buyer of the first buyer's response. If the first buyer fulfills or waives the contingency, the second sales agreement terminates and the seller will return the second buyer's earnest money. On the other hand, if the first buyer does not fulfill or waive the contingency, the first sale will terminate and the second sale will proceed.

BUMP NOTICE. An example of a bump notice—the seller's notice to the first buyer about the second offer—is shown in Figure 8.6. This notice states that the seller has accepted another offer as a backup, and gives the first buyer a certain amount of time to satisfy or waive the contingency. The notice also states that if the first buyer fails to remove the contingency, her purchase and sale agreement will terminate.

Upon receiving the seller's bump notice, the first buyer must decide fairly quickly whether to waive the contingency or terminate the agreement. (It's unlikely that the buyer will be able to satisfy the contingency in such a short time.) If the buyer decides to terminate the agreement, he is entitled to a refund of the earnest money. If the buyer decides to waive the contingency, he must proceed with the transaction whether or not his home sells.

BUMP REPLY. Once the first buyer makes his decision, he then gives the seller notice of what he intends to do. This is sometimes called a bump reply. A form such as the one shown in Figure 8.7 may be used for this purpose.

RESCISSION

When a purchase and sale agreement is terminated because a contingency was neither satisfied nor waived, the seller usually wants to put the property back on the market. In some cases, the seller has already entered into a backup agreement that is conditioned on the termination of the first agreement. But uncertainties about the rights and obligations of the buyer and seller under the first agreement may cause problems for a subsequent sale. Thus, a second sale should not proceed until the first agreement has been officially terminated and it is clearly established that the first buyer has no right to enforce that earlier agreement. This is done by having the first buyer and the seller sign a rescission agreement.

As explained in Chapter 6, a rescission agreement formally terminates a purchase and sale agreement. It should authorize the designated broker or other party who is keeping the earnest money in trust to disburse it to the appropriate party. If a dispute arises over the earnest money, the law requires the designated broker holding the deposit to give all parties notice of her intent to disburse the deposit, and then distribute the funds within 30 days of that notice. An example of a rescission agreement is shown in Chapter 6 (Figure 6.5).

CHAPTER SUMMARY

1. Most purchase and sale agreements are contingent on the occurrence of a specified event (or events). Unless the event occurs, the party benefiting from the contingency (usually the buyer) is not obligated to follow through with the transaction. The party benefiting from the contingency has an obligation to make a good faith effort to fulfill it.

2. A contingency provision should include a statement of what the condition is and what has to occur to fulfill it, the procedure for notifying the other party of satisfaction or waiver of the condition, the time limit for fulfilling or waiving the condition, and what happens if the condition is not fulfilled or waived.

3. The three most common types of contingencies in residential purchase and sale agreements are financing contingencies, inspection contingencies, and sale of the buyer's home contingencies.

4. A financing contingency gives the buyer the right to be released from the agreement without forfeiting her deposit if she can't get the financing she needs. Sometimes, the financing contingency will specify in detail the terms of the loan the buyer will apply for.

5. An inspection contingency conditions the sale on a satisfactory structural, pest, soil, geological, or hazardous substances inspection. The inspection contingency should state who is responsible for ordering and paying for the inspection, when and how the buyer will notify the seller of disapproval of the report, the seller's option to perform any necessary repairs, and the time limit for reinspection if the seller makes repairs.

6. An offer may be conditioned on the sale of the buyer's current home. The contingency provision should state whether the condition will be fulfilled by the acceptance of an offer or when the sale of the buyer's home closes; the deadline for fulfillment or waiver of the contingency; the notification requirements; what happens if the contingency is not met or waived; and what happens if the seller gets another offer during the contingency period.

7. A bump clause allows the seller to continue actively marketing her property during the contingency period. If the seller intends to accept another offer, the seller notifies the first buyer and gives the first buyer a short time to either meet or waive the contingency, or the first contract will terminate.

8. If a contingent transaction fails, the buyer and the seller should sign a rescission agreement. A rescission agreement formally terminates the purchase and sale agreement, authorizes the disbursement of the earnest money deposit, and may provide for a commission to be paid if the buyer and seller enter into another sales agreement within a specified period. Once a rescission agreement has been signed by the first buyer and the seller, the seller can safely enter into a purchase and sale agreement with another buyer.

CHAPTER QUIZ

1. If a contingency clause benefits both parties to a contract, it:
   a. can only be waived with the consent of both parties
   b. cannot be waived by either party
   c. can be waived by either party
   d. can be waived by the buyer, but not by the seller

2. All of the following are typically found in contingency provisions except:
   a. a procedure for notifying the other party that the condition has been waived or satisfied
   b. a deadline for waiving or satisfying the condition
   c. statutorily required language advising the parties to seek legal advice
   d. the rights of the parties if a condition isn't waived or satisfied

3. Which of the following is usually not included in a financing contingency provision?
   a. The parties' options in case of a low appraisal
   b. The amount of the buyer's downpayment
   c. The terms of the seller financing arrangement
   d. A clause making the sale dependent on the buyer's ability to get homeowner's insurance

4. If an inspection reveals building code violations, which of the following is true?
   a. The buyer's lender may require the seller to correct the violations as a condition of loan approval
   b. The buyer may require the seller to correct the violations before proceeding with the contract
   c. Public authorities may order the seller to correct the violations whether or not the transaction closes
   d. All of the above

5. An inspection contingency provision will often contain a/an:
   a. hidden contingency
   b. instruction to the designated broker to wait until the inspection contingency period has ended before depositing the earnest money
   c. schedule of adjustments in the purchase price for different problems that may be found during the inspection
   d. bump clause allowing the seller to keep the property on the market and accept other offers

6. After an inspection, the buyer requests that the seller make certain repairs. Which of the following is not one of the ways in which the seller can respond?

   a. Waiving the inspection contingency

   b. Refusing to make the requested repairs

   c. Offering to modify the contract

   d. Offering to make only some of the requested repairs

7. A sale of buyer's home contingency will usually state:

   a. a price at which the buyer will be required to accept an offer on his current home

   b. that the seller may continue to market her property until the contingency is waived or fulfilled

   c. that all contingencies must be waived on any offer on the buyer's current home

   d. a deadline for applying for a swing loan

8. With a sale of buyer's home contingency, the common approaches to resolving the conflicting needs of the buyer and seller do not include:

   a. having the buyer get the funds to close the purchase of the seller's home with a swing loan

   b. making the contract contingent on the buyer's acceptance of an offer, but allowing the buyer to terminate if the sale of the buyer's home fails to close

   c. a bump clause

   d. a rescission agreement

9. The purpose of a second buyer's addendum is to:

   a. inform a second buyer that the seller's property is already subject to a contingent purchase and sale agreement

   b. notify the contingent buyer of the seller's intention to accept another offer

   c. create a contingency for secondary financing

   d. notify the seller that the sale of buyer's home contingency has been satisfied

10. A rescission agreement commonly contains a safety or extender clause for the protection of the:

   a. first buyer

   b. second buyer

   c. real estate agent

   d. seller

ANSWER KEY

1. a. When a contingency clause benefits both parties to a contract, the condition can only be waived with the consent of both parties. If the condition isn't satisfied, either party can terminate the contract.

2. c. Generally, contingency provisions don't require language advising the parties to seek counsel, although obtaining legal advice is often a good idea.

3. c. If the seller is going to provide financing for the buyer, the terms should be set forth in another addendum, and the financing forms that will be used must be attached. (Seller financing is not ordinarily treated as a contingency.)

4. d. If an inspection reveals violations of the building code or other laws, public authorities could order the seller to correct the violations, regardless of whether the sale to the buyer proceeds.

5. b. In many transactions, the designated broker is instructed to wait until after the inspection contingency period has ended before depositing the buyer's earnest money check. (An inspection contingency provision could include a bump clause, but ordinarily does not.)

6. a. The inspection contingency is for the benefit of the buyer, so only the buyer has the ability to waive it.

7. b. A typical sale of buyer's home contingency will include a bump clause, which allows the seller to keep her property on the market and consider other offers.

8. d. A rescission agreement terminates a purchase and sale agreement, so it would only be used if the contingency is not fulfilled.

9. a. A seller uses a second buyer's addendum to inform the second buyer that the property is subject to a prior contingent purchase agreement. It requires the second buyer to waive certain contingencies before the seller will send the first buyer a bump notice.

10. c. A rescission agreement may include an extender clause (safety clause), which obligates the seller to pay the commission if the seller sells the property to the same buyer within a certain period of time.

PREAPPROVAL

- The preapproval process
- Prequalification

THE UNDERWRITING PROCESS

- Income analysis
  - Stable monthly income
  - Acceptable types of income
  - Unacceptable types of income
  - Verifying income
  - Calculating monthly income
  - Using income ratios
- Net worth
- Credit reputation
- Low-documentation loans
- Subprime lending

CHOOSING A LOAN

- Comparing loan costs
- Other considerations

PREDATORY LENDING

INTRODUCTION

Many buyers, especially first-time buyers, have only a vague idea of what they can afford to pay for a home. Other buyers think they know exactly how much they can afford to pay for housing on a monthly basis, but they don't realize that the percentage of income they're prepared to spend on a mortgage payment would be unacceptably high to a lender.

While financing the sale is the buyer's responsibility, and judging the creditworthiness of the buyer is the lender's responsibility, it's still a good idea for you to be familiar with the loan approval process so that you can discuss financing options with your buyers. In this chapter, we will explain the loan preapproval process. We'll also review the underwriting process lenders use to evaluate the creditworthiness of mortgage loan applicants, and how a loan applicant can compare different loans.

PREAPPROVAL

A couple finds a house that they are thrilled with. It costs more than they planned to spend, but it's perfect for them. They immediately make a full-price offer, and the seller accepts it. The buyers apply for a loan and happily make arrangements to move into the house. Unfortunately, their loan application is rejected. The sale, which was contingent on financing, is terminated, and the seller is very upset. The buyers are mortified. In fact, they feel so bad that they postpone looking for another house indefinitely.

This scenario could have been prevented if the buyers had found out how large a mortgage loan they could qualify for before they started house-hunting. Their maximum loan amount, together with the money they have available for a downpayment and closing costs, determines the upper limit of their price range. If they'd known their maximum loan amount, they would have focused their search on homes that they could afford. This is why loan preapproval is now so common.

THE PREAPPROVAL PROCESS

A homebuyer can find out in advance how large a mortgage loan he'll be able to obtain by getting preapproved for a loan. **Preapproval** is a formal process that involves working with a lender. To get preapproved, buyers must complete a loan application and provide the required supporting documentation, just as if they were applying for a loan after finding a house. The lender evaluates an application for preapproval in the same way as an ordinary loan application, with this exception: there's no property appraisal or title report at this point, since the buyers have not yet chosen a home to buy. If the buyers are creditworthy, the lender uses their income and net worth information to set a maximum loan amount. The lender gives the buyers a **preapproval letter**, agreeing to loan them up to the specified amount when they find the home they want to buy, as long as the property meets the lender's standards. The preapproval letter will expire at the end of a specified period—for example, after one or two months. If the buyers haven't found the house they want by then, the lender may agree to an extension.

A preapproval letter can be an extremely useful tool in negotiating with a seller. It gives the seller confidence that if he accepts the buyers' offer, the financing contingency won't be a problem; the buyers are ready, willing, and able to buy. In an active market, a listing agent might advise her sellers to consider offers only from preapproved buyers. Certainly, a seller weighing two or more offers should always take into account whether each buyer has been preapproved or not.

In negotiations with sellers, there's one potential disadvantage to a preapproval letter from a lender. The lender's letter will ordinarily state the *maximum* amount that the buyer is preapproved for. This is fine if the buyer is looking for a home near the upper limit of her price range, but it can be a drawback if she is making an offer on a home that's well within the limit.

EXAMPLE: The buyer has a preapproval letter that says she's financially qualified to purchase property worth up to $285,000. But the buyer is interested in a home that's listed for only $252,000, and she wants to make a starting offer of $240,000. The seller will be able to tell from the buyer's preapproval letter that the buyer could easily afford to pay the full listing price for his home. That's likely to make the seller much less inclined to accept a lower offer than he might otherwise be.

There is a way around this problem. To make an offer on this property, the buyer could ask her lender for a special version of the preapproval letter indicating that the buyer is preapproved to purchase a $255,000 home. This would assure the seller that the buyer is financially qualified to buy his home, without revealing the buyer's full purchasing power.

In addition to its value in negotiations, preapproval helps streamline the closing process. The lender has already fully evaluated the buyers, and only the appraisal and title report remain to be done. For buyers who are sure that they're ready to buy, preapproval can be terrific. Getting preapproved for a loan has become a very popular choice.

PREQUALIFICATION

Until fairly recently, some buyers used the **prequalification** process instead of (or in addition to) preapproval. Prequalifying is an informal process that may be performed by a real estate agent or a lender. It involves sitting down with a buyer, asking her a variety of questions about her income, assets, debts, and credit history, and then using that information to determine a range of affordable home prices.

Although prequalifying a buyer used to be a fairly common procedure, today's real estate agents rarely take this step. For one thing, many real estate websites have calculators that allow buyers to perform a basic prequalification for themselves. Also, the widespread use of automated underwriting systems (which we'll discuss in the next section) has made the preapproval process straightforward enough that many buyers simply get preapproved before beginning a home search in earnest.

THE UNDERWRITING PROCESS

Before you can discuss financing options with your buyers, you must understand the criteria a lender will use to qualify a buyer for a loan. These criteria are referred to as **qualifying standards** or **loan underwriting standards**.

Loan underwriting is the process a lender goes through to evaluate the buyer and the property to determine whether the proposed loan would be a good risk. The lender has employees called loan underwriters (or credit underwriters) who carry out the underwriting process and decide whether to accept or reject the loan application.

Every loan carries some degree of risk. In fact, every time a lender makes a loan, the lender assumes two risks:

1. the risk that the borrower will not pay off the loan as agreed; and
2. the risk that, if the borrower does default, the property will be worth less than what the borrower owes the lender.

If a loan underwriter feels that these events are likely to occur, the loan is considered too risky, and the application will be rejected.

To evaluate the lender's risk, the underwriter tries to answer two questions during the underwriting process:

1. Can the borrower be expected to make the monthly loan payments on time, based on her overall financial situation?
2. If the borrower defaults, will the security property generate enough money in a foreclosure sale to pay off the loan balance?

To help answer these two questions, the underwriter applies underwriting standards to both the buyer and the property. The underwriter's evaluation of the property is based on an appraisal. The appraisal process is similar to the process you go through when you price property (discussed in Chapter 4), but it is more rigorous. In this chapter, we will focus on the standards that are applied to the buyer.

Although lenders may establish their own qualifying standards, the standards set by the major secondary market agencies (Fannie Mae and Freddie Mac) have been very influential. Lenders want to be able to sell their loans on the secondary market, and conventional loans that don't meet the standards set by Fannie Mae and Freddie Mac (referred to as **nonconforming** loans) are more difficult to sell. Also, lenders who want to make loans through a particular loan program are required to comply with the program's qualifying standards. For example, a loan will only be eligible for FHA insurance or a VA guaranty if it meets FHA or VA standards.

While qualifying standards vary, the underwriting process is basically the same no matter what type of loan the buyer has applied for. This section will focus on the basic underwriting process. The specific qualifying standards for the major loan programs will be discussed in the next chapter.

Nowadays, of course, lenders handle many aspects of the underwriting process by computer. This is known as **automated underwriting**. Fannie Mae and Freddie Mac each have an automated underwriting system (AUS) that lenders can use for loans they're planning to sell on the secondary market, and some large lenders have their own systems. An AUS can analyze a borrower's loan application and credit report and provide a recommendation for or against approval.

However, while computer programs can speed up the underwriting process, the analysis of a loan application can't be entirely automated. As a general rule, the ultimate decision—whether or not to approve the loan—is still made by human beings, not computers.

When qualifying a buyer, a lender examines the information included in the loan application, plus additional information acquired from a credit report and verification forms. The lender uses all this information to evaluate the buyer's complete financial situation. This information can be broken down into three basic categories:

1. income,
2. net worth, and
3. credit reputation.

INCOME ANALYSIS

An underwriter analyzes a loan applicant's income to see if the applicant can really afford the monthly payment that would be required to pay off the requested loan. This analysis is a two-step process. First, the underwriter will decide how much of the applicant's income is acceptable income, generally referred to as **stable monthly income**. Next, the underwriter will decide if the loan applicant has enough stable monthly income to make the monthly mortgage payment reliably.

CHARACTERISTICS OF STABLE MONTHLY INCOME. To be counted as stable monthly income, a loan applicant's income must be of a high quality, and it must also be durable.

QUALITY. To evaluate the quality of an applicant's income, the underwriter looks at the source. High-quality income comes from a dependable source. For example, if the income is salary income, the more established the employer, the higher the quality of the income.

EXAMPLE: Your buyer, Hathaway, has applied for a loan. She works for the U.S. Postal Service. Because the Postal Service is a government agency, it is considered a very dependable source of income. Therefore, Hathaway's salary will be considered high-quality income.

The less dependable the source of income, the lower the quality of that income.

EXAMPLE: Suppose instead that Hathaway works for a new construction company that is struggling to make ends meet. The underwriter might decide that the company is not a dependable source of income, and therefore consider Hathaway's salary low-quality income.

DURABILITY. Income is considered durable if it can be expected to continue for a long period of time. Durable income typically includes wages from permanent employment, disability benefits, and interest on established investments. An example of a type of income that isn't considered durable is income from unemployment benefits. Unemployment benefits, by their very nature, are not expected to continue for a long period of time.

ACCEPTABLE TYPES OF INCOME. Lenders have general rules of thumb that they follow when determining what is or is not stable monthly income. Let's take a look at some of those general rules.

PERMANENT EMPLOYMENT. Lenders will accept a loan applicant's income from permanent employment as stable monthly income only if he has a history of continuous, stable employment. As a general rule, a loan applicant should have continuous employment for at least two years in the same field. However, each of your buyers is unique. Even without a two-year work history, there may be extenuating circumstances that would warrant loan approval; for example, having recently finished college or left the armed services. Special training or education can also make up for minor weaknesses in job history.

Another point to keep in mind: if your buyer has changed jobs once or twice within the last few years to advance within the same line of work, this is a good sign. However, if she has changed jobs persistently without any advancement, the lender will probably see this as a problem.

SELF-EMPLOYMENT. Special rules apply if the loan applicant's primary income source is self-employment. Self-employment income is considered less durable and dependable than other types of employment income, so lenders are more reluctant to count it as stable monthly income.

A self-employed buyer will have to meet rigorous qualifying standards. If he has been self-employed for less than two years, he may have a hard time qualifying for a loan. And if he has been in business for less than one year, it will be even more difficult. A lender will only count the income of a self-employed buyer who has been in business for a short time if the buyer has a history of employment in the same field and can document a reasonable chance for success based on market feasibility studies and pro forma financial statements. This is difficult to do, but not impossible.

OTHER EMPLOYMENT INCOME. In addition to a salary or wages from a full-time job, a buyer can use other types of employment income to qualify for a loan. Bonuses, commissions, and part-time earnings can be considered stable monthly income if they've been a regular part of a loan applicant's overall earnings pattern for at least one, but preferably two, years. Lenders prefer not to consider overtime stable income, but they will if overtime is clearly a regular part of the applicant's earnings.

> **EXAMPLE:** Schwinn's salary is $3,500 a month. Over the last three months, she worked many hours of overtime. She averaged an additional $1,000 a month in overtime during those three months. A lender will not count that additional $1,000 a month as stable income, because Schwinn only earned it for three months.
>
> If, however, Schwinn could show that she earned an average of $1,000 a month in overtime over the previous 14 months, the lender would probably consider that part of her stable monthly income. Or if Schwinn could show that she earned an average of $3,000 a year in seasonal overtime from September to November every year for the past three years, and that this pattern is likely to continue, the lender would probably be willing to count the overtime as stable income.

SECONDARY INCOME SOURCES. There are other acceptable income sources besides employment income. For example, pension and social security payments are also considered part of a loan applicant's stable monthly income.

Alimony or spousal maintenance payments are only considered stable monthly income if the payments are reliable. So the underwriter will look to see whether the payments are required by a court decree, how long the loan applicant has been receiving the payments, the financial status of the ex-spouse, and the applicant's ability to compel payment.

Child support payments are accepted as stable monthly income under the same conditions: if they are required by a court decree and there is proof of regular payment. If payments are missed, or regularly late, the underwriter may decide to exclude the child support from the loan applicant's stable monthly income. Also, child support payments typically stop when the child turns 18. So the closer the child is to age 18, the less durable the child support income is. If the child is over 15, the underwriter probably won't count the support payments as part of the loan applicant's stable monthly income.

> **EXAMPLE:** Martinez gets court-ordered child support for her daughter, who is 16, and for her son, who is 13. Martinez has received the child support regularly for three years. The lender will probably consider only the child support for her son as part of her stable monthly income. The child support for the daughter will only last another two years, so it isn't durable.

Income from public assistance programs may also be acceptable income. The Equal Credit Opportunity Act prohibits lenders from discriminating against loan applicants just because all or part of their income is from a public assistance program, such as welfare or food stamps. Public assistance payments are considered stable monthly income if they are durable—that is, if they are expected to continue for a long period of time. If the loan applicant's eligibility for the program will terminate shortly, the lender is unlikely to consider the income as part of the loan applicant's stable monthly income.

> **EXAMPLE:** A loan applicant receives monthly income from a public assistance program. Although the lender generally will consider public assistance payments as stable monthly income, the loan applicant's eligibility for this particular program is expected to run out in a year and a half. From the lender's point of view, the payments are not durable enough to be counted in calculating the applicant's stable monthly income.

Dividends or interest on investments are also part of stable monthly income, unless the loan applicant will need to cash in the investment to have enough funds for a downpayment or to pay for closing costs.

Net income from **rental property** can count as stable monthly income. This may be property the loan applicant already owns or the property being purchased. When possible, the lender will generally use detailed information about the property's income and expenses to determine a monthly net income figure. In other cases, the lender may use a certain percentage (typically 75%) of the gross rent as a rough estimate of the net income.

> **EXAMPLE:** Your buyer is purchasing a duplex. She'll occupy one unit; the other is currently leased for $2,000 per month. To allow for maintenance expenses and possible vacancy or rent collection losses, the lender will count only 75% of the gross rent, or $1,500, as stable monthly income.

Sometimes it's very clear that a buyer won't have enough income to support the loan application. In that case, a **co-mortgagor** can be used. A co-mortgagor is simply a co-borrower—someone who signs the mortgage and note and is obligated to pay off the loan along with the primary borrower. For instance, parents often use their income history and financial status to help their children qualify for a loan.

Like the primary borrower, a co-mortgagor must have an income, net worth, and credit reputation that are acceptable to the lender. To help the borrower, the co-mortgagor must be able to support both his own housing expense and a proportionate share of the borrower's new housing expense.

UNACCEPTABLE TYPES OF INCOME. Some types of income are not considered to be stable monthly income. As mentioned earlier, unemployment benefits last only for a limited period of time, so they are virtually never considered stable monthly income.

Also, lenders are generally not interested in the earnings of family members other than the loan applicants themselves. For instance, if a married couple is applying for a loan, the lender will take into account the income of both the husband and the wife. However, income that the couple's teenage children earn will not be considered, because the children won't necessarily be sharing their parents' home for much longer.

Income from a full- or part-time temporary job is not considered stable monthly income. Income from a temporary job does not pass the test of durability. Note that a job does not have to have a termination date for the lender to consider it temporary. Other factors can be taken into account, such as the nature of the work itself.

> **EXAMPLE:** A recent flood has damaged a large portion of an industrial complex. The property manager has hired several full-time workers to help clean up the mess left by the flood and repair the damage. These jobs have no termination date, but are by their nature temporary. The income generated by these jobs wouldn't be considered stable monthly income.

However, income from temporary work may be accepted if the loan applicant has supported herself through a particular type of temporary work for years. The income from temporary work is then considered self-employment income.

> **EXAMPLE:** Ingraham works in the computer industry as a temporary employee. She goes from job to job, helping to set up databases. Each job is temporary. However, Ingraham has supported herself for four years with this kind of temporary work. At this point, a lender might regard these temporary jobs as a form of self-employment and consider Ingraham's earnings to be stable monthly income.

VERIFYING INCOME. Lenders need to verify the income information given to them by loan applicants. A lender may send an income verification form directly to the applicant's employer. The employer fills out the form and then sends it directly back to the lender. The verification form is never handled by the loan applicant at all.

In many cases a lender will use an alternative income verification method. The loan applicant gives the lender W-2 forms for the previous two years, and payroll stubs or vouchers for the previous 30-day period. The lender then confirms the employment and income information with a phone call to the employer.

The lender will also verify other types of income. For example, if the applicant is relying on commission income, the lender will require copies of the applicant's federal income tax returns for the previous two years.

A self-employed loan applicant will have to give the lender audited financial statements and federal income tax statements for the two years prior to the loan application.

For alimony or child support income, the lender will require a copy of the court decree and proof that the payments are received. A bank statement showing that the checks have been deposited into the applicant's account may be good enough. However, some lenders may require photocopies of the deposited checks.

To verify rental income, the loan applicant will usually have to submit copies of recent income tax returns. The lender may also require additional documentation, such as copies of current leases.

In some cases a lender may be willing to approve a loan application with less documentation than is usually required. Low-documentation loans are discussed later in this chapter.

CALCULATING MONTHLY INCOME. The lender will want to know the amount of the loan applicant's income in monthly terms. If a buyer works full-time for an hourly wage, monthly income is calculated by multiplying the hourly wage by 173.33.

> **EXAMPLE:** Your buyer makes $17.50 an hour. To find her monthly earnings, multiply $17.50 by 173.33. $17.50 × 173.33 = $3,033.28. Her monthly earnings are $3,033.

If a buyer gets paid twice a month, simply multiply the amount of the paycheck by two.

> **EXAMPLE:** Your buyer gets paid $2,700 twice a month. $2,700 × 2 = $5,400. His monthly income is $5,400.

It's a little more complicated if the buyer gets paid every two weeks. First, you must multiply the payment by 26 to get the annual income figure, and then you must divide that figure by 12 to get the monthly income figure.

> **EXAMPLE:** Your buyer gets paid $2,700 every two weeks. $2,700 × 26 = $70,200. His annual income is $70,200. Now divide $70,200 by 12. $70,200 ÷ 12 = $5,850. His monthly income is $5,850.

USING INCOME RATIOS. Now you have a rough idea of how much stable monthly income your buyer has. Next comes the second part of the income analysis—determining if that income is enough.

The lender will usually use two numbers, called **income ratios** or **qualifying ratios**, to measure the buyer's income. The rationale behind income ratios is that if a loan applicant's regular monthly expenses exceed a certain percentage of his monthly income, the applicant may have a difficult time making loan payments. The lender wants to be sure that the applicant can make the mortgage payment and still have enough income left over for other expenses, such as food, clothing, medical bills, car payments, and other necessities.

There are two types of income ratios:

1. a debt to income ratio, and
2. a housing expense to income ratio.

A debt to income ratio measures the monthly mortgage payment plus any other regular debt payments against the monthly income. A housing expense to income ratio measures the monthly mortgage payment alone against the monthly income. For the purposes of income ratios, the monthly mortgage payment includes principal, interest, property taxes, and hazard insurance, plus mortgage insurance and homeowners association dues, if any. (This is sometimes referred to as the PITI payment. **PITI** stands for principal, interest, taxes, and insurance.)

Each ratio is expressed as a percentage. For instance, a loan applicant's housing expense to income ratio would be 29% if her proposed mortgage payment represented 29% of her monthly income.

Each loan program has its own income ratio requirements. For example, the maximum acceptable debt to income ratio might be 36% or 41%, depending on the program. We'll discuss the specific income ratio limits used for various loan programs in the next chapter. For now, we'll just use the common rule of thumb that the monthly mortgage payment should not exceed 28% of the loan applicant's income.

EXAMPLE: Robinson's annual salary is $42,000. During the last four months, she made an extra $300 per month in overtime. For the past three years, she has received an annual bonus of $600. She recently inherited a rental house that rents for $1,100 a month.

First determine which portions of Robinson's employment income would be considered stable. Her salary is stable monthly income, but you should exclude the overtime, because it hasn't been a regular part of her earnings history. You can include her annual bonuses, because she has received them for the past three years. So add $600 to her annual income of $42,000.

$$\$42,000 + \$600 = \$42,600$$

To calculate Robinson's stable monthly income from employment, divide this annual figure by 12 to arrive at a monthly figure.

$$\$42,600 \div 12 = \$3,550$$

Now take 75% of her regular rental income (to allow for maintenance expenses and vacancy or rent collection losses) and add that to her monthly employment income.

$$\$1,100 \times .75 = \$825$$
$$\$825 + \$3,550 = \$4,375$$

All together, Robinson's stable monthly income is about $4,375. To get a rough idea of the maximum loan payment she would qualify for, multiply her stable monthly income by 28%.

$$\$4,375 \times .28 = \$1,225$$

Robinson could probably qualify for a monthly housing payment of $1,225. About 15% of that ($185) would go to taxes and insurance; the rest ($1,040) is her maximum principal and interest payment.

NET WORTH

Along with income, a lender will also analyze the buyer's net worth. Net worth is the buyer's "bottom line"—the value of his total financial holdings, in dollars and cents. To calculate his net worth, you simply subtract his liabilities (debts) from his assets.

EXAMPLE: Brown owns a house, a car, and some furniture, and he has $2,900 in savings. The total value of all of these items (or assets) is $177,000. Brown owes $5,000 on the car and $143,000 on the house; he owns the furniture free and clear.

To determine Brown's net worth, subtract the money he owes (his liabilities) from the value of his assets. $177,000 − $148,000 = $29,000. Brown has a net worth of $29,000.

Net worth is important to lenders for a number of reasons. First, lenders feel that if a loan applicant has accumulated a significant amount of net worth, that's a sign that she will be a good credit risk. A healthy net worth is especially important if the loan application is weak in another area. For instance, if a loan applicant's income is marginal, an above-average net worth can mean the difference between loan approval and rejection.

EXAMPLE: Carter has been out of college for four years. She makes $3,800 a month. She paid cash for her car, which is worth about $10,000. She has $9,600 in an IRA account, $4,200 in mutual funds, and $6,500 in a savings account set aside for the downpayment and closing expenses. Her monthly bills consist of a revolving charge card payment of $45 and a college loan payment of $55. She's applied for a loan that would require monthly payments of $1,178.

Using the lender's income ratios, the highest payment Carter can qualify for is $1,064. However, because Carter has managed to accumulate a significant amount of assets in a short period of time, the lender may approve the loan anyway. Carter's accumulation of assets shows that she's an able money manager and a good credit risk.

Significant net worth—particularly cash—also tells the lender that the loan applicant will have sufficient funds to complete the purchase. The applicant will need enough cash to cover the downpayment, the closing costs, and any other expenses involved in buying the property.

Also, some lenders require a loan applicant to have **reserves** left over after making the downpayment and paying the closing costs. For example, an applicant might be required to have enough money in reserve to cover two or three months' mortgage payments. Reserves give the lender confidence that the applicant could handle a temporary financial emergency without defaulting on the loan.

Thus, a significant net worth tells the lender that the loan applicant:

1. knows how to manage money,
2. has enough cash to close the transaction, and
3. can weather a financial emergency without missing a loan payment.

TYPES OF ASSETS. A buyer should list all of his assets on the loan application. An asset is anything of value, including real estate, cars, furniture, jewelry, stocks, bonds, or the cash value in a life insurance policy.

LIQUID ASSETS. Liquid assets are generally more important to an underwriter than non-liquid assets. Liquid assets include cash and any other assets that can be quickly converted to cash. For example, stocks (which can easily be sold) are preferred over real estate. And cash in the bank is best of all.

A loan applicant will be required to give the lender all the pertinent information about her bank accounts, including the name of the bank, the account number, and the balance. This information enables the lender to verify the applicant's cash deposits.

VERIFYING ACCOUNT INFORMATION. The lender may use a "Request for Verification of Deposit" form to verify that the loan applicant actually has the money in his bank accounts that he claims to have. This form is sent directly to the bank and returned directly to the lender. In many cases, lenders are willing to accept a faster, alternative method of verification: the loan applicant is asked to submit original bank statements for the previous three months.

The lender looks for four things when it verifies deposits:

1. Does the verified information agree with the amounts claimed in the loan application?
2. Does the loan applicant have enough money in the bank to meet the expenses of purchasing the property?
3. Has the bank account been opened only recently (within the last couple of months)?
4. Is the present balance significantly higher than the average balance?

If the account was opened recently or has a higher balance than normal, the lender may become suspicious. These are strong indications that the loan applicant borrowed the funds for the downpayment and closing costs, which generally is not allowed. However, if the funds are a gift, the lender may find this acceptable. (See the discussion of gift funds, below.)

REAL ESTATE. Often, a buyer is selling one home in order to buy another (usually more expensive) home. In that case, the buyer can use her **net equity** in the first home as a liquid asset. Net equity is the difference between the market value of the property and the sum of the liens against the property, plus the selling expenses. In other words, net equity is the money the buyer expects to receive from the sale of her current home.

To estimate the amount of equity your buyer can apply toward the new purchase, take the appraised value of the current home (or the sales price, if a sale is already pending), subtract any outstanding mortgages or other liens, and then subtract the estimated selling costs (which are commonly between 10% and 13% of the sales price).

Example: The market value of the buyer's current home is $350,000. There's a mortgage with a $294,000 balance to be paid off when the home is sold. To calculate the buyer's gross equity, subtract the mortgage balance from the market value.

$$\$350,000 - \$294,000 = \$56,000$$

The gross equity is $56,000. From the gross equity, deduct the estimated selling expenses, which are $38,500.

$$\$56,000 - \$38,500 = \$17,500$$

Your buyer will have approximately $17,500 in net equity to apply to the purchase of a new home.

Sometimes equity in other property is the primary source of the cash that the buyer will use to purchase the new property. In this situation, the lender will probably require proof that the property has been sold and that the buyer has received the sale proceeds before it will make the new loan.

If it looks as though the buyer will not be able to sell his other property right away, then he may be able to arrange a swing loan, as we explained in Chapter 8. The swing loan provides the cash to close the buyer's purchase transaction, and when the other property eventually sells, the buyer will pay the swing loan off out of the sale proceeds.

Your buyer may also own real estate that she is not planning to sell. The property may be a rental house, a small apartment building, or vacant land. In any case, the property must be included in the loan application. Again, it is the equity in this other real estate that is important, not just the appraised value. If the buyer has little or no equity in the property, the lender may view it as a liability rather than an asset.

Liabilities. As we explained earlier, to determine net worth, the lender subtracts liabilities from assets. So after listing all his assets on the loan application, a buyer must then list all his liabilities.

Liabilities include balances owing on credit cards, charge accounts, student loans, car loans, and other installment debts. Other types of debts, such as income taxes that are currently payable, are also considered liabilities.

GIFT FUNDS. Sometimes a buyer has enough income to qualify for a loan, but lacks the liquid assets necessary to close the loan. In that case, the buyer's family may be willing to make up the deficit. This is acceptable to most lenders, as long as the money supplied by the family is a gift and not a loan.

A gift of money from a relative must be confirmed with a gift letter. The letter should clearly state that the money is a gift to the buyer and does not have to be repaid, and it must be signed by the donor. Lenders often have their own form for gift letters and may require the donor to use their form.

The lender will have to verify the gift funds, so the donor should give them to the buyer as soon as possible. It's best if the lender can verify the gift funds when it verifies the buyer's other bank deposits.

Many loan programs have limits on the amount of gift funds that can be used in a transaction. These limits are intended to ensure that the buyer invests at least a small amount of his own money in the property he's buying.

CREDIT REPUTATION

The third part of the qualifying process is analyzing the loan applicant's credit reputation. The lender does this by obtaining a credit report from one or more credit reporting agencies. The applicant (the buyer) normally pays the fee for the credit report(s).

A personal credit report includes information about an individual's debts and repayment history for the preceding seven years. A credit report primarily covers credit cards and loans. Other bills, such as utility bills, usually aren't listed unless they were turned over to a collection agency.

DEROGATORY CREDIT INFORMATION. If a loan applicant's credit report shows a history of slow payment or other credit problems, the loan application could be declined. Derogatory credit information includes all of the following.

- **Slow payments.** If the applicant is chronically late in paying bills, this will show up on the credit report. Slow payments may be a sign that the applicant is unable to pay on time, perhaps because she is already financially overextended. Or they may be a sign that she does not take debt repayment seriously.

- **Debt consolidation and refinancing.** A pattern of continually increasing liabilities and periodic "bailouts" through refinancing and debt consolidation is a red flag to a lender. It suggests that the loan applicant has a tendency to live beyond a prudent level.

- **Collections.** After several attempts to get a debtor to pay a bill, a frustrated creditor may turn the bill over to a collection agency. Collections show up on the debtor's credit report for seven years.

- **Repossessions.** If someone purchases an item on credit and fails to make the payments, the creditor may be able to repossess the item. Repossessions stay on the debtor's credit report for seven years.

- **Foreclosure.** A real estate foreclosure stays on the debtor's credit report for seven years. (Some alternatives to foreclosure, such as a short sale, will also tarnish a borrower's credit history.)

- **Judgments.** If someone successfully sued the loan applicant, that, too, will show up on the credit report. A judgment is listed on a credit report for seven years after it is entered in the public record.

- **Bankruptcy.** Not surprisingly, lenders look at bankruptcy with disfavor. A bankruptcy also stays on the debtor's credit report longer than other credit problems—for ten years instead of seven.

CREDIT SCORES. Underwriters use credit scores to help evaluate a loan applicant's credit reputation. A credit reporting agency calculates an individual's credit score using the information that appears in his credit report and a quantitative model developed by a national credit scoring company. Credit scoring models, which are based on statistical analysis of large numbers of mortgages, are designed to predict the likelihood of successful repayment of or default on a mortgage. In general, someone with a poor credit score is much more likely to default than someone with a good credit score.

There are a variety of credit scoring models in use. The most widely used credit scores are FICO® scores. FICO® scores range from under 300 to over 800. A relatively high FICO® score (for example, over 700) is a positive sign.

HOW CREDIT SCORES ARE USED. In some cases, underwriters use credit scores to decide what level of review to apply to a loan applicant's credit history. For example, if an applicant has a very good credit score, the underwriter might perform a basic review, simply confirming that the information in the credit report is complete and accurate without investigating further. The underwriter probably won't question the applicant about any derogatory information in the report, because it's already been taken into account in calculating the credit score. On the other hand, if the applicant has a mediocre or poor credit score, the underwriter will perform a more complete review, looking into the circumstances that led to credit problems.

A loan applicant's credit score may also be a factor in determining the interest rate that will apply if the loan is approved. If the credit score is mediocre, instead of rejecting the application altogether, the lender may approve the loan but charge a higher interest rate to make up for the increased risk of default.

MAINTAINING A GOOD CREDIT SCORE. Any information that appears on a person's credit report may affect his credit score, but credit activity within the last two years has the greatest impact.

While most people would expect chronically late payments and collection problems to hurt someone's credit rating, they might be surprised at some of the other factors that can. For example, with a revolving credit card, maintaining a balance near the credit limit ("maxing out" the card) will have a negative impact on the cardholder's credit score, even if she always makes the minimum monthly payment on time.

Applying for too much credit can also have a negative effect. Each time a person applies for credit (a store charge card, a car loan, a home equity loan, and so on), the creditor makes a "credit inquiry" that becomes part of the applicant's credit history. Occasional inquiries are fine, but more than a few inquiries within the past year can detract from the applicant's credit score. From a lender's point of view, too many credit inquiries may be an indication that the applicant is becoming overextended.

A special rule applies when a number of credit inquiries are made within a two-week period. This could happen, for example, if someone were applying for a car loan or mortgage loan from various lenders, intending to compare loan offers and accept the best one. To allow for that type of situation, all of the credit inquiries within a certain period (ranging from 14 to 45 days) are treated as a single inquiry when the applicant's credit score is calculated.

OBTAINING CREDIT INFORMATION. It's a good idea for prospective homebuyers to obtain their credit reports and find out their credit scores well before they apply for a mortgage. (Obtaining a copy of your own credit report does not count as a credit inquiry.) A credit report may contain incorrect information, and the Fair

Credit Reporting Act, a federal law, requires credit reporting agencies to investigate complaints and make corrections. This process can take a month or more.

There are three major credit reporting agencies: Equifax, Experian, and TransUnion. A buyer should obtain a credit report from each of the three agencies. Credit scores should also be requested; they are not automatically part of the credit report.

EXPLAINING CREDIT PROBLEMS. A negative credit report or a poor credit score won't necessarily prevent a buyer from getting a loan at a reasonable interest rate. Credit problems can often be explained. If the lender is convinced that the past problems don't reflect the buyer's overall attitude toward credit and that the circumstances leading to the problems were temporary and are unlikely to recur, the loan application may well be approved. By obtaining her credit report before applying for a mortgage loan, the buyer can be prepared to discuss any problems with the lender.

Most people try to meet their credit obligations on time; when they don't, there's usually a reason. Loss of a job, divorce, hospitalization, prolonged illness, or a death in the family can create extraordinary financial pressures and adversely affect bill-paying habits. If a buyer has a poor credit score, it may be possible to show that the credit problems occurred during a specific period for an understandable reason, and that the buyer has handled credit well both before and since that period. The buyer should put this explanation in writing and be prepared to provide supporting documentation (such as hospital records) from a third party.

When a buyer explains a credit problem to a lender, it's a mistake to blame the problem on the creditor. Lenders hear too many excuses from loan applicants who refuse to accept responsibility for their own actions. The lender's reaction is predictable: skepticism and rejection of the loan application. The lender will reason that someone who won't take responsibility for previous credit problems won't take responsibility for future ones, either.

Even serious credit problems can be resolved with time. When buyers tell you they have had credit problems in the past, don't simply assume that they can't qualify for a good loan. Refer them to a lender and get an expert's opinion.

LOW-DOCUMENTATION LOANS

At times, some lenders have been willing to make low-documentation ("low-doc") loans to certain buyers. For example, if a buyer with a high credit score could make a large downpayment, a lender might waive some of the requirements for

---

FIG. 9.1   MORTGAGE LOAN UNDERWRITING

INCOME ANALYSIS
- STABLE MONTHLY INCOME: QUALITY AND DURABILITY
- INCOME VERIFICATION
- INCOME RATIOS MEASURE ADEQUACY OF STABLE
  MONTHLY INCOME

NET WORTH
- ASSETS MINUS LIABILITIES
- LIQUID VS. NON-LIQUID ASSETS
- ASSET VERIFICATION
- RESERVES AFTER CLOSING
- GIFT FUND LIMITS

CREDIT REPUTATION
- CREDIT REPORT (COVERS UP TO TEN YEARS)
- CREDIT SCORES
- MITIGATING CIRCUMSTANCES FOR PAST PROBLEMS

---

proof of income and assets, in exchange for a higher interest rate. This is convenient for self-employed buyers and others with complicated financial situations.

However, the practice got out of hand in recent years. Some lenders made low-doc and even "no doc" loans to less creditworthy buyers, including some who claimed income and assets they didn't actually have. Many of these borrowers eventually defaulted, and low-doc loans are much less common now as a result.

SUBPRIME LENDING

Buyers who won't qualify for a loan under standard underwriting requirements may be able to obtain a subprime mortgage. Subprime lenders apply more flexible underwriting standards, taking on riskier borrowers and riskier loans. To offset the increased risk, subprime lenders charge significantly higher interest rates and fees. In addition, subprime loans are more likely to involve prepayment penalties, balloon payments, and negative amortization.

Many subprime borrowers are buyers with poor or limited credit histories. However, subprime financing has also been used by buyers who:

- can't (or would rather not have to) meet the income and asset documentation requirements of prime lenders;
- have good credit but carry more debt than prime lenders allow; or
- want to purchase nonstandard properties that prime lenders don't regard as acceptable collateral.

Beginning in the late 1990s, the mortgage industry experienced a boom in subprime lending, enabling many subprime borrowers to buy homes. However, by 2008 and even earlier, a significant number of these borrowers were defaulting on their loans. The resulting wave of foreclosures hurt housing prices generally and the economy as a whole. It is now much more difficult to get subprime loans.

CHOOSING A LOAN

In many cases, a homebuyer will be offered a choice of different loans, either by a single lender or by competing lenders. Comparing the loans and choosing between them can be a challenge. The buyer must compare the cost of the loans and also consider how the structure of each loan (the downpayment, repayment period, and other features) would affect his financial situation in both the short term and the long term.

COMPARING LOAN COSTS

To tell which of two or more possible loans is the least expensive, it isn't enough to compare the quoted interest rates. Loan fees and other financing charges also need to be taken into account.

The **Truth in Lending Act**, a federal law, requires lenders to disclose information about loan costs in consumer credit transactions. The disclosures help loan applicants compare credit costs and shop around for the best terms.

The Truth in Lending Act is implemented by the Federal Reserve's **Regulation Z**. Regulation Z does not set limits on interest rates or other finance charges, but it does regulate the disclosure of these charges.

The most important disclosure required under Regulation Z is the loan's **annual percentage rate** (APR). The APR expresses the relationship of the total finance charges to the total amount financed expressed as a percentage. The total finance charges include interest, the loan origination fee, any discount points that will be paid by the borrower, and mortgage insurance costs (see Chapter 10).

Because it takes into account the other finance charges as well as the interest, the APR for a real estate loan is virtually always higher than the quoted interest rate. For example, a loan that bears an annual interest rate of 6% might have a 6.25% APR, because of the origination fee and mortgage insurance.

In a residential mortgage transaction, Regulation Z requires the lender to give the loan applicant a disclosure statement listing good faith estimates of the finance charges within three business days after receiving the written loan application. Most lenders give the disclosure statement to the applicant at the time of application. If any of the estimated figures change over the course of the transaction, new disclosures must be made before closing.

It is only by comparing the APRs quoted by different lenders that the least expensive loan can be found. By comparing only the interest rates, a buyer could easily be misled. A lender may quote a very low interest rate, but charge a large origination fee or several discount points. In that case, the total cost of the loan may actually be greater than the total cost of a loan from a competitor with a higher interest rate. The APRs of the two loans will reveal this difference in cost.

While a buyer won't get a Truth in Lending disclosure statement before actually applying for a loan, it's possible to find out the estimated APR of a loan with a phone call to the lender.

RATE LOCK-INS. If a buyer chooses a lender because of a low interest rate, she should ask whether the lender will **lock in** the rate for a certain period. If the rate is not locked in, the lender may change it at any time before closing. So even if the rate is 6.25% when the loan application is submitted, by the time the loan closes, the rate could be 6.5%. The buyer might end up with a much higher monthly loan payment than originally anticipated—even an unaffordable payment.

A buyer who wants to lock in the interest rate will usually be required to pay a lock-in fee; for example, the lender might charge 0.25% of the loan amount. The fee is typically applied to the buyer's closing costs if the transaction closes. If the lender rejects the loan application, the lock-in fee is refunded. But if the buyer withdraws the application, the fee is forfeited to the lender.

If the buyer thinks market interest rates may drop in the next few weeks, it probably doesn't make sense to lock in the rate. The lender may charge the buyer the locked-in rate even if market rates have gone down in the period before closing.

OTHER CONSIDERATIONS IN CHOOSING A LOAN

The interest rate and the overall cost of a loan are important considerations for any buyer, but they are by no means the only ones. In comparing different financing options, buyers should think about a variety of other issues: How much money will they have left in savings after the loan closes? How much spending money will they have left over each month after making their mortgage payment? How long do they plan to stay in the home they're buying? With income ratios and other qualifying standards, a lender takes certain aspects of the buyers' situation into account before agreeing to make a loan. But only the buyers themselves can decide which financing alternative is most comfortable for them and fits in best with their own financial plans.

Some buyers are only planning to live in the house they're purchasing for a few years. These buyers generally want to minimize the short-term cost of the property, and they're less concerned with the potential long-term cost. For example, a buyer who expects to sell the property in less than five years might be a candidate for an adjustable-rate mortgage with a five-year fixed-rate period at the outset. He can take advantage of the lower starting interest rate without worrying about how high market rates may rise in the future.

Buyers who hope to retire early or reduce their workload may be most concerned with building equity and paying off their mortgage as soon as possible. They might prefer a loan with a 15-year or 20-year term, rather than the standard 30-year term, even though it means they will qualify for a smaller loan amount and have to buy a less expensive home than they otherwise would.

Some first-time buyers with limited buying power want to purchase the largest home they can afford. They may be interested in financing arrangements that can boost their price range: an adjustable interest rate, a high loan-to-value ratio, a 40-year loan term, discount points, secondary financing, and so on.

On the other hand, some buyers don't want to borrow as much money for a house as lenders would allow. They may want to invest their money differently, or they may simply prefer to avoid the financial stress that the maximum monthly mortgage payment would represent for them.

In short, buyers must evaluate every potential loan in light of their own goals and preferences. The downpayment and other cash requirements, a fixed or adjustable interest rate, the monthly payment amount, and the loan term are all variables to consider in choosing a loan. We'll be discussing these and other loan features in the next chapter.

FIG. 9.2   BUYER'S CONSIDERATIONS IN CHOOSING A LOAN

- INTEREST RATE AND LOAN FEES

- SHORT-TERM COST OF FINANCING VS. OVERALL LONG-TERM COST

- SAVINGS REMAINING AFTER HOME PURCHASE

- SPENDING MONEY REMAINING AFTER MONTHLY MORTGAGE PAYMENT

- HOW LONG DOES THE BUYER INTEND TO OWN THIS HOME?

- HOW RAPIDLY WILL EQUITY BUILD?

- HOW SOON WILL THE MORTGAGE BE PAID OFF?

- HOW MUCH HOUSE WILL THIS FINANCING ENABLE THE BUYER TO PURCHASE?

- WHAT ALTERNATIVE INVESTMENT OPPORTUNITIES ARE AVAILABLE?

PREDATORY LENDING

We can't end our discussion of loan qualifying without mentioning predatory lending. The term predatory lending is used to describe an array of mortgage practices used to take advantage of unsophisticated borrowers. Predatory lenders tend to target elderly or minority borrowers, especially those with limited income or limited English skills.

Examples of predatory lending practices include:

- **Predatory steering.** Steering a buyer toward a more expensive loan when the buyer could qualify for a less expensive one.
- **Fee packing.** Charging interest rates, points, or processing fees that far exceed the norm and aren't justified by the cost of the services provided.
- **Loan flipping.** "Stripping away" a homeowner's equity by charging high fees on repeated refinancings.
- **Disregarding borrower's ability to pay.** Making a loan based on the property's value, without using appropriate qualifying standards to determine the borrower's ability to afford the loan payments.

- **Balloon payment abuses.** Making a partially amortized or interest-only loan with low monthly payments, without disclosing to the borrower that a large balloon payment will be required after a short period.
- **Fraud.** Misrepresenting or concealing unfavorable loan terms or excessive fees, falsifying documents, or using other fraudulent means to induce a prospective borrower to enter into a loan agreement.

Predatory lending is often associated with subprime mortgages, and is considered to have contributed to the subprime mortgage crisis. Many states now have anti-predatory lending laws, including Washington. The state Mortgage Broker Practices Act (MBPA), which regulates mortgage brokers, contains provisions that are intended to help prevent certain fraudulent practices in lending.

The Mortgage Broker Practices Act prohibits mortgage brokers (who now have a fiduciary duty to borrowers) from a number of actions, including:

- defrauding or misleading borrowers, lenders, or third parties;
- engaging in unfair or deceptive practices;
- obtaining property by fraud or misrepresentation;
- contracting with a borrower to receive fees even when the borrower doesn't actually obtain a loan;
- misrepresenting available rates, points, or financing terms;
- failing to make required disclosures to loan applicants and other parties;
- bribing an appraiser;
- advertising an interest rate without disclosing the APR (or otherwise violating the Truth in Lending Act);
- failing to pay third-party service providers within 30 days of recording loan closing documents; or
- acting as a mortgage broker in her own transaction or a transaction handled by another licensee working for the same brokerage.

A violation of the MBPA is a misdemeanor. An individual harmed by a violation of the law may bring a civil action against the mortgage broker's bond for actual damages suffered. In addition, a violation of the MBPA is considered an unfair or deceptive act or practice and unfair method of competition in violation of the Consumer Protection Act (CPA). Individuals may bring actions under the CPA for up to three times the amount of actual damages, up to a maximum of $25,000.

CHAPTER SUMMARY

1. Homebuyers usually obtain preapproval from a lender before beginning their house hunt. Preapproval is a formal process that requires submission of a loan application and all supporting documentation.

2. When a mortgage loan application is submitted to a lender, the lender's underwriters evaluate it to determine whether the applicant is a good credit risk and can afford the proposed loan. The underwriter analyzes the applicant's income, net worth, and credit reputation.

3. Stable monthly income is income that meets the lender's standards of quality (how dependable the source is) and durability (how long the income is likely to continue). Verified income from employment, pensions, social security, spousal maintenance, child support, public assistance, dividends, interest, and rental property may be counted as stable monthly income.

4. Income ratios are used to measure the adequacy of a loan applicant's income. In many cases, the underwriter will apply both a debt to income ratio and a housing expense to income ratio. A debt to income ratio states the applicant's monthly mortgage payment, plus any other monthly obligations, as a percentage of her stable monthly income. A housing expense to income ratio states the mortgage payment alone as a percentage of stable monthly income.

5. Net worth is calculated by subtracting liabilities from assets. A loan applicant's net worth indicates to a lender whether the applicant knows how to manage money, has the cash required for closing, and has adequate reserves in case of a financial emergency. Liquid assets are generally more helpful to a loan application than non-liquid assets. If the loan applicant owns real estate, the lender will be concerned with the applicant's net equity. Lenders place limits on the amount of gift funds a buyer can use to close the transaction.

6. A credit report lists credit problems that have occurred within the past seven years (ten years for a bankruptcy). A loan applicant's credit score provides an overall measure of creditworthiness and may be used to determine the level of review applied to the application. It may also be a factor in setting the loan's interest rate.

7. Subprime lending involves making riskier loans, usually in exchange for higher interest rates and fees. Many subprime borrowers have poor or limited credit histories; others simply want to purchase very expensive homes or non-standard properties that prime lenders don't regard as acceptable collateral.

8. The Truth in Lending Act requires lenders to provide loan applicants with a disclosure statement within three days after receiving a written application. The statement must include the annual percentage rate (APR) of the proposed loan, as well as good faith estimates of all finance charges. When comparing loans, it's more accurate to consider their respective APRs rather than the interest rates alone.

9. Remember that it is not always a good idea for buyers to borrow the maximum loan amount and buy the most expensive home they can. Buyers need to consider their entire financial situation, short-term and long-term, when choosing a home to buy and a loan to finance the purchase.

10. Predatory lenders take advantage of unsophisticated borrowers, often targeting elderly or minority borrowers. Predatory lending practices include predatory steering, fee packing, loan flipping, disregarding a borrower's ability to pay, balloon payment abuses, and fraud.

CHAPTER QUIZ

1. When a potential buyer approaches a lender prior to looking for a house, in order to obtain a promise of a loan up to a certain amount, this is known as:

    a. prequalification

    b. predetermination

    c. preapproval

    d. prepayment

2. A buyer may find it useful to have a preapproval letter because it:

    a. does not commit the lender to making a loan

    b. gives the seller confidence that the financing contingency won't be a problem

    c. tells the seller the maximum amount the buyer can afford

    d. allows the buyer to extend the closing process

3. If a loan applicant's primary source of income is self-employment, the lender will consider this stable monthly income if the loan applicant:

    a. does not have any other source of income

    b. also has secondary sources of income

    c. has been self-employed for at least five years

    d. has a history of employment in the same field and can document a reasonable chance for success

4. Which of the following would a lender consider an acceptable secondary income source?

    a. Rental income, with a percentage deducted for vacancies or uncollected rent

    b. Interest on investments that the loan applicant will cash in to pay for closing costs

    c. Child support payments for the loan applicant's 17-year-old daughter

    d. Regular monthly income from a public assistance program, if the loan applicant's eligibility will expire at the end of the year

5. A housing expense to income ratio differs from a debt to income ratio because:

    a. a housing expense to income ratio takes into account principal and interest on the mortgage, but not taxes and insurance

    b. a housing expense to income ratio is based on the monthly mortgage payment alone, not on all of the loan applicant's debt payments

    c. a debt to income ratio doesn't include the proposed monthly mortgage payment

    d. a housing expense to income ratio takes into account the loan applicant's net worth as well as monthly income

6. Which of the following is true about how a lender evaluates net worth?

   a. When verifying bank accounts, the lender wants the present balance to be significantly higher than the average balance in the past

   b. The lender will prefer non-liquid assets to liquid assets

   c. The lender is primarily concerned with the appraised value of the real estate that the loan applicant owns

   d. If the loan applicant's income is marginal, the lender may approve the loan anyway if the applicant has significant net worth

7. How would a lender calculate the net equity in real estate the loan applicant owns?

   a. Take the market value of the property and deduct the sum of the liens against the property, plus the selling expenses

   b. Subtract the existing mortgage debt from the assessed value of the property

   c. Take the market value of the property and subtract between 10% and 13% for the estimated selling costs

   d. Add the buyer's downpayment to the market value of the property, then subtract the sum of the liens against the property

8. Which of the following would be most likely to have a negative effect on an individual's credit rating?

   a. Obtaining a copy of his own credit report

   b. Unemployment

   c. Debt consolidation

   d. A high FICO® score

9. The APR for a real estate loan:

   a. must be disclosed before a loan application is submitted

   b. expresses the relationship of the total finance charges to the total amount financed

   c. includes interest, points, lock-in fees, closing costs, and the downpayment

   d. is usually lower than the quoted interest rate

10. Fee packing, loan flipping, and balloon payment abuses are all examples of:

    a. preapproval techniques

    b. derogatory credit information

    c. rate lock-ins

    d. predatory lending practices

ANSWER KEY

1. c. A buyer who would like to be preapproved will go directly to a lender and submit a loan application. Prequalification, by contrast, can be performed by a real estate agent and is merely a determination of an appropriate price range.

2. b. Preapproval makes a buyer's offer more attractive because the seller can be confident that the buyer will qualify for financing.

3. d. A lender will count the income of a self-employed loan applicant who has been in business for a short time, but only if the loan applicant has a history of employment in the same field and can document a reasonable chance for success with pro forma financial statements and market feasibility studies.

4. a. Income from sources besides employment must still be reliable and durable. Rental income is acceptable if the loan applicant can prove that rental payments are made regularly, but the lender will usually only consider a certain percentage because vacancies and rent collection problems are unpredictable.

5. b. A housing expense to income ratio measures the adequacy of the loan applicant's income using only the monthly mortgage payment (principal, interest, taxes, and insurance). A debt to income ratio also takes payments on other debts into account.

6. d. Above-average net worth can mean the difference between approval and rejection if the loan applicant's income is marginal.

7. a. Net equity is the amount of money the loan applicant can expect to receive from the sale of the property. This is often the primary source of cash that will be used to buy the new property.

8. c. A pattern of increasing liabilities followed by debt consolidation suggests that the individual tends to live beyond his means.

9. b. The annual percentage rate (APR) helps loan applicants compare the overall cost of different loans by expressing the total finance charges as a percentage of the loan amount.

10. d. These are all examples of predatory lending practices.

CHAPTER 10

FINANCING PROGRAMS

BASIC LOAN FEATURES

- Repayment period
- Amortization
- Loan-to-value ratios
- Secondary financing
- Loan fees
- Fixed and adjustable interest rates

CONVENTIONAL LOANS

- Conventional loans and the secondary market
- Characteristics of conventional loans
- Underwriting conventional loans
- Making conventional loans more affordable

GOVERNMENT-SPONSORED LOAN PROGRAMS

- FHA-insured loans
- VA-guaranteed loans
- Rural Housing Service loans

SELLER FINANCING

- How seller financing works
- Types of seller financing
- Other ways sellers can help

INTRODUCTION

As discussed in the previous chapter, the size of loan a particular buyer can get depends on the buyer's income, net worth, and credit reputation. But it also depends on the features of the loan and the way it's structured. How long is the repayment period? How much of a downpayment does the lender require? Is the interest rate fixed or adjustable? The types of loans that residential lenders offer change over time to reflect changing conditions in the mortgage finance market. Lenders want to make loans that will enable buyers to purchase homes, but they have to structure the loans to control the risk of default and protect their investments. The mortgage loans that make business sense to a lender vary with the state of the market: Are interest rates high or low, and are they headed up or down? Is this a buyer's market or a seller's market?

As a real estate agent, you can help your buyers get the financing they need by keeping abreast of currently available options. Lenders will frequently send you information about their latest loan programs, and you should keep an eye out for new developments. First-time buyers are especially likely to benefit from special programs. This chapter will provide you with the background information needed to understand the various types of loans lenders offer. In the first part of the chapter, we'll review the basic features of a mortgage loan; it is differences in these features that distinguish the various loan programs. In the second part of the chapter, we'll look at the main categories of mortgage loan programs: conventional loans and government-sponsored loans. We'll also discuss seller financing.

BASIC LOAN FEATURES

The basic features of a mortgage loan include the repayment period; the amortization; the loan-to-value ratio; a secondary financing arrangement (in some cases); the loan fees; and a fixed or adjustable interest rate.

REPAYMENT PERIOD

The repayment period of a loan is the number of years the borrower has to repay the loan. The repayment period may also be referred to as the loan term.

Thirty years is generally considered the standard repayment period for a residential mortgage, but many lenders also offer 15-year and 20-year loans. In some programs a term as short as 10 years or as long as 40 years is allowed.

The length of the repayment period affects two important aspects of a mortgage loan:

1. the amount of the monthly payment, and
2. the total amount of interest paid over the life of the loan.

To see the impact that the repayment period has on the monthly payment and the total interest paid, let's compare a 30-year loan with a 15-year loan.

MONTHLY PAYMENT AMOUNT. The main reason 30 years became the standard term for a residential mortgage is that a longer repayment period reduces the amount of the monthly payment. Thus, a 30-year loan is more affordable than a 15-year loan.

> **EXAMPLE:** The monthly payment on a $100,000 30-year loan at 7% interest is $665.30. The monthly payment on the same loan amortized over a 15-year period is $898.83.

The higher monthly payment required for a 15-year loan means that the borrower will build equity in the home much faster. But the higher payment also makes it much more difficult to qualify for a 15-year loan than for the same size loan with a 30-year term. A buyer who wants a 15-year loan and has sufficient funds might decide to make a larger downpayment and borrow less money in order to make the monthly payment amount more affordable. Or the buyer might choose instead to buy a much less expensive home than what he could afford with a 30-year loan.

TOTAL INTEREST. The biggest advantage of a shorter repayment period is that it substantially decreases the amount of interest paid over the life of the loan. With a 15-year mortgage, a borrower will end up paying less than half as much interest over the life of the loan as a 30-year mortgage would require.

> **EXAMPLE:** Let's look at our $100,000 loan at 7% interest again. By the end of a 30-year loan term, the borrower will pay a total of $239,509. But by the end of a 15-year term, the borrower will pay only $161,789. After deducting the original $100,000 principal amount, you can see that the 30-year loan will require $139,509 in interest, while the 15-year loan will require only $61,789 in interest.
>
> So the 30-year mortgage has affordable payments, but requires the borrower to pay a lot more interest over the life of the loan. On the other hand,

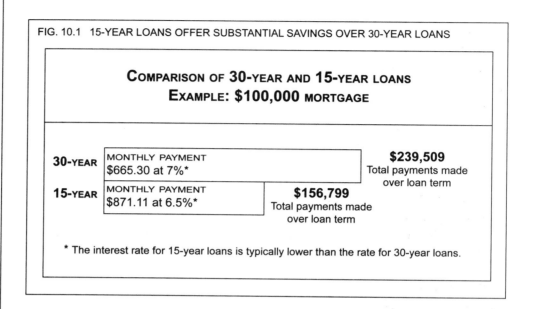

FIG. 10.1   15-YEAR LOANS OFFER SUBSTANTIAL SAVINGS OVER 30-YEAR LOANS

COMPARISON OF 30-YEAR AND 15-YEAR LOANS
EXAMPLE: $100,000 MORTGAGE

30-YEAR   MONTHLY PAYMENT
$665.30 at 7%*

$239,509
Total payments made
over loan term

15-YEAR   MONTHLY PAYMENT
$871.11 at 6.5%*

$156,799
Total payments made
over loan term

* The interest rate for 15-year loans is typically lower than the rate for 30-year loans.

the 15-year loan has much higher monthly payments, but allows the borrower to pay far less interest over the life of the loan.

INTEREST RATES FOR 15-YEAR LOANS. To simplify our comparison of a 15-year loan and a 30-year loan, we applied the same interest rate—7%—to both loans. In fact, however, a lender is likely to charge a significantly lower interest rate on a 15-year loan than it charges for a comparable 30-year loan. That's because a 15-year loan represents less of a risk for the lender.

The interest rate on a 15-year loan might be half a percentage point lower than the rate on a 30-year loan. If the interest rate on the 15-year loan in our example were only 6.5% instead of 7%, the monthly payment would be $871.11. The total interest paid over the life of the loan would be $56,799.

AMORTIZATION

The amortization of a loan refers to how the principal and interest are paid over the repayment period. Most loans made by institutional lenders like banks and savings and loans are **fully amortized**. A fully amortized loan is completely paid off by the end of the repayment period by means of regular monthly payments. The amount of the monthly payment remains the same throughout the repayment period. Each monthly payment includes both a principal portion and an interest portion. As each payment is made, the principal amount of the debt is reduced. With each succeeding payment, a slightly smaller portion of the payment is applied to interest and a slightly larger portion is applied to the principal, until at last the final payment pays off the loan completely.

In the early years of a fully amortized loan, the principal portion of the payment is quite small, so it takes several years for the borrower's equity to increase significantly through debt reduction. But toward the end of the loan period, the borrower's equity increases more rapidly.

> **EXAMPLE:** A fully amortized, 30-year $100,000 loan at 6% interest calls for monthly payments of $599.55. Only $99.55 of the first payment is applied to the principal. But by the twentieth year of the loan term, $327.89 of the $599.55 payment is applied to the principal.

The alternatives to fully amortized loans include partially amortized loans and interest-only loans. Like a fully amortized loan, a **partially amortized** loan requires monthly payments of both principal and interest. However, the monthly payments are not enough to completely pay off the debt by the end of the repayment period. At the end of the repayment period, some principal remains unpaid. It must then be paid off in one lump sum called a **balloon payment**.

FIG. 10.2 PAYMENTS FOR A FULLY AMORTIZED LOAN

EXAMPLE: **$100,000** LOAN @ **6%**, **30**-YEAR TERM, MONTHLY PAYMENTS

PAYMENT NUMBER	BEGINNING BALANCE	TOTAL PAYMENT	INTEREST PORTION	PRINCIPAL PORTION	ENDING BALANCE
1	$100,000.00	$599.55	$500.00	$99.55	$99,900.45
2	$99,900.45	$599.55	$499.50	$100.05	$99,800.40
3	$99,800.40	$599.55	$499.00	$100.55	$99,699.85
4	$99,699.85	$599.55	$498.50	$101.05	$99,598.80
5	$99,598.80	$599.55	$497.99	$101.56	$99,497.24

EXAMPLE: A partially amortized $100,000 loan might have a $71,000 balance at the end of the loan term. The borrower will have to make a balloon payment of $71,000 to pay off the loan.

In most cases, the borrower comes up with the funds for the balloon payment by refinancing. (Refinancing means using the funds from a new mortgage loan to pay off an existing mortgage.)

The term **interest-only loan** may be used in two different ways. In the first of these, an interest-only loan is one that calls for payments during the loan term that cover only the interest accruing on the loan, without paying off any of the principal. The entire principal amount—the amount originally borrowed—is due at the end of the term. For example, in this sense, someone who borrows $100,000 on an interest-only basis will make monthly interest payments to the lender during the loan term; at the end of the term, the borrower will be required to repay the lender the entire $100,000 principal amount as a lump sum.

In the alternative usage, an interest-only loan is one that allows the borrower to make interest-only payments for a specified period at the beginning of the loan term. At the end of this period, the borrower must begin making amortized payments that will pay off all of the principal, along with the additional interest that accrues, by the end of the term. (This use of the term has been more common in recent years than the first one.)

LOAN-TO-VALUE RATIOS

A **loan-to-value ratio** (LTV) expresses the relationship between the loan amount and the value of the home being purchased. If a buyer is purchasing a $100,000 home with an $80,000 loan and a $20,000 downpayment, the loan-to-value ratio is 80%. If the loan amount were $90,000 and the downpayment were $10,000, the LTV would be 90%. The higher the LTV, the larger the loan amount and the smaller the downpayment.

A loan with a low LTV is generally less risky than one with a high LTV. The borrower's investment in her home is greater, so she'll try harder to avoid defaulting on the loan and losing the home. And if the borrower does default, the outstanding loan balance is less, so it's more likely that the lender will be able to recoup the entire amount in a foreclosure sale.

Lenders use LTVs to set maximum loan amounts. For example, under the terms of a particular loan program, the maximum loan amount might be 95% of the sales price or appraised value of the property, whichever is less. The borrower would be required to make a downpayment of at least 5%.

SECONDARY FINANCING

Sometimes a buyer may want to get two loans at the same time. One of the loans is a **primary loan** for most of the purchase price, and the other is used to pay part of the downpayment or closing costs required for the first loan. The second loan is referred to as **secondary financing**.

Secondary financing can come from a variety of sources. It may come from the same lender who is making the primary loan, it may come from a second lender, it may come from the seller, or it may come from a private third party.

A lender making a primary loan will usually place restrictions on the type of secondary financing arrangement the borrower may enter into. The borrower generally must be able to qualify for the combined payment on the primary and secondary loans. And in most cases the borrower will still be required to make at least a minimum downpayment out of his own funds.

LOAN FEES

Of course, lenders don't loan money free of charge. For mortgage loans, lenders not only charge borrowers interest on the principal, they also charge points. The term "point" is short for "percentage point." A point is one percentage point (1%) of the loan amount. For example, on a $100,000 loan, one point would be $1,000; six points would be $6,000. Any lender charges that are a percentage of the loan amount may be referred to as points; the chief examples are loan origination fees and discount points.

ORIGINATION FEES. A loan origination fee is designed to pay administrative costs the lender incurs in processing a loan; it is sometimes called a service fee, an administrative charge, or simply a loan fee. An origination fee is charged in virtually every residential loan transaction. It is usually paid by the buyer.

DISCOUNT POINTS. Discount points are used to increase the lender's upfront yield, or profit, on the loan. By charging discount points, the lender not only gets interest throughout the loan term, it collects an additional sum of money up front, when the loan is funded. As a result, the lender is willing to "discount" the loan—that is, make the loan at a lower interest rate than it would have without the discount points. In effect, the lender is paid a lump sum at closing so the borrower can avoid paying more interest later. A lower interest rate also translates into a lower monthly payment.

Discount points are not charged in all loan transactions, but they are quite common. The number of discount points charged usually depends on how the loan's interest rate compares to market interest rates. Typically, a lender that offers an especially low rate charges more points to make up for it.

FIXED AND ADJUSTABLE INTEREST RATES

A loan's interest rate can be either fixed or adjustable. With a fixed-rate loan, the interest rate charged on the loan remains constant throughout the entire loan term. If a borrower obtains a 30-year home loan with a 7% fixed interest rate, the interest rate remains 7% for the whole 30-year period, no matter what happens to market interest rates during that time. If market rates increase to 9%, or if they drop to 5%, the interest rate charged on the loan will still be 7%.

Until the early 1980s, virtually all mortgage loans had fixed interest rates. During the 1980s, however, market interest rates rose dramatically and fluctuated constantly. Suddenly, many borrowers could no longer afford a home loan. And many lenders, unable to predict future interest rates, became uncomfortable lending money for 30 years at a fixed rate. The **adjustable-rate mortgage** (ARM) was introduced as the solution to both of these problems.

An ARM allows the lender to periodically adjust the loan's interest rate to reflect changes in market interest rates. The lender's ability to change the loan's interest rate during the loan term passes on the risk of interest rate increases to the borrower. Because of this shift in risk, lenders are often willing to charge a lower rate on ARMs. For example, if a borrower could get a fixed-rate loan at 6%, he might be able to get an ARM at an initial rate between 5% and 5½%.

FIG. 10.3 BASIC FEATURES OF MORTGAGE LOANS

BASIC LOAN FEATURES

- REPAYMENT PERIOD
- AMORTIZATION
- LOAN-TO-VALUE RATIO
- SECONDARY FINANCING (IN SOME CASES)
- LOAN FEES
  - ORIGINATION FEE (NEARLY ALWAYS)
  - DISCOUNT POINTS (IN SOME CASES)
- INTEREST RATE: FIXED OR ADJUSTABLE

Of course, while a lower initial interest rate may make an adjustable-rate loan attractive, the borrower is assuming the risk that he'll have to pay a significantly higher rate later on. If market rates go up, the borrower's interest rate and monthly payment amount will also go up. On the other hand, there's also the possibility of a lower rate later on: if market rates decrease, the borrower's interest rate and monthly payment will also decrease.

ARM FEATURES. The special features of an adjustable-rate loan include the note rate, the index, the margin, the rate adjustment period, and the payment adjustment period. There may also be rate caps, a payment cap, a negative amortization cap, and a conversion option.

NOTE RATE. The note rate is the ARM's initial interest rate. It's commonly referred to as the note rate because it's the rate stated in the promissory note.

INDEX. An index is a widely published statistical report that is considered a reliable indicator of changes in the cost of money. Examples include the one-year Treasury securities index, the Eleventh District cost of funds index, and the LIBOR index.

Some indexes are more responsive to changes in the cost of money than others. For example, the one-year Treasury securities index is very responsive to economic fluctuations, while the cost of funds index is more stable. Most lenders choose the more responsive indexes. A borrower may want a more responsive index if she thinks rates will decrease, but a more stable index if she thinks rates will increase. This way, if the borrower is right and rates decrease, the borrower's interest rate will quickly reflect that change. On the other hand, if rates are increasing and a more stable index is used, the borrower's interest rate will increase more slowly.

MARGIN. An ARM's margin is the difference between the index rate and the interest rate the lender charges the borrower. The margin is how the lender earns a profit on the loan. A typical margin is between two and three percentage points.

EXAMPLE: Suppose the current index rate is 4% and the lender's margin is 2%. 4% + 2% = 6%. The lender charges the borrower 6% on the loan. The 2% margin is the lender's income from the loan.

RATE ADJUSTMENT PERIOD. An ARM's rate adjustment period determines how often the lender has the right to adjust the loan's interest rate. The most common rate adjustment period is one year. But the rate adjustment period may be every six months, every three years, or some other time period. At the end of each period, the lender checks the index. If the index rate has increased, the lender can increase the borrower's interest rate. If the index rate has decreased, the lender must decrease the borrower's interest rate.

Some ARMs have a two-tiered rate adjustment structure. They provide for a longer initial period before the first rate adjustment, with more frequent rate adjustments after that.

EXAMPLE: The borrowers are financing their home with a 30-year ARM that has an initial rate adjustment period of three years, with annual rate adjustments from then on. The interest rate charged on their loan won't change during the first three years of the repayment period, but it will change each year after that.

The loan in the example would be called a 3/1 ARM. There are also 5/1 ARMs, 7/1 ARMs, and 10/1 ARMs. In each case, the first number is the number of years in the initial rate adjustment period, and the second number means that subsequent rate adjustments will occur once a year. Some borrowers who choose these types of loans intend to sell or refinance their home before the end of the initial adjustment period. As a general rule, the longer the initial adjustment period, the higher the initial interest rate. Still, the initial rate will often be lower than the rate for a comparable fixed-rate loan.

MORTGAGE PAYMENT ADJUSTMENT PERIOD. An ARM's mortgage payment adjustment period determines when the lender changes the amount of the borrower's monthly payment to reflect a change in the interest rate charged on the loan. For most ARMs, the payment adjustment period coincides with the interest rate adjustment period. In that case, when the lender increases the interest rate on the loan, the payment amount immediately goes up as well. And when the lender decreases the loan's interest rate, the payment amount immediately goes down.

RATE CAPS. ARM borrowers may run the risk of "payment shock." Payment shock occurs when interest rates rise so rapidly that an ARM borrower can no longer afford her monthly mortgage payment.

To help borrowers avoid payment shock, lenders generally include interest rate caps in their ARMs. A rate cap limits how much the interest rate on the loan can go up, regardless of what its index does; and limiting interest rate increases prevents the monthly payment from increasing too much.

Many ARMs have two kinds of rate caps. One limits the amount that the interest rate can increase in any one adjustment period. The other limits the amount that the interest rate can increase over the entire life of the loan. For example, rate caps might be 2% per year and 6% over the life of the loan.

FIG. 10.4   COMMON FEATURES OF ADJUSTABLE-RATE MORTGAGES

ARM FEATURES

- NOTE RATE: INITIAL INTEREST RATE
- INDEX: CHANGES IN ARM'S INTEREST RATE ARE TIED TO INDEX
- MARGIN: DIFFERENCE BETWEEN INDEX RATE AND ARM RATE
- RATE ADJUSTMENT PERIOD: HOW OFTEN ARM INTEREST RATE MAY CHANGE
- PAYMENT ADJUSTMENT PERIOD: HOW OFTEN PAYMENT AMOUNT MAY CHANGE
- RATE CAPS: LIMIT RATE INCREASES (PER ADJUSTMENT AND LIFE-OF-LOAN)
- PAYMENT CAP: DIRECTLY LIMITS INCREASES IN MONTHLY PAYMENT AMOUNT
- NEGATIVE AMORTIZATION CAP: LIMITS HOW MUCH INTEREST CAN BE ADDED TO PRINCIPAL BALANCE
- CONVERSION OPTION: ALLOWS BORROWER TO CONVERT TO FIXED RATE

PAYMENT CAP. A mortgage payment cap serves the same purpose as a rate cap: limiting how much the borrower's monthly mortgage payment can increase. A payment cap directly limits how much the lender can raise the monthly mortgage payment, regardless of what is happening to the mortgage interest rate. For example, a payment cap might limit payment increases to 7.5% annually. However, many ARMs have only rate caps, with no direct cap on payment increases, since rate caps provide protection against payment shock without creating the possibility of negative amortization (see below).

NEGATIVE AMORTIZATION CAP. If an ARM has a payment cap but no rate cap, payment increases don't always keep up with increases in the loan's interest rate. The same thing can happen if the payment adjustment period differs from the rate adjustment period. As a result, the monthly payments don't cover the full amount of the interest that has accrued. So the lender adds the unpaid interest to the loan's principal balance. This is called **negative amortization**. A loan's principal balance ordinarily declines steadily over the loan term, but negative amortization makes the balance go up instead of down. The borrower can end up owing the lender more money than the original loan amount.

A negative amortization cap limits the amount of unpaid interest that can be added to the principal balance. A typical negative amortization cap might limit the total amount a borrower can owe to 110% of the original loan amount (although caps can go as high as 125%). Most ARMs today are structured to prevent negative amortization in the first place.

CONVERSION OPTION. An ARM may have a conversion option that allows the borrower to convert it to a fixed-rate loan. Most conversion options give the borrower a limited time in which to convert. For example, the borrower may be able to convert the ARM to a fixed-rate loan anytime between the first and fifth year of the loan term. Conversion is usually considerably less expensive than refinancing the loan.

ARM CHECKLIST. Adjustable-rate loans are complicated. To help your buyers understand ARMs and get all the information they need, you should give them the following list of questions to ask the lender:

- What will my initial interest rate be?
- How often will my interest rate change? Is the first rate adjustment period longer than later adjustment periods?
- How often will my payment change?
- Is there any limit to how much my interest rate can be increased?
- Is there any limit to how much my payment can be increased at any one time?
- Is negative amortization a possibility with my loan?
- Can my ARM be converted to a fixed-rate loan?

CONVENTIONAL LOANS

Now let's turn our attention to loan programs. Loans made by institutional lenders (such as banks, savings and loans, or mortgage companies) can be divided into two main categories: conventional loans and government-sponsored loans. A **conventional loan** is any institutional loan that is not insured or guaranteed by a government agency. For example, a loan that is made by a commercial bank and insured by a private mortgage insurance company is a conventional loan. A loan that is insured by the FHA (Federal Housing Administration) or guaranteed by the VA (Department of Veterans Affairs) is not a conventional loan. We'll discuss conventional loans first, and then look at the FHA, VA, and Rural Housing Service loan programs.

CONVENTIONAL LOANS AND THE SECONDARY MARKET

Lenders sometimes make conventional "portfolio" loans. A portfolio loan is one that the lender plans on keeping in its own portfolio of investments, as opposed to selling it on the secondary market. With some limitations, portfolio loans can be made according to the lender's own underwriting standards.

However, lenders generally want to have the option of selling their loans on the secondary market instead of keeping them in portfolio. Conventional loans are much easier to sell if the lender makes them in accordance with the underwriting standards and other rules set by the major secondary market agencies, Fannie Mae and Freddie Mac. Loans that conform to the rules of Fannie Mae and/or Freddie Mac are called **conforming loans**; by contrast, loans that don't meet Fannie Mae or Freddie Mac's standards are **nonconforming loans**. Because the standards of the secondary market agencies have been very influential, our discussion of conventional loans is primarily based on rules set by Fannie Mae and Freddie Mac.

CHARACTERISTICS OF CONVENTIONAL LOANS

A conventional loan's characteristics are determined by rules concerning loan amounts, loan-to-value ratios, private mortgage insurance, risk-based loan fees, secondary financing, prepayment penalties, and assumption.

CONVENTIONAL LOAN AMOUNTS. In order for a loan to be eligible for purchase by Fannie Mae or Freddie Mac, the loan amount must not exceed the applicable **conforming loan limit**. Conforming loan limits for dwellings with one, two, three, or four units are set by the Federal Housing Finance Agency (the agency that oversees the secondary market agencies) based on median housing prices nationwide. The limits may be adjusted annually to reflect changes in median prices.

For 2013, the conforming loan limit for single-family homes and other one-unit dwellings in most parts of the country is $417,000. In high-cost areas—areas where housing is more expensive—there are higher limits based on area median housing prices, up to a maximum of $625,500 (most of these high-cost areas are in Alaska, Hawaii, Guam, and the Virgin Islands, where homes are exceptionally expensive).

Although they're generally ineligible for sale to the major secondary market agencies, conventional loans that exceed the conforming loan limits are also available in many areas. For these larger loans, sometimes called **jumbo loans**, lenders generally charge higher interest rates and fees and apply stricter underwriting standards.

CONVENTIONAL LTVs. Traditionally, the standard conventional loan-to-value ratio was 80%. A mortgage loan for 80% of the property's sales price or appraised value is generally regarded as a very safe investment. The 20% downpayment gives the borrower a substantial incentive to avoid default, and if foreclosure becomes necessary, the lender is likely to recover the full amount owed.

At one time, very few lenders were willing to make conventional loans with LTVs over 80%. That started changing in the 1980s. More and more lenders became comfortable making conventional loans with higher LTVs, and soon they were widely available. By the late 1990s they had become more common than 80% loans. Lenders routinely made conventional loans with LTVs up to 95%, requiring only a 5% downpayment.

Conventional loans with even higher loan-to-value ratios—97% or above—became widespread in the early 2000s. Some lenders even made 100% conventional loans, requiring the borrowers to put no money down. Unfortunately, these loans with little or no downpayment played a role in the recent mortgage foreclosure crisis. In 2007 and 2008, when home values began dropping around the country, many borrowers who had started out with very little equity suddenly had none. As values continued to decline, these borrowers soon had "negative equity"—in other words, they owed their lenders more than their homes were worth. If borrowers in that situation can no longer afford to pay their mortgage, their lenders usually incur serious losses. As a result of the foreclosure crisis, conventional loans with LTVs over 95% are no longer common, although some lenders still offer them through special programs. (See the discussion of low downpayment programs later in the chapter.)

Conventional loans with loan-to-value ratios up to 95% are still generally available. Applicants for conventional loans with LTVs over 90% typically must meet stricter qualifying standards than they'd have to for a lower-LTV loan, and they can expect to pay a higher interest rate and higher loan fees. Some lenders also require these loans to have a fixed interest rate, because the unpredictability of changes in the interest rate and monthly payment amount of an adjustable-rate mortgage makes default more likely with an ARM than with a fixed-rate loan.

PRIVATE MORTGAGE INSURANCE. With a conventional loan, if the downpayment is less than 20% of the property's value, the lender requires the borrower to purchase private mortgage insurance (PMI). The mortgage insurance protects the lender against the extra risk that a higher loan-to-value ratio represents. Fannie Mae and Freddie Mac both require PMI on all conventional loans they purchase that have loan-to-value ratios over 80%.

With PMI, the mortgage insurance company insures the lender against losses that might result if the borrower defaults on the loan. The mortgage insurance covers only the upper portion of the loan amount—for example, it might cover the upper 25%. In this way, the insurance company assumes only part of the risk of loss rather than the entire risk.

> **EXAMPLE:** Wilson is buying a $200,000 home. She's financing the purchase with a $180,000 loan, so the loan-to-value ratio is 90%. Because the LTV is over 80%, the lender requires Wilson to purchase PMI. In exchange for the PMI premiums, the mortgage insurance company insures the top 25% of the loan amount, or $45,000. The insurance company is assuming the risk that the lender may lose up to $45,000 on a foreclosure sale in the event that Wilson defaults.

If the borrower defaults on a loan covered by PMI, the lender has two options. The lender can foreclose on the property, and if the foreclosure sale results in a loss, file a claim with the insurance company to cover the loss, up to the policy amount. Or the lender can simply relinquish the property to the insurer and make a claim for actual losses up to the policy amount. Most lenders choose the first option.

PREMIUMS. The premiums for private mortgage insurance can be paid by the lender or another party, but they are usually paid by the borrower. (As in the example above, the lender requires the borrower to purchase the insurance as a condition of making the loan.) Mortgage insurers offer various payment plans, such as:

- a flat monthly premium amount added to the monthly mortgage payment;
- an initial premium paid at closing, plus annual renewal premiums; or
- a one-time premium paid at closing or financed along with the loan amount.

CANCELLATION OF PMI. If all goes well, the borrower will gradually pay off the principal. And unless the property depreciates in value, as the principal balance goes down, the loan-to-value ratio will decrease. Eventually the mortgage insurance should no longer be necessary.

A federal law called the Homeowners Protection Act requires lenders to cancel a conventional loan's PMI and refund any unearned premium to the borrower once certain conditions are met. The cancellation rules apply to loans closed on or after July 29, 1999.

Here are the basic rules for standard loans covered by PMI (different rules apply to loans classified as high-risk and outside standard guidelines):

- The lender must automatically cancel the PMI when the loan's principal balance is scheduled to reach 78% of the home's original value, unless the borrower is delinquent on the payments.
- The borrower may send the lender a written request to cancel the PMI earlier, when the principal balance is scheduled to reach 80% of the original value. The request must be granted if the borrower's payment history is good, the value of the home has not decreased, and the borrower has not taken out any other loans on the home.

Although these rules don't apply to loans closed before July 29, 1999, the borrower can often get the PMI canceled on an earlier loan once the loan-to-value ratio has decreased sufficiently. Also, the Homeowners Protection Act requires lenders to send all borrowers with PMI (regardless of when their loans were closed) an annual notice concerning their PMI cancellation rights.

Risk-based Loan Fees. Conventional borrowers are nearly always expected to pay an origination fee, and they may also agree to pay discount points. In addition, if their loan is going to be sold to Fannie Mae or Freddie Mac, the lender will probably be charged one or more **loan-level price adjustments** (LLPAs) that the lender will pass on to the borrower. Loan-level price adjustments shift some of the risk (that is, the cost) of mortgage defaults to borrowers. As a general rule, the riskier the loan, the more the borrower is required to pay in LLPAs.

Nearly all loans sold to the secondary market agencies are subject to an LLPA. The amount of the LLPA varies depending on the borrower's credit score and the loan-to-value ratio; the riskier the loan, the larger the LLPA. For instance, a borrower with a credit score of 650 and an 80% loan-to-value ratio might be required to pay an LLPA of 3.00% of the loan amount at closing, while a borrower with a credit score of 710 and a 90% loan might be charged only 1.00%.

There are also LLPAs for certain types of transactions that involve more risk, such as investor loans, loans with secondary financing, and interest-only loans. One or more of these LLPAs may be charged in addition to the one that's based on the credit score and loan-to-value ratio.

FIG. 10.5 FEATURES OF CONVENTIONAL LOANS

CONVENTIONAL LOAN FEATURES

- LOAN-TO-VALUE RATIOS UP TO 95% GENERALLY AVAILABLE

- PRIVATE MORTGAGE INSURANCE REQUIRED IF LTV IS OVER 80%

- BORROWERS MAY BE REQUIRED TO PAY RISK-BASED LOAN FEES (LOAN-LEVEL PRICE ADJUSTMENTS)

- SECONDARY FINANCING ALLOWED IF CERTAIN RULES ARE MET

- PREPAYMENT PENALTIES NOT STANDARD, BUT IN SOME LOANS

- ASSUMPTION: LENDER'S PERMISSION USUALLY REQUIRED

SECONDARY FINANCING AND CONVENTIONAL LOANS. Secondary financing can be used in conjunction with conventional loans, but most lenders require a series of rules to be met. These rules are designed to keep the borrower from overextending himself, thus reducing the risk that he will default on the primary loan. For example, a second loan generally isn't allowed to have a repayment period of less than five years. This prevents the second lender from requiring the borrower to make a balloon payment in the first five years of the loan term, when the risk of default on the primary loan is the greatest. If your buyer is interested in secondary financing, he should check with the lender to see what types of secondary financing arrangements are acceptable.

PREPAYMENT PENALTIES. Some mortgage loan agreements allow the lender to charge the borrower a prepayment penalty if the borrower pays off all of the principal, or a substantial portion of it, before it is due. A prepayment penalty is not considered a standard provision in a conventional loan. However, some lenders offer reduced loan fees or a lower interest rate in exchange for including a prepayment penalty provision in the loan agreement. While this can be a reasonable arrangement, the borrower should carefully consider the consequences before agreeing to a prepayment penalty.

A prepayment penalty is usually charged only if the loan is prepaid during the first few years of the loan term. The borrower should find out how many years the prepayment penalty provision will be in effect. She also needs to ask under what circumstances the penalty will be charged. Will she have to pay the penalty if the loan is paid off early because she has sold the property, or only if she refinances? And how much will the penalty be? Imposing a heavy prepayment penalty with unreasonable terms is a predatory lending practice, and borrowers should beware.

The Dodd-Frank Act of 2010 placed new limitations on prepayment penalties. High-cost refinances and home equity loans subject to the Home Ownership and Equity Protection Act may no longer contain prepayment penalties. And prepayment penalties for all "higher-priced" loans (those that exceed average rates and fees by a certain amount) are prohibited during the first two years of the loan, or if the loan payment amount changes, during the first four years of the loan.

Assumption. A conventional loan usually includes a due-on-sale clause (alienation clause), which means it can be assumed only with the lender's permission. The lender will evaluate the new buyers to make sure they are creditworthy. The buyers will be expected to pay an assumption fee, and the lender may also raise the interest rate on the loan.

Underwriting Conventional Loans

In recent years, with the advent of automated underwriting systems (see Chapter 9), Fannie Mae and Freddie Mac significantly changed their prescribed procedures for evaluating the creditworthiness of applicants for conventional loans. Most of the changes apply not only to loans underwritten through an AUS, but also to loans that are underwritten manually. Income, net worth, and credit reputation are still considered, but there are new methods for weighing that information in order to decide whether or not to make a loan.

Fannie Mae treats the applicant's credit reputation, as reflected in his credit score, as one of two primary risk factors. The other is the cash investment the applicant will be making, measured by the loan-to-value ratio. Based on the credit score and the LTV, a proposed loan is ranked as having a low, moderate, or high primary risk, and that determines the level of review applied to the rest of the loan application. Fannie Mae treats the other aspects of the application, such as the applicant's total debt to income ratio and cash reserves, as contributory risk factors that may increase or decrease the risk of default.

Freddie Mac's approach involves a separate evaluation of each of the main components of creditworthiness—credit reputation, capacity to repay (income and net worth), and collateral (the value of the property)—and an evaluation of the "overall layering of risk." This means that strength in one component of the

FIG. 10.6 UNDERWRITING CONVENTIONAL LOANS

CONVENTIONAL UNDERWRITING

- CREDIT SCORE AND LTV MAY BE TREATED AS PRIMARY RISK FACTORS TO DETERMINE LEVEL OF REVIEW, WITH OTHER ASPECTS OF APPLICATION AS CONTRIBUTORY RISK FACTORS
- UNDERWRITER EVALUATES OVERALL RISK
- INCOME RATIOS
  - BENCHMARK TOTAL DEBT TO INCOME RATIO: 36%
  - BENCHMARK HOUSING EXPENSE TO INCOME RATIO: 28%
  - HIGHER RATIOS ALLOWED WITH COMPENSATING FACTORS
- RESERVES TO COVER AT LEAST TWO MONTHS OF MORTGAGE PAYMENTS ARE DESIRABLE BUT NOT NECESSARILY REQUIRED
- GIFT FUNDS ALLOWED BUT LIMITED IF LTV IS OVER 80%

application may compensate for weakness in another. But even if each of the main components seems acceptable on its own, the combined risk factors in the application as a whole may amount to excessive layering of risk. In that case, the loan should be denied.

The differences between Freddie Mac's approach and Fannie Mae's aren't as great as they may sound; there's a lot of common ground. In both, each aspect of the application is to be considered as part of the overall picture, and negative factors may be offset by positive ones.

CREDIT SCORES. Both Fannie Mae and Freddie Mac expect lenders to use applicants' credit scores as a key tool in evaluating creditworthiness. In addition, as explained earlier, credit scores are used in determining the risk-based loan fees (loan-level price adjustments) that borrowers will be charged.

Fannie Mae won't buy loans made to borrowers with credit scores below 620. Depending on the type of loan and the LTV, Freddie Mac will consider borrowers with scores below 620, although many Freddie Mac loan programs require higher scores. Loans made to borrowers with lower credit scores have higher delivery fees.

INCOME RATIOS. As with any type of loan, the first step in the income analysis for a conventional loan is calculating the applicant's stable monthly income.

(See Chapter 9.) The next step is measuring the adequacy of the stable monthly income using income ratios. Traditionally, two income ratios have been used for conventional underwriting: the total debt to income ratio and the housing expense to income ratio.

The total debt to income ratio measures the relationship between the loan applicant's monthly income and his total monthly debt. The total monthly debt is made up of the proposed housing expense (which includes PITI: principal, interest, property taxes, hazard insurance, and any mortgage insurance or homeowners association dues), plus any other recurring liabilities. These other recurring liabilities fall into three categories:

- installment debts (which have a definite beginning and ending date and fixed monthly payments);
- revolving debts (such as credit card payments); and
- other obligations (such as child support or spousal maintenance).

Note that an installment debt usually counts as part of the applicant's monthly obligations only if there are more than ten payments remaining.

EXAMPLE: George has applied for a conventional loan. Among other debts, he has a student loan that requires payments of $108 per month. However, he only has to make ten more payments to pay off the loan. As a result, the $108 payment won't be included in George's total monthly debt.

That rule also applies to child support or spousal maintenance (alimony): if the required payments will end in ten months or less, they don't count as part of the loan applicant's monthly obligations.

There is an exception to the ten-payment rule, however. Even if there are no more than ten payments remaining on a debt, if the payment amount is large enough to potentially interfere with the borrower's ability to pay the mortgage, then the debt should be counted in calculating the total debt to income ratio.

The standard or benchmark total debt to income ratio for conventional loans is 36%. In other words, a loan applicant's income is generally considered adequate for a conventional loan if the total monthly debt does not exceed 36% of the applicant's stable monthly income.

EXAMPLE: The Browns' stable monthly income is $4,800. Their monthly debts include a $40 minimum payment on a credit card, a $250 car loan payment, and a $150 personal loan payment.

To estimate how large a mortgage payment the Browns might qualify for if they apply for a conventional loan, first multiply $4,800 by 36%.

$4,800 \times .36 = \$1,728$. The benchmark 36% total debt to income ratio would allow them to have up to $1,728 in monthly obligations, including their housing expense.

Now subtract the Browns' monthly payments on their debts from that figure: $1,728 – $40 charge card payment – $250 car loan payment – $150 personal loan payment = $1,288. So $1,288 is the maximum monthly housing expense the Browns could afford under the 36% total debt to income ratio guideline.

The second ratio that lenders have traditionally used for conventional loans is the housing expense to income ratio. The proposed housing expense generally should not exceed 28% of the borrower's stable monthly income.

EXAMPLE: Let's go back to the Browns' situation. Their stable monthly income is $4,800. To apply the housing expense to income ratio, simply multiply $4,800 by 28%, or .28. $4,800 $\times$ .28 = $1,344. So $1,344 is the maximum housing expense the Browns could afford under the 28% housing expense to income ratio guideline.

The maximum housing expense figure arrived at with the total debt to income ratio is compared to the one arrived at with the housing expense to income ratio, and the smaller of the two figures is treated as the maximum allowable housing expense. In our example, the Browns' maximum housing expense would be $1,288 (the figure indicated by the total debt to income ratio) rather than $1,344.

Lenders consider the total debt to income ratio a more reliable indicator than the housing expense to income ratio, because the total debt to income ratio takes all of the loan applicant's monthly obligations into account. In fact, Fannie Mae no longer sets a benchmark housing expense to income ratio; the monthly housing expense is now considered only as one of the components of the total debt to income ratio in Fannie Mae's underwriting.

It's important to understand that both Fannie Mae and Freddie Mac consider their income ratios as benchmarks or guidelines rather than rigid limits. They may be willing to purchase a loan even though the borrower's total debt to income ratio exceeds 36%, as long as there are compensating factors that justify making the loan in spite of the higher income ratio. For example, one or more of the following factors (especially either of the first two) might offset the extra risk:

- a large downpayment;
- substantial net worth;
- demonstrated ability to incur few debts and accumulate savings;
- ability to devote extra income to housing expenses;

- education, job training, or employment history that indicates strong potential for increased earnings; or
- significant energy-efficient features in the home being purchased.

On the other hand, when a proposed loan would involve other factors that represent increased rather than decreased risk, then a total debt to income ratio in excess of 36% is generally unacceptable. For example, many lenders would be unwilling to accept a high total debt to income ratio for a loan with a loan-to-value ratio over 90% or for an adjustable-rate loan.

In a case where compensating factors make a total debt to income ratio over 36% acceptable, how much higher than the benchmark can the ratio be? If the loan application is manually underwritten, neither Fannie Mae nor Freddie Mac will accept a debt to income ratio over 45%, no matter how many compensating factors are present. If the application is submitted to an automated underwriting system, there's no set maximum; the AUS will decide whether the high ratio is acceptable in the context of the overall default risk that the application presents.

Reserves. Conventional loan applicants generally should have the equivalent of at least two months of mortgage payments in reserve after making the down-payment and paying all closing costs. That's not necessarily treated as a strict requirement, but less than that in reserve will weaken an application, and more will strengthen it. Some lenders do require at least two months of reserves, and some require even more for riskier loans. For example, a lender might require three months of reserves for a 95% loan for a principal residence or six months for an investor loan. The reserves must be cash or liquid assets that could easily be converted to cash if necessary (for example, the cash value of a life insurance policy, or the vested portion of a retirement account).

Gift Funds. Lenders also apply a number of rules regarding the use of gift funds to close a transaction financed with a conventional loan. The donor usually must be someone who has a particular connection with the borrower—for example, a family member, domestic partner, fiancé, or employer. A nonprofit organization or a municipality may also be an acceptable donor. The donor is usually required to sign a gift letter to confirm that the funds are a gift and not a loan. And for high-balance loans or for loans to buy a non-principal residence property, the borrower must make a downpayment of at least 5% out of her own funds.

This 5% requirement typically isn't applied if the loan-to-value ratio is 80% or less. So if the gift funds are at least 20% of the sales price, the borrower generally isn't required to contribute any of her own funds.

MAKING CONVENTIONAL LOANS MORE AFFORDABLE

Sometimes a buyer can't qualify for a standard fixed-rate loan and wouldn't be comfortable with an adjustable-rate loan. There are quite a few other options that can make a conventional loan more affordable. These include buydowns, loans with lower initial payments, low-downpayment programs, and programs targeted at first-time buyers, public employees, low-income borrowers, or low-income neighborhoods.

BUYDOWN PLANS. One of the easiest ways to make a loan less expensive is with a buydown. A buydown lowers the borrower's monthly payment and can make it easier to qualify for the loan. When the loan is made, the seller or a third party pays the lender a lump sum that is used to reduce the borrower's payments either early in the loan term or throughout the loan term.

A buydown has the same effect as discount points (mentioned earlier in the chapter). The lump sum payment at closing increases the lender's upfront yield on the loan, and in return the lender charges a lower interest rate, which lowers the amount of the borrower's monthly mortgage payment. But a buydown is typically proposed to the lender by the parties; unlike ordinary discount points, it's not a component of the lender's initial rate quote.

Note that when a seller agrees to pay for a buydown, he doesn't have to come up with cash to do so. The amount of the buydown is simply deducted from the seller's net proceeds at closing and transferred to the lender. As you might expect, buydowns are especially popular when market interest rates are high.

A buydown can be permanent or temporary. With a permanent buydown, the borrower pays the lower interest rate (and a lower monthly payment) for the entire loan term. With a temporary buydown, the interest rate and the monthly payment are reduced only during the first years of the loan term.

PERMANENT BUYDOWNS. If a borrower's interest rate is bought down permanently, the buydown reduces the note rate, which is the interest rate stated in the promissory note. The cost of a permanent buydown depends on how much the interest rate is reduced; the greater the rate reduction, the higher the cost.

> **EXAMPLE:** Bowen needs to borrow $150,000 to buy Sanderson's property. The lender quoted a 10% interest rate, and Bowen can't quite qualify for the loan at that rate. Sanderson offers to buy down Bowen's interest rate by 1% to help her qualify for the loan.
>
> Based on market conditions, the lender estimates it will take about six points to increase the yield on a 30-year loan by 1%. So the lender

agrees to make the buydown for six points, or 6% of the loan amount. To determine how much the buydown will cost Sanderson, multiply the loan amount by 6%. $150,000 × .06 = $9,000. At closing, the lender will withhold approximately $9,000 from the loan funds, reducing Sanderson's proceeds from the sale.

The 1% buydown will reduce Bowen's mortgage payment by almost $100 per month, enabling her to qualify for the loan. The lender will charge Bowen 9% interest instead of 10% throughout the 30-year loan term, which will save Bowen nearly $35,800 over the life of the loan.

As the example indicates, the cost of a buydown is affected by market conditions, including market interest rates and the average time loans are outstanding before they are paid off. The amount that the lender will actually charge should be confirmed before the parties sign an agreement.

TEMPORARY BUYDOWNS. A temporary buydown reduces the buyer's monthly payment in the early years of the loan. Temporary buydowns appeal to buyers who believe they can grow into a larger payment, but need time to get established. They also cost sellers less than permanent buydowns.

There are two types of temporary buydown plans: level payment and graduated payment. A **level payment plan** calls for an interest reduction that stays the same throughout the buydown period. For example, a seller might buy a buyer's interest rate down by 2% for two years. The buyer would pay the lower interest rate during the first two years, and then the lender would begin charging the note rate at the start of the third year.

With a **graduated payment plan**, the interest rate reduction changes at set points during the buydown period. For example, one graduated payment plan is the 3-2-1 buydown. It calls for a 3% reduction in the interest rate during the first year, 2% during the second year, and 1% during the third year. The lender begins charging the note rate in the fourth year. This gives the buyer the chance to get used to higher payments gradually.

With a temporary buydown, because the buyer will eventually have to afford a larger payment based on the full note rate, the lender may not be willing to qualify the buyer at the buydown rate. Instead, the lender may use a rate somewhere between the note rate and the buydown rate for qualifying. For instance, in the case of a 3% buydown, the lender might use a rate only 1% or 2% below the note rate to qualify the buyer. This would give the lender some assurance that the buyer will be able to handle the payment increase when the time comes. Alternatively, the lender might qualify the buyer at the buydown rate, but apply stricter income ratios to control the risk of default.

LIMITS ON BUYDOWNS AND OTHER CONTRIBUTIONS. Fannie Mae and Freddie Mac limit the financial contributions a buyer may accept from the seller or another interested party, such as the builder or a real estate agent involved in the transaction. The limits are based on a percentage of the property's sales price or appraised value, whichever is less. These limits apply to buydowns, to payment of closing costs ordinarily paid by the buyer, and to similar contributions.

In addition, Fannie Mae and Freddie Mac both limit the amount of the interest rate reduction for buydowns. For example, Fannie Mae limits temporary buydowns to a maximum 3% rate reduction, while Freddie Mac has similar limits that vary depending on the loan type. Fannie Mae does not limit the total dollar amount of an interest rate buydown, but Freddie Mac does.

LOANS WITH LOWER INITIAL PAYMENTS. Many first-time homebuyers are just starting out in their careers. They expect their incomes to increase steadily, so that they'll eventually be able to afford a higher mortgage payment than they can now. These buyers may be able to buy a more expensive home without waiting if they get a loan that has lower payments at first and higher payments later on. This type of payment plan doesn't always work out well; buyers run the risk that they'll experience payment shock later on, especially if their incomes don't increase as expected. But under some circumstances, a loan with lower initial payments may be a reasonable choice.

As we just discussed, a temporary buydown is one way of making a loan more affordable in the first years of the repayment period. Earlier in the chapter we also discussed adjustable-rate mortgages with two-tiered rate adjustment schedules. One example is the 5/1 ARM: the interest rate and payment amount start out lower than the rate and payment for a fixed-rate loan, and they don't change during the first five years; the lender makes annual adjustments after that. Other types of conventional loans with two-tiered structures that offer lower payments in the initial years than comparable fixed-rate loans include:

- two-step mortgages,
- balloon/reset mortgages, and
- interest-only mortgages.

TWO-STEP MORTGAGES. A two-step mortgage offers some of the advantages of an ARM, with less uncertainty for the borrower. A two-step mortgage is a 30-year loan that allows the lender to adjust the loan's interest rate at only one point during the term. Common two-step programs include the 5/25 plan and the 7/23 plan.

The interest rate of a 5/25 loan is automatically adjusted after five years to the current market rate, and the monthly payment is adjusted accordingly. The interest rate and payment then stay at that level for the remaining 25 years of the loan term.

> **EXAMPLE:** When your buyer obtained a loan, the current fixed interest rate was 6%. The buyer was able to get a 5/25 two-step loan at a 5.75% initial interest rate. Five years later, the market rate has increased by 2%, so the buyer's rate increases to 7.75%. The lender will continue to charge 7.75% interest for the remainder of the loan term, 25 years.

A "7/23" loan automatically adjusts after seven years to the current market rate, and then stays at that rate for the remaining 23 years of the loan term.

Because the lender will have an opportunity to adjust the loan's interest rate to reflect changes in the market rate, two-step mortgages may be offered at a lower initial rate than fixed-rate loans. And while the borrower assumes the risk that interest rates will increase in the next five or seven years, he also gets to take advantage of lower rates without refinancing if market rates decrease during that five- or seven-year period. Because the interest rate on a two-step loan changes only once, many borrowers feel more comfortable with this type of loan than with an ARM.

BALLOON/RESET MORTGAGES. Balloon/reset mortgages are similar to two-step mortgages, with some key differences. Like two-step mortgages, balloon/reset mortgages come in two versions, 5/25 and 7/23. With a balloon/reset mortgage,

---

FIG. 10.7 MAKING CONVENTIONAL LOANS MORE AFFORDABLE

CONVENTIONAL AFFORDABILITY PLANS AND PROGRAMS

- BUYDOWNS: PERMANENT OR TEMPORARY
- LOW INITIAL PAYMENT PROGRAMS
  - TWO-STEP MORTGAGES
  - BALLOON/RESET MORTGAGES
  - INTEREST-ONLY MORTGAGES
- LOW-DOWNPAYMENT PROGRAMS
  - TYPICALLY ALLOW LTVS UP TO 97%
  - BORROWER MAY USE SOME FUNDS FROM ALTERNATIVE SOURCES
  - TARGETED PROGRAMS: PUBLIC EMPLOYEES, FIRST-TIME BUYERS, LOW- OR MODERATE-INCOME BUYERS, OR LOW-INCOME NEIGHBORHOODS

however, the initial five- or seven-year period is actually the term of the loan. Although the payment amount is based on a 30-year amortization schedule, the entire mortgage balance becomes due at the end of the five- or seven-year term. In other words, a balloon/reset mortgage is a partially amortized loan.

At the end of the five- or seven-year term, the borrower may have to refinance in order to make the balloon payment. Alternatively, she may be allowed to "reset" the loan. Under the reset option, the loan stays in place and the interest rate is adjusted to the current market rate. The rate and payment are then level for 25 or 23 years.

By exercising the reset option, the borrower can avoid refinancing charges. To be entitled to reset the loan, the borrower has to meet certain conditions. For example, she must not have been delinquent on the mortgage payments during the preceding year. And she must not have placed other liens against the security property.

INTEREST-ONLY MORTGAGES. As we said earlier in the chapter, some loans allow the borrower to make interest-only payments for a specified period at the beginning of the loan term. The borrower isn't required to start paying off the principal until that period expires. Let's look an example of a typical interest-only plan.

> **EXAMPLE:** Ann's loan has a 30-year term, with a 10-year interest-only period. She won't have to begin paying off the principal until the 11th year. The interest rate will remain fixed throughout the 30-year term. When it's time for Ann to begin paying off the principal, the entire loan amount will be fully amortized over the remaining 20 years of the term.

Because the principal is amortized over the remainder of the term, the amount of the required monthly payment is likely to rise sharply at the end of the interest-only period, making payment shock a serious risk. However, the borrower is usually allowed to make prepayments of principal at any time during the initial interest-only period. Any prepayments will reduce the amount of the monthly payment later on.

LOW-DOWNPAYMENT PROGRAMS. For many potential homebuyers, especially first-time buyers, coming up with enough cash is the biggest challenge in buying a home. They have a steady, reliable income, but they don't have the savings to cover the downpayment, closing costs, and reserves required for a standard conventional loan. Even the 5% downpayment required for a 95% loan may be beyond their means. Buyers in this situation may want to consider special programs that have reduced cash requirements and allow them to draw on alternative sources for the cash they need.

The details of these programs vary. But here are examples of the types of loans that buyers can look for:

- A loan with a 95% LTV that requires a 3% downpayment from the borrower's own funds, with 2% from alternative sources.
- A loan with a 97% LTV that requires a 3% downpayment from the borrower's own funds, plus a 3% contribution to closing costs that may come from alternative sources.

Depending on the program, the allowable alternative sources of funds may include gifts, grants, or unsecured loans. The funds may come from a relative, an employer, a public agency, a nonprofit organization, or a private foundation. More than one source may be tapped to get the necessary funds together.

Some of these programs don't require the borrower to have any reserves after closing. Others require only one month's mortgage payment in reserve.

TARGETED PROGRAMS. Although some conventional low-downpayment programs are open to any prospective homebuyer, many are specifically targeted at low- and moderate-income buyers. As a general rule, a buyer can qualify for one of these targeted programs if his stable monthly income does not exceed the median income in the metropolitan area in question. (An increased income limit applies in a high-cost area such as Seattle.) To make it even easier for low- and moderate-income buyers to get a mortgage, these programs may allow a total debt to income ratio of 38% or even 40% without compensating factors, and may have no maximum housing expense to income ratio.

To encourage neighborhood revitalization, the targeted programs often waive their income limits for buyers who are purchasing homes in low-income or run-down neighborhoods. Thus, a buyer whose income is well above the area median could still qualify for a targeted low-downpayment program if she's buying a home in a neighborhood that meets the program's standards.

Other conventional low-downpayment programs are offered to groups such as teachers, police officers, and firefighters. These programs encourage public employees to live in the communities where they work. Special programs for first-time buyers are generally meant to stimulate the housing market.

GOVERNMENT-SPONSORED LOAN PROGRAMS

Now let's turn to government-sponsored mortgage loan programs. The two major programs established by the federal government are the FHA-insured loan program and the VA-guaranteed loan program. We'll look at each of these in turn, and then briefly examine Rural Housing Service loans.

FHA-INSURED LOANS

The federal government created the Federal Housing Administration (FHA) in 1934, during the Great Depression, to help people with low and moderate incomes buy homes. For much of the twentieth century, the FHA-insured loan program was the main source of low-downpayment mortgage loans for U.S. homebuyers.

The program became less important in the last years of the century and in the early 2000s. During that period (as we discussed earlier) buyers could obtain a conventional loan with a very small downpayment, or even no downpayment at all. At the same time, home prices increased dramatically, and FHA loan amounts were so limited that the program was no longer useful in areas where housing was expensive. Now, however, conventional loans with very high LTVs are no longer widely available, and FHA maximum loan amounts have been significantly increased in high-cost areas. As a result, many buyers with limited funds for a downpayment are once again turning to the FHA-insured loan program.

The FHA is an agency within the U.S. Department of Housing and Urban Development. The FHA does not make loans; it insures loans made by banks and other institutional lenders. In effect, the FHA is a giant mortgage insurance agency. Its insurance program, the Mutual Mortgage Insurance Plan, is funded with premiums paid by FHA borrowers. If a lender that makes an FHA-insured loan suffers a loss because the borrower defaults, the FHA will compensate the lender for its loss.

In exchange for insuring a loan, the FHA regulates most of the loan's terms and conditions. The FHA has various programs for specific types of mortgage loans, such as home rehabilitation loans and energy efficiency loans. But the central program for single-family home purchase loans is the 203(b) program. The rules we'll be discussing here apply to loans made through the 203(b) program.

CHARACTERISTICS OF FHA LOANS. Here are some of the key characteristics of FHA loans:

- An FHA loan requires a comparatively small downpayment, and the loan fees and other charges may be lower than they would be for a typical conventional loan. Overall, an FHA borrower may need significantly less cash for closing.

- FHA loan amounts can't exceed specified maximums that are based on median housing prices. In some areas, the FHA maximum loan amounts are considerably lower than the maximums for conforming conventional loans.
- The qualifying standards for an FHA loan are not as strict as those for a standard conventional loan.
- Although FHA programs are intended to help homebuyers with low or moderate incomes, there are no maximum income limits. (Instead, the maximum loan amount rules ensure that FHA loans can generally only be used to purchase relatively modest homes.)
- The property purchased with an FHA loan may have up to four dwelling units. The borrowers must intend to occupy it as their primary residence. The FHA does not insure loans made to investors, as opposed to owner-occupants.
- If there are any other mortgage liens against the property, the FHA loan must have first lien position.
- The interest rate on an FHA loan may be fixed or adjustable.
- Most FHA loans have 30-year terms, although 15-year loans are also available. (However, if the interest rate is adjustable, the term must be 30 years.)
- In addition to an origination fee, an FHA borrower may be charged discount points, which can be paid by either the borrower or the property seller.
- Mortgage insurance is required on all FHA loans.
- FHA loans never call for a prepayment penalty. They can be paid off at any time with no penalty.

FHA LOAN AMOUNTS. The loan amount for a transaction financed with an FHA loan can't exceed the local limit that applies in the area where the property is located. Local limits are based on median housing prices and tied to the conforming loan limits for conventional loans. They may be adjusted annually.

For 2013, the FHA maximum loan amount for single-family homes and other one-unit dwellings is generally $271,050, but it can be as much as $729,750 in high-cost areas. (As with conventional loans, there are higher limits for Alaska, Hawaii, Guam, and the Virgin Islands.) The ceiling is the same as the conventional conforming loan limit for high-cost areas, and it represents a significant increase in the FHA maximum loan amount. The increase is designed to make the FHA program useful again for buyers in high-cost areas.

LOAN-TO-VALUE RATIOS. The loan amount for a particular transaction is determined not just by the FHA loan ceiling for the local area, but also by the FHA's rules concerning loan-to-value ratios.

The maximum loan-to-value ratio for an FHA loan depends on the borrower's credit score. If the borrower's credit score is 580 or above, the maximum LTV is 96.5%. If his score is 500 to 579, the maximum LTV is 90%. Someone with a score below 500 isn't eligible for an FHA loan.

MINIMUM CASH INVESTMENT. The difference between the maximum loan amount and the appraised value or sales price (whichever is less) is called the borrower's **minimum cash investment.** In effect, the minimum cash investment is the required downpayment for an FHA loan. In a transaction with maximum financing (a 96.5% LTV), the borrower must make a minimum cash investment of 3.5%.

At one time, certain closing costs paid by the borrower could be used to fulfill the FHA's minimum cash investment requirement, but that's no longer true. Now neither closing costs nor discount points paid by the borrower count toward the minimum cash investment. And neither do "prepaid expenses," which include interim interest on the loan and impounds for property taxes and hazard insurance.

FHA INSURANCE PREMIUMS. The mortgage insurance premiums for FHA loans are called the MIP. Usually, an FHA borrower pays both a one-time premium and annual premiums.

UPFRONT PREMIUM. The one-time premium is called the **upfront MIP**. Either the borrower or the seller can pay the upfront premium in cash at closing. The borrower also has the option of financing the upfront premium over the loan term. When the upfront premium is financed, it's simply added to the base loan amount (the amount determined by the maximum loan amount and minimum cash investment rules). The monthly payments are then set to pay off the total amount financed by the end of the loan term. When the upfront premium is financed in this way, the total loan amount (the base loan amount plus the upfront premium) can't exceed 100% of the property's appraised value. Currently, the upfront premium for FHA purchase loans is 1.75% of the loan amount.

ANNUAL PREMIUM. In addition to the upfront MIP, an annual premium is also required for most FHA loans. The annual premium ranges from 0.45% to 1.55% of the loan balance, depending on the principal balance, loan term, and the loan-to-value ratio. The annual premium is paid in monthly installments: one-twelfth of the annual premium is added to each monthly payment.

With most loans made before June 3, 2013, the annual premium is charged until the borrower pays the loan balance down to 78% of the original sales price or appraised value, whichever is lower. For newer loans, however, the rules have changed. If the original LTV is over 90%, the annual MIP must be paid for the entire loan term; if the original LTV is 90% or less, the annual MIP gets canceled after 11 years. (The mortgage insurance remains in effect throughout the life of the loan, however.)

SELLER CONTRIBUTIONS. As you've seen, to make the home more affordable, sometimes a seller agrees to buy down the buyer's interest rate. Or the seller might help pay all or part of the buyer's closing costs or discount points. When the sale is financed with an FHA loan, contributions from the seller—or from another interested party, such as a real estate agent—may not exceed 6% of the sales price or the appraised value, whichever is less. Any amount over that limit must be subtracted from the sales price before applying the loan-to-value ratio and calculating the minimum cash investment.

SECONDARY FINANCING. Secondary financing is allowed in conjunction with FHA loans. In fact, the amount of the first and second mortgages added together can exceed the FHA's local loan ceiling, so in some cases secondary financing makes it possible to buy a more expensive house. As a general rule, however, the combined loan-to-value ratio can't exceed the FHA's maximum allowable LTV. That means secondary financing ordinarily can't be used for the minimum cash invest-

FIG. 10.8 FEATURES OF FHA-INSURED LOANS

FHA LOAN FEATURES

- FOR RESIDENTIAL PROPERTIES WITH ONE TO FOUR UNITS
- BORROWER MUST OCCUPY PROPERTY AS PRIMARY RESIDENCE
- FHA MORTGAGE INSURANCE (MIP) ON ALL LOANS
- MAXIMUM LOAN AMOUNT BASED ON LOCAL MEDIAN HOUSING PRICES
- BORROWER'S MINIMUM CASH INVESTMENT: 3.5% OF PRICE OR VALUE, OR 10% IF CREDIT SCORE IS BELOW 580
- MINIMUM CREDIT SCORE 500
- SECONDARY FINANCING ALLOWED
- INCOME RATIO GUIDELINES:
  - 43% DEBT TO INCOME RATIO
  - 31% HOUSING EXPENSE TO INCOME RATIO
- ASSUMPTION: LENDER'S APPROVAL REQUIRED

ment. (There are exceptions to this rule when the secondary financing is provided by a family member, nonprofit, or a governmental agency, or when the borrower is 60 or older.)

A number of other restrictions apply to secondary financing supplementing an FHA loan. For example, the second loan can't require a balloon payment within a certain number of years after closing, and it can't have a prepayment penalty.

UNDERWRITING FHA LOANS. To qualify a buyer for an FHA loan, the lender will examine both the creditworthiness of the loan applicant and the value of the property. As with conventional loans, examining the creditworthiness of the loan applicant involves analyzing his credit reputation, income, and net worth. However, it's important to note that the FHA's underwriting standards are not as strict as the standards used for conventional loans. The less stringent FHA standards make it easier for low- and moderate-income homebuyers to qualify for a mortgage.

INCOME RATIOS. The FHA's term for stable monthly income is **effective income**. An FHA loan applicant's effective income is his monthly gross income from all sources that can be expected to continue for the first three years of the loan term.

Two ratios are applied to evaluate the adequacy of the applicant's effective income. These are the debt to income ratio and the housing expense to income ratio. As a general rule, an FHA loan applicant's debt to income ratio may not exceed 43%. In addition, the applicant's housing expense to income ratio may not exceed 31%. The applicant must qualify under both ratios.

The debt to income ratio takes into account the proposed monthly housing expense plus all recurring monthly charges. The housing expense includes principal and interest (based on the total amount financed), property taxes, hazard insurance, one-twelfth of the annual premium for the FHA mortgage insurance, and any dues owed to a homeowners association. Recurring monthly charges include the monthly payments on any debt with ten or more payments remaining. Alimony and child support payments, installment debt payments, and payments on revolving credit accounts are all counted.

> **EXAMPLE:** Miriam is applying for an FHA loan. She has a reliable monthly salary of $2,750. She also receives $740 a month in Social Security payments for her young children, which began when their father died three years ago. Miriam's effective income totals $3,490 a month. She pays the following monthly recurring charges: a $235 car payment, a $50 minimum Master-Card payment, and a $125 personal loan payment.

To get a general idea of how large a house payment Miriam can qualify for with FHA financing, use the FHA's two income ratios. First multiply her effective income by 43% to see how much she can spend per month on her total monthly obligations. $3,490 × .43 = $1,501. Then subtract her recurring monthly charges from her maximum monthly obligations. $1,501 – $235 car payment – $50 MasterCard payment – $125 personal loan payment = $1,091. Miriam could qualify for a $1,091 monthly housing expense under the debt to income ratio.

Next, apply the housing expense to income ratio by multiplying Miriam's effective income by 31%. $3,490 × .31 = $1,082. So $1,082 is the maximum monthly housing expense Miriam could qualify for under this ratio. Since Miriam must qualify under both ratios, $1,082 is her maximum monthly housing expense for an FHA loan.

If a loan applicant's income ratios exceed the 43% and 31% limits, he might not qualify for an FHA loan. However, the loan can be approved if there are compensating factors that will reduce the risk of default. For example, if the applicant has a conservative attitude toward credit and has at least three months' mortgage payments in reserve after closing, the underwriter could approve the loan in spite of a debt to income ratio over 43%.

A temporary buydown can be used with an FHA loan, as long as the loan has a fixed interest rate. However, the FHA underwriter will use the note rate to qualify the borrower. So even if the interest rate on the loan were bought down from 11% to 9% for the first two years of the loan term, the buyer would still be required to qualify for the loan at 11%, the note rate.

FUNDS FOR CLOSING. At closing, an FHA borrower must have enough cash to cover the minimum cash investment, discount points, prepaid expenses, and other out-of-pocket expenses. Ordinarily, no reserves are required. The borrower may use gift funds to help close the transaction. The donor of the gift funds must be the borrower's employer or labor union, a close relative, a close friend with a clearly defined interest in the borrower, a charitable organization, or a government agency.

An FHA borrower also has other options for coming up with the necessary funds. As we discussed earlier, a close family member may provide secondary financing to cover the minimum cash investment and other funds needed for closing. Alternatively, a close family member may simply loan the funds to the borrower without requiring a second mortgage or any form of security in return.

Also, the borrower may be permitted to borrow the cash needed for closing from someone other than a family member, as long as the loan is secured by collateral other than the property being purchased with the FHA mortgage. For example, if the applicant can borrow money against his car or vacation property, the loan funds may be used to close the sale. Note that this loan must be from an independent third party, not from the seller or a real estate agent involved in the transaction. It must be clear that the loan is a bona fide business transaction and that the collateral is truly worth the loan proceeds.

ASSUMPTION. FHA loans contain due-on-sale clauses, and various limitations on assumption apply. With some exceptions, the buyer must intend to occupy the property as his primary residence. The lender will review the creditworthiness of the buyer before agreeing to the assumption.

VA-GUARANTEED LOANS

The VA home loan program allows veterans to finance the purchase of their homes with low-cost loans that offer a number of advantages over conventional and FHA loans. A VA loan, like an FHA loan, is made by an institutional lender, not a government agency. However, the loan is guaranteed by the Department of Veterans Affairs (VA), and that significantly reduces the lender's risk. If the borrower defaults, the VA will reimburse the lender for its losses, up to the guaranty amount.

A VA loan can be used to finance the purchase or construction of an owner-occupied single-family residence, or a multifamily residence with up to four units, as long as the veteran will occupy one of the units.

CHARACTERISTICS OF VA LOANS. One of the biggest advantages of VA financing is that, unlike most loans, a typical VA loan does not require a downpayment. Within certain limitations, a VA loan can equal the sales price or appraised value of the home, whichever is less. This allows many veterans who would otherwise be unable to buy homes to do so.

Equally important to many veterans, the underwriting standards for VA loans are more relaxed than the standards for conventional loans. So not only will a veteran need less cash to buy a home with a VA loan, it will also be easier to qualify for the loan.

There are no income limits on VA borrowers, nor are there official restrictions on the size of a VA loan. This means that VA loans aren't limited to low- or moderate-income buyers.

VA loans are fully amortized and typically have 30-year terms. The lender may not impose any prepayment penalties.

The VA doesn't set a maximum interest rate for VA loans; the interest rate is negotiable between the lender and borrower. The lender may charge the borrower a flat fee of no more than 1% of the loan amount to cover administrative costs (the equivalent of an origination fee). The lender may also charge reasonable discount points, which can be paid by the borrower, the seller, or a third party.

VA loans do not require mortgage insurance. The borrower doesn't have to pay for the private mortgage insurance required for many conventional loans, or the MIP required for all FHA-insured loans. However, a VA borrower usually has to pay a **funding fee**, which the lender will remit to the VA. (Veterans with service-connected disabilities are exempt.) In 2013, for a member of the regular military obtaining a no-downpayment loan, the funding fee is 2.15% of the loan amount; it's 2.4% for a member of the National Guard or Reserves. If the borrower makes a downpayment of 5% or more, the fee is reduced. The funding fee can be paid at closing or financed along with the loan amount.

Another important feature of VA loans is the leniency extended to VA borrowers who are experiencing temporary financial difficulties, such as illness, injury, unemployment, or the death of a spouse. A VA loan officer can help a borrower whose loan becomes delinquent to negotiate a repayment plan.

ELIGIBILITY. To obtain a VA loan, a veteran must have a Certificate of Eligibility issued by the VA. To be eligible, the veteran must have served at least a minimum amount of active duty service. This minimum amount varies depending on when the veteran served, and it ranges from 90 days to two years of active duty. A buyer who is unsure about his eligibility should check with the local VA office.

VA GUARANTY. Like private mortgage insurance, the VA guaranty covers only a portion of the loan amount. The guaranty amount available for a particular transaction depends on the loan amount. For larger loans, it also depends on median home prices in the county where the property being purchased is located.

For example, for loan amounts over $144,000 and up to $417,000, the guaranty amount is 25% of the loan amount. (So that's a $104,250 guaranty for a $417,000 loan.) For loan amounts over $417,000, the guaranty is 25% of the loan amount, up to the maximum specified for the county.

In Washington, the 2013 maximum guaranty ranges from $104,250 (for most counties) up to $125,000 (for the most expensive counties).

LOAN AMOUNT. The amount of a VA loan can't exceed the appraised value of the home or the sales price. The VA puts no other restrictions on the loan amount. However, most lenders do have rules about VA loan amounts. The most common rule is that for a no-downpayment VA loan, most lenders require the guaranty amount to equal at least 25% of the value or sales price of the property, whichever is less. For example, with a guaranty amount of $104,250 (the 2013 maximum in most places that don't have high housing prices), this restriction means that most lenders won't make a no-downpayment VA loan for more than $417,000 ($104,250 ÷ 25% = $417,000).

Lenders who follow that rule will still approve a larger loan if the borrower can make a downpayment. They typically want the total of the guaranty amount and the veteran's downpayment to equal 25% of the value or the sales price, whichever is less. This 25% rule means that the downpayment a veteran may have to make is still likely to be fairly modest.

> **EXAMPLE:** Sharon Vincent is eligible for a VA loan. She wants to buy a home for $430,000. The maximum guaranty amount in her county is $104,250, so her lender won't make a no-downpayment VA loan larger than $417,000. That means Sharon will have to make a downpayment in order to purchase the home.
>
> However, because of the lender's 25% rule, Sharon doesn't have to pay the difference between the $430,000 sales price and $417,000 to get the loan. Her downpayment only has to equal 25% of the difference. The combination of the guaranty and the downpayment must equal 25% of the sales price. 25% of $430,000 is $107,500. $107,500 − $104,250 guaranty amount = $3,250. Sharon only has to make a $3,250 downpayment in order to purchase the home.

The other situation in which a VA borrower has to make a downpayment is when the property's sales price exceeds its appraised value. The borrower must make up the difference out of his own funds.

SECONDARY FINANCING. If he doesn't have enough cash, a VA borrower can obtain secondary financing to cover a downpayment required by the lender. The total financing (the VA loan plus the secondary financing) can't exceed the appraised value of the property, the borrower must be able to qualify for the payments on both loans, and the second loan cannot have more stringent conditions than the VA loan.

Secondary financing that meets these standards can be used for the borrower's closing costs, as well as for a downpayment required by the lender. But secondary financing cannot be used when the downpayment is required because the sales price exceeds the property's appraised value.

SELLER CONCESSIONS. When a sale is financed with a VA loan, the seller is allowed to make certain concessions to help the buyer purchase the property. The seller's concessions generally must be no more than 4% of the property's value. But payment of the buyer's closing costs and normal discount points don't count toward the 4% limit. For example, suppose a lender would ordinarily charge two points on a loan, and the seller has offered to pay five points. The three extra points would be counted against the 4% limit on seller concessions.

ASSUMPTION AND RELEASE OF LIABILITY. A VA loan can be assumed by anyone, either a veteran or a non-veteran, as long as the person is creditworthy. Generally, the VA must give prior approval. The interest rate on a VA loan is not changed on assumption. The VA will charge a 0.5% funding fee, and the lender may charge limited processing and underwriting fees.

The original borrower is released from further liability in connection with the loan if the following conditions are met:

1. the loan payments are current,
2. the new buyer is an acceptable credit risk, and
3. the new buyer contractually assumes the veteran's obligations on the loan.

RESTORATION OF ENTITLEMENT. The guaranty amount available to a particular veteran is sometimes called the veteran's "entitlement." After using his entitlement, a veteran can obtain another VA loan only if the entitlement is restored.

> **EXAMPLE:** Joe McDowell used a VA loan to buy a home in 2002. This year Joe decided to sell the property. He paid off his VA loan out of the sale proceeds. When he repaid the loan, Joe's guaranty entitlement was restored. If Joe decides to buy another home, he can use his entitlement to get another VA loan.

It's possible for a veteran to have his entitlement restored even if the loan is assumed instead of paid off when the home is sold. For this to work, the new homebuyer must also be a veteran who agrees to substitute her entitlement for the seller's entitlement. The loan payments must be current, and the buyer must also

FIG. 10.9 FEATURES OF VA-GUARANTEED LOANS

VA LOAN FEATURES

- FOR RESIDENTIAL PROPERTIES WITH ONE TO FOUR UNITS
- BORROWER MUST OCCUPY PROPERTY AS PRIMARY RESIDENCE
- 100% FINANCING ALLOWED — NO DOWNPAYMENT REQUIRED
- 1% ORIGINATION FEE (DISCOUNT POINTS ALSO ALLOWED)
- FUNDING FEE, BUT NO MORTGAGE INSURANCE
- NO MAXIMUM LOAN AMOUNT
- MAXIMUM GUARANTY IS TIED TO COUNTY MEDIAN HOME PRICE AND VARIES WITH LOAN AMOUNT
- LENDER MIGHT REQUIRE DOWNPAYMENT IF GUARANTY IS LESS THAN 25% OF LOAN AMOUNT
- SECONDARY FINANCING ALLOWED FOR DOWNPAYMENT
- LOAN CAN BE ASSUMED BY CREDITWORTHY VETERAN OR NON-VETERAN (WITH LENDER'S APPROVAL)
- RESTORATION OF ENTITLEMENT: LOAN MUST BE PAID OFF UNLESS ASSUMED BY ANOTHER VETERAN
- INCOME RATIO GUIDELINE: 41% TOTAL DEBT TO INCOME RATIO
- RESIDUAL INCOME REQUIREMENTS

be an acceptable credit risk. If all of these conditions are met, the veteran can formally request a substitution of entitlement from the VA.

QUALIFYING FOR A VA LOAN. To qualify for a VA loan, a veteran must meet the underwriting standards set by the Department of Veterans Affairs. A VA loan applicant's income is analyzed with two different methods, an income ratio method and a residual income method. The veteran must qualify under both methods.

The income ratio method for analyzing a veteran's income is very similar to the method used for conventional and FHA loans. However, only one ratio—the total debt to income ratio—is used, instead of two ratios. As a general rule, the vet's total debt to income ratio should not be more than 41%.

EXAMPLE: Robert Garcia is eligible for a VA loan. He makes $2,800 a month, and his total monthly obligations add up to $375 a month. To estimate how large a house payment he can qualify for, multiply $2,800 by 41%. $2,800 × .41 = $1,148. Now subtract his monthly obligations of $375 from $1,148. $1,148 – $375 = $773. Robert could qualify for a $773 monthly housing expense under the total debt to income ratio.

The second method used to qualify a VA loan applicant is the **residual income method**, also called cash flow analysis. The proposed housing expense (the PITI payment), estimated property maintenance and utility costs, all other recurring obligations, and certain taxes (including federal income tax, any state or local income tax, Social Security tax, Medicare tax, and any other taxes deducted from the veteran's paychecks) are subtracted from the veteran's gross monthly income to determine his residual income. The monthly maintenance and utility cost estimate is calculated by multiplying the number of square feet of living area in the house by 14 cents. (The VA refers to the borrower's PITI payment plus the maintenance and utility cost estimate as the **monthly shelter expense**.)

The loan applicant's residual income should be at least one dollar more than the VA's minimum requirement. The minimum requirement varies, depending on where the veteran lives, his family size, and the size of the proposed loan (see Figure 10.10). For example, the residual income required for a family of three living in Washington State when the loan amount is less than $80,000 is $859. The residual income required for a family of four living in Washington when the loan amount is $80,000 or more is $1,117.

EXAMPLE: Robert lives in Washington; he's divorced and has one child. He wants to buy a 1,500 square-foot home that costs $107,000. The VA requires him to have at least $823 in residual income to qualify for a loan.

To calculate Robert's residual income, start with his monthly gross income, $2,800. Subtract his federal income tax, which is $350. There's no state or local income tax where he lives, but Social Security and Medicare taxes do have to be subtracted; they total $214. Next, subtract his recurring monthly obligations, which are $375. Calculate the monthly maintenance and utility costs ($0.14 × 1,500 square feet = $210) and subtract that figure. Then subtract Robert's proposed housing expense (PITI), which is, at most, $773 (the figure obtained from applying the 41% total debt to income ratio).

$$2,800 – $350 – $214 – $375 – $210 – $773 = $878$$

Robert's residual income is above his required minimum ($823) so he should have no problem qualifying for the loan.

The VA emphasizes that its minimum residual income figures are only guidelines. If the veteran fails to meet the guidelines, it should not mean an automatic rejection of the loan application. The lender should take other factors into consid-

FIG. 10.10 VA RESIDUAL INCOME REQUIREMENTS

Table of Residual Incomes by Region For loan amounts of $79,999 and below				
Family Size	**Northeast**	**Midwest**	**South**	**West**
1	$390	$382	$382	$425
2	$654	$641	$641	$713
3	$788	$772	$772	$859
4	$888	$868	$868	$967
5	$921	$902	$902	$1,004
Over 5: Add $75 for each additional member up to a family of 7.				

Table of Residual Incomes by Region For loan amounts of $80,000 and above				
Family Size	**Northeast**	**Midwest**	**South**	**West**
1	$450	$441	$441	$491
2	$755	$738	$738	$823
3	$909	$889	$889	$990
4	$1,025	$1,003	$1,003	$1,117
5	$1,062	$1,039	$1,039	$1,158
Over 5: Add $80 for each additional member up to a family of 7.				

eration, such as the applicant's ability to accumulate a significant net worth, and the number and ages of any dependents.

The VA's 41% income ratio is also flexible. A lender can approve a VA loan even though the applicant's income ratio is above 41% if the application presents other favorable factors, such as an excellent credit reputation, a substantial amount of reserves, a substantial downpayment, or significantly more residual income than the minimum amount required by the VA. Extra residual income is an especially important compensating factor. If the applicant's residual income is at least 20% over the required minimum, the lender can approve the loan even though the income ratio is well over 41% and there are no other compensating factors.

Rural Housing Service Loans

The Rural Housing Service (RHS) is a federal agency within the U.S. Department of Agriculture that makes and guarantees loans used to purchase, build, or rehabilitate homes in rural areas. (These loans are often referred to as rural development (or RD) loans.) A rural area is generally defined as open country or a town with a rural character and a population of 10,000 or less. However, an area with a population of up to 20,000 may be considered rural if it falls outside a metropolitan area and suffers a serious lack of mortgage credit (even a population up to 25,000 may be eligible under certain circumstances).

To qualify for an RHS program, a borrower must currently be without adequate housing. The borrower must also be able to afford the proposed mortgage payments and have a reasonable credit history. A home purchased, built, or improved with a rural development loan must be modest in both size and design.

DIRECT LOANS. Low-income borrowers (whose income is no more than 80% of the area median income) may obtain financing from RHS for 100% of the purchase price. The loan term may be as long as 38 years, depending on the borrower's income level. The interest rate is set by RHS, and the loan is serviced by RHS.

GUARANTEED LOANS. The Rural Housing Service also guarantees loans made by approved lenders to borrowers whose income is no more than 115% of the area median income. Approved lenders include any state housing agency, FHA- and VA-approved lenders, and lenders participating in RHS-guaranteed loan programs. The loan amount may be 100% of the purchase price. The loan term is 30 years, and the interest rate is set by the lender.

SELLER FINANCING

Institutional lenders such as banks, savings and loans, and mortgage companies are not the only sources of residential financing. In some cases, the home seller may also be a source. When a seller helps a buyer finance the purchase of a home, it's called **seller financing**. Seller financing can take a variety of forms, ranging from the simple to the complex.

HOW SELLER FINANCING WORKS

As you know, institutional lenders require both a promissory note and a security instrument (a mortgage or a deed of trust) when they make a loan. The promissory note is evidence of the debt, and the security instrument makes the property collateral for the loan. In many cases, these same documents are used in seller financing. The homebuyer signs a promissory note, promising to pay the seller the amount of the debt, and then signs a mortgage or deed of trust that gives the seller a security interest in the home being purchased. This kind of seller financing arrangement is often called a **purchase money loan** or a carryback loan.

Purchase money loans are quite different from institutional loans. With an institutional loan, the lender gives the borrower cash, which is then given to the seller in return for the deed to the property. With a purchase money loan, the seller simply extends credit to the buyer. Essentially, the buyer is allowed to pay off the purchase price in installments over time, instead of having to pay the total purchase price in cash at closing.

In some instances, the seller may choose to use a land contract instead of the promissory note and mortgage or deed of trust. With a land contract, the buyer takes immediate possession of the land, but does not acquire legal title until the entire purchase price is paid off. A land contract is another way a seller can offer credit to the buyer.

In a seller-financed transaction, the seller usually decides which type of financing documents to use. If your seller is unsure about which type to use, you should recommend that she speak to an attorney. Never advise a seller about the legal consequences of using the various types of documents. And always recommend that an attorney prepare any documents used in a seller-financed transaction. If your seller wishes to prepare the documents herself, strongly recommend that an attorney review them before they are signed by the parties.

Why Use Seller Financing? Setting up a seller-financed transaction can be complicated. The seller has to decide what kinds of documents to use and, typically, one or more attorneys get involved somewhere along the way. But there are several good reasons to use seller financing. One important reason is to make the property more marketable. This is especially true when market interest rates are high

FIG. 10.11   ADVANTAGES OF SELLER FINANCING

Why Use Seller Financing?

- May make property more marketable
- Seller can help buyer qualify for institutional loan
- Buyer may save money on financing costs
- Buyer may be willing to pay more for home
- Possible tax benefits for seller (installment sale reporting)

or loans are difficult to obtain. When interest rates are high, mortgage payments are also high. Potential buyers may have a difficult time qualifying for a loan with high mortgage payments, or they may be simply unwilling to take on a long-term loan at such high interest rates. By offering seller financing at a lower-than-market interest rate, a seller can make his home more attractive to potential buyers.

Seller financing can also help a buyer who could not qualify for institutional financing to complete the purchase of a home. With seller financing, the buyer avoids some of the costs of borrowing money from a lender, such as the loan origination fee and any discount points. Also, the seller may agree to a smaller downpayment than an institutional lender would require. Both of these factors mean a buyer can close a seller-financed sale with much less cash than would be required for an institutional loan.

Because of the potential advantages that seller financing has for buyers, the seller may be able to get more for her home. For example, if the seller was asking $150,000 cash, a buyer might be willing to pay $157,000 for the property and attractive seller financing terms. In essence, the buyer would pay an additional $7,000 for the property to get the advantages of a low downpayment, fewer closing costs, a favorable interest rate, and lower monthly payments.

Seller financing can also provide the seller with important tax benefits. Because the buyer will be paying the purchase price of the home in installments, over a period of years, the seller is allowed to spread out her profit from the sale over that same period. In other words, the seller does not have to report the full profit from the sale on her tax return in the year of sale. Only the amount of profit actually received in a given year is taxed in that year. The seller can spread the tax payments out over a longer period, and may be able to take advantage of a lower tax rate as a result.

Always advise a seller to consult an accountant or attorney about the tax implications of seller financing. There may be some tax disadvantages to a particular transaction that the seller may not be aware of.

CONCERNS OF THE PARTIES. When structuring a seller financing arrangement, it's important to pay close attention to the particular needs of the buyer and the seller. The buyer will be concerned with the cost of the financing, especially the interest rate and the amount of the downpayment. If the seller requires a balloon payment in a few years, the buyer should have some idea where he is going to get the money to make that payment. Will the buyer have the cash to make the balloon payment, or will he have to refinance the transaction? Financing that involves a

---

FIG. 10.12   POTENTIAL ISSUES WITH SELLER FINANCING

SELLER FINANCING CONCERNS

- BALLOON PAYMENT: HOW WILL BUYER PAY IT WHEN THE TIME COMES?

- HOW MUCH IMMEDIATE CASH DOES SELLER NEED FROM SALE?

- IS INTEREST RATE CHARGED A GOOD RATE OF RETURN FOR SELLER?

- COULD THE SALE CREATE TAX PROBLEMS FOR SELLER?

- PRIORITY OF SELLER'S LIEN

---

balloon payment always presents a risk for the buyer. This kind of arrangement often works out fine, but the buyer should make plans about the balloon payment sooner rather than later.

Seller financing raises different concerns for the seller. Obviously, the seller doesn't want to extend financing to a buyer who can't afford the monthly payments. And the seller should also be concerned about whether the buyer will be able to make any required balloon payment. But there are other equally important issues for the seller to consider.

First of all, the seller needs to decide whether she can really afford to offer seller financing, or whether she needs to be cashed out. For example, if the seller is purchasing a new home, she may need all of her equity from the old home in cash at closing. And even if the seller does not need all of the equity immediately, will the buyer's anticipated downpayment be enough cash to meet the seller's needs?

Most sellers who offer seller financing do so because they don't need the cash right away and a steady monthly income is attractive. Is the mortgage payment the buyer is going to pay on the seller financing enough to meet the seller's monthly needs? Is the interest rate charged on the seller financing a good rate of return? If the seller would charge 5% interest on the second mortgage, but could get a 7% return from investing in a mutual fund, the seller may want to rethink the transaction. And depending on the rate of interest charged, the seller could be faced with tax penalties based on the "imputed interest" rule. Under the imputed interest rule, if a seller charges an interest rate that is below a specified minimum, the IRS will treat some of the principal received in each installment payment as interest, and thus taxable. If the seller runs afoul of the imputed interest rule, many of the benefits the seller thought he was getting by offering seller financing could be eliminated. Again, it is imperative to advise your sellers to seek competent tax advice before they enter into a seller-financed transaction.

Finally, lien priority is an important consideration in any seller financing arrangement. It is almost certain that any new or existing institutional loan will have a higher priority than the seller's loan. In the event of default, the higher priority loan will be repaid first. If there is nothing left after the institutional loan has been repaid, the seller will get nothing. Thus, like an institutional lender, the seller must consider the relationship between the liens and the property's value. Would the property sell for enough at a foreclosure sale to pay off the seller financing as well as the liens with higher priority?

TYPES OF SELLER FINANCING

Seller financing can be used alone or in conjunction with institutional financing.

SELLER SECONDS. One of the most common forms of seller financing is the seller second. With a seller second, the buyer pays most of the purchase price with an institutional loan, and the seller finances some of what would normally be the buyer's downpayment with a second mortgage.

> **EXAMPLE:** Schmidt is buying Earnshaw's home for $200,000. She is getting an institutional loan for $170,000. However, she doesn't have enough cash to make a $30,000 downpayment, so Earnshaw agrees to take back a second mortgage in the amount of $15,000. Now Schmidt only has to come up with $15,000 for the downpayment.

There are several advantages to a seller second. As in this example, a seller second allows the buyer to make a smaller downpayment than she might otherwise have to make. A seller second can also help a marginal buyer qualify for an institutional loan. Institutional lenders have certain rules that must be followed when the buyer is going to use secondary financing. The lender should always be consulted to make sure the seller second is acceptable.

As long as the parties stay within the institutional lender's guidelines, they can come up with virtually unlimited ways to structure their financing package.

PRIMARY SELLER FINANCING. Seller financing may also be used as the main or only source of financing. This is called primary seller financing. Seller financing is at its most flexible when it is the only financing. Lender guidelines for secondary loans no longer have to be followed, and qualifying standards can be virtually ignored if the parties choose to do so.

UNENCUMBERED PROPERTY. Seller financing can be used when the property is either encumbered by a previous mortgage or unencumbered. Property is unencumbered when the seller owns it free and clear of any liens. When the property is unencumbered, seller financing is usually very straightforward. All the buyer and seller have to do is negotiate the sales price and the terms of the financing, and then have the appropriate finance documents prepared.

If the seller financing is the only source of financing, the seller will have first lien position, as long as she properly records the loan documents. However, the seller still has to be prepared to protect her security interest. A first mortgage does not have priority over all other liens. For example, real property tax liens and special assessment liens take priority over mortgages, no matter what the recording date. If the buyer fails to pay the property taxes, the property could be foreclosed on and the seller could take a loss at the foreclosure sale.

Destruction of the premises is another danger. Suppose the buyer fails to keep the property insured and the house burns down. The buyer then defaults on the loan, and the seller has to foreclose. Since the property is now probably worth much less than the amount of the remaining debt, the seller is likely to lose a great deal of money in the foreclosure sale.

The seller can protect her interest in the property by setting up an impound account for taxes and insurance, just as many institutional lenders do. Along with the loan payment, the buyer would make monthly tax and insurance payments, which would be deposited into the impound account. The funds in the impound account would then be used to pay off the property taxes and insurance premiums when they become due. Many banks, savings and loans, and mortgage companies are willing to provide and service impound accounts for private parties.

ENCUMBERED PROPERTY. It's relatively uncommon for a seller to own his property free and clear of any other mortgage liens. Typically, the seller financed the purchase of the property and still owes money on that loan when he decides to sell. When the property is encumbered with a mortgage loan, it is a rare seller who can pay off the first loan with savings or the proceeds of the downpayment alone.

For instance, suppose Brown is selling his home for $260,000. He would prefer to finance the sale and receive payments on an installment basis. However, there's a first mortgage on the property in the amount of $125,000. Brown doesn't have enough cash to pay off a $125,000 loan at closing, and a buyer is unlikely to have that much cash to invest in the home as a downpayment. It's possible that the buyer could assume the seller's existing mortgage, and Brown could finance the rest of the purchase price with a seller second. But there is another alternative that may be more attractive: wraparound financing.

With a **wraparound loan**, the buyer does not assume the seller's mortgage. Nor does the seller try to pay off this mortgage at closing. Instead, the buyer takes the property "subject to" the existing mortgage. This means the seller remains primarily responsible for making the payments on this mortgage. The seller finances the complete purchase price for the buyer, less the downpayment. The seller then uses part of the monthly payment received from the buyer to make the monthly payment on the existing mortgage (referred to as the **underlying mortgage**), and keeps the balance.

> **EXAMPLE:** Brown owes $125,000 on his house. The mortgage payment is $1,200. Brown sells his house to Morgan for $300,000. Morgan pays Brown a $35,000 downpayment, and Brown finances the remaining $265,000 purchase price at 7% interest. Morgan's monthly payment is $1,900. Brown uses part of the $1,900 to make the $1,200 payment on the underlying mortgage, then keeps the remaining $700 for himself.

Wraparound financing is only possible if the underlying loan does not have a due-on-sale clause. If there's a due-on-sale clause, the lender may call the underlying note, and it will become immediately due and payable.

When there is a due-on-sale clause in the underlying mortgage, it is dangerous to try to get away with a wraparound loan by keeping the lender in the dark about the sale. This is called a "silent" wrap, and it could easily backfire. Real estate agents should never get involved in silent wraps.

With wraparound financing, the buyer typically needs a little extra protection. If the seller fails to make the payments on the underlying loan, the institutional lender could foreclose, and the buyer could lose the property as well as all the monthly payments she has already made.

The best way to protect the buyer is to set up an escrow account for the loan payments. An independent third party in charge of the escrow account uses part of the buyer's payment to make the underlying loan payments and sends the remainder to the seller. Thus, the buyer is assured that the underlying loan payments will always be made in a timely manner. The seller can require the buyer to deposit tax and hazard insurance payments into the same account, thus protecting the seller's security interest in the property as well.

OTHER WAYS SELLERS CAN HELP

In many cases a seller can't afford to offer seller financing to a buyer, usually because the seller can't wait several years to be cashed out. However, there are a number of other ways in which a seller can help a buyer close the transaction, including all of the following:

- **Buydowns.** As we discussed earlier, the seller can help the buyer by agreeing to a buydown. To buy down the interest rate on the buyer's institutional loan, the seller doesn't have to pay the lender a lump sum at closing. Instead, the seller's net proceeds from the sale are reduced by the amount of the buydown. From the seller's point of view, a buydown is similar to a price reduction. However, a buydown may help the buyer more than a straight price reduction, by enabling him to qualify for an institutional loan more easily.
- **Contributions to closing costs.** By paying for some of the closing costs that are typically the buyer's responsibility, the seller enables the buyer to close the transaction with less cash. Remember, however, that lenders place limitations on the amount a seller can contribute toward the buyer's closing costs.
- **Equity exchanges.** Instead of cash, the seller may be willing to accept another asset, such as recreational property, a car, or a boat, as all or part of the downpayment. Again, this kind of transaction enables the buyer to close the sale with significantly less cash.
- **Lease/options.** Sometimes a prospective buyer may simply not be ready to purchase a home. The buyer may need time to save up for a downpayment, pay off debts, or improve her credit rating. Or perhaps the buyer needs more time to sell a property she already owns. In these circumstances, a lease/option arrangement may help the buyer purchase the seller's home. A lease/option is a combination of a lease and an option to buy. The seller leases the property to a prospective buyer for a specific period of time. At the same time, the seller gives the buyer an option to purchase the property at a certain price during the lease period.

Whenever you're handling a sale that involves seller financing, you should make sure that both parties understand the ramifications of the transaction. While you can't give them legal advice, it's appropriate to raise the concerns we've discussed here, such as the seller's lien priority and the importance of escrow accounts. As a real estate agent, you should never prepare the documents used in a seller-financed transaction, and you should always recommend that both the buyer and the seller get competent advice from their attorneys or accountants, or both.

CHAPTER SUMMARY

1. Conventional loans may be 30-year or 15-year, fixed- or adjustable-rate, and fully or partially amortized. Conventional loans with loan-to-value ratios up to 95% are generally available. Private mortgage insurance is required for conventional loans with LTVs over 80%.

2. Lenders charge an origination fee to cover their administrative costs, and may charge discount points to increase the upfront yield on the loan. A seller may pay for a buydown to help the buyer qualify for financing.

3. As a general rule, a conventional loan applicant's total debt to income ratio shouldn't exceed 36%, and the housing expense ratio shouldn't exceed 28%.

4. FHA loans are characterized by less stringent qualifying standards, a low downpayment (minimum cash investment) requirement, and mortgage insurance (both a one-time premium and annual premiums).

5. An FHA loan applicant's debt to income ratio should not exceed 43%, and the housing expense to income ratio should not exceed 31%.

6. VA loans generally require no downpayment and no mortgage insurance. VA qualifying standards are lenient. The maximum guaranty for VA loans is adjusted annually. Although the VA does not set a maximum loan amount, most lenders require the guaranty to cover at least 25% of the loan amount.

7. A VA loan applicant is generally required to have a total debt to income ratio of 41% or less, and also have residual income that meets VA standards.

8. When a seller helps the buyer finance the transaction, it's called seller financing. The most common form of seller financing is the seller second: the buyer pays most of the purchase price with an institutional loan, and the seller finances some of the buyer's downpayment.

9. Seller financing may also be used as the only source of financing. If the property is already encumbered by a mortgage, the parties may decide to use wraparound financing. In a wraparound arrangement, the buyer takes the property subject to the first mortgage, and the seller uses part of the monthly payment received from the buyer to make the payment on the underlying mortgage. Wraparound financing can't be used if there is a due-on-sale clause in the underlying mortgage.

CHAPTER QUIZ

1. A loan that requires monthly payments of both principal and interest, but leaves some of the principal to be paid off in a balloon payment at the end of the loan term, is:

    a. fully amortized

    b. negatively amortized

    c. non-amortized

    d. partially amortized

2. A lender will usually charge a higher interest rate in which of the following situations?

    a. The borrower wants an ARM instead of a fixed-rate mortgage

    b. The seller is offering a buydown

    c. The borrower wants a 5/1 ARM instead of an ARM with a one-year initial rate adjustment period

    d. The borrower wants a two-step mortgage instead of a fixed-rate mortgage

3. A portfolio loan is a loan that:

    a. the lender plans to keep as an investment

    b. conforms to the rules of Fannie Mae and Freddie Mac

    c. is insured or guaranteed by a government agency

    d. is sold on the secondary market

4. To compensate for the extra risk, a lender making a conventional loan with a high loan-to-value ratio:

    a. might apply stricter qualifying standards

    b. might charge higher loan fees

    c. will require private mortgage insurance

    d. All of the above

5. The Homeowners Protection Act requires:

    a. borrowers to send a written request to their lender in order to cancel private mortgage insurance

    b. all loans closed on or after July 29, 1999, to be covered by private mortgage insurance

    c. lenders to send all borrowers with private mortgage insurance an annual notice concerning their PMI cancellation rights

    d. lenders to automatically cancel the PMI when a loan's principal balance reaches 78% of the home's current appraised value

6. All of the following factors might justify making a loan when the borrower's income ratios exceed the standard benchmarks, except:

    a. substantial net worth
    b. significant energy-efficient features in the home being purchased
    c. a high loan-to-value ratio
    d. education that indicates strong potential for increased earnings

7. With a graduated payment buydown plan, what rate will a lender probably use to qualify the buyer for the loan?

    a. A rate somewhere between the initial rate the borrower will pay and the full note rate
    b. The index rate
    c. A rate 1% or 2% above the note rate
    d. The buydown rate

8. Which of the following can the borrower count as part of the minimum cash investment required for an FHA loan?

    a. Discount points
    b. Closing costs
    c. Prepaid expenses
    d. None of the above

9. Jack, a veteran who wants to buy a house with a VA loan, has full guaranty entitlement. Which of the following is true?

    a. The VA guaranty will cover only a portion of the loan amount
    b. The VA guaranty will cover the entire loan amount
    c. Jack cannot be required to make a downpayment, regardless of the loan amount
    d. Jack is guaranteed a VA loan, so the VA's usual qualifying standards will be waived

10. If a seller wants to help a prospective buyer qualify for a conventional loan, which of the following options may reduce the interest rate used to qualify the buyer for the loan?

    a. Buydown
    b. Lease/option
    c. Silent wrap
    d. Equity exchange

ANSWER KEY

1. d. With a partially amortized loan, not all of the principal is paid off through the monthly payments, and the borrower must make a balloon payment at the end of the loan term.

2. c. With adjustable-rate loans, as a general rule, the longer the initial rate adjustment period, the higher the interest rate. The interest rate on a 5/1 ARM is not adjusted during the first five years, but may be adjusted annually after that.

3. a. If a lender plans to keep a loan as an investment instead of selling it on the secondary market, the lender is keeping the loan "in portfolio."

4. d. For a high-LTV conventional loan, many lenders apply stricter qualifying standards and charge a higher interest rate and loan fees. Private mortgage insurance is generally required on any conventional loan with an LTV over 80%.

5. c. The Homeowners Protection Act requires lenders to send an annual notice to borrowers with PMI, regardless of whether their loans are subject to the other provisions of the act. (PMI must be canceled automatically when the principal balance reaches 78% of the home's original value, not 78% of the current appraised value.)

6. c. If the borrower exceeds the income ratio guidelines, the lender may consider other factors that indicate the borrower will be able to make the monthly payments. A high loan-to-value ratio, however, means the borrower has less invested in the property and is more likely to default.

7. a. Because a buyer with a graduated payment buydown will eventually have to pay interest at the full note rate, the lender wants to make sure the buyer will be able to handle the increased monthly payments. As a result, the lender will often qualify the buyer using a rate that is lower than the full note rate but higher than the initial buydown rate.

8. d. Discount points paid by the borrower do not count towards the minimum cash investment, nor do the closing costs or prepaid expenses.

9. a. The VA guaranty covers only a portion of the loan amount. Even veterans who have full guaranty entitlement must meet the VA's qualifying standards in order to obtain a VA-guaranteed loan.

10. a. With a buydown, the seller can lower the interest rate on the buyer's loan, which may allow the buyer to get a loan he might not otherwise qualify for.

CLOSING THE TRANSACTION AND REAL ESTATE MATH

THE CLOSING PROCESS

- Escrow
- Steps in closing a transaction
  - Overview
  - Inspections
  - Financing
  - Appraisal
  - Hazard insurance
  - Title insurance
- Real estate agent's role

CLOSING COSTS

- Costs and credits
- Estimating the buyer's net cost
- Estimating the seller's net proceeds

FEDERAL LAWS THAT AFFECT CLOSING

- Income tax regulations
  - Form 1099 reporting
  - Form 8300 reporting
  - Foreign Investment in Real Property Tax Act
- Real Estate Settlement Procedures Act

REAL ESTATE MATH

INTRODUCTION

You helped your buyers find an affordable house that suits their needs. They made an offer on the house, and the sellers accepted it. The buyers must now order inspections, apply for or finalize their financing, and obtain a preliminary title report. The sellers must pay off the liens against the property, arrange for required repairs, and execute the deed. In other words, the buyers and the sellers must go through the closing process.

As a real estate agent, you will be shepherding your buyers and sellers through closing. Many of your clients will be unfamiliar with the process; you'll need to calm their anxieties and answer their questions. How long will it take to close the sale? What responsibilities does each party have? How much cash will the buyer need to close the sale? How much cash will the seller receive at closing?

In this chapter, we will discuss the closing process, closing costs and which party usually pays them, and how to estimate the buyer's net cost and the seller's net proceeds. We'll also cover some federal laws that affect closing, including the Real Estate Settlement Procedures Act. We'll end the chapter with a quick look at some common math problems you're likely to encounter in your real estate practice.

THE CLOSING PROCESS

The phrase "closing a sale" actually has two meanings in the real estate field. Sometimes it refers to getting a buyer to make an offer. For instance, a seller's agent can "close a sale" by overcoming the buyer's objections and convincing the buyer that it's the right time to make an offer on the house. Here, however, we'll be using "closing the sale" in its other sense, to mean completing all the tasks that have to be taken care of before title can be transferred to the buyer and the purchase price can be disbursed to the seller.

For every sale you handle as a real estate agent, it's part of your job to make sure that all of the closing requirements are met on time. You probably won't be completing all, or even most, of the necessary tasks yourself, but you have to know what needs to be done, who's responsible for doing it, and whether it's being done in a timely manner. If the closing process doesn't go smoothly, it can cause considerable delay and inconvenience, and in some cases the transaction will fall apart altogether.

FIG. 11 .1   CHECKLIST FOR CLOSING

Closing Checklist

Property: _____

Buyer: _____

Seller: _____

Other party's agent: _____

Financing		Inspection 1	
Lender: _____		Company: _____	
Loan application submitted	_____	Inspection ordered	_____
Appraisal ordered	_____	Inspection report issued	_____
Appraisal completed	_____	Approval or disapproval	_____
Loan package submitted	_____	Seller's response	_____
Loan approved	_____	Repairs completed	_____
Loan documents signed	_____	Repairs reinspected	_____
Loan funds disbursed	_____	Reinspection approved	_____

Closing Requirements		Inspection 2	
Earnest money deposited	_____	Company: _____	
Escrow opened	_____	Inspection ordered	_____
Escrow instructions	_____	Inspection report issued	_____
Seller's information	_____	Approval or disapproval	_____
Title search ordered	_____	Seller's response	_____
Preliminary title report	_____	Repairs completed	_____
Demand for payoff	_____	Repairs reinspected	_____
All conditions fulfilled	_____	Reinspection approved	_____
All documents signed	_____		
Buyer deposits funds	_____	**Moving**	
Hazard insurance policy	_____	Seller's belongings out	_____
Documents recorded	_____	Yard cleanup	_____
Title policies issued	_____	Interior cleaning	_____
Settlement statements	_____	Keys for buyer	_____

To help keep track of the steps in the closing process and make sure that everything's getting done, you might want to use a closing checklist, such as the one shown in Figure 11.1. Review the purchase and sale agreement to remind yourself of the basic terms and any unusual provisions; add any special requirements to the checklist. As the days go by, refer to your list on a regular basis, check off what has been accomplished and fill in the date of completion, and note what still needs to be done.

ESCROW

Most transactions in Washington are closed through the escrow process. The closing is handled by a neutral third party called an **escrow agent** or **closing agent**. The escrow agent holds money and documents on behalf of the buyer and seller in accordance with their written **escrow instructions**. The agent will release the money and documents to the appropriate parties only when all of the conditions set forth in the escrow instructions have been fulfilled.

There are two major benefits to closing a transaction through escrow. First, escrow helps ensure that both parties will go through with the transaction as agreed. For example, once a signed deed has been placed in escrow, it's much more difficult for the seller to change his mind at the last moment and refuse to transfer title to the buyer. The escrow agent has legally binding instructions to deliver the deed to the buyer when the buyer pays the purchase price. The seller can't just demand the deed back from the escrow agent. So if the seller changes his mind, a lawsuit may be required to resolve the matter.

The second benefit of escrow is convenience. It isn't necessary for everyone involved in the transaction to be present at the same time for the sale to close.

ESCROW AGENTS. In addition to holding items on behalf of the parties and disbursing them at the proper time, the escrow agent or closing agent is also responsible for seeing that legal documents are prepared and recorded, prorating the settlement costs, preparing the settlement statements, and various other tasks.

LICENSING AND EXEMPTIONS. In Washington, escrow agents must be licensed and registered with the Department of Financial Institutions. However, there are several exemptions from the escrow licensing requirements. Attorneys, title companies, banks, savings and loans, credit unions, insurance companies, federally approved lenders, and those acting under court supervision (such as probate administrators) may provide escrow services without fulfilling the licensing and registration requirements. Real estate agents who provide escrow services for transactions they are handling are also exempt, as long as they don't charge a fee for their escrow services.

EXAMPLE: Yamamoto is buying Farley's house. You are the real estate agent representing Farley. You agree to act as the closing agent free of charge. You may do so, even if you are not a licensed escrow agent. But if you charged Yamamoto and Farley an escrow fee in addition to your regular commission, you would be violating the escrow registration law.

Although it's legal for real estate licensees to handle escrow in their own transactions, it isn't necessarily a good idea; the arrangement may create a conflict of interest. A licensee usually represents either the buyer or the seller and owes a duty of loyalty to her client. But a closing agent is supposed to be neutral and act on behalf of both parties.

TERMINOLOGY. Sometimes the term "escrow agent" is reserved for a registered independent escrow company or a licensed escrow agent, while "closing agent" is used as a general term that refers to any person or entity providing escrow services in a real estate transaction (whether that's a lawyer, a bank, a real estate licensee, or a licensed escrow agent). In other cases, the two terms are used interchangeably in the more general sense, to mean any person or entity that is providing escrow services in a real estate transaction. Thus, when a lawyer or a real estate licensee is performing the same tasks as an independent escrow company, you may hear the lawyer or the licensee referred to either as the closing agent or as the escrow agent for the transaction.

STEPS IN CLOSING A TRANSACTION

Certain steps must be completed during the closing process in almost every residential transaction. We'll give you an overview of these steps, and then consider some of them in more detail.

OVERVIEW. If the sale is contingent on one or more inspections—for example, a home inspection and a pest inspection—the inspections should be ordered as soon as possible after the purchase and sale agreement is signed. This is usually done by the buyer or the buyer's real estate agent.

BUYER'S LOAN. Another step that should be taken as soon as possible is arranging for financing. The buyer must either apply for a loan or, if he has been preapproved for a loan, fulfill any additional requirements set by the lender. In any case, the lender will order a property appraisal before issuing a final loan commitment.

OPENING ESCROW. Escrow may be opened when the buyer's lender delivers a copy of the purchase and sale agreement to its escrow department. Alternatively, a real estate agent may open escrow by delivering a copy of the agreement to the escrow agent specified by the parties. Either way, the escrow agent uses the purchase and sale agreement as the basis for preparing the escrow instructions for the buyer and seller to sign. The conditions and deadlines in the instructions must match the terms of the agreement.

APPRAISAL. The appraisal report is sent to the buyer's lender, because the lender is the appraiser's client. To find out what the appraiser concluded, the parties or their real estate agents usually have to ask the lender.

TITLE REPORT. The escrow agent orders a preliminary title report, if the lender has not already done so. This report, which describes the current condition of the seller's title to the property, is sent to the lender and the buyer for approval. Any unexpected title problems revealed in the report must be addressed.

LOAN PAYOFF. In most transactions, the seller has a mortgage or deed of trust on the property that will be paid off at closing. The closing agent requests a final payoff figure from the seller's lender. A form called a "Demand for Payoff" or a "Request for Beneficiary's Statement" is used to make this request. The closing agent will also need to obtain exact figures for any other liens that must be removed or judgments that must be paid.

INSPECTION REPORTS. After an inspection has been completed, the inspection report may be sent to the buyer or the buyer's real estate agent, who in turn may be expected to provide a copy to the buyer's lender. If the report shows that repairs are needed, there may be negotiations between the buyer and the seller about which of them will pay for the repairs (see Chapter 8). For any lender-required repairs, the lender will want proof that the repairs have been completed.

LOAN APPROVAL. When the buyer's loan is approved, the lender informs the buyer of the exact terms on which it was approved and the date on which the loan commitment will expire. The lender also gives the buyer an updated good faith estimate of her closing costs. The lender sends all of the new loan documents—the promissory note and the mortgage or deed of trust—to the escrow agent, who arranges for the buyer to review and sign them. Once the loan documents have been signed, they are returned to the lender, who then coordinates loan funding with the escrow agent.

BUYER'S FUNDS. When all of the contingencies listed in the purchase and sale agreement (such as the inspections, the financing arrangements, or the sale of the buyer's home) have been satisfied, the buyer deposits the downpayment and the closing costs into escrow. Some lenders disburse the loan funds to the escrow agent at this point, but many lenders wait until the title has been transferred and the buyer's deed and mortgage or deed of trust have been recorded. It is the title company that files the documents with the county clerk for recording.

FIG. 11.2 STEPS IN THE CLOSING PROCESS

- INSPECTIONS ORDERED BY BUYER OR REAL ESTATE AGENT
- FINANCING APPLIED FOR OR FINALIZED BY BUYER
- APPRAISAL ORDERED BY LENDER
- ESCROW OPENED BY LENDER OR REAL ESTATE AGENT
- ESCROW INSTRUCTIONS PREPARED BY CLOSING AGENT
- PRELIMINARY TITLE REPORT ORDERED BY CLOSING AGENT
- LOAN PAYOFF AMOUNT REQUESTED FROM SELLER'S LENDER BY CLOSING AGENT
- LOAN DOCUMENTS SIGNED BY BUYER
- DOWNPAYMENT AND CLOSING COSTS DEPOSITED BY BUYER
- LOAN FUNDS DEPOSITED BY LENDER
- SETTLEMENT STATEMENTS PREPARED BY CLOSING AGENT
- FUNDS DISBURSED BY CLOSING AGENT
- TITLE POLICY ISSUED BY TITLE COMPANY
- DOCUMENTS FILED FOR RECORDING BY TITLE COMPANY
- HAZARD INSURANCE POLICY ISSUED TO BUYER

SETTLEMENT STATEMENTS. After learning from the title company how much the recording fees will come to and how much the owner's and lender's title insurance policies cost, the escrow agent prepares the final settlement statements and disburses the funds held in escrow to the seller, the real estate licensee, and other individuals or entities that are entitled to payment. The title insurance policies are issued, as is the buyer's hazard or homeowner's insurance policy. Once this has all been done, the sale has officially closed.

Next, let's look at certain aspects of the closing process in more detail. We'll discuss property inspections, financing and the appraisal, hazard insurance, and title insurance.

INSPECTIONS. As we discussed in Chapter 8, many residential purchase and sale agreements have one or more inspection contingency provisions. For the benefit of the buyer, the sale is conditioned on a satisfactory inspection of the property by an expert. In addition, many lenders make one or more satisfactory inspections a condition of loan approval. Thus, inspections are a key part of the closing process.

For each inspection required by the parties' agreement or by the lender, not only must an initial inspection be ordered, but the inspection report must be approved or rejected by the buyer or the lender, repairs must be completed and reinspected, and the parties must be notified about the results of the reinspection. (For more information about the types of addenda and notice forms that can be used for inspection contingencies, see Chapter 8.) It's very important for inspections to be ordered early in the closing process; if repairs are required, they need to be completed early enough so that they don't delay the closing.

TYPES OF INSPECTIONS. There are many different types of real estate inspections. Here are brief descriptions of the inspections most commonly required in residential transactions. The first three on the list may be carried out by a single expert, a licensed home inspector.

- **Structural inspection.** The inspector identifies the materials used in the construction, the type of construction, and the accessibility of the various areas that are to be inspected. In addition, the inspector checks for major and minor problems in the structural systems of the building, including the foundation and the floor, wall, and roof framing.
- **Electrical and plumbing inspection.** The inspector checks the existing electrical and plumbing systems for capacity, safety, and life expectancy. Plumbing systems are also checked for unsanitary conditions. Upgrades and repairs may be recommended. If the property's water source is a private well, it may also be inspected for water quality and quantity.
- **Interior inspection.** The inspector checks the walls, floors, and ceilings for signs of water damage, settling, fire hazards, or other problems. Ventilation and energy conservation issues are noted. Appliances may also be examined for operational problems.
- **Pest inspection.** A pest inspector checks for damage caused by wood-eating insects such as termites, wood-boring beetles, and carpenter ants.
- **Soil inspection.** A soil inspector or geologist examines the soil conditions to see if there are existing or potential settling or drainage problems.
- **Environmental inspection.** An environmental inspection addresses concerns about radon, urea formaldehyde, asbestos, lead-based paint, underground

storage tanks, or contaminated water. (These problems are discussed in more detail in Chapter 3.)

CHOOSING AN INSPECTOR. For a particular inspection, your buyer may have an inspector in mind, or he may ask you to recommend someone reputable. When referring home inspectors, you must be sure to follow your brokerage firm's policy on referrals. State law requires every firm to have a written policy on referring home inspectors. This policy must address the buyers' or sellers' right to pick a home inspector of their own choosing and prohibit any collusion between a home inspector and a real estate licensee. Keep in mind that if you refer someone to a home inspector with whom you have (or had) any type of relationship, then full disclosure of the relationship must be provided in writing prior to the buyer or seller using the services of the home inspector.

Many firms will suggest that you give the buyer at least three names to choose from. (Ask other agents in your office for suggestions, if necessary.) To help a buyer make the selection, you can suggest that he ask the home inspector the following questions:

1. How long has the firm (or individual inspector) been in business? (A minimum of five years' experience is recommended.)
2. Does the firm belong to the American Society of Home Inspectors? (Membership requires actual experience, passing a written examination, inspection reviews, and continuing education.)
3. Has the firm changed its name recently? If so, why?
4. What type of report does the firm prepare? How long does it take to complete the report and get it back to the client?
5. How many inspectors does the firm have? Are they full-time or part-time?
6. Does the firm engage in other businesses in addition to inspections? (In other words, is home inspection only a sideline?)
7. Does the firm also offer to make any of the repairs recommended by the inspection? (Inspection companies that also make repairs may not give unbiased reports.)
8. Does the firm provide references? If the buyer requests them, an inspector should be willing to give several references.

You must check the state licensing database to make sure any home inspector you recommend is licensed. It is also a good idea to check with the Department of Licensing and the Better Business Bureau to see if any complaints have been lodged against the inspection firm.

Inspection reports. After an inspection is completed, the inspector prepares an inspection report. The report should summarize the major points of concern and state which problems need to be repaired or otherwise addressed promptly. This should include information about substandard workmanship and also about deterioration, such as dry rot or old wiring.

The report should put the property into perspective by comparing it to similar properties. A 15-year-old house can't be expected to be in the same condition as a brand new one.

In addition, the report should project a five-year budget for anticipated repair work and identify potential remodeling problems. For instance, if the buyer were to add rooms onto the house, the entire electrical system might need to be up-graded. Or the septic system might only be adequate for a three-bedroom house, and if another bedroom were added, a new septic tank would be required.

Repairs. After an inspection report has been issued, the party who request-ed it (the buyer or the lender) must either approve or disapprove the report. Depending on the terms of the inspection contingency provision, the buyer may have the right to disapprove the report for any reason and terminate the transac-tion without giving the seller the opportunity to make repairs. Or the contingency provision may require the buyer to identify which items in the report are unsat-isfactory and need to be repaired if the transaction is to continue. (See Chapter 8.) If the buyer's lender ordered the inspection, the repairs may be a condition of loan approval.

Ideally, the parties will already have agreed who will pay for any required repairs, but that isn't always the case. The purchase and sale agreement may commit the seller to paying up to a specified amount, but no more than that. If the repair costs significantly exceed that amount, it may be necessary for the seller to negotiate a price adjustment or some other concession to persuade the buyer to go forward.

In many cases, the repairs have to be completed and reinspected—and the buyer or lender has to approve the reinspection report—before the sale can close or the loan can be funded. In some circumstances, however, the closing can take place even though the repairs won't be completed by the closing date.

Financing. A home sale can't close unless the buyers have enough money to pay the purchase price. The buyers nearly always borrow the money they need from a bank or other lender. As explained in Chapter 9, it's now common for buyers to get preapproved for financing. Before choosing a house to buy, the buyers submit a fully completed loan application and the supporting documentation. The lender performs a credit analysis and qualifies the buyers for a certain loan amount at a specified interest rate. If they find a house that can be purchased with that loan amount, and if the property meets the lender's standards, the lender will issue a final loan commitment. By taking care of many matters beforehand, loan preapproval can streamline the closing process.

Employees of the buyer's lender are actively involved in closing the transaction. Even if the buyer has been preapproved for a loan, the lender's team orders and evaluates the appraisal, reviews the preliminary title report, and may also order inspections and require repairs. They prepare the financing documents for the buyer to sign, and they are responsible for funding the loan—that is, depositing the loan amount into escrow so that it can be disbursed at closing. As we indicated earlier, in many cases the entire closing is handled by the lender's escrow department.

Because of their role, the loan officer and other employees of the lender can have a big impact on the closing. If they're reputable and competent, they'll make sure that the loan process is completed smoothly and quickly, with a minimum of errors. Find out which lenders have good or bad reputations by asking experienced real estate agents, and pass that information along to your buyers before they choose their lender.

APPRAISAL. The buyer's lender orders the appraisal as part of the loan underwriting process. The property as well as the buyer must be qualified for the requested loan. Regardless of the buyer's financial situation, it's the property that serves as the security for the debt. If the loan is not repaid as agreed, the lender will foreclose on the property to recover the money owed. Before approving the loan, the lender must be certain that the property is worth enough to protect the lender's investment in case the borrower defaults.

The residential appraisal process has a lot in common with the competitive market analysis that real estate agents use to help price a home (see Chapter 4). In fact, the CMA method is based on the sales comparison approach to appraisal, which is the most important approach for residential appraisals.

You should understand the basic appraisal process well enough to give a brief explanation of the process to the buyer and seller. They are often anxious about the appraisal, since their transaction depends on the appraiser's opinion.

HAZARD INSURANCE. Virtually all lenders require the escrow agent to make sure that the mortgaged property is insured up to the property's replacement cost before the loan funds are disbursed. In most cases the minimum insurance policy is the HO-3 policy. This type of policy provides coverage against most perils, but does exclude floods and earthquakes, as well as some less common perils (such as war and nuclear hazard).

In addition to insuring the real property, these policies usually provide coverage for personal property on the premises. They also provide a limited amount of liability coverage for personal injury and property damage that the policy holder causes.

As mentioned, the HO-3 policy does not cover damage resulting from floods or earthquakes. A buyer who is concerned about floods or earthquakes should consider buying supplemental coverage. However, this type of coverage can be expensive, and it isn't available in all areas or for all properties.

Applying for hazard insurance used to be a part of the closing process that was taken for granted. Buyers rarely had trouble obtaining ordinary coverage. However, because of stricter insurance underwriting standards, it's no longer so unusual for a buyer to be turned down. As a result, some purchase and sale agreement forms now have a hazard insurance contingency provision, which makes the sale contingent on whether the buyer can obtain adequate coverage. The hazard insurance contingency may be regarded as part of the financing contingency. (See Chapter 8.)

TITLE INSURANCE. Title insurance insures the buyer or the buyer's lender against financial losses that could result from as yet undiscovered problems with the seller's title. As we said earlier, the escrow agent or the lender orders a preliminary title report on the property.

The title report should be ordered early in the closing process to allow time for problems to be resolved. For example, if the title report indicates that there is a judgment lien against the property, the seller will have to clear away the lien so that marketable title can be transferred to the buyer at closing. Depending on the circumstances, the seller may simply arrange to pay the lienholder at closing. Or the seller may need to prove to the title company's satisfaction that there is no lien against the property. Perhaps the title searcher overlooked a recorded release, or the lien might be against a completely different person who has the same name as the seller.

TYPES OF TITLE POLICIES. As a condition of the buyer's loan, the lender will require the buyer to purchase a **lender's title insurance policy** for the lender. The lender's policy (sometimes referred to as a mortgagee's policy) protects the lender's security interest.

EXAMPLE: After closing, it comes to light that there's a lien against the property that has higher priority than the lender's deed of trust. That other lien was not discovered by the title searcher and listed in the title report. As a result, the lien was not paid off before closing; but it also wasn't listed as an exception to coverage in the title policy. If the lender suffers a financial loss because it doesn't have first lien position, the title company will have to reimburse the lender, up to the face amount of the policy.

The purchase and sale agreement usually requires the seller to purchase an **owner's title insurance policy** for the buyer. This policy will protect the buyer's ownership interest against undiscovered title problems, such as a forged deed or a gap in the chain of title. It will cover the legal fees paid to defend the buyer's title against a covered claim, and it will also pay off successful claims, up to the face amount of the policy.

It's never wise for a buyer to purchase a home without an owner's title insurance policy. (Keep in mind that the lender's policy offers no protection to the buyer.) The coverage is not particularly expensive, and although title problems are unlikely to surface, they could be very costly if they did.

STANDARD COVERAGE. Standard coverage title insurance protects the policy holder against title problems that concern matters of record—that is, deeds and liens and other interests that appear in the public record.

EXTENDED COVERAGE. Extended coverage protects against all of the same problems that a standard coverage policy does, plus problems that should be discovered in an actual inspection of the property. These include encroachments, adverse possession, construction that may result in a lien that hasn't been recorded yet, and other problems that do not show up in the public record. The title company sends an inspector to the property to look for indications that there may be one of these problems.

HOMEOWNER'S COVERAGE. In recent years, a third type of title insurance, homeowner's coverage, has become available in transactions involving residential property with up to four units. A homeowner's coverage policy covers most of the same matters as an extended coverage policy, as well as some additional issues such as violations of restrictive covenants.

Lenders require lender's policies to be extended coverage policies. Traditionally, owner's policies provided standard coverage, but it's more common now for buyers to obtain homeowner's coverage. In Washington, most residential purchase agreement forms now provide for this type of policy to be obtained for the buyer, unless the parties specifically agree on another type.

THE REAL ESTATE AGENT'S ROLE IN THE CLOSING PROCESS

As your sale progresses toward closing, it's important to keep track of the details. Don't assume that everything's going smoothly while you turn your attention to other listings and other buyers.

COMMUNICATION. Throughout the closing process, keep your client up to date on what's happening. Let her know when the appraisal is completed, when the loan is approved, and so on. This will ease her anxieties and reassure her that someone—you—is looking after her interests. Communication is especially important when problems crop up. If there's a delay in getting a preliminary title report or the pest inspection looks bad, tell your client immediately. Explain the problem, suggest what can be done about it, and then work with the client to find a solution.

Communication with the other party's agent is also very important. You need to promote your client's interests, but you should always do your best to get along with the other agent and the other party. Although their interests will sometimes conflict with those of your client, in most cases all of you ultimately want the sale to close. Don't agree to unreasonable demands, but work with the other agent to complete the transaction successfully.

PREVENTING PROBLEMS. Here is a list of questions and suggestions that will help you prevent problems and make the closing process smoother. Of course, what you do in a particular transaction will depend in part on whether you're representing the buyer or the seller.

PREPARING THE PURCHASE AND SALE AGREEMENT. Have the forms used for the buyer's offer and any counteroffers been filled out carefully? Do the parties understand the terms of their agreement? Is the legal description of the property complete and correct? Consider whether the deadlines in the agreement make sense under all of the current conditions. How long will it take to fulfill the contingencies in this market? The contingencies may include inspections, financing, and even the sale of the buyer's current home. When does the buyer need to move? Is it realistic to expect that the seller can be completely moved out by that date?

OPENING ESCROW. Does the escrow agent have a copy of every addendum and amendment as well as a copy of the purchase and sale agreement itself? Do the escrow instructions prepared by the agent accurately reflect all the terms of the purchase and sale agreement? The parties can sign amended instructions if necessary.

INSPECTIONS. Are you responsible for ordering any inspections? If so, do it right away. And if someone else has that responsibility, make sure they take care of it as soon as possible. Later, check to see whether the inspection report has been delivered to the appropriate parties. Does the report seem thorough and accurate? If the report recommends repairs, do the recommendations seem reasonable? If the transaction is contingent on the results of this inspection, help your client prepare or respond to the inspection notice (see Chapter 8). If repairs are agreed to, they should be ordered and completed as soon as possible. Have arrangements for a timely reinspection been made?

FINANCING. If the buyer hasn't been preapproved for a loan, has she gathered all of the personal information that she'll need for the loan application? Has she chosen a competent lender? Check with the lender periodically to find out how the loan process is going.

APPRAISAL. Was the property listed at a reasonable price? Is the sales price in line with local property values? If the appraisal comes in low, does a request for reconsideration of value seem appropriate? (See Chapter 4.)

SPECIAL PROVISIONS. Are there any special provisions in the purchase and sale agreement that require your attention? Are both parties clear on which personal property items and fixtures are included in the sale, and which the seller is going to take with him?

TITLE INSURANCE. Has a preliminary title report been ordered? When the report becomes available, find out whether there are any title problems that need to be cleared up.

HAZARD INSURANCE. Has the buyer applied for and obtained a new homeowner's insurance policy? Has a copy of the policy been delivered to the escrow agent or the lender?

MOVING OUT. Is the seller packing his belongings and preparing to move out on time? Has he arranged for his mail to be forwarded? When the seller leaves, will the house be reasonably clean? Will the yard be in reasonably good shape? Many sellers will be glad to pay to have junk hauled away, or to have a team of house cleaners go over the house once it's empty. You should be able to recommend junk hauling services and house cleaning services. Ask the other agents in your office which companies they recommend.

MOVING IN. If the buyer wants to move in before closing, has an interim rental agreement been prepared and signed? (See Chapter 7.) Whenever the buyer moves in, will the seller have all of the house keys ready to turn over to the buyer? If the buyer finds personal property that may have been left behind accidentally, or if there's unforwarded mail for the seller, it's usually more appropriate to contact the seller's agent rather than the seller himself.

LAST-MINUTE PROBLEMS. In the closing process, the risk that the transaction will fall apart is usually greatest before the contingencies have been fulfilled, but something can go wrong at any point, right up through the last few days before closing.

EXAMPLE: The sale of your client's house to the Friedmans has been going well. The seller and the buyers have been taking care of their responsibilities on time, and the financing contingency and inspection contingencies have been satisfied.

But just a week before the date set for closing, you get a call from the seller. He says that there's a problem with the house that he never told you about. There's some dry rot in one of the crawl spaces. He should have listed this in the seller disclosure statement, but he decided not to. The home inspector apparently missed the problem. Now the seller's conscience (and fear of liability) has prompted him to let you know about it. He wants to know what he should do.

How you handle this situation may mean the difference between closing the sale on time and not closing it at all. The problem must be disclosed to the buyers, and they could use it as grounds for canceling the contract. You should do whatever you can to prevent that. For instance, you might go to the house and investigate the extent of the problem, consult with your designated broker or a licensed home inspector, help the seller decide on an appropriate price concession to offer the buyers, and then call the buyers' agent. By dealing with this problem in a straightforward and professional manner, you can make it much more likely that the sale will go through.

To summarize, always stay on top of the closing process. Keep in touch with your client, with the other party's agent, and with the escrow agent. Handle any problems that come up as promptly as you can. Your role in getting the transaction to close can be just as important as your role in negotiating the sale in the first place.

CLOSING COSTS

One of your primary tasks as a real estate agent is explaining the various costs of closing a real estate transaction to your clients. Some examples of closing costs are inspection fees, title insurance fees, recording fees, escrow fees, and loan fees. Some of these are paid by the buyer, some are paid by the seller, and some are split between the two parties.

The closing costs, along with the other financial details of the transaction, are set forth in a **settlement statement** (also called a **closing statement**). The final settlement statement prepared for the buyer shows exactly how much money the buyer must pay at closing. The final statement for the seller shows exactly how much the seller will take away from closing.

Preliminary and final settlement statements are prepared for the parties by the closing agent. As a real estate agent, you might never be responsible for filling out a settlement statement form. Even so, you should be able to read one. And you need to be able to give the buyers and sellers you work with a reasonable estimate of how much their closing costs will be. For a seller, even before he lists his property, one of the most important pieces of information is the answer to the question, "How much money will I get from this sale?"

To explain the seller's estimated **net proceeds** (the amount of cash the seller will walk away with) and the buyer's estimated **net cost** (the amount of cash the buyer must pay at closing), you have to know how the various closing costs are typically allocated on a settlement statement. Many agents use worksheets to help them calculate—and explain—the net costs and net proceeds. A buyer's estimated net cost worksheet is shown later in the chapter, in Figure 11.4. A seller's estimated net proceeds worksheet is shown in Figure 11.5. Your designated broker or branch manager may have similar worksheets available for you to use.

You'll need to do some math to calculate the amount of certain closing costs. And some expenses will have to be **prorated** between the buyer and the seller. To prorate an expense is to divide and allocate it proportionately between two or more parties, according to time, interest, or benefit. Figure 11.3 shows the steps involved in proration.

COSTS AND CREDITS

On a settlement statement, the costs that a party must pay at closing are referred to as that party's **debits** (the opposite of credits). The buyer's debits increase the amount of money the buyer will have to bring to closing. The seller's debits decrease the seller's net proceeds.

In addition to their debits, each party will usually have some credits that also must be taken into account (and in some cases prorated). Credits are payments

FIG. 11.3   PRORATING AN EXPENSE

STEP 1
Divide the expense by the number of days it covers to find the per diem (daily) rate.
- Divide annual expenses by 365 (or by 360, for an estimate).
- Divide monthly expenses by the number of days in the month in question (or by 30, for an estimate).

STEP 2
Determine the number of days for which one party is responsible for the expense.

STEP 3
Multiply the number of days by the per diem rate to find that party's share of the expense.

Expense paid in arrears (overdue):
- Seller's share is a debit for the seller.

Expense paid in advance:
- Seller's share is a credit for the seller.

Expense continues after closing:
- Buyer's share is a credit for the buyer if paid in arrears.
- Buyer's share is a debit for the buyer if paid in advance.

that will be made to the buyer or the seller at closing. The buyer's credits decrease the buyer's net cost. The seller's credits increase the seller's net proceeds.

Note that some closing costs are charges that one party owes the other party. At closing, each of these will be treated as a debit for the party that must pay it and as a credit for the other party. For example, the buyer may be required to pay the seller a prorated share of the annual property taxes, because the seller paid the taxes in advance. The prorated amount is a debit for the buyer and a credit for the seller on the settlement statement. On your worksheets, add it to the buyer's net cost, and also add it to the seller's net proceeds.

Other closing costs are charges that one party must pay to a third party. For example, the seller will have to pay the brokerage firm a sales commission. This is a debit for the seller (subtracted from the net proceeds), but it does not affect the buyer.

Also, some of the credits a party receives at closing come from a third party. For example, the seller's lender must refund any unused tax and insurance reserves to the seller at closing. This is a credit for the seller (added to the net proceeds), and it does not affect the buyer.

Residential transactions involve many standard closing costs. Some are allocated according to custom, some are allocated according to the terms of the purchase and sale agreement, and a few are allocated according to law. We'll first go through the process of estimating a buyer's net cost. After that, we'll turn to the seller's net proceeds.

ESTIMATING THE BUYER'S NET COST

Certain costs are the buyer's responsibility in every transaction, or almost every transaction. Responsibility for other costs—whether they'll be paid by the buyer or by the seller, or shared between them—may vary. To estimate a buyer's net cost, you add up all of the charges the buyer will have to pay to close the sale and offset them with the credits owed to the buyer.

PURCHASE PRICE. Of course, the purchase price is the major cost for the buyer in every transaction. Use this as the starting point on your buyer's net cost worksheet. The price is offset by the buyer's earnest money deposit and the financing.

EARNEST MONEY. In most transactions, the buyer provides an earnest money deposit. The deposit is applied to the purchase price if the sale closes. Since the buyer has already paid the earnest money, it is treated as a credit for the buyer on the settlement statement. On the net cost worksheet, subtract the amount of the earnest money from the purchase price.

FINANCING. Most buyers pay a large part of the purchase price with borrowed money. Any financing arrangement—a new loan, the assumption of the seller's loan, or seller financing—is treated as a credit for the buyer. On the buyer's worksheet, subtract the loan amount and/or the amount of other financing from the purchase price.

LOAN COSTS. Borrowing money isn't free. In addition to the interest the buyer will have to pay over the life of the loan, she will incur a number of closing costs in the course of obtaining the loan. Unless the seller has agreed to pay some of them, the buyer will pay all of the closing costs associated with the loan. That means you should add these closing costs to the purchase price on your buyer's net cost worksheet.

APPRAISAL. The appraisal is required by the buyer's lender, so the appraisal fee is ordinarily paid by the buyer.

CREDIT REPORT. The buyer's lender charges the buyer for the credit investigation, so this is also a cost for the buyer.

ORIGINATION FEE. This is the lender's one-time charge to the borrower for setting up the loan (see Chapter 10). It's almost always paid by the buyer. If the buyer is assuming the seller's loan, an assumption fee will be charged instead of an origination fee.

DISCOUNT POINTS. The discount points are paid by the buyer, unless the seller has agreed to pay for a buydown (see Chapter 10). In that case, some or all of the points are paid by the seller.

PREPAID INTEREST. As a general rule, the first payment date of a new loan is not the first day of the month immediately following closing, but rather the first day of the next month after that. For instance, if a sale closes on March 15, the first payment on the new loan is due on May 1 instead of April 1. This gives the buyer a chance to recover a little from the financial strain of closing.

Even though the first loan payment isn't due for an extra month, interest begins accruing on the loan on the closing date. Interest on a real estate loan is almost always paid in arrears. In other words, the interest that accrues during a given month is paid at the end of that month. For instance, a loan payment that is due on September 1 includes the interest that accrued during August. So if the transaction closes on March 15, the first payment will be due on May 1, and that payment will cover the interest accrued in April. However, it won't cover the interest accrued between March 15 and March 31. Instead, the lender will require the buyer to pay the interest for those 17 days in March at closing. This is called **prepaid interest** or **interim interest**. It is almost always paid by the buyer.

EXAMPLE: The buyer is borrowing $166,500 at 6.5% interest to finance the purchase. The annual interest on the loan during the first year will be $10,822.50 ($166,500 × .065 = $10,822.50). The escrow agent divides that annual figure by 365 to determine the per diem interest rate.

$$\$10,822.50 \div 365 = \$29.65 \text{ per diem}$$

FIG. 11.4   BUYER'S ESTIMATED NET COST WORKSHEET

Buyer's Estimated Net Cost	
Purchase Price	**$185,000.00**
Earnest money deposit (credit)	− 5,000.00
Financing (credit)	− 166,500.00
Remainder (price less offsets)	**$13,500.00**
Buyer's Closing Costs	
Appraisal fee	+ 275.00
Credit report	+ 40.00
Origination fee	+ 1,665.00
Discount points	+ 4,995.00
Prepaid interest	+ 504.05
Lender's title insurance	+ 600.00
Inspection fees	+ 400.00
Hazard insurance	+ 375.00
Attorney's fees	+ 350.00
Recording fees	+ 50.00
Escrow fee	+ 250.00
Property taxes	+ 960.68
Estimated Net Cost	**$23,964.73**

There are 17 days between the closing date (March 15) and the first day of the following month, so the lender will expect the buyer to prepay 17 days' worth of interest at closing.

$$\$29.65 \times 17 \text{ days} = \$504.05 \text{ prepaid interest}$$

The escrow agent will enter $504.05 as a debit to the buyer on the settlement statement. When you are preparing your estimated net cost worksheet for the buyer, you can go through the same process to come up with a figure for the prepaid interest. Add it to the buyer's net cost.

LENDER'S TITLE INSURANCE PREMIUM. As explained earlier, the lender requires the buyer to provide a policy to protect the lender's lien priority. The premium for the lender's policy is paid by the buyer, unless otherwise agreed.

INSPECTION FEES. The cost of an inspection is allocated by agreement between the parties. Customarily, the buyer pays for the inspection fees.

HAZARD INSURANCE. The lender generally requires the buyer to pay for one year of hazard insurance coverage in advance, at closing.

ATTORNEY'S FEES. A buyer who is represented by an attorney in the transaction is responsible for her own attorney's fees. (The same is true for the seller.) In many transactions, the attorney's fees are not handled through escrow. Instead, each lawyer simply bills his or her client directly.

RECORDING FEES. The fees for recording the various documents involved in the transaction are usually charged to the party who benefits from the recording. The fees for recording the deed and the new mortgage or deed of trust are normally paid by the buyer.

ESCROW FEE. Also called a settlement fee or closing fee, this is the escrow agent's charge for her services. The buyer and the seller commonly agree to split the escrow fee, so that each of them pays half.

PROPERTY TAXES. The seller is responsible for the property taxes up to the day of closing; the buyer is responsible for them on the day of closing and thereafter. If the seller has already paid some or all of the property taxes in advance, he is entitled to a prorated refund from the buyer at closing. The amount of the refund is a debit for the buyer and a credit for the seller.

> **EXAMPLE:** The sale is closing on March 15. This year the property taxes on the house are $1,200.85. The escrow agent determines the per diem rate by dividing that figure by 365, the number of days in the year.

$$\$1,200.85 \div 365 = \$3.29 \text{ per diem}$$

The seller is responsible for the property taxes from January 1 through March 14—in other words, for the first 73 days of the year. The buyer's responsible for them from March 15 to the end of the year.

The seller has already paid the full year's taxes, so at closing he will be entitled to a credit for the share that is the buyer's responsibility. The escrow agent multiplies the number of days for which the seller is responsible by the per diem rate to determine the seller's share of the taxes. The escrow agent subtracts the seller's share from the annual figure to find the buyer's share.

$$73 \text{ days} \times \$3.29 = \$240.17 \text{ (Seller's share)}$$

$$\$1,200.85 - \$240.17 = \$960.68 \text{ (Buyer's share)}$$

This $960.68 will appear on the buyer's settlement statement as a debit and on the seller's statement as a credit. Again, you can do a similar proration for your net cost and net proceeds estimates. Add the buyer's debit to the buyer's net cost, and add the seller's credit to the seller's net proceeds.

ESTIMATED TOTAL COST. When all of the appropriate items on your net cost worksheet have been filled in, you're ready to calculate the buyer's estimated net cost. Subtract the buyer's credits from the purchase price, and then add all of the buyer's costs. The result is the net cost, the amount of money that the buyer will have to pay the escrow agent in order to close the sale.

Be sure your buyer knows what kind of check the escrow agent will accept. A certified check or cashier's check, rather than a personal check, is often required.

ESTIMATING THE SELLER'S NET PROCEEDS

Now let's look at the costs and credits that you should take into consideration when estimating a seller's net proceeds.

SALES PRICE. The largest credit for the seller is, naturally, the sales price. It should be the starting point in your net proceeds calculation. You'll add any other credits that the seller will receive at closing to the price, then you'll subtract the costs that the seller must pay.

REFUNDS. The seller may be entitled to certain refunds at closing. As you've already seen, if the seller has paid the property taxes in advance, the buyer will have to refund the share that she's responsible for to the seller. That will increase the seller's net proceeds. (On the other hand, if the seller hasn't paid the taxes yet, he will have to pay a prorated share of them at closing, which will decrease the net proceeds.)

Another possible credit for the seller is a refund of funds remaining in the reserve account (or impound account) for the seller's loan. A seller often has reserves on deposit with his lender to cover future property taxes and hazard insurance premiums. When the seller's loan is paid off, the unused balance in the reserve account is refunded to the seller by the lender. If your seller will receive this type of refund, add it to the seller's net proceeds. The seller's lender can help you determine how much the refund of reserves will be.

Any other refunds that the seller will receive at closing should be treated in the same way.

TOTAL PROCEEDS. On your net proceeds worksheet, add all of the seller's credits to the sales price to determine the seller's total proceeds. You'll be subtracting the seller's costs from this figure.

SELLER FINANCING OR LOAN ASSUMPTION. We explained earlier that any type of financing is a credit for the buyer. Thus, just like a new loan, seller financing or an assumed loan is subtracted from the buyer's net cost. But unlike a new loan, seller financing or an assumed loan is also subtracted from the seller's net proceeds. That's because either of these financing arrangements will reduce the amount of cash the seller will receive at closing. (Note, however, that if the buyer obtains a new loan from a bank or other third-party lender, the loan amount has no effect on the seller's net proceeds.)

PAYOFF OF SELLER'S LOAN. If, like most sellers, your seller will have to pay off his existing mortgage loan, his net will be reduced by the payoff amount. This is the unpaid principal balance, plus any unpaid interest, as of the closing date. Even if you don't yet know when the closing date will be, you can calculate a good estimate of the payoff amount by asking the seller's lender for the current principal balance.

The actual payoff amount will probably be somewhat less than the estimated payoff (because the principal balance will be less), but you don't need to worry about the difference. Since your estimate of the seller's net proceeds won't match the actual net proceeds exactly, it's better if the estimate turns out to be a little lower than the actual figure, rather than a little higher. That way, the seller will be pleased rather than disappointed at closing. (For the same reason, it's better if the buyer's estimated net cost is a little higher than the actual figure.)

INTEREST ON SELLER'S LOAN. Because interest on a real estate loan is paid in arrears, when a transaction closes in the middle of the payment period, the seller owes his lender some interest after paying off the principal balance.

> **EXAMPLE:** The closing date is March 15. Although the seller made a mortgage payment on his loan on March 1, that payment did not include any of the interest that is accruing during March. The seller owes the lender interest for the period from March 1 through March 15. The escrow agent prorates the interest, charging the seller only for those days, rather than for the whole month.
>
> Suppose the remaining principal balance is $78,000 and the annual interest rate is 7%. First find the per diem amount.
>
> $$\$78,000 \times .07 = \$5,460 \text{ annual interest}$$
> $$\$5,460 \div 365 = \$14.96 \text{ per diem interest}$$
> $$\$14.96 \times 15 \text{ days} = \$224.40$$
>
> The seller owes the lender $224.40 in interest. Subtract this from the seller's net proceeds.

Suppose the seller in this example had arranged for the buyer to assume his loan. In that case, the buyer's first payment to the lender would be due April 1, and it would pay all of the interest for March. The seller would be debited for the interest owed up to March 15, and the buyer will be credited for the same amount.

Note that the FHA loan program does not allow proration of interest when a loan is paid off in the middle of a payment period. The seller must pay for a full month's interest regardless of the closing date.

PREPAYMENT PENALTY. This is a charge the seller's lender may impose on the seller for paying the loan off before the end of its term. If the seller must pay a prepayment penalty, contact the lender to determine approximately how much the penalty will be. Subtract the estimated penalty from the seller's net proceeds.

SALES COMMISSION. The real estate commission is almost always paid by the seller. The amount of the commission is usually determined by multiplying the sales price by the commission rate.

> **EXAMPLE:** Your listing agreement states that the seller will pay a commission of 7% of the sales price. The property sells for $185,000. $185,000 × .07 = $12,950. The amount of the brokerage commission is $12,950.

FIG. 11.5   SELLER'S ESTIMATED NET PROCEEDS WORKSHEET

Seller's Estimated Net Proceeds	
Sales Price	**$185,000.00**
Prorated property taxes (credit)	+ 960.68
Reserve account (credit)	+ 500.32
Total Proceeds to Seller	**+ 186,461.00**
Seller's Closing Costs	
Loan payoff	– 78,000.00
Interest due on loan	– 224.40
Prepayment penalty	– 0.00
Other liens and assessments	– 0.00
Brokerage commission	– 12,950.00
Owner's title insurance	– 725.00
Seller-paid discount points	– 0.00
Excise tax	– 2,830.50
Repairs	– 500.00
Attorney's fees	– 0.00
Recording fees	– 24.00
Escrow fee	– 250.00
Estimated Net Proceeds	**$90,957.10**

Since the commission is one of the seller's costs, you should subtract it from the sales price when you're calculating the seller's net proceeds.

OWNER'S TITLE INSURANCE PREMIUM. As explained earlier, the premium for the owner's title insurance policy (which protects the buyer) is customarily paid by the seller.

DISCOUNT POINTS. If the seller has agreed to pay discount points or other costs involved in the buyer's loan, these will be a debit for the seller on the settlement statement. Subtract them from the seller's net proceeds.

EXCISE TAX. An excise tax is imposed on most sales of real property in Washington. The amount of the tax varies depending on the location of the property. The state's share of the tax is 1.28% of the selling price, and an additional percentage is owed to the city or county government. The excise tax is customarily paid by the seller. (However, if for some reason the tax is not paid at closing, it will become a lien against the property now owned by the buyer.)

REPAIR COSTS. The cost of repairs that the seller agreed to pay for will be deducted from the seller's proceeds at closing, unless the seller has already paid for them.

ATTORNEY'S FEES. The seller will pay his own attorney's fees if he is represented by a lawyer. These will not necessarily be handled through the closing process.

RECORDING FEES. The seller will pay the recording fees for the documents that are recorded for his benefit. For instance, the seller customarily pays the fee for recording a deed of reconveyance to release the property from the lien of the deed of trust he has paid off.

ESCROW FEE. As mentioned earlier, the seller customarily pays half of the escrow fee.

ESTIMATED NET PROCEEDS. When you subtract the seller's loan payoff and all of the seller's closing costs from the seller's total proceeds, you arrive at the seller's estimated net proceeds, the amount he can expect to take away from the closing. The escrow agent may offer the seller different options for receiving these funds, such as a cashier's check or direct deposit.

FEDERAL LAWS THAT AFFECT CLOSING

To end the chapter, we'll discuss some federal laws that must be complied with in closing a real estate transaction. These include certain income tax laws and the Real Estate Settlement Procedures Act.

INCOME TAX REGULATIONS

There are some income tax requirements connected with closing that you should be familiar with. The escrow agent (or other closing agent) is primarily responsible for ensuring that these requirements are met.

FORM 1099 REPORTING. The person responsible for closing a real estate sale generally must report the sale to the Internal Revenue Service. IRS Form 1099-S is used to report the seller's name and social security number and the gross proceeds from the sale. In most cases, the gross proceeds figure is the same as the property's sales price.

There are several exemptions to this reporting requirement. Most significantly, the form isn't required in the sale of a principal residence if: 1) the seller certifies in writing that none of the gain is taxable; and 2) the sale is for $250,000 or less ($500,000 or less if the seller is married).

Note that the closing agent is not permitted to charge an extra fee for filling out the 1099-S form.

FORM 8300 REPORTING. If a closing agent receives more than $10,000 in cash, she must report the cash payment on IRS Form 8300. This is true even if the cash isn't received all at once.

> **EXAMPLE:** ABC Escrow is handling the closing for buyer Sam. As part of the process, Sam will bring $12,000 cash to closing. He gives ABC Escrow $8,000 on Thursday, and the remaining $4,000 on Friday. Although the individual amounts are less than $10,000, ABC Escrow will need to submit Form 8300 to the IRS because the transactions are related.

The closing agent must file Form 8300 within 15 days of receiving the cash, and a copy of the form should be kept on file for five years.

FIRPTA. The Foreign Investment in Real Property Tax Act (FIRPTA) was passed in 1980 to help prevent foreign investors from evading tax liability on income generated from the sale of U.S. real estate. To comply with FIRPTA, the buyer must determine whether the seller is a "foreign person" (someone who is not a U.S. citizen or a resident alien). If the seller is a foreign person, then the buyer must withhold 10% of the amount realized from the sale and forward that amount to the Internal Revenue Service. Usually, the amount realized is simply the sales price. In most cases, the closing agent handles these requirements on behalf of the buyer.

Many purchase and sale agreement forms have a provision concerning FIRPTA compliance. It requires the closing agent to prepare a certification stating that the seller is not a foreign person under the terms of this law, and the seller agrees to sign the certification. However, if the seller is a foreign person, the closing agent is directed to withhold the required amount and comply with the law, unless the sale is exempt from FIRPTA.

FIRPTA's exemptions cover various types of transactions. Most notably for our purposes, some residential transactions are exempt from the law. For the exemption to apply, the buyer must be purchasing the property for use as her home, and the purchase price must be $300,000 or less.

REAL ESTATE SETTLEMENT PROCEDURES ACT

The Real Estate Settlement Procedures Act (RESPA) affects how closing is handled in most residential transactions financed with institutional loans. The law has two main goals:

- to provide borrowers with information about their closing costs; and
- to eliminate kickbacks and referral fees that unnecessarily increase the costs of purchasing a home.

TRANSACTIONS COVERED BY RESPA. RESPA applies to "federally related" loan transactions. A loan is federally related if:

1. it will be secured by a mortgage or deed of trust against:
   - property on which there is (or on which the loan proceeds will be used to build) a dwelling with four or fewer units;
   - a condominium unit or a cooperative apartment;
   - a lot with (or on which the loan proceeds will be used to place) a mobile home; and
2. the lender is federally regulated, has federally insured accounts, is assisted by the federal government, makes loans in connection with a federal program, sells loans to Fannie Mae, Ginnie Mae, or Freddie Mac, or makes real estate loans that total more than $1,000,000 per year.

In short, the act applies to almost all institutional lenders and to most residential loans.

EXEMPTIONS. RESPA does not apply to the following loan transactions:

- a loan used to purchase 25 acres or more;
- a loan primarily for a business, commercial, or agricultural purpose;
- a loan used to purchase vacant land, unless there will be a one- to four-unit dwelling built on it or a mobile home placed on it;
- temporary financing, such as a construction loan; and
- an assumption for which the lender's approval is neither required nor obtained.

Note that RESPA also does not apply to seller-financed transactions, since they are not federally regulated.

RESPA REQUIREMENTS. RESPA has these requirements for federally related loan transactions:

1. Within three days of receiving a written loan application, the lender must give every applicant:
   - a copy of a settlement booklet (that meets HUD standards), which explains RESPA, closing costs, and the uniform settlement statement;
   - a good faith estimate (GFE) of all closing costs the borrower is expected to pay; and
   - a mortgage servicing disclosure statement, to inform the borrower about the likelihood that the lender may or may not be transferring the loan to another lender during the loan term.
2. If a lender or other settlement service provider requires the borrower to use a particular appraiser, title company, or other service provider, that requirement must be disclosed to the borrower at the time of the loan application or service agreement.
3. If any settlement service provider is in a position to refer a borrower to an "affiliated" provider, that joint business relationship must be fully disclosed as well, along with fee estimates and language that the referral is optional.
4. The closing agent is required to itemize all loan settlement charges on a uniform settlement statement form (discussed below).
5. If the borrower will have to make deposits into an impound account to cover taxes, insurance, and other recurring costs, the lender cannot require excessive deposits (more than necessary to cover the expenses when they come due, plus a two-month cushion).
6. A lender or other settlement service provider (such as a title company) may not:
   - pay or accept kickbacks or referral fees (a payment from one settlement service provider to another provider for referring customers);
   - pay or accept unearned fees (a charge that one settlement service provider shares with another provider who hasn't actually performed any services in exchange for the payment); or

- charge a fee for the preparation of the uniform settlement statement, an impound account statement, or the disclosure statement required by the Truth in Lending Act.

7. The seller may not require the buyer to use a particular title company.

RESPA's prohibition on kickbacks and unearned fees (number 6 above) is intended to prevent practices that were once widespread and that generally benefited real estate agents, lenders, and other settlement service providers at the expense of homebuyers. Note that this prohibition doesn't apply to referral fees that one real estate licensee pays to another for referring potential brokerage customers or clients, or to commission sharing agreements between real estate licensees, as long as all of the licensees are acting in a real estate brokerage capacity and not providing other services.

GOOD FAITH ESTIMATE AND UNIFORM SETTLEMENT STATEMENT. Lenders and mortgage brokers must provide the required good faith estimate of closing costs on a standardized form developed by HUD. (See Figure 11.6.) The good faith estimate form corresponds very closely to the uniform settlement statement form. (See Figure 11.7.) HUD believes these forms will provide consumers with more accurate information about their transaction costs, making it easier for borrowers to shop for the least costly loans and avoid unnecessary and unexpected costs at closing.

Under RESPA, lenders and mortgage brokers are encouraged to give borrowers a GFE form as early in the lending process as possible, so borrowers have the time to obtain multiple GFEs (from different lenders) to compare the pros and cons of various options. Lenders may only charge for the cost of the credit report and a minor administrative fee at the time of a loan application (so borrowers can afford to shop around for loans).

The new GFE form also imposes limits on the amount certain categories of loan costs can increase from the time a GFE is given to a borrower and the closing date. These limits on increases are called "tolerances," and they have been imposed by HUD to prevent bait and switch tactics, in which low estimates of closing costs are later increased at closing, once a borrower is locked in with a specific lender. Loan originators can avoid being penalized for excessive increases in the initial cost estimates by amending the GFE form, disclosing the new information to the borrower, and issuing a refund to the borrower within 30 days of closing (if excessive costs were paid).

FIG. 11.6   GOOD FAITH ESTIMATE OF CLOSING COSTS

OMB Approval No. 2502-0265

Good Faith Estimate (GFE)

Name of Originator		Borrower	
Originator Address		Property Address	
Originator Phone Number			
Originator Email		Date of GFE	

Purpose

This GFE gives you an estimate of your settlement charges and loan terms if you are approved for this loan. For more information, see HUD's *Special Information Booklet* on settlement charges, your *Truth-in-Lending Disclosures*, and other consumer information at www.hud.gov/respa. If you decide you would like to proceed with this loan, contact us.

Shopping for your loan

Only you can shop for the best loan for you. Compare this GFE with other loan offers, so you can find the best loan. Use the shopping chart on page 3 to compare all the offers you receive.

Important dates

1. The interest rate for this GFE is available through _____. After this time, the interest rate, some of your loan Origination Charges, and the monthly payment shown below can change until you lock your interest rate.

2. This estimate for all other settlement charges is available through _____.

3. After you lock your interest rate, you must go to settlement within ☐ days (your rate lock period) to receive the locked interest rate.

4. You must lock the interest rate at least ☐ days before settlement.

Summary of your loan

Your initial loan amount is	$
Your loan term is	years
Your initial interest rate is	%
Your initial monthly amount owed for principal, interest, and any mortgage insurance is	$ per month
Can your interest rate rise?	☐ No ☐ Yes, it can rise to a maximum of %. The first change will be in .
Even if you make payments on time, can your loan balance rise?	☐ No ☐ Yes, it can rise to a maximum of $
Even if you make payments on time, can your monthly amount owed for principal, interest, and any mortgage insurance rise?	☐ No ☐ Yes, the first increase can be in and the monthly amount owed can rise to $. The maximum it can ever rise to is $.
Does your loan have a prepayment penalty?	☐ No ☐ Yes, your maximum prepayment penalty is $.
Does your loan have a balloon payment?	☐ No ☐ Yes, you have a balloon payment of $ due in years.

Escrow account information

Some lenders require an escrow account to hold funds for paying property taxes or other property-related charges in addition to your monthly amount owed of $ _____ .
Do we require you to have an escrow account for your loan?
☐ No, you do not have an escrow account. You must pay these charges directly when due.
☐ Yes, you have an escrow account. It may or may not cover all of these charges. Ask us.

Summary of your settlement charges

A	Your Adjusted Origination Charges (See page 2.)	$
B	Your Charges for All Other Settlement Services (See page 2.)	$
A + B	Total Estimated Settlement Charges	$

Good Faith Estimate (HUD-GFE) 1

Understanding your estimated settlement charges

Your Adjusted Origination Charges	
1. Our origination charge This charge is for getting this loan for you.	
2. Your credit or charge (points) for the specific interest rate chosen ☐ The credit or charge for the interest rate of [＿＿] % is included in "Our origination charge." (See item 1 above.) ☐ You receive a credit of $[＿＿＿] for this interest rate of [＿＿] %. This credit **reduces** your settlement charges. ☐ You pay a charge of $[＿＿＿] for this interest rate of [＿＿] %. This charge (points) **increases** your total settlement charges. The tradeoff table on page 3 shows that you can change your total settlement charges by choosing a different interest rate for this loan.	
A Your Adjusted Origination Charges	$

Some of these charges can change at settlement. See the top of page 3 for more information.

Your Charges for All Other Settlement Services	
3. Required services that we select These charges are for services we require to complete your settlement. We will choose the providers of these services. *Service*　　　　　　　　*Charge*	
4. Title services and lender's title insurance This charge includes the services of a title or settlement agent, for example, and title insurance to protect the lender, if required.	
5. Owner's title insurance You may purchase an owner's title insurance policy to protect your interest in the property.	
6. Required services that you can shop for These charges are for other services that are required to complete your settlement. We can identify providers of these services or you can shop for them yourself. Our estimates for providing these services are below. *Service*　　　　　　　　*Charge*	
7. Government recording charges These charges are for state and local fees to record your loan and title documents.	
8. Transfer taxes These charges are for state and local fees on mortgages and home sales.	
9. Initial deposit for your escrow account This charge is held in an escrow account to pay future recurring charges on your property and includes ☐ all property taxes, ☐ all insurance, and ☐ other [＿＿＿].	
10. Daily interest charges This charge is for the daily interest on your loan from the day of your settlement until the first day of the next month or the first day of your normal mortgage payment cycle. This amount is $[＿＿＿] per day for [＿＿] days (if your settlement is [＿＿＿]).	
11. Homeowner's insurance This charge is for the insurance you must buy for the property to protect from a loss, such as fire. *Policy*　　　　　　　　*Charge*	
B Your Charges for All Other Settlement Services	$
A + B Total Estimated Settlement Charges	$

 Good Faith Estimate (HUD-GFE) 2

Instructions

Understanding which charges can change at settlement

This GFE estimates your settlement charges. At your settlement, you will receive a HUD-1, a form that lists your actual costs. Compare the charges on the HUD-1 with the charges on this GFE. Charges can change if you select your own provider and do not use the companies we identify. (See below for details.)

These charges **cannot increase** at settlement:	The total of these charges **can increase up to 10%** at settlement:	These charges **can change** at settlement:
■ Our origination charge ■ Your credit or charge (points) for the specific interest rate chosen *(after you lock in your interest rate)* ■ Your adjusted origination charges *(after you lock in your interest rate)* ■ Transfer taxes	■ Required services that we select ■ Title services and lender's title insurance *(if we select them or you use companies we identify)* ■ Owner's title insurance *(if you use companies we identify)* ■ Required services that you can shop for *(if you use companies we identify)* ■ Government recording charges	■ Required services that you can shop for *(if you do not use companies we identify)* ■ Title services and lender's title insurance *(if you do not use companies we identify)* ■ Owner's title insurance *(if you do not use companies we identify)* ■ Initial deposit for your escrow account ■ Daily interest charges ■ Homeowner's insurance

Using the tradeoff table

In this GFE, we offered you this loan with a particular interest rate and estimated settlement charges. However:

■ If you want to choose this same loan with **lower settlement charges,** then you will have a **higher interest rate.**
■ If you want to choose this same loan with a **lower interest rate,** then you will have **higher settlement charges.**

If you would like to choose an available option, you must ask us for a new GFE.

Loan originators have the option to complete this table. Please ask for additional information if the table is not completed.

	The loan in this GFE	The same loan with lower settlement charges	The same loan with a lower interest rate
Your initial loan amount	$	$	$
Your initial interest rate[1]	%	%	%
Your initial monthly amount owed	$	$	$
Change in the monthly amount owed from this GFE	No change	You will pay $ **more** every month	You will pay $ **less** every month
Change in the amount you will pay at settlement with this interest rate	No change	Your settlement charges will be **reduced** by $	Your settlement charges will **increase** by $
How much your total estimated settlement charges will be	$	$	$

[1] *For an adjustable rate loan, the comparisons above are for the initial interest rate before adjustments are made.*

Using the shopping chart

Use this chart to compare GFEs from different loan originators. Fill in the information by using a different column for each GFE you receive. By comparing loan offers, you can shop for the best loan.

	This loan	Loan 2	Loan 3	Loan 4
Loan originator name				
Initial loan amount				
Loan term				
Initial interest rate				
Initial monthly amount owed				
Rate lock period				
Can interest rate rise?				
Can loan balance rise?				
Can monthly amount owed rise?				
Prepayment penalty?				
Balloon payment?				
Total Estimated Settlement Charges				

If your loan is sold in the future

Some lenders may sell your loan after settlement. Any fees lenders receive in the future cannot change the loan you receive or the charges you paid at settlement.

 Good Faith Estimate (HUD-GFE) 3

FIG. 11.7   UNIFORM SETTLEMENT STATEMENT

OMB Approval No. 2502-0265

A. Settlement Statement (HUD-1)

B. Type of Loan

| 1. ☐ FHA | 2. ☐ RHS | 3. ☐ Conv. Unins. | 6. File Number: | 7. Loan Number: | 8. Mortgage Insurance Case Number: |
| 4. ☐ VA | 5. ☐ Conv. Ins. | | | | |

C. Note: This form is furnished to give you a statement of actual settlement costs. Amounts paid to and by the settlement agent are shown. Items marked "(p.o.c.)" were paid outside the closing; they are shown here for informational purposes and are not included in the totals.

| D. Name & Address of Borrower: | E. Name & Address of Seller: | F. Name & Address of Lender: |

| G. Property Location: | H. Settlement Agent: | I. Settlement Date: |
| | Place of Settlement: | |

J. Summary of Borrower's Transaction		K. Summary of Seller's Transaction	
100. Gross Amount Due from Borrower		**400. Gross Amount Due to Seller**	
101. Contract sales price		401. Contract sales price	
102. Personal property		402. Personal property	
103. Settlement charges to borrower (line 1400)		403.	
104.		404.	
105.		405.	
Adjustment for items paid by seller in advance		**Adjustments for items paid by seller in advance**	
106. City/town taxes to		406. City/town taxes to	
107. County taxes to		407. County taxes to	
108. Assessments to		408. Assessments to	
109.		409.	
110.		410.	
111.		411.	
112.		412.	
120. Gross Amount Due from Borrower		**420. Gross Amount Due to Seller**	
200. Amounts Paid by or in Behalf of Borrower		**500. Reductions In Amount Due to Seller**	
201. Deposit or earnest money		501. Excess deposit (see instructions)	
202. Principal amount of new loan(s)		502. Settlement charges to seller (line 1400)	
203. Existing loan(s) taken subject to		503. Existing loan(s) taken subject to	
204.		504. Payoff of first mortgage loan	
205.		505. Payoff of second mortgage loan	
206.		506.	
207.		507.	
208.		508.	
209.		509.	
Adjustments for items unpaid by seller		**Adjustments for items unpaid by seller**	
210. City/town taxes to		510. City/town taxes to	
211. County taxes to		511. County taxes to	
212. Assessments to		512. Assessments to	
213.		513.	
214.		514.	
215.		515.	
216.		516.	
217.		517.	
218.		518.	
219.		519.	
220. Total Paid by/for Seller		**520. Total Reduction Amount Due Seller**	
300. Cash at Settlement from/to Borrower		**600. Cash at Settlement to/from Seller**	
301. Gross amount due from borrower (line 120)		601. Gross amount due to seller (line 420)	
302. Less amounts paid by/for borrower (line 220)	( )	602. Less reductions in amount due seller (line 520)	( )
303. Cash ☐ From ☐ To Borrower		**603. Cash** ☐ To ☐ From Seller	

The Public Reporting Burden for this collection of information is estimated at 35 minutes per response for collecting, reviewing, and reporting the data. This agency may not collect this information, and you are not required to complete this form, unless it displays a currently valid OMB control number. No confidentiality is assured; this disclosure is mandatory. This is designed to provide the parties to a RESPA covered transaction with information during the settlement process.

Previous editions are obsolete   Page 1 of 3   HUD-1

L. Settlement Charges					
700. Total Real Estate Broker Fees					
Division of commission (line 700) as follows:				Paid From Borrower's Funds at Settlement	Paid From Seller's Funds at Settlement
701. $		to			
702. $		to			
703. Commission paid at settlement					
704.					
800. Items Payable in Connection with Loan					
801. Our origination charge		$	(from GFE #1)		
802. Your credit or charge (points) for the specific interest rate chosen $			(from GFE #2)		
803. Your adjusted origination charges			(from GFE A)		
804. Appraisal fee to			(from GFE #3)		
805. Credit report to			(from GFE #3)		
806. Tax service to			(from GFE #3)		
807. Flood certification			(from GFE #3)		
808.					
900. Items Required by Lender to Be Paid in Advance					
901. Daily interest charges from to @ $ /day			(from GFE #10)		
902. Mortgage insurance premium for months to			(from GFE #3)		
903. Homeowner's insurance for years to			(from GFE #11)		
904.					
1000. Reserves Deposited with Lender					
1001. Initial deposit for your escrow account			(from GFE #9)		
1002. Homeowner's insurance months @ $		per month $			
1003. Mortgage insurance months @ $		per month $			
1004. Property taxes months @ $		per month $			
1005. months @ $		per month $			
1006. months @ $		per month $			
1007. Aggregate Adjustment		−$			
1100. Title Charges					
1101. Title services and lender's title insurance			(from GFE #4)		
1102. Settlement or closing fee		$			
1103. Owner's title insurance			(from GFE #5)		
1104. Lender's title insurance		$			
1105. Lender's title policy limit $					
1106. Owner's title policy limit $					
1107. Agent's portion of the total title insurance premium		$			
1108. Underwriter's portion of the total title insurance premium		$			
1200. Government Recording and Transfer Charges					
1201. Government recording charges			(from GFE #7)		
1202. Deed $ Mortgage $		Releases $			
1203. Transfer taxes			(from GFE #8)		
1204. City/County tax/stamps Deed $		Mortgage $			
1205. State tax/stamps Deed $		Mortgage $			
1206.					
1300. Additional Settlement Charges					
1301. Required services that you can shop for			(from GFE #6)		
1302.		$			
1303.		$			
1304.					
1305.					
1400. Total Settlement Charges (enter on lines 103, Section J and 502, Section K)					

Comparison of Good Faith Estimate (GFE) and HUD-1 Charges		Good Faith Estimate	HUD-1
Charges That Cannot Increase	**HUD-1 Line Number**		
Our origination charge	# 801		
Your credit or charge (points) for the specific interest rate chosen	# 802		
Your adjusted origination charges	# 803		
Transfer taxes	#1203		

Charges That in Total Cannot Increase More Than 10%		Good Faith Estimate	HUD-1
Government recording charges	# 1201		
	#		
	#		
	#		
	#		
	#		
	#		
Total			
Increase between GFE and HUD-1 Charges		$ or	%

Charges That Can Change		Good Faith Estimate	HUD-1
Initial deposit for your escrow account	#1001		
Daily interest charges	# 901 $ /day		
Homeowner's insurance	# 903		
	#		
	#		
	#		

Loan Terms

Your initial loan amount is	$
Your loan term is	____ years
Your initial interest rate is	____ %
Your initial monthly amount owed for principal, interest, and and any mortgage insurance is	$ ____ includes ☐ Principal ☐ Interest ☐ Mortgage Insurance
Can your interest rate rise?	☐ No. ☐ Yes, it can rise to a maximum of ____%. The first change will be on ____ and can change again every ____ after ____. Every change date, your interest rate can increase or decrease by ____%. Over the life of the loan, your interest rate is guaranteed to never be **lower** than ____ % or **higher** than ____ %.
Even if you make payments on time, can your loan balance rise?	☐ No. ☐ Yes, it can rise to a maximum of $ ____.
Even if you make payments on time, can your monthly amount owed for principal, interest, and mortgage insurance rise?	☐ No. ☐ Yes, the first increase can be on ____ and the monthly amount owed can rise to $ ____. The maximum it can ever rise to is $ ____.
Does your loan have a prepayment penalty?	☐ No. ☐ Yes, your maximum prepayment penalty is $ ____.
Does your loan have a balloon payment?	☐ No. ☐ Yes, you have a balloon payment of $ ____ due in ____ years on ____.
Total monthly amount owed including escrow account payments	☐ You do not have a monthly escrow payment for items, such as property taxes and homeowner's insurance. You must pay these items directly yourself. ☐ You have an additional monthly escrow payment of $ ____ that results in a total initial monthly amount owed of $ ____. This includes principal, interest, any mortgage insurance and any items checked below: ☐ Property taxes ☐ Homeowner's insurance ☐ Flood insurance ☐ ____ ☐ ____

Note: If you have any questions about the Settlement Charges and Loan Terms listed on this form, please contact your lender.

The closing agent must provide a completed Uniform Settlement Statement to the buyer and seller at closing. By law, the buyer has a right to be given a copy of the statement a day before closing, upon request. Although the same form is used for both the seller and buyer, in most cases a separate statement is prepared for each party. The form summarizes the costs that have been paid outside of closing (by each party), and also summarizes the cash that must be paid to and from the seller and buyer at closing.

REAL ESTATE MATH

Real estate agents use math constantly: to determine the square footage of homes they are listing or selling, to prorate closing costs, and so on. Calculators make all of these tasks much easier than they once were, but it is still necessary to have a basic grasp of the math involved. Earlier in this chapter, we showed you how to prorate expenses at closing. In this section, we'll provide step-by-step instructions for solving a variety of real estate math problems.

DECIMALS AND PERCENTAGES

To carry out a calculation, it's easier to work with decimal numbers than with fractions or percentages. So if a problem presents you with fractions or percentages, you'll usually convert them into decimal numbers.

CONVERTING FRACTIONS. To convert a fraction into decimal form, divide the top number of the fraction (the numerator) by the bottom number of the fraction (the denominator).

> **EXAMPLE:** To change ¾ into a decimal, divide 3 (the top number) by 4 (the bottom number): $3 \div 4 = .75$.

CONVERTING PERCENTAGES. To solve a problem involving a percentage, you'll first convert the percentage into a decimal number, then convert the decimal answer back into percentage form.

To convert a percentage to a decimal, remove the percent sign and move the decimal point two places to the left. It may be necessary to add a zero.

EXAMPLE: 5% becomes .05   32.5% becomes .325

To convert a decimal into a percentage, do just the opposite. Move the decimal point two places to the right and add a percent sign.

EXAMPLE: .08 becomes 08%   .095 becomes 09.5% (9.5%)

The percent key on a calculator performs the conversion of a percentage to a decimal number automatically. On most calculators, you can key in the digits and press the percent key, and the calculator will display the percentage in decimal form.

DECIMAL CALCULATIONS. Calculators handle decimal numbers in exactly the same way as whole numbers. If you enter a decimal number into the calculator with the decimal point in the correct place, the calculator will do the rest. But if you're working without a calculator, you'll need to apply the following rules.

To add or subtract decimals, put the numbers in a column with their decimal points lined up.

EXAMPLE: To add 3.755, 679, and 1.9, put the numbers in a column with the decimal points lined up as shown below, then add them together.

```
    3.755
  679.0
+   1.9
  ─────
  684.655
```

To multiply decimal numbers, first do the multiplication without worrying about the decimal points. Then put a decimal point into the answer in the correct place. The answer should have as many decimal places (that is, numbers to the right of its decimal point) as the total number of decimal places in the numbers that were multiplied. So count the decimal places in the numbers you are multiplying and put the decimal point the same number of places to the left in the answer.

EXAMPLE: Multiply 24.6 times 16.7. The two numbers contain a total of two decimal places.

```
    24.6
×  16.7
  ─────
  410.82
```

In some cases, it will be necessary to include one or more zeros in the answer to have the correct number of decimal places.

EXAMPLE: Multiply .2 times .4. There is a total of two decimal places.

$$
\begin{array}{r}
.2 \\
\times\ .4 \\
\hline
.08
\end{array}
$$

A zero has to be included in the answer in order to move the decimal point two places left.

To divide by a decimal number, move the decimal point in the denominator (the number you're dividing the other number by) all the way to the right. Then move the decimal point in the numerator (the number that you're dividing) the same number of places to the right. (In some cases it will be necessary to add one or more zeros to the numerator in order to move the decimal point the correct number of places.)

EXAMPLE: Divide 26.145 by 1.5. First move the decimal point in 1.5 all the way to the right (in this case, that's only one place). Then move the decimal point in 26.145 the same number of places to the right.

26.145 ÷ 1.5 becomes 261.45 ÷ 15

Now divide. 261.45 ÷ 15 = 17.43

Remember, these steps are unnecessary if you're using a calculator. If the numbers are keyed in correctly, the calculator will automatically give you an answer with the decimal point in the correct place.

AREA PROBLEMS

A real estate agent often needs to calculate the area of a lot, a building, or a room. Area is usually stated in square feet or square yards. The formula to be used for the calculation depends on the shape of the area in question. It may be a square, a rectangle, a triangle, or some combination of those shapes.

SQUARES AND RECTANGLES. The formula for finding the area of a square or a rectangle is $A = L \times W$.

EXAMPLE: If a rectangular room measures 15 feet along one wall and 12 feet along the adjoining wall, how many square feet of carpet would be required to cover the floor?

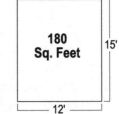

A = L × W

A = 15′ × 12′

To find A, multiply L times W: 15′ × 12′ = 180 Sq. ft. 180 square feet of carpet are needed to cover the floor.

TRIANGLES. The formula for finding the area of a triangle is:

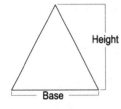 or Area = ½ Base × Height

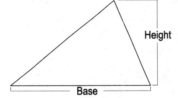

EXAMPLE: If commercial building lots in a certain neighborhood are selling for approximately $5 per square foot, approximately how much should the lot pictured below sell for?

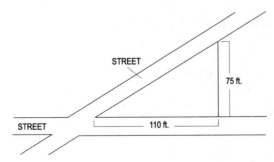

A = ½ B × H
Area = 55′ (½ of 110) × 75′
75′ × 55′ = 4,125 Sq. ft.

The lot contains 4,125 square feet. If similar lots are selling for about $5 per square foot, this lot should sell for about $20,625.

$$
\begin{array}{ll}
4,125 & \text{Square feet} \\
\underline{\times\ \$5} & \text{Per square foot} \\
\$20,625 & \text{Selling price}
\end{array}
$$

ODD SHAPES. The best approach to finding the area of an odd-shaped figure is to divide it up into squares, rectangles, and triangles. Find the areas of those figures and add them all up to arrive at the area of the odd-shaped lot, room, or building in question.

EXAMPLE: If the lot pictured below is leased on a 50-year lease for $3 per square foot per year, with rental payments made monthly, how much would the monthly rent be?

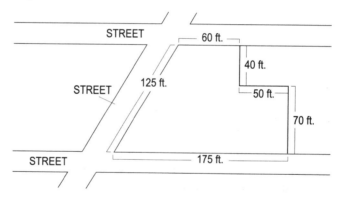

First, divide the lot up into rectangles and triangles.

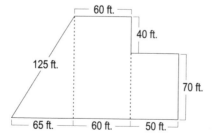

The next step is to find the area of each of the following figures. The height of the triangle is determined by adding together the 70-foot border of the small rectangle and the 40-foot border of the large rectangle.

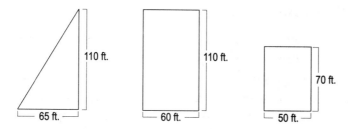

First, find the area of the triangle.

A = ½ Base × Height
A = 32.5′ (½ of 65′) × 110′
32.5′ × 110′ = 3,575 Sq. ft.

Then, find the area of the large rectangle.

A = Length × Width
A = 110′ × 60′
110′ × 60′ = 6,600 Sq. ft.

Next, find the area of the small rectangle.

A = Length × Width
A = 70′ × 50′
50′ × 70′ = 3,500 Sq. ft.

Finally, add the three areas together to find the area of the entire lot: 3,575 + 6,600 + 3,500 = 13,675 Total square feet.

The lot contains 13,675 square feet. At $3 per square foot per year, the annual rent would be $41,025.

13,675	Square feet
× $3	Rent per square foot
$41,025	Annual rent

The monthly rental payment would be one-twelfth of the annual rent: $41,025 ÷ 12 = $3,418.75. Thus, the monthly rental payment for this odd-shaped lot is $3,418.75.

PERCENTAGE PROBLEMS

Many real estate math problems, including problems about mortgage loan interest, involve percentages. To solve percentage problems, you'll usually convert the percentage into a decimal number, calculate, and then convert the answer back into percentage form. As explained earlier, a percentage is converted into a decimal number by removing the percent sign and moving the decimal point two places to the left. If the percentage is a single digit (for example, 7%), it will be necessary to add a zero (.07). To convert a decimal number into a percentage, you reverse those steps: move the decimal point two places to the right and add the percent sign.

In a math problem, whenever something is expressed as a percentage "of" another number, that indicates that you should multiply that other number by the percentage. For instance, what is 75% of $40,000?

<u>Step 1</u>	<u>Step 2</u>
75% becomes .75	$40,000
	× .75
	$30,000

Basically, percentage problems ask you to find a part of a whole. The whole is a larger figure, such as a property's sales price. The part is a smaller figure, such as a broker's commission. The general formula might be stated thus: A percentage of the whole equals the part. This can be written as an equation: Part = Whole × Percentage.

> **EXAMPLE:** A house is listed for sale at a price of $172,000, with an agreement to pay a commission of 6% of the sales price. The property sells for $170,000. How much is the commission?

$P = W \times \%$

Change the percentage (6%) into a decimal number (.06) first: $P = $170,000 \times .06$.

$170,000	Sales price
× .06	Commission rate
$10,200	Commission

The commission is $10,200.

In some percentage problems, the part is given and you're asked to calculate either the whole or the percentage. For those problems, you'll need to rearrange the percentage formula into a division problem. If the whole is the unknown, divide the part by the percentage: Whole = Part ÷ Percentage.

If the percentage is the unknown, divide the part by the whole: Percentage = Part ÷ Whole.

Notice that in either case, you'll be dividing the value of the part by either the whole (to determine the percentage) or by the percentage (to determine the whole).

LOAN PROBLEMS. Loan problems can be solved using the general percentage formula: Part = Whole × Percentage. Here, the part is the amount of the interest, the whole is the loan amount or principal balance, and the percentage is the interest rate.

> **EXAMPLE:** Henry borrows $5,000 for one year and agrees to pay 7% interest. How much interest will he be required to pay?
>
> $P = W \times \%$
> $P = \$5,000 \times .07$
>
> | $5,000 | Loan amount |
> |---|---|
> | × .07 | Interest rate |
> | $350 | Interest |
>
> Henry will pay $350 in interest.

INTEREST RATES. Interest rates are expressed as annual rates—a certain percentage per year. Some problems present you with monthly, quarterly, or semi-annual interest payments instead of the annual amount. In that case, you'll need to multiply the payment amount stated in the problem to determine the annual amount before you substitute the numbers into the formula.

> **EXAMPLE:** If $450 in interest accrues on a $7,200 interest-only loan in six months, what is the annual interest rate?
>
> You're asked to find the annual interest rate, but the interest amount given in the problem ($450) accrued in only six months. The annual interest amount would be double that, or $900.

P = W × %

For the part (the interest amount), be sure to use the annual figure ($900): $900 = $7,200 × Percentage.

Rearrange the formula to isolate the unknown (in this case, the percentage). The part is divided by the whole to determine the percentage: $900 ÷ $7,200 = .125.

Convert the decimal number back into a percentage: .125 becomes 12.5%. Thus, the annual interest rate is 12½%.

CHAPTER SUMMARY

1. Most real estate transactions in Washington are closed through the escrow process. Money and documents are given to a neutral third party (the escrow agent), who holds them until they can be disbursed or delivered to the proper parties. The escrow agent may also handle a variety of other tasks, such as preparing documents for the parties to execute, ordering the preliminary title report, calculating and prorating closing costs, and preparing settlement statements.

2. Some of the most important aspects of the closing process are inspections and repairs, approval of the buyer's loan, the appraisal, and the purchase of hazard insurance and title insurance. As a real estate agent, you should have a checklist of what needs to be done and make sure everything is getting done in time for the closing date. It's part of your job to keep the sale on track.

3. You should be able to provide good estimates of the buyer's net cost and the seller's net proceeds. To do this, you need to be familiar with the standard closing costs and who typically pays them. You must also be able to prorate certain expenses, such as property taxes and hazard insurance.

4. The federal income tax regulations that apply to real estate closings include Form 1099 and 8300 reporting and rules, and the Foreign Investment in Real Property Tax Act. In some transactions, FIRPTA requires the escrow agent to withhold a portion of the seller's proceeds and send the money to the IRS.

5. The Real Estate Settlement Procedures Act, another federal law, helps home buyers and sellers understand their closing costs. RESPA applies to most residential real estate transactions financed with institutional loans. Key requirements include the Good Faith Estimate of closing costs and the uniform settlement statement. The prohibition on kickbacks and referral fees is another important aspect of RESPA.

6. Real estate agents should know the mathematical formulas for converting fractions to decimals, percentages to decimals, and decimals to percentages. They should also know the formulas for calculating area, volume, and percentages.

CHAPTER QUIZ

1. Although the terms are often used interchangeably, the technical difference between an escrow agent and a closing agent is that:

    a. an escrow agent is an independent escrow company or a licensed escrow agent, while a closing agent is anyone providing escrow services

    b. a closing agent represents the interests of only one party to a transaction, while an escrow agent acts on behalf of both parties and is supposed be neutral

    c. the term "closing agent" refers specifically to a real estate licensee who is providing escrow services

    d. None of the above; there is no difference

2. Which of the following is not one of the steps in the inspection process?

    a. Ordering the inspection

    b. Approval or disapproval of the inspection report

    c. Appraisal of the property

    d. Reinspection of any required repairs

3. When choosing a home inspector, a buyer should look for a firm that:

    a. has recently changed its name

    b. will offer to make the repairs recommended by the inspection

    c. belongs to the American Society of Home Inspectors

    d. does other business in addition to inspections

4. An HO-3 hazard insurance policy will cover damages resulting from:

    a. floods

    b. vehicles

    c. earthquakes

    d. encroachments

5. If the buyer is concerned about title problems that do not show up in the public record, he should:

    a. make sure there are no problems on the preliminary title report

    b. require the seller to purchase a standard coverage title insurance policy

    c. rely on the lender's title insurance policy

    d. get a homeowner's coverage title insurance policy

6. On a settlement statement, the debits represent:

  a. the amount of financing in the transaction

  b. amounts that are owed to a party at closing

  c. costs that a party must pay at closing

  d. costs that the buyer must pay to the seller

7. The earnest money deposit is:

  a. retained by the brokerage firm at closing in lieu of a commission

  b. applied toward the purchase price at closing

  c. a credit for the buyer on the settlement statement

  d. Both b and c

8. Prepaid interest refers to:

  a. the charge that the buyer must pay at closing to cover interest that will accrue on his loan during the last part of the month in which closing occurs

  b. the refund to the seller of reserves on deposit in an impound account with her lender

  c. the interest owed by the seller at closing after paying off the principal balance of her loan

  d. the fact that mortgage interest is usually paid in advance

9. The seller customarily pays the fee for recording the:

  a. deed of reconveyance

  b. deed from the seller to the buyer

  c. new mortgage or deed of trust

  d. None of the above

10. A loan secured by a deed of trust on the home the buyer is purchasing will be considered a "federally related" loan if the:

  a. person responsible for closing must report the sale to the IRS

  b. lender makes real estate loans that total more than $1,000,000 per year

  c. closing agent is required to withhold part of the proceeds under FIRPTA

  d. loan is used to purchase more than 25 acres

ANSWER KEY

1. a. The two terms are often used interchangeably, but technically the term "escrow agent" refers to an independent escrow company or licensed escrow agent. "Closing agent" refers to anyone providing escrow services—a lawyer, an independent escrow company, a real estate licensee, a lender, etc.

2. c. During the closing process, the initial inspection needs to be ordered, and then the inspection report must be approved or rejected by the buyer and/or the lender. If the seller makes repairs, a reinspection will be necessary. (The appraisal is a separate matter, not part of the inspection process.)

3. c. Membership in the American Society of Home Inspectors requires actual experience, passing a written examination, inspection reviews, and continuing education.

4. b. Floods and earthquakes are not covered by a typical hazard insurance policy, although supplemental coverage may be available. (Protection against encroachments would be provided by extended coverage title insurance, not by hazard insurance.)

5. d. A homeowner's title insurance policy will protect the buyer against problems that do not appear in the public record, such as an encroachment or adverse possession.

6. c. Debits are costs that a party must pay at closing, either to the other party or to a third party. The buyer's debits increase the amount of money the buyer will need to pay at closing. The seller's debits decrease the seller's net proceeds.

7. d. The earnest money deposit is applied toward the purchase price at closing; it's part of the buyer's downpayment. Because the buyer has already paid the earnest money, it is treated as a credit for the buyer on his settlement statement.

8. a. The buyer's first payment on a new loan is not due the first day of the month immediately after closing, but the first day of the month after that. To cover the interest that accrues during the remainder of the month in which closing occurs, the buyer must pay prepaid or interim interest at closing.

9. a. The seller would pay the fee for recording a deed of reconveyance to release the property from the lien of a deed of trust. The recording fee for a document is generally paid by the party who benefits most from having that document recorded.

10. b. For RESPA purposes, a loan is federally related if the lender is federally regulated, has federally insured accounts, is assisted by the federal government, makes loans in connection with a federal program, sells loans to secondary market agencies, or makes real estate loans that total more than $1,000,000 per year.

GLOSSARY

The definitions given here explain how the listed terms are used in the real estate field. Some of the terms have additional meanings, which can be found in a standard dictionary.

ABSTRACT OF TITLE—*See:* Title, Abstract of.

ACCELERATION CLAUSE—A provision in a promissory note or security instrument allowing the lender to declare the entire debt due immediately if the borrower breaches one or more provisions of the loan agreement. Also referred to as a call provision.

ACCEPTANCE—1. Agreeing to the terms of an offer to enter into a contract, thereby creating a binding contract. 2. Taking delivery of a deed from the grantor.

ACCEPTANCE, QUALIFIED—*See:* Counteroffer.

ACCRUED ITEMS OF EXPENSE—Expenses that have been incurred but are not yet due or payable; in a settlement statement, the seller's accrued expenses are credited to the buyer.

ACQUISITION COST—The amount of money a buyer was required to expend in order to acquire title to a piece of property; in addition to the purchase price, this might include closing costs, legal fees, and other expenses.

ACRE—A measure of area for land; one acre is 43,560 square feet.

ADJUSTABLE-RATE MORTGAGE—*See:* Mortgage, Adjustable-Rate.

Administrator's Deed—*See*: Deed, Administrator's.

Ad Valorem—A Latin phrase that means "according to value," used to refer to taxes that are assessed on the value of property.

Affiliated Licensees—The individual real estate agents licensed under a particular brokerage.

Agency—A relationship of trust created when one person (the principal) grants another (the agent) authority to represent the principal in dealings with third parties.

Agency, Apparent—When third parties are given the impression that someone who has not been authorized to represent another is that person's agent, or else given the impression that an agent has been authorized to perform acts which are in fact beyond the scope of her authority. Also called ostensible agency.

Agency, Dual—When an agent represents both parties to a transaction, as when a real estate agent represents both the buyer and the seller.

Agency, Exclusive—*See:* Listing, Exclusive.

Agency, Ostensible—*See:* Agency, Apparent.

Agency Coupled with an Interest—When an agent has a claim against the property that is the subject of the agency, so that the principal cannot revoke the agent's authority.

Agency, Inadvertent Dual—Providing agency services to one party without disclosing that you already represent the other party; you unintentionally create a dual agency.

Agency, Non-—When a licensee limits herself to the role of neutral intermediary in a transaction. Non-agency is typically limited to commercial transactions, but may occur in residential transactions as well.

Agent—A person authorized to represent another (the principal) in dealings with third parties.

Agent, Dual—*See:* Agency, Dual.

Agent, General—An agent authorized to handle all of the principal's affairs in one area or in specified areas.

Agent, Special—An agent with limited authority to do a specific thing or conduct a specific transaction.

Agent, Universal—An agent authorized to do everything that can be lawfully delegated to a representative.

AGREEMENT—*See:* Contract.

ALIENATION—The transfer of ownership or an interest in property from one person to another, by any means.

ALIENATION, INVOLUNTARY—Transfer of an interest in property against the will of the owner, or without action by the owner, occurring through operation of law, natural processes, or adverse possession.

ALIENATION, VOLUNTARY—When an owner voluntarily transfers an interest to someone else.

ALIENATION CLAUSE—A provision in a security instrument that gives the lender the right to declare the entire loan balance due immediately if the borrower sells or otherwise transfers the security property. Also called a due-on-sale clause.

ALL-INCLUSIVE TRUST DEED—*See:* Mortgage, Wraparound.

ALTA—American Land Title Association, a nationwide organization of title insurance companies. An extended coverage title policy is sometimes referred to as an ALTA policy.

AMENITIES—Features of a property that contribute to the pleasure or convenience of owning it, such as a fireplace, a beautiful view, or its proximity to a good school.

AMERICANS WITH DISABILITIES ACT—A federal law requiring facilities that are open to the public to ensure accessibility to disabled persons, even if that accessibility requires making architectural modifications. The ADA also requires employers to make reasonable accommodations for disabled employees.

AMORTIZATION, NEGATIVE—When unpaid interest on a loan is added to the principal balance, increasing the amount owed.

AMORTIZE—To gradually pay off a debt with installment payments that include both principal and interest. *See also:* Loan, Amortized.

ANNUAL PERCENTAGE RATE (APR)—All of the charges that the borrower will pay for the loan (including the interest, loan fee, discount points, and mortgage insurance costs), expressed as an annual percentage of the loan amount.

ANTICIPATION, PRINCIPLE OF—An appraisal principle which holds that value is created by the expectation of benefits to be received in the future.

ANTITRUST LAWS—Laws that prohibit any agreement that has the effect of restraining trade, including conspiracies.

APPRAISAL—An estimate or opinion of the value of a piece of property as of a particular date. Also called valuation.

APPRAISER—One who estimates the value of property, especially an expert qualified to do so by training and experience.

APPRECIATION—An increase in value; the opposite of depreciation.

APPURTENANCES—Rights that go along with ownership of a particular piece of property, such as air rights or mineral rights; they are ordinarily transferred with the property, but may, in some cases, be sold separately.

APR—*See:* Annual Percentage Rate.

AREA—The size of a surface, usually in square units of measure, such as square feet or square miles. The area of a piece of land may also be stated in acres.

ARM—*See:* Mortgage, Adjustable-Rate.

ARM'S **L**ENGTH **T**RANSACTION—A transaction in which there is no family or business relationship between the parties.

ARTIFICIAL **P**ERSON—A legal entity such as a corporation, which the law treats as an individual with legal rights and responsibilities; as distinguished from a natural person, a human being. Sometimes called a legal person.

ASSESSMENT—The valuation of property for purposes of taxation.

ASSESSOR—An official who determines the value of property for taxation.

ASSET—Anything of value that a person owns.

ASSETS, **L**IQUID—Cash and other assets that can be readily liquidated (turned into cash), such as stock.

ASSIGN—To transfer rights (especially contract rights) or interests to another.

ASSIGNEE—One to whom rights or interests have been assigned.

ASSIGNMENT—1. A transfer of contract rights from one person to another. 2. In the case of a lease, when the original tenant transfers her entire leasehold estate to another. *Compare:* Sublease.

ASSIGNMENT OF **C**ONTRACT AND **D**EED—The instrument used to substitute a new vendor for the original vendor in a land contract.

ASSIGNOR—One who has assigned his rights or interest to another.

ASSUMPTION—When a buyer takes on personal liability for paying off the seller's existing mortgage or deed of trust.

ASSUMPTION FEE—A fee paid to the lender, usually by the buyer, when a mortgage or deed of trust is assumed.

ATTORNEY IN FACT—Any person authorized to represent another by a power of attorney; not necessarily a lawyer (an attorney at law).

AUTHORITY, ACTUAL—Authority actually given to an agent by the principal, either expressly or by implication.

AUTHORITY, APPARENT—Authority to represent another that someone appears to have and that the principal is estopped from denying, although no actual authority has been granted.

AUTHORITY, IMPLIED—An agent's authority to do everything reasonably necessary to carry out the principal's express orders.

BAD DEBT/VACANCY FACTOR—A percentage deducted from a property's potential gross income to determine the effective gross income, estimating the income that will probably be lost because of vacancies and tenants who don't pay.

BALLOON PAYMENT—A payment on a loan (usually the final payment) that is significantly larger than the regular installment payments.

BANKRUPTCY—1. When the liabilities of an individual, corporation, or firm exceed the assets. 2. When a court declares an individual, corporation, or firm to be insolvent, so that the assets and debts will be administered under bankruptcy laws.

BARGAIN AND SALE DEED—*See*: Deed, Special Warranty.

BENEFICIARY—1. One for whom a trust is created and on whose behalf the trustee administers the trust. 2. The lender in a deed of trust transaction. 3. One entitled to receive real or personal property under a will; a legatee or devisee.

BILL OF SALE—A document used to transfer title to personal property from one person to another.

BINDER—1. An instrument providing immediate insurance coverage until the regular policy is issued. 2. Any payment or preliminary written statement intended to make an agreement legally binding until a formal contract has been drawn up.

BLIND AD—An advertisement placed by a real estate licensee that does not include the name of her real estate firm, as licensed.

BLOCKBUSTING—Attempting to induce owners to list or sell their homes by predicting that members of another race or ethnic group, or people suffering from some disability, will be moving into the neighborhood; this violates antidiscrimination laws. Also called panic selling.

BLUE SKY LAWS—Laws that regulate the promotion and sale of securities in order to protect the public from fraud.

BOARD OF DIRECTORS—The body responsible for governing a corporation on behalf of the shareholders, which oversees the corporate management.

BONA FIDE—In good faith; genuine; not fraudulent.

BREACH—Violation of an obligation, duty, or law; especially an unexcused failure to perform a contractual obligation.

BRANCH MANAGER—A managing broker who is responsible for the operations of a firm's branch office; the branch manager is authorized to perform branch management duties under the supervision of the firm's designated broker.

BROKER—A licensed individual acting on behalf of a real estate firm to perform real estate brokerage services, under the supervision of a designated and/or managing broker.

BROKER, DESIGNATED—*See:* Designated Broker.

BROKER, MANAGING—*See:* Managing Broker.

BROKERAGE—*See:* Real Estate Brokerage.

BROKERAGE FEE—The commission or other compensation charged for a real estate firm's services.

BROKER'S PRICE OPINION—Under Washington law, any oral or written report of property value, prepared by a real estate licensee. A CMA is a broker's price opinion.

BUMP CLAUSE—A provision in a purchase and sale agreement that allows the seller to keep the property on the market while waiting for a contingency to be fulfilled; if the seller receives another good offer in the meantime, she can require the buyer to either waive the contingency clause or terminate the contract.

BUSINESS OPPORTUNITY—A business that is for sale.

BUYDOWN—When discount points are paid to a lender to reduce (buy down) the interest rate charged to the borrower; especially when a seller pays discount points to help the buyer/borrower qualify for financing.

BUYER REPRESENTATION AGREEMENT—A representation agreement between a prospective property buyer and a real estate firm. The buyer hires the firm to locate a suitable property for the buyer to purchase.

CALL PROVISION—*See:* Acceleration Clause.

CANCELLATION—Termination of a contract without undoing acts that have been already performed under the contract. *Compare:* Rescission.

CAPACITY—The legal ability or competency to perform some act, such as enter into a contract or execute a deed or will.

CAPITAL—Money (or other forms of wealth) available for use in the production of more money.

CAPITALIZATION—A method of appraising real property by converting the anticipated net income from the property into the present value. Also called the income approach to value.

CAPITALIZE—1. To provide with cash, or another form of capital. 2. To determine the present value of an asset using capitalization.

CARRYBACK LOAN—*See:* Loan, Purchase Money.

CARRYOVER CLAUSE—*See:* Extender Clause.

CASH FLOW—The residual income after deducting all operating expenses and debt service from gross income. Also called spendable income.

CERTIFICATE OF ELIGIBILITY—A document issued by the Department of Veterans Affairs as evidence of a veteran's eligibility for a VA-guaranteed loan.

CERTIFICATE OF SALE—The document given to the purchaser at a mortgage foreclosure sale, instead of a deed; replaced with a sheriff's deed only after the redemption period expires.

CHAIN OF TITLE—*See:* Title, Chain of.

CHANGE, PRINCIPLE OF—An appraisal principle which holds that property values are in a state of flux, increasing and decreasing in response to social, economic, and governmental forces.

CIVIL LAW—The body of law concerned with the rights and liabilities of one individual in relation to another; includes contract law, tort law, and property law. *Compare:* Criminal Law.

CIVIL RIGHTS—Fundamental rights guaranteed to individuals by the law. The term is primarily used in reference to constitutional and statutory protections against discrimination or government interference.

CIVIL SUIT—A lawsuit in which one private party sues another private party (as opposed to a criminal suit, in which an individual is sued—prosecuted—by the government).

CLIENT—One who hires a real estate agent, lawyer, or appraiser. A real estate agent's client can be a seller, a buyer, a landlord, or a tenant.

CLOSING—The final stage in a real estate transaction, when the seller receives the purchase money, the buyer receives the deed, and title is transferred. Also called settlement.

CLOSING COSTS—Expenses incurred in the transfer of real estate in addition to the purchase price; for example, the appraisal fee, title insurance premium, brokerage commission, and excise tax.

CLOSING DATE—The date on which all the terms of a purchase and sale agreement must be met, or the contract is terminated.

CLOSING STATEMENT—*See:* Settlement Statement.

CLOUD ON TITLE—A claim, encumbrance, or apparent defect that makes the title to a property unmarketable. *See:* Title, Marketable.

CMA— *See*: Competitive Market Analysis.

CODE OF ETHICS—A body of rules setting forth accepted standards of conduct, reflecting principles of fairness and morality; especially one that the members of an organization are expected to follow.

COLLATERAL—Anything of value used as security for a debt or obligation.

COLOR OF TITLE—*See:* Title, Color of.

COMMINGLING—Mixing personal or business funds with client funds for any reason. Commingling funds violates the license law.

COMMISSION—1. The compensation paid to a brokerage for services in connection with a real estate transaction (usually a percentage of the sales price). 2. A group of people organized for a particular purpose or function; usually a governmental body, such as the Real Estate Commission.

COMMISSION SPLIT—A compensation arrangement in which listing and selling firms share the commission paid by the seller.

COMMITMENT—In real estate finance, a lender's promise to make a loan. A loan commitment may be "firm" or "conditional"; a conditional commitment is contingent on something, such as a satisfactory credit report on the borrower.

COMMUNITY PROPERTY—In Washington and other community property states, property owned jointly by a married couple, as distinguished from each spouse's separate property; generally, any property acquired through the labor or skill of either spouse during marriage.

CO-MORTGAGOR—Someone (usually a family member) who accepts responsibility for the repayment of a mortgage loan along with the primary borrower, to help the borrower qualify for the loan.

COMPETENT—1. Of sound mind, for the purposes of entering into a contract or executing an instrument. 2. Both of sound mind and having reached the age of majority.

COMPETITION, PRINCIPLE OF—An appraisal principle which holds that profits tend to encourage competition, and excess profits tend to result in ruinous competition.

COMPETITIVE MARKET ANALYSIS (CMA)—A comparison of homes that are similar in location, style, and amenities to the subject property, in order to set a realistic listing price. Similar to the sales comparison approach to value.

COMPLIANCE INSPECTION—A building inspection to determine, for the benefit of a lender, whether building codes, specifications, or conditions established after a prior inspection have been met before a loan is made.

CONDITION—1. A provision in a contract that makes the parties' rights and obligations depend on the occurrence (or non-occurrence) of a particular event. Also called a contingency clause. 2. A provision in a deed that makes title depend on compliance with a particular restriction.

CONDITIONAL COMMITMENT—*See:* Commitment.

CONFORMING LOAN—*See:* Loan, Conforming.

CONFORMITY, PRINCIPLE OF—An appraisal principle which holds that the maximum value of property is realized when there is a reasonable degree of social and economic homogeneity in the neighborhood.

CONSIDERATION—Anything of value (such as money, goods, services, or a promise) given to induce another to enter into a contract. Sometimes called valuable consideration.

CONSPIRACY—An agreement or plan between two or more persons to perform an unlawful act.

CONSTRUCTION LIEN—*See:* Lien, Construction.

CONTINGENCY CLAUSE—*See:* Condition.

CONTRACT—An agreement between two or more persons to do or not do a certain thing, for consideration.

CONTRACT, BILATERAL—A contract in which each party has made a binding promise to perform (as distinguished from a unilateral contract).

CONTRACT, BROKERAGE AND AFFILIATED LICENSEE—A contract between a brokerage and an affiliated licensee, outlining their mutual obligations.

CONTRACT, CONDITIONAL SALES—*See:* Contract, Land.

CONTRACT, EXECUTED—A contract in which both parties have completely performed their contractual obligations.

CONTRACT, EXECUTORY—A contract in which one or both parties have not yet completed performance of their obligations.

CONTRACT, EXPRESS—A contract that has been put into words, either spoken or written.

CONTRACT, IMPLIED—A contract that has not been put into words, but is implied by the actions of the parties.

CONTRACT, INSTALLMENT SALES—*See:* Contract, Land.

CONTRACT, LAND—A contract for the sale of real property in which the buyer (the vendee) pays in installments; the buyer takes possession of the property immediately, but the seller (the vendor) retains legal title until the full price has been paid. Also called a conditional sales contract, installment sales contract, real estate contract, or contract for deed.

CONTRACT, ORAL—A spoken agreement that has not been written down. Also called a parol contract.

CONTRACT, REAL ESTATE—1. Any contract pertaining to real estate. 2. A land contract.

CONTRACT, SALES—*See:* Purchase and Sale Agreement.

CONTRACT, UNENFORCEABLE—An agreement that a court would refuse to enforce; for example, because its contents can't be proven or the statute of limitations has run out.

CONTRACT, UNILATERAL—A contract that is accepted by performance; the offeror has promised to perform her side of the bargain if the other party performs, but the other party has not promised to perform. *Compare:* Contract, Bilateral.

CONTRACT, VALID—A binding, legally enforceable contract.

CONTRACT, VOID—An agreement that is not an enforceable contract, because it lacks a required element (such as consideration) or is defective in some other respect.

CONTRACT, VOIDABLE—A contract that one of the parties can disaffirm without liability, because of lack of capacity or a negative factor such as fraud or duress.

CONTRACT FOR DEED—*See:* Contract, Land.

CONTRACT OF ADHESION—A contract that is one-sided and unfair to one of the parties; a "take it or leave it" contract, in which the offeror had much greater bargaining power than the offeree.

CONTRACT OF SALE—*See:* Purchase and Sale Agreement.

CONTRIBUTION, PRINCIPLE OF—An appraisal principle which holds that the value of real property is greatest when the improvements produce the highest return commensurate with their cost (the investment).

CONVENTIONAL FINANCING—*See:* Loan, Conventional.

CONVERSION—Misappropriating property or funds belonging to another; for example, converting trust funds to one's own use.

CONVEYANCE—The transfer of title to real property from one person to another by means of a written document, especially a deed.

COOPERATIVE SALE—A sale in which the buyer and the seller are brought together by licensees working for different real estate firms.

CORPORATION—An association organized according to certain laws, in which individuals may purchase ownership shares; treated by the law as an artificial person, separate from the individual shareholders. *Compare:* Partnership.

CORRECTION DEED—*See*: Deed, Correction.

COST—The amount paid for anything in money, goods, or services.

COST, REPLACEMENT—In appraisal, the current cost of constructing a building with the same utility as the subject property using modern materials and construction methods.

COST, REPRODUCTION—In appraisal, the cost of constructing a replica (an exact duplicate) of the subject property, using the same materials and construction methods that were originally used, but at current prices.

COST APPROACH TO VALUE—One of the three main methods of appraisal, in which an estimate of the subject property's value is arrived at by estimating the cost of replacing (or reproducing) the improvements, then deducting the estimated accrued depreciation and adding the estimated market value of the land.

COUNTEROFFER—A response to a contract offer, changing some of the terms of the original offer; it operates as a rejection of the original offer (not as an acceptance). Also called qualified acceptance.

COVENANT—1. A contract. 2. A promise. 3. A guarantee (express or implied) in a document such as a deed or lease. 4. A restrictive covenant.

COVENANT, RESTRICTIVE—A promise to do or not do an act relating to real property, especially a promise that runs with the land; usually an owner's promise not to use the property in a specified manner.

CREDIT—A payment receivable (owed to you), as opposed to a debit, which is a payment due (owed by you).

CREDITOR—One who is owed a debt.

CREDITOR, SECURED—A creditor with a security interest in or a lien against specific property; if the debt is not repaid, the creditor can repossess the property or (in the case of real estate) foreclose on the property and collect the debt from the sale proceeds.

CRIMINAL LAW—The body of law under which the government can prosecute an individual for crimes, wrongs against society. *Compare:* Civil Law.

CUL-DE-SAC—A dead end street, especially one with a semi-circular turnaround at the end.

CUSTOMER—From the point of view of a listing agent, a prospective property buyer.

DAMAGES—In a civil lawsuit, an amount of money the defendant is ordered to pay the plaintiff.

DAMAGES, COMPENSATORY—Damages awarded to a plaintiff as compensation for injuries (personal injuries, property damage, or financial losses) caused by the defendant's act or failure to act.

DAMAGES, LIQUIDATED—A sum that the parties to a contract agree in advance (at the time the contract is made) will serve as full compensation in the event of a breach.

DAMAGES, PUNITIVE—In a civil lawsuit, an award added to compensatory damages, to punish the defendant for outrageous or malicious conduct and discourage others from similar conduct.

DEBIT—A charge or debt owed to another.

DEBTOR—One who owes money to another.

DEBT SERVICE—The amount of money required to make the periodic payments of principal and interest on an amortized debt, such as a mortgage.

DEED—An instrument which, when properly executed and delivered, conveys title to real property from the grantor to the grantee.

DEED, ADMINISTRATOR'S—A deed used by the administrator of an estate to convey property owned by the deceased person to the heirs.

DEED, BARGAIN AND SALE—*See*: Deed, Special Warranty.

DEED, CORRECTION—A deed used to correct minor mistakes in an earlier deed, such as misspelled names or typographical errors in the legal description. Also called a deed of confirmation or a reformation deed.

DEED, GENERAL WARRANTY—A deed in which the grantor warrants the title against defects that might have arisen before or during his period of ownership.

DEED, GIFT—A deed that is not supported by valuable consideration; often lists "love and affection" as consideration.

DEED, GRANT—A deed that uses the word "grant" in its words of conveyance and carries certain implied warranties; rarely used in Washington.

DEED, QUITCLAIM—A deed that conveys any interest in a property that the grantor has at the time the deed is executed, without warranties.

DEED, REFORMATION—*See:* Deed, Correction.

DEED, SHERIFF'S—A deed delivered, on court order, to the holder of a certificate of sale when the redemption period after a mortgage foreclosure has expired.

DEED, SPECIAL WARRANTY—A deed in which the grantor warrants title only against defects that may have arisen during her period of ownership.

DEED, STATUTORY WARRANTY—A short form of the general warranty deed, in which the covenants are implied (by the use of language specified in the state statute) rather than spelled out.

DEED, TAX—A deed given to a purchaser of property at a tax foreclosure sale.

DEED, TRUST—*See:* Deed of Trust.

DEED, TRUSTEE'S—A deed given to a purchaser of property at a trustee's sale.

DEED, WARRANTY—1. A general warranty deed. 2. Any type of deed that carries warranties.

DEED, WILD—A deed that won't be discovered in a standard title search, because of a break in the chain of title.

DEED EXECUTED UNDER COURT ORDER—A deed that is the result of a court action, such as judicial foreclosure or partition.

DEED IN LIEU OF FORECLOSURE—A deed given by a borrower to the lender, relinquishing ownership of the security property, to satisfy the debt and avoid foreclosure.

DEED OF PARTITION—Deed used by co-owners (such as tenants in common or joint tenants) to divide up the co-owned property so that each can own a portion in severalty.

DEED OF RECONVEYANCE—The instrument used to release the security property from the lien created by a deed of trust when the debt has been repaid.

DEED OF TRUST—An instrument that creates a voluntary lien on real property to secure the repayment of a debt, and which includes a power of sale clause permitting nonjudicial foreclosure; the parties are the grantor or trustor (borrower), the beneficiary (the lender), and the trustee (a neutral third party).

DEED RELEASE PROVISION—*See:* Release Clause.

DEED RESTRICTIONS—Provisions in a deed that restrict use of the property, and which may be either covenants or conditions.

DEFAULT—Failure to fulfill an obligation, duty, or promise, as when a borrower fails to make payments, or a tenant fails to pay rent.

DEFENDANT—1. The person being sued in a civil lawsuit. 2. The accused person in a criminal lawsuit.

DEFERRED MAINTENANCE—Depreciation resulting from maintenance or repairs that were postponed, causing physical deterioration of the building.

DELEGATION AGREEMENT—A written agreement in which a designated broker transfers some of her authority and duties to another managing broker (such as a branch manager). However, the agreement doesn't relieve the designated broker of the ultimate responsibility for the delegated function.

DELIVERY—The legal transfer of a deed from the grantor to the grantee, which results in the transfer of title.

DEPARTMENT OF LICENSING—The state agency in charge of administering the real estate license law in Washington.

DEPOSIT—Money offered as an indication of commitment or as a protection, and which may be refunded under certain circumstances, such as an earnest money deposit or a tenant's security deposit.

DEPOSIT RECEIPT—*See:* Purchase and Sale Agreement.

DEPRECIATION—1. A loss in value (caused by deferred maintenance, functional obsolescence, or external obsolescence). 2. For the purpose of income tax deductions, apportioning the cost of an asset over a period of time.

DESIGNATED BROKER—A managing broker who registers with the state to have a designated broker endorsement added to their license. May represent one or more firms, and will have ultimate responsibility for all firm activities.

DISBURSEMENTS—Money paid out or expended.

DISCLAIMER—A denial of legal responsibility.

DISCOUNT—1. (verb) To sell a promissory note at less than its face value. 2. (noun) An amount withheld from the loan amount by the lender when the loan is originated; discount points.

DISCOUNT POINTS—A percentage of the principal amount of a loan, collected by the lender at the time a loan is originated, to reduce the interest rate and give the lender an additional upfront yield.

DISCRIMINATION—Treating people unequally because of their race, religion, sex, national origin, age, or some other characteristic.

DISTRESSED PROPERTY LAW—A state law intended to help protect financially distressed homeowners from foreclosure scams.

DONATIVE INTENT—The intent to transfer title immediately and unconditionally; required for proper delivery of a deed.

DOWNPAYMENT—The part of the purchase price of property that the buyer is paying in cash; the difference between the purchase price and the financing.

DRAINAGE—A system to draw water off land, either artificially (e.g., with pipes) or naturally (e.g., with a slope).

DUAL AGENCY—*See:* Agency, Dual.

DUE-ON-SALE CLAUSE—*See:* Alienation Clause.

DURESS—Unlawful force or constraint used to compel someone to do something (such as sign a contract) against his will.

EARNEST MONEY—A deposit that a prospective buyer gives the seller as evidence of her good faith intent to complete the transaction.

EARNEST MONEY AGREEMENT—*See:* Purchase and Sale Agreement.

EASEMENT—An irrevocable right to use some part of another person's real property for a particular purpose.

ELEMENTS OF COMPARISON—In the sales comparison approach to appraisal, considerations taken into account in selecting comparables and comparing comparables to the subject property; they include date of sale, location, physical characteristics, and terms of sale.

EMPLOYEE—Someone who works under the direction and control of another. *Compare:* Independent Contractor.

ENCUMBER—To place a lien or other encumbrance against the title to a property.

ENCUMBRANCE—A nonpossessory interest in real property; a right or interest held by someone other than the property owner, which may be a lien, an easement, a profit, or a restrictive covenant.

ENCUMBRANCE, FINANCIAL—A lien.

ENCUMBRANCE, NONFINANCIAL—An easement, a profit, or a restrictive covenant.

EQUITABLE REMEDY—In a civil lawsuit, a judgment granted to the plaintiff that is something other than an award of money (damages); an injunction, rescission, and specific performance are examples.

EQUITY—1. An owner's unencumbered interest in his property; the difference between the value of the property and the liens against it. 2. A judge's power to soften or set aside strict legal rules, to bring about a fair and just result in a particular case.

ESCROW—An arrangement in which something of value (such as money or a deed) is held on behalf of the parties to a transaction by a disinterested third party (an escrow agent) until specified conditions have been fulfilled.

ESTATE—1. An interest in real property that is or may become possessory; either a freehold or a leasehold. 2. The property left by someone who has died.

ESTOPPEL—A legal doctrine that prevents a person from asserting rights or facts that are inconsistent with her earlier actions or statements.

ESTOPPEL CERTIFICATE—A document that prevents a person who signs it from later asserting facts different from those stated in the document. Also called an estoppel letter.

ETHICS—A system of accepted principles or standards of moral conduct. *See:* Code of Ethics.

EXCLUSIVE LISTING—*See:* Listing, Exclusive.

EXCULPATORY CLAUSE—A clause in a contract that relieves one party of liability for certain defaults or problems; such provisions are not always enforceable.

EXECUTE—1. To sign an instrument and take any other steps (such as acknowledgment) that may be necessary to its validity. 2. To perform or complete. *See:* Contract, Executed.

EXEMPTION—A provision holding that a law or rule does not apply to a particular person or group; for example, a person entitled to a tax exemption is not required to pay the tax.

EXPRESS—Stated in words, whether spoken or written. *Compare:* Implied.

EXTENDER CLAUSE—A clause in a listing agreement providing that for a specified period after the listing expires, the listing agent will still be entitled to a commission if the property is sold to someone that agent dealt with during the listing term. Also called a safety clause or carryover clause.

EXTERNAL OBSOLESCENCE—*See:* Obsolescence, External.

FAILURE OF PURPOSE—When the intended purpose of an agreement or arrangement can no longer be achieved; in most cases, this releases the parties from their obligations.

FANNIE MAE—Popular name for the Federal National Mortgage Association (FNMA).

FED—The Federal Reserve.

Fee—*See:* Fee Simple.

Fee, Qualified—A fee simple estate that is subject to termination if a certain condition is not met or if a specified event occurs. It may be a fee simple determinable or a fee simple subject to condition subsequent. Also called a conditional fee or defeasible fee.

Fee Simple—The highest and most complete form of ownership, which is of potentially infinite duration. Also called a fee or a fee simple absolute.

FHA—Federal Housing Administration. *See also:* Loan, FHA.

Fiduciary Relationship—A relationship of trust and confidence, where one party owes the other (or both parties owe each other) loyalty and a higher standard of good faith than is owed to third parties. For example, an agent is a fiduciary in relation to the principal; husband and wife are fiduciaries in relation to one another.

Finance Charge—Any charge a borrower is assessed, directly or indirectly, in connection with a loan. *See also:* Total Finance Charge.

Financial Statement—A summary of facts showing the financial condition of an individual or a business, including a detailed list of assets and liabilities. Also called a balance sheet.

Financing Statement—A brief instrument that is recorded to perfect and give constructive notice of a creditor's security interest in an article of personal property.

Finder's Fee—A referral fee paid to someone for directing a buyer or a seller to a real estate agent.

Firm Commitment—*See:* Commitment.

First Lien Position—The position held by a mortgage or deed of trust that has higher lien priority than any other mortgage or deed of trust against the property.

Fixed-Rate Loan—*See:* Loan, Fixed-Rate.

Fixed Term—A period of time that has a definite beginning and ending.

Foreclosure—When a lienholder causes property to be sold against the owner's wishes, so that the unpaid lien can be satisfied from the sale proceeds.

Foreclosure, Judicial—1. The sale of property pursuant to court order to satisfy a lien. 2. A lawsuit filed by a mortgagee or deed of trust beneficiary to foreclose on the security property when the borrower has defaulted.

FORECLOSURE, NONJUDICIAL—Foreclosure by a trustee under the power of sale clause in a deed of trust.

FORFEITURE—Loss of a right or something else of value as a result of failure to perform an obligation or fulfill a condition.

FOR SALE BY OWNER—A property that is being sold by the owner without the help of a real estate agent. Also called a FSBO (often pronounced "fizz-bo").

FRANCHISE—A right or privilege granted by a government to conduct a certain business, or a right granted by a private business to use its trade name in conducting business.

FRAUD—An intentional or negligent misrepresentation or concealment of a material fact, which is relied upon by another, who is induced to enter a transaction and harmed as a result.

FRAUD, ACTUAL—Deceit or misrepresentation with the intention of cheating or defrauding another.

FRAUD, CONSTRUCTIVE—A breach of duty that misleads the person the duty was owed to, without an intention to deceive; for example, if a seller gives a buyer inaccurate information about the property without realizing that it is false, that may be constructive fraud.

FREDDIE MAC—Popular name for the Federal Home Loan Mortgage Corporation (FHLMC).

FREE AND CLEAR—Ownership of real property completely free of any liens.

FREEHOLD—A possessory interest in real property that has an indeterminable duration; it can be either a fee simple or an estate for life. Someone who has a freehold estate has title to the property (as opposed to someone with a leasehold estate, who is only a tenant).

FRONTAGE—The distance a property extends along a street or a body of water; the distance between the two side boundaries at the front of the lot.

FRONT FOOT—A measurement of property for sale or valuation, with each foot of frontage presumed to extend the entire depth of the lot.

FUNCTIONAL OBSOLESCENCE—*See*: Obsolescence, Functional.

GENERAL WARRANTY DEED—*See*: Deed, General Warranty.

GIFT DEED—*See*: Deed, Gift.

GIFT FUNDS—Money that a relative (or other third party) gives to a buyer who otherwise would not have enough cash to close the transaction.

GINNIE MAE—Popular name for the Government National Mortgage Association (GNMA).

GOOD FAITH ESTIMATE (GFE)—RESPA requires loan originators to disclose accurate estimates of anticipated closing costs, using a standard GFE form published by HUD.

GRANT—To transfer or convey an interest in real property by means of a written instrument.

GRANT DEED—*See*: Deed, Grant.

GRANTEE—One who receives a grant of real property.

GRANTING CLAUSE—Words in a deed that indicate the grantor's intent to transfer an interest in property.

GRANTOR—One who grants an interest in real property to another.

GROUP BOYCOTT—An agreement between two or more real estate agents to exclude other agents from equal participation in real estate activities.

GUARDIAN—A person appointed by a court to administer the affairs of a minor or an incompetent person.

HABENDUM CLAUSE—A clause included after the granting clause in many deeds; it begins "to have and to hold" and describes the type of estate the grantee will hold.

HEIR—Someone entitled to inherit another's property under the laws of intestate succession.

HEIRS AND ASSIGNS—A phrase used in legal documents to cover all successors to a person's interest in property; assigns are successors who acquire title in some manner other than inheritance, such as by deed.

HIGHEST AND BEST USE—The use which, at the time of appraisal, is most likely to produce the greatest net return from the property over a given period of time.

HOLDER IN DUE COURSE—A person who obtains a negotiable instrument for value, in good faith, without notice that it is overdue or notice of any defenses against it.

HUD—The U.S. Department of Housing and Urban Development.

HYPOTHECATE—To make property security for an obligation without giving up possession of it. *Compare:* Pledge.

IMPLIED—Not expressed in words, but understood from actions or circumstances. *Compare:* Express.

IMPOUND ACCOUNT—A bank account maintained by a lender for payment of property taxes and insurance premiums on the security property; the lender requires the borrower to make regular deposits, and then pays the expenses out of the account when they are due. Also called a reserve account.

IMPROVEMENTS—Man-made additions to real property.

IMPROVEMENTS, MISPLACED—Improvements that do not fit the most profitable use of the site; they can be overimprovements or underimprovements.

INCOME, DISPOSABLE—Income remaining after income taxes have been paid.

INCOME, EFFECTIVE GROSS—A measure of a rental property's capacity to generate income; calculated by subtracting a bad debt/vacancy factor from the economic rent (potential gross income).

INCOME, GROSS—A property's total income before making any deductions (for bad debts, vacancies, operating expenses, etc.).

INCOME, NET—The income left over after subtracting the property's operating expenses (fixed expenses, maintenance expenses, and reserves for replacement) from the effective gross income. In the income approach to value, it is capitalized to estimate the subject property's value.

INCOME, POTENTIAL GROSS—A property's economic rent; the income it could earn if it were available for lease in the current market.

INCOME, RESIDUAL—The amount of income that an applicant for a VA loan has left over after taxes, recurring obligations, and the proposed housing expense have been deducted from his gross monthly income.

INCOME, SPENDABLE—The income that remains after deducting operating expenses, debt service, and income taxes from a property's gross income. Also called net spendable income or cash flow.

INCOME APPROACH TO VALUE—One of the three main methods of appraisal, in which an estimate of the subject property's value is based on the net income it produces; also called the capitalization method or investor's method of appraisal.

INCOME PROPERTY—Property that generates rent or other income for the owner, such as an apartment building. In the federal income tax code, it is referred to as property held for the production of income.

INCOME RATIO—A standard used in qualifying a buyer for a loan, to determine whether she has sufficient income; the buyer's debts and proposed housing expense should not exceed a specified percentage of her income.

INCOMPETENT—Not legally competent; not of sound mind.

INDEPENDENT CONTRACTOR—A person who contracts to do a job for another, but retains control over how he will carry out the task, rather than following detailed instructions. *Compare:* Employee.

INDEX—A published statistical report that indicates changes in the cost of money; used as the basis for interest rate adjustments in an ARM.

INDEX, TRACT—An index of recorded documents in which all documents that carry a particular legal description are grouped together.

IN-HOUSE SALE—A sale in which the buyer and the seller are brought together by licensees working for the same brokerage firm.

INJUNCTION—A court order prohibiting someone from performing an act, or commanding performance of an act.

INSTALLMENT SALE—Under the federal income tax code, a sale in which less than 100% of the sales price is received in the year the sale takes place.

INSTRUMENT—A legal document, usually one that transfers title (such as a deed), creates a lien (such as a mortgage), or establishes a right to payment (such as a promissory note or contract).

INSURANCE, HAZARD—Insurance against damage to real property caused by fire, flood, theft, or other mishap. Also called casualty insurance.

INSURANCE, HOMEOWNER'S—Insurance against damage to a homeowner's real property and personal property.

INSURANCE, MORTGAGE—Insurance that protects a lender against losses resulting from the borrower's default.

INSURANCE, MUTUAL MORTGAGE—The mortgage insurance provided by the FHA to lenders who make loans through FHA programs.

INSURANCE, PRIVATE MORTGAGE (PMI)—Insurance provided by private companies to conventional lenders for loans with loan-to-value ratios over 80%.

INSURANCE, TITLE—Insurance that protects against losses resulting from undiscovered title defects. An owner's policy protects the buyer, while a lender's policy protects the lien position of the buyer's lender.

INSURANCE, TITLE, EXTENDED COVERAGE—Title insurance that covers problems that should be discovered by an inspection of the property (such as encroachments and adverse possession), in addition to the problems covered by standard coverage policies. Sometimes referred to as an ALTA (American Land Title Association) policy.

INSURANCE, TITLE, HOMEOWNER'S COVERAGE—Title insurance that is available only in residential one- to four-unit transactions; covers the same issues as an extended coverage policy, plus some additional issues.

INSURANCE, TITLE, STANDARD COVERAGE—Title insurance that protects against latent title defects (such as forged deeds) and undiscovered recorded encumbrances, but not against problems that would only be discovered by an inspection of the property.

INTEREST—1. A right or share in something (such as a piece of real estate). 2. A charge a borrower pays to a lender for the use of the lender's money.

INTEREST, COMPOUND—Interest computed on both the principal and the interest that has already accrued. *Compare:* Interest, Simple.

INTEREST, INTERIM—*See:* Interest, Prepaid.

INTEREST, PREPAID—Interest on a new loan that must be paid at the time of closing; covers the interest due for the first month of the loan term. Also called interim interest.

INTEREST, SIMPLE—Interest that is computed on the principal amount of the loan only, which is the type of interest charged in connection with real estate loans. *Compare:* Interest, Compound.

INTERPLEADER—A court action filed by someone who is holding funds that two or more people are claiming. The holder turns the funds over to the court; the court resolves the dispute and delivers the funds to the party who is entitled to them.

INVALID—Not legally binding or legally effective; not valid.

JOINT TENANCY—A form of co-ownership in which the co-owners have unity of time, title, interest, and possession and the right of survivorship. *Compare:* Tenancy in Common.

JUDGMENT—1. A court's binding determination of the rights and duties of the parties in a lawsuit. 2. A court order requiring one party to pay the other damages.

JUDGMENT, **D**EFICIENCY—A personal judgment entered against a borrower in favor of the lender if the proceeds from a foreclosure sale of the security property are not enough to pay off the debt.

JUDGMENT **C**REDITOR—A person who is owed money as a result of a judgment in a lawsuit.

JUDGMENT **D**EBTOR—A person who owes money as a result of a judgment in a lawsuit.

JUDGMENT **L**IEN—*See:* Lien, Judgment.

JUDICIAL **F**ORECLOSURE—*See:* Foreclosure, Judicial.

KICKBACK—A fee paid for a referral (for example, to an appraiser or inspector). The Real Estate Settlement Procedures Act prohibits kickbacks in most residential mortgage loan transactions.

LAND **C**ONTRACT—*See:* Contract, Land.

LANDLORD—A landowner who has leased his property to another (a tenant). Also called a lessor.

LATENT **D**EFECT—A defect that is not visible or apparent. *Compare:* Patent Defect.

LAWFUL **O**BJECT—An objective or purpose of a contract that does not violate the law or a judicial determination of public policy.

LEASE—A conveyance of a leasehold estate from the fee owner to a tenant; a contract in which one party pays the other rent in exchange for the possession of real estate. Also called a rental agreement.

LEASEBACK—*See:* Sale-Leaseback.

LEGAL **D**ESCRIPTION—A precise description of a parcel of real property that would enable a surveyor to locate its exact boundaries. It may be a lot and block description, a metes and bounds description, or a government survey description.

LENDER, **I**NSTITUTIONAL—A bank, savings and loan, or similar organization that invests other people's funds in loans; as opposed to an individual or private lender, which invests its own funds.

LESSOR—A landlord.

LESSEE—A tenant.

LEVERAGE—The effective use of borrowed money to finance an investment such as real estate.

LEVY—To impose a tax.

LIABILITY—1. A debt or obligation. 2. Legal responsibility.

LIABILITY, JOINT AND SEVERAL—A form of liability in which two or more persons are responsible for a debt both individually and as a group.

LIABILITY, LIMITED—When a business investor is not personally liable for the debts of the business, as in the case of a limited partner or a corporate shareholder.

LIABILITY, VICARIOUS—A legal doctrine holding that a principal can be held liable for harm to third parties resulting from an agent's actions. (This rule usually does not apply to real estate agency relationships in Washington.)

LIABLE—Legally responsible.

LICENSE—1. Official permission to do a particular thing that the law does not allow everyone to do. 2. Revocable, non-assignable permission to use another person's land for a particular purpose. *Compare:* Easement.

LIEN—A nonpossessory interest in real property, giving the lienholder the right to foreclose if the owner doesn't pay a debt owed to the lienholder; a financial encumbrance on the owner's title.

LIEN, ATTACHMENT—A lien intended to prevent transfer of the property pending the outcome of litigation.

LIEN, CONSTRUCTION—A lien on property in favor of someone who provided labor or materials to improve it. Also called a mechanic's lien or materialman's lien.

LIEN, EQUITABLE—A lien arising as a matter of fairness, rather than by agreement or by operation of law.

LIEN, GENERAL—A lien against all the property of a debtor, rather than a particular piece of her property. *Compare:* Lien, Specific.

LIEN, INVOLUNTARY—A lien that arises by operation of law, without the consent of the property owner. Also called a statutory lien.

LIEN, JUDGMENT—A general lien against a judgment debtor's property, which the judgment creditor creates by recording an abstract of judgment in the county where the property is located.

LIEN, MATERIALMAN'S—A construction lien in favor of someone who supplied materials for a project (as opposed to labor).

LIEN, MECHANIC'S—*See:* Lien, Construction.

LIEN, PROPERTY TAX—A specific lien on property to secure payment of property taxes.

LIEN, SPECIFIC—A lien that attaches only to a particular piece of property. *Compare:* Lien, General.

LIEN, STATUTORY—*See:* Lien, Involuntary.

LIEN, TAX—A lien on property to secure the payment of taxes.

LIEN, VOLUNTARY—A lien placed against property with the consent of the owner; a deed of trust or a mortgage.

LIENHOLDER, JUNIOR—A secured creditor whose lien is lower in priority than another's lien.

LIEN PRIORITY—The order in which liens are paid off out of the proceeds of a foreclosure sale.

LIEN THEORY—The theory holding that a mortgage or deed of trust does not involve a transfer of title to the lender, but merely creates a lien against the property in the lender's favor. *Compare:* Title Theory.

LIMITED LIABILITY—*See:* Liability, Limited.

LIQUIDATED DAMAGES—*See:* Damages, Liquidated.

LIQUIDITY—The ability to convert an asset into cash quickly.

LISTING—A written agency contract between a seller and a real estate firm, stipulating that the firm will be paid a commission for finding (or attempting to find) a buyer for the seller's property. Also called a listing agreement.

LISTING AGENT—The agent who takes a listing, and thus represents the seller.

LISTING, EXCLUSIVE—Either an exclusive agency listing or an exclusive right to sell listing.

LISTING, EXCLUSIVE AGENCY—A listing agreement that entitles the agent to a commission if anyone other than the seller finds a buyer for the property during the listing term.

LISTING, EXCLUSIVE RIGHT TO SELL—A listing agreement that entitles the agent to a commission if anyone—including the seller—finds a buyer for the property during the listing term.

LISTING, MULTIPLE—A listing (usually an exclusive right to sell listing) that includes a provision allowing the agent to submit the listing to the multiple listing service for dissemination to cooperating licensees.

LISTING, NET—A listing agreement in which the seller sets a net amount he is willing to accept for the property; if the actual selling price exceeds that amount, the agent is entitled to keep the excess as her commission. Net listings are illegal in Washington.

LISTING, OPEN—A nonexclusive listing, given by a seller to as many agents as she chooses. If the property is sold, an agent is entitled to a commission only if he was the procuring cause of the sale.

LOAN, AMORTIZED—A loan that requires regular installment payments of both principal and interest (as opposed to an interest-only loan). It is fully amortized if the installment payments will pay off the full amount of the principal and all of the interest by the end of the repayment period. It is partially amortized if the installment payments will cover only part of the principal, so that a balloon payment of the remaining principal balance is required at the end of the repayment period.

LOAN, CALLED—A loan that has been accelerated by the lender. *See:* Acceleration Clause.

LOAN, CARRYBACK—*See:* Loan, Purchase Money.

LOAN, CONFORMING—A loan made in accordance with the standardized underwriting criteria of the major secondary market agencies, Fannie Mae and Freddie Mac, and which therefore can be sold to those agencies.

LOAN, CONSTRUCTION—A loan to finance the cost of constructing a building, usually providing that the loan funds will be advanced in installments as the work progresses. Also called an interim loan.

LOAN, CONVENTIONAL—An institutional loan that is not insured or guaranteed by a government agency.

LOAN, FHA—A loan made by an institutional lender and insured by the Federal Housing Administration, so that the FHA will reimburse the lender for losses that result if the borrower defaults.

LOAN, FIXED-RATE—A loan on which the interest rate will remain the same throughout the entire loan term. *Compare:* Mortgage, Adjustable-rate.

LOAN, GUARANTEED—A loan in which a third party has agreed to reimburse the lender for losses that result if the borrower defaults.

LOAN, HOME EQUITY—A loan secured by the borrower's equity in a home that she already owns. *Compare:* Loan, Purchase Money.

LOAN, INTEREST-ONLY—A loan that requires the borrower to pay only the interest during the loan term, with the principal due at the end of the term.

LOAN, INTERIM—*See:* Loan, Construction.

LOAN, JUMBO—A conventional loan that exceeds the conforming loan limit; typically involves higher interest rate and fees and stricter underwriting standards.

LOAN, PARTICIPATION—A loan in which the lender receives some yield on the loan in addition to the interest, such as a percentage of the income generated by the property, or a share in the borrower's equity.

LOAN, PERMANENT—*See:* Loan, Take-out.

LOAN, PURCHASE MONEY—1. When a seller extends credit to a buyer to finance the purchase of the property, accepting a deed of trust or mortgage instead of cash. Sometimes called a carryback loan. 2. In a more general sense, any loan the borrower uses to buy the security property (as opposed to a loan secured by property the borrower already owns).

LOAN, ROLLOVER—A loan in which the interest rate is renegotiated at specified intervals.

LOAN, TAKE-OUT—Long-term financing used to replace a construction loan (an interim loan) when construction has been completed. Also called a permanent loan.

LOAN, VA-GUARANTEED—A home loan made by an institutional lender to an eligible veteran and guaranteed by the Department of Veterans Affairs. The VA will reimburse the lender for losses if the borrower defaults.

LOAN CORRESPONDENT—An intermediary who arranges loans of an investor's money to borrowers, and then services the loans.

LOAN FEE—A loan origination fee, an assumption fee, or discount points.

LOAN-LEVEL PRICE ADJUSTMENT (LLPA)—A risk-based loan fee that varies depending on the borrower's credit score and the loan-to-value ratio (or on certain other factors that affect risk); charged on some conventional conforming loans.

LOAN-TO-VALUE RATIO (LTV)—The relationship between the loan amount and either the sales price or the appraised value of the property (whichever is less), expressed as a percentage.

LOAN WORKOUT—An alternative to foreclosure in which a lender agrees to a new payment plan for a loan, or to reduction of the loan's interest rate or principal amount.

LOCK-IN CLAUSE—A clause in a promissory note or land contract that prohibits pre-payment before a specified date, or prohibits it altogether.

LTV—*See:* Loan-to-Value Ratio.

M.A.I.—Member of the Appraiser's Institute. The initials identify a member of the American Institute of Real Estate Appraisers of the National Association of Realtors.®

MAJORITY, AGE OF—The age at which a person becomes legally competent; in Washington, 18 years old. *See:* Minor.

MAKER—The person who signs a promissory note, promising to repay a debt. *Compare:* Payee.

MANAGING BROKER—A licensed individual with at least three years' experience as a broker who has passed the managing broker exam; a managing broker performs brokerage services for a firm, under the supervision of a designated broker.

MARGIN—In an adjustable-rate mortgage, the difference between the index rate and the interest rate charged to the borrower.

MARKETABLE TITLE—*See:* Title, Marketable.

MARKET DATA APPROACH—*See:* Sales Comparison Approach.

MARKET PRICE—1. The current price generally being charged for something in the marketplace. 2. The price actually paid for a property. *Compare:* Value, Market.

MASTER/SERVANT RELATIONSHIP—A legal term for a standard employer/employee relationship.

MATERIAL FACT—Information that has a substantial negative impact on the value of the property, on a party's ability to perform, or on the purpose of the transaction.

MATURITY DATE—The date by which a loan is supposed to be paid off in full.

MEETING OF MINDS—*See:* Mutual Consent.

MINOR—A person who has not yet reached the age of majority; in Washington, a person under 18.

MIP—Mortgage insurance premium; especially a premium charged in connection with an FHA-insured loan.

MISREPRESENTATION—A false or misleading statement. *See:* Fraud.

MLS—*See:* Multiple Listing Service.

MONOPOLY—When a single entity or group has exclusive control over the production or sale of a product or service.

MORTGAGE—1. An instrument that creates a voluntary lien on real property to secure repayment of a debt, and which (unlike a deed of trust) ordinarily does not include a power of sale, so it can only be foreclosed judicially; the parties are the mortgagor (borrower) and mortgagee (lender). 2. The term is often used more generally, to refer to either a mortgage or a deed of trust—i.e., to any loan secured by real property. *Note: If you do not find the specific term you are looking for here under "Mortgage," check the entries under "Loan."*

MORTGAGE, **A**DJUSTABLE-**R**ATE (ARM)—A loan in which the interest rate is periodically increased or decreased to reflect changes in the cost of money. *Compare:* Loan, Fixed-Rate.

MORTGAGE, **B**ALLOON—A partially amortized mortgage loan that requires a large balloon payment at the end of the loan term.

MORTGAGE, **B**LANKET—A mortgage that is a lien against more than one parcel of property.

MORTGAGE, **B**UDGET—A loan in which the monthly payments include a share of the property taxes and insurance, in addition to principal and interest; the lender places the money for taxes and insurance in an impound account.

MORTGAGE, **C**LOSED—A loan that cannot be paid off early.

MORTGAGE, **C**LOSED-**E**ND—A loan that does not allow the borrower to increase the balance owed; the opposite of an open-end mortgage.

MORTGAGE, **D**IRECT **R**EDUCTION—A loan that requires a fixed amount of principal to be paid in each payment; the total payment becomes steadily smaller, because the interest portion becomes smaller with each payment as the principal balance decreases.

MORTGAGE, **F**IRST—The mortgage on a property that has first lien position; the one with higher lien priority than any other mortgage against the property.

MORTGAGE, HARD MONEY—A mortgage given to a lender in exchange for cash, as opposed to one given in exchange for credit.

MORTGAGE, JUNIOR—A mortgage that has lower lien priority than another mortgage against the same property. Sometimes called a secondary mortgage.

MORTGAGE, LEVEL PAYMENT—An amortized loan with payments that are the same amount each month, although the portion of the payment that is applied to principal steadily increases and the portion of the payment applied to interest steadily decreases. *See:* Loan, Amortized.

MORTGAGE, OPEN-END—A loan that permits the borrower to reborrow money he has repaid on the principal, usually up to the original loan amount, without executing a new loan agreement.

MORTGAGE, PACKAGE—A mortgage that is secured by certain items of personal property (such as appliances) in addition to the real property.

MORTGAGE, SATISFACTION OF—The document a mortgagee gives the mortgagor when the mortgage debt has been paid in full, acknowledging that the debt has been paid and the mortgage is no longer a lien against the property.

MORTGAGE, SECONDARY—*See:* Mortgage, Junior.

MORTGAGE, SENIOR—A mortgage that has higher lien priority than another mortgage against the same property; the opposite of a junior mortgage.

MORTGAGE, WRAPAROUND—A purchase money loan arrangement in which the seller uses part of the buyer's payments to make the payments on an existing loan (called the underlying loan); the buyer takes title subject to the underlying loan, but does not assume it. When the security instrument used for wraparound financing is a deed of trust instead of a mortgage, it may be referred to as an all-inclusive trust deed.

MORTGAGE BANKER—An intermediary who originates real estate loans.

MORTGAGE BROKER—An intermediary who brings real estate lenders and borrowers together and negotiates loan agreements between them.

MORTGAGE BROKER PRACTICES ACT—A state law that regulates the mortgage broker business and contains provisions intended to help prevent fraudulent lending practices.

MORTGAGE COMPANY—A type of real estate lender that originates and services loans on behalf of large investors (acting as a mortgage banker) or for resale on the secondary mortgage market.

MORTGAGE LOAN—Any loan secured by real property, whether the actual security instrument used is a mortgage or a deed of trust.

MORTGAGEE—A lender who accepts a mortgage as security for repayment of the loan.

MORTGAGING CLAUSE—A clause in a mortgage that describes the security interest given to the mortgagee.

MORTGAGOR—A property owner (usually a borrower) who gives a mortgage to another (usually a lender) as security for payment of an obligation.

MULTIPLE LISTING SERVICE (MLS)—An organization of real estate firms and licensees who share their exclusive listings.

MUTUAL CONSENT—When all parties freely agree to the terms of a contract, without fraud, undue influence, duress, menace, or mistake. Mutual consent is achieved through offer and acceptance; it is sometimes referred to as a "meeting of the minds."

NAR—National Association of Realtors.®

NARRATIVE REPORT—A thorough appraisal report in which the appraiser summarizes the data and the appraisal methods used, to convince the reader of the soundness of the estimate; a more comprehensive presentation than a form report or an opinion letter.

NATIONAL MARKET—*See:* Secondary Mortgage Market.

NEGLIGENCE—Conduct that falls below the standard of care that a reasonable person would exercise under the circumstances; carelessness or recklessness.

NEGOTIABLE INSTRUMENT—An instrument containing an unconditional promise to pay a certain sum of money, to order or to bearer, on demand or at a particular time. It can be a check, promissory note, bond, draft, or stock.

NET INCOME—*See:* Income, Net.

NET LISTING—*See:* Listing, Net.

NET WORTH—An individual's personal financial assets, minus her personal liabilities.

NOMINAL INTEREST RATE—The interest rate stated in a promissory note. Also called the note rate or coupon rate. *Compare:* Annual Percentage Rate.

NONCONFORMING LOAN—*See:* Loan, Conforming.

NORMAL MARKET CONDITIONS—A sale taking place in a competitive and open market, with informed parties acting prudently, and at arm's length, without undue stimulus (such as an urgent need to sell the property immediately)

NOTARIZE—To have a document certified by a notary public.

NOTARY PUBLIC—Someone who is officially authorized to witness and certify the acknowledgment made by someone signing a legal document.

NOTE—*See:* Note, Promissory.

NOTE, DEMAND—A promissory note that is due whenever the holder of the note demands payment.

NOTE, INSTALLMENT—A promissory note that calls for regular payments of principal and interest until the debt is fully paid.

NOTE, JOINT—A promissory note signed by two or more persons with equal liability for payment.

NOTE, PROMISSORY—A written promise to repay a debt; it may or may not be a negotiable instrument.

NOTE, STRAIGHT—A promissory note that calls for regular payments of interest only, so that the entire principal amount is due in one lump sum at the end of the loan term.

NOTICE, ACTUAL—Actual knowledge of a fact, as opposed to knowledge imputed by law (constructive notice).

NOTICE, CONSTRUCTIVE—Knowledge of a fact imputed to a person by law. A person is held to have constructive notice of something when she should have known it (because she could have learned it through reasonable diligence or an inspection of the public record), even if she did not actually know it.

NOTICE OF DEFAULT—A notice sent by a secured creditor to the debtor, informing the debtor that he has breached the loan agreement.

NOTICE OF SALE—A notice stating that foreclosure proceedings have been commenced against a property.

NOVATION—1. When one party to a contract withdraws and a new party is substituted, relieving the withdrawing party of liability. 2. The substitution of a new obligation for an old one.

OBSOLESCENCE—Any loss in value (depreciation) due to reduced desirability and usefulness.

OBSOLESCENCE, EXTERNAL—Loss in value resulting from factors outside the property itself, such as proximity to an airport. Also called economic obsolescence or external inadequacy.

OBSOLESCENCE, FUNCTIONAL—Loss in value due to inadequate or outmoded equipment, or as a result of poor or outmoded design.

OFFER—When one person (the offeror) proposes a contract to another (the offeree); if the offeree accepts the offer, a binding contract is formed.

OFFER, TENDER—*See:* Tender.

OFFEREE—One to whom a contract offer is made.

OFFEROR—One who makes a contract offer.

OFFICER—In a corporation, an executive authorized by the board of directors to manage the business of the corporation.

OFF-SITE IMPROVEMENTS—Improvements that add to the usefulness of a site but are not located directly on it, such as curbs, street lights, and sidewalks.

ONE-TIME AGENCY AGREEMENT—An agreement entered into by a FSBO seller and a buyer's agent: the seller agrees to compensate the agent for bringing him a particular buyer.

OPEN HOUSE—Showing a listed home to the public for a specified period of time.

OPTION—A contract giving one party the right to do something, without obligating her to do it.

OPTIONEE—The person to whom an option is given.

OPTIONOR—The person who gives an option.

OPTION TO PURCHASE—An option giving the optionee the right to buy property owned by the optionor at an agreed price during a specified period.

ORDINANCE—A law passed by a local legislative body, such as a city or county council. *Compare:* Statute.

ORIENTATION—The placement of a house on its lot, with regard to its exposure to the sun and wind, privacy from the street, and protection from outside noise.

ORIGINATION FEE—A fee that a lender charges a borrower upon making a new loan, to cover the administrative costs of making the loan. Also called a loan fee or points.

"OR MORE"—A provision in a promissory note that allows the borrower to prepay the debt.

OWNERSHIP—Title to property, dominion over property; the rights of possession and control.

OWNERSHIP, CONCURRENT—When two or more individuals share ownership of one piece of property, each owning an undivided interest in the property (as in a tenancy in common or joint tenancy, or with community property). Also called co-ownership or co-tenancy.

OWNERSHIP IN SEVERALTY—Ownership by a single individual.

PANIC SELLING—*See:* Blockbusting.

PARCEL—A lot or piece of real estate, especially a specified part of a larger tract.

PARTIAL RECONVEYANCE—The instrument given to the borrower when part of the security property is released from a blanket deed of trust under a partial release clause.

PARTIAL RELEASE CLAUSE—*See:* Release Clause.

PARTIAL SATISFACTION—The instrument given to the borrower when part of the security property is released from a blanket mortgage under a partial release clause.

PARTNER, GENERAL—A partner who has the authority to manage and contract for a general or limited partnership, and who is personally liable for the partnership's debts.

PARTNER, LIMITED—A partner in a limited partnership who is essentially only an investor; as long as he does not participate in the management of the business, a limited partner is not personally liable for the partnership's debts.

PARTNERSHIP—An association of two or more persons to carry on a business for profit. The law regards a partnership as a group of individuals, not as an entity separate from its owners. *Compare:* Corporation.

PARTNERSHIP, GENERAL—A partnership in which each member has an equal right to manage the business and share in the profits, as well as equal responsibility for the partnership's debts.

PARTNERSHIP, LIMITED—A partnership made up of one or more general partners and one or more limited partners.

PARTNERSHIP PROPERTY—All property that partners bring into their business at the outset or later acquire for their business.

PATENT **D**EFECT—A problem that is readily observable in an ordinary inspection of the property. *Compare:* Latent Defect.

PAYEE—In a promissory note, the party who is entitled to be paid; the lender. *Compare:* Maker.

PERCOLATION **T**EST—A test to determine the ability of the ground to absorb or drain water; used to determine whether a site is suitable for construction, particularly for installation of a septic tank system.

PERSONAL **P**ROPERTY—Any property that is not real property; movable property not affixed to land. Also called chattels or personalty.

PERSONALTY—Personal property.

PHYSICAL **D**ETERIORATION—Loss in value (depreciation) resulting from wear and tear or deferred maintenance.

PLAINTIFF—The party who brings or starts a civil lawsuit; the one who sues.

PLEDGE—When a debtor transfers possession of property to the creditor as security for repayment of the debt. *Compare:* Hypothecate.

PMI—*See:* Insurance, Private Mortgage.

POINT—One percent of the principal amount of a loan.

POINTS—*See:* Discount Points; Origination Fee.

PORTFOLIO—The mix of investments owned by an individual or company.

POSSESSION—1. The holding and enjoyment of property. 2. Actual physical occupation of real property.

POWER OF **A**TTORNEY—An instrument authorizing one person (the attorney in fact) to act as another's agent, to the extent stated in the instrument.

POWER OF **S**ALE **C**LAUSE—A clause in a deed of trust giving the trustee the right to foreclose nonjudicially (sell the debtor's property without a court action) if the borrower defaults.

PREDATORY **L**ENDING—Lending practices used by lenders and mortgage brokers to take advantage of unsophisticated borrowers.

PREPAYMENT—Paying off part or all of a loan before payment is due.

PREPAYMENT **P**ENALTY—A penalty charged to a borrower who prepays.

PREPAYMENT PRIVILEGE—A provision in a promissory note allowing the borrower to prepay.

PREVENTIVE MAINTENANCE—A program of regular inspection and care of a property and its fixtures, allowing the prevention of potential problems or their immediate repair.

PRICE FIXING—The cooperative setting of prices by competing firms. Price fixing is an automatic violation of antitrust laws.

PRIMARY MORTGAGE MARKET—The market in which mortgage loans are originated, where lenders make loans to borrowers. *Compare:* Secondary Mortgage Market.

PRIME RATE—The interest rate a bank charges its largest and most desirable customers.

PRINCIPAL—1. One who grants another person (an agent) authority to represent him in dealings with third parties. 2. One of the parties to a transaction (such as a buyer or seller), as opposed to those who are involved as agents or employees (such as a real estate or escrow agent). 3. In regard to a loan, the amount originally borrowed, as opposed to the interest.

PROCURING CAUSE—The real estate agent who is primarily responsible for bringing about a sale; for example, by negotiating the agreement between the buyer and seller.

PROFIT—A nonpossessory interest; the right to enter another person's land and take something (such as timber or minerals) away from it.

PROGRESSION, PRINCIPLE OF—An appraisal principle which holds that a property of lesser value tends to be worth more when it is located in an area with properties of greater value than it would be if located elsewhere. The opposite of the principle of regression.

PROMISEE—Someone who has been promised something; someone who is supposed to receive the benefit of a contractual promise.

PROMISOR—Someone who has made a contractual promise to another.

PROMISSORY NOTE—*See:* Note, Promissory.

PROPERTY—1. The rights of ownership in a thing, such as the right to use, possess, transfer, or encumber it. 2. Something that is owned.

PROPERTY TAX—*See:* Tax, Property.

PROPRIETORSHIP, INDIVIDUAL OR SOLE—A business owned and operated by one person.

Proration—The process of dividing or allocating something (especially a sum of money or an expense) proportionately, according to time, interest, or benefit.

Public Record—The official collection of legal documents that individuals have filed with the county recorder in order to make the information contained in them public.

Puffing—Superlative statements about the quality of a property that should not be considered assertions of fact.

Purchase and Sale Agreement—A contract in which a seller promises to convey title to real property to a buyer in exchange for the purchase price. Also called an earnest money agreement, deposit receipt, sales contract, or contract of sale.

Purchaser's Assignment of Contract and Deed—The instrument used to assign the vendee's equitable interest in a contract to another.

Qualifying Standards—The standards a lender requires a loan applicant to meet before a loan will be approved. Also called underwriting standards.

Quitclaim Deed—*See*: Deed, Quitclaim.

Ratify—To confirm or approve after the fact an act that was not authorized when it was performed.

Real Estate—*See:* Real Property.

Real Estate Brokerage—A business entity that offers real estate brokerage services; it is licensed by the Department of Licensing and must have a designated broker who represent its interests. Also known as a real estate firm.

Real Estate Commission—A commission appointed by the Governor, consisting of the Director of the Department of Licensing and six commissioners; responsible for preparing and conducting the real estate licensing examinations.

Real Estate Contract—1. A purchase and sale agreement. 2. A land contract. 3. Any contract having to do with real property.

Real Estate Firm—*See:* Real Estate Brokerage.

Real Estate Investment Syndicate—A group of people or companies who join together to purchase and develop a piece of real estate.

Real Estate Investment Trust (REIT)—A real estate investment business with at least 100 investors, organized as a trust and entitled to special tax treatment under IRS rules.

Real Estate Settlement Procedures Act—*See:* RESPA.

REAL PROPERTY—Land and everything attached to or appurtenant to it. Also called realty or real estate. *Compare:* Personal Property.

REALTOR—A real estate agent who is an active member of a state and local real estate board that is affiliated with the National Association of Realtors.®

REALTY—*See:* Real Property.

RECONCILIATION—The final step in an appraisal, when the appraiser assembles and interprets the data in order to arrive at a final value estimate. Also called correlation.

RECONVEYANCE—Releasing the security property from the lien created by a deed of trust, by recording a deed of reconveyance.

RECORDING—Filing a document at the county recorder's office, so that it will be placed in the public record.

RECORDING NUMBERS—The numbers stamped on documents when they're recorded, used to identify and locate the documents in the public record.

REDEMPTION—1. When a defaulting borrower prevents foreclosure by paying the full amount of the debt, plus costs. 2. When a mortgagor regains the property after foreclosure by paying whatever the foreclosure sale purchaser paid for it, plus interest and expenses.

REDLINING—When a lender refuses to make loans secured by property in a certain neighborhood because of the racial or ethnic composition of the neighborhood.

REDUCTION CERTIFICATE—A signed statement from a lender certifying the present balance on the loan, the rate of interest, and the maturity date. A form of estoppel certificate.

REFORMATION—A legal action to correct a mistake, such as a typographical error, in a deed or other document. The court will order the execution of a correction deed.

REFORMATION DEED—*See*: Deed, Reformation.

REGRESSION, PRINCIPLE OF—An appraisal principle which holds that a valuable property surrounded by properties of lesser value will tend to be worth less than it would be in a different location; the opposite of the principle of progression.

REGULATION Z—The Federal Reserve Board's regulation that implements the Truth in Lending Act.

REINSTATE—To prevent foreclosure by curing the default.

RELEASE—1. To give up a legal right. 2. A document in which a legal right is given up.

RELEASE CLAUSE—1. A clause in a blanket mortgage or deed of trust which allows the borrower to get part of the security property released from the lien when a certain portion of the debt has been paid or other conditions are fulfilled. Often called a partial release clause. 2. A clause in a land contract providing for a deed to a portion of the land to be delivered when a certain portion of the contract price has been paid. Also known as a deed release provision.

RENT—Compensation paid by a tenant to the landlord in exchange for the possession and use of the property.

REPLACEMENT COST—*See:* Cost, Replacement.

REPRODUCTION COST—*See:* Cost, Reproduction.

RESCISSION—When a contract is terminated and each party gives anything acquired under the contract back to the other party. (The verb form is rescind.) *Compare:* Cancellation.

RESERVE ACCOUNT—*See:* Impound Account.

RESERVE REQUIREMENTS—The percentage of deposits commercial banks must keep on reserve with the Federal Reserve Bank.

RESERVES FOR REPLACEMENT—For income-producing property, regular allowances set aside to pay for the replacement of structures and equipment that are expected to wear out.

RESPA—The Real Estate Settlement Procedures Act; a federal law that requires lenders to disclose certain information about closing costs to loan applicants.

RESPONDEAT SUPERIOR, DOCTRINE OF—A legal rule holding that an employer is liable for torts committed by an employee within the scope of her employment.

RESTITUTION—Restoring something (especially money) that a person was unjustly deprived of.

RESTRICTION—A limitation on the use of real property.

RESTRICTION, DEED—A restrictive covenant in a deed.

RESTRICTION, PRIVATE—A restriction imposed on property by a previous owner, a neighbor, or the subdivision developer; a restrictive covenant or a condition in a deed.

RESTRICTION, PUBLIC—A law or regulation limiting or regulating the use of real property.

RESTRICTIVE COVENANT—*See:* Covenant, Restrictive.

RISK ANALYSIS—*See:* Underwriting.

RURAL HOUSING SERVICE LOAN—A loan made by the Rural Housing Service, a federal agency, to purchase, build, or rehabilitate homes in rural areas.

SAFETY CLAUSE—*See:* Extender Clause.

SALE-LEASEBACK—A form of real estate financing in which the owner of industrial or commercial property sells the property and leases it back from the buyer. In addition to certain tax advantages, the seller/lessee obtains more cash through the sale than would normally be possible by borrowing and mortgaging the property, since lenders will not often lend 100% of the value.

SALES COMPARISON APPROACH—One of the three main methods of appraisal, in which the sales prices of comparable properties are used to estimate the value of the subject property. Also called the market data approach.

SATISFACTION OF MORTGAGE—*See:* Mortgage, Satisfaction of.

SECONDARY FINANCING—Money borrowed to pay part of the required downpayment or closing costs for a first loan, when the second loan is secured by the same property that secures the first loan.

SECONDARY MORTGAGE MARKET—The market in which investors (including Fannie Mae, Freddie Mac, and Ginnie Mae) purchase real estate loans from lenders; also called the national market.

SECRET PROFIT—A financial benefit that an agent takes from a transaction without informing the principal.

SECURITY AGREEMENT—Under the Uniform Commercial Code, a document that creates a lien on personal property being used to secure a loan.

SECURITY INSTRUMENT—A document that creates a voluntary lien, to secure repayment of a loan; for debts secured by real property, it is either a mortgage or a deed of trust.

SECURITY INTEREST—The interest a creditor may acquire in the debtor's property to ensure that the debt will be paid.

SECURITY PROPERTY—The property that a borrower gives a lender a voluntary lien against, so that the lender can foreclose if the borrower defaults.

SELLING AGENT—The agent responsible for procuring a buyer for real estate; may represent either the seller or the buyer.

SEPARATE PROPERTY—Property owned by a married person that is not community property; includes property acquired before marriage or by gift or inheritance after marriage.

SERVANT—*See:* Master/Servant Relationship.

SETTLEMENT—1. An agreement between the parties to a civil lawsuit, in which the plaintiff agrees to drop the suit in exchange for money or the defendant's promise to do or refrain from doing something. 2. Closing.

SETTLEMENT STATEMENT—A document that presents a final, detailed accounting for a real estate transaction, listing each party's debits and credits and the amount each will receive or be required to pay at closing. Also called a closing statement.

SEVERALTY—*See:* Ownership in Severalty.

SHAREHOLDER—An individual who holds ownership shares (shares of stock) in a corporation, and has limited liability in regard to the corporation's debts. Also called a stockholder.

SHERIFF'S DEED—*See:* Deed, Sheriff's.

SHERIFF'S SALE—A foreclosure sale held after a judicial foreclosure. Sometimes called an execution sale.

SHORT SALE—Selling a home for less than the amount owed, with the lender's consent. The lender receives the sale proceeds and, typically, releases the borrower from the remaining debt.

SPECIAL ASSESSMENT—A tax levied only against the properties that have benefited from a public improvement (such as a sewer or a street light), to cover the cost of the improvement; creates a special assessment lien. Also called an improvement tax.

SPECIAL WARRANTY DEED—*See:* Deed, Special Warranty.

SPECIFIC PERFORMANCE—A legal remedy in which a court orders someone who has breached to actually perform the contract as agreed, rather than simply paying money damages.

STABLE MONTHLY INCOME—A loan applicant's gross monthly income that meets the lender's tests of quality and durability.

STATUTE—A law enacted by a state legislature or the U.S. Congress. *Compare:* Ordinance.

STATUTE OF FRAUDS—A law that requires certain types of contracts to be in writing and signed in order to be enforceable.

STATUTE OF LIMITATIONS—A law requiring a particular type of lawsuit to be filed within a specified time after the event giving rise to the suit occurred.

STATUTORY WARRANTY DEED—*See*: Deed, Statutory Warranty.

STEERING—Channeling prospective buyers or tenants to or away from particular neighborhoods based on their race, religion, national origin, or ancestry.

STOCKHOLDER—*See:* Shareholder.

SUBAGENT—A person that an agent has delegated authority to, so that the subagent can assist in carrying out the principal's orders; the agent of an agent.

SUBCONTRACTOR—A contractor who, at the request of the general contractor, provides a specific service, such as plumbing or drywalling, in connection with the overall construction project.

SUBJECT TO—When a purchaser takes property subject to a trust deed or mortgage, he is not personally liable for paying off the loan; in case of default, however, the property can still be foreclosed on.

SUBLEASE—When a tenant grants someone else the right to possession of the leased property for part of the remainder of the lease term; as opposed to a lease assignment, where the tenant gives up possession for the entire reminder of the lease term. Also called a sandwich lease. *Compare:* Assignment.

SUBORDINATION CLAUSE—A provision in a mortgage or deed of trust that permits a later mortgage or deed of trust to have higher lien priority than the one containing the clause.

SUBPRIME LENDING—Making riskier loans to borrowers who are otherwise unable to qualify for a loan, often charging higher interest rates and fees to make up for the increased risk.

SUBROGATION—The substitution of one person in the place of another with reference to a lawful claim or right. For instance, a title company that pays a claim on behalf of its insured, the property owner, is subrogated to any claim the owner successfully undertakes against the former owner.

SUBSTITUTION, PRINCIPLE OF—A principle of appraisal holding that the maximum value of a property is limited by the cost of obtaining another equally desirable property, assuming that there would not be a long delay or significant incidental expenses involved in obtaining the substitute property.

Substitution of Liability—A buyer wishing to assume an existing loan may apply for the lender's approval; once approved, the buyer assumes liability for repayment of the loan, and the original borrower (the seller) is released from liability.

Survey—The process of precisely measuring the boundaries and determining the area of a parcel of land.

Syndicate—An association formed to operate an investment business. A syndicate is not a recognized legal entity; it can be organized as a corporation, partnership, or trust.

Tax, Ad Valorem—A tax assessed on the value of property.

Tax, Excise—A state tax levied on every sale of real estate, to be paid by the seller.

Tax, General Real Estate—An annual ad valorem tax levied on real property.

Tax, Improvement—*See:* Special Assessment.

Tax, Property—1. The general real estate tax. 2. Any ad valorem tax levied on real or personal property.

Tax Deed—*See:* Deed, Tax.

Tax Sale—Sale of property after foreclosure of a tax lien.

Tenancy in Common—A form of concurrent ownership in which two or more persons each have an undivided interest in the entire property, but no right of survivorship. *Compare:* Joint Tenancy.

Tenant—Someone in lawful possession of real property; especially, someone who has leased the property from the owner (also called a lessee).

Tender—An unconditional offer by one of the parties to a contract to perform her part of the agreement; made when the offeror believes the other party is breaching, it establishes the offeror's right to sue if the other party doesn't accept it. Also called a tender offer.

Term—A prescribed period of time; especially, the length of time a borrower has to pay off a loan, or the duration of a lease.

Third Party—1. A person seeking to deal with a principal through an agent. 2. In a transaction, someone who is not one of the principals.

Tie-in Arrangement—An agreement to sell one product, only on the condition that the buyer also purchases a different product. This is an antitrust violation.

TIGHT MONEY MARKET—When loan funds are scarce, leading lenders to charge high interest rates and discount points.

TILA—Truth in Lending Act.

TIME IS OF THE ESSENCE—A clause in a contract that means performance on the exact dates specified is an essential element of the contract; failure to perform on time is a material breach.

TITLE—Lawful ownership of real property. Also, the deed or other document that is evidence of that ownership.

TITLE, ABSTRACT OF—A brief, chronological summary of the recorded documents affecting title to a particular piece of real property.

TITLE, AFTER-ACQUIRED—Title acquired by a grantor after she attempted to convey property she didn't own.

TITLE, CHAIN OF—1. The chain of deeds (and other documents) transferring title to a piece of property from one owner to the next, as disclosed in the public record. 2. A listing of all recorded documents affecting title to a particular property; more complete than an abstract.

TITLE, CLEAR—A good title to property, free from encumbrances or defects; marketable title.

TITLE, COLOR OF—Title that appears to be good title, but which in fact is not; commonly based on a defective instrument, such as an invalid deed.

TITLE, EQUITABLE—The vendee's interest in property under a land contract. Also called an equitable interest.

TITLE, LEGAL—The vendor's interest in property under a land contract.

TITLE, MARKETABLE—Title free and clear of objectionable liens, encumbrances, or defects, so that a reasonably prudent person with full knowledge of the facts would not hesitate to purchase the property.

TITLE COMPANY—A title insurance company.

TITLE INSURANCE—*See:* Insurance, Title.

TITLE REPORT, PRELIMINARY—A report issued by a title company, disclosing the condition of the title to a specific piece of property, before the actual title insurance policy is issued.

Title Search—An inspection of the public record to determine all rights and encumbrances affecting title to a piece of property.

Title Theory—The theory holding that a mortgage or deed of trust gives the lender legal title to the security property while the debt is being repaid. *Compare:* Lien Theory.

Topography—The contours of the surface of the land (level, hilly, steep, etc.).

Tort—A breach of a duty imposed by law (as opposed to a duty voluntarily taken on in a contract) that causes harm to another person, giving the injured person the right to sue the one who breached the duty. Also called a civil wrong (in contrast to a criminal wrong, a crime).

Total Finance Charge—Under the Truth in Lending Act, the total finance charge on a loan includes interest, any discount points paid by the borrower, the loan origination fee, and mortgage insurance costs.

Tract—1. A piece of land of undefined size. 2. In the rectangular survey system, an area made up of 16 townships; 24 miles on each side.

Trust—A legal arrangement in which title to property (or funds) is vested in one or more trustees, who manage the property on behalf of the trust's beneficiaries, in accordance with instructions set forth in the document establishing the trust.

Trust Account—A bank account maintained by a brokerage for depositing client funds. Most trust accounts must be interest-bearing, with the exception of trust accounts for property management funds.

Trust Deed—*See:* Deed of Trust.

Trust Funds—Money or things of value received by an agent, not belonging to the agent but being held for the benefit of others.

Trustee—1. A person appointed to manage a trust on behalf of the beneficiaries. 2. A neutral third party appointed in a deed of trust to handle the nonjudicial foreclosure process in case of default.

Trustee in Bankruptcy—An individual appointed by the court to handle the assets of a person in bankruptcy.

Trustee's Deed—*See:* Deed, Trustee's.

Trustee's Sale—A nonjudicial foreclosure sale under a deed of trust.

Trustor—The borrower in a deed of trust. Also called the grantor.

TRUTH IN LENDING ACT—A federal law that requires lenders and credit arrangers to make disclosures concerning loan costs (including the total finance charge and the annual percentage rate) to consumer loan applicants.

UNDERWRITING—In real estate lending, the process of evaluating a loan application to determine the probability that the applicant would repay the loan, and matching the risk to an appropriate rate of return. Sometimes called risk analysis.

UNDUE INFLUENCE—Exerting excessive pressure on someone so as to overpower the person's free will and prevent him from making a rational or prudent decision; often involves abusing a relationship of trust.

UNENFORCEABLE—*See:* Contract, Unenforceable.

UNIFORM COMMERCIAL CODE—A body of law adopted in slightly varying versions in most states (including Washington), which attempts to standardize commercial law dealing with such matters as negotiable instruments and sales of personal property. Its main applications to real estate law concern security interests in fixtures and bulk transfers.

UNIFORM SETTLEMENT STATEMENT—A settlement statement required for any transaction involving a loan that is subject to the Real Estate Settlement Procedures Act (RESPA).

UNIFORM STANDARDS OF PROFESSIONAL APPRAISAL PRACTICE—Guidelines for appraisers adopted by the Appraisal Foundation, a nonprofit organization of professional appraiser associations.

UNILATERAL CONTRACT—*See:* Contract, Unilateral.

UNJUST ENRICHMENT—An undeserved benefit; a court generally will not allow a remedy (such as forfeiture of a land contract) if it would result in the unjust enrichment of one of the parties.

USURY—Charging an interest rate that exceeds legal limits.

VA—Department of Veterans Affairs (formerly the Veterans Administration).

VACANCY FACTOR—*See:* Bad Debt/Vacancy Factor.

VALID—The legal classification of a contract that is binding and enforceable in a court of law.

VALUABLE CONSIDERATION—*See:* Consideration.

VALUATION—*See:* Appraisal.

V<small>ALUE</small>—The present worth of future benefits.

V<small>ALUE</small>, **A**<small>SSESSED</small>—The value placed on property by the taxing authority (the county assessor, for example) for the purposes of taxation.

V<small>ALUE</small>, **F**<small>ACE</small>—The value of an instrument, such as a promissory note or a security, that is indicated on the face of the instrument itself.

V<small>ALUE</small>, **M**<small>ARKET</small>—The most probable price which a property should bring in a competitive and open market under all conditions requisite to a fair sale, the buyer and seller each acting prudently and knowledgeably, and assuming the price is not affected by undue stimulus. (This is the definition from the Uniform Standards of Professional Appraisal Practice.) Market value is also called fair market value, value in exchange, or objective value. *Compare:* Market Price.

V<small>ALUE</small>, **S**<small>UBJECTIVE</small>—The value of a property in the eyes of a particular person, as opposed to its market value (objective value).

V<small>ALUE</small>, **U**<small>TILITY</small>—The value of a property to its owner or to a user. (A form of subjective value.) Also called value in use.

V<small>ALUE IN</small> **E**<small>XCHANGE</small>—*See:* Value, Market.

V<small>ALUE IN</small> **U**<small>SE</small>—*See:* Value, Utility.

V<small>ARIABLE</small> **I**<small>NTEREST</small> **R**<small>ATE</small>—A loan interest rate that can be adjusted periodically during the loan term, as in the case of an adjustable-rate mortgage.

V<small>ENDEE</small>—A buyer or purchaser; particularly, someone buying property under a land contract.

V<small>ENDOR</small>—A seller; particularly, someone selling property by means of a land contract.

V<small>ERIFY</small>—1. To confirm or substantiate. 2. To confirm under oath.

V<small>OID</small>—Having no legal force or effect.

V<small>OIDABLE</small>—*See:* Contract, Voidable.

W<small>AIVER</small>—The voluntary relinquishment or surrender of a right.

W<small>ARRANTY</small>, **I**<small>MPLIED</small>—In a sale or lease of property, a guarantee created by operation of law, whether or not the seller or landlord intended to offer it.

W<small>ARRANTY</small> **D**<small>EED</small>—*See:* Deed, Warranty.

WASHINGTON LAW AGAINST DISCRIMINATION—A state law that is stricter than the Fair Housing Act in its prohibition against discrimination in housing and other transactions on the basis of race, creed, color, national origin, sex, marital status, familial status, disability, military status, or use of a service animal.

WASTE—Destruction, damage, or material alteration of property by someone in possession who holds less than a fee estate (such as a life tenant or lessee), or by a co-owner.

WATER TABLE—The level at which water may be found, either at the surface or underground.

WILD DEED—*See*: Deed, Wild.

WRAPAROUND FINANCING—*See:* Mortgage, Wraparound.

YIELD—The return of profit to an investor on an investment, stated as a percentage of the amount invested.

ZONE—An area of land set off for a particular use, such as agricultural, residential, industrial, or commercial.

ZONING—Government regulation of the uses of property within specified areas.

INDEX

A

Acceptance. *See* Offer and acceptance
Accounting. *See* Trust accounts and trust
    funds
ADA 87–89
Adjustable-rate mortgages 326–330
  affordable alternatives to 341, 344
  and income ratios 340
  and LTV rules 332
  low starting interest rate 310, 326
  two-tiered rate schedule 328, 343
Adverse possession 385
Advertising 77, 83–84, 93–94
  on the Internet 157
  newspaper 157
  open houses 160
Agency. *See* Real Estate Brokerage Relation-
    ships Act
  agency authority 45
  agency disclosures 10, 16, 22, 31–32, 154,
    168, 182, 238
  agency law pamphlet 10
  agent and principal 5
  creation of agency 13–14, 20, 23, 25
  disclosure form 17
  duties to all parties 6, 31–32
  duties to principal 6, 11
  inadvertent agency 14, 17–18
  in-house transactions 26, 30–31, 45, 54
  non-agency 14, 23, 31
  notifying principal through agent 195
  subagency 20, 32
  termination of agency 14, 46–47
  types of agency relationships 19–32
Alienation (due-on-sale) clauses 336, 353,
    366

Alimony (spousal maintenance) 294, 297,
    338, 351
American Society of Home Inspectors 381
Americans with Disabilities Act 87–89
Amortization 322, 329–330, 345
  negative 307, 329–330
Annual percentage rate 159, 308–309, 312
Antidiscrimination laws. *See* Civil rights
Antitrust laws 46, 89, 93
Appraisal
  and closing 377–378, 383–384
  and underwriting 291, 377, 383
  appraiser as agent of lender 137, 378
  appraiser's fee 392
  distinguished from CMA 111, 383
  for FHA or VA loan 260
  low appraisal 135–138, 263, 355, 387
  methods of appraisal 113, 137, 383
  request for reconsideration of value
    136–138, 387
  value (concept of) 111
APR 159, 308–309, 312
Area of lot 116–118
Area problems 412–422
ARMs. *See* Adjustable-rate mortgages
Asbestos 97, 380
"As is" sales 269
Assets 301, 306–307
Assumption of mortgage or other lien 356
  and purchase and sale agreement 217, 226,
    230
  and RESPA 401
  assumption fee 392
  conventional loans 336
  FHA loans 353
  on settlement statement 391, 396–397
  VA loans 356

Attachments. *See* Fixtures
Attorney at law. *See* Lawyers
Attorney in fact 225
Automated underwriting 336, 340

B

Backup offers 185–190, 279
Balloon payments 307–308, 312, 323–324, 335, 351
Balloon/reset mortgages 344–345
Bank accounts 301
Bankruptcy 304
Bathrooms 119, 122
Bedrooms 119–120, 122
Blind ad 158
Blockbusting 78, 81, 83
Bonuses as income 293, 299
Branch office 3
Bridge loan (swing loan) 273, 302
Broker 2
Brokerage firm 3
   affiliation required 3
   choosing a 3–5
Building analysis 118
Building codes 269
Building moratoriums 244
Bump clauses 274–279
Buydowns 341, 350, 352, 367, 392
Buyer agency 23
   buyer's duty to inspect property 26
   compensation 25–30
   creation of buyer agency 14, 25
   history of buyer agency 20
   no duty to look for additional properties 12
   ordering inspections 377
   presenting offers 182, 184, 192
   representation agreement 25, 75
Buyer's net cost
   decreased by credits 390
   estimating net cost 391–395
   worksheet for buyer 180, 192, 389

C

Cancellation of PMI 333–334
Caps (ARM) 328–329
Carryback loan 361
Carryover clause. *See* Extender clause
Cash equivalent financing 124
Cash flow analysis 358
Casualty loss 365. *See also* Hazard insurance
CC&Rs 57, 230
CERCLA 96
Certificate of Eligibility (VA) 354
Chain of title 385
Child support 294, 297, 338, 351
Civil rights 77
   actions that do not violate fair housing laws 86–87
   affirmative marketing plan 87
   Americans with Disabilities Act 87–89
   blockbusting 78, 81, 83
   complying with fair housing laws 82, 183, 206–208
   discriminatory advertising 84
   discriminatory intent not required 82, 206
   discriminatory listing practices 83
   discriminatory sales practices 206–208
   enforcement of laws 79
   exemptions from laws 79, 81
   Fair Housing Act 77
   HIV/AIDS 79
   lending discrimination 77–78, 80
   real estate license law provisions 82
   redlining 78
   steering 78, 87, 207
   Washington Law Against Discrimination 79
Cleaning services 387
Clean Water Act 96
Closing 374–388. *See also* Closing costs; Escrow agents; Settlement statements
   brokerage providing closing services 376–377
   closing date 183, 190, 217, 232

disbursements and funding 376, 378–379, 383–384

documents 376, 378

escrow 376–377, 386

last-minute problems 388

lender's role in closing 383

real estate agent's role 374–375, 377, 383–384, 386–388

RESPA 401–418

streamlined by preapproval 289, 383–382

who may provide closing services 376–377

Closing agents. *See* Escrow agents

Closing costs 388–399. *See also* Prorations

allocation of 389, 391

and listing agreement 49

buyer's costs 180, 391–395

credits and debits 389–391

FHA loans 260

in purchase agreement 233, 391

loan costs 391–394

seller contribution limits 343, 350, 367

seller's costs 396

source of funds 325, 343, 345–346, 350–352, 356

VA loans 260

Closing statements. *See* Settlement statements

CMA. *See* Competitive market analysis

Cold calls 147

Collection of debts 304

Commercial facilities 88

Commingling 10

Commission 4. *See also* Compensation of real estate agents

Commission income (loan applicant's) 293, 297

Common areas or elements 63

Community property 223–224

Co-mortgagor 295

Comparable properties

choosing comparables for CMA 122, 130

expired listings 133

in request for reconsideration of value 137

making adjustments 125, 131–132

primary elements of comparison 123–125

reliability of comparables 132

Compensating factors (in underwriting) 339–340, 352, 358–359

Compensation of real estate agents 4

buyer's agents 25–30

commission splits 27, 50, 74–75, 90, 237

depending on type of listing 39–40

dual agents 12, 31

earnest money as compensation 50, 196, 237

extender clause 47–48

fixed in listing agreement 41, 46–47

license law rules 74

on settlement statement 397–398

price fixing 46, 90, 93

provided for in purchase agreement 243

ready, willing, and able buyer 41, 47

seller's agents 20, 26

who pays does not affect agency 27, 50

without closing 41, 196

written agreement required 42, 75

Competence (mental) 46, 223, 225

Competitive market analysis 111, 113–114, 152

analyzing seller's property 114, 130

choosing comparables 122, 130

CMA form 133–135

distinguished from appraisal 111, 383

estimating market value 128, 132–133

expired listings 133

making adjustments 125, 131–132

presenting to seller 152–154

value (concept of) 111

Computers and underwriting 291

Conditions. *See* Contingencies

Condominiums 401

Confidential information 11, 21, 23. *See also* Disclosures
    after agency ends 23
    in dual agency 30
Conflicts of interest 11, 93
Conforming loan limits 331
Conforming loans 291, 331
Consideration for contract 216
Conspiracy (antitrust) 89
Construction. *See also* Development; *See also* Vacant land
    and ADA 89
    and Consumer Protection Act 94
    and RESPA 401
    and seller disclosure statement 63
    construction costs and feasibility 244
    construction loan 401
    unrecorded liens 385
Constructive fraud 7
Consumer Protection Act 93, 312
Contingencies 181, 183, 217
    and closing 231–232, 274, 378, 386, 388
    and earnest money 204–205, 256, 259, 263, 273, 279
    backup offers 185–190
    basic elements of 258–259, 272–273
    benefiting one party 256–257
    bump clauses 274–279
    contingent counteroffers 185
    financing contingencies 135, 226, 259, 384
    general or specific terms 259–260
    good faith effort required 258
    hazard insurance contingencies 384
    hidden contingencies 269–272
    how contingencies work 256
    inspection contingencies 264–279, 377, 379, 382, 387–386
    mold contingencies 101
    notification 259–260, 274–279
    rescission agreement 198, 279–280
    sale of buyer's home 269–279
    waiver 256–257, 259–260, 268, 279

Contracts. *See also* Offer and acceptance
    adding special clauses 180, 196, 238
    amending or modifying 55, 196
    basic requirements for validity 216, 223
    breach (default) 46, 187–188, 201, 205, 236–237
    contractual capacity 223
    land contracts 226, 264, 361
    rescission 64–65, 196, 279
    statute of frauds (writing requirement) 42, 195, 243
    time is of the essence clause 237
    tortious interference with 187
    who may prepare 179–180, 238
Contributory risk factors 336
Conventional loans 291, 330
    affordable loan programs 341–346
    assumption 336
    conforming loan limits 331
    jumbo loans 331
    loan-to-value ratios 332
    mortgage insurance 332, 354
    secondary financing 335
    underwriting standards 336
Conversion option 330
Conveyance. *See* Deeds
Cooperating agents 27, 45, 49–50
Cooperatives 401
Co-owners signing contract 51–55, 223–224
Copy of document provided 55, 180, 192, 196
Corporations 224
Cost vs. price or value 112–113
Counteroffers 190
    contingent 185
    counteroffer terminates offer 192, 241
    deadline for acceptance 241
    modified acceptance is counteroffer 196
    revocation of counteroffer 194
Credit inquiries 305
Credit reports and credit scores 303, 336, 351, 392
    and risk-based loan fees 334

Credits on settlement statement 389
Criminal activity on property 8–9

D

Death of agent or principal 46, 75
Death on property 8
Debits on settlement statement 389–390
Debt consolidation 304
Debts (liabilities) 299–300, 302–303,
       338, 351
Debt to income ratio 298
    affordable housing programs 346
    as contributory risk factor 336
    conventional loans 338, 346
    FHA loans 351
    VA loans 357, 359
Decimal numbers 410–422
Deed of reconveyance 399
Deeds 217, 230–231, 378, 385
Deeds of trust 226, 264, 360, 378, 399
Delivery fee. *See* Risk-based pricing
       (loan fees)
Demand for Payoff 378
Deposit. *See* Earnest money
Depth of lot 116
Description. *See* Property description
Design and layout of house 120–122
Designated broker 3
    liability for affiliated licensee's
       actions 32
    temporary permit 75
Development. *See also* Construction
    and environmental issues 95–97
    development costs 244
    subdivision regulations 243
    vacant land 66, 77, 243, 401
Disabilities
    Americans with Disabilities Act 87–89
    antidiscrimination laws 77, 79, 86
Disciplinary action
    for agency disclosure violation 17, 31
    for failing to disclose form of deposit
       199
    for violation of antidiscrimination laws
       82

Disclosures. *See* Confidential information
    agency 10, 16, 22, 31–32, 154, 168,
       182, 238
    amount and form of deposit 199
    closing costs 401
    conflicts of interest 11, 93
    distressed property/short sales 48
    environmental problems 63, 99, 101,
       106
    home inspector referral 381
    information that need not be disclosed
       8–9
    latent defects 8, 12, 65, 101, 388
    lead-based paint 63, 99, 238–241
    licensed status 19
    material facts 8, 65, 93, 231
    seller disclosure statement 55, 388
    sex offenders 9
    third party's information disclosed to
       principal 21
    Truth in Lending Act 158–159,
       308–309, 403
Discount points 309–310, 325–326
    and FHA loans 348–350, 352
    and VA loans 354, 356
    on settlement statement 392, 398
Discrimination. *See* Civil rights
Distressed property law 48–55, 76–77,
       225
    20-day occupancy rule 77
    distressed home consultant 76
    distressed home consultant agreement
       76
    distressed home conveyance 76–78
    distressed home definition 76
    effect on real estate agents 76–77
Dividends 295
Dodd-Frank Act 336
Do-Not-Call Registry 148
Downpayment
    and buyer's price range 288
    and earnest money 198
    and gift funds 340
    and LTV 135, 324
    as buyer's investment 303, 324, 332,
       336

(Downpayment, continued)
FHA loans 347, 350, 352
for seller financing 362–364
funds for closing 300, 303, 310, 325,
　345–346, 362, 378
in financing contingency 226, 260
low-downpayment loan programs
　345–347
personal property used for 367
source of 269, 295, 325, 340, 345–346,
　355, 364
VA loans 353, 355–356
Drug lab on property 9, 100
Dual agency 11, 30
compensation 12, 31
confidential information 30
dual agency agreement 14, 23
inadvertent 14, 17–18
in-house transactions 26, 30, 45
loyalty 11, 30
Due-on-sale (alienation) clauses 336,
　353, 366
Durability of income 292, 296

E

Earnest money 198. *See also* Contingen-
　cies
5% limit 205, 236–237
after rescission 64, 196
applied to downpayment 198, 391
as liquidated damages 50, 205, 236
authority to accept 45
bounced or stopped check 204
brokerage responsibilities 203, 205
forfeiture of 198, 204–206, 237, 258,
　273
form of deposit 199, 226
handling the deposit 201
held by someone other than brokerage
　203
holding check without depositing 203
in cash 200, 226
in trust account or pooled account 203
not required by law 198
on settlement statement 391
personal check for 200–204, 226–230

personal property as 201
promissory note for 201
purpose of 178, 198–199
receipt for deposit 226–230
refunded 64, 203–206, 237, 256, 263,
　273
shared by agents 196
shared by seller and agent(s) 50
shared by seller and brokerage(s) 206,
　237
size of deposit 190, 198
Earthquakes 102, 384
Easements 57, 230
Ecology, Dept. of 97
Effective income (FHA) 351
Electrical system in house 63, 380
Employment income 293–294, 297
Encroachments 57, 385
Encumbrances
and seller financing 365–366
listed in purchase agreement 217, 230
undisclosed 230
Endangered Species Act 97
Energy efficiency 120, 347, 380
Environmental issues 94–102, 244
agent's responsibilities 102
CERCLA 96
contingency clauses 264
environmental hazards 97, 238, 380
environmental impact statements 95
environmental inspection 380
environmental laws 95
EPA 97
liability for cleanup 96, 102
on seller disclosure statement 63
wetlands 96
Equal Credit Opportunity Act 295
Equal Housing Opportunity logo 86
Equifax 306
Equity 301–302, 323, 363
Equity exchanges 367
Escrow account for underlying loan 366
Escrow agents (closing agents) 232,
　376–377
and IRS requirements 399–401
designated in purchase agreement 232

escrow fee 233, 376, 394, 399
   independent escrow companies 377
   kickbacks (referral fees) 402–403
   lender providing escrow services 232,
      376–377
   licensing and exemptions 376–377
   unearned fees 402
Escrow instructions 376–378, 386
Estoppel 13
Eviction 236
Excise tax 399
Exclusive listings 39–40, 46
Executor of estate 224, 376
Experian 306
Expert advice 12
Extended coverage title policy 385
Extender clause 47–48, 198
Extension agreement 232

F

Facilitator 31. *See also* Non-agency
Fair Credit Reporting Act 305
Fair Housing Act 77, 79, 87. *See*
      also Civil rights
Familial status 77, 79
Family earnings 296
Fannie Mae. *See* Secondary market agen-
      cies
Farming 146–147
Federal Fair Housing Act. *See* Civil
      rights; *See also* Fair Housing Act
Federal Housing Administration.
      See FHA loans
Federal Housing Finance Agency 331
Federally related loan transactions 401
FHA loans 330, 347
   203(b) program 347
   appraisal provisions 260, 263
   assumption 353, 401
   characteristics of FHA loans 347
   closing costs 260, 349–350
   contingency provisions 260
   final month's interest not prorated 397
   funds for closing 352
   income ratios 351–352

loan fees 348–349, 352
   maximum loan amount 347–349
   minimum cash investment 349, 352
   mortgage insurance (MIP) 347, 349
   owner-occupancy requirement 348, 353
   secondary financing 350–352
   underwriting standards 291, 348,
      351–353
FICO bureau scores 304
Fiduciary 6
Fifteen-year loans 310, 320–322, 348
Financing
   and closing 377–378, 380, 382–383,
      387, 391
   and sale of buyer's home 269–273
   basic loan features 320
   choosing a loan 308–312, 387
   cost of financing 308–309, 362
   federally related loans 401
   financing addendum 260
   financing contingencies 135, 226, 259,
      384
   financing documents 378, 383
   fixed or adjustable rate 310, 326–330,
      332, 341, 343–344
   preapproval 288, 377, 383
   terms in purchase and sale agreement
      190
FIRPTA 232, 400–401
Fish and Wildlife Service 97
Fixed payment to income ratio (FHA)
      351–352
Fixtures 190, 230, 387
Flooding 101, 384
Floor duty 164
Floor plan. *See* Design and layout of house
Foreclosure 333, 383
   foreclosure crisis 312, 332
   on credit report 304
   seller financing 365, 366
Foreign Investment in Real Property Tax
      Act 232, 400–401
Forged document 385
Form 1099 reporting 399–400
Form 8300 reporting 400

Formaldehyde gas 98
Forms
  Agency Disclosure 17, **18**
  Amendment to Exclusive Sale and Listing Agreement 55, **56**
  Backup Addendum 185, **186**
  Buyer Representation Agreement 26, **28**
  Counteroffer Addendum 190, **191**
  Earnest Money Promissory Note 201, **202**
  Exclusive Sale and Listing Agreement **43**, 45
  Financing Addendum 260, **261**
  Inspection Contingency addenda **265**, 267, 268–269
  Lead-based Paint Disclosure 241, **242**
  Listing Input Sheet 51, **52**
  Notice from Contingent Buyer (bump reply) **277**, 279
  Notice to Backup Buyer 188, **189**
  Notice to Remove Contingency (bump notice) **276**, 279
  Optional Clauses Addendum 196, 238, **239**
  Payment Terms Addendum 226, **227**, 264
  preparation of forms 180, 217–223, 367
  Rental Agreement 233, **234**
  Rescission of Purchase and Sale Agreement 196, **197**
  Residential Purchase and Sale Agreement 217, **218**
  Sale of Buyer's Property Contingency **270**, 273
  Second Buyer's Addendum 274, **275**
  Seller Disclosure Statement 57, **58**
  sources of legal forms 217
  Uniform Settlement Statement **404**, 407
  use only as intended 223, 243
  Vacant Land Listing Input Sheet 66, **67**
  Vacant Land Purchase and Sale Agreement 243, **245**
  Withdrawal of Offer or Counteroffer **193**, 194

For sale by owner properties 25, 30, 148–150
Forty-year loans 310, 320
Fractions 410–411
Fraud 7, 312
Freddie Mac. *See* Secondary market agencies
Frontage 116
FSBOs 25, 30, 148–150
Fully amortized loan 322–323
Funding fee (VA loans) 354

G

Gap loan (swing loan) 273, 302
Geologic hazards 101–102, 264, 384
Gift funds 301, 303, 340, 346, 352
Good faith and continuous effort 12
Good faith deposit. *See* Earnest money
Good faith effort to fulfill contingency 226, 258
Good faith estimate of closing costs 378, 403–418
  tolerances 403
Good faith estimate of finance charges 309
Government-sponsored loans 330, 346. *See also* FHA loans; VA loans
Graduated payment buydown 342
Group boycotts 91, 93
Growth mitigation 244
Guardian signing contracts 223
Guest logs 160
Guide or service dog 79

H

Habitability, implied warranty of 94
Habitat Conservation Plan 97
Handicap. *See* Disabilities
Hazard insurance 383, 387, 394
  and financing contingency 383–384
  and liability coverage 384
  HO-3 policy 384–386
  impound accounts 349, 365–366, 402

*Boldface page numbers indicate the page(s) on which the form itself appears, as opposed to pages on which the form is discussed.

policy issued 379
proration of 217
Hazardous waste 96, 99, 264
HIV/AIDS 79
Hold harmless clause 50, 64
Home inspectors 380–381
Homeowners association 63, 233
Home Ownership and Equity Protection Act 336
Homeowner's insurance. *See* Hazard insurance
Homeowners Protection Act 334
Housing and Urban Development, Dept. of 79, 347
Housing expense to income ratio 298–299
    affordable housing programs 346
    conventional loans 338–339, 346
    FHA loans 351–352
HUD 79, 347
Human Rights Commission 79, 81

I

Implied warranty of habitability 94
Impound (reserve) accounts 349, 365–366, 391, 402–403
Imputed interest rule 363
Inadvertent agency 14, 17–18
Included items 183, 230, 387
Income analysis 292
    acceptable types of income 293
    and buydowns 342, 352
    calculating monthly income 297
    conventional loans 336–337
    FHA loans 348, 351–352
    income verification 296, 306–307
    low-downpayment programs 346
    marginal income 300, 339–340
    stable monthly income 292–296, 351
    unacceptable types of income 293, 296
    VA loans 357–360
Income approach to value 113
Income ratios 298–299, 310
    affordable housing programs 346
    as contributory risk factor 336

conventional loans 338, 342
    FHA loans 351–352
    VA loans 357, 359
Income taxation
    1099 reporting 399–400
    foreign sellers (FIRPTA) 232, 400
    Form 8300 400
    imputed interest rule 363
    installment sales 362–363
    IRS form W-9 203
Incompetence (mental) 46, 223, 225
Independent contractor vs. employee status 4
Index for ARM 327
In-house transactions 26, 30–31, 45
Input sheets 51, 66
Inspections 379
    approval or disapproval of report 264, 268, 380, 382
    "as is" sales 269
    buyer's duty to inspect property 26, 64, 269
    choosing an inspector 381
    for title company 385
    inspection contingencies 264, 377, 379, 382, 386–387
    inspection reports 378, 381–382, 386–387
    lender-required 263, 379–380, 382
    mold 101
    no duty to inspect or investigate 9
    notification 264, 268, 380, 386–387
    ordering 264, 377, 380, 383, 386
    reinspection 264, 380, 382, 387
    repairs 264–268, 378, 380–382, 386–387
    types of inspections 380
    waiver 268
    who pays for 263–264, 382
Installment debts 338, 351
Installment sale tax benefit 362–363
Institutional lenders and loans 364, 383
Insulation (UFFI) 98
Insurance. *See* Hazard insurance; Mortgage insurance; Title insurance

Interest and interest rates 417–418
  15-year loans 322
  and credit scores 305
  and discount points 325–326
  buydowns 341–343, 350, 352
  FHA loans 348
  fixed or adjustable rate 310, 326–330,
    332, 341, 343–344
  high-LTV loans 332
  imputed interest rule 363
  interest-only loans 324, 345
  interest on seller's loan 397
  interim or prepaid interest 349
  market rates 326–327, 341–342, 361
  negative amortization 329–330
  paid in arrears 392, 397
  prepaid (interim) interest 349,
    392–394
  proration of interest 392–394, 397
  rate lock-ins 309
  total interest over loan term 321
  VA loans 354
Interim or prepaid interest 349, 392–394
Intermediary 31. *See also* Non-agency
Internet advertising 157
Investment income 295
Investor loans 340, 348

J

Joinder (community property) 223
Joint tenancy 224
Judgments 304, 378, 384
Junk hauling services 387

K

Keyboxes 49, 156
Kickbacks (referral fees) 401–403

L

Land contracts 226, 264, 361
Land description. *See* Property description
Landslides 101
Latent defects 8, 12, 65, 94, 101

Lawyers (attorneys)
  attorneys' fees 51, 201, 237, 394, 399
  drafting and preparing legal documents
    180–181, 238
  giving expert advice 181, 183, 224,
    231, 236, 361–362
  providing closing services 376–377
  unauthorized practice of law 180, 196
Layout. *See* Design and layout of house
Lead-based paint 63, 98, 238, 241, 380
Lease/options 367
Legal description 46. *See also* Property
    description
Legal guardian signing contracts 223
Legal title 361
Lenders and lending
  and government-sponsored loans 347,
    353
  competence 387
  institutional lenders 330, 360
  lender's role in closing 376, 383
  lending discrimination 77–78, 80
  mortgagee's title policy 384–385, 394
Lender's title policy 384–385
Level payment buydown 342
Liabilities (debts) 299, 302, 338, 351
Liability coverage 384
Liability (tort) 7, 13, 32, 180, 187
Liens
  lien priority 348, 364–365, 385, 394
  listed in purchase and sale agreement
    217
  paid off at closing 230, 232, 378,
    384–385
Liquid assets 301, 340
Liquidated damages 50, 205–206,
    236–237
List-back agreements 92
Listing agreements 38. *See also* Compensation of real estate agents
  agency relationship created by 13, 45,
    50
  agent's right to market property 49
  basic legal requirements 41
  discriminatory listing practices 83
  duration, expiration, termination 46–47,
    75, 133

elements of 40
exclusive listings 39–40, 46
listing input sheet 51, 66
listing price 110–111, 128, 130, 133
modification of 55, 161
net listings 41–42
open listings 25, 39
ownership of listing 75
prepared and signed by broker 45
preventing automatic buyer agency 14,
    23
property description 41, 46
provision concerning earnest money
    237
required to be in writing 42, 75, 243
seller's warranties 50
signatures 51–55
types of listings 38
typical provisions 42
vacant land listings 66
Listing practices
cold calls 147
expired listings 148
farming 146–147
listing presentations 151–155
referrals 150–151
servicing the listing 155–162
LLPA. *See* Risk-based pricing (loan fees)
Loan amount
and loan-to-value ratio 324
and preapproval 288
conventional loans 331
FHA loans 348
maximum loan amount 288–289, 324
VA loans 353, 355
Loan application 291–292
and closing process 377, 387
good faith estimate of closing costs 309
preapproval 288, 377, 383
verification of applicant's information
    296, 301–303, 306, 308
Loan commitment 377–378, 383
Loan fees 308, 325, 392
and seller financing 362
for FHA loans 348–350, 352

for high-LTV loans 332
for VA loans 354
risk-based 334
Loan flipping 311
Loan-level price adjustment. *See* Risk-
    based pricing (loan fees)
Loan payment amount 328–329
and buydown or points 325, 341–342
and length of repayment period 321
buyer's ability to afford payment 292,
    298, 310–311, 361–362
for ARM 327–328
for fully amortized loan 322
lower initial payments 342–343
maximum monthly payment 310
Loan term. *See* Repayment period
Loan-to-value ratios 135, 324
97% and 100% loans 346, 353
and risk-based loan fees 334
and underwriter's level of review 336
conventional loans 332
FHA loans 348
high-LTV loans 332, 340, 345–347, 353
Loan underwriting. *See* Underwriting
Lock-ins 309
Low appraisal 135–138, 263, 355, 387
Low-documentation loans 297, 306
Low-downpayment loan programs
    345–346
Loyalty to principal 11, 21, 23, 30
LTVs. *See* Loan-to-value ratios

M

Mailbox rule 194
Managing broker 2
Manual underwriting 336, 340
Manufactured or mobile homes 63, 401
Margin (ARM) 327
Marital property 223–224
Marital status 79, 86
Marketable title 230, 384
Market allocation 92–93
Market price 112
Market value 112, 128, 132
Material facts 8, 65, 93, 231

Math problems
  area 412–422
  converting to decimals 410–412
  percentages 416–422
Mental competence or incompetence 46, 223, 225
Minimum cash investment (FHA) 349–350, 352
Mining and subsidence 102
Minors 223
MIP (FHA) 349, 354
Misrepresentation 7, 272
MLS. *See* Multiple listing services
Mobile homes 63, 401
Model homes 89
Modifying contracts 55, 196, 232
Mold 100
Money orders 200–201, 226
Mortgage Broker Practices Act 312–317
Mortgagee's (lender's) title policy 385, 394
Mortgage insurance 309, 354
  FHA 347–348
  PMI 332
Mortgage payment. *See* Loan payment amount
Mortgage payment adjustment period 328
Mortgage payment cap 329
Mortgages 360. *See also* Financing
  financing documents 378, 383
  payoff of seller's loan 378, 396
Moving 387
Multiple listing services 19, 49–51, 55, 123, 154, 217
Mutual consent. *See* Offer and acceptance

N

National Environmental Protection Act 95
Negative amortization 329–330
Negative equity 332
Negligence 7, 180
Negotiations 24–25, 167, 190, 289

Neighborhoods
  CC&Rs 230
  neighborhood analysis 114, 130
  neighborhood's effect on property values 114–115, 123
  revitalization 346
  targeted loan programs 346
NEPA 95
Net cost (buyer's) 180, 192, 389–395
Net equity 301–302
Net listings 41–42
Net proceeds (seller's) 155, 389–391, 395–399
Net worth in underwriting 299
  conventional loans 340
  FHA loans 351
  funds for closing 300–301
  liabilities 302–303
  reserves 340
  types of assets 301
  VA loans 359
  verification 301, 306–307
Non-agency 14, 23, 31
Nonconforming loans 291, 331
Nonstandard forms, agency disclosure 17
Note rate 327, 341
Notice from Contingent Buyer (bump reply) 279
Notice to Backup Buyer 188
Notice to Remove Contingency (bump notice) 279

O

Offer and acceptance 166–167, 216
  acceptance cannot change terms 196
  acceptance creates contract 188, 196, 243
  acceptance of purchase agreement 241
  additional offers after contract signed 8, 12, 185, 274
  and agent's authority 45
  and earnest money 203
  backup offers 185–190, 279
  bump clauses 274

communication to agent 195
counteroffers 185, 190, 196, 241
legal requirements for acceptance 194
legal requirements for offer 180
mailbox rule 194
manner of acceptance 195, 241
multiple offers 167–168, 183, 185, 289
must be in writing 195
negotiations 24, 167
preparing an offer 178
presenting offers 8, 182
revocation of offer 188–190, 194
termination of offer 188–190, 192
Open houses 159–161
Open listings 25, 39
Optional Clauses Addendum 196
Origination fees 309, 325, 348, 354, 392
Overtime pay 294, 299
Owner-occupancy 348, 353
Owner's title policy 385, 398

P

Panic selling (blockbusting) 78, 81, 83
Partially amortized loan 323–324, 345,
    362
Partnerships 224
Part-time jobs 293
Payment amount. *See* Loan payment
    amount
Payment caps 329
Payment shock 328, 343, 345
Payment Terms Addendum 226, 264
Payoff of seller's loan 378, 396
Pension payments 294
Percentage problems 416–422
  approach to solving 416–422
  loans and interest 417–422
Percolation problems and tests 244
Personal property 201, 387
Pests and pest control 264, 380
PITI 298, 338
Plats and platted property 66, 243–244
Plottage 118
Plumbing system in house 63, 380
PMI 330, 332, 354

Points. *See* Discount points; *See
    also* Origination fees
Portfolio loans 331
Possession 181, 183, 190, 217, 233, 387
Postdated check 200
Power of attorney 224–225
Preapproval 164, 288, 377, 383
Predatory lending 311, 336
Prepaid expenses 349
Prepaid (interim) interest 349, 392–394
Preparing property 155–156, 160
Prepayment 335, 345, 348, 354, 397
  penalties 307
Prequalifying 164, 290
Presentation of offers 8, 182
Previewing property 166
Price
  as gross sale proceeds 400
  higher than appraised value 135–138,
      263, 355, 387
  in initial offer 190
  in purchase and sale agreement 217,
      226
  listing price 110–111, 128, 130, 133
  market price 112
  on settlement statement 391, 395
  price vs. value or cost 112
Price fixing 46, 90, 93
Principal or client. *See* Agency
Private mortgage insurance 332, 354
Probate administrator or executor 376
Procuring cause 39–40
Promissory notes 378
  as earnest money 201, 226
  for seller financing 226, 264, 360
  note rate 327, 341
Property description
  added to contract later 41
  for platted property 243
  in listing agreement 41, 46
  in purchase and sale agreement 181,
      216, 225, 386
Property taxes
  and lien priority 365
  impound accounts 349, 365–366, 396
  proration of 217, 233, 390, 394–395

Prorations 233, 376, 389–390
  interest on seller's loan 397
  prepaid (interim) interest 392–394
  property taxes 217, 233, 390, 394–395
Public accommodation 88
Public assistance income 295
Purchase and sale agreements. *See
    also* Contingency clauses; Con-
    tracts
  addenda 196, 238, 386
  adding special clauses 180–181, 196,
    238
  agency disclosure 17, 238
  and opening escrow 377
  basic legal requirements 216
  default or breach 236–237, 264
  form used for buyer's offer 178
  for vacant land 243
  method of payment 181, 217, 226
  modifying 232
  must be in writing 195, 216
  parties and signatures 223, 243
  prepared by real estate agents
    180–181, 386
  properties in bankruptcy or foreclosure
    225
  property description 181, 216, 225,
    386
  purpose of 216
  receipt for deposit 226–230
  rescission 64–65, 196, 279–280
  termination of 232, 279–280
  typical provisions 217
  unenforceable 190, 195, 223, 232
Purchase money loan 361

Q

Qualifying standards. *See* Underwriting
Quality and durability of income
    292–293

R

Radon 98, 100, 380
Rate adjustment period 327–328, 343
Rate caps 328–329
Rate lock-ins 309

Ratification 13
Ready, willing, and able buyer 38, 47,
    198, 272
Real estate agent
  affiliation and termination 75
  may only be paid by designated broker
    74–75
  preparing and signing contract forms 75
  reimbursement for costs 50
Real estate as asset (loan application)
    301–302
Real estate assistants 170–172
Real estate broker. *See* Compensation of
    real estate agents
  as agent of firm 32
Real estate brokerage
  authority under listing agreement 45
  handling earnest money 201–203, 205
  policy on home inspector referrals 381
  providing closing services 376–377
  represented by licensee 181
Real Estate Brokerage Relationships Act
    6. *See also* Agency
  agency duties 6, 31
  agency law pamphlet 10
  creation of real estate agency 13–14,
    20, 23, 25
  no duty to inspect or investigate 9
  vicarious liability 13, 32
Real estate contracts (land contracts) 226,
    264, 361
Real estate license 2–3
Real estate licensee
  as agent of brokerage 181
  as independent contractor 4
  brokerage affiliation required 3
  budgeting and planning 5
  handling earnest money deposit 201,
    205
  preparing and signing contract forms
    181, 386
  selling or buying property for self 19
Real estate license law
  and advertising 158
  and real estate assistants 170
  antidiscrimination provisions 82
  commissions 74–75

disclosure of licensed status 19
loss of license terminates agency 46, 75
Real Estate Settlement Procedures Act.
    See RESPA
Real estate transfer disclosure statement.
    See Seller disclosure statement
Reasonable care and skill 7
Receipt for deposit 226–230
Reconsideration of value 136–138, 387
Reconveyance deed 399
Recording documents 378
  on closing date 231
  recording fees 379, 394, 399
Redlining 78
Referral fees (kickbacks) 401–403
Referrals 150–151
Refinancing 330, 336, 345
Regulation Z 308–309
Reinspection 264, 380, 382, 387
Remodeling 382
Rental agreement 233, 387
Rental income 233, 295, 297, 299
Renunciation 15
Renunciation of agency 46
Repairs
  and inspection contingency 380, 382
  recommended in inspection report 263,
      382, 386–387
  seller's opportunity to repair 264–268
  who pays for 382, 399
Repayment period 310, 320, 335
Repossessions 304
Representation agreement (buyer agency)
    25, 75
Representations. *See* Misrepresentation;
    See also Warranties
Request for Beneficiary's Statement 378
Request for reconsideration of value
    136–138, 387
Request for Verification of Deposit 301
Rescission of purchase agreement 64–65,
    196, 279–280
Reserve (impound) accounts 349,
    365–366, 391, 402–403
Reserves after closing 300, 336, 340,
    346, 352, 359

Reset option 345
Residual income (VA) 358–360
RESPA 401–418
  covered transactions 401
  exemptions 401
  good faith estimate of closing costs 403
  kickbacks 401–403
  requirements 402–418
  unearned fees 402
Retainer for buyer's agent 30
Retirement income 294
Revocation 15
Revocation of agency 46
Revocation of offer 188–190, 194
Revolving debts 338, 351
Risk-based pricing (loan fees) 334, 337
Risk of casualty loss 365
Risk of default on loan 352
  and credit score 304, 336
  and loan-to-value ratio 324, 332, 336
  and secondary financing rules 335
  and underwriting 290–291, 336, 352
  ARM vs. fixed-rate loan 332
  buyer's effort to avoid default 332
  compensating factors 352
  contributory risk factors 336
Risk of foreclosure loss 290–291, 324,
    332, 347

S

Safety clause. *See* Extender clause
Sale of buyer's home contingencies
    269–279
Sales comparison approach to appraisal
    113, 383
Secondary financing 310, 325
  conventional loans 335
  FHA loans 350–352
  seller seconds 364
  VA loans 355–356
Secondary market agencies 331
  and conventional underwriting 291, 339
  and federally related loans (RESPA)
      401
  seller contribution limits 343
  underwriting software 291

Second Buyer's Addendum 274
Secret profits 11
Security instruments. *See* Deeds of trust;
    See also Mortgages
Seismic retrofitting 102
Seizure of property 100
Self-employment income 293, 297,
    306–307
Seller agency 13, 20. *See also* Listing
    agreements
  compensation 20, 26
  pre-existing relationship with buyer
    22–23
  presenting offers 182–185
  setting listing price 110–111, 133
  working with buyers 21–23
Seller contribution limits 343, 356, 367
Seller disclosure statement 55, 94
  amending 65, 388
  buyer's rescission rights 64–65
  changed circumstances 64
  latent defects 65
  no warranties from seller or agent 65
  waiver of rights 64
Seller financing 124, 226, 360–367
  addendum and attached documents
    264, 360
  and RESPA 402
  and underwriting standards 362, 365
  buyer's concerns 362
  land contracts 226, 264, 361
  on settlement statement 391, 396
  other ways to help buyer 367
  purpose and advantages of 361–362
  seller's concerns 362–364
  types of seller financing 364
  wraparounds 366
Seller seconds 364
Seller's net proceeds
  buydown deducted from 341, 367
  decreased by debits 391
  estimating seller's net 395–399
  increased by credits 390
  net listings 41
  worksheet for seller 155, 183, 389
Selling agent. *See* Buyer agency

Selling practices
  determining needs 164–165
  finding buyers 162–164
SEPA 95
Separate property 224
Septic systems 57
Settlement statements 376, 379, 389
  credits and debits 389–391
  uniform settlement statement 402–403
Sewer system 57, 244
Shelter expense 358
Sherman Antitrust Act 89
Shoreline Management Act 95–96
Short sales 48–50, 77
Showing property 161, 165–166
  access and keyboxes 49, 169
  discriminatory sales practices 206, 208
  safety issues 169–170
Signatures on contracts 51–55, 223, 243
Silent wrap 366
Site analysis 116
Social media regulations 157
Social security payments 294
Soil inspection 380
Special assessment liens 365
Spousal maintenance payments 294, 297,
    338, 351
Square footage 119
Stable monthly income 292, 292–296,
    337, 351
Standard coverage title policy 385
State Environmental Policy Act 95
Statute of frauds 42, 195, 243
Steering 78, 87, 207
Storage tanks 99, 100, 102, 380
Structural components of a house 63
Structural inspections 380
Subagency 14, 20, 23, 32
Subdivision. *See* Development; *See*
    also Neighborhoods
Subprime lending 307–308, 312
Subsidence 102
Substantial development permit 95
Superfund 96
Swing loan 273, 302

T

Targeted loan programs 346
Taxes and taxation. *See* Excise tax;
      See also Income taxation; *See
      also* Property taxes
Temporary buydowns 342, 352
Temporary work 296
Tenancy in common 224
Ten-year loans 320
Termination
   of affiliation with brokerage firm 75
   of listing 46–47, 75
   of offer 188–190, 192
   of purchase agreement 232, 279–280
Thirty-year loans 310, 320–322, 326,
      348, 354
Tie-in arrangements 92–93
Time is of the essence 237
Title
   affected by legal action 231
   issues in seller disclosure statement 57
   issues in site analysis 118
   legal title 361
   marketable title 230, 384
   provisions in purchase agreement 217,
      230
   transfer of 378
Title insurance 384–385
   exceptions to coverage 385
   extended vs. standard coverage 385
   homeowner's coverage 385
   lender's (mortgagee's) policy
      384–385, 394
   matters of record 385
   owner's policy 385, 398
   policies issued 379
   preliminary title report 231, 378,
      383–385, 387
   problems discovered by inspection 385
   provided for in purchase and sale
      agreement 230
   title companies 376, 378–379,
      402–403
   title search 384–385
   who pays for 384–385, 394, 398

Tolerances 403
Topography 115, 118
Tortious interference with contract 187
Tort liability 7, 13, 32, 180, 187
Total debt to income ratio. *See* Debt to
      income ratio
Total finance charge 308
Toxic mold 100
Transfer disclosure statement. *See* Seller
      disclosure statement
TransUnion 306
Trust accounts and trust funds 10, 201,
      203. *See also* Earnest money
Trusts and trustees 224–225
Truth in Lending Act 158–159, 308–
      309, 312, 403
Twenty-year loans 310, 320
Two-step mortgages 343–344
Two-tiered loans 328, 343–345

U

UFFI 98, 380
Unauthorized practice of law 180, 196
Underground storage tanks 99–100, 102,
      380
Underlying mortgage 366
Underwriting 290, 310
   affordable housing programs 346
   automated 291
   compensating factors 339–340, 352,
      358–359
   computer software for 291
   contributory risk factors 336
   conventional loans 336
   credit reputation 303, 351
   FHA loans 291, 348, 351–353
   gift funds 301, 303, 340, 346, 352
   high-LTV loans 332, 340, 345–346
   income analysis 292, 337, 351–352,
      357–359
   level of review 304
   low-documentation loans 297, 306
   net worth 299, 351
   preapproval 288, 382–383
   reserves after closing 300, 336, 340,
      346, 352

(Underwriting, continued)
   seller financing 362, 365
   standards 291, 331–332, 348, 351, 353
   VA loans 291, 353, 357–360
   verification of information 296,
      301–303, 306, 308
   with a buydown 342, 352
Unearned fees 402
Unemployment benefits 293
Unfair business practices 93
Uniform settlement statement 402–403
Upfront premiums (FHA) 349
Urea formaldehyde 98, 380
Utilities 66, 244

V

Vacant land. *See* Development
  and fair housing laws 77
  and RESPA 401
  listing agreements 66
  property condition report 66
  purchase and sale agreements 243
VA loans 330, 353–360
  25% rule 355
  appraisal provisions 260
  assumption 356
  characteristics of 353
  closing costs 260
  eligibility 354
  guaranty 354–356
  income analysis 357–359
  interest rate 354
  loan amount 355
  loan fees 354
  no downpayment 353–355
  owner-occupancy requirement 353
  restoration of entitlement 356
  secondary financing 355–356
  shelter expense 358
  underwriting standards 291, 353,
     357–360
  with downpayment 354–356, 359
Value 111
Veterans Affairs, Dept. of. *See* VA loans
Vicarious liability 13, 32

W

Waiver of contingency 256–257,
   259–260, 268, 279
Warranties
  agent's disclaimer of 26, 65
  implied warranty of habitability 94
  seller's warranties in listing agreement
   50
  statutory warranty deed 230
Washington Law Against Discrimination
   79, 85
Washington Unfair Business Practices
   and Consumer Protection Act 93
Water
  Clean Water Act 96
  contaminated water 100, 381
  issues in seller disclosure statement 57
  water damage and flooding 101
  wells 100, 380
Wetlands 96
Wheelchair ramps 88
Wraparound financing 366

Z

Zoning 66, 244, 269